对话式设计
gmp建筑师事务所建筑作品

Designing in Dialogue
The Architecture of von Gerkan,
Marg and Partners

 UED magazine

德国冯·格康，玛格及合伙人建筑师事务所 《城市·环境·设计》杂志社　主编

对话式设计

gmp建筑师事务所建筑作品

Designing in Dialogue

The Architecture of von Gerkan,
Marg and Partners

"建筑是艺术的社会化应用"

"Architecture is the social application of art"

gmp

对话式设计——gmp建筑师事务所建筑作品

"建筑是艺术的社会化应用。"

这句话阐述的不仅是gmp的建筑方式,甚至是gmp的建筑风格在语言学层面的表达。gmp的建筑作品具有明确的功能性和标志性的简约风格,并将建筑美学与社会责任有效连接。尽管这句话是gmp建筑事务所于1965年在汉堡成立时由创始人创造的,但语句中传达的方法论恰恰是曼哈德·冯·格康和福尔克温·玛格将这一理论沿用至今,并借此表达自己的建筑理念和方式的原因。

这一理念的可贵之处在于它与好建筑一样,都能经受住时间的考验。数十年来,它的含义一直没有发生改变,但被赋予了全新的和不同的解读方式。一方面,它的准确性被广泛认可,具备了建筑语言所应有的可持续性;另一方面,它的涵盖领域广泛,适用于任何情况和个人,和好建筑一样,可以从多种不同的角度进行解读。

然而,这里的"艺术"和"社会化"意味着什么?"应用"意在传达什么?换而言之,怎样的建筑构造才是对这一开放性语句的恰当解读?当然,可能没有也不必有明确答案能够解答这些问题。责任性与"艺术"(美学责任)和"社会化应用"(社会责任)息息相关,是建筑赖以生存的建筑文脉中的首要和最重要的考量因素与评价标准。建筑师从这些不断变化的文脉中探寻自己的答案,在找到真正的问题之所在后也就有了自己的解答。

这一过程是gmp所倡导的"对话式设计"的核心。设计是从建筑命题与特定场地之间的对话中产生的。它们与具体的生态、地形、经济、社会和政治情况休戚相关,因此需要找到可持续性的建筑方式。gmp认为建筑的可持续性意味着它必须在满足气候条件的同时,选用适合的材料进行设计。真正的可持续建筑是令形形色色的人们都能自由地安居乐业的设计。因此gmp追求传统的简洁性,在自然的基础上进行简化,融入自然,克服建筑冲突。

在"传统的简洁性"中,"传统"的概念在gmp的设计中扮演着特殊的角色,是建筑师独一无二的社会责任背后的关键因素。然而,gmp认为自身的责任不仅在于不断实现建筑理念,还包括留给后世属于自己的建筑"遗产"。曼哈德·冯·格康和福尔克温·玛格多年的建筑设计与教育经历使gmp事务所注定走上知识的传递与交流之路。为此,2007年成立了gmp基金会,其使命是为学生和毕业生提供支持与教育,并促进国内外建筑、景观建筑和景观保护领域的研究与发展。

建筑文化学院(acc)为杰出的德国及海外学生提供工作场所,在它的支持下,基金会成为实现目标的工具。建筑文化学院的指导以多样化的主题和教学方法而独树一帜,讲求直接、实际以及国际视野。gmp在海外尤其是远东地区开展的长期的多层面的活动回流到建筑文化学院,惠泽学生,为他们提供了在国际舞台开展建筑实践的极有价值的信息。

对话式设计还意味着建立建筑现状与建筑师之间的对话。对话参与者深入这一过程,互相影响。每个建筑师依据个人的喜好与能力以不同的方式展开对话,建筑也就从中产生。

建筑师在这一过程中开展的对话避免了专业局限性使设计停滞不前状况的发生,使建筑概念得到更广阔的发展。因此,建筑师能够以成熟、理性和恰如其分的方式进行管理,承担从概念图到最终施工完成全过程中的责任。gmp是少数进行全方位设计的建筑师事务所之一,对建筑项目从方案设计到施工建造直至室内装修全面负责。

这种姿态使gmp成为德国最大的建筑事务所之一,并为之赢得全球性的成功。自从gmp成立以来,曼哈德·冯·格康和福尔克温·玛格与合作伙伴胡贝特·尼恩霍夫、尼古劳斯·格茨、于尔根·希尔默、斯特凡·胥茨和吴蔚一道,在全球10个事务所地点的500名员工的支持下,在德国的重点城市和全球除澳洲外的所有大洲进行着设计与建筑实践。gmp的项目涵盖范围极其广泛,包括私人别墅、公共、交通和商业建筑以及城市设计等。公司的专业领域,尤其是大规模项目在不断扩大,包括博览中心、体育馆、火车站和机场等。

想到gmp所涉猎的建筑类型之广,建筑挑战之大,也就不难理解建筑师为什么必须不断追求新的建筑答案。然而,建筑师并不一定要一直寻求新方法。gmp在对话式设计中遵循以下理念:

简洁性
寻找最清晰明了的设计方案。追求最完美的简约设计。

结构秩序
赋予设计以条理分明的秩序。将功能组织成清晰的建筑形式。

融合多样性与统一性
在多样性中寻求统一性,在统一性中体现多样性。

个性设计
从具体的场地与项目条件中创造具有鲜明的形象特色的设计。

这其中呈现的每个项目都被打上了这种建筑理念的烙印。此外,无论项目命题如何不同,建筑师无时无刻不在面临着相似的主题。伴随这些理念的是定义项目选择和分类的建筑主题或主题领域。"多样性与统一性"部分表现了如何将主题式和系统式思考在建筑中连接起来,这既是指导原则也是主题。我们挑选的主题包括:

- 多样性和统一性
- 社会和责任
- 传统与现代
- 创新与自我风格
- 都市性
- 流动性

与这些主题相关的问题由来已久,自建筑出现之日起就已存在。为了找到正确答案,需要进行不断的创新,迸发新的思维方式。这里呈现的是gmp已经探索到的一小部分答案。

/

Designing in Dialogue – The Architecture of von Gerkan, Marg and Partners

"Architecture is the social application of art."

This sentence describes more than just the architectural approach of gmp. In its own architecture – with its clear functionality and iconic austerity, it efficiently and inextricably ties together architecture aesthetics and social responsibility – the sentence even projects gmp's approach linguistically. Although they coined this phrase while establishing their architectural office of von Gerkan, Marg and Partners (gmp) in Hamburg in 1965, the methodology expressed in and by this sentence is the reason why Meinhard von Gerkan and Volkwin Marg still use it today to describe their approach to architecture.

The sentence functions so well because, like good architecture, it never ages. Its meaning remains unchanged, yet, over the decades, it is always interpreted anew and differently. Its precision is generally understood – just as good and sustainable architectural language should be. On the other hand, it is also general in a very precise way – in the sense of being universal, available to everyone, interpretable in different ways without ever being arbitrary. Just like good architecture.

Yet, what do "art" and "social" mean here? What is meant by "application"? In other words: How must architecture be constituted in order to do justice to that opening sentence? Of course, there can and must not be any blanket answers to these questions. Since this responsibility, which goes hand in hand with the word "art" (aesthetic responsibility) as well as the phrase "social application" (social responsibility), is first and foremost a consideration and evaluation of the particular contexts within which architecture is created. The architect seeks his or her answers in these ever changing contexts, finding them only when he or she asks the right questions.

This process lies at the heart of the "dialogical design" that gmp represents. Designs emerge in dialogue between the building task at hand and its particular site. They are responsive to ever specific conditions of ecology, topography, economy, society and politics, and thereby find a way to ensure architectural sustainability. gmp considers architecture to be sustainable if it meets both the require-

ments of the climatic conditions and is designed with the appropriate materials. So true sustainability only occurs if something is designed as a place for the diversity of human existence to flourish in the most natural way possible. gmp therefore strives for traditional simplicity, for a reduction based on plausibility and naturalness able to integrate and overcome architectural conflicts.

"Traditional simplicity" – the concept of "tradition" plays a special role at gmp because it is one of the key concepts behind the unique social responsibility of the architect. gmp sees this responsibility, however, not only in the consistent realization of its architectural concepts, but also in its own "legacy". The many years of experience acquired by Meinhard von Gerkan and Volkwin Marg in both architectural design and education have predestined the firm to play a role in the transfer and exchange of knowledge. For this purpose the gmp Foundation was established in 2007. Its mission is to support and educate students and graduates, as well as to promote research, in the fields of architecture, landscape architecture, and landscape conservation at home and abroad.

The instrument for achieving these objectives is the Foundation-supported Academy for Architectural Culture (aac) in Hamburg, which offers workshops for outstanding German and foreign students. Instruction at aac is distinguished by its thematic and methodological variability, its direct, practical relevance, and, not least, its international focus: The long-term, multifaceted activities of gmp abroad – especially in the Far East – flow back into the aac and provide students with valuable information for practicing architecture on an international stage.

Dialogical design also means establishing a dialogue between the conditions for architecture and the architects themselves. It is a process into which dialogue partners enter with each other and thus mutually influence one another. Each architect will conduct this dialogue differently due to his or her personal inclinations and abilities, but architecture is always the result of such a dialogue.

The dialogue, which the architect conducts during this process, avoids the deadlocks of one-sided specialization by enabling the concept of architecture to be developed in its higher dimension. They allow the architect – in a mature, rational and appropriate manner – to manage and take responsibility for a project from concept to realization. gmp is one of the few agencies with a generalist stance, meaning that it feels responsible for a project from concept and implementation up to and including interior design.

This stance has made gmp one of the largest architectural offices in Germany – and brought it worldwide success. Since founding gmp, Meinhard von Gerkan and Volkwin Marg, along with their partners, Hubert Nienhoff, Nikolaus Goetze, Jürgen Hillmer, Stephan Schütz and Wu Wei – as well as over 500 employees in ten offices worldwide – have designed and built structures in nearly all of Germany's major cities and on all continents except Australia. gmp's portfolio includes almost every construction task imaginable: private, public, transport and commercial buildings and urban design. The company's expertise, especially in large-scale projects, is constantly growing (exhibition centers, stadiums, railway stations, airports).

One only has to imagine this extreme range of architectural challenges to understand that the architect must always be on the search for new architectural answers. However, he or she does not always have to look for new methods. gmp adheres to the following guidelines in dialogical design:

"建筑是艺术的社会化应用"

Simplicity.
Search for the clearest solution for your design.
Strive for the best of simplicity.

Structural order.
Render a structural order to the design.
Organize functions as clear building forms.

Diversity and unity.
Create unity within diversity.
Create diversity within unity.

Distinctiveness.
Develop an identity of the design from the specific conditions of location and task.

Each project presented in this catalogue is stamped by these methodological guidelines. Additionally, no matter how different the tasks may be, the architect is constantly confronted with similar thematic aspects. Alongside these guidelines, there are architectural themes or thematic fields that define project selection and classification in this catalogue. The "diversity and unity" section shows how closely thematic and methodical thinking in architecture can be linked – it is both the guiding principle and theme. Our selection of themes includes:

· Diversity and unity
· Society and responsibility
· Tradition versus moderne
· Innovation and identity
· Urbanity
· Mobility

The questions connected to these themes are as old as architecture itself. To find the right answers for you, architecture constantly requires new creativity and new thinking. This catalogue presents a small selection of the answers that gmp has discovered.

简洁性
Simplicity

结构秩序
Structural order

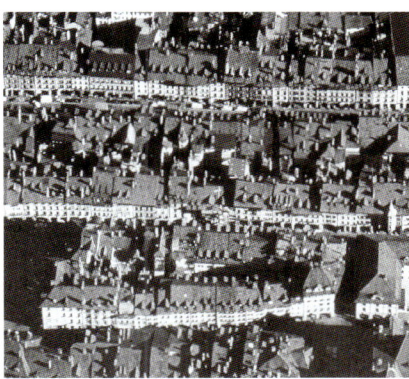
融合多样性与统一性
Diversity and unity

个性设计
Distinctiveness

"Architecture is the social application of art"

团队

Team

创始合伙人
Founding Partners

合伙人
Partners

中国区合伙人
Partner China

项目合伙人
Associate Partners

创始合伙人	Founding Partners
教授，荣誉博士，工程硕士，建筑师（BDA） 曼哈德·冯·格康	Prof. Dr. h. c. mult. Dipl.-Ing. Architect BDA Meinhard von Gerkan
教授，荣誉博士，工程硕士，建筑师（BDA） 福尔克温·玛格	Prof. Dr. h. c. Dipl.-Ing. Architect BDA Volkwin Marg

合伙人 / Partners

建筑师，工程硕士　胡贝特·尼恩霍夫	Dipl.-Ing. Architect Hubert Nienhoff
建筑师，工程硕士　尼古劳斯·格茨	Dipl.-Ing. Architect Nikolaus Goetze
建筑师，工程硕士　于尔根·希尔默	Dipl.-Ing. Architect Jürgen Hillmer
建筑师（BDA），工程硕士　斯特凡·胥茨	Dipl.-Ing. Architect BDA Stephan Schütz

中国区合伙人 / Partner China

建筑师，瑞士联邦高等工业大学(ETH)工程硕士 吴蔚	Dipl. Arch. ETH Wu Wei

项目合伙人 / Associate Partners

建筑师，工程硕士　玛德琳·唯斯	Dipl.-Ing. Architect Magdalene Weiss
建筑师，工程硕士　施蒂芬·瑞沃勒	Dipl.-Ing. Architect Stephan Rewolle
建筑师，工程硕士　德克·海勒	Dipl.-Ing. Architect Dirk Heller
建筑师，工程硕士　尼古拉斯·博兰克	Dipl.-Ing. Architect Nicolas Pomränke
建筑师，工程硕士　福克玛·西弗斯	Dipl.-Ing. Architect Volkmar Sievers
建筑师，工程硕士　马克·西蒙斯	Dipl.-Ing. Architect Marc Ziemons
建筑师，工程硕士　伯恩德·高斯曼	Dipl.-Ing. Architect Bernd Gossmann
建筑师，工程硕士　克里斯蒂安·霍夫曼	Dipl.-Ing. Architect Christian Hoffmann
建筑师，工程硕士　约翰·科恩	Dipl.-Ing. Architect Jochen Köhn
建筑师（BDA），工程硕士　汉斯·约阿希姆·帕普	Dipl.-Ing. Architect BDA Hans-Joachim Paap

多样性与统一性

临港新城　上海，中国
中国航海博物馆　临港新城，上海，中国
南汇行政中心　临港新城，上海，中国
上海东方体育中心　上海，中国

Diversity and Unity

Lingang New City Shanghai, China
China Maritime Museum Lingang New City, Shanghai, China
Nanhui Administration Center Lingang New City, Shanghai, China
Shanghai Oriental Sports Center Shanghai, China

gmp"对话式设计"建筑方向的指导原则之一就是"在多样性中寻求统一性,在统一性中体现多样性"。这一建筑视角只有当设计者将项目视为一个整体进行创作时才能够实现:从抽象的概念出发,专注细节,找到兼容多样性和统一性的解读方式。对于一座独立建筑而言这无疑是真理,需要传达明确的定位和表现内在的一致性;在此类建筑中,所有的建筑因素从美学和功能两方面都彼此呼应,不言自明。

但通常情况下人们期待建筑不只有一种"功能",而是能够同时发挥不同作用。公共建筑必须提供多样化的功能,并能够均衡实现不同的美学价值。仅仅做到"吸引人"还远远不够,其美学特征必须有特殊的象征意义,凸显社会性或暗示功能性。如果说将这些看似矛盾的方面组合到一个设计中是不可能完成的任务,那么成功就无从谈起。设计必须对多样性和统一性的课题有所回应,使建筑不仅是若干独立部件的简单组合。因此,建筑绝不能过于单调或简化。对于建筑群而言更是如此,在其中,各个独立建筑应该像建筑中的独立因素一样彼此相关联。设想一下,倘若建筑群中的每栋建筑都各自具有独特的功能将会怎样?那么在满足多样化的功能需求的同时,体现更加强烈的一致性将显得愈发重要和具有挑战性。

除了现实中可明确分配的功能,建筑或多或少被赋予了社会属性。gmp将建筑定义为"艺术的社会化应用"。这测试了是否能以另一种方式将多样性与统一性连接起来:建筑中存在不同的美学和功能层面,同时建筑与自己赖以生存的多样化的社会文脉相互影响,如何使两者相统一?设计和建筑任务中的多样性与统一性的课题在城市建设和整体城市规划中是最普遍、最重要、最具挑战性的,但同时又是最有回报性的。这是因为城市不仅是建筑或建筑群的混乱叠加,而是一个有机体。或换而言之,城市是构建社会。因此,关于建筑与社会的关系问题是城市规划中至关重要的一环。

与赋予独立建筑以多样化特色的理念类似,gmp在中国的临港新城项目中也做到了举一反三,从零开始打造一座城市:首先,就城市形态而言,临港新城是gmp负责的最大的项目和建筑史上最大的项目之一。其次,临港新城的部分设计更加具体地回答了多样性和统一性的问题。城市建于水上,且以水为中心展开设计;多样性体现在建筑元素中,而统一性则恰似水滴落到平静的水面上时激起的一圈圈波纹。位于临港的航海博物馆在中国同类建筑中尚属首例。其中,多样性和统一性相融合的集中体现在于创造同样具备标志性、代表性和功能性的建筑设计。临港的行政区域力求实现整体的统一性与各个独立建筑的多样性之间的平衡。

→ 98

中国航海博物馆,临港新城,上海
China Maritime Museum,
Lingang New City, Shanghai

/

临港新城，上海
Lingang New City, Shanghai

One of the guiding principles of gmp's architectural approach – designing in dialogue – is to "Create unity in diversity. Create diversity in unity." This guiding vision can only be fulfilled by a designer who conceives and builds a project as a whole, someone who takes it from an abstract idea all the way down to the details and can explain it from both directions. This is certainly true for an individual building, which has to take a clear position and show an inherent consistency; a building in which all elements refer to each other in self-evident ways, both aesthetically and functionally.

But often a building is also expected to "function" in more than just one way and to serve different purposes at the same time. A public building has to provide for diverse uses and also be able to fulfill different aesthetic aspects equally. "Appealing" may not be enough; its aesthetics might also have to stand for something particular, emphasize its importance for society or denote its function. If bringing all of these sometimes contradictory aspects together in a consistent design isn't feasible, then it can never be successful. A design has to answer to the issue of diversity and unity in a way that will allow the building to be more than just the sum of its individual parts. Because of this, it should never be too monotonous or overly reduced. This is even more true for a building ensemble, where the individual buildings are supposed to relate to each other like the individual elements in each building. And what if every building is supposed to have its own distinct function within the ensemble? Then it will be even more important – and challenging – to meet the diversity of functions with an even stronger consistency of design.

Beyond clearly assignable functions in a practical sense architecture always has a more or less strongly pronounced social dimension to it as well. gmp defines architecture as an "art applied to society". This tests the issue of how diversity and unity connect in another way: How can the many different aesthetic and functional aspects of building be brought in line with the diverse social and societal contexts from which a building emerges – and to which it is mutually related? The issues of diversity and unity in design and building tasks are nowhere more numerous, significant, and more challenging or rewarding than in urban construction or when planning an entire city.

Diversity and Unity

This is because a city is more than just a jumble of buildings or building ensembles – it is an organism. It is, so to speak, built society. Because of this, the question of how architecture and society relate is of utmost importance when it comes to urban planning.

Analogous to the idea of diversity in the individual, we offer three answers in one: first in form of a city, the largest project gmp has ever taken on and one of the largest projects ever in the history of architecture. The other two examples are parts of this city and answer more specific questions about diversity and unity. Lingang New City in China – the singular task of building a city from scratch. A city on the water and centered around water; a city as diverse as the element to which it is dedicated, and as consistent as the circles emanating from a drop of water that has fallen onto a tranquil, liquid surface. The Maritime Museum in Lingang is the first of its kind in China. Here, the connection between diversity and unity is characterized mainly by the task of creating an equally iconic, representative and functional architectural design. The Lingang's administrative area is informed by the idea of striking a balance between the unity of the entire complex and the diversity of its individual buildings.

→ 202

上海东方体育中心，上海
Shanghai Oriental Sports Center, Shanghai

→ 114

南汇行政中心，临港新城，上海
Nanhui Administration Center, Lingang New City, Shanghai

Diversity and Unity

临港新城
上海，中国

如何构建一座城市？
为什么最好的市中心是不存在高楼大厦的？

在这片土地上，曾遍布淤泥和海水，而目前一个海港却正在开发中。在上海附近长江河口一个拥有130万人口的港口城市——临港新城正在日益发展壮大。在近海32km处建造中的临港将成为全球最大深水港的行政中心。

临港在传承传统欧洲城市的理想特征外，还体现了革命性：市中心内包含了一个直径2.5km的环形湖，成为向全体市民开放的休闲放松中心，如同城市中的科巴卡巴那海滩。通常地价昂贵的市中心被9km的海岸线取而代之，成为众多城市建筑的首选之地。

临港的建设以人类活动为基础，而不是依赖技术强度。项目旨在打造一个工作、休闲和居住等功能和谐共生之地。举例而言，城市的组织结构摆脱了对长途驾车的依赖。整体形态的设计灵感来源于水滴落入湖中时水面上泛起的一圈圈涟漪。功能单元依据罗盘式分布原则，从中心按照环形向四周展开：步行区、商业区、500m长的类似环形的城市公园依次展开，几座独栋公用建筑屹立其中；坐落在放射式道路旁的居住区，每个可容纳13 000人。自然景观以楔形扩展至二环，而居住区内则有溪流和小湖穿过。

/

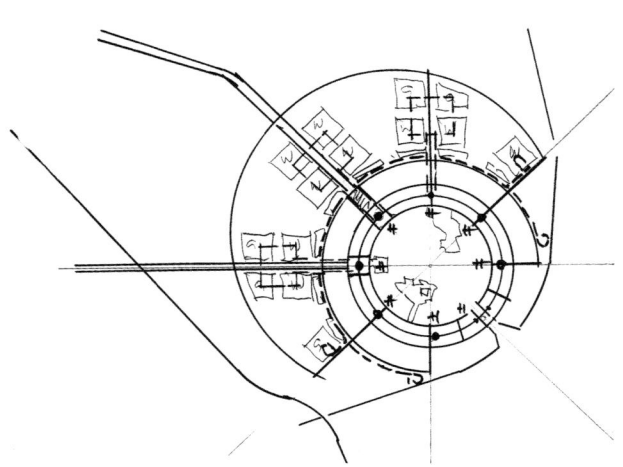

Lingang New City
Shanghai, China

How do you build a city?
And why is the best city center one without buildings?

Once there was only silt and the sea here, but now a seaport is being developed on this spot. A port city for 1.3 million inhabitants, near Shanghai, on the Yangzi estuary is growing: Lingang New City. Lingang is to be the administrative center for the largest deepwater port in the world, which is being constructed 32 km offshore.

Lingang picks up on the ideals of the traditional European city while adding one, revolutionary idea: The city center consists of a circular lake some 2.5 km in diameter: a center for everyone, a Copacabana in the city, unobstructable and relaxing. The usual dense, expensive downtown has been replaced by nine kilometers of shoreline, thereby providing many of the city's buildings with a prime address.

Lingang is based not on technical mobility, but on the scale of the human body. The goal is a symbiosis of work, leisure and habitation. The city, for example, is structured in such a way that there is no need for long car drives. The metaphorical model for this overall design is the image of concentric waves spreading out from the impact of a drop of water on the water surface. The functions are organized as series of rings from the center to the outside: promenade, business district, a 500-meters-wide, likewise ring-shaped city park with a few stand-alone public buildings in it and block-like residential areas – each able to house 13,000 people – situated along radial roads, following the principle of a compass rose. Wedges of natural landscape penetrate up to the second ring, while residential areas are traversed by streams and smaller lakes.

中国航海博物馆
临港新城，上海，中国

如何使建筑同时具备功能性和标志性？
如何使建筑脱颖而出却又不觉突兀？

中国的第一个航海博物馆坐落于临港湖岸边。塔状的设计借鉴了风中张开的风帆的建筑类别，在几英里范围内便清晰可见，使博物馆成为临港的地标，突出了港口城市与大海及海运的关系。

巨大的古老船只（比如有完备风帆的中国帆船）在位于58m高的"风帆"下方如同大厅般宽敞的空间内展出。交错的风帆屹立在中央庭院的独立基座上，博物馆运营所需要的全部功能设施都位于此。游客们被吸引到宽阔的楼梯上休憩停留，建立了与博物馆场地景观设计的直接联系。

屋顶表现力十足的形态设计面临着建筑上与结构上的双重挑战。巨大的风帆形状设计还需要经受住同等的压力：博物馆紧邻开放的海平面，使其极易受到高气压大风的攻击和侵害。在完成之前，设计在上海同济大学的一个风洞试验中经过了抗压率和抗风力测试。

航海博物馆不仅将象征意义和功能需求完美融合于一项设计中，并且在不打乱城市多样化与统一性并存的复合结构的同时，将一个极富挑战性的地标性建筑植入其中，为城市发展增砖添瓦。

/

China Maritime Museum
Lingang New City, Shanghai, China

How can a building be both functional and iconic at the same time?
And how does it stand out without protruding?

China's first maritime museum is situated on the shore of Lingang Lake. Its towering design – an architectural analogy of two sails swelled by the wind – is visible for miles around and makes the museum a Lingang landmark, emphasizing the port city's relationship to the sea and to shipping.

Very large historic ships (fully rigged Chinese junks, for example) can be exhibited in the ample hall-sized space beneath the 58 meters high "sails". The crossed sails stand in the central courtyard, erected on a freestanding plinth that contains all the functions necessary for operating the museum. Visitors are invited to linger on the wide flights of stairs, which form an immediate relationship with the landscape design of the museum grounds.

The challenge of the roof's expressive form was not only architectural, but structural as well. Anything in the shape of a gigantic sail should also be able to withstand comparable stresses: The museum's close proximity to the open sea leaves it especially vulnerable to high-pressure winds. Before completion, the design was tested for pressure ratios and wind loads in a wind tunnel trial at Tongji University of Shanghai.

The Maritime Museum not only brings its representative and functional tasks together in one design; it also integrates the additional challenge of setting a landmark in this complex structure of diversity and unity – the city! – without disturbing it.

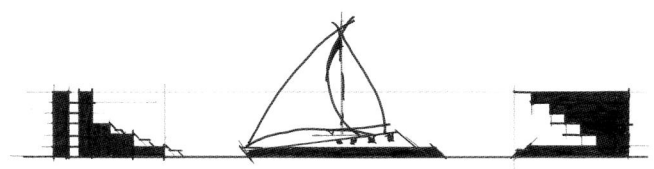

Diversity and Unity

南汇行政中心
临港新城，上海，中国

如何将组合体转化成单一实体？
即使有河流流过依然能够成形？

临港新城总部嵌入环绕市中心的第一个城市绿化带，一条河流将综合体一分为二。场地位于主要的入口公路，显著的位置与对区域和城市的重要功能需要独立建筑同样无掩蔽的严密组合，合并成为更大的统一体。大面积的天然石立面（依据用途而变化）和建筑两个长长的平行体块潜在的象征表达了同一主题，保证了组合体的统一性。院落中的水域和绿色空间以及两架人行桥将综合体的两部分连接起来。

在市政厅案例中，多样化与统一性之间的相互关系可以被解读为对自然和建筑二元性的探索，而这也正是临港新城的基本主题——将城市融入景观中。项目目标旨在以一种明智有机的方式将北部景观花园、流经区域的河流以及强有力的市政大楼连接起来。

/

Nanhui Administration Center
Lingang New City, Shanghai, China

How can an ensemble become a single unit?
Even with a river running through it?

Lingang's city headquarters is embedded in the first green belt circling the city center. A river divides the complex into two parts. Both the site's prominent location on one of the main access highways and its important function for the area and the city call for a simultaneously exposed and rigorous architectural composition of the individual buildings, which would merge to form a larger, unified ensemble.

The unity of this ensemble is ensured by both the common theme of a generous natural stone facade (which varies according to use) and the underlying typology of two long, parallel blocks of buildings. In the courtyard, with its water basins and green spaces, two footbridges connect the two parts of the complex.

In the case of the City Hall, the tension between diversity and unity can also be understood as an investigation of the duality of nature and architecture – the basic theme of Lingang New City, a city man has crafted into the landscape. The aim was to connect the landscape park in the north, the river that cuts through the area and the municipal building's powerful form and garden in sensible, organic ways.

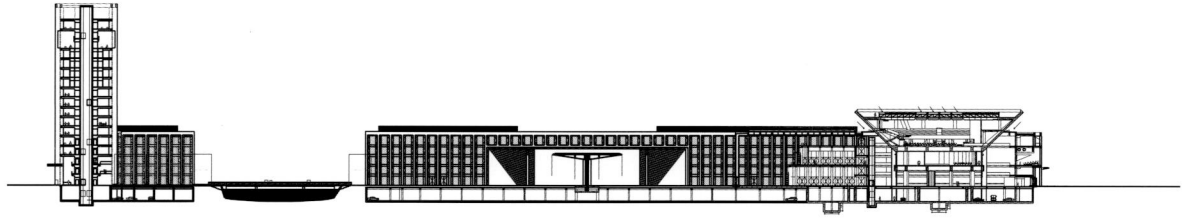

上海东方体育中心
上海，中国

上海东方体育中心（SOSC）建造于黄浦江岸边，作为2011年国际泳联世界游泳锦标赛的比赛场馆，是将多功能性与文化多样性完美融合于一个统一的开发项目中的典范。首先令人注目的是多样化的功能：该综合性运动场馆的设计依照公园形式展开，由一个可以举办多种体育项目和文化活动的主场馆、一个室内游泳池、一个室外跳水池以及一个媒体中心组成。

多样性与统一性的关系在城市设计中同样有所体现：在黄浦江沿岸，为了实现土地的可持续性利用，上海东方体育中心建造于弃用的工业区，体育中心和2010年世博会场地一样是构成一体化城市开发区的众多环节之一。

公园和建筑的整体概念主题设计参照了水、波浪和桥梁等因素。所有的建筑位于人工湖内抬高的平台上，开发项目中心内的大片水域间接将建筑连为一体，而直接的连接方式则是桥梁。此外，所有建筑采用统一的建筑特征、形式语言和材料，象征意义超越了单一性。双曲面三角形面板令人联想到风中飘扬的风帆，与大跨度的钢管拱架形成鲜明对比。

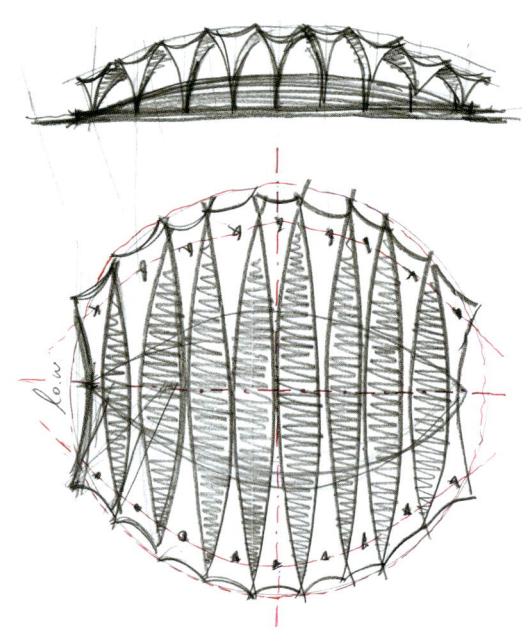

Shanghai Oriental Sports Center
Shanghai, China

The Shanghai Oriental Sports Center (SOSC), which was built on the banks of the Huangpu River on the occasion of the 2011 FINA World Aquatic Championships, is a prime example of how one can unify multiple functions and introduce multiplicity into a uniform development. What catches the eye at first is the functional diversity: the sports complex has been laid out in the form of a park and comprises a pool stadium for several sports disciplines and cultural events, an indoor swimming pool, an outdoor swimming pool and a media center.

The relationship between multiplicity and unity also exists in an urban design sense: in order to make more sustainable use of the land, the SOSC was developed on industrial brownfield sites along the Huangpu River, and the Center, as well as the site of the 2010 World EXPO, is one of many components aimed at creating an integrated urban development.

The overall conceptual theme of the park and the architecture consists of references to water, waves and bridges. All buildings are placed on raised platforms within artificially created lakes – the generous expanse of water at the heart of the development creates an indirect link between the buildings, while the direct connections are formed by bridges. Furthermore, the buildings share construction features, a pattern language and materials, and thus form a symbolic whole that is beyond the suggestion of uniformity. This is exemplified by the wide-spanning steel arches contrasted with large triangular panels with double-sided curvature that are reminiscent of sails billowing in the wind.

社会与责任

基督教会海淀堂　北京，中国
青岛大剧院　青岛，中国
万向大厦　上海，中国
2000年汉诺威世博会基督教馆　沃尔肯罗达，德国
德意志银行双塔　法兰克福，德国
国家体育场　华沙，波兰

Society and Responsibility

Christian Church Beijing, China
Qingdao Grand Theater Qingdao, China
Wanxiang Plaza Shanghai, China
Christ Pavilion, Expo 2000 Volkenroda, Germany
Deutsche Bank Twin Towers Frankfurt, Germany
National Stadium Warsaw, Poland

随着建筑的深入发展，价值也越来越高。古典派建筑、罗马式建筑和哥特式建筑分别出现在5欧元、10欧元和20欧元的纸币上。50欧元、100欧元和200欧元的纸币上的建筑图案则分别为文艺复兴、巴洛克和19世纪的风格。当代建筑是最"昂贵"的，价值500欧元。因此可以说欧元纸币的图案揭示了许多关于建筑的故事。欧元纸币透露了很多有关建筑设计的信息，其正反两面均有相关图像显示，一面是典型的建筑艺术，另一面是反映工程技术的桥梁构筑，这从根本上反映了建筑设计的重要性。欧元纸币也说明，其重要性也与建筑设计的身份打造相关：桥梁联系了欧洲，共同的传统建筑语汇或与其产生交互作用的技术进步亦如此。显然，建筑艺术具有巨大的社会影响力，它定义了整个欧洲大陆的特殊品质。建筑艺术不仅代表自身，这也代表了其所应该代表的事物。凡是存在这种影响力的地方，也要求担负起重大的责任，这种责任是多方面的，包括美学的、功能的、社会的、经济、政治和当今被视为重要的环境责任。

基督教会海淀堂，北京
Christian Church, Beijing

建筑是筑造而成的环境。它围绕着我们，我们与它一起共存。它同货币一样，无处不在，具有公开性和必不可少的特性。它一旦建成，就不会再挪动，当然，我们可以把它拆除，但要花钱，而花钱并不是决定性的因素。关键是要耗费能源，而建成它已经耗费了不少能源。付出代价的不是所筑造的环境，而是自然环境。今天，地球上的所有建筑物的能源消耗已占世界全部能源消费的40%左右，如不进行可持续发展的建设，就是不负责任的浪费。500欧元钞票也可能向我们传达了这样的信息：低劣建筑的成本从来没有像今天那样高。或者说，现代建筑必须最昂贵，因为它决定了我们的未来。

可持续建设不仅意味着设计可节省资源的房屋。我们不再欣赏的建筑（因为它们的审美仅属于短暂的潮流）和我们不再需要的建筑（因为它们的功能不足以适应时代）给我们和我们的环境造成负担。我们是否应当拆除它们？或者尽管我们不喜欢它们，但是为了环境是否不得不忍受那些变得丑陋的建筑？（具有讽刺意味的是，拆迁可能是环境不幸中之小的不幸。）那些被证明功能不足的建筑应该怎么办？其功能一开始没有考虑可扩建或可改变之可能，以致不能吸收社会或技术上的变化。我们不再需要或看不下去的建筑从任何角度上看都是不可持续的，因为它给我们和我们的环境造成了负担。

更重要的是，如何在城市建设中让建筑同时担负起生态环保的责任和政治责任。正如社会准则和法律规范能够使我们和睦相处一样，对于公共的更大更高层次的结构也应有一个如何设计如何建造的约定。否则，我们的和睦相处难免会恶化。建筑作为公共事务，具有深刻的政治性，只有表现出良好社会品质和文化品质的建筑才是好建筑。建筑如果要获得社会意义，必须是政治性的，而它只有是负责任的，才能获得社会意义。这一点在城市建设中很难实现，因为经济、政治，尤其是技术条件的变化快于人类社会的文化接受能力。如果对未来负责的城市建设不能成功地协调先进的技术与传统的生活习惯，必定会产生审美、社会与功能上的各种问题。请设想一下你在拥堵的城市交通中寸步难行，或者想方设法寻找停车位，或者骑着自行车或作为行人在汽车中间艰难地穿梭而行。

万向大厦，上海
Wanxiang Plaza, Shanghai

为了应对这些挑战，没有客观的、一成不变和明确无疑的解决方案。每一个挑战都不同，每一个建筑师也是不同的。但是任务总是相同的：以可持续的方式将审美、社会和功能相互结合。只有这样，建筑才能架构人与人之间的联系。gmp认为负责任的建筑设计就是对话式设计，它将建筑及其条件之间的复杂关联问题置于设计工作之首和中心地位。如果问题提得正确，那么建筑设计的回答也是好的。

建筑具有凝聚作用的社会影响力首先也是一种文化影响力。因此，文化建筑对建筑师来说是特别具有吸引力的建筑任务。青岛大剧院和在北京和河内的各类博物馆是对不同的文化问题包括艺术和民族历史问题所做的答案。北京的基督教堂协调了文化和宗教之间的联系。世博会的基督教馆打造了同一宗教各个教会之间的纽带。华沙国家体育场在困难的过去和乐观向上的现在之间找到了一种平衡。德意志银行的改造工程也遵循了这一理念：它克服了对环境有害的原有建筑和现代资源节约型的建筑之间的鸿沟。

→ 90

青岛大剧院，青岛
Qingdao Grand Theater, Qingdao

/

The more architecture develops, the more it costs. Roman architecture is worth 5 euros, Romanesque 10, Gothic 20. The architecture of the Renaissance costs 50 euro. Baroque: 100, 19th century: 200. Contemporary architecture is the most expensive, at 500 euros. The euro banknotes reveal a lot about architecture. Its depiction on both sides of the bills – typical buildings on the one side and bridges more exemplary for engineering feats on the other – is a testament to its importance. The bills also prove that this importance stems from architecture's powers of providing identity: The bridges seem to connect Europe, as does its shared traditional language of architecture or the technological progress interacting with it. If it can define the identity of a whole continent, architecture quite obviously has a great influence on society. It does more than simply stand for itself. It also represents what we stand for. The wielding of such influence demands responsible behavior, and that goes for all aspects of architecture: the aesthetic, functional, social, financial, political and, today more than ever, the environmental aspects.

Architecture is built environment. It surrounds us, we surround ourselves with it. It is – and it has this trait in common with money – ubiquitous, public, and inevitable. Once it exists it will remain. Of course we can demolish it. But that also has its cost. And the financial cost isn't even the critical factor. More than anything, it costs energy. And the energy to build is also an expense in itself. Here, it's not the man-made environment that pays the price, but the natural

Society and Responsibility

would be wastefully irresponsible behavior not to build sustainably. The message of the 500 euro bill could thus be: Never has the price paid for bad designs been higher than today. Or: Contemporary architecture must be dear to us, because it is a critical factor in our future.

Sustainable building includes more than energy-saving and resource-efficient buildings. What about the aesthetics of buildings that follow short-lived trends? Do we demolish them when we don't like them anymore? Or do we grin and bear, for the sake of our natural environment, how the built environment has become ugly? (Ironically, demolishing sometimes can be the more environ-mentally-friendly solution.) What about buildings that turn out to function poorly? Or when a building's functionality leaves no room for extension or flexible use, so it isn't able to react to changes in society and technology? Buildings we no longer need or can no longer bear to look at are unsustainable in every respect, because they are a burden to our environment and to us.

Responsible building is even more important in urban development, particularly with regards to the environment. But also in a political respect: Just as there are social rules and legal regulations that facilitate our coexistence, there has to be public and higher-level agreements on how architecture is developed and implemented. As a public art, architecture is inherently political and only ever good when it exhibits social and cultural quality. If it is to be relevant to society, then it has to be political and can only serve society if it acts responsibly. But this is no easy task, particularly in urban development, because economic, political and especially technological factors change urban conditions much more rapidly than society is able to adapt to culturally. If urban development and architecture are unable to reconcile technological changes with settled habits, then aesthetic, social and functional problems are bound to occur. One is easily reminded of this when stuck in a traffic jam or looking for a parking spot in the city. Or as a cyclist or pedestrian, when trying to find a way between the cars.

There is no such thing as an objectively correct, always applicable, obvious solution for these challenges. Every challenge is different, just as every architect is different. The task is always the same: connect the aesthetic, social and functional in a sustainable way. This is the only way architecture can connect with people. gmp understands responsible design as designing in dialogue, an approach

德意志银行双塔，法兰克福
Deutsche Bank
Twin Towers, Frankfurt

2000年汉诺威世博会基督教馆，沃尔肯罗达
Christ Pavilion, Expo 2000, Volkenroda

This is the only way architecture can connect with people. gmp understands responsible design as designing in dialogue, an approach that puts the issue of the complicated interactions between a design and its conditions at the starting point and center of their work. And if you ask the right kind of questions, you will get good architectural answers.

Architecture's connecting power in society is also a cultural one. That is why cultural buildings are a particularly rewarding architectural task. The opera in Qingdao and the museums in Beijing and Hanoi are answers to widely diverging questions of culture – in an artistic but also a historic-national sense. Architecture can also provide a cultural understanding. The Christian Church in Beijing acts as an intermediary between cultures and religions, the Christ Pavilion at EXPO 2000 between different orientations of the same faith. The National Stadium in Warsaw acts as an intermediary between a difficult past and contemporary optimism. In a way, the retrofitted Deutsche Bank does the same: It stands for a polluting, old building made new with the help of today's resource-efficient construction methods.

国家体育场，华沙
National Stadium, Warsaw

Society and Responsibility

基督教会海淀堂
北京，中国

如何以一个非传教士的身份在中国这样一个非基督教国家进行教堂设计？

在中国的首都北京修建一座基督教堂并不是一件轻松的事。中国没有基督教传统，所以设计中必须凸显基督文脉。但是，出于对其他各宗教传统以及城市特有的发展现状的尊重，基督教堂的建造必须谨小慎微。

教堂自由弯曲的形状是对建筑双重职责的集中体现，从周围的商业建筑中脱颖而出，同时完美融入"书城"和中关村文化大厦之间的景观空间。教堂的弯曲形状指引了一条视觉轴线。教堂的艺术性在结构因素中有所体现：表皮采用白色弯曲立面搭配细而长的玻璃窗，既保证了连贯性，又为教堂建立了视觉联系。这为教堂内部营造了特殊的光照氛围，与建筑的宗教功能相契合。

巨大的十字架明确标示教堂主入口，辨识度极高。入口从立面有机扩展而来，它之于建筑如同建筑之于周围城市环境。它脱颖而出，但又是整体的有机组成部分。因此设计中彰显了教堂的社会和（跨）文化属性：既保有自我意识又不失好客姿态，既具独立精神又不失合作态度。

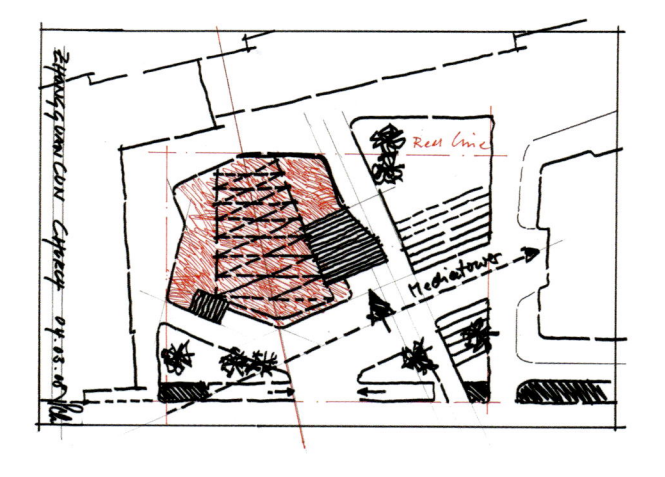

/

Christian Church
Beijing, China

How do I promote Christ in a non-Christian country without acting like a missionary?

Building a Christian church in China's capital – and the country's largest at that – is no ordinary assignment. China has no Christian tradition, so the church had to emphasize this context all the more. However, out of respect for the other tradition in general and the specific urban situation in particular, it also had to be as subtle as possible.

The freely-curved shape of the church fulfills this double responsibility. It marks the building as individual and distinguishes it from the surrounding commercial buildings. At the same time, it fits perfectly into the park-like space between the so-called "book city" and the Zhongguancun Cultural Tower, towards which the church's curved shape directs a visual axis. Artistic expression confines itself to a structural element: the white mullions of the facade alternating with narrow, slender glass windows. It creates coherence and allows the building to "breathe" in a visual sense. This makes for a special atmosphere of light on the inside, very appropriate to the building's religious function.

A gigantic cross marks the entry in which it stands as clearly as it identifies the church as such. By developing organically from the facade, it relates to the building just as the building relates to its urban surroundings: It stands out, yet seems a natural part of the whole. Thus the social, (cross-)cultural gesture of the church is clearly represented in the design: self-conscious but inviting; individual but well-integrated.

青岛大剧院
青岛，中国

如何在山地地区中实现经济效益？

经济的腾飞使中国的大都市跃跃欲试，希望建造宏大的歌剧院和音乐厅以获得更大的经济发展。但是在中国，"大剧院"不仅仅是用作表演的独立舞台的简单结合，更多的是要成为集展览、购物、住宿等生活休闲于一体的综合性建筑，目的是实现经济利益的最大化。这种现象并不是中国独有的。换句话说，建筑除了获得经济效益，还要承担起一系列社会责任，包括营造美学价值和社会人文价值。而青岛大剧院正是这样一个典范，已经成为青岛的城市地标，包括歌剧院、音乐厅、多功能厅、媒体中心和酒店，独特的建筑实体是城市景观向连贯的建筑隐喻转变而来的结果。

青岛大剧院选址海边，崂山地区云雾缭绕，赋予了景观一抹神秘的氛围。如同一个小山丘，大剧院从自然景观中升腾而出，云一样的屋顶环绕山一样的建筑。大剧院的公共露台从周围的景观中升起，为民众打造了一个宽敞的露天广场。

大剧院略微高于景观轴线，提供了俯瞰周围壮观的自然景色的视野，并再一次印证了如何使经济利益与建筑设计相结合才能真正造福社会。

/

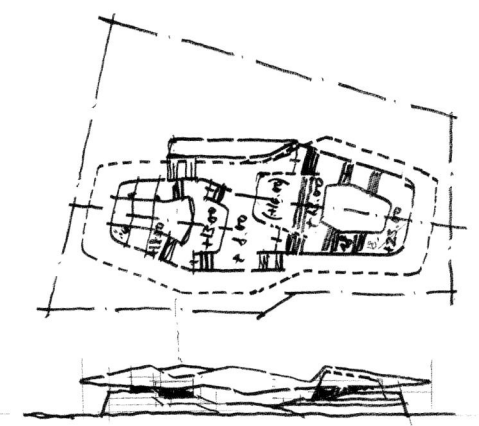

Qingdao Grand Theater
Qingdao, China

How do you connect economic interests and a mountainous region?

The economic boom has created a new desire in China's metropolises to build spectacular operas and concert halls. But in China, "Grand Theater" often means a combination of not only at least two separate stages, but also of a museum and a shopping mall, a hotel etc. This cluster is for economic optimization. This phenomenon is neither exclusive to China nor a critical point per se – so long as architecture is able to transform commercial tendencies into a consistent ensemble, give it an identity and also creates an aesthetic and social benefit for society besides economic profit. The Grand Theater achieves this is an exemplary way – and is also becoming a landmark for Qingdao. It includes an opera, a concert and multi-purpose hall, a media center and a hotel. A unique ensemble emerges from the translation of the city's landscape into coherent architectural metaphors.

Because of its unique seaside location, the Laoshan Mountain region is often veiled in mist, lending the landscape a mystical atmosphere. Just like a mountain massif, the building complex arises from the landscape while a cloud-like roof surrounds the again mountain-like buildings. Just like a mountain massif, a public patio arises from the surrounding park, creating space for an ample plaza. Slightly raised and offset from the park's axis, it offers abundant views of the landscape and again illustrates how economic and architectural interests can be unified to benefit society.

万向大厦
上海，中国

万向大厦办公大楼显示负责任的建筑是如何一方面采用含蓄克制的设计，同时又取得了独特不凡的效应。鉴于场地特殊的城市环境，要完成设计任务需要独特的解决方案：建筑坐落于黄浦江畔，与外滩码头相对，大楼与相邻的一些大厦共同构成了当地独具一格的天际线。

虽然设计旨在彰显公司的自信和立场，而且任何位于城市特色如此鲜明的地点的建筑都必须风格独具，但同时要融入当地周围环境和建筑文脉，这是任何建筑都需要遵循的法则。换句话说，仅仅通过与周边建筑形成鲜明对比而彰显出自身的特点是行不通的。有时候，为了实现自身的与众不同必须依靠一种看似保守、低调的设计方法。或许可将该方法称之为低调的张扬。

本案中建筑目标的达成得益于两方面。首先，斜截面、凸面和凹面，特别是立面的设计引人注目。建筑被白色天然石材覆盖，赋予了立面独特的雕塑般的深邃感。外部的垂直金属元素则凸显了两层楼高的开窗。

另一方面，大楼又以一种朴素、雅致、有序的姿态与整个建筑文脉相契合。同时，各个建筑体量聚合在一起而不显拥挤，独特的排列方式有助于建筑与周边环境的融合。

/

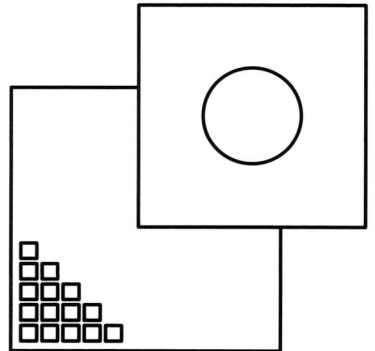

Wanxiang Plaza
Shanghai, China

The Wanxiang Plaza office building demonstrates how responsible building can involve restraint, and yet achieve an identity. Owing to the particular location in the urban setting, the design task required an exceptional solution: the building is situated directly at the Huangpu River and opposite the magnificent "Bund" waterfront, and some tower blocks in the direct neighborhood of the development form a distinctive skyline.

Although the design aimed to express the company's self-confidence – in keeping with its standing – and any building in such a prominent urban situation has to have a certain presence, a highly expressive architecture that competes with the neighboring and opposite buildings was out of the question. Sometimes, uniqueness has to be achieved with the help of a certain understatement, and a subtleness of the design, in order to achieve the desired added value for the community. One might call the solution: being conspicuously inconspicuous.

In this case, the objective was achieved on the one hand by a design which, with its truncations, projections and recesses – and above all, its facade – is anything but inconspicuous. The building is clad in white natural stone, which gives a distinct sculptural depth to the facade, with external vertical metal elements accentuating the two-story high window openings.

On the other hand, the building merges quietly, elegantly and organically into the architectural context. This is supported by the arrangement of the building volumes, which huddle together and yet do not touch.

2000年汉诺威世博会基督教馆
沃尔肯罗达，德国

如何在两个不同的地点建造一座教堂并表现出两种不同的宗教信仰？

为汉诺威世博会设计的基督馆对于gmp来说是个小项目，但却最有趣味性。建造教堂总能有一些新的发现，为世博会服务更是如此。但将基督教和天主教两个不同的宗教信仰融入到一个教堂中，使其成为一个世界级的标志性教堂，对gmp来说责任重大，同时也倍感荣幸。

以上只是设计的很小一部分：对话式设计需要一个特定的建造地点，而该场馆却是为两个截然不同的地点而建造的：既要体现出世博会作为公共场所的熙熙攘攘，同时也要保持即将在世博会后重建的沃尔肯罗达修道院的静谧。这一特殊的要求并未改变我们设计的初衷：一座宗教建筑必须彰显其宁静、平和及冥思的特点。

基督教馆的设计采用一种可拆卸和装配的组合模块体系的概念，并通过细部的处理得以体现。所选用的材料极其简单朴素，如大理石、钢、玻璃、清水混凝土、砾石和水景等。整个基督教馆在3.4m宽、6.8m高的走廊设计下呈聚合状展开。北面最底端是一个祈祷室，自然光透过垂直角度的大玻璃照射进来，增加了静谧的氛围。走廊中的窗棂设计将自然与科技相融合（比如煤、罂粟壳、点火器、齿轮等），有极高的美学价值，并迎合了世博会"人–自然–技术"的主题。

/

Christ Pavilion, Expo 2000
Volkenroda, Germany

How do you build one church for two different religious orientations and two different places?

Designed for the Expo 2000 in Hanover, the Christ Pavilion is a rather small gmp project but nonetheless one of its most interesting. Of course it is always something special to be able to build a church, all the more so at a World's fair! But to design the place of presentation for both German Christian churches, an ecumenical house for the whole of the world – is a great honor, and a great responsibility.

And that wasn't all: The method of designing in dialogue usually seeks a dialogue with a specific place, but the pavilion was planned for two places that couldn't have been more different: the bustle of the extremely public Expo and the secluded Volkenroda Abbey, where it was to be rebuilt after the Expo. This unique condition doesn't change the basic premise: A religious building must above all serve as a symbol of its purpose – tranquility, spirit, contemplation.

Emerging from these conditions was a simple, evident design that reveals the constructive details of its dismountable modular system and confines itself to just a few materials: steel, glass, concrete, marble, gravel and water. An ambulatory 3.4 meters wide and 6.8 meters tall bounds the whole of the complex and also a ceremonial room at the north end, the atmosphere of which is enhanced by natural lighting and a special verticality. The idea of filling the ambulatory's window-panes with objects of nature and technology (e.g. coal, poppy seed capsules, fire lighters, cogs) is of great aesthetic value, but also encourages contemplation of the Expo 2000's motto "Mensch, Natur, Technik" (humanity, nature, technology).

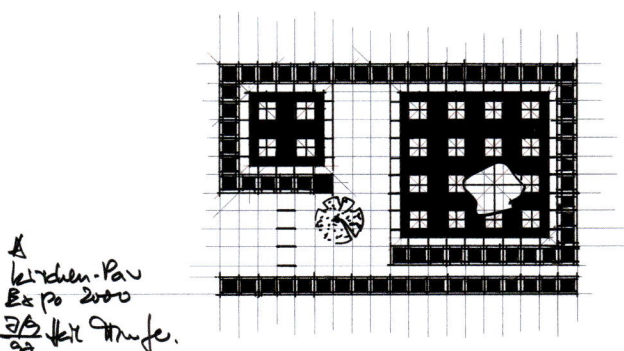

德意志银行双塔
法兰克福，德国

您如何将传统塔楼设计成环保双塔？

德意志银行的双子塔已经成为法兰克福市的地标建筑。用户对设计的要求是既要彰显出德意志银行总部的现代感以及对城市生态改造的重视，同时也要保留建筑外观的历史厚重感。

gmp为总部大楼设计了一个全新的立面，整个立面看起来与之前的没有任何区别，保温性能更好的三层玻璃折页窗立面是唯一的不同。这些折页窗一方面降低了夜晚制冷系统的消耗，同时也给整日与空调为伍的工作人员提供了呼吸新鲜空气的机会。总之，所有的措施都是为了降低能耗——二氧化碳能耗减少89%，空调能耗减少67%，电消耗减少55%，水消耗减少74%，材料再利用提高98%。建筑设备机房尺度减小，从而使得整个银行获得了额外的850m^2的办公区域。双子塔符合美国LEED白金认证以及德国DGNB可持续建筑金奖认证，这座"绿色双子塔"被公认为目前世界上最环保的摩天大楼。

事实证明，这种可持续的环保型建筑用材不但提高了环境质量，同时对整个公司及其员工都产生了极佳的效果。建筑翻新中所节省的建筑用材不但减少了工程造价，同时也提高了整栋大楼的建筑价值。

Deutsche Bank Twin Towers
Frankfurt, Germany

How do you convert conventional towers into Green Towers?

The twin towers of the Deutsche Bank have become an icon of Frankfurt's cityscape. The renewal and modernization of the company's headquarters aimed for an ecological retrofitting that would set new standards while leaving the exterior of the almost historic architectural icon unchanged.

gmp provided the towers with a completely new facade that is virtually indistinguishable from the old one. Foldout windows in the considerably better isolated triple-glazing facade are the only evidence. They serve for an energy-efficient night cooling of the building and are a blessing for those of the staff who had previously suffered from full air conditioning and a hermetically closed facade. All in all, the various measures have produced the following savings: carbon dioxide savings – 89%, cooling and heating energy – 67%, electric energy – 55%, water consumption – 74%, material recycling 98%. The scale of the building services could be reduced so much that the buildings gained an additional 850 m² of office space. With American LEED Platinum certification and a German DGNB gold certificate, the rightly so-called "Green Towers" are now considered among the most environmentally friendly skyscrapers in the world.

The fact that this was possible with an existing building shows how sustainable and responsible architectural approaches can be, even when applied to innovative modernization. It also makes clear that this is profitable in several respects: the environment benefits, but also the people in the building and the company it houses. The savings achieved through renovation quickly redeem construction costs, and the building's value even increases.

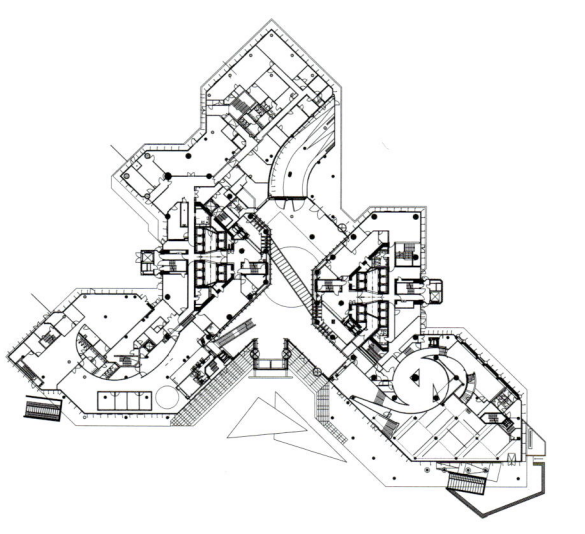

国家体育场
华沙，波兰

如何使当下的建筑永葆过去的辉煌？

如果从一开始就可以预知建筑将不仅成为一个城市的伟大象征，甚至对整个国家都举足轻重，那么"社会与责任"就将会是建筑师在设计过程中首先且重点考虑的问题。华沙的新国家体育场位于Dziesięciolecia国家体育场的山脊上。场地在二战中德国军队镇压华沙起义中被摧毁后获得了新生。深厚的民族价值要求必须维持这一地点的原貌，而其社会环境和寓意从某种角度而言也是对柏林奥林匹克体育场的一种补充。

体育场建造在旧建筑中空平台的顶部，如同加注在历史之上的皇冠。厚重的历史根基由石头堆砌而成，而新建筑则由钢、玻璃和PTFE（聚四氟乙烯）薄膜建造而来，这种二元性赋予了体育场以别具一格的形象特征，可容纳55 000名观众观看比赛。此外，由大型金属面板制作的立面采用红白两种民族色彩。体育场的另一项社会和可持续优势是可闭合屋顶，保证了在任何天气条件下都能够正常举办活动和音乐会。体育场还包括一个大办公区及相关的会议设施、一个博物馆和餐饮区。

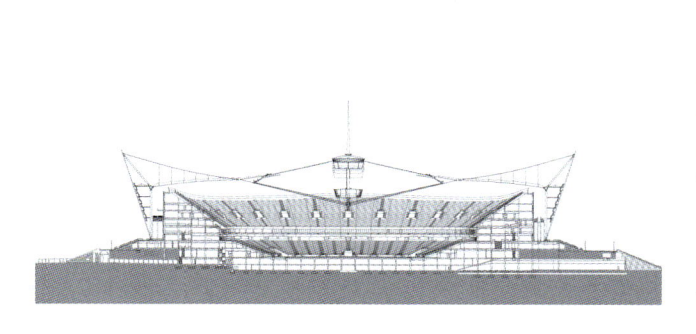

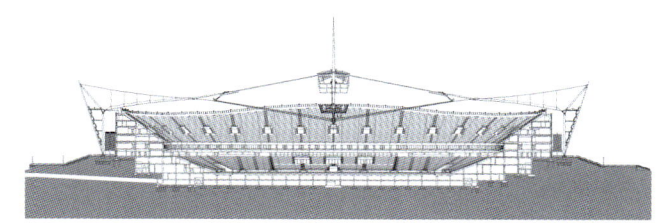

/

National Stadium
Warsaw, Poland

How does one make the present the crown of the past?

If it is obvious from the beginning that a building will have great symbolic significance not just for a city, but also for a whole country, then "society and responsibility" will have to be the architect's most important reference points when it comes to design. The new National Stadium in Warsaw is located on the ridge of the Dziesięciolecia national stadium. This had been heaped up after the war from the rubble of the old town, which was destroyed during German troops' suppression of the Warsaw Uprising in the Second World War. Due to its national significance, this mound had to remain unaffected. Considering its social conditions and implications, the stadium is – in a way – complementary to the Berlin Olympic Stadium.

The stadium has now been erected respectfully atop the terrace hollow of the old one, and thus rests on the past like a crown. The duality of the massive historic base built of stone and the new building made of steel, glass and PTFE membranes gives the soccer stadium with room for 55,000 spectators a distinctive identity. This is added to significantly by the braided facade of expanded metal panels in the national colors of red and white. The translucent layer makes a whole of the different parts within the stadium. The stadium has another social and sustainable benefit based completely in the economic present: A closable roof allows events and concerts in all weather conditions. It also includes a large office and conference facilities, a museum, and catering.

传统与现代

中国国家博物馆　北京，中国
河内博物馆　河内，越南
国家议会大厦　河内，越南
曼海姆美术馆　曼海姆，德国

Tradition versus Moderne

National Museum of China Beijing, China
Hanoi Museum Hanoi, Vietnam
Parliament House Hanoi, Vietnam
Kunsthalle Mannheim Mannheim, Germany

gmp对话式设计指导原则中最重要的对话存在于新与旧、传统与现代之间。进步是必需的，因为任何社会的需求和认知都是不断变化的。对变化无动于衷意味着停滞不前。然而，停滞不前的对立面同样是未知数。当社会加速前进，以致于切断了与历史的所有关联，丢弃了文化记忆，那么社会也将失去自我。毫无疑问，这不是进步，而是退化。哲学家保罗·维利里奥将其称之为"疾速停滞"，而避免这两种情况发生的灵丹妙药就是传统。

这些问题涉及到建筑和城市设计所扮演的双重角色，并以独特的方式表达了对美学和社会的敬意。从这一角度而言，传统对于建筑而言具有核心重要性。建筑中的创新和身份认同只有通过以负责任的态度对待传统因素才能实现。这一点放诸四海而皆准。建筑的全球化创造了许多机会，但随之而来的还有风险和隐患。举例来说，为满足全球标准而牺牲本土建筑传统和历史财富的案例屡见不鲜；老生常谈的"更大、更高、更快"的象征意义使全球的建筑和天际线都像克隆产品，而对于有深厚历史根基的与众不同的建筑语言则不加理解或不闻不问。在这种文脉下，建筑语言是否与民族和地方特色相关，是否有艺术和美学传统渊源都显得不再重要。

另一方面，不计任何代价的强迫式保护传统也是错误的解读。作曲家古斯塔夫·马勒曾经说过"传统是星火相传，而不是灰烬崇拜"。哲学家和物理学家卡尔·冯·魏茨泽克表达过同样的观点，他说"传统是有保留的进步；进步是对好传统的延续"。对于以改扩建原有老建筑为职责的建筑师而言，这样的隐喻和格言并不像乍看上去那样抽象晦涩。原因在于如果建筑师不直接、明确和公开介入历史、现在、未来之间以及新旧之间的对话，而只考虑到其中一两个方面，那么他将看不到现存事物的价值；或者在缺乏周密计划的情况下，草率地投入到历史建筑的保护过程中。他将不会有任何创作，也不会对任何事物起到保护作用。在历史城区或与靠近历史城区的场地构建新事物的建筑师面临着同样的问题。新建筑必须融入文脉，同时又不能隐藏自己的锋芒。它必须找到适合自己的表达方式，同时成为群体里的一部分。否则，建筑将不会形成自己独有的身份特征，而是会自我毁灭。

传统是动态的过程；同时"传统"也在不断地"转变"。"现代"就是从这一转化过程中衍生而来的，而不是传统的对立面。"传统"与"现代"之间有千丝万缕的联系，如果传统持续演变，那么现代也必须经历同样的过程。在今天看似是未来世界中的并因此被称之为"现代"的事物，在明天也将成为传统的一部分。20世纪20年代，社会美学运动的倡导者们创造了"现代"一词，他们绝对不会想到在几十年后，他们将被称之为"古典现代派"的代表。

涉及传统因素的建筑文脉是最多面化和最吸引人的，但同时也问题重重。好的建筑师不会对这些视而不见，而是将其视为设计的动力。许多趣味十足的矛盾体迫使建筑师在具体的传统文脉中以十足的敬意和创意进行创作，而这些矛盾体在以下案例中也有明确而独特的体现。比如，新的曼海姆艺术馆的

→ 106

河内博物馆，河内
Hanoi Museum, Hanoi

设计缓和了保存老建筑的欲望和创造新事物与开启新传统的动力之间的潜在冲突,成为典范之作。与之相反,河内博物馆则以顶部着地的方式"颠覆"了国家历史,生动的形象使年轻一代也能够理解传统之美。河内的另一建筑越南国家会议中心表明了民族传统和有代表性的象征性元素可以有独特的呈现方式,并融入意义更加宏大的文脉中。中国国家博物馆的扩建工程在扩建纪念性建筑的同时,为了传承历史,加入新元素,两者看似互相冲突,但完美融合。

/

One of the most important dialogues involved in gmp's principle of dialogue in design is the dialogue between old and new, tradition and Moderne. Progress is a necessity, because the needs and understanding of society – any society – are subject to constant change. Failing to react means stagnation. However, the opposite of stagnation can be equally as dangerous. When a society accelerates so fast that it cuts off all historic ties and loses its cultural memory, it will also lose its identity. That is not progression, but regression; or, in the words of philosopher Paul Virilio, "hurtling stagnation". The idea that helps to avoid both of these is that of tradition.

These problems concern the dual role of architecture and urban design in a special way with respect to aesthetic and social discipline. To that extent, tradition is of central importance to architecture. Innovation and identity in architecture are not possible without a responsible approach to tradition. This is as true on the global stage as it is on the regional one. The globalization of architecture offers many opportunities, but it also brings with it many dangers. For example, when a global standard architecture is created at the expense of the historic wealth of regional building traditions. When the banal symbolism of "bigger, higher, faster" produces worldwide clone-like buildings and skylines, and a differentiated architectural language that has its roots in history is no longer understood and heard. In that context it does not matter whether this architectural language is related to a national or regional identity in a social sense, or whether it has an affinity with a certain artistic, aesthetic tradition.

On the other hand, compulsive preservation at any cost is misunderstanding the issue. "Tradition is passing on the fire, not revering the ash", said the composer Gustav Mahler. The philosopher and physicist, Carl-Friedrich von Weizsäcker, expressed the same thought in this way: "Tradition is progress preserved, progress is tradition continued."

→ 82

中国国家博物馆,北京
National Museum of China, Beijing

For an architect whose task it is to extend or convert an old existing building, such metaphors and maxims sound much less abstract than they might at first appear. Because, if this architect does not enter directly, visibly and publicly into the dialogue between history, the present and the future, between old and new, when he thinks only of one or the other – he will either devalue what is existing, or engage in ill-conceived historic building preservation. He will not create anything, nor will he preserve anything. An architect who is building something new in, or adjacent to, a historically grown ensemble faces a similar problem. His building must fit in, but without keeping its head down. It must have its own expression, and yet be part of a group. Otherwise, it will not have an identity, but simply de(sturb) stroy it.

Tradition is a dynamic process; "tradition" is always also, and always already, "transformation". "Moderne" is what results from that transformation process – rather than the antithesis of tradition. The two terms are inextricably linked; if tradition keeps evolving on an ongoing basis, the Moderne, of necessity, will have to do the same. What today seems to encapsulate the future – and for this reason is called "modern" – will tomorrow have become part of tradition. In the 1920s, the protagonists of the socio-aesthetic movement who coined the term "Moderne" would not have dreamt that a few decades later they would be called representatives of the "classical Moderne".

There is no context that is more multi-faceted and attractive, but also problematic, than that resulting from having to deal with tradition. A good architect will not ignore it, but consider it a driver of his design. The many interesting contradictions which force the architect to be respectful and creative when he builds in specific contexts of tradition become evident in their own way in the examples collected here. The design for the new Kunsthalle in Mannheim moderates in an exemplary way the potential conflict between the desire to preserve the old and the drive to create something new and start a new tradition. By contrast, the architecture of the National Museum in Hanoi literally turns the country's history on its head – and thereby makes it accessible and graphically comprehensible again to the younger generation. The Vietnamese parliament building – another design for Hanoi – shows how national tradition and representative symbolism can be distinctly represented and, at the same time, integrated in a larger context of meaning. The extension to the Chinese National Museum involved the seemingly conflicting task of expanding a building of monumental architecture and, in order to succeed, of imposing a new restraint.

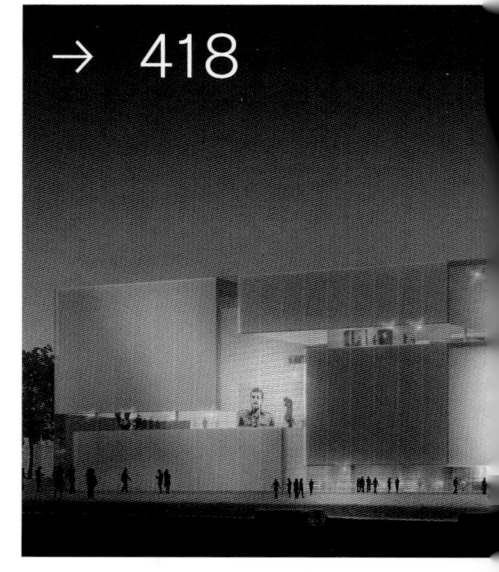

→ 418

曼海姆美术馆，曼海姆
Kunsthalle Mannheim, Mannheim

→ 184

国家议会大厦，河内
Parliament House, Hanoi

Tradition versus Moderne

中国国家博物馆
北京，中国

如何做到在尊重历史建筑形式语言的同时，将丰富的传统转化为更适宜的建筑形式？

这一问题也是位于北京天安门广场的中国国家博物馆项目中所面临的挑战之一。它需要牺牲中央建筑，将现有的南北侧翼连接为一个充满凝聚力的建筑综合体，因为不加筛选全面保留现有传统的风格来进行博物馆扩建将使建筑整体美学显得夸张而充满争议。这与试图打动人心的传统是背道而驰的，因为有争议性的美学在任何传统中都不会令人印象深刻。

260m的长廊提供了进入新的综合体的通道，中部外扩，将广场和原有建筑入口联系起来。新建的"会场大厅"充当门厅和多功能场馆，提供了通往所有公共设施的入口。

新建筑面积达192 000m²，是目前全球最大的博物馆。然而，尽管规模庞大，但博物馆并不令人感觉"高不可攀"。明亮的建筑强调公共特性，白色花岗岩、方格天花板和棕色木材饰面间的和谐对话进一步凸显了这一点。新建筑檐口简约的设计显示了如何以负责任的方式缓和了建筑严肃的氛围。

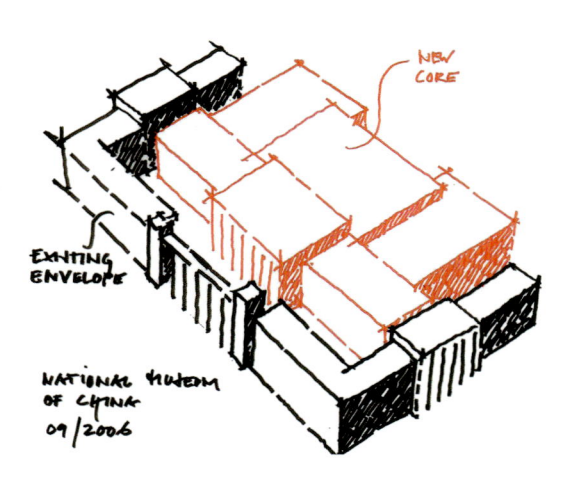

/

National Museum of China
Beijing, China

How is it possible to respect a monumental architectural pattern language with a rich tradition and at the same time to translate it into a more moderate architecture?

This question arises as part of the task of linking the existing northern and southern wings of the Chinese National Museum in Beijing at Tiananmen Square into a cohesive building complex – while sacrificing the center building. Because simply extending the already huge museum by perpetuating the existing tradition of the monumental style without any filter would result in a questionable – because exaggerated – overall aesthetic. And that would also be contrary to a tradition that wants to impress, because a questionable aesthetic never achieves such an aim in any tradition.

A 260 meter long hall provides access to the new complex. It widens out in the center and thereby establishes a relationship between the square and the portal of the existing building. The newly created "forum" serves as foyer and multi-functional venue which provides access to all functions relevant to the public.

Today, with its 192,000 sqm, the Museum is one of the largest in the world. However, in spite of its size, the Museum does not feel intimidating. With its brightness, the building emphasizes its public character, which is further supported by the harmonious dialogue between the white granite, the coffered ceiling and the brown timber cladding in the gallery. The rather simpler design of the parapets on the new buildings is another example of how it is possible to tone down the tradition of the monumental in a responsible way.

河内博物馆
河内，越南

如何打造新的形式以保存历史？

"对于从父辈那里继承而得的遗产，必须做到真正地消化吸收，并将其转化为自己源源不断的财富。"歌德的《浮士德》所表达的精髓是，文化传承的责任不仅仅是简单的保留，而是应该开辟新的表现方式。

河内博物馆外形独特，既采用又保留了历史和文化传统。建筑形状以极其抽象的方式"创造"了历史——头顶着地。倒置的阶梯状金字塔形成了宇庙式的氛围，悬挑屋顶平台同样令人联想到越南宝塔。建筑本身提供了阴凉遮蔽，既节能又有利于展品的保护。此外，建筑看上去给人悬浮空中之感，参观者向外看去也获得同样的体验。典型的越南装饰风格在立面形态中重现，体现了越南文化传统的传承。

建筑楼梯间的形态在主题公园中重现：铺设有梯形水阶的湖泊一路直达建筑，展品装点着基底，直接联系内外。秉持着轻松、开放的心态，通过抽象化和多样化的处理保留了建筑的历史性。

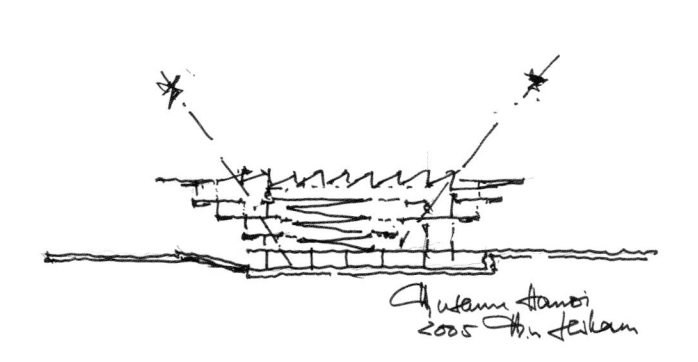

/

Hanoi Museum
Hanoi, Vietnam

How does one preserve history by giving it a new form?

"What from your father you've inherited, You must earn again, to own it straight." What Goethe's Faust essentially says is that responsibility towards cultural heritage has to consist of more than just its preservation. It should also be made accessible in a new way.

With its characteristic form, the Hanoi Museum both adapts and preserves its historic and cultural heritage. The building's shape "earns" history by – in a very abstract way – literally standing on its head. The upside down, terraced pyramid creates a temple-like pathos and, with its overhanging roof platform, also evokes associations of a Vietnamese pagoda. The building provides shadow for itself, not only saving energy, but also creating a conservational benefit for the exhibits. Another effect: Looking at the building, you get the impression that it is hovering, as does the visitor peering out from inside. While the concept of weightlessness is varied on the interior with the spiral form of a sweeping visitor ramp, Vietnamese cultural heritage reappears in the facade in form of the stylized ornamentation that is characteristic for the country.

The building's staircase shape reappears in the museum park: A lake with water steps seems to extend right up to the building, exhibits adorning its base and creating a direct connection between inside and out. History is preserved by dealing with it in an easy and open-minded way, and by making it accessible through abstraction and variation.

国家议会大厦

河内，越南

没有任何一种建筑类型比议会建筑更需要以极大的敬意全面表现民族传统和象征意义。这意味着对于gmp来说，设计位于河内的越南国家会议中心的任务既是无上的光荣，也是重大的责任。

对象征性表达的探索不流于浮夸，而体现在深深植根于越南传统中的精妙的形式语言中，比如圆形代表"太阳父亲"，方形代表"地球母亲"。

建筑体量的基础为圆形，与方形建筑相结合。庭院式的进凹空间提供了通向所有房间的便捷的通道，并保证了高质量的日光照射。同时，封闭空间的结构充满律动，与铺满植被的室内庭院共同定义了建筑外观，而不是由办公室开窗的重复性设计决定的。

议会大厦不可过于张扬的原因之一在于环绕其四周的景观。尽管由于功能使然，建筑必然是独一无二的，但会议中心依然巧妙融入博物馆公园中。通过采用公园基本的网格设计和庭院式的进凹空间与自然之间的互动，国家会议中心成为整体环境中和谐存在的一部分。而这又成为对传统本质的强有力的注解：不是为了传统而传统，而是以整体为重。

/

Parliament House

Hanoi, Vietnam

Hardly any type of building must architecturally represent national tradition and symbolism more thoroughly and more respectfully than a parliament building. This meant that the commission to design the Vietnamese parliament building in Hanoi was as honoring as it was a responsibility.

Symbolic expression is not sought with a grand gesture, but with the subtle means of a pattern language that is deeply anchored in Vietnam's tradition: the elementary shapes of a circle (representing "sun/father") and a square ("earth/mother").

The building volume is based on the shape of a circle which is bounded by a square building. Recesses in the form of courtyards provide efficient access to all rooms, as well as good quality daylight. At the same time, they create an external appearance which is not determined by the repetition of office window fenestration, but by the rhythmic structure of enclosed spaces and planted inner courtyards.

One reason for not allowing the parliament building to become too dominant is the landscape which surrounds it. Although the building is unique – which it has to be given its function – it also deliberately blends in with the Museum Park. By adopting the basic grid of the park in the design, and through the interaction with nature by way of the courtyard-like recesses, the parliament building becomes a harmonious part of the entire whole. In turn, this makes a strong statement on the nature of this tradition: it is not serving itself, but a greater whole.

曼海姆艺术馆
曼海姆，德国

在新建曼海姆艺术馆的过程中，gmp着力在发扬传统的同时开拓创新。曼海姆的珍贵传统在现有展馆的映衬下显得愈发举足轻重。新建筑四周被古铜色的金属结构环绕，既与区域内普遍存在的红色沙岩建筑形成对话，又彰显了对历史的无限敬意。在现有的建筑中，沙岩是曼海姆建筑传统的集中体现。另一方面，建筑设计独树一帜，标志着新纪元的开始，并在城市发展史中留下深刻印记，作为一个值得纪念的场馆影响几代人。

这一深远意义的形成还得益于艺术馆的发展与曼海姆内城的棋盘式布局之间的紧密联系。这一结构在新的艺术馆中得到了淋漓尽致的体现：设计由若干个立方体组合而成，高度和宽度各异，打破了规则的外形，开放的空间形成广场。虽说艺术馆的立面是最鲜明的特色，并使建筑成为独一无二、极具辨识度的城市地标，但建筑宽度和屋檐高度的设计又建立了与周围历史建筑的紧密联系。

这些特点意味着艺术馆将曼海姆传统中的艺术性、城市设计风格和建筑特色融为一体，三位一体的呼应关系为新传统的到来奠定了基础。

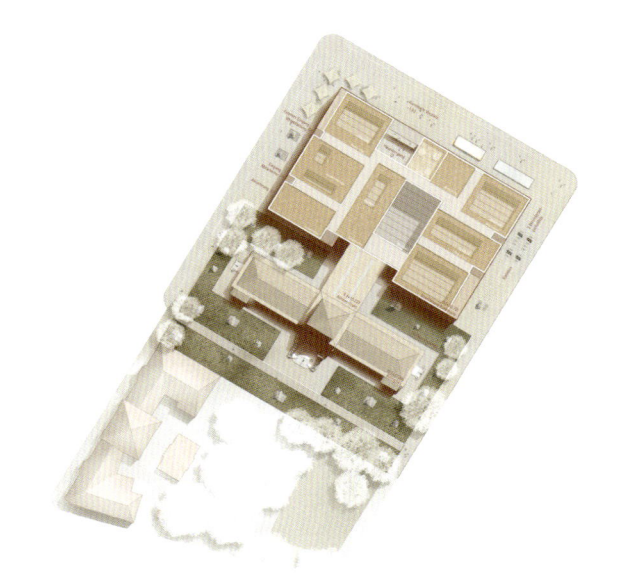

/

Kunsthalle Mannheim
Mannheim, Germany

With its design for the new construction of Kunsthalle Mannheim, gmp intended to continue a tradition and also starts a new one. Mannheim's important tradition, highlighted by the existing exhibition building, is honored by the copper-colored metal fabric that encloses the new building, which enters into a respectful dialogue with the red sandstone that is common in the region – the very sandstone which, in the existing building, reaches the pinnacle of Mannheim's architectural tradition. On the other hand, the building is intended to be distinct enough to mark the beginning of a new era and to make its imprint on the city as a memorable venue that straddles generations.

This is also achieved by relating the development to a special feature of Mannheim's inner city, the layout of which is designed in the manner of a chess board. This structure is taken up by the new Kunsthalle: the design is a composition of cubes, the regularity of which is broken up by offsetting them by height and width and by opening up spaces to form squares. While the facade of the Kunsthalle is its significant identification characteristic and makes the building into a unique and recognizable landmark, the design also picks up a relationship with the historic neighboring buildings, for example in the width and eaves height of the building.

All these characteristics mean that the Kunsthalle negotiates three of Mannheim's traditions all at once: an artistic one, an urban design one and an architectural one. And the result of these negotiations will hopefully lay the foundations for a new tradition.

创新与自我风格

摩西·马布海达体育场　德班，南非
莱比锡新会展中心　莱比锡，德国
柏林奥林匹克体育场改建和屋顶加建工程　柏林，德国
古纳别墅　丘马拉，拉脱维亚
亚马逊体育场　马瑙斯，巴西
国家体育场　巴西利亚，巴西

Innovation and Identity

Moses Mabhida Stadium Durban, South Africa
New Leipzig Trade Fair Leipzig, Germany
Berlin Olympic Stadium, Reconstruction and Roofing Berlin, Germany
Guna Villa Jurmala, Latvia
Arena da Amazônia Manaus, Brazil
Estádio Nacional Brasilia, Brazil

建筑与人具有共同的特点，或换言之，应该具有同一个共同特征，即自我风格。缺乏个性的人虽不一定是坏人，但可能会无趣、缺乏激情与态度或不善言谈。没有人能够或乐于与缺乏自我风格的人相识相交，甚至都不会注意到他的存在。对于建筑而言也是如此。没有鲜明形象特征的建筑不是好建筑，因为它可以被其他任何形式取而代之。好的建筑一定是具体的，并且能够传达一定的信息。这种信息可以有不同的呈现形式。建筑可以表达个人、团体、城市或一个国家的理念；可以讲述传统与现代、文化与自然、技术与功能以及美学之间的关系和故事。功能是创造建筑形象特色的一部分，而纯功能性的设计则忽略了这一事实。自我风格并不仅仅意味着与众不同。其最高尚也是最重要的任务是创造显而易见的形象特征。

建筑是艺术的社会化应用，建筑是为人而建造，而不是为了建造而建造。为了在建筑周围活动或使用建筑的人考量，建筑必须具备两方面的特质：首先，人们必须认可建筑是特别的存在（独一无二），可以与建筑展开充满趣味性的谈话；其次，人们必须认同建筑及其所传达的信息。形象创造对话，对话激活形象。"建筑的自我风格"所蕴含的深意绝不是无中生有，而是特殊文脉的产物。自我的特征不能够被创造，只能在找寻之后被挖掘出来。像gmp一样通过对话式设计，从任务的本质中、从文化背景中、从特殊的功能和独特的施工方式中探寻形象特征。建筑特色不是可以短期速成或随意发生的，而且与发展趋势无关，其本质是更加可持续和复杂的。

通过保留复杂的理念可以形成独特的自我风格，这一定是所有建筑师对原有建筑进行加建或改建时所坚持的核心思想。如果建筑师不建立新旧建筑之间的对话，而是仅仅关注其中某一方面，那么将导致两种后果的发生：其一，他将抹杀原有建筑的价值；或者，他将误读保护历史遗迹的真正含义，从而与其背道而驰，渐行渐远。他将不会有任何创作，也不会对任何事物起到保护作用。在历史城区或靠近历史城区的场地内构建新事物的建筑师同样应该扪心自问，他们所构建的新建筑必须融入文脉，同时又不能隐藏自己的锋芒。它必须找到适合自己的表达方式，同时成为群体里的一部分。否则，建筑将不会形成自己独有的形象特征，而是会自我毁灭。作曲家古斯塔夫·马勒曾经说过"传统是星火相传，而不是灰烬崇拜"。从这个角度来说，创新就是在现有事物的基础上创造新事物，而这也正是创新的原则。（拉丁语中的"创新"等同于"更新"，"innovare"="renew"）

今天，创新主要与科技相关。事实上，人们经常将建筑特色与技术进步联系起来。除了老生常谈的更高、更大和更加壮丽恢弘的建筑，许多经久不衰的标志性设计必须以不断的进步为前提，才能成为现实。社会进步改变着人们对于建筑与自我风格之间关系的看法。举例来说，没有技术创新，可持续性和环境友好型设计基本是无法实现的。而这些价值观现在已经成为构成建筑特色的一部分。创新与自我风格的关系问题由来已久，自从有建筑之日起就已存在。哥特式教堂中的天花板拱顶令一种"非人间"的距离感油然而生，彩虹般五颜六色的光源照射着墙壁，预示着神圣的耶路撒冷。但这背后的石材结构在中世纪时期还属于构造工艺领域的高科技，令人印象深刻。将施工艺术与工程艺术分隔开来的理念绝对是错误的，它们如同一枚硬币的两面，两相结合才能形成完整的结构。

→ 252

摩西·马布海达体育场，德班
Moses Mabhida Stadium, Durban

→ 338

柏林奥林匹克体育场改建和屋顶加建工程，柏林
Berlin Olympic Stadium,
Reconstruction and Roofing, Berlin

针对创新与科技而言，有两种特殊的建筑类型是建筑特性的最佳代言，即体育场和商品交易中心。这两种建筑需要建筑师、工程师等多方面的努力，并都与社会有独特的联系。体育场通常被赋予了更深层次的象征意义，而贸易中心则有明确的建造目标，那就是展示、介绍、支持和销售各种创新产品。如果说柏林奥林匹克体育场建立了建筑与历史的对话，亚马逊体育场建立了建筑与周围环境的对话，巴西利亚国家体育场建立了建筑与现有建筑体块的对话，迪拜摩西·马布海达体育场建立了建筑与特别的象征意义之间的对话，莱比锡和里米尼博览会展馆应用的创新型施工手段之间形成了对话，那么将产生关于创新与形象特色之间独立而新颖别致的观点。就这一点而言，古纳别墅或许可以作为小型结构的代表，但就形象特色而言，它建立了最密切的对话，即主人与自己的住宅之间的对话。

/

→ 296

莱比锡新会展中心，莱比锡
New Leipzig Trade Fair, Leipzig

Buildings and people have a common trait: an identity. At least, they should have one. A person lacking individual character isn't necessarily a bad person. But he is boring, uninspiring, lacking attitude and a dull conversation partner. Without an identity, no one can or wants to identify with him. More than likely, you wouldn't even notice him in the first place. The same goes for buildings. A building lacking identity is a bad one, architecturally speaking, because it could just as well be a different one. A good building is always specific. It carries a message. This type of message can take various forms. Architecture can relate something about an individual person, a group, a city, or a country. It can tell a story about the relations between tradition and modernity, culture and nature, aesthetics, technology and function. Purely functional design overlooks the fact that it is part of architecture's role to create identity. And this isn't only about being distinctive. One of its noblest and most important tasks is to create an outward identity.

Architecture is art applied to society; it is made for people, not for its own sake. In order to create an identity not just for the building itself, but also for the people around it or using it, two kinds of identity are necessary: People have to be able to identify the building as something special (by its distinctiveness) or as an interesting dialogue partner, so to speak. But they must also be able to identify with it and with its message. Identity creates dialogue, and dialogue creates identity. Whatever is meant by "architectural identity" does not come from nowhere. There is always a context, something to relate to. Identity cannot be invented, only be found. You have to look

for it first. Designing in dialogue, as gmp does, searches for identity in the nature of the task, on site, in the cultural context, in special functions and particular ways of construction. Without this dialogue, no more than a simulation of identity is possible. Built identity isn't short-lived or random, and it has nothing to do with trends. It is more sustainable and complex in nature.

A complex idea could, for example, be the concept of creating identity by preserving it. This must be the central idea of every architect adding on to or converting an existing building. If he or she does not engage this dialogue between new and old, but instead concentrates on only on one or the other, then he will either de-value the existing building or pursue a misunderstood kind of monument -protection. He will create nothing and preserve nothing. Architects who build something new within or next to a historical ensemble have to ask themselves a similar question. Their buildings have to fit in without "ducking". They have to be individual and yet part of a group. If not, they will not create identity, but disturb or even destroy it. "Tradition is passing the fire, not worshipping the ashes," composer Gustav Mahler said. In this sense, the novel and the creator of identity is always something that creates new things from the existing. This is the principle of innovation (Lat.: "innovare" = "renew").

Today, innovation is mainly associated with technology. As a matter of fact, architectural identity is often connected to technological progress. Beyond the banal higher, bigger, and more spectacular, many lasting iconic designs have only become feasible by progress in the first place. Progress also changes ideas concerning the relation between architecture and identity itself. Sustainability and environmental friendliness, for example, are often impossible to achieve without technical innovations. At the same time, these values now constitute an integral part of architectural identity. The connection between innovation and identity, however, is as old as architecture itself. The ceiling vaults of Gothic cathedrals evoke a feeling of superhuman distance and, in connection with the dissolved walls re-

→ 430

亚马逊体育场，马瑙斯
Arena da Amazônia, Manaus

→ 370

古纳别墅，丘马拉
Guna Villa, Jurmala

Jerusalem. But the stone structure behind this is the medieval high technology of an impressive constructive logic. It would be a misunderstanding to separate between the art of constructing and the art of engineering. They are two sides of the same coin, and together, they form the structure's identity.

Concerning innovation and technology, two particular types of building projects are especially suitable for illustrating the identity of and through architecture: stadiums and trade fair halls. Both types of building require sophisticated efforts from architects and engineers alike, and both are relevant to society in special ways. Stadiums are often loaded with a stronger symbolic significance while trade fair halls are built explicitly to present, explain, support and sell innovations of all kinds.

If a building enters into dialogue with history, such as the Berlin Olympic Stadium, and with its surroundings, such as the Arena da Amazônia in Manaus, and with the existing building stock, such as the Estádio Nacional in Brasília – or if a dialogue develops between a special symbolic significance and a building such as the Moses Mabhida Stadium in Durban, and if a dialogue develops from innovative construction means used at the trade fairs in Leipzig and Rimini, then individual, original statements on innovation and identity emerge. Guna Villa may stand here as an example of buildings at the smaller end of the scale, and it holds the most intimate dialogue of all when it comes to identity: the one between a person and his or her own house.

→ 434

国家体育场，巴西利亚
Estádio Nacional, Brasilia

Innovation and Identity

摩西·马布海达体育场
德班，南非

如何从一个标志性符号中创造出多个衍生符号？

为了迎接2010年南非世界杯，在开普敦和德班分别建造了体育场。但是两地所面临的实际工作却完全不同。在城市风光和自然风光的大背景下，开普敦的体育场低调亮相。而德班市长的态度却截然相反："我们的体育场要成为地图上显著的一笔！"摩西·马布海达体育场要成为德班的象征，好比悉尼歌剧院之于悉尼的意义。

象征联系的拱形设计在建筑上并不是首次出现，但不同的是，此次gmp建筑师事务所为其附加了另外两个标志性符号，并与施莱希工程设计咨询公司的设计师们竭诚合作，以纯概念性设计和技术创新满足其基本的功能性。织物顶棚悬架于拱形部分之上，纵向对称地横跨整个总长超过350m的椭圆形体育场，以此构成了数里以外就能看到的地标性建筑。拱形部分在南端一分为二，朝向城市开放。该分叉设计既充当体育馆的主入口，又是风格独具城市大门。从空中鸟瞰，不禁让人联想起南非的国旗。

此外，体育场本身还为观众提供了鸟瞰的机会，拱形结构的底部备有缆车，可升至高达105m的顶部平台，一览印度洋和德班的风光。德班居民抬头仰望巨大的拱形结构即可辨别出他们的城市，但是当他们低头从拱形结构向下俯视城市时，将会获得全新的体验。

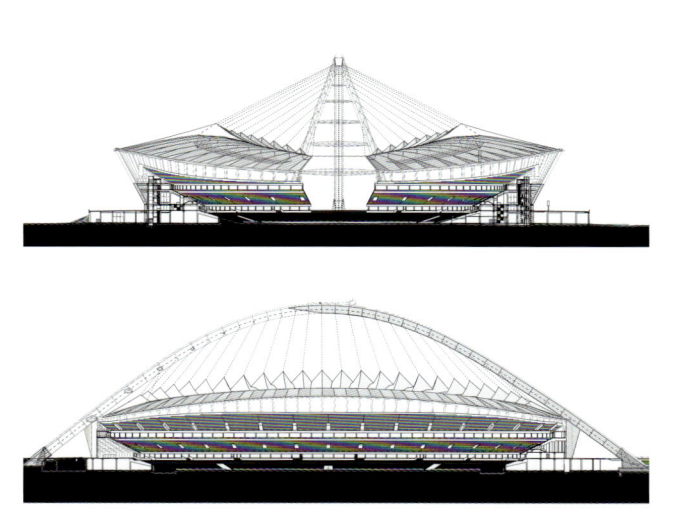

/

Moses Mabhida Stadium
Durban, South Africa

How do I create many symbols from one symbol?

The occasion for building the stadiums in Cape Town and Durban was the same: the 2010 Soccer World Cup in South Africa. But the task could not have been more different. While the stadium in Cape Town won its identity by keeping a low profile against the backdrop of the urban and natural landscape, the mayor of Durban asked for exactly the opposite: "Put us on the map!" The Moses Mabhida Stadium was supposed to become for Durban what the Opera is for Sydney: the emblem.

The arch as a symbol of connection is not new. But the way that gmp loaded it with two additional symbols and, in a tried and trusted collaboration with the structural engineers at schlaich bergermann und partner, made it an elementary functional element – this is pure conceptual and technical innovation. The arch, from which the textile tent roof is suspended and which also diminishes its weight, spans the oval of the stadium symmetrically over the 350-meter longitudinal direction and constitutes a landmark that is visible for miles around. The arch forks at the south end, thus opening towards the city: Its opening acts as both a main entrance to the stadium and a stylized city gate. Seen from a bird's-eye view, it also reminiscent of the South African flag.

Moreover, it offers a bird's-eye view of visitors themselves: Moving from the arch's foot is a cable car that ascends to a platform at its apex which, with 105 meters in height, offers an unrivaled panorama view of the Indian Ocean and Durban. This is more than just a joke: The inhabitants of Durban can identify with their city when raising their eyes up towards the arch – but they can also literally identify the city anew when looking down from the arch.

莱比锡新会展中心
莱比锡，德国

如何构建天堂？

不言而喻，一个展会大厅应该具备功能完善、运营高效和交通便利等特点。但是，考虑到博览会的开放度和参加人群摩肩接踵的境况，展厅除具备以上特点外，必须做到更好。关于这一点，莱比锡是最佳代言。

"构筑天堂之梦"是德国一家大报社对综合体的玻璃主厅的设想和形容，80m的大跨度和240m长的结构辉煌华丽。巨大的木框架拱形结构横跨大厅，玻璃外壳悬浮于拱形结构之上，而没有任何一个接点。每个1.5m×3m大小的玻璃嵌板四点固定，一起构成了一个巨大的玻璃桶，平坦光滑。这种结构令人感觉置身在开放的天空下，而且在全球也尚属首例，这再次说明建筑的天堂往往只能借助创意十足的工程设计才能够实现。展厅的环境务必是具有实用性的：博览会主要是为众人提供见面和沟通的场所，鼓励开展有建设性的对话交流。

这座20世纪末期的水晶宫迅速成为莱比锡的里程碑。这与在两德统一后不久组织有序和快速施工的博览会不无关系，并成为所有德国人寻求身份认同感的主要来源。

/

New Leipzig Trade Fair
Leipzig, Germany

How do you build heaven?

It goes without saying that a trade fair hall must be functional, logistically efficient, easy to reach etc. But it can be so much more – must be so much more if one considers how public a trade fair is and how many people gather there – and the Neue Messe Leipzig can demonstrate this like maybe no other in the world.

"The dream of a built heaven" is how a large German newspaper seems to have perceived the complex's glass main hall, with its resplendent 80 meter span and 240 meters in length. It is spanned by large, timber-framed arches, from which a glass shell is suspended without a single joint. Each of the 1.5×3 meters-large glass panels is attached at four points; together they result in a gigantic glass barrel that is completely smooth and lacking any profile on the inside. This structure generates the impression of being under an open sky and was a world premiere, which once again goes to show that the architectural heavens can often only be reached with the help of creative, innovative engineering. The hall's atmosphere, though, is by all means functional: A trade fair is mainly a place for lots of people to meet and communicate, and a meeting in the open encourages communication conducted in a constructive spirit.

The Crystal Palace of the late 20th century quickly became Leipzig's landmark. And not least due to the extremely well-organized, rapid construction of the trade fair shortly after the German reunification, it has also become a source of overall German identity.

柏林奥林匹克体育场改建和屋顶加建工程
柏林，德国

如何实现宣传性建筑向歌剧院的完美蜕变？

2006年足球世界杯赛场——柏林奥林匹克体育场在改扩建过程中遇到的最大问题莫过于历史问题：如何将希特勒在1936年奥运会时用以宣传其势力的舞台，在70年后转换成具有积极意义的全球性赛事竞技场，与全世界人民共襄盛举，并且在毫不隐藏或否定其复杂历史的情况下完成身份的转换。

而技术上同样面临严峻的挑战：如何将一个几近破损且配备有混凝土长椅的露天竞技场改造成现代体育场？足球赛事特有的氛围能否在这样一个宽阔的、多功能体育场中得到展现？这无疑是将一个希腊式圆形露天剧场转化为米兰的斯卡拉歌剧院。

出于对历史设计的尊重，所有必要的新建筑都建于场馆外的地下区域。比赛场地降低了2.65m，如此一来原有的老旧的下层看台可以一层层更换成更加靠近比赛场地的新座椅，加强观赛体验。而最重要的改变是顶部，和体育场本身一样，它并不是封闭的，而是一端开放。这样，从东门穿过体育场到达场外钟楼的视觉轴线即使在改造之后也依然存在。精妙的结构和表层材料刻意将其与历史建筑的固体构造区分开来。顶部还有独特的照明系统，使内部产生如斯卡拉歌剧院般的剧院效果。

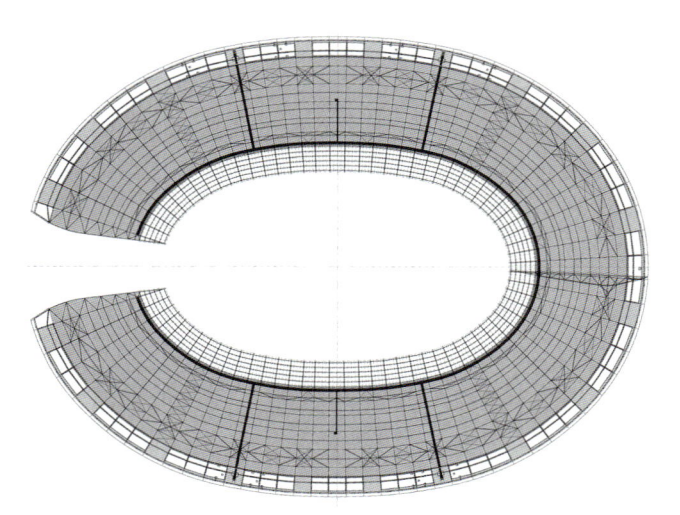

/

Berlin Olympic Stadium, Reconstruction and Roofing
Berlin, Germany

How do you convert propaganda architecture into an opera with a happy end?

The biggest problem in the conversion and extension of the Berlin Olympic Stadium for the 2006 Soccer World Cup was a historical one: How could the identity of the arena, which Hitler used to great effect for his propaganda during the Olympic Games of 1936, be transformed in such a way that, 70 years later, it would radiate the absolutely positive identity of a global event that brings the world's people together? And this without hiding or denying its difficult history?

The technical challenge was no less tremendous: How do you convert a half-rotten, open-air arena with concrete benches into a modern stadium? And can a proper soccer atmosphere even develop in such a spacious, multipurpose-stadium? Just imagine converting a Greek amphitheater into Milan's La Scala.

Out of respect for the historic design, all necessary new buildings were erected underground outside the stadium. The playing field was lowered by 2.65 meters so that, step-by-step, the non-restorable, old lower stand could be replaced with a new one closer to the playing field, intensifying the experience of the game. But the most important aspect of the conversion was the roof, which, like the stadium itself, is not a closed circle but open at one end. Thus the visual axis from the east gate across the stadium towards the bell tower outside was preserved even after conversion. Its delicate structure and the choice of surface materials deliberately set it apart from the solid tectonics of the historic building. The roof also contains a unique lighting system that can make the interior appear almost as theatrical as La Scala.

古纳别墅
丘马拉,拉脱维亚

如何创造自由随意的张力?

建筑是一种承担着社会和功能职责的艺术形式。这几方面的完美融合是形成建筑特质的基础。但有时建筑就是单纯的艺术。位于拉脱维亚尤尔马拉波罗的海海岸的古纳别墅就体现了这一点,深入人心。它是对经典现代主义的全新解读,并表现了满腔敬意,作为一座自给自足的雕塑住宅屹立在常绿松木林中。

建筑形状之间以及建筑与周边环境之间的对话赋予了别墅艺术特性。古纳别墅代表着将对比性元素和谐融入一个形象中的艺术,而不是消解这种差异性。深绿色的森林和亮白的室内环境通过差异比对,带给人全新的感受。分明的棱角和弯曲因素的对比赋予了立方体建筑独特的魅力,比如15m高的观察台提供了俯瞰大海的视野,建筑南侧的阳台以U形开放。这种对比还形成了别墅内部全新的张力,令人神清气爽。室内组织沿不同楼层展开,由一系列坡道相连接。周围房间朝向中央空间开放,提供了观看周围自然环境的持续变换的视野,带给人以独特的空间体验。

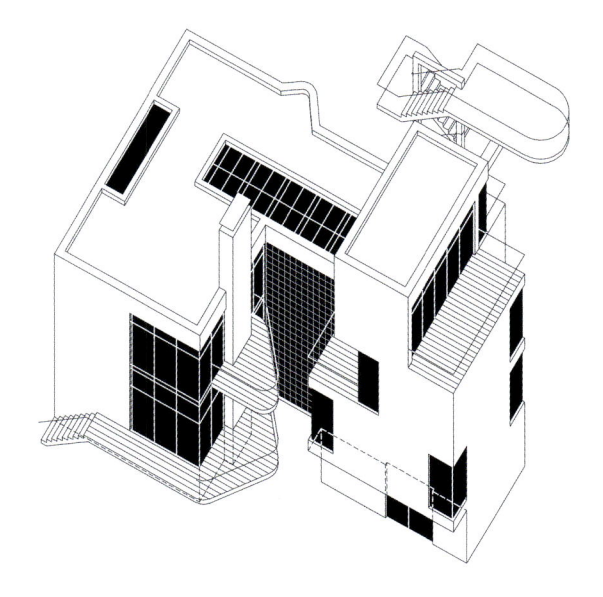

/

Guna Villa
Jurmala, Latvia

How does one build a relaxing tension?

Architecture is art with a social and a functional task. Its identity is based on the successful fusion of these aspects. But sometimes architecture is also art. Guna Villa, on the shore of the Baltic Sea in Jurmala, Latvia demonstrates this quite impressively. It is a fresh and radiating homage to Classic Modernism and yet stands as an autonomous sculpture of a house in an evergreen pinewood.

The Villa's artistic identity is again the result of dialogue: between architectural shapes on the one hand, and the building and its surroundings on the other. Guna Villa stands for the art of incorporating contrast into an identity harmoniously, without dissolving it. The dark green of the forest, the radiant white within: a pairing that, through its differences, appears all the more fresh. The cubical building itself derives a special charm from the contrast of angular and curved elements, such as the 15 meters high observation deck with a view overlooking the Sea or the balconies on the building's south side, which open into a U-shape. The contrast also creates a refreshing tension on the villa's inside. The interior is organized on split levels connected via a series of ramps. This central space, onto which the neighboring rooms open, offers constantly changing views of the natural surroundings, becoming a spatial experience in its own right.

The villa is named after its owner Guna Eglite, a friend of Latvian-born Meinhard von Gerkan's. The individual expressiveness, which lends the house its strong identity, is caused not least by the character of its owner – and the talks the architect had with her.

亚马逊体育场
马瑙斯，巴西

怎样才能令建筑在融入周边自然环境的同时不受其影响？

玛瑙斯市位于世界最大的保护区亚马逊雨林的腹地。那里常年极度炎热潮湿，使得修建这座2014年世界杯足球赛场馆成为了一项巨大挑战。基于对当地环境的尊重，一方面，建筑师和工程师们必须尽最大的可能提出环境友好型的创新建筑构思。另一方面，他们也要确保体育场内的温度能达到令人舒适的观赛环境。同样重要的还有，这样一座巨大的标志性建筑物势必要以一种标志性美学的方式来体现出其周边自然环境的壮丽恢弘。

巧妙的屋顶设计解决了这两个问题，也成为了将创新与形象特征相结合的典范。屋顶似乎编织在体育场四周，形状灵感来源于热带雨林多样化的生命形态和结构。编条式设计精美至极，排水管道的复杂和高效程度在全球范围内也是首屈一指。它担负着整个体育场45%的耗水量，并降低了建筑的湿度。弯曲的几何形屋顶延伸至建筑立面，在立面上形成自身的阴影。体育场屋顶和立面表面为半透明玻璃纤维。这一材质增强了建筑的阴影效果，但同时充分利用了日光。与立面开窗的互动形成自然的通风和舒适的微环境，温暖而不炎热。

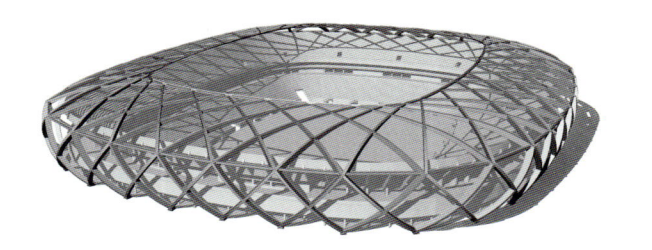

/

Arena da Amazônia
Manaus, Brazil

How can a building celebrate its natural surroundings while providing shelter from them at the same time?

In Manaus, it is hot and humid all year round – very hot and very humid. The proximity of the world's largest preserve, the Amazon Rainforest, makes building the Arena da Amazônia for the 2014 Soccer World Cup in Brazil a special challenge. Out of respect for its location, architects and engineers must on the one hand come up with innovative ideas for building that is as environmentally friendly as possible. But then again, they also have to ensure that temperatures inside of the stadium are as bearable as possible for spectators. Last but not least, such a grand building with a correspondingly great potential for identification cannot be erected without honoring its great natural surroundings in a symbolic-aesthetic way.

The answer to both problems is given in the roof design, which is exemplary for how innovation and identity come together. It seems to be woven around the stadium and takes its shape from the tropical rainforest's diverse forms and structures. This wattle work is the most beautiful, complicated and efficient gutter in the world. It delivers 45% of the stadium's water consumption and protects the building from humidity. The curved geometry of the roof merging into the facade in turn creates a self-shadowing effect on the facade. Roof and facade surfaces consist of a translucent glass fiber fabric that adds to the shadowing effect, but also makes perfect use of the daylight. The interplay with the facade openings provides for natural ventilation and a comfortable microclimate that is hot, but not too hot.

国家体育场
巴西利亚，巴西

如何使建筑设计星火相传，而木材与混凝土成为完美搭档？

"传统是火种传承，而非灰烬崇拜"。古斯塔夫·马勒十分认可并且尊重以创新的手段来处理音乐传统。同样，这种理念也适用于建筑传统。2014年世界杯将在巴西举行，针对巴西国家体育场的设计，gmp建筑师事务所和施莱希工程设计公司的结构工程师们确实拥有两把火种用来照亮其路程。

由奥斯卡·尼迈耶和卢西奥·科斯塔设计的巴西利亚城是现代主义建筑和都市化的标志性建筑。城市中最大的和公众使用率最高的宏伟公共建筑必须体现城市文脉。体育场直接坐落于巴西利亚城恢弘的城市中轴线旁，被赋予一个更为具体并且权威的文脉：该体育场并非新建项目，而是对Ícaro Castro Mello设计的马内·加林查体育场的改建与扩建。目前，爱德华多·卡斯特·罗梅洛正在与gmp建筑师事务所合作，赋予父亲的原作以崭新的面貌。

体育场下层的新增看台正在建设中，现存的上层看台片段也在修复之中。国家体育场有独特的环形散步区域使人们可以环绕体育场散步。巨大的环形悬索屋顶栖息在独特的"柱群"之上，完美的环形几何设计成为一大特色。其太阳能电池板为场馆提供全部能量需要。体育场的设计简单明了，这一点在独立部件的极简至原始化的设计中得到了进一步强化，同时也表达了尼迈尔的设计理念。体育场的主要建筑材料正是巴西的传统建筑材料——混凝土。

/

Estádio Nacional
Brasilia, Brazil

How can fire be passed on and the woods and concrete become friends?

"Tradition is passing the fire, not worshipping the ashes": Gustav Mahler considers it right and respectful to deal with musical tradition in an innovative way. The same applies to tradition in architecture. For the design of the Estádio Nacional Brazil in Brasília on occasion of the 2014 Soccer World Cup in Brazil, gmp and the structural engineers at schlaich bergermann und partner did indeed have two torches to light their way.

Brasilia, designed by Oscar Niemeyer and Lúcio Costa, is an iconic manifesto of Modernist architecture and urbanism. The design of the largest and most public building in this city dominated by monumental public buildings must reflect this context – the more so as the stadium is situated directly next to the central axis of Brasília's grand urban design. This is added to by a more concrete and equally authoritative context: The stadium is not a new building, but the conversion and extension of the Mané Garrincha Stadium originally designed by Ícaro Castro Mello. His son, Eduardo Castro Mello, together with gmp is giving a new shape to his father's fire.

A new lower stand is being built and the present upper stand fragment is being completed. With its unique circulatory esplanade, the Estádio Nacional also allows people to stroll around the stadium. A gigantic suspension roof of perfect circular geometry rests on a characteristic "cluster of supports." With its solar modules, it provides for the stadium's complete energy needs. This clear and simple gesture is underlined by the reduced, almost archetypal design of the individual components and clearly refers to Niemeyer's design vocabulary. The main building material used is, as typical for Brazil, concrete.

都市性

期货广场双子大厦　大连，中国
保利大廈　上海，中国
天津大剧院　天津，中国
开普敦体育场　开普敦，南非

Urbanity

Twin Towers, Commodity Exchange Plaza Dalian, China
Poly Plaza Shanghai, China
Tianjin Grand Theater Tianjin, China
Cape Town Stadium Cape Town, South Africa

政治、经济和技术之间的界限在近几十年来已经越发模糊，或者说三者之间的互相渗透愈发明显。早在互联网时代还未到来之前，媒介理论家马歇尔·麦克卢汉就已经创造了被广泛应用的"地球村"一词。但是乡村的时代已经过去。现在更加合适的语汇是"城市地球"：世界人口正在以与城市人口相同的速度增长。2007年，城市人口在历史上首次超过农村人口。

就人口而言，世界在日益壮大，人们的居住距离越来越近。"密度"或许是理解都市化及其必然衍生物"流动性"最重要的关键词。这两个词语紧密相关。交通密度、人口密度、发展密度都在急速增长。在许多发展项目中界限逐渐模糊，但同时也创造了新的制约因素。一个城市系统最多能够容纳多少人？限制城市化和全球交通的环境可持续性发展的因素有哪些？技术可行性与社会期望度之间的差异在哪里？

归根结底，这些问题探讨的都是民众管理及其引发的密度课题。这是政治家、社会学家和科学家面临的共同课题，对建筑师而言同样是严峻的挑战。尤其在亚洲，城市人口众多，并且在人口的不断涌入下持续增长。创造空间和最大化地利用可能性空间是城市设计面临的主要任务之一。以高效和节省空间的方式进行城市建设，而不是单纯构建拥挤密集的功能性建筑需要美学和社会创造力。城市是居住空间，建筑是构建居住空间和环境。然而，由于需求、限制因素和现实状况的多样化，人们经常忽略这一事实。城市发展的另一个重要条件是利用开放空间点缀建筑密集区的需求，因为有开放空间的存在才称得上是真正的居住空间。

塔式大楼是大都市特色建筑类型的最佳代言人。天际线使城市在远方即可清晰可辨；无可争议，塔式大楼是实现城市密度的主要手段，将办公、居住和其他空间以垂直叠加而非水平延展的方式汇聚到建筑中。因此城市也向上发展。但如果塔式大楼与现有的城市建筑和公共空间文脉相隔离，垂直维度与水平的城市特征之间毫无关联，那么城市空间将在发展过程中日益暗淡。上海的保利大厦彰显了在不损害高层建筑所必须具备的独有特色的前提下可以做到两者的完美融合。大连期货广场双子大厦提供了对密度、高层建筑和空间关系的全然不同但相互关联的解读。可以说它们将外部空间包容进垂直堆叠的体量内，从而抵消了垂直形态密度过于集中的印象。

功能建筑中有些特殊形态是为大众特别设计的，塑造城市并且也被城市塑造，比如体育场，这是对大量人群进行管理的一种特殊方式。与火车站和机场等设施一样，体育场必须四通八达，并且以直接高效而安全的方式指引数以千计的游客在建筑内外通行。然而，体育场设施内，全体观众在同一时间内存在于同一地点，这不仅对建筑提出了功能和技术要求，同时还需要有美学考量。体育场的设计不仅涉及到管理人群的问题，同时还有编排问题。从某种意义上说，人群就是建筑美学特色的组成部分之一。因此建筑师必须将体育场打造成为区域地标。出于这一考量，建筑应该创造一种城市文脉或融入现有文脉，同时保留自身"不同凡响"的风格特色。这一点在gmp为2012世界杯设计的开普敦球场中得到了完美体现。

→ 154

保利大厦，上海
Poly Plaza, Shanghai

同理，城市性和流动性如同一枚硬币的两面，城市和文化生活也是一脉相承的。从精神和美学维度而言，自由空间是城市中的必备因素；人们需要没有界限和拥有自由视野的空间。天津大剧院使城市和文化的相互关系通过建筑得以明确的体现，并且具备实际的使用价值。它不仅是城市中的文化场所，而且是城市文化的代表。

/

Politics, the economy and technology have removed many boundaries in recent decades, or made them more penetrable. Long before the advent of the internet, media theorist Marshall McLuhan coined the often-used term "global village". But the days of the village have gone. Nowadays it is more appropriate to talk about the "urban globe": the world population is growing at the same pace as that of the cities. In 2007, for the first time in history, more people lived in cities than in rural areas.

In terms of its population, the world is becoming bigger – and people are living closer together. The word 'density' is perhaps the most important keyword for understanding urbanity and its corollary: mobility. The two terms are closely interrelated. Traffic density, population density, density of development – all of these are increasing rapidly. In many instances, this development has much to do with the removal of boundaries, but it also creates new limitations. How many people can a city support without its systems breaking down? What are the limits of the environmental sustainability of urbanization and of worldwide traffic? Where are the limits of what is technically feasible and what is desirable for society?

Every single one of these questions boils down to the same issue: management of the masses and the resulting density. It is a problem for politicians, sociologists and scientists. But it is also a key challenge for any architect. In Asia in particular, the populations in cities are enormous and are continually growing due to the influx of people. Creating space, and using up space where there is little: that is one of the main tasks of urban design. The need to build as efficiently and in as space-saving a manner as possible without building purely functional buildings that look crammed together requires aesthetic and social creativity. Because the city is a living space. Architecture is built living space, built environment.

Nevertheless, that is often forgotten – especially in cities where this aspect of architecture is absolutely central – owing to the multitude

→ 54

期货广场双子大厦，大连
Twin Towers,
Commodity Exchange Plaza, Dalian

Urbanity

of demands, limitations and conditions. And yet one of the most important conditions of urban development is the need to intersperse dense building zones with open spaces, because living space does not exist unless there is also open space.

No building typology is more characteristic of a metropolis than the tower block. The skyline makes a city recognizable as such from afar; it is an indisputable fact that the tower block is the key means for achieving urban density: it is used to create office, residential and other space in a vertically stacked fashion, rather than horizontally. The city grows – also upwards. But when tower blocks are built in isolation, without context within the existing city architecture and public spaces, when they fail to establish a relationship between their vertical dimension and the horizontal urban features, then the urban space will become desolate to the same degree as it grows. The Poly Plaza in Shanghai demonstrates how such integration can succeed without detriment to the specific character that comes of necessity with high-rise buildings. A very different, and yet related interpretation of the relationship between density, high-rise building and space is provided by the Dalian Twin Towers: one might say that they include the outside space in their stacked envelope and thereby counteract the very impression of excessive density in vertical form.

→ 244

开普敦体育场，开普敦
Cape Town Stadium, Cape Town

都市性

→ 214

天津大剧院，天津
Tianjin Grand Theater, Tianjin

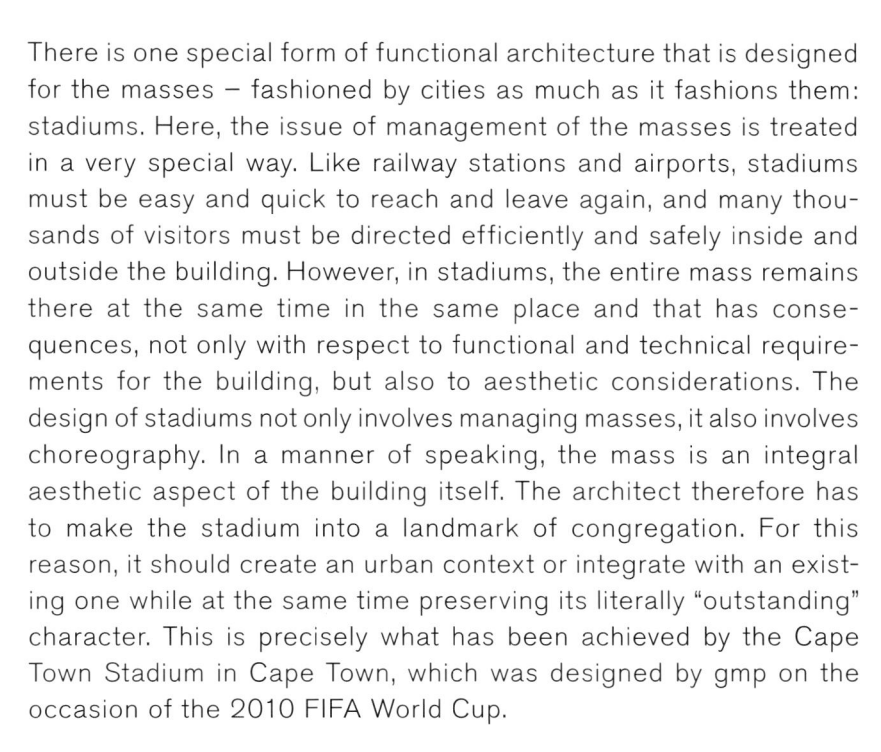

There is one special form of functional architecture that is designed for the masses — fashioned by cities as much as it fashions them: stadiums. Here, the issue of management of the masses is treated in a very special way. Like railway stations and airports, stadiums must be easy and quick to reach and leave again, and many thousands of visitors must be directed efficiently and safely inside and outside the building. However, in stadiums, the entire mass remains there at the same time in the same place and that has consequences, not only with respect to functional and technical requirements for the building, but also to aesthetic considerations. The design of stadiums not only involves managing masses, it also involves choreography. In a manner of speaking, the mass is an integral aesthetic aspect of the building itself. The architect therefore has to make the stadium into a landmark of congregation. For this reason, it should create an urban context or integrate with an existing one while at the same time preserving its literally "outstanding" character. This is precisely what has been achieved by the Cape Town Stadium in Cape Town, which was designed by gmp on the occasion of the 2010 FIFA World Cup.

In the same way that urbanity and mobility are two sides of the same coin, urban and cultural life also belong together. Free spaces are a mandatory requirement for cities — also in terms of a spiritual and an aesthetic dimension; there is a need for spaces without boundaries and with free horizons. The Opera House in Tianjin makes the interrelationship between city and culture architecturally visible and usable; it is not just a place of culture in the city: it is a place of city culture.

Urbanity

期货广场双子大厦
大连，中国

在地面，通过诸如公园、广场的开放空间就能够打破城市延续性的空间密度。这对于高层建筑是否同样适用？

尽管由于城市缺乏空间使得建筑不得不纵向发展，但这并不意味着在高层建筑中就必然存在大量可供使用的空间。事实恰恰相反。在大连期货中心双塔项目中，尝试采用了在纵向建筑结构中开辟开放和绿色空间，打破城市空间密度的设计方法。

大连期货中心双塔是大连高科技中心的一部分。基座部分为酒店，双塔则包括银行、股票交易和行政管理的办公设施。项目共53层，总高度达到了惊人的240m。利用这一高度，项目设置了8层高（32m）的被称之为"空中大厅"的类温室种植区域。这些大厅同样为上层宽敞的接待区提供了一种舒适的环境，使得到此的访客能够受到宾至如归的接待。然而，它们的功能不是虚有其表，而是希望尽管人们身处100m左右的高空，但依然感觉如同置身于底层大厅。如果从大连期货中心双塔俯视整个城市，能够感受到这座建筑在任何高度所展现出的与城市的互动，充满生机。尽管塔楼令人印象深刻，但与城市空间形成独特、亲密对话的形式是通过基座建筑实现的：通过与双塔的组合，它们形成了一个延伸至步行区的矩形公共的绿色开放空间。

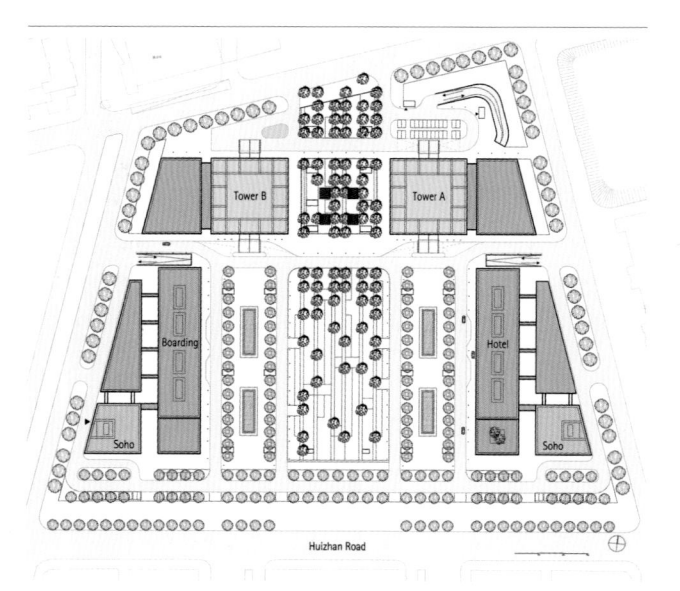

Twin Towers, Commodity Exchange Plaza
Dalian, China

On the ground, it is possible to break up the density of urban continuity – with open spaces, parks and squares. Would that also be possible for high-rise blocks?

Because even though it is the lack of space in cities that has brought about the necessity of building vertically, this doesn't mean that there is a large amount of space available in high-rise buildings. Quite the opposite. With the Dalian Twin Towers however, an attempt has been made to apply the urban design tool of breaking up urban density with open and green spaces in the vertically built structure itself.

The Dalian Twin Towers are part of a high-tech center in Dalian. While the plinth accommodates a hotel, the two towers contain office accommodation for banks, the stock exchange and general administration. Their 53 stories add up to an impressive total height of 240 meters. This height has been used to install so-called "sky lobbies", conservatory-like planted areas that are eight stories high (32 meters). These lobbies provide a suitable ambiance for generous reception areas also on the upper floors, so that visitors can be received in an appropriate setting. However, their function is more than just representative, because the feeling is that of entering a high foyer like those on the ground floor, even though it may be at a height of some 100 meters. The Dalian Twin Towers bring this interaction between building and city to life at any height, while one is already looking down at the city. This original and – in spite of the impressiveness of the towers – virtually intimate dialogue with the urban space is prepared by the plinth buildings: together with the Towers, they form a rectangular public and planted open space which extends to the pedestrian zone.

保利大厦
上海，中国

如何在城市密集区创造空间感？

上海作为经济繁荣发展的典范在中国是首屈一指的，大都市的发展与进化在黄浦江东岸的浦东开发区体现得淋漓尽致。在此，诸多的新兴城市发展项目巩固了城市与河流之间的联系。

保利大厦以独特的方式与周围环境展开交流，它包括了由四座不同高度的小型办公楼组成的建筑实体以及高143m的30层楼高的办公住宅两用大厦。该高层建筑由一高一低两种结构组成。建筑的形式、排列和方位由观景视野决定，北侧的外滩亲水长廊、西侧浦东经济中心独特的天际线以及东侧杨浦大桥和河口的美景尽收眼底。建筑立面及高低错落的体量形成多样化和丰富的视角和空间。为表现对直接语境水域的敬意，视线以独特的方式沿建筑流动，如同水面的一条条波纹。整个基地被划分为三层阶梯状平面，实现了公共空间最大化的通达性。保利大厦的建筑概念创造了与周围环境间的视觉对话。它体现了开放性和丰富性可以在有限的空间内展开，并且以独特的方式解决了城市致密化趋势的问题。

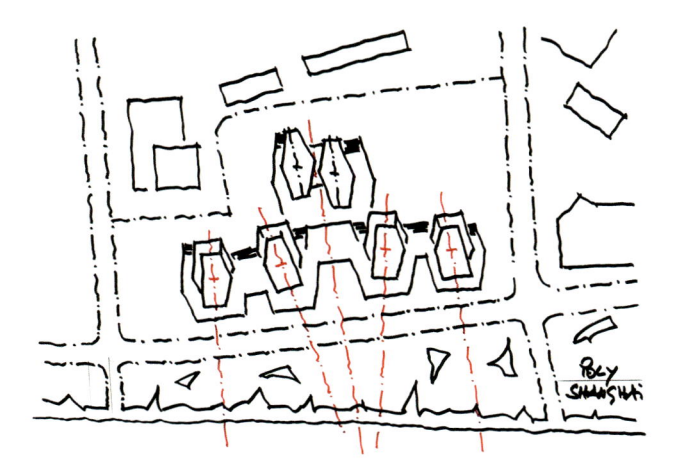

/

Poly Plaza
Shanghai, China

How do you create a feeling of space in a dense area?

Shanghai stands for the country's economic boom like no other city in China. The metropolis' growth and transformation is clearly visible in the district of Pudong on the east bank of the Huangpu River, where many urban development projects are emerging with the goal of reinforcing the connection between city and river. Poly Plaza achieves this by communicating with its surroundings in a very special way. It consists of an ensemble of four smaller buildings of varying heights (offices) and a 143 meters tall high-rise with 30 stories (offices and apartments), which again consists of a twin structure with a lower and a taller part. Form, array and orientation of the buildings are determined by the view north across the water – to the "Bund" waterside promenade – the view west towards the economic center of Pudong's distinctive skyline, and the view east towards Yangpu Bridge and the river mouth.

Emerging from the buildings' offset array, their angled form, their offset facades and their staggered height come a network of diverse, generous perspectives and spaces. As homage to the immediate situation on the river, the view lines are defined in such a way that they flow around the buildings like the lines on the water. The complex is also terraced across three levels, which makes for maximum accessibility of the public spaces. The architectural concept for Poly Plaza creates a visual dialogue with the surroundings: It sees where openness and generosity can develop, even with limited space, and solves the problem of the urban tendency to densification in its own way.

Urbanity

天津大剧院
天津，中国

城市生活与文化生活息息相关。这意味着一方面为艺术打造的建筑必须与其自身所服务的城镇相关联，必须与当代城市发展的要求相适应；另一方面，它独特的文化功能同样需要在自身的概念设计中找到正确的表达方式——成为有目共睹的延展、打破和丰富日常城市生活的场所。

剧院占据了天津新文化中心的核心位置，屋顶的圆形结构与现有的自然历史博物馆屋顶相呼应，这使地面的博物馆与仿佛悬浮的剧院屋顶之间形成建筑对话。

舞台的主要理念同样体现在室外，户外台阶从水面一直通向较高的入口处，形成了如同外部舞台的平台空间。从字面理解，只要有需求，这些外部区域就可以成为户外表演场所。总而言之，项目创造的所有空间都充当着城市生活的舞台。这里是城市的交会点和交流场所，吸引过路者落座，稍憩片刻，提供遍及湖泊和文化中心的广阔视野。文化生活和城市生活水乳交融的理念恰如其分地表现在外部区域的建筑之中。

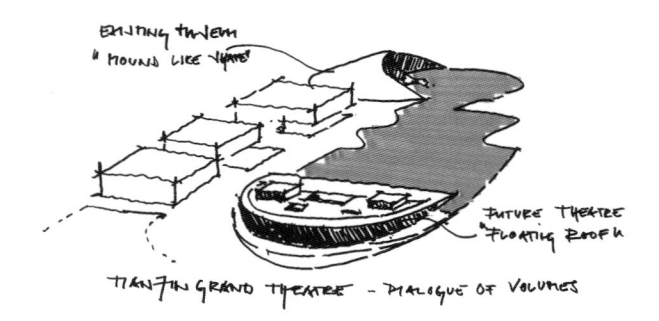

/

Tianjin Grand Theater
Tianjin, China

Urban lifestyle is closely linked with cultural lifestyle. This means that, on the one hand, a building for the arts has to relate to the town or city it serves and has to be compliant with the requirements of contemporary urban development. On the other hand, its special cultural function also needs to find expression in its conceptual design: it is a place that extends, interrupts and enriches normal everyday urban life. And that must be visible.

The theater occupies the key position in Tianjin's new Cultural Center. The circular form of the roof structure corresponds to that of the existing Natural History Museum. This creates an architectural dialogue between the earthbound museum and the seemingly floating roof of the theater.

The key idea of the stage is replicated on the outside: open-air flights of steps lead from the water edge to the raised entrance level and form something like an outside stage. In a quite literal sense: when there is a need for it, these outside areas can be used for open-air performances. But above all the space created serves as a stage for urban life. It is an urban meeting point and place of communication, it invites passers-by to sit down and relax and offers an expansive vista across the lake and the Cultural Center. The idea that cultural and urban life belong together is fittingly expressed in the architecture of the outside areas.

开普敦体育场
开普敦，南非

如何将建筑"大而化小"，使其成为旷世巨作？

在南非，橄榄球曾一度被认为是"白人的"运动，而足球是"黑人的"运动。位于开普敦的开普敦球场虽然是为举办2010年世界杯而建，但却是人民的球场。它坐落于"绿点公共绿地"公园，而"公共"即意味着它向所有人开放。体育场被赋予了体现团结、活力并凝结多样化的城市有机体的使命，在诸如南非的国度里尤其如此。

体育场显示了这一特色，另一方面，它以超然独立的姿态融入周围的公园和城市景观文脉。圆形建筑充满活力的轮廓和轻质型的外观与城市的两个自然地标桌山的水平线和信号山的尖端完美契合。建筑半透明的表皮与当地典型多变的光照环境交错互动。比赛场地植入人为抬高的高地，使其看上去相对较低。

三层看台叠加设计，可容纳68 000名观众，最顶层的看台依据圆形几何设计上下旋转。从技术角度而言，体育场轻质的美学设计与顶端的屋顶设计交相辉映。悬索屋顶面积为36 000m²，重4 500t，极致轻薄。这表明开普敦球场不事张扬而自成一派，以低调而绚丽的方式成为开普敦城市和社会景观中浓墨重彩的一笔。

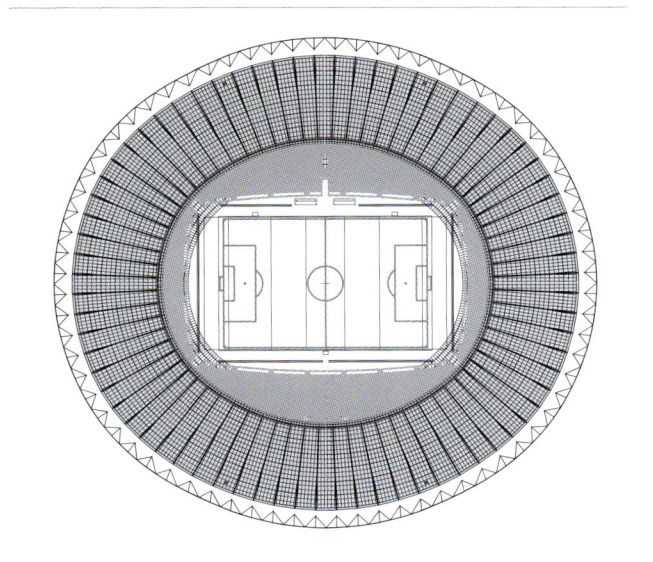

/

Cape Town Stadium
Cape Town, South Africa

How do I make something big small, so that it becomes great?

There was a time in South Africa when rugby was regarded as a "white" sport and soccer as "black." The Cape Town Stadium in Cape Town, built for the 2010 World Cup, is a stadium for all people. It is situated in "Green Point Common" park, and the word "common" would imply that it is for everyone. A stadium – particularly in a country like South Africa – has to emphasize its unifying aspect, animating and bringing together the heterogeneous mass of the urban organism.

This character is demonstrated by the stadium itself, which on the one hand takes a striking stand-alone form while discretely blending into the surrounding park and wider landscape context of the city. The vibrant contours and lightweight look of the circular building, the translucent skin of which plays with the typically variable local lighting conditions, harmonize perfectly with the city's two natural landmarks: Table Mountain's horizontal line and the tip of Signal Hill. True to scale, the arena was also inserted into an artificially-elevated plateau, making it appear lower.

Three tiers were erected above each other to accommodate 68,000 spectators, the upper-most tier of which swings up and down according to circle geometry. The stadium's aesthetic lightness is echoed technically in a roof design mounted on cables: The suspension roof, which has a surface of 36,000 m² and weighs 4,500 tons, is extremely lightweight. This also shows: The Cape Town Stadium is spectacular without having to flaunt it – the only way it could have become a valuable part of Cape Town's urban and social landscape.

流动性

天津西站 天津，中国
柏林泰格尔机场和TXL⁺总体规划 柏林，德国
柏林中央火车站 柏林，德国
柏林勃兰登堡机场 柏林，德国

Mobility

Tianjin West Railway Station Tianjin, China
Berlin-Tegel Airport and TXL⁺ Berlin, Germany
Berlin Central Station Berlin, Germany
Berlin Brandenburg Airport Berlin, Germany

借助现代运输技术和物流，几乎每个人都可到达世界任意角落。任何时候都有大量人群在流动中，他们相逢于城市的交通枢纽，会聚在火车站或者机场。

与流动性相关的建筑设计堪称最复杂的建设项目任务。设计必须将纷纭多样的功能有机地结合在一起，并使各种不同的流程相互协调，而所有这一切均应在一个相对狭小的空间内并以最高的效率完成。车站和机场连接各个城市，就其方方面面的多样性和复杂性（有时也包括规模）而言，可以和一座城市相媲美。在设计时，仅考虑安全、物流、休闲、消费、餐饮、管理等方面是不够的，建筑师必须同时充当道路系统的设计者，包括通往和离开建筑综合体的道路和建筑综合体内部各个设施之间的道路。的确，为数百万人口城市建造机场或火车站对建筑师来讲是充满极限的挑战。建筑设计是整个规划设计的许多组成部分之一，而这样大规模的建设任务在世界上只有少数几个建筑设计事务所能够承担。

作为功能性交通枢纽建筑，火车站和机场一个潜在风险是空间的千篇一律并可任意对换。所以，人类学家Marc Augé 使用了"非地点"这一概念，所指的城市和城郊的大面积单功能空间，例如购物中心，尤其是交通设施，如机场或（新）火车站。它们没有历史，只产生"孤独和相似性"。尽管这些建设项目的建筑师受到全球化现代社会强制性约束（强调功能、效率、商业性等），但他们还是必须尽量赋予这些建筑以个性特征和独有风格，也就是赋予它们建筑学意义上的人性面孔，他们的责任是为大众设计，但应不惜一切代价避免大众化设计。

但是，对于"流动性"建筑设计和城市规划的思考不仅仅只意味着对交通建筑的思考。像gmp这样的建筑设计事务所为流动性设计了大量的建筑，诸如机场或火车站。然而，它经常需要不顾，有时甚至针对"流动性结构"而进行设计。例如，当规划建筑综合体与一条多车道道路毗邻时，建筑设计的个性化问题将重新提出。对话式设计要求并寻求与城市文脉对话。在这种情况下，需要通过对话考虑是否以及如何在大量道路竞争条件下保持设计构思，以发展自身一贯的个性。当然，这样的城市规划对话过程只有在其追求创造一种整体的个性架构才是有益的，也就是说，由道路和建筑共同组成的个性架构才是理想的结局。如此一来，建筑设计不再是用一种结构挑战另一种结构，也不是孤芳自赏，互不相干，而是负责任地力求使原有的各个城市要素在美学和功能上相互配合，达到和谐统一。

对话，顾名思义，不是单行线，而是双向交流。办公建筑、居住建筑或多功能建筑为了发挥其功能需要与交通建筑或交通网络进行对话，对话有时可能是很艰难。反之亦然，火车站必须被看作是城市的有机部分并按此进行设计。即使机场建在城区以外的地方，也应发展其同城区的有机联系。它是城市的使者或延伸，在任何情况下，它属于城市，而不是其他地方。

由gmp设计并于2006开始运营的柏林中央火车站面对独特的历史背景，满足了这一要求：它创建了一个充满象征力和活力的令人瞩目的整合架构，填补了城市中心在柏林墙坍塌后而形成的一片无人之地。火车站自身变成了一

→ 272

柏林泰格尔机场和TXL⁺总体规划，柏林
Berlin-Tegel Airport and TXL⁺, Berlin

个城市空间，它不仅仅是交通技术设施，同时也是城市的链接要素。在这方面，新的天津火车站也是一个明证。

20世纪70年代柏林泰格尔机场因其短距架构而对机场建设产生了革命性影响，而它自身已成为柏林的地标。今天，在同一个城市，gmp建筑设计事务所以一种非常不同的方式成功地设计了柏林勃兰登堡机场，在个性化、功能性和城市关联之间达到了综合平衡，gmp同时还提出了柏林泰格尔机场再利用的具体设计方案，这是对今日城市建设一个最重要方面的认同，即保证其生态和社会功能意义上的可持续发展。

/

→ 188

天津西站，天津
Tianjin West Railway Station, Tianjin

Thanks to modern transport technology and logistics, today almost anyone can reach almost any place on earth. Masses of people are on the move at any point in time and meet each other, in particular, at urban intersections: in railway stations and airports.

Today, mobility-related architecture is one of the most complicated building tasks there is. It has to combine the most diverse functions and coordinate a wide range of processes – and all that in a relatively small space and with maximum efficiency. Railway stations and airports link cities with each other and – with respect to their diversity and complexity, and even sometimes their dimension – are themselves comparable to cities. It is not enough to include aspects of security, safety, logistics, leisure, consumption, gastronomy, administration and technology in the design, to mention but a few. The architect also has to deal with the circulation issues: the access routes to and from the building complex and the routes between the various facilities within the complex itself. In fact, the task of building airports or railway stations for large conurbations pushes architecture beyond its implied defining limits: designing has become just one part of the many components in the overall planning and design process which, at such a scale, can only be managed by very few practices in the world.

With its orientation towards functionality, the architecture of railway stations and airports is in danger of becoming faceless and replaceable. In this context, the ethnologist Marc Augé coined the expression: "non-place", with which he referred to large (sub)urban mono-functionally used areas such as shopping malls and, particularly, spaces of transience such as airports or (new) railway stations without history, which only produce "loneliness and similarity", but no identity. In spite of all the demands imposed on the architect by modern,

globalized society with respect to such building projects (functionality, efficiency, commercial viability etc.), he has to try to give them their own identity and to make them unique – one might say human, in an architectural sense. It is his responsibility to design architecture for the masses, but to avoid mass architecture at all costs.

But reflecting on "mobility" in architecture and urban design involves more than thinking about transport buildings. Architectural practices such as gmp are involved in many projects serving mobility, such as airports and railway stations. On the other hand, many of the projects also involve designing "against" such mobility structures. For example, when a building or development has to be designed next to a multi-lane highway, the question of architectural identity arises again. Designing in dialogue needs and seeks the interaction with the urban context. In this case, one would have to discuss whether, and in what manner, the design would have to stand up against the imposing presence of the road in order to be able to develop its own conclusive identity. However, such a discussion would not make sense from the urban design point of view unless it also intends to create an overall identity, i.e. ideally that of an ensemble that includes both the road and buildings. That would be an architectural solution which, instead of pitting one structure against the other and creating both in isolation, attempts to harmonize the existing context with as much responsibility as possible – both in terms of aesthetics, and functionality.

To expand the image, one could say that a dialogue is not a one-way street. In order for their buildings to function appropriately, the designers of offices, housing or multi-purpose buildings often have to carry out difficult negotiations with those of transport buildings and structures. The reverse is also true. A railway station has to be understood and designed as part of the city. Even when an airport is built outside the urban area, it has to develop a relationship with the city. It is the city's ambassador, or its extension; it belongs exactly where it is, and nowhere else.

→ 330

柏林勃兰登堡机场，柏林
Berlin Brandenburg Airport, Berlin

→ 302

柏林中央火车站，柏林
Berlin Central Station, Berlin

The main railway station in Berlin, which was designed by gmp and opened in 2006, meets these requirements in the context of a unique historic background: it fills the site in the center of the city, which had become a no-man's land after the fall of the Berlin Wall, with a distinctive structure that links East and West, with symbolism and life. The fact that a railway station itself can become an urban space and a place of interconnection not only in a transport technology, but also in an urban design sense, is demonstrated by the new railway station in Tianjin.

The Berlin-Tegel airport, which was created in the 1970s, has revolutionized airport design with its structure of short circulation routes – and has become a Berlin landmark in itself. Today, with the Berlin-Brandenburg airport, the practice is succeeding in quite a different way in the same city to strike a balance between its own identity, function and urban context. At the same time, gmp is presenting detailed plans for the possible uses of Berlin-Tegel, which reflect a strong commitment to perhaps the most important aspect of current urban design: sustainability in an ecological and social/functional sense.

Mobility

天津西站
天津，中国

大型交通建筑不能只是默默无闻的功能巨人，而要表现、丰富和提升自我，成为城市的一部分。这一信念在新的天津西站的设计过程中发挥了关键作用。新的火车站已经成为京沪高铁线路上必不可少的一环。作为区域间的交通集中地，它肩负着连接当地和长距离铁路运输以及陆路城市公交的职责，是基础设施建设中至关重要的一部分。

火车站贯通城市南北，在城市设计中所扮演的角色同等重要。从象征意义来说，这一点在57m高和长约400m的桶形拱状屋顶中得到了体现，并将中央经济区（CBD）和北部的天津老城连接起来。弯曲的屋顶传达了巨大的城市大门的印象，而下方的空间则代表了古典意义上的广场。屋顶钻石形状的花边设计保证了广场内充盈的日光照射，一方面，提供了更好的方向性和清晰度，另一方面，令人感觉更加舒适和幸福安乐。此外，火车站南侧的前方空地形成了一个大型连贯的开放空间，不仅将车站与城市有机结合，而且可以被大众用来举办多种活动。如此一来，火车站成为交通工具与城市生活之间密切联系的具体体现，并促进两者的发展。

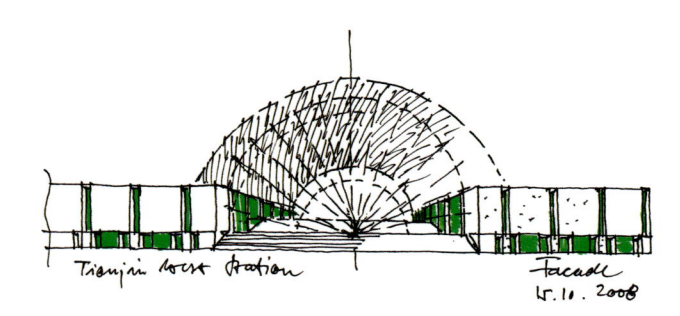

/

Tianjin West Railway Station
Tianjin, China

The conviction that large mobility buildings must not be anonymous functional monsters but must present themselves as part of the city and enrich and strengthen its identity – this conviction played a vital role in the design of the new Tianjin railway station. The new railway station had become necessary as part of the new high-speed rail link between Beijing and Shanghai. As an inter-regional transport intersection linking local and long-distance rail traffic as well as overland coaches and city buses, the railway station is a hugely important part of the infrastructure.

But the role it plays in the urban design is of at least equal importance: the railway station links the north and the south of the city. Symbolically, this is expressed by a 57 meter high and almost 400 meter long barrel vault roof which links the Central Business District (CBD) to the north with Tianjin's old city. The curved shape of the roof conveys the impression of an enormous city gate, while the space beneath represents a concourse in the classical sense. The diamond-shaped lacework of the roof structure allows daylight to flood the concourse providing better orientation and clarity on the one hand, and a greater sense of comfort and well-being on the other. In addition, the southern forecourt of the railway station forms a large continuous open space, which not only links the railway station organically with the city, but which can also be used by the general public in many different ways. In this way, the railway station becomes a visible expression of the close connection between mobile and urban life – and supports both.

柏林泰格尔机场和TXL⁺总体规划
柏林，德国

如何将城市历史转化为城市的未来？

时代在变化。回想20世纪60年代，当gmp通过柏林泰格尔机场项目声名鹊起时，大众对于全球恐怖主义和全球商业化还闻所未闻。当机场在1974年正式投入使用时，没有人想到了大门和大型购物中心的设立，只想到尽量缩短距离和避免不必要的时间流失。gmp的理念在当时看来具有开天辟地的意义：环形航站楼和六边形建筑为停靠在外环的飞机创造了大片空间，同时缩短了内环乘客的步行距离。

当时，几乎没有人考虑过重新利用和可持续性，而这些词汇却是当下城市规划中最关键的词汇。柏林泰格尔机场将荣耀不再，而gmp找到了解决其未来发展之路的多种途径。其中，最引人注目的答案叫做TXL⁺正能源城市。这是项目的暂定名称，意在先前的跑道间建造一座生态城，自给自足。要实现目标，需要将所有的现有信息融合到新社区内的节能、可持续性和与生态相关的建筑设计中，同时保留六边形建筑物的中央地位。

在该案例中，可持续性还意味着创造新的城市文脉。这恰恰是TXL⁺所要完成的，将调研、工作和生活融为一体。此外，如果在机场围栏拆除之后机场仍然是一个公共地点，那么它将成为连接赖尼肯多夫和施潘道区的桥梁。TXL⁺不仅将成为柏林城内的重大项目，还将为全球范围内相似社区的建设提供范本。

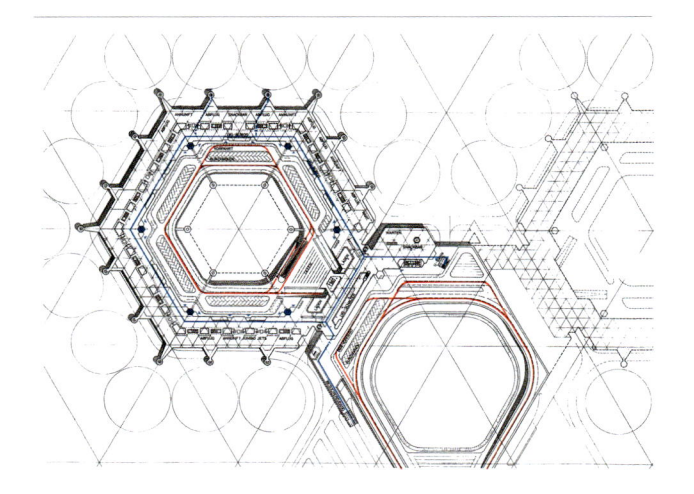

/

Berlin-Tegel Airport and TXL⁺
Berlin, Germany

How do you transform the history of a city into its future?

The times, they are a-changin': Back in the 1960s, when gmp established its reputation with Berlin Tegel Airport, there was no such thing as either global terrorism or global commercialization. When it opened in 1974, no one was thinking of gates or shopping malls, only about keeping distances as short as possible and avoiding unnecessary loss of time. The firm's concept was groundbreaking for the requirements at that time: The closed-circle, hexagonal form allowed plenty of space for airplanes berthing on the outer ring while shortening the walking distance for passengers on the inner ring.

In those days, few had even considered about reuse and sustainability, which are now among the most critical aspects of urban planning. Berlin Tegel Airport will be decommissioned, and gmp found manifold answers to the question of the future of its own built past. The most spectacular answer is called TXL⁺. This is the working title for building an eco-city between the former runways that will produce its own energy. The aim is to pool all available knowledge on energy-saving as well as sustainable and eco-related building together in this new neighborhood, keeping the hexagon at its center.

In this case, sustainable also means creating new urban contexts. That is exactly what TXL⁺ would do, since it would bring together the functions of research, work and living. Moreover, if it remains a public place after the airport fences are taken down, it would act as a connection between the neighborhoods of Reinickendorf and Spandau. TXL⁺ would not only be an important project for Berlin; it would serve as a model for similar communities around the world.

Mobility

柏林中央火车站
柏林，德国

如何以及为何将罗盘上上下下所有的点连接起来？

以前，火车站代表的是全世界人民追求进步工具和环球旅行的梦想。因此，火车站的建筑角色与教堂同等重要。然而，时过境迁。gmp在设计德国柏林中央火车站时，抓住了重新改造欧洲首都中央车站的历史机遇，以高度现代化的方式重现往日辉煌，这也是火车站之所以四通八达的另一原因。

建筑位于东西柏林中间一处曾经"无人问津"的场地上，是重获统一后的城市的象征。作为欧洲最大的换乘站，每天搭载300 000名铁路乘客。它将上层和下层区域连为一体，从321m长的玻璃棚顶到首层以下15m的平台，横跨三个楼层。连通南北的同时，屋顶下方的平台也服务了东西向的客流。中间层辅助本地公共交通。两个4米高的玻璃建筑如同一架桥梁横跨东西大厅，包含服务、办公和酒店区。在这中间，玻璃门厅沿南北方向延展。

建筑部分的叠加明确高效地区划了不同的交通层，同时创造了其他的功能空间。从这个层面来说，项目是遵守交通和城市建筑原则的典范。此外，不容忽视的是玻璃十字架强烈的美学效果归功于两个大厅，如同教堂的中殿和十字形翼部相互交叉，暗指历史上火车站所扮演的崇高神圣的建筑角色。

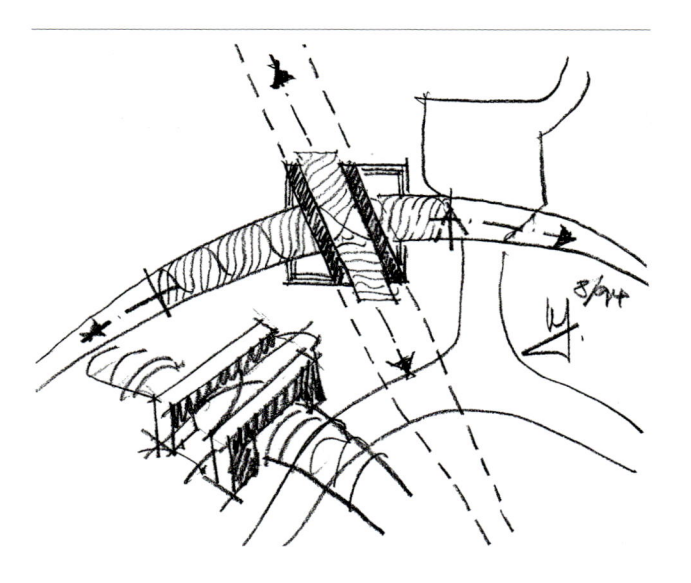

/

Berlin Central Station
Berlin, Germany

How and why do you tie all points of the compass, top and bottom together?

In former times, train stations stood for the dream of progressive and cosmopolitan mobility. Accordingly, their architectural role was on par with that of cathedrals. This has long since changed. Designing the Berlin Central Station, gmp seized on a historic opportunity to reinvent the central station of a European capital city, reinstating its former grandeur in a highly modern way – another reason why the train station has so many connections.

Situated in the former "no man's land" between East and West Berlin, it is a symbol of the reunified city. Europe's largest interchange station connects 300,000 rail passengers on any given day. It ties upper and lower areas together, stretching across three levels from the 321 meters long, vaulted glass roof down to the platform 15 meters below ground level. This connects north and south, while the platforms below the roof serve the east-west direction. The middle level facilitates local public transport. Two 4 meters high glass buildings span the east-west hall like bridges. They contain service, office and hotel functions. Between them, stretching out in north-south direction, is the glass foyer.

This superposition of building parts layers the different traffic levels transparently and efficiently while also providing space for other functions. In this way, it is exemplary of the principles to which architecture of mobility and urbanity must adhere. And, not least, the glass cross owes its strong aesthetic effect to the two halls, which intersect like the nave and transept of a church, thus alluding to the once lofty architectural role of train stations in history.

柏林勃兰登堡机场
柏林，德国

如何在航空业未来发展状况还未可知的情况下进行机场设计？

今天的许多重大的现代化机场项目都是大型结构，并成为推动区域经济增长的主要力量。所以新的柏林勃兰登堡机场（以前柏林市长和德国总理威利·勃兰特的名字命名）同样具有城市维度也就不足为奇。14.7km²的面积等同于2 000个足球场的大小。机场每年将服务2 700万乘客，扩建后乘客数量将达到4 500万人。

机场被设定为由若干个独立模块组成的系统，众多个体依旧美学和功能组织，融合成为一个完整的城市结构。南侧跑道和北侧跑道之间植入了一个所谓的"中场航站楼"。这一中央轴线几乎将所有的重要空间和区域都集中于此。结构分明的立面和清晰的几何形式赋予了航站楼独特的建筑因素，从辛克尔到包豪斯都有所体现。所有的功能融合在六个楼层中，由平坦的49 000平方米的屋顶覆盖。离境层或主楼层面积宽阔，长220米的大厅沐浴在阳光下。

材料、色彩和景观设计的选择都以促进机场独特个性的形成为原则，与"籍籍无名"的地点截然相反。但即使单纯从功能层面来讲，机场仍然是城市设计的范本。今天的机场如同城市一样，瞬息万变。但是柏林勃兰登堡机场适应性强的模块化设计早已对航空业的未来发展胸有成竹，坚信万变不离其宗。

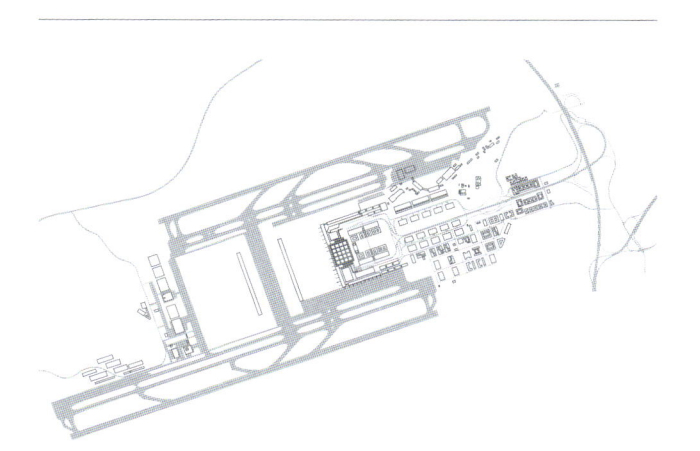

/

Berlin Brandenburg Airport
Berlin, Germany

How do you design the future of aviation without knowing it yet?

Today's modern, major airports are mega structures and economic driving forces in their regions. So it's no wonder the new Berlin Brandenburg Airport – named after former Berlin mayor and German chancellor Willy Brandt – also has a city's dimensions: At 14.7 km², its area covers the equivalent of 2,000 soccer fields. It will serve up to 27 million passengers a year and be expanded to include up to 45 million passengers.

The airport is conceived as a system of individual modules, which merge into an overall urban structure organized by aesthetic and functional aspects. The terminal, a so-called midfield terminal, is embedded between a north and a south runway. This central axis condenses almost all important spaces and areas into one line. With its structured facades and clear, geometric forms, the terminal picks up on architectural elements from Schinkel to Bauhaus. All functions have been integrated onto six floors covered by the flat, 49,000 m² roof. The departure level, or main level, is a generous, 220 meters long hall bathed in light.

The choice of material, color, and landscape design all contribute to the airport's individual identity, making it the opposite of a "non-place." But even with regards to function, it stands as a model for urban design: Today's airport, like the city itself, is increasingly subject to a transformation. But with its adaptable, modular design, Berlin Brandenburg Airport is already thinking ahead to the future of aviation – without necessarily having to know it.

本书为《对话式设计》巡展中国站展览目录册，与媒体伙伴《城市·环境·设计》杂志社合作出版。

感谢Verseidag Coating and Composite公司的友好支持。

《对话式设计》—— gmp建筑师事务所建筑作品

www.gmp-architekten.de
www.uedmagazine.net
www.verseidag.de

gmp | URBAN ENVIRONMENT DESIGN | **VERSEIDAG** COATING AND COMPOSITE

德国gmp建筑师事务所 北京代表处
北京市东城区东直门南大街5号中青旅大厦1212室
Tel. +86 10 58156161
Fax. +86 10 58156365
beijing@gmp-architekten.de

德国gmp建筑师事务所 上海代表处
上海市徐汇区汾阳路138号轻科大厦10楼
Tel. +86 21 5465 5151
Fax. +86 21 5465 5131
shanghai@gmp-architekten.de

德国gmp建筑师事务所 深圳代表处
深圳市福田区金田路4028号荣超经贸中心3706室
Tel.+86 755 8257 7766-87
Fax.+86 755 8257 7799
www.gmp-architekten.de

This catalog is published to accompany a touring exhibition in China in cooperation with UEDmagazine.

The exhibitions were produced with the kind support of Verseidag Coating and Composite.

Designing in Dialogue – The Architecture of von Gerkan, Marg and Partners

www.gmp-architekten.de
www.uedmagazine.net
www.verseidag.de

gmp Beijing
CYTS Plaza, No.1212
No. 5 Dongzhimen South Avenue
Dongcheng District
100007 Beijing
P. R. China
T: +86.10.5815 6161
F: +86.10.5815 6365
beijing@gmp-architekten.de

gmp Shanghai
Qing Ke Mansion, 10th Floor
No. 138 Fen Yang Road
Xu Hui District
200031 Shanghai
P. R. China
T: +86.21.5465 5151
F: +86.21.5465 5131
shanghai@gmp-architekten.de

gmp Shenzhen
Landmark Building, Unit 3706
No. 4028 Jintian Road
Futian District
518035 Shenzhen
P. R. China
T: +86.755.8257 7766
F: +86.755.8257 7799
shenzhen@gmp-architekten.de

Exhibition

Curator: Michael Kuhn (gmp)
Hinerant exhibation promoter in China: Michael Kuhn (gmp),
Peng Lixiao (UED)
Project management: Hanne Banduch, Heidi Knaut
Project management China: Zheng Shanshan (gmp)
Graphic design: ON Grafik, Hamburg, Germany
Digital image processing: Beatrix Hansen (gmp)
Editing and proofreading: Joachim Otte,
Bettina Ahrens (gmp), Fang Xiaoshi (gmp)
Translation: Fang Xiaoshi (gmp), Hartwin Busch, Li Xuan (gmp),
Xu Xuelai (gmp), Wei Shaochen
Exhibition installation: Wilking Metallbau GmbH, Berlin, Germany
Production of exhibition graphics and print:
Reproplan graphics GmbH, Hamburg, Germany
Architectural model construction: Monath+Menzel Architekturmodellbau Berlin, Germany, Werner Modellbau Braunschweig, Germany
Logistics: BTG Messespedition, Germany, Dieke Eiben (gmp)
Media and Public Relations: UEDmagazine,
Fang Xiaoshi (gmp), Zheng Shanshan (gmp), Christian Füldner (gmp)
Exhibition films: Hans Georg Esch (HG Esch Photography) and
Oliver Schwabe
Film interviews: Julia Ackermann, Film editor: Markus
Carlsen (gmp), Editor: Claudia Tiesler (gmp)
We would like to thank all of the team
at gmp for their dedication and support with
this exhibition project.

Publication

Publisher: gmp · von Gerkan, Marg
and Partners Architects, UEDmagazine
Coordination: Michael Kuhn (gmp), Liu Qing (UED)
Editing and proofreading: Joachim Otte, Bettina Ahrens (gmp),
Fang Xiaoshi (gmp), Heidi Knaut, Hanne Banduch, Liu Ran (UED)
Jiang Siqi (UED), Feng Yuanyue (UED)
Translation: Fang Xiaoshi (gmp), Hartwin Busch, Li Xuan (gmp),
Xu Xuelai (gmp), Wei Shaochen, Feng Yuanyue (UED), Han
Miao (UED), Gong Qiushan (UED), Liu Ran (UED)
Graphic design and typesetting: ON Grafik,
Hamburg with Hendrik Sichler, Felix Heining
Cover design: ON Grafik, Hamburg, Germany
Cover photos: (from top to bottom) Christian Gahl, Marcus
Bredt, Marcus Bredt, Portal da Copa/Tomás Faquini

展览

策展人：迈克尔·库恩 (gmp)
巡展中国站发起人：迈克尔·库恩 (gmp)、彭礼孝 (UED)
展览总体负责人：汉娜·班度、海迪·克劳特
展览中国协调：郑珊珊 (gmp)
平面设计：欧恩平面设计公司（德国汉堡）
数字图片处理：贝阿特里希·汉森 (gmp)
编辑/审校：约阿希姆·奥特、贝蒂娜·阿伦斯 (gmp)、方小诗 (gmp)
翻译：方小诗 (gmp)、海德威·布赫、李萱 (gmp)、徐雪莱 (gmp)、韦劭辰
展览设备：威尔金金属制品有限公司（德国柏林）
展览印刷：莱普布兰平面设计有限公司（德国汉堡）
建筑模型：莫纳特及门采尔建筑模型公司（德国柏林）；韦尔纳建筑模型公司（德国布伦瑞克）
展览物流：迪耶克·艾本巴伐利亚运输集团，德国 (gmp)
新闻及公共事务：《城市·环境·设计》杂志社、方小诗 (gmp)、郑珊珊 (gmp)、克里斯蒂安·富伦德 (gmp)
展览影片：汉斯·乔治·艾施摄影工作室和奥利弗·施瓦博
影片采访：尤莉亚·阿克曼
影片剪辑：马库斯·卡尔森 (gmp)
影片编辑：克劳迪亚·蒂斯勒 (gmp)
在此诚挚感谢所有为展览成功举办付出心血的同事们！

展览目录册

主编：德国冯·格康，玛格及合伙人建筑师事务所，《城市·环境·设计》杂志社
总策划：迈克尔·库恩 (gmp)、柳青 (UED)
编辑/审校：约阿希姆·奥特、贝提娜·阿伦斯 (gmp)、方小诗 (gmp)、海迪·克劳特、汉娜·班度、刘然 (UED)、姜思琪 (UED)、冯元玥 (UED)
翻译：方小诗 (gmp)、海德威·布赫、李萱 (gmp)、徐雪莱 (gmp)、韦劭辰、冯元玥 (UED)、韩苗 (UED)、宫秋姗 (UED)、刘然 (UED)
版式设计：亨德里克·西什莱和菲利克斯·海宁，欧恩平面设计公司（德国汉堡）
封面设计：欧恩平面设计公司（德国汉堡）
封面照片（由上至下）：克里斯蒂安·盖尔、马库斯·布莱特、波特尔·科布/托马斯·方琼

对话式设计
gmp建筑师事务所建筑作品

Designing in Dialogue
The Architecture of von Gerkan,
Marg and Partners

gmp　　**UED**magazine

德国冯·格康，玛格及合伙人建筑师事务所　《城市·环境·设计》杂志社　主编

辽宁科学技术出版社
·沈阳·

图书在版编目（CIP）数据

对话式设计：gmp建筑师事务所建筑作品 / 德国冯·格康，玛格及合伙人建筑师事务所，《城市·环境·设计》杂志社主编. —— 沈阳：辽宁科学技术出版社，2013.8
　ISBN 978-7-5381-8192-0
　Ⅰ.①对　Ⅱ.①德　②城　Ⅲ.①建筑设计–作品集–世界–现代 Ⅳ.①TU206
中国版本图书馆CIP数据核字(2013)第176124号

主　　编：德国冯·格康，玛格及合伙人建筑师事务所(gmp)，《城市·环境·设计》杂志社(UEDmagazine)
总 策 划：迈克尔·库恩(gmp)，柳青(UED)
策　　划：约阿希姆·奥特、贝提娜·阿伦斯(gmp)、方小诗(gmp)、郑珊珊(gmp)、孙思瑶(UED)、刘然(UED)、付蓉(UED)
版式设计：亨德里克·西什莱和菲利克斯·海宁，欧恩平面设计公司（德国汉堡）
封面设计：欧恩平面设计公司（德国汉堡）
公司地址：德国汉堡易北大道139,22763
网　　址：www.gmp-architekten.de　www.uedmagazine.net

出版发行：辽宁科学技术出版社
　　　　　（地址：沈阳市和平区十一纬路29号 邮编：110003）
印 刷 者：北京雅昌彩色印刷有限公司
经 销 者：各地新华书店
幅面尺寸：196mm×255mm
印　　张：32.75
插　　页：4
字　　数：400千字
印　　数：1~3000
出版时间：2013年8月第1版
印刷时间：2013年8月第1次印刷
责任编辑：刘　然
文字编辑：姜思琪　冯元玥
美术编辑：龙　洋
责任校对：王玉宝

书　　号：ISBN 978-7-5381-8192-0
定　　价：580.00元

对话式设计

gmp建筑师事务所建筑作品

Designing in Dialogue

The Architecture of von Gerkan,
Marg and Partners

前言
Preface

在过去的45年中，冯·格康，玛格及合伙人建筑师事务所已经在全球范围内建成了超过350栋建筑。
本书选择了gmp极具代表性的作品，很好地诠释了gmp对于建筑艺术在社会中的责任的理解，这同时也是gmp所遵循的基本原则。

In the past 45 years, the architects von Gerkan, Marg and Partners have realized over 350 buildings worldwide.
This cataloge is an exemplary selection of gmp buildings which describe us and our understanding of architectural art in social responsibility as well as the guiding principles under which they are arranged.

亚洲
Asia

非洲
Africa

欧洲
Europe

南美洲
South America

→ 8

→ 234

→ 258

→ 426

亚洲
Asia

中国 China
北京 Beijing
长春 Changchun
重庆 Chongqing
大连 Dalian
佛山 Foshan
淮安 Huai'an
南宁 Nanning
青岛 Qingdao
深圳 Shenzhen
上海 Shanghai
天津 Tianjin
郑州 Zhengzhou

印度 India
新德里 New Delhi
海得拉巴 Hyderabad

越南 Vietnam
河内 Hanoi

→

26

34

南宁国际会议展览中心
南宁，中国

设计竞赛：1999年，一等奖　**方案设计**：曼哈德·冯·格康，尼古劳斯·格茨　**项目负责人**：德克·海勒，卡伦·施罗德　**中方合作设计单位**：广西建筑设计研究院　**业主**：南宁国际会展中心有限公司　**建设周期**：2000—2003年，扩建工程至2005年　**建筑面积**：130 000m²

基地45m的高差赋予坐落其上的会展中心以独特的外部空间形象。半透明的圆顶使人联想起盛开的花朵，也必将成为南宁城市的地标。高70m的折叠拱顶覆盖着直径48m的多功能大厅，构成了建筑的开端。来访者可通过由展览广场延伸而出的步行桥到达展厅入口处。从这里开始，舒适的大型阶梯和自动扶梯将引领人们进入四层功能各不相同的展厅。

Nanning International Convention & Exhibition Center
Nanning, China

International competition 1999 – 1st Prize　**Design** Meinhard von Gerkan and Nikolaus Goetze　**Project leaders** Dirk Heller, Karen Schroeder　**Chinese partner practice** Guangxi Architectural Comprehensive Design & Research Institute　**Client** Nanning International Convention & Exhibition Co., Ltd.　**Construction period** 2000–2003, extension up until 2005　**Gross floor area** 130,000 m²

The external quality of the exhibition center is generated with the location on a slope with an altitude difference of approximately 45 meters. The shape of the translucent dome is reminiscent of an opening blossom, which has become the symbol of Nanning, and therefore defines a new symbol of the city. The multi-functional large hall with its folded domical roof and an overall height of 70 meters and a hall diameter of 48 meters forms the head of the complex. The access from the center is provided via a pedestrian bridge from the exhibition square. Starting from the entrances, comfortable flights of stairs and escalators lead to the four flexibly usable exhibition levels.

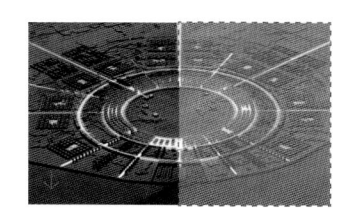

临港新城
上海，中国

设计竞赛：2002/2003年，一等奖　**方案设计**：曼哈德·冯·格康　**合伙人**：尼古劳斯·格茨　**业主**：上海城市规划局　**面积**：74km²　**规划人口规模**：800 000人　**建设周期**：2003—2020年

临港新城的方案源于欧洲的理想城市理念，并赋予其革新性的思想内容：城市的中心是一片直径2.5km的圆形湖泊。一滴水珠落在平静的湖面上，泛起一道道同心涟漪——这个充满诗意的画面隐喻了整个新城的结构逻辑。城市的各个功能设施呈放射状从中心向外扩散：湖畔林荫大道，高密度的商务区，500m宽的环形城市公园，以及可供13 000人居住的块状街区住宅群，都以罗盘射线状分布。楔形的绿地景观向城市内部延伸，直至第二道内环处。河道及小型湖泊贯穿点缀于所有区域中。

Lingang New City
Shanghai, China

Competition 2002/2003 – 1st Prize　**Design** Meinhard von Gerkan　**Partner** Nikolaus Goetze　**Client** Shanghai Urban Planning Administration Bureau　**Construction period** since 2003　**Area** 74 km²　**Future inhabitants** 800,000

The concept adopts the ideals of the traditional European city, combining them with a revolutionary idea: A circular lake with a 2.5 km diameter forms the core. The image of concentric waves, produced by a drop hitting the water surface, is the principle metaphoric image of the overall city structure. The use structure is divided into radial rings from the inside to the outside: promenade, business district with high density, 500 meter wide ring-shaped city park, block-like residential districts for 13,000 people each situated along radial roads according to the principle of a compass card. Wedges of landscape reach into the city as far as the second ring. Watercourses and small lakes penetrate all districts.

42

48

世纪莲体育公园
佛山，中国

设计竞赛： 2003年，二等奖，委托设计　**方案设计：** 福尔克温·玛格　**合伙人：** 尼古劳斯·格茨　**项目负责人：** 克里斯蒂安·霍夫曼　**中方合作设计单位：** 华南理工大学建筑设计研究院　**业主：** 佛山市第十二届省运动会场馆建设中心　**建设周期：** 2004—2006年　**体育场座席数：** 36 000个　**游泳馆座席数：** 2 800个

体育中心宛如出水芙蓉，在公园里绽放。它坐落在小山岗上，是河畔公园的新地标，更是新佛山南部的城市风景线。体育馆顶棚覆盖白色薄膜，如同灿烂盛开的莲花。其张开时的面积达到120m×180m，是世界上最大的可折叠顶棚。当它展开时，一座体育场只需12分钟即可变成一座室内竞技场。当顶棚收合时，又会变成一个巨大的电视屏幕，悬浮于体育场上空。游泳馆作为体育中心附属的竞技场馆，造型上采用了同质化的建筑语言，强调两座体育馆为一个整体的同时避免了喧宾夺主。

Century Lotus Sports Park with Stadium and Swimming Hall
Foshan, China

Competition 2003 – 2nd Prize and Commission **Design** Volkwin Marg **Partner** Nikolaus Goetze **Project leader** Christian Hoffmann **Chinese partner practice** South China University, Architectural Design and Research Institute **Client** Foshan Sports Site Construction Center for the 12th Provincial Sports Event **Construction period** 2004 – 2006 **Seats, stadium** 36,000 **Seats, swimming hall** 2,800

The stadium is situated in the park like a flourishing water rose in a lake. Being situated on a hill, it forms the new landmark of the park on the river and adds an imposing and monumental shape to the southern cityscape of the new Foshan. The stadium roof unfolds itself with its white membrane like a radiant bloom. With 120×180 meters being the biggest retractable roof in the world it turns the stadium into one of the biggest fully-covered arenas in the world within twelve minutes. The second venue in the sports park, the swimming pool, reflects the architectural language of the stadium, allowing the two buildings to appear as an ensemble without undermining the unquestioned dominance of the stadium.

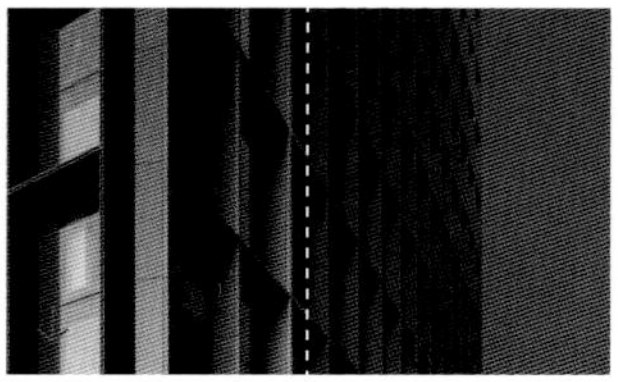

中青旅大厦
北京，中国

方案设计： 曼哈德·冯·格康和斯特凡·胥茨以及多莉丝·谢夫勒，2003年　**中方合作设计单位：** 中国建筑科学研究院　**业主：** 中国中青旅控股有限公司　**建设周期：** 2004—2005年　**建筑面积：** 65 000m²　**高度：** 75m

北京中青旅集团作为现代化，面向世界开放的集团公司，希望将其清晰、透明、高效的企业管理理念通过建筑的语汇加以传达。两座75m高的中庭内设有空中连廊和电梯，访客以及大厦各层的办公人员均能在此领略壮丽的北京城市景观。在大厦两个交通核心中间的每4层都设有一个公共活动空间，作为举办活动、休憩以及交流的区域，同样享有俯瞰城市的美好视野。葱郁繁茂的绿色植物营造出宜人的氛围。立面素雅的大尺度的网格结构使建筑从周边的环境中凸现出来，并赋予建筑强有力的均衡感。2007年7月，规模不断壮大中的gmp建筑事务所北京分部迁入了位于中青旅大厦12层的新办公室。

CYTS Plaza
Beijing, China

Design Meinhard von Gerkan with Stephan Schütz and Doris Schäffler, 2003 **Chinese partner practice** CABR **Client** China CYTS Tours Holding Co., Ltd. **Construction period** 2004–2005 **Gross floor area** 65,000 m² **Height** 75 m

The clear structural order of this scheme is directly related to the "CYTS-philosophy": clear and transparent, but innovative and efficient at the same time. Bridges and observer elevators are placed within the two 75 meters high atriums so that the space and the view on the city landscape can be physically experienced by both visitors and employees. The center part of the building is determined by four-story high halls. These spaces serve as communication zones for all the people working in this CYTS building and also grant a view of the city. By lush green these zones provide a pleasant atmosphere. The building's facade consists of a dark aluminum structure, giving the building a strong proportion. In July 2007 the expanding Beijing dependence of gmp architects moved into their new office on the 12th floor of CYTS Plaza.

54

期货广场双子大厦
大连，中国

设计竞赛：2003年，一等奖 **方案设计**：曼哈德·冯·格康 **合伙人**：尼古劳斯·格茨 **项目负责人**：德克·海勒，卡伦·施罗德 **中方合作设计单位**：华东建筑设计研究院有限公司 **业主**：大连商品交易所，中铁建工集团有限公司 **建设周期**：2005—2010年 **建筑面积**：353 000m² **高度**：240m **楼层数**：53层

双子大厦从地面算起53层，总高240m。两栋大厦均由一个矩形平面发展而来，通高的中庭作为建筑的玻璃暖房位于两楼各自中心的凹进处。中庭内每八层设有阳光暖房，被称为"空中大堂"，使高层办公空间均能拥有开阔的前厅空间。大楼采用复合式结构；钢筋混凝土结构在内，网格如外壳包裹于外，承受荷载。大厦的外立面正是这种构造的忠实反映。

Twin Towers, Commodity Exchange Plaza
Dalian, China

Competition 2003 – 1st Prize **Design** Meinhard von Gerkan **Partner** Nikolaus Goetze **Project leaders** Dirk Heller, Karen Schroeder **Chinese partner practice** ECADI **Clients** Dalian Commodity Exchange, China Railway Construction Engineering Group **Construction period** 2005–2010 **Gross floor area** 353,000 m² **Height** 240 m **Floors** 53

With 53 floors above ground the Twin Towers reach an overall height of 240 meters. Both towers are based on rectangular floor plans, with full height conservatories recessed into the center of each. Within the conservatories sky lobbies span the height of eight floors each, allowing for spacious lobby and entrance situations on all floors. The design of the facade is based on the structural composition of the building: The concrete core within and the grid-like shell outside are load bearing.

60

重庆大剧院
重庆，中国

设计竞赛：2004年，一等奖 **方案设计**：曼哈德·冯·格康和克劳斯·伦茨 **合伙人**：尼古劳斯·格茨 **项目负责人**：福克玛·西弗斯 **中方合作设计单位**：华东建筑设计和研究院有限公司 **业主**：重庆城建投资发展股份有限公司 **建设周期**：2005—2009年 **建筑面积**：100 000m²

临水而立的大剧院如同漂浮在长江之上的巨轮。一个石材基座支撑着这座如玻璃雕塑般的建筑。看似随意却极富表现力的建筑造型隐喻着巨轮，但这丝毫不影响建筑的平面和立面与功能之间的高度契合。位于长轴之上的两座演出厅和与其配套的前厅构成巨轮的"龙骨"，并在首尾两端形成建筑的入口空间。入口空间的中间或所谓"舯舱"是展览厅，它同时与所有的剧院前厅相连接。

Chongqing Grand Theater
Chongqing, China

Competition 2004 – 1st Prize **Design** Meinhard von Gerkan and Klaus Lenz **Partner** Nikolaus Goetze **Project leader** Volkmar Sievers **Chinese partner practice** ECADI **Client** Chongqing Urban Construction Investment **Construction period** 2005–2009 **Gross floor area** 100,000 m²

With its close proximity to the water, the "Grand Theater" seems to hover above the River Yangtze. A stone platform base supports the glass sculpture; the ground plan and elevation are subject to strict functional requirements despite their seemingly arbitrary expressiveness and maritime analogy. Two concert halls with their respective foyers are situated in the longitudinal axis, similar to the "keel line" of a ship, thus forming entrance areas at the bow anc the stern. In the center, in other words "midship" of these entrance areas, is the exhibition hall, which joins all the theater foyers together.

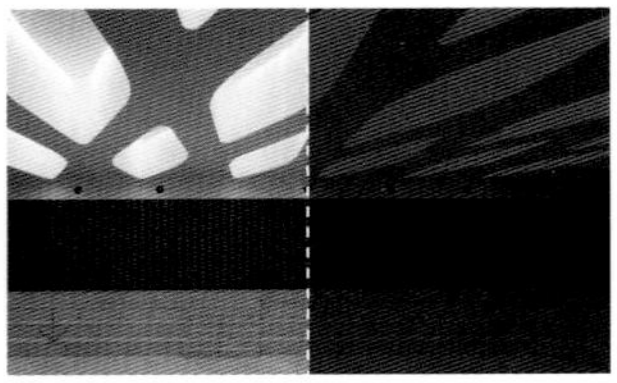

68

基督教会海淀堂
北京，中国

设计竞赛：2004年，一等奖　**方案设计**：曼哈德·冯·格康和斯特凡·胥茨　**中方合作设计单位**：三磊建筑设计有限公司　**业主**：中国中关村文化发展股份有限公司　**建筑周期**：2005—2006年　**建筑面积**：4 000m²

中国特有的"3P"原则是：公众-个人-合作关系，这座中国最大的基督教堂便在这一原则下设计完成，建筑包括了一个做商业用途的一层以及其引人瞩目的竖条外观。建筑流线型的外立面强调着其教堂身份，并刻意与周遭的商用建筑在审美情趣上拉开距离，这是设计思想的重点所在。交错的实体与空隙在室内形成了奇妙的光线效果，营造出宗教仪式所需的神圣氛围。

Christian Church
Beijing, China

Competition 2004 – 1st Prize **Design** Meinhard von Gerkan and Stephan Schütz **Chinese partner practice** Sunlight **Client** China Zhongguancun Culture Development Co., Ltd. **Construction period** 2005–2006 **Gross floor area** 4,000 m²

A Chinese version of "Triple P": A Public-Private-Partnership characterizes this design for the largest Christian Church in China. It comprises of a ground floor with commercial use and a distinctive facade. The primary aim of this design concept is the aesthetic differentiation of the building with its curved form from the surrounding commercially used buildings, in order to emphasize its special function as a church. The interplay of openings and solid areas in the facade's structure generates a special interior lighting atmosphere that is appropriate to the sacral use.

74

国家会议中心
河内，越南

设计竞赛：2004年，一等奖　**方案设计**：曼哈德·冯·格康　**合伙人**：尼古劳斯·格茨　**项目负责人**：克劳斯·伦茨　**合作设计**：Inros Lackner　**业主**：越南社会主义共和国　**建设周期**：2004—2006年　**建筑面积**：65 000m²

建筑整个镶嵌在一片园林景观之中，将主题性和象征性的含义与越南文化与传统相结合。国家会议中心、酒店和博物馆的新建筑就根植在这大片园林景观的怀抱中。国家会议中心的屋顶悠然起伏，极富表现力，一路伴随来宾进入前厅；屋顶向上耸立，甚至覆盖了最高的大会堂，进而成为河内城市的显著地标。

National Conference Center
Hanoi, Vietnam

Competition 2004 – 1st Prize **Design** Meinhard von Gerkan **Partner** Nikolaus Goetze **Project leader** Klaus Lenz **Co-operation with** Inros Lackner **Client** Socialist Republic of Vietnam **Construction period** 2004–2006 **Gross floor area** 65,000 m²

The whole complex is embedded in a park landscape, which integrates thematic and symbolic references to the Vietnamese culture and traditions. The new buildings for the National Conference Center, the hotel and museum have been positioned in this landscape garden. The expressive undulating roof of the whole NCC accompanies the visitors on their way into the foyer. It rises up to an even greater height above the large congress hall, thus creating a distinctive landmark for the NCC Hanoi.

82

中国国家博物馆
北京，中国

设计竞赛： 2004年，一等奖 **方案设计：** 曼哈德·冯·格康，斯特凡·胥茨，施蒂芬·瑞沃勒，多莉丝·舍弗勒 **项目负责人：** 马提亚斯·魏格曼，帕特里克·弗雷德尔 **中方合作设计单位：** 中国建筑科学研究院 **业主：** 中国国家博物馆
建设周期： 2005—2010年 **建筑面积：** 192 000m²

中国国家博物馆由中国历史博物馆和中国革命博物馆合并而成。扩建的新馆为一个嵌入式的建筑体，向东面延伸，大部分内部空间用于展览。老馆的中央大厅和东翼被拆除，这就使得改建后的老馆旧建筑从三面围合着新馆。参观者经由两个主入口可到达博物馆的中心区域，这是一个260m长的入口大厅，它将新老馆沿着原有的对称轴线接榫在一起。拱廊的尺度和体量在新老馆之间创造出一种崭新的空间体验。

National Museum of China
Beijing, China

Competition 2004 – 1st Prize **Design** Meinhard von Gerkan and Stephan Schütz with Stephan Rewolle and Doris Schäffler **Project leaders** Matthias Wiegelmann, Patrick Pfleiderer **Chinese partner practice** CABR **Client** National Museum of China **Construction period** 2005–2010 **Gross floor area** 192,000 m²

National Museum of China represents the merger of the former Chinese History Museum and Chinese Revolutionary Museum. The museum was expanded with a sequence of buildings towards the east containing a large proportion of the exhibition area. The former central structure and east wing of the old building were removed, so that the remaining parts of the refurbished old building enclose the new building on three sides. From the two main entrances, visitors pass into the core area – a 260 meter long forum that dovetails the new building with the old building on its original symmetrical axis. In their scale and dimensions, the arcades are typologically a cross between old and new architecture.

90

青岛大剧院
青岛，中国

设计竞赛： 2004年，一等奖 **方案设计：** 曼哈德·冯·格康和斯特凡·胥茨以及尼古拉斯·博兰克 **中方合作设计单位：** 上海华东建筑设计研究院有限公司 **业主：** 青岛国信大剧院有限公司
建设周期： 2005—2010年 **建筑面积：** 59 000m²

青岛大剧院选址于青岛崂山区，位于新规划出的从崂山山脚延伸至海边的园林景观中。如此非凡的地理位置，促使人们将天然的美景引入建筑语汇，从而塑造出一座继承了场所精神并且独一无二的建筑综合体。如同山峰一般的建筑体拔地而起，浮云般的屋顶轻盈地环绕其四周。

Qingdao Grand Theater
Qingdao, China

Competition 2004 – 1st Prize **Design** Meinhard von Gerkan and Stephan Schütz with Nicolas Pomränke **Chinese partner practice** ECADI **Client** Qingdao Conson Industrial Corporation **Construction period** 2005–2010 **Gross floor area** 59,000 m²

Located in the Laoshan district of Qingdao the Grand Theater is placed along a newly created park, which stretches from the sea to the foot of the Laoshan Mountains. In view of this extraordinary location it is highly attractive to implement the genius loci into architectural appearance. Like a mountain landscape the building is growing from the ground, and a roof that is similar to a light and floating cloud surrounds this "architectural landscape".

98

中国航海博物馆

临港新城，上海，中国

咨询设计：2005年　**方案设计**：曼哈德·冯·格康　**合伙人**：尼古劳斯·格茨　**项目负责人**：克劳斯·伦茨，马库斯·汤臣　**中方合作设计单位**：上海建筑设计研究院　**业主**：上海港城开发（集团）有限公司　**建设周期**：2006—2009年　**建筑面积**：46 400m²

中国首个航海博物馆坐落于一个5km²的人工湖湖畔——这是临港新城的中心区域，由填海造地而得。在博物馆广场中央，矗立着两座58m高的"风帆"，进一步隐喻着港口中扬帆待发的船只。如大教堂般的内部空间陈列着一艘仿真明代帆船。

China Maritime Museum

Lingang New City, Shanghai, China

Consultancy 2005　**Design** Meinhard von Gerkan
Partner Nikolaus Goetze　**Project leaders** Klaus Lenz, Marcus Tanzen　**Chinese partner practice** SIADR
Client Shanghai Harbour City Development Group Co., Ltd.
Construction period 2006–2009　**Gross floor area** 46,400 m²

China's first ever Maritime Museum is situated on the shore of a five square kilometer artificial lake that has been reclaimed from the Sea – the lake being the core piece of the new city development. The analogy of a ship in a port is developed further in the symbolism of the two "sails" with a height of 58 meter each, located almost in the middle of the museum square. The enormous cathedral-like interior space allows the display of a fully rigged junk.

106

河内博物馆

河内，越南

设计竞赛：2005年，一等奖　**方案设计**：曼哈德·冯·格康，尼古劳斯·格茨和克劳斯·伦茨　**项目负责人**：马库斯·汤臣，文宣承　**联合设计**：Inros Lackner　**业主**：河内文化信息部　**建设周期**：2008—2010年　**总建筑面积**：30 000m²
屋面：92.4m×92.4m

在正方形的建筑体中庭内，一座圆形的挑空大厅将入口层面与其上的三层展览空间连接起来。建筑体如同倒置的金字塔，上方悬挑出的楼层在其下方楼层处形成阴影，是为节能设计的一部分。因为博物馆的内部空间不受阳光直射，这也对文物展品起到了保护作用。而这样的空间构成让人们从室内向外观望时，仿佛"漂浮"于周边的景观之上。作为该建筑显著特征的螺旋形坡道将参观者引入更高的楼层，走在上面，能从多个视角一览入口大厅和展览区域。

Hanoi Museum

Hanoi, Vietnam

Competition 2005 – 1st Prize　**Design** Meinhard von Gerkan and Nikolaus Goetze with Klaus Lenz　**Project leaders** Marcus Tanzen, Tuyen Tran Viet　**Co-operation with** Inros Lackner　**Client** Hanoi Culture and Information Department　**Construction period** 2008–2010
Gross floor area 30,000 m²　**Roof** 92.4 m × 92.4 m

Within the square building, a central circular atrium links the entrance level with the three exhibition levels. The upwardly projecting stories cause in each of the layers below a shading, which is part of the energy efficiency concept. Since the interior spaces are protected from direct sunlight, also a conservative impact is created for the exhibits. For visitors, the effect is that, when looking out, they seem to be floating over the landscape. Visitors to the museum reach the upper levels via a spiral ramp. As the dominant feature, the ramp offers perspectives into the entrance hall and exhibition areas.

114

118

南汇行政中心
临港新城，上海，中国

设计竞赛：2005年，一等奖　方案设计：曼哈德·冯·格康　合伙人：尼古劳斯·格茨　项目负责人：约恩·奥特曼　中方合作设计单位：上海建筑设计研究院　业主：南汇区政府　建设周期：2006—2008年　建筑面积：100 860m²

规划地块位于临港新城的一条主干道旁的显著位置，这要求行政办公中心的各个主楼和辅楼的设计同样具有显著性和明朗性，使其成为一个和谐统一的整体。位于西面正对主干道的高层建筑将成为城市的地标。两座长型的办公楼组成一个闭合的街区，东部以圆形体块收尾。内庭中设有水景和绿化带，两座步行桥连接了建筑群的两个部分。

Nanhui Administration Center
Lingang New City, Shanghai, China

Competition 2005 – 1st Prize **Design** Meinhard von Gerkan **Partner** Nikolaus Goetze **Project leader** Jörn Ortmann **Chinese partner practice** SIADR **Client** Government of the Nanhui District **Construction period** 2006 – 2008 **Gross floor area** 100,860 m²

The prominent position of the plot by one of the main access roads and the important function for the district and the city demands a similarly exposed as well as strict architectural composition for the two individual buildings, which are grouped together to form a super-ordinate ensemble. The high-rise at the west side of the site – facing the main entrance axis of the city – is designed as a landmark for Lingang New City. Two linear office buildings are forming an elongated block. At the eastern end they are joined to a round closure. In between the inner courtyard with its water basins and green trees two pedestrian bridges connect both parts of the complex.

万向大厦
上海，中国

设计竞赛：2005年，一等奖　方案设计：曼哈德·冯·格康　合伙人：尼古劳斯·格茨　项目负责人：福克玛·西福斯　业主：万向控股集团　建设周期：2007—2010年　建筑总面积：42 000m²　建筑高度：79m　楼层：19层

万向控股集团的区域总部坐落于上海浦东黄浦江畔，地理位置得天独厚。白色的天然石材幕墙饰面赋予建筑立面犹如雕塑般的立体感。每两层被划分为一个立面单元，由通高的幕墙窗覆盖。通风窗位于竖直方向的金属网板构件之后。这一设计凸显了两层高窗带的纤细瘦长。建筑的裙楼通过高大的柱廊和退后的幕墙延续了建筑外形的雕塑感，柱廊的交会处构成三层高的大厦主入口。大厦的外立面和裙楼各层的地面均采用浅色的天然石材铺装。

Wanxiang Plaza
Shanghai, China

Competition 2005 – 1st Prize **Design** Meinhard von Gerkan **Partner** Nikolaus Goetze **Project leader** Volkmar Sievers **Chinese partner practice** HAS **Client** Wanxiang Holding **Construction period** 2007 – 2010 **Gross floor area** 42,000 m² **Height** 79 m **Floors** 19

The site in Shanghai-Pudong, on which the regional headquarters of the Wanxiang Holding was built, is impressive with its location on the Huangpu River. Its facade, faced in white natural stone, has a consciously intense sculptural depth. Tall window openings extend over two stories each. On the outside they have vertical metal mesh elements, behind which on the inside are placed ventilation windows. As slender two story high elements, they accentuate the window openings. The sculptural form of the facade is continued on the building's base by the deeply recessed windows and a high colonnade, which leads into the three story high main entrance. Light-colored natural stone is the material used throughout on the facade and the floors of the lower base levels.

124

128

内政部大厦
河内，越南

设计竞赛：2006年，一等奖　**方案设计**：曼哈德·冯·格康和尼古劳斯·格茨　**项目负责人**：乌铎·迈耶　**合作设计**：Inros Lackner　**越方合作设计单位**：越南国家建设咨询部（VNCC）　**业主**：越南社会主义共和国　**建设周期**：2007—2010年　**建筑面积**：180 000m²

在这座引人注目的建筑中设有公共职能机构。主建筑由两组高八层，面对中轴线对称展开的锯齿状的建筑组成，在中轴线的中点处，跨越轴线的横向建筑将两组建筑结合在一起，自然地构成整个部门的入口。中轴两侧建筑通过锯齿状布置形式，使自由的外部空间和建筑主体得以紧密衔接，并各自产生一个半开放式的中央庭院。

Headquarters of the Ministry of the Interior
Hanoi, Vietnam

Competition 2006 – 1st Prize **Design** Meinhard von Gerkan and Nikolaus Goetze **Project leader** Udo Meyer **Co-operation with** Inros Lackner AG **Vietnamese partner practice** Vietnamese National Construction Consultants (VNCC) **Client** Social Republic of Vietnam **Construction period** 2007–2010 **Gross floor area** 180,000 m²

The most important and principal public functions of the ministry are housed in this prominent building. The ground plan figure of the central complex is formed by two comb-shaped eight-story blocks arranged along a central axis. Transverse to this central axis is an elevated block, so as to mark the obvious entrance to the whole ministerial complex. As a result of the comb-shape of the office levels, there is an excellent intermeshing of open space and buildings, with a small, semi-open interior courtyard in each recess.

会议展览中心
淮安，中国

设计竞赛：2006年，一等奖　**方案设计**：曼哈德·冯·格康和斯特凡·胥茨以及施蒂芬·瑞沃勒　**项目负责人**：帕特里克·弗莱德勒　**中方合作设计单位**：中国建筑科学研究院建筑设计院　**业主**：淮安市园林部　**建设周期**：2007—2010年　**建筑面积**：125 000m²

设计方案的宗旨为将会展中心塑造为城市独一无二的地标性建筑。对与其他城市中已建成的展览和会议中心雷同的建筑形式，设计予以刻意的回避。会展中心屋面起伏如嶙峋的岩石，极富表现力，延续了广场网轴的划分肌理，同时强调了建筑的雕塑感。封闭的表皮与开放的玻璃错落有致，如同凝固的旋律，中和了建筑群相对巨大的体量感。双层玻璃幕墙结构作为保温层则起到了节能的作用。

Convention & Exhibition Center
Huai'an, China

Competition 2006 – 1st Prize **Design** Meinhard von Gerkan and Stephan Schütz with Stephan Rewolle **Project leader** Patrick Pfleiderer **Chinese partner practice** CABR **Client** Huai'an City Gardening Bureau **Construction period** 2007–2010 **Gross floor area** 125,000 m²

The major architectural goal was to design the center as a unique landmark. Therefore any analogy to existing trade fair halls or convention centers in other cities or countries had to be clearly avoided. The expressive shape of the buildings is produced by folded surfaces which continue the grid of the plaza and develop a sculptural idea of architecture. Clad surfaces alter with glass areas so that a clear rhythm is produced which provide structure to the comparatively big building. At the same time the building is energy saving by highly insulated cladding structures as well as double-skin glass structures.

134

贾瓦哈拉尔·尼赫鲁体育场
新德里，印度

设计竞赛： 2006年，一等奖　**方案设计：** 福尔克温·玛格和胡贝特·尼恩霍夫　**项目负责人：** 斯温·施莫德、马库斯·福斯特　**合作设计：** 施莱希工程设计公司、CES工程顾问公司、IG科技　**业主：** 中央公共工程部（CPWD）　**建设周期：** 2007—2010年　**座席数：** 57 000个

在2012年英联邦运动会举行期间，尼赫鲁体育场将作为开幕式、闭幕式以及橄榄球和田径赛事场地投入使用。体育场最引人瞩目的是经过重新设计的碗状看台结构以及新屋面，其重现了印度传统历史根源的同时赋予了建筑现代的形象。一个钢结构框架环围合了整座体育场，将看台分割成两层独立的看台，在原有的场地结构上构成了一个内环和一个外环。

Jawaharlal Stadium, Commonwealth Games 2010
New Delhi, India

Competition 2006 – 1st Prize **Design** Volkwin Marg and Hubert Nienhoff **Project leaders** Sven Schmedes, Markus Pfisterer **Co-operation with** schlaich bergermann und partner; CES Consulting Engineering Services; IG Tech **Client** Central Public Works Department (CPWD) **Construction period** 2007–2010 **Seats** 57,000

The Jawaharlal Nehru Stadium, the venue for the opening and closing ceremony, as well as for the rugby and athletics events, was the center of attention during the Commonwealth Games 2010. The redesign of the existing bowl structure and the new roof created a modern stadium, which reflects its tradition and historical roots at the same time. A rotating steel grid spins around the stadium bowl in two separated layers, forming an inner and outer ring around the existing stand construction.

138

嘉铭中心
北京，中国

设计竞赛： 2006年，一等奖　**方案设计：** 曼哈德·冯·格康和斯特凡·胥茨以及尼古拉斯·博兰克　**项目负责人：** 托斯顿·贝瑟尔、陈澜　**中方合作设计单位：** 中国建筑科学研究院　**业主：** 嘉铭投资（集团）有限公司　**建设周期：** 2008—2011年　**建筑面积：** 57 600m²　**高度：** 100m　**楼层数：** 20层

项目位于北京东三环，紧邻中央商务区，建筑由两个前后相互平行错开的体块构成。两座形式单一的建筑体略微地错位在北面的城市空间中形成了一个街角广场。这座前广场位置显要，并呈现出迎接的姿态，而在基地南面与之完全对称的位置上坐落着一个80m高的玻璃中庭。外立面延续了方案简洁、清晰的设计理念，极其简化的材料语言、大规格的石材和玻璃幕墙的使用保证了双层"可呼吸"式幕墙结构的实现，建筑表皮可通过被覆盖于其内的开窗进行自然通风。

Jiaming Center
Beijing, China

Competition 2006 – 1st Prize **Design** Meinhard von Gerkan and Stephan Schütz with Nicolas Pomränke **Project leaders** Torsten Bessel, Chen Lan **Chinese partner practice** CABR **Client** Jiaming Investment (Group) Co., Ltd. **Construction period** 2008–2011 **Gross floor area** 57,600 m² **Height** 100 m **Floors** 20

Sited on the eastern Ring 3 close to Beijing's Central Business District, the building consists of two slender blocks placed parallel to each other. The slight displacement of the two monoliths relative to each other creates an urban space in the north that is a response to the position at the corner of a major junction. As a forecourt to the building, the space is prominent and inviting, and is matched by a more intimate counterpart on the south side in the form of a completely glazed, 80 meters high atrium. The conceptual simplicity and clarity continue in the facade. This takes the form of a double-shell, climate-active facade that allows a complete reduction to large-format stone and glass surfaces, permitting natural ventilation via concealed apertures.

146

154

科技文化综合中心
长春，中国

设计竞赛：2006年，一等奖　**方案设计**：曼哈德·冯·格康　**合伙人**：尼古劳斯·格茨　**项目负责人**：亨里希·缪勒，马克·西蒙斯　**中方合作设计单位**：吉林省建筑设计院有限责任公司　**业主**：长春科学文化中心项目领导组　**建设周期**：2007—2010年　**建筑面积**：107 500m²　**三座博物馆平面**：81m×81m

"长春科技文化综合中心"由三座博物馆组成。三个石质的立方体如同风车的翼板般将一个公共的前厅建筑围合于中央。三座立方体在建筑体态的雕塑感以及外立面细节上富于变化，色彩和材质则保持相对统一，成为城市东南新规划社区的基石。三座博物馆均采取了相同的内部交通组织形式：所有外侧的展览空间均避免了阳光的直射，为循环的参观流线串联起来。展厅之间由开放的空中桥梁相连接。

保利大厦
上海，中国

设计竞赛：2006年，一等奖　**方案设计**：曼哈德·冯·格康和玛德琳·唯斯　**合伙人**：尼古劳斯·格茨，吴蔚　**项目负责人**：亚里山大·肖伯，郝艳丽，安妮卡·施罗德　**中方合作设计单位**：华东建筑设计研究院有限公司　**业主**：上海保利房地产有限公司　**建设周期**：2007—2010年　**建筑面积**：65 000m²　**建筑高度**：143m　**楼层数**：30层

保利广场位于上海浦东黄浦江畔。一座塔楼和四座临江建筑构成了整个办公综合体，其外立面为双层呼吸式幕墙。整个基地被划分为三层阶梯状平台，从下沉式庭院可直达地下层，并从那里前往商业区域。从第二层的平台上可一览黄浦江的壮观景致。四座较低的临江建筑体沿岸依次排开，错落有致，直接面对黄浦江边的公共绿地和林荫道。

Museum for Culture, Fine Arts and Science
Changchun, China

Competition 2006 – 1st Prize　**Design** Meinhard von Gerkan　**Partner** Nikolaus Goetze　**Project leaders** Hinrich Müller, Marc Ziemons　**Chinese partner practice** JPADI　**Client** Changchun Science and Culture Center Project Leading Team　**Construction period** 2007–2010　**Gross floor area** 107,500 m² 3 Museums à 81 × 81 m edge length

Three museums form the "Changchun Museum for Culture, Fine Arts and Science". The three stone cubes, housing the three museums, are positioned around a common foyer in shape of a windmill. Different in its expression, and sculptural facade detail, the same in color and material, the museum laid the foundation for a new neighborhood in the southeast of the city. The three museums have the same site development idea: sunscreened exhibition spaces arranged along the visitors' tour. The rooms are linked by open bridges.

Poly Plaza
Shanghai, China

Competition 2006 – 1st Prize　**Design** Meinhard von Gerkan with Magdalene Weiss　**Partners** Nikolaus Goetze, Wu Wei　**Project leaders** Alexander Schober, Hao Yan Li, Annika Schröder　**Chinese partner practice** ECADI　**Client** Shanghai Poly Xin Real Estate Co., Ltd.　**Construction period** 2007–2010　**Gross floor area** 65,000 m²　**Height** 143 m　**Floors** 30

The Poly Plaza project is situated on the prominent shore of the Huangpu River in Pudong. One high-rise and four waterfront buildings with an outer ventilated double facade provide office spaces. The site is terraced over three levels, giving direct basement access through cut out deep yards leading into the commercial area. The terrace on the second level provides a magnificent outlook on the riverside. The lower waterfront buildings create a rhythm along the shore, which will host a public park and green promenade along the Huangpu.

162

2011年世界大学生运动会体育中心
深圳，中国

设计竞赛：2006年，一等奖 **方案设计**：曼哈德·冯·格康和斯特凡·胥茨以及尼古拉斯·博兰克 **项目负责人**：Ralf Sieber **中方合作设计单位**：深圳市建筑设计研究院（体育场），中国建筑东北设计研究院（多功能厅），中建国际设计公司（游泳馆），深圳市北林苑景观及建筑规划设计院（景观设计） **业主**：深圳市建筑工务署 **建设周期**：2007—2011年 **建筑面积**：870 000m² **体育场座席数**：60 000个 **多功能厅座席数**：18 000个 **游泳馆座席数**：3 000个

深圳大运会体育中心在功能设置上除可满足举办国际体育赛事的有关要求外还可用于举行各种规模的演出活动。设计构想源于其所处群山环抱的地理环境。一个人工湖使山脚下的体育场与北面圆形多功能中心以及西面呈长方形的游泳馆连接起来。通过一个被抬高的林荫大道人们可从各体育场馆到达位于中央的体育广场。

Universiade 2011 Sports Center
Shenzhen, China

Consultancy 2006 – 1st Prize **Design** Meinhard von Gerkan and Stephan Schütz with Nicolas Pomränke **Project leader** Ralf Sieber **Chinese partner practices** SADI (stadium), CNADRI (multi-function hall), CCDI (swimming hall), BLY (landscape design) **Client** Bureau of Public Works of Shenzhen Municipality **Construction period** 2007–2011 **Planning area** 870,000 m² **Seats, stadium** 60,000 **Seats, multi-function hall** 18,000 **Seats, swimming hall** 3,000

The Universiade sports center has to satisfy the functional requirements of both international sports events and the organization of other smaller and larger-scale events and concerts. The design is inspired by the surrounding undulating landscape. An artificial lake connects the stadium at the foot of the mountain with the circular multifunctional hall in the north and the rectangular swimming hall west thereof. The central sports plaza is accessed via a raised promenade from the individual stadia.

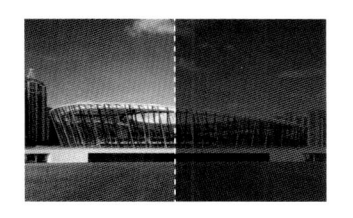

170

宝安体育场
深圳，中国

设计竞赛：2007年，一等奖 **方案设计**：曼哈德·冯·格康，斯特凡·胥茨和大卫·申科 **项目负责人**：大卫·申科，李然 **结构设计**：施莱希工程设计咨询公司 **照明设计**：Schlotfeldt Licht, 柏林 **中方合作设计单位**：中国华南理工大学 **业主**：深圳市宝安区体育局 **建设周期**：2009—2011年 **座席数**：40 050个

体育馆坐落于深圳宝安区内，设计目标为一座可容纳四万多人的田径体育馆，在2011年世界大学生运动会召开之际将被委以重任，作为足球赛场投入使用。场馆的设计灵感来源于极具华南地区风情的竹林场景，其在重现了华南的地域特色的同时还构成了看台以及大跨度屋面的结构支承系统。 观众看台上部的屋面为拉索固定的张拉膜结构，通过一个位于中心的张力环和呈放射状的辐条结构支撑。

Bao'an Stadium
Shenzhen, China

Competition 2007 – 1st Prize **Design** Meinhard von Gerkan and Stephan Schütz with David Schenke **Project leaders** David Schenke, Li Ran **Structural concept and design, roof** schlaich bergermann und partner **Chinese partner practice** SCUT **Client** The Sports Bureau of Bao'an District **Construction period** 2009–2011 **Seats** 40,050

The stadium was designed as an athletics stadium holding 40,050 spectators and was used for football matches during the 2011 Universiade. The extensive bamboo forests of southern China were the inspiration for the design. The bamboo look serves two purposes: it reflects the character of the region, and thus creates identity. And it serves as a structural concept for both the load-bearing frame of the stadium stands and the supports for the wide-span roof structure.

178

华为科研中心办公楼
深圳，中国

方案设计：曼哈德·冯·格康和斯特凡·胥茨以及施蒂芬·瑞沃勒，2007年 **项目负责人：**卡提纳·罗洛夫 **中方合作设计单位：**上海建筑设计研究院 **业主：**华为技术有限公司 **建设周期：**2008—2011年 **建筑面积：**226 000m²

华为技术有限公司是一家领先的新一代通信设备生产销售公司，其深圳科技园由六栋办公楼和两栋职工餐厅楼组成。建筑师在力求优化工作环境的同时，亦强调了建筑与自然的关系。科技园以多个方形、四层高的单元建筑组成，每个单元环抱着一个内庭：该内庭既是人流集散区域，也是景观庭院。这个古典的内廊式建筑无论在内部功能还是流线设计上，都体现出其高效性。办公楼的外立面为双层玻璃幕墙：外层为隔热玻璃，内层为夹胶玻璃。两层玻璃之间有一个30cm宽的夹层，空气在其中通过机械送风的方式流通。

Huawei Development & Research Office Buildings
Shenzhen, China

Design Meinhard von Gerkan and Stephan Schütz with Stephan Rewolle, 2007 **Project leader** Katina Roloff **Chinese partner practice** SIADR **Client** Huawei Technologies Co., Ltd. **Construction period** 2008–2011 **Gross floor area** 226,000 m²

The six office building complexes and two canteen buildings for Huawei – a company in providing next generation telecommunications networks – create an optimized working environment with a strong relationship to the surrounding landscape. The shape of all office buildings is based on a square, four-story building module. Every module frames a courtyard, which serves as an entrance yard and landscape garden respectively. The facades of the office buildings consist of a fixed outer insulated glass layer and an interior layer of tempered glass. The characteristic of the facade is the 30 cm wide air cavity between the two facade layers, which is ventilated mechanically.

184

国家议会大厦
河内，越南

设计竞赛：2007年，一等奖 **方案设计：**曼哈德·冯·格康 **合伙人：**尼古劳斯·格茨 **项目负责人：**德克·海勒（项目合伙人），约恩·奥特曼，马库斯·汤臣，Duc Tran Cong **合作设计：**Inros Lackner **业主：**越南社会主义共和国建设部 **建设周期：**2009—2014年 **建筑面积：**36 000m²

新的国家议会大厦位于河内的一块充满历史沉淀的基地上，正对人民英雄胡志明的纪念堂，在城市中占据了无与伦比的重要地位，被誉为"世纪之作"。设计的隐喻表达通过深深扎根于越南文化中的象征性得以展现：基本的圆形和方形的使用，即天圆地方的概念。议会大厦可容纳800名议员的会议厅是一个圆柱形体块，基底为圆形，外墙向外倾斜，由一个宏大的入口大厅所围合，从这里可以直接俯瞰巴亭广场以及其对面的胡志明纪念堂。

Parliament House Hanoi
Hanoi, Vietnam

Competition 2007 – 1st Prize **Design** Meinhard von Gerkan **Partner** Nikolaus Goetze **Project leaders** Dirk Heller (Associate Partner), Jörn Ortmann, Marcus Tanzen, Duc Tran Cong **Co-operation with** Inros Lackner **Client** Ministry of Construction of the Socialist Republic of Vietnam **Construction period** 2009–2014 **Gross floor area** 36,000 m²

The new parliament building in Hanoi, designated to be the "building of the century", is situated on the historic land of the ancient sunken city and located opposite the mausoleum of Ho Chi Minh, thus occupying an incomparably prominent position within the city. The symbolic expression of the design is achieved by making use of the subtle means of a traditional symbolism, deeply anchored in Vietnam's history: through the basic forms of the circle and square, with the circle representing the heavens and the square the earth. The parliament building's plenary hall, which accommodates 800 delegates, is characterized by a circle functioning as a cylindrical body with outward inclined walls, surrounded by an expansive entrance hall that provides an unimpeded view of Ba Dinh Square, as well as of the mausoleum opposite it to the west.

188

天津西站
天津，中国

设计竞赛：2007年，一等奖　方案设计：曼哈德·冯·格康，斯特凡·胥茨和施蒂芬·瑞沃勒　项目负责人：施蒂芬·瑞沃勒，姜琳琳　业主：北京铁道局　建设周期：2009—2011年
总建筑面积：179 000m²

天津西站的重要性在于它将城市的北区与南区相连接。其57m高、400m长的筒形穹顶把北面的市中心商业区与天津老城区联系起来。拱形结构的屋面如一座宏伟的城门，而候车大厅也令人瞩目，它构建出一条古典主义风格的走道。穿插交织的菱形屋面结构使日光照射到大厅内部，创造出清晰的秩序感和舒适宜人的氛围。

Tianjin West Railway Station
Tianjin, China

Competition 2007 – 1st Prize **Design** Meinhard von Gerkan and Stephan Schütz with Stephan Rewolle **Project leaders** Stephan Rewolle, Jiang Lin Lin **Chinese partner practice** TSDI **Client** Beijing Railroad Bureau **Construction period** 2009 – 2011 **Gross floor area** 179,000 m²

The main significance of Tianjin West Railway Station is to link the northern half of the city with the southern half. The link is symbolized by the 57 meter high, 400 meter long barrel roof linking the central business district on the north side with Tianjin old city. The arched roof shape comes across as a grand gateway, while the impressive concourse constitutes a classic passage thoroughfare. The lozenge-weave pattern of the roof structure admits natural daylight into it, facilitating orientation and providing clarity while also making for an agreeable ambience that is a pleasure to be in.

196

临港投资公司标准厂房"条码"外立面
临港新城重工业区，上海，中国

咨询设计：2008年　方案设计：曼哈德·冯·格康　合伙人：尼古劳斯·格茨　项目负责人：马库斯·汤臣，朱宏昊　业主：上海漕河泾新兴技术开发区股份有限公司　建设周期：2008—2009年　建筑面积：1号厂房：11 170m²，119m×72m；2号厂房：7 150m²，117m×48m

临港新城内的工业区与近海的深水港洋山港同时面临着急速的发展。为了赋予生产大厅统一又不失个性的企业识别形象，设计构思展现了一个条纹编码的意象，垂直黑色条状开洞构成立面的肌理，建筑的门窗集中于此处。抹灰外立面作为极为简洁并且经济的施工方式，除未与其近旁的高科技园区外还在这里得到了进一步的运用。

"Barcode" Halls, Standard Facades for Manufacturing Buildings
Heavy Industry Zone of Lingang New City, Shanghai, China

Consultancy 2008 **Design** Meinhard von Gerkan **Partner** Nikolaus Goetze **Project leaders** Marcus Tanzen, Zhu Honghao **Client** Shanghai Caohejing Hi-Tech Park New Economic Zone Development Co., Ltd. **Construction period** 2008 – 2009 **Gross floor area** Hall 1: 11,170 m², 119 m × 72 m; Hall 2: 7,150 m², 117 m × 48 m

The industrial plants in the city of Lingang are growing at breakneck speed to keep pace with the development of the offshore deep-sea port Yangshan. In order to create a corporate identity of the manufacturing buildings, a facade structure was developed analogous to barcode labels. The facades are articulated by patterns of black vertical strips integrating windows and doors. The very simple and inexpensive design with rendered facades in the adjoining high tech park was continued.

202

上海东方体育中心
上海，中国

设计竞赛： 2008年，一等奖　**方案设计：** 曼哈德·冯·格康，尼古劳斯·格茨以及玛德琳·唯斯　**项目负责人：** 陈缨　**中方合作设计单位：** 上海建筑设计研究院，同济大学建筑设计研究院　**业主：** 上海市体育局　**建设周期：** 2009—2011年　**综合体育馆座席数：** 18 000个　**室内游泳馆座席数：** 5 000个　**室外跳水馆座席数：** 5 000个

上海东方体育中心坐落于黄浦江沿岸工业区的旧址之上，为第14届国际泳联世界游泳锦标赛的比赛场地。体育中心包括一座室内游泳馆、一座综合体育馆、一座室外跳水馆和一个媒体中心。公园景观、运动场馆以及媒体中心中贯穿始终的设计元素——水、浪、沙滩和桥梁——都折射出其中心主题：水。三座体育场馆相似的结构，共同的造型手法及类似的材质选用，令整个建筑群成为一个和谐统一的整体。

Shanghai Oriental Sports Center
Shanghai, China

Competition 2008 – 1st Prize　**Design** Meinhard von Gerkan and Nikolaus Goetze with Magdalene Weiss　**Project leader** Chen Ying　**Chinese partner practices** SIADR, Architectural Design & Research Institute of Tongji University　**Client** Shanghai Administration of Sports　**Construction period** 2009–2011　**Capacity** Hall stadium 18,000 seats, Natatorium 5,000 seats, Outdoor swimming pool 5,000 seats

The Shanghai Oriental Sports Center (SOSC) was built on industrial brownfield land along the Huangpu River as a venue for the 14th FINA World Swimming Championships in 2011. It consists of a swimming stadium, a sports stadium, an outdoor swimming pool for outdoor high-diving competitions, and a media center. Recurrent design motifs – water and waves, beaches and bridges – in both the park and the architecture of the stadiums and media center reflect the overall theme of water. A similar design, a common structural idiom and use of materials produce structural unity among all the stadiums.

210

三一重工奉贤产业中心概念规划
上海，中国

方案设计： 曼哈德·冯·格康和尼古劳斯·格茨以及玛德琳·唯斯，2009年　**项目负责人：** 任允平　**中方合作设计单位：** 联创国际设计集团　**业主：** 三一重工集团　**建设周期：** 2010—2014年　**建筑面积：** 473 000m²

总体规划的目标，是为三一集团这样知名且成功的重型机械制造厂商打造集机械制造、管理、研发中心、培训中心以及员工宿舍于一体的现代化的产业园区。三一上海产业中心位于新成立的奉贤–临港工业园区的中心地带，规划用地面积235hm²，是临港重工业基地最早期也最大型的项目之一。基地东侧设置景观公园，作为本设计的"软性边界"。通过绿地景观以及散布其间的小型建筑物，在营造生态且符合人体尺度的环境的同时，创造宜人的停留和展示空间。基地西侧的"硬性边界"主要为生产和物流服务：面积充裕的堆场，高效的交通流线——各种生产机械和制造厂房形成清晰的建筑和空间界限。

Sany Fengxian Master Plan
Shanghai, China

Design Meinhard von Gerkan and Nikolaus Goetze with Magdalene Weiss, 2009　**Project leader** Ren Yunping　**Chinese partner practice** UDG　**Client** Sany Group　**Construction period** 2010–2014　**Gross floor area** 473,000 m²

This master planning is developing an industrial estate for Sany, a construction machine manufacturer. It includes large production buildings, office accommodations, research facilities, canteens and housing. The site is located in a central position on the newly designated Fengxian/Lingang industrial zone and, with 235 ha, it is the first and largest project, launching the development of this expansion area of Lingang's heavy industry zone. Towards the east, the design includes a "soft edge" in the form of a landscaped park with small-scale buildings. Towards the west, the "hard edge" is defined by large production facilities, which are characterized by a uniform design in terms of proportion, volume and facade design.

214

天津大剧院
天津，中国

设计竞赛：2009年，一等奖　**方案设计**：曼哈德·冯·格康，斯特凡·胥茨以及尼古拉斯·博兰克　**项目负责人**：大卫·申科，徐山　**中方合作设计单位**：华东建筑设计研究院有限公司　**业主**：天津文化中心项目建设办公室　**建设周期**：2010—2012年　**建筑面积**：59 000m²　**歌剧厅座席数**：1 600个　**音乐厅座席数**：1 200个　**多功能厅座席数**：400个

天津大剧院占据了新建天津文化公园内的显著位置。呈碟形的屋面结构回应了其身后的自然历史博物馆。自然历史博物馆可看成是扎根于大地的建筑，而大剧院的造型则更多地与天空产生了联系。而天（天津大剧院）和地（自然历史博物馆）则是中国哲学和文化中的一对重要元素。三座相互独立的演出大厅坐落于一个石质基座上。宽阔的台阶将人们连接了水面和高处的平台，构成一个上演城市生活情境的舞台，人们可在此休憩，同时欣赏湖景，一览文化公园全貌。

Tianjin Grand Theater
Tianjin, China

Competition 2009 – 1st Prize　**Design** Meinhard von Gerkan and Stephan Schütz with Nicolas Pomränke　**Project leaders** David Schenke, Xu Shan　**Chinese partner practice** ECADI　**Client** Tianjin Culture Center Project and Construction Head Office　**Construction period** 2010–2012　**Gross floor area** 59,000 m²　**Seats, opera hall** 1,600　**Seats, concert hall** 1,200　**Seats, small multifunctional hall** 400

The building occupies the key position in Tianjin's new Culture Park. The roof structure's circular shape matches that of the existing Museum of Natural History, creating an architectural dialog between the earth-bound museum and the "floating" roof. The duality between the two elements earth (Museum of Natural History) and sky (Grand Theater) reflects a fundamental theme in Chinese philosophy. The Theater's three venues are designed as freestanding volumes on a stone base. Broad stairways connect the water level to the raised plaza, creating a sort of stage for urban life overlooking the lake and the Culture Park.

222

郑东绿地中心
郑州，中国

设计竞赛：2010年，一等奖　**方案设计**：曼哈德·冯·格康和斯特凡·胥茨以及尼古拉斯·威尔克　**项目负责人**：杰恩·威尔和尼古拉斯·威尔克　**中方合作设计单位**：同济大学建筑设计研究院，上海　**业主**：上海绿地集团中原房地产事业部　**建设周期**：2010—2016年　**建筑面积**：746 000m²　**高度**：284m　**楼层数**：63层

郑东绿地中心坐落于城市主轴线上，面向市中心，直指新建郑州东站，并在其西侧临近公共公园一侧构成大门的意象。这组多功能建筑综合体由两座布局对称的办公塔楼构成，两栋塔楼面向公共绿化广场的一侧由具有辅助商业功能的裙楼围合。郑东绿地中心的设计灵感来自郑州的自然景观风貌，黄河水流的冲刷塑造了郑州绵缓的地势以及蜿蜒的河岸线。塔楼的造型如同缠绕的丝带，同时也令人联想到逶迤的黄河。

Greenland Central Plaza
Zhengzhou, China

Competition 2010 – 1st Prize　**Design** Meinhard von Gerkan and Stephan Schütz with Nicolas Pomränke　**Project leaders** Jens Weiler, Niklas Veelken　**Chinese partner practice** TJADRI　**Client** Zhongyuan Real Estate Business Department of Shanghai Greenland Group　**Construction period** 2010–2016　**Gross floor area** 746,000 m²　**Height** 284 m　**Floors** 63

The Greenland Central Plaza Project is located on the urban axis pointing from the new East Station towards Zhengzhou City Center, forming a gate to the public park in the west of the project. The multifunctional complex consisting of two symmetrical office towers being flanked by supporting commercial podium buildings is organized on both sides of a landscaped public plaza. The design of the Zhengzhou Central Plaza draws its inspiration from the Zhengzhou landscape of gentle slopes and soft turns, being shaped by the waters of the Yellow River nearby. The towers are conceived as continuous winding bands as an analogy to the meandering Yellow River.

226

印度理工学院
海得拉巴，印度

设计竞赛：2011年，一等奖　**方案设计**：福尔克温·玛格和胡贝特·尼恩霍夫以及克里斯汀·斯潘　**项目负责人**：玛格丽特·勃斯　**业主**：ITT，海得拉巴　**建设开始**：2012年
建筑面积：83 000m²

项目包括一座设有会议大厅的校园行政大楼、由八幢建筑组成的学生宿舍以及一座食堂。行政大厦楼位于理工大学校园的中心位置。两座呈弧线的多功能建筑对峙而建，在其间形成了一个阴凉的庭院。学生宿舍综合体之间点缀有可供休憩的凉亭以及丰富的绿色植物，将景观引入建筑体内。两层高的食堂大厅由宽大的屋面覆盖，在树荫遮蔽的公共广场一侧构成一个开放大气的入口。

Indian Institute of Technology
Hyderabad, India

Competition 2011 – 1st Prize **Design** Volkwin Marg and Hubert Nienhoff with Kristian Spencker **Project leader** Margret Böthig **Client** ITT Hyderabad **Construction started** 2012 **Gross floor area** 83,000 m²

The project comprises a campus administration building with meeting hall, a students' hostel complex of eight buildings and a dining hall. The administration building area occupies the central position in the technology park. Two curved shaped multi-story building wings, shifted against each other, form a shaded courtyard. The residential complex for students, supplemented by common pavilions for recreation, is imbedded in the central richly planted common green, which connects the buildings with the landscape. The 2-story dining hall building with its roof-covered, shady open spaces create a generous entry gesture and opens towards a tree-covered public plaza.

230

国家会展中心
天津，中国

设计竞赛：2013年，一等奖　**方案设计**：曼哈德·冯·格康，斯特凡·胥茨以及尼古拉斯·博兰克　**竞赛项目负责人**：西蒙·舍特，帕特里克·弗莱德　**中方合作设计单位**：中国建筑科学研究院建筑设计院　**业主**：天津市规划局　**建筑面积**：1 200 000m²

即将兴建的天津国家会展中心将以其总面积120万平方米、净展览面积40万m²晋身世界最大会展中心之列，也将成为中国东部最大的会展中心。方案由两个几乎完全相同的建设周期构成。每期工程都包括一个中央大厅，大厅入口处由巨大的具有金属编制感的伞状顶棚覆盖，大厅两侧设有8个展厅以及一条中央轴线，连接了展厅与中央大厅。室外展览空间、一个会议中心、若干酒店和写字楼以及管理机构设施对会展中心功能进行了全面补充。

National Convention and Exhibition Center
Tianjin, China

Competition 2013 – 1st Prize **Design** Meinhard von Gerkan and Stephan Schütz with Nicolas Pomränke **Chinese partner practice** CABR **Client** Tianjin Planning Bureau **Gross floor area** 1,200,000 m²

With a total square area of 1.2 million square meters and dedicated exhibition floor space of 400,000 square meters, one of the world's largest exhibition centers will be created in the east of China over the next few years. The design concept proposes two almost identical construction phases. They both consist of a central entrance hall roofed over by filigree canopies, eight exhibition halls on both sides and a main central thoroughfare that connects the entrance halls with the exhibition halls. The functions of the exhibition center are rounded off with open-air exhibition space, a congress center, hotels, offices and administration facilities. The entire exhibition floor space is located on one level.

26 ¹⁰ ↑

南宁国际会议展览中心
南宁，中国

**Nanning International
Convention & Exhibition Center**
Nanning, China

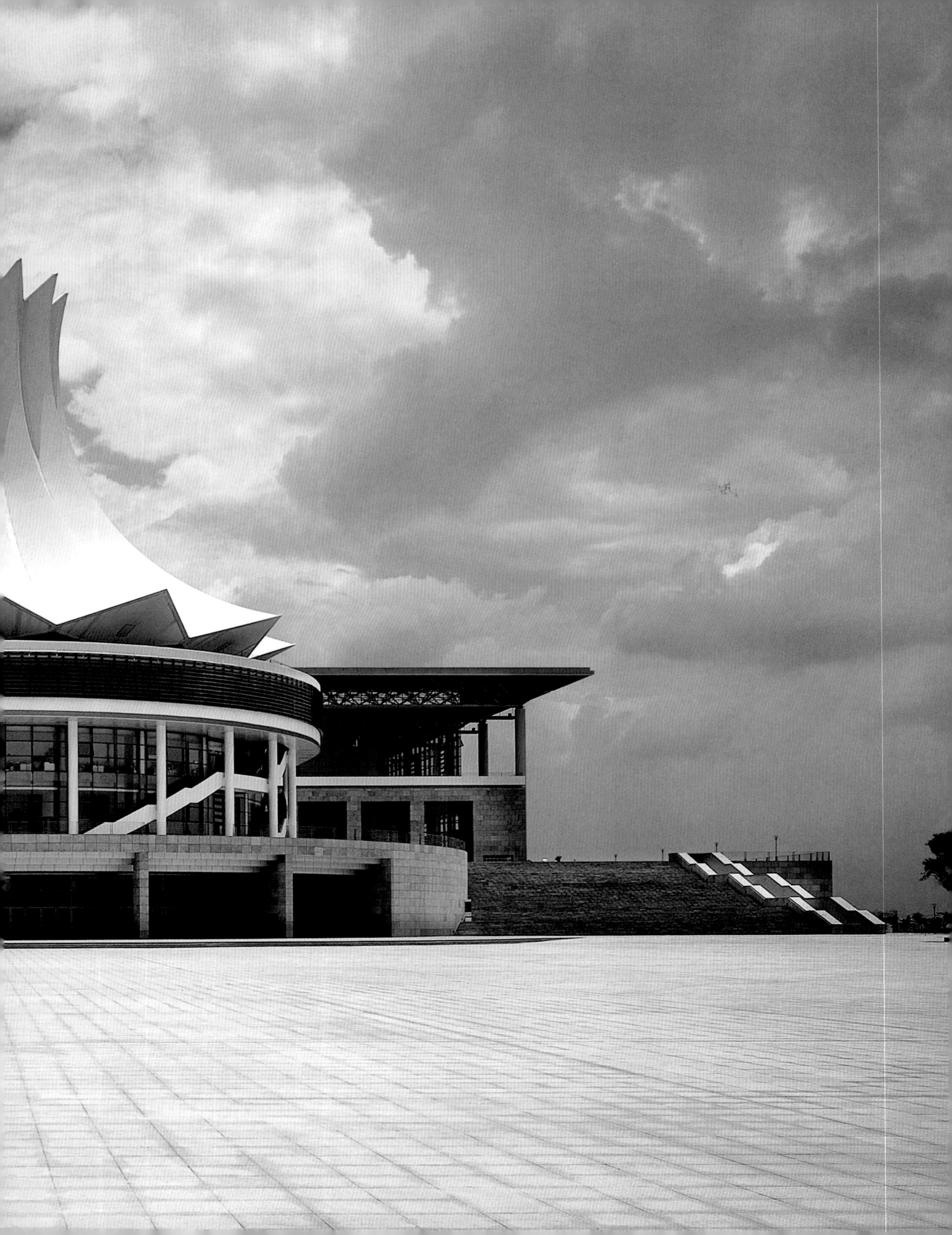

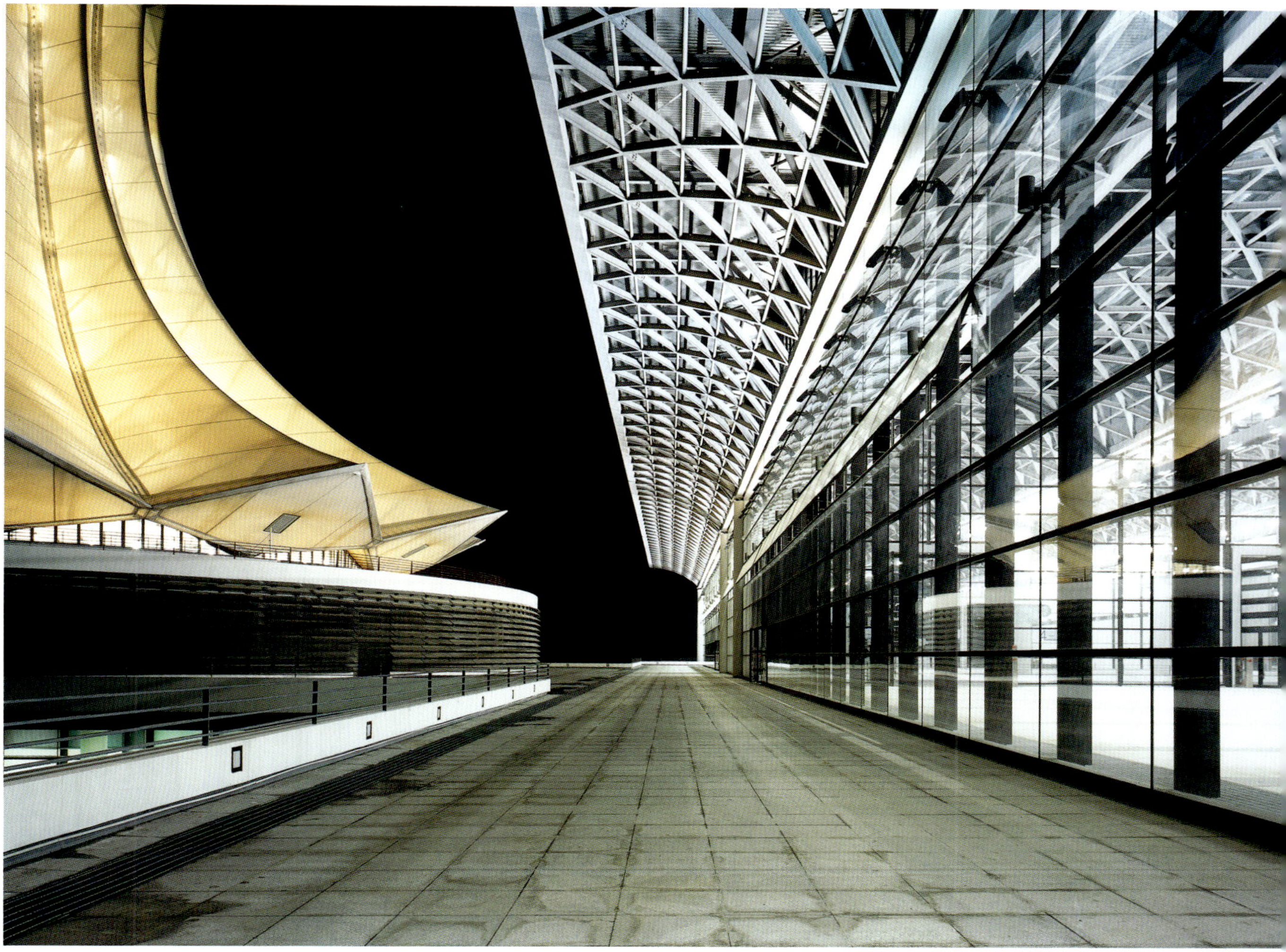

南宁国际会议展览中心　南宁

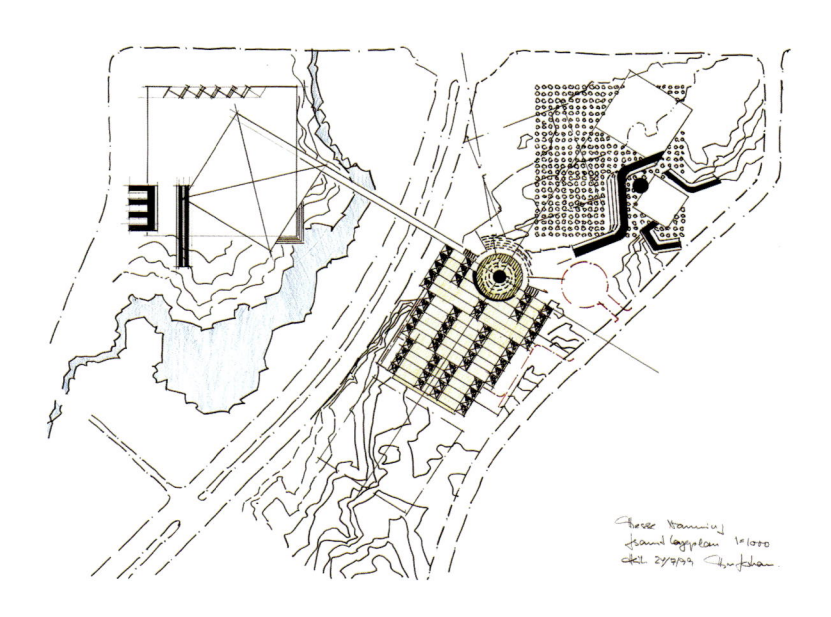

Nanning International Convention & Exhibition Center Nanning

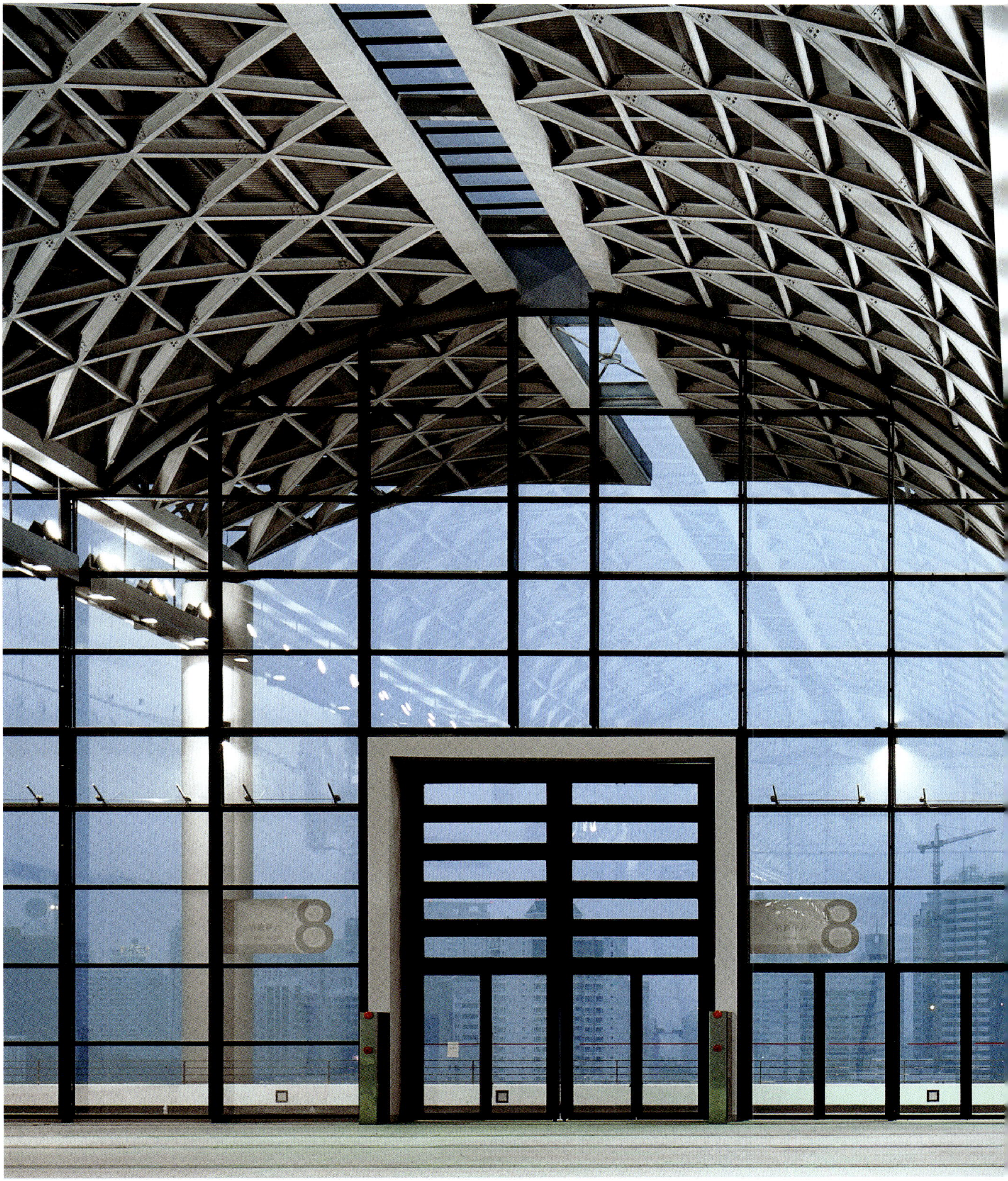

南宁国际会议展览中心　南宁

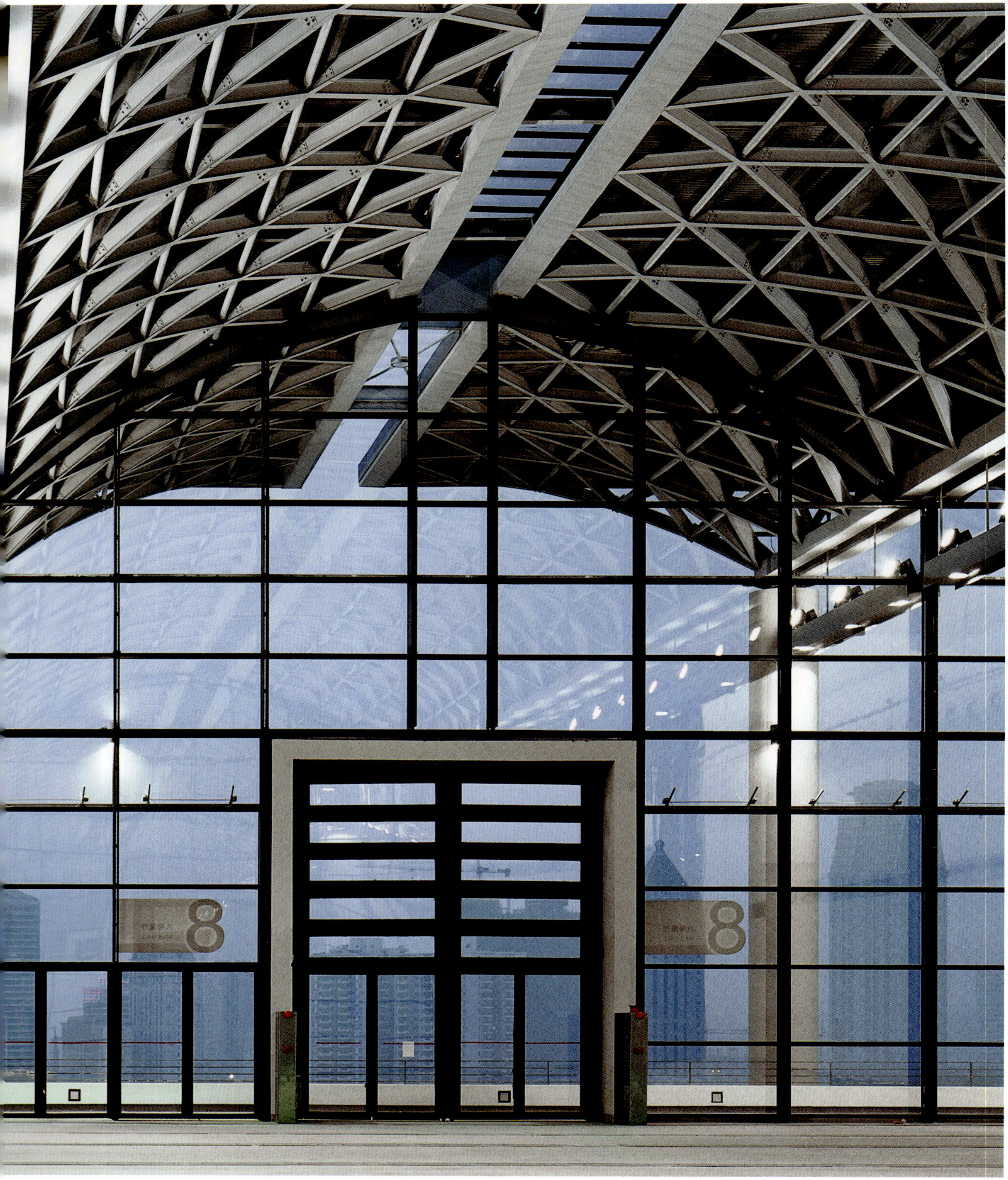
8
8

32　南宁国际会议展览中心　南宁

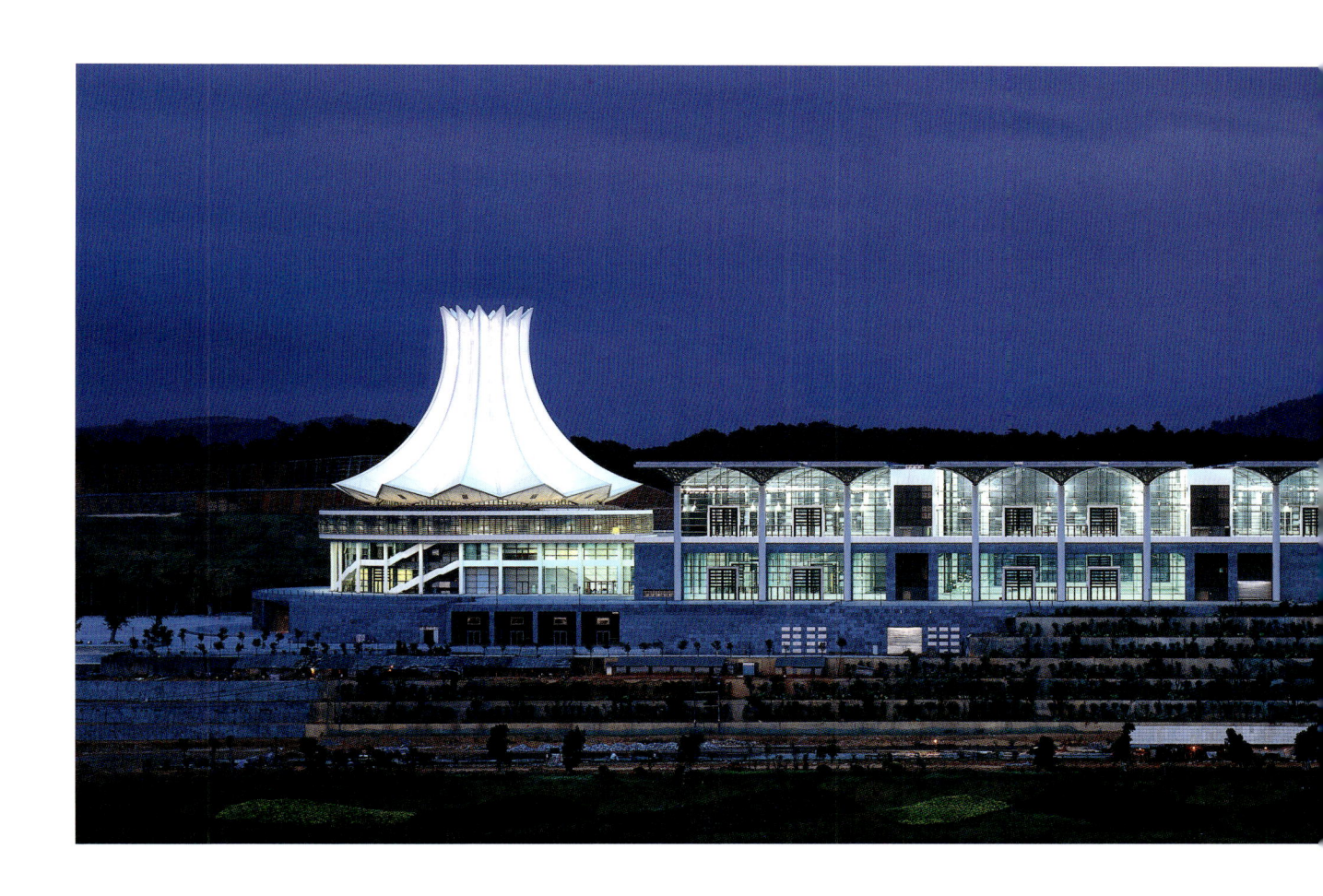

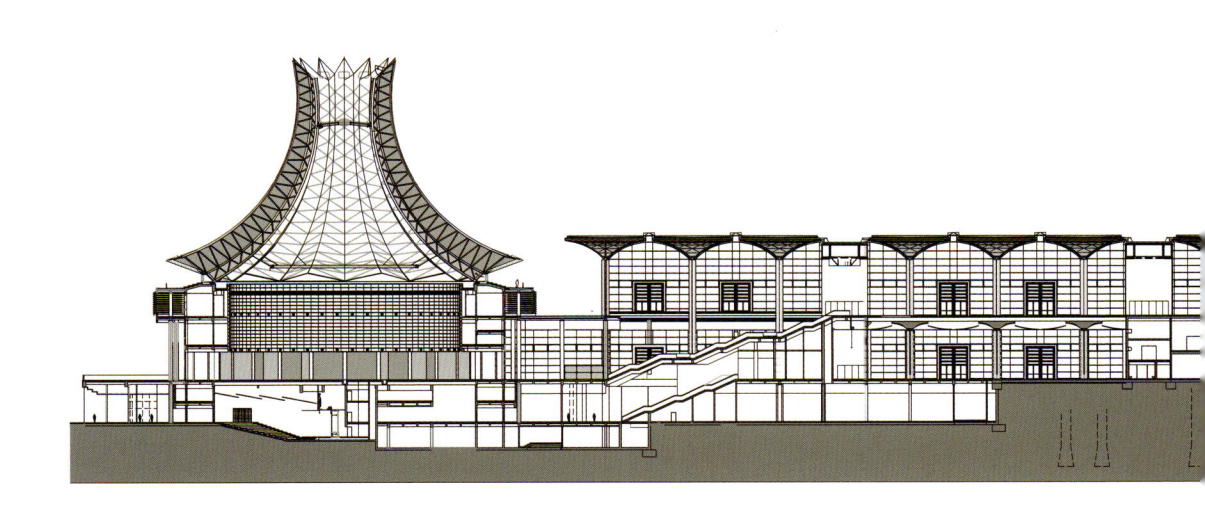

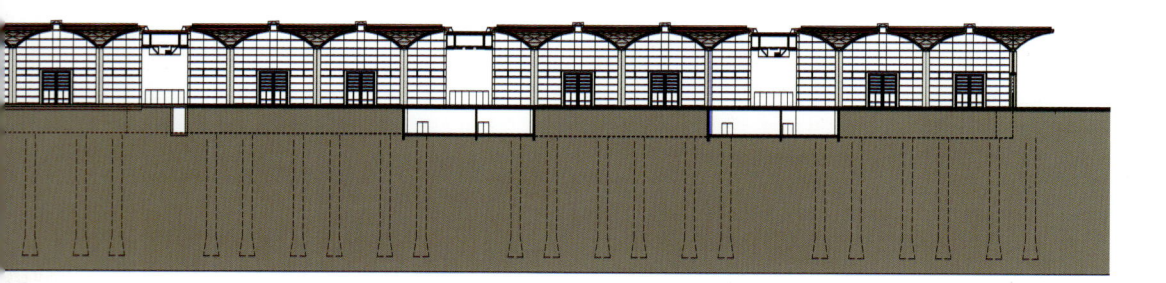

Nanning International Convention & Exhibition Center Nanning   33

34 ^{10} ↑

临港新城
上海，中国

Lingang New City
Shanghai, China

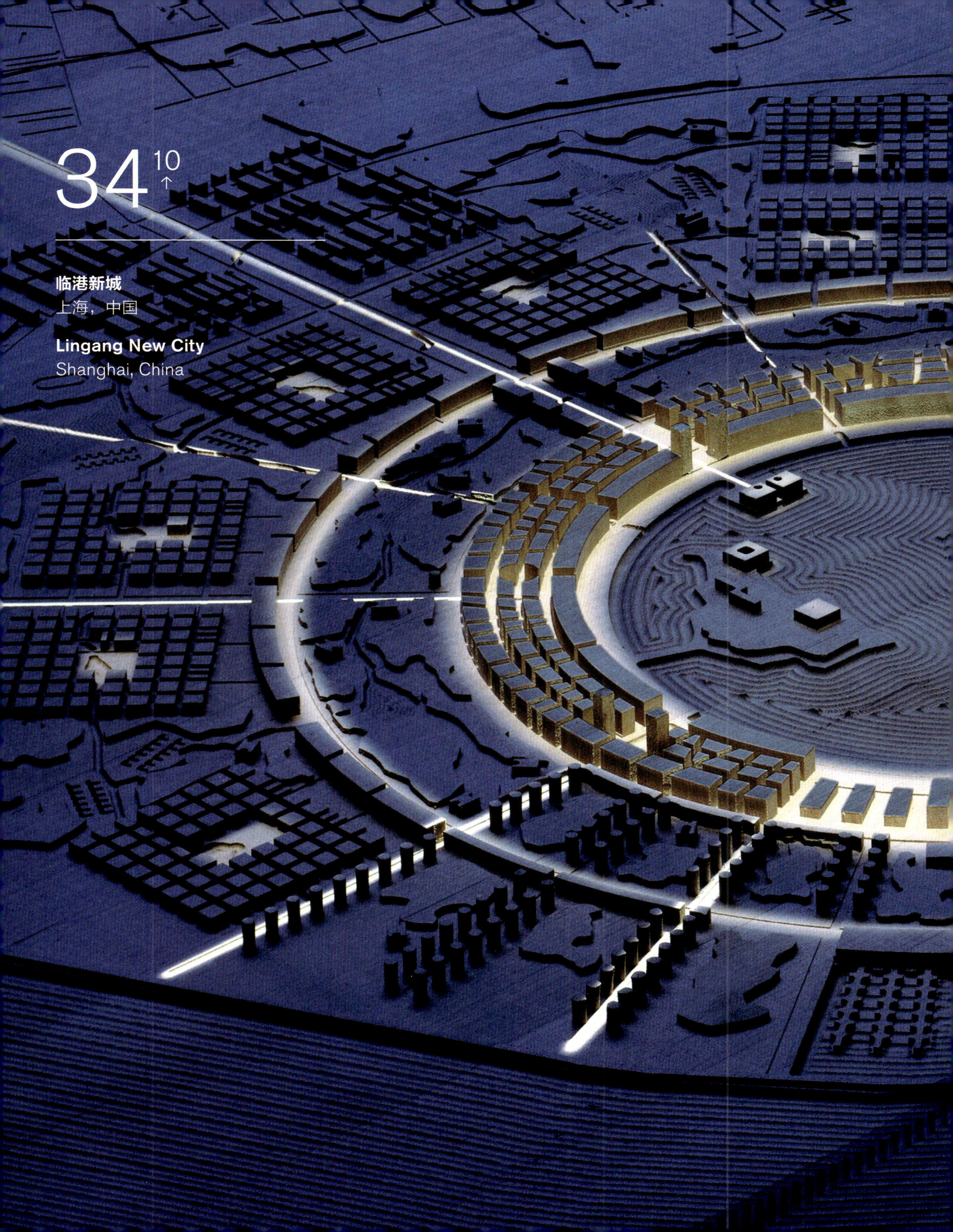

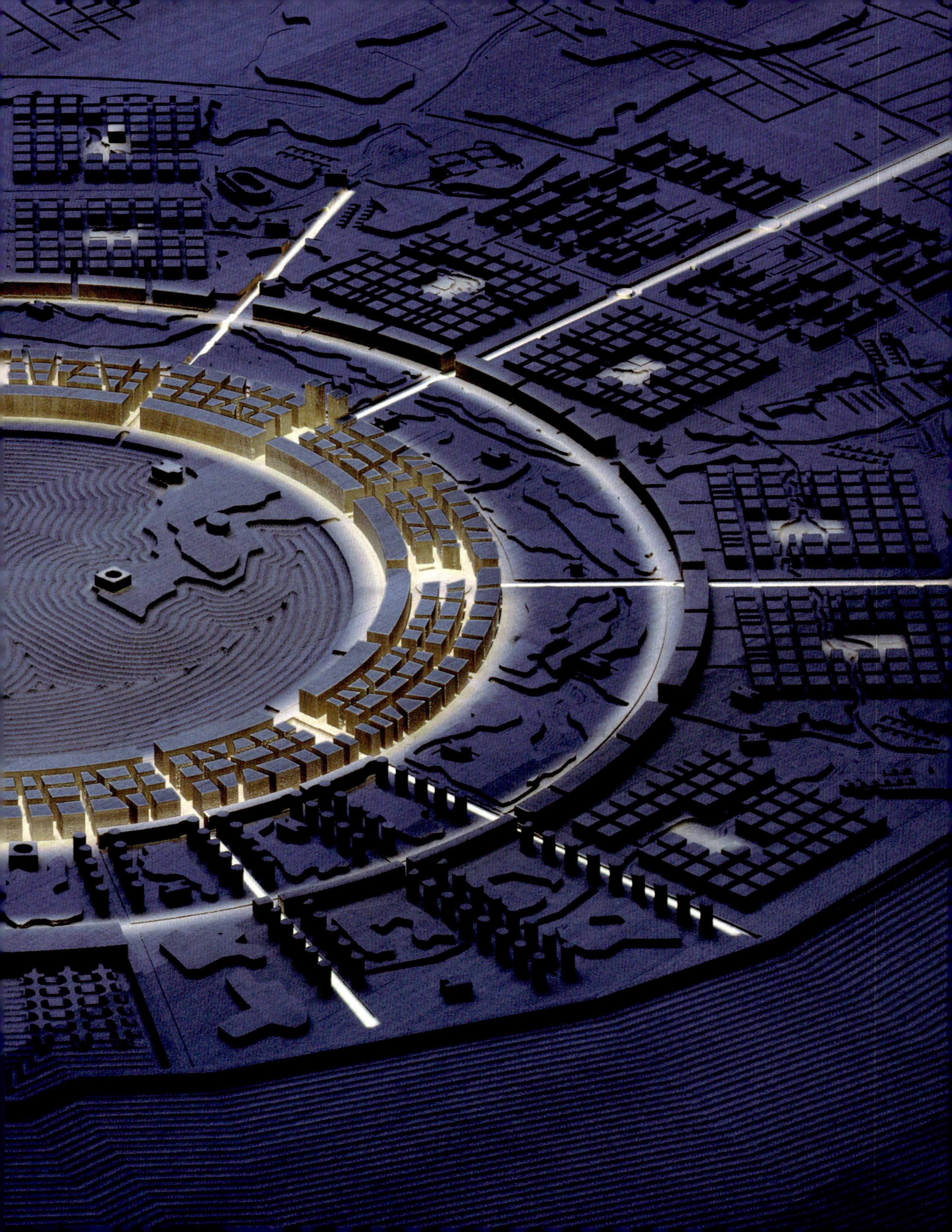

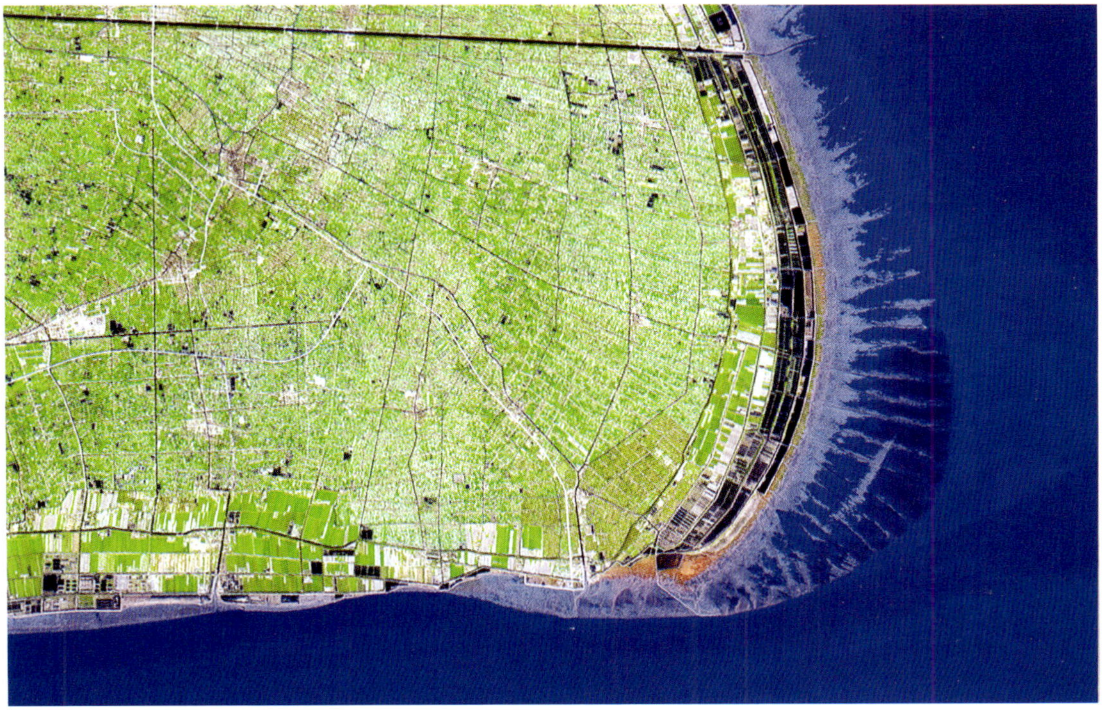

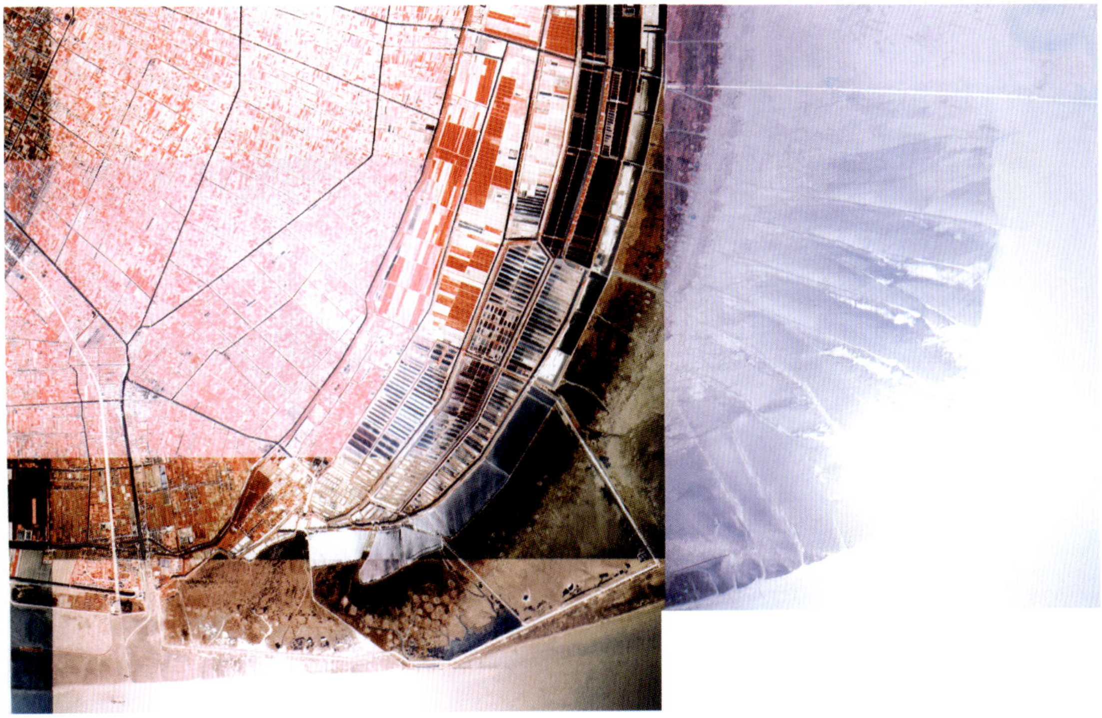

36　临港新城　上海

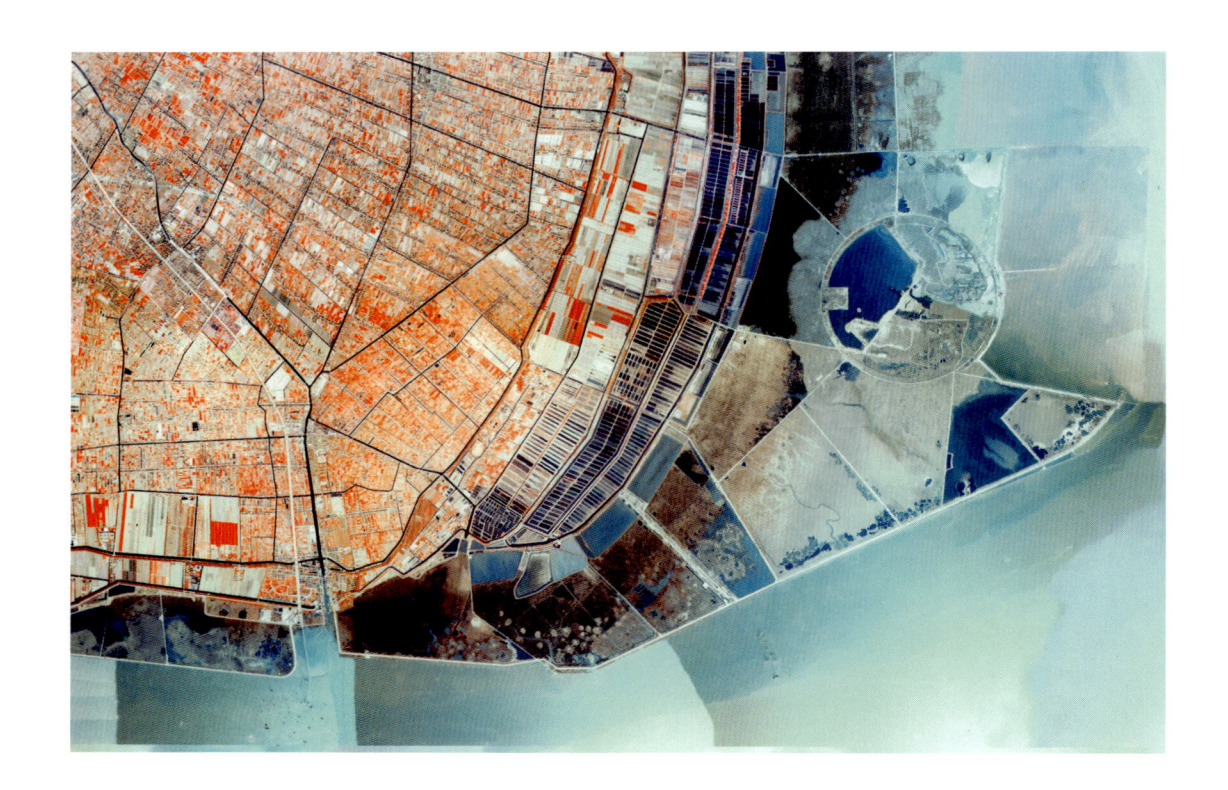

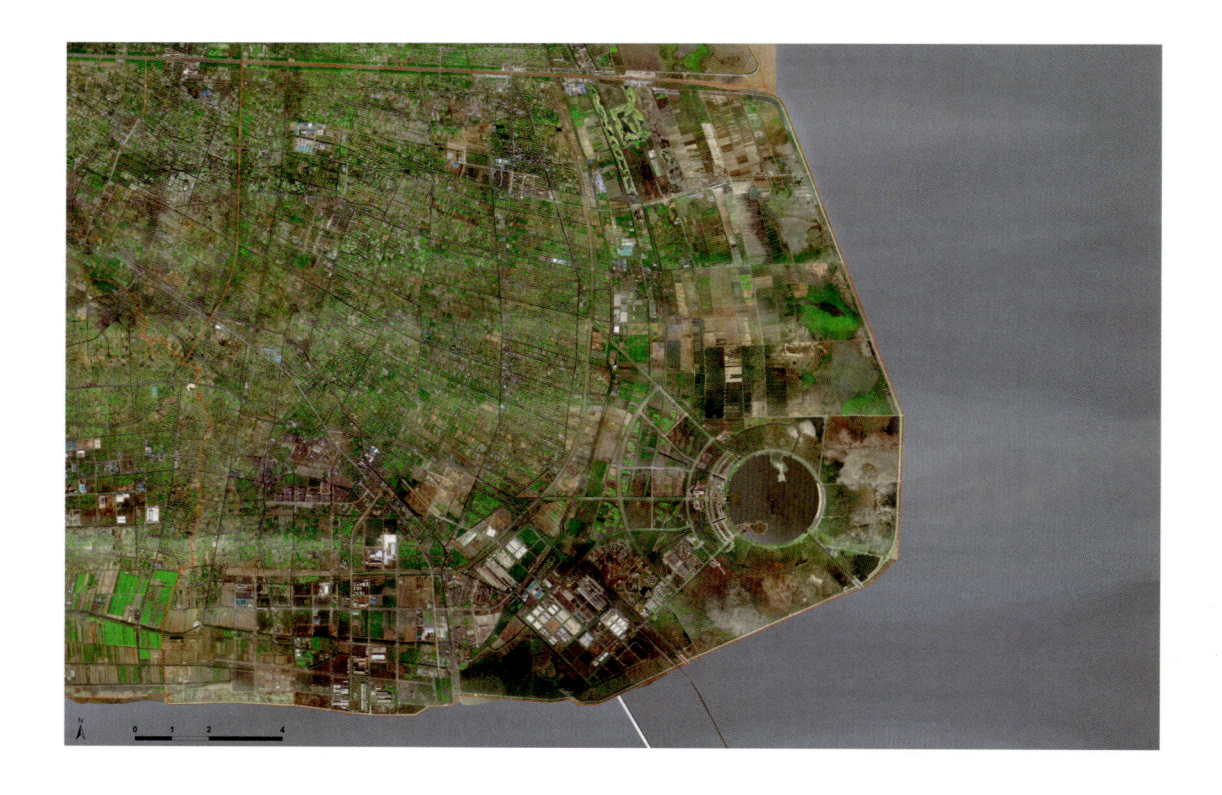

Lingang New City Shanghai

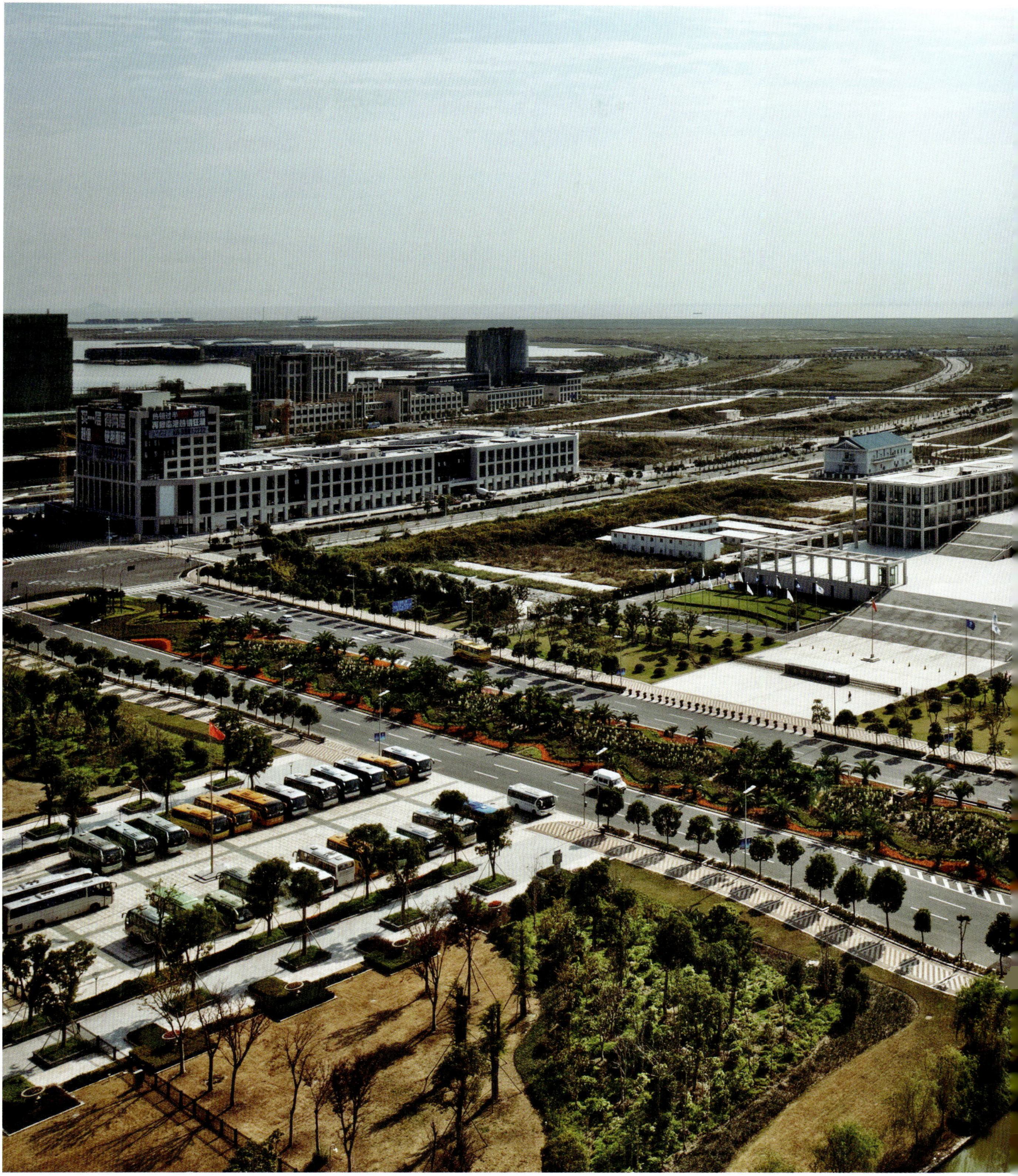

临港新城 上海

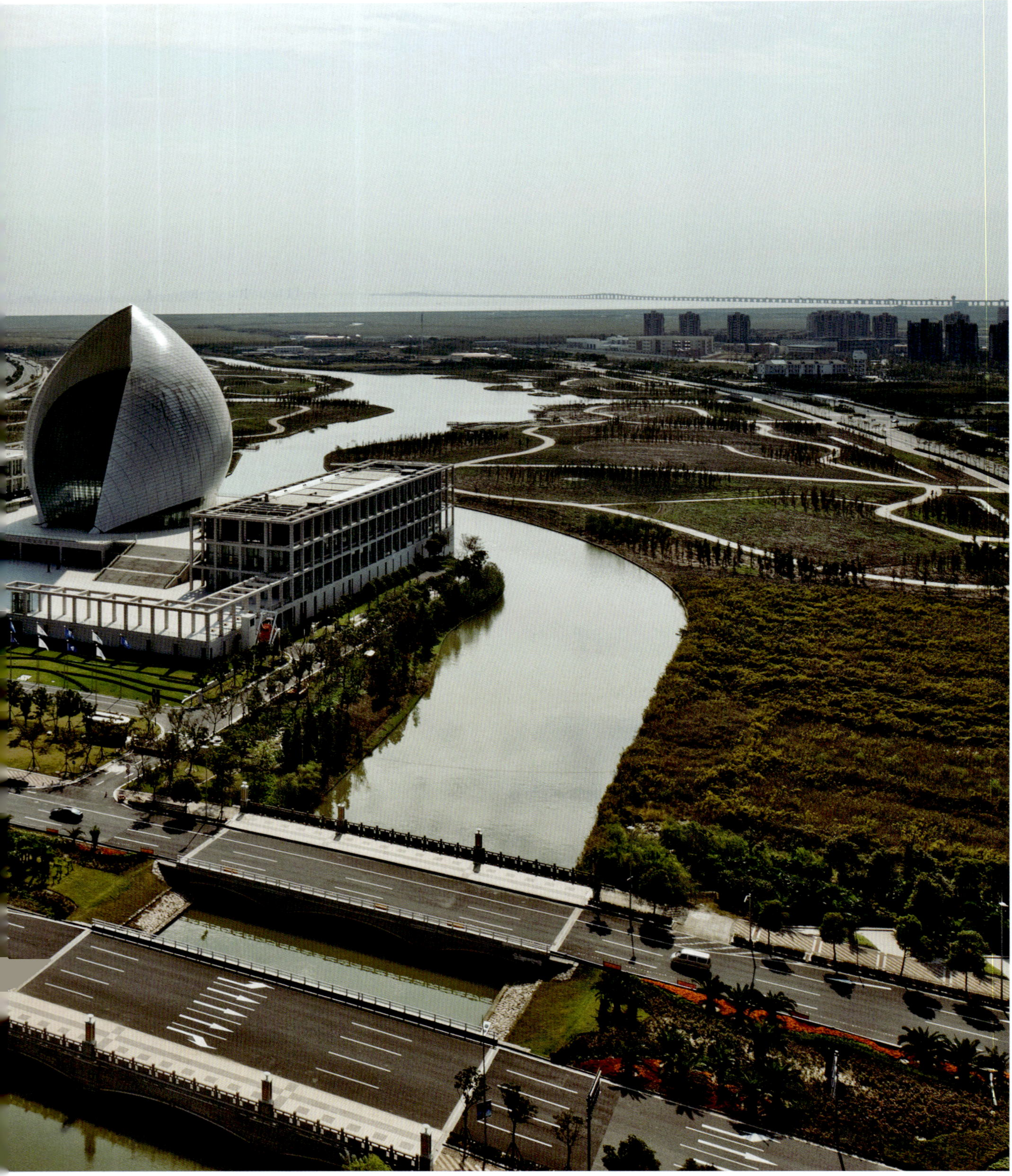

Lingang New City Shanghai

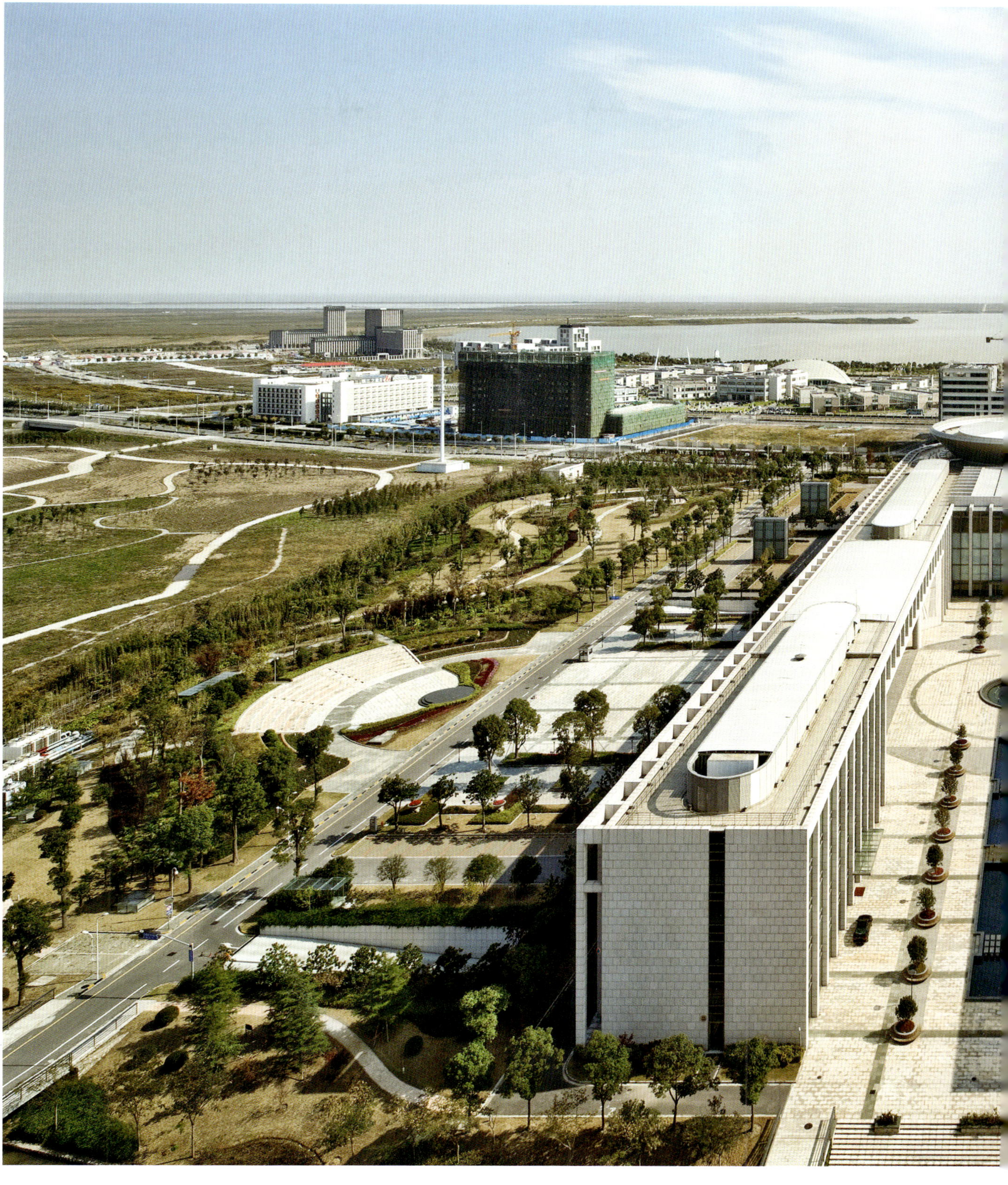

临港新城　上海

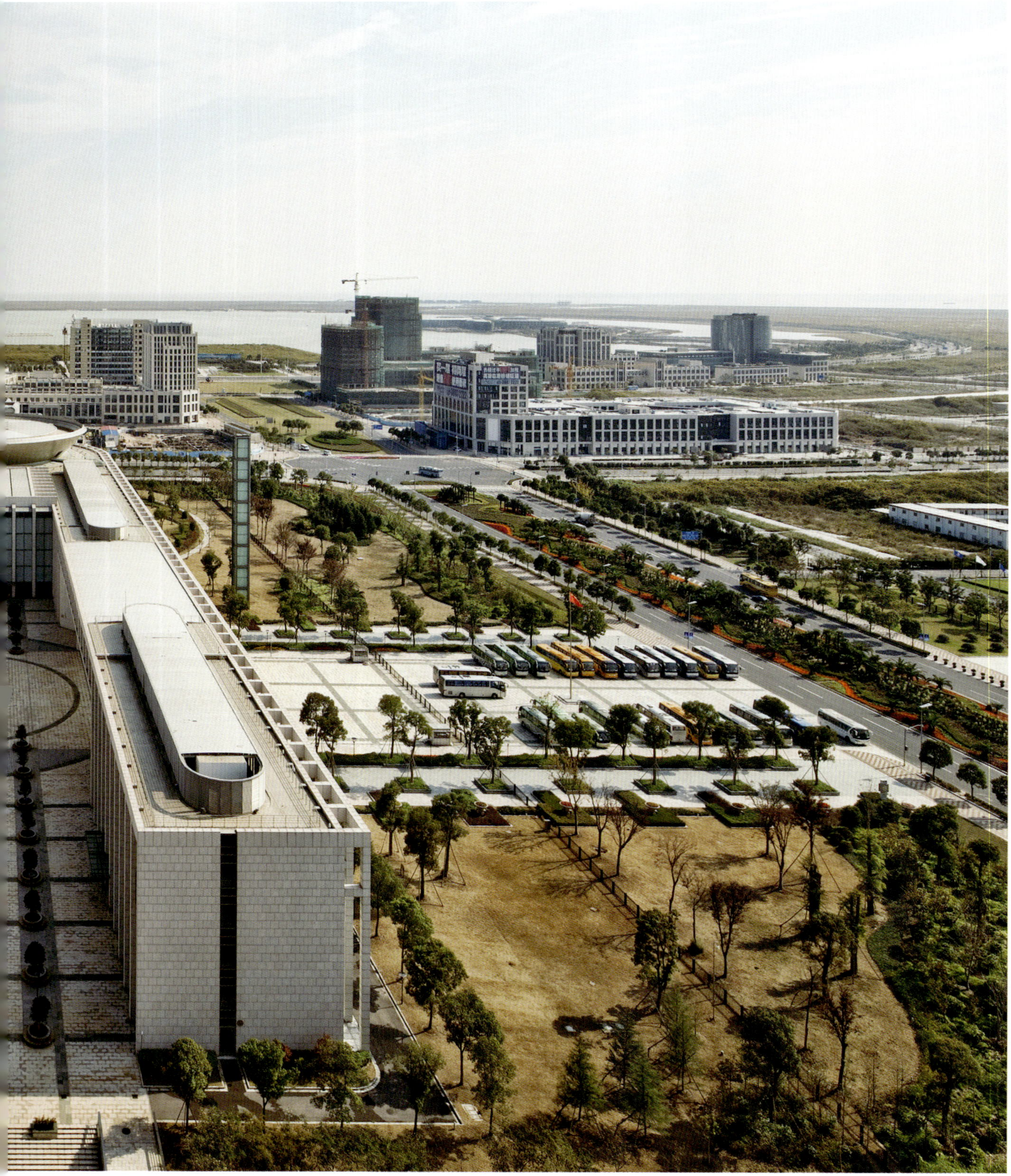

Lingang New City Shanghai

42 ^11 ↑

世纪莲体育公园
佛山，中国

**Century Lotus Sports Park with
Stadium and Swimming Hall**
Foshan, China

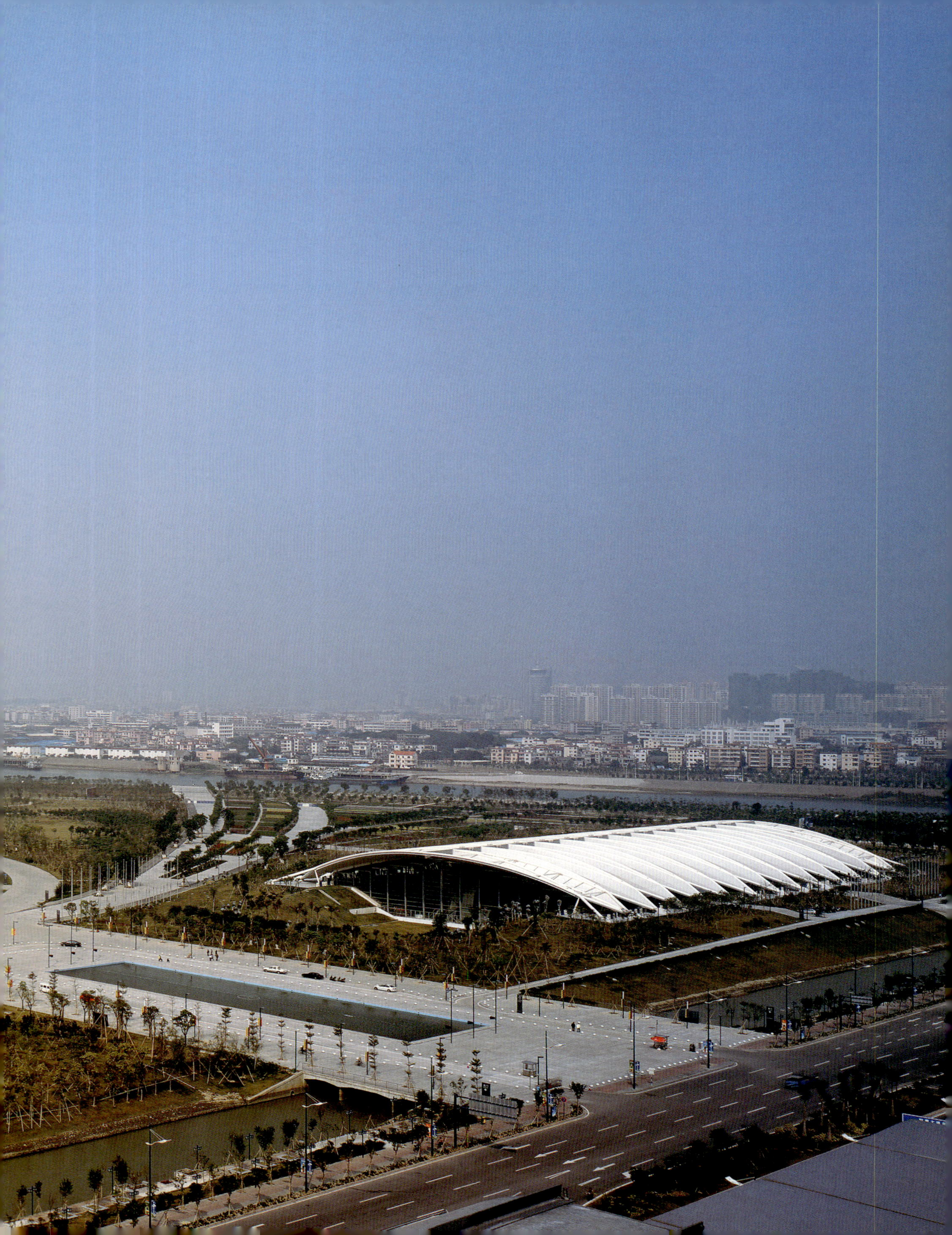

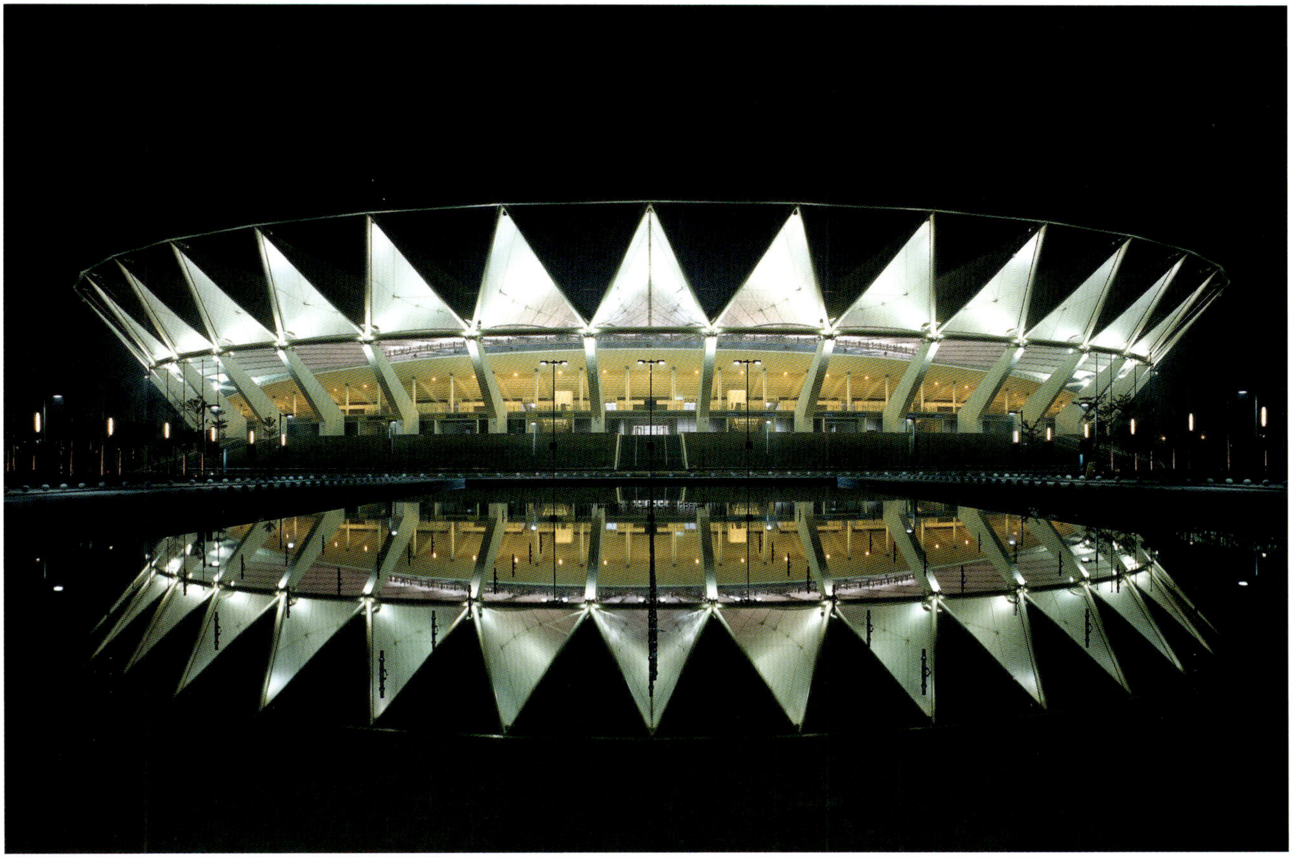

世纪莲体育公园　佛山

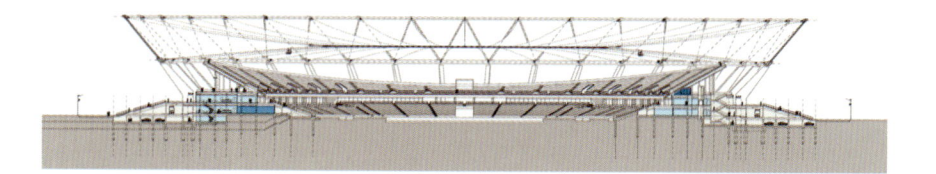

Century Lotus Sports Park with Stadium and Swimming Hall Foshan

46　世纪莲体育公园　佛山

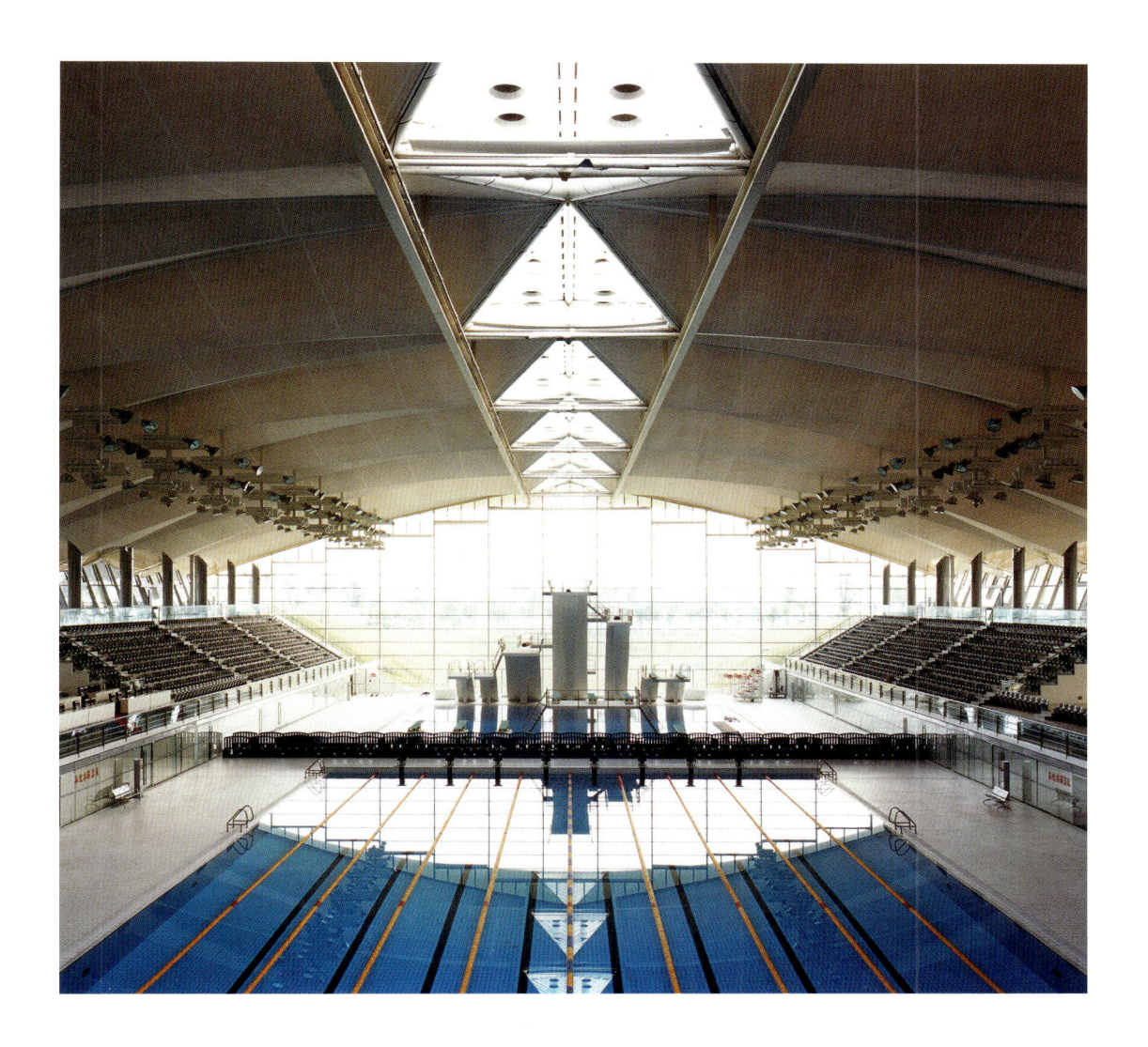

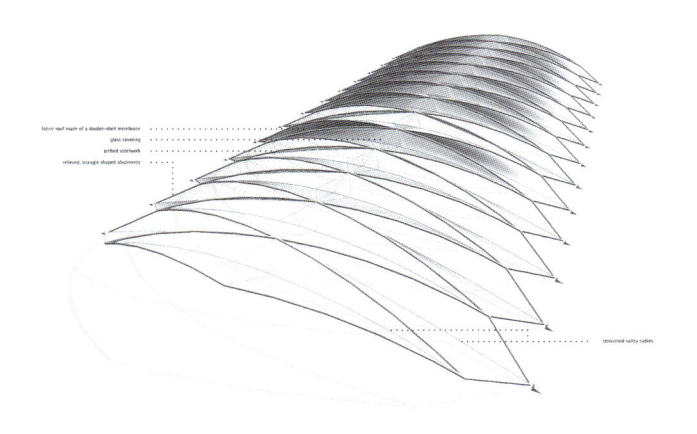

Century Lotus Sports Park with Stadium and Swimming Hall Foshan

48 ¹¹
↑

中青旅大厦
北京，中国
CYTS Plaza
Beijing, China

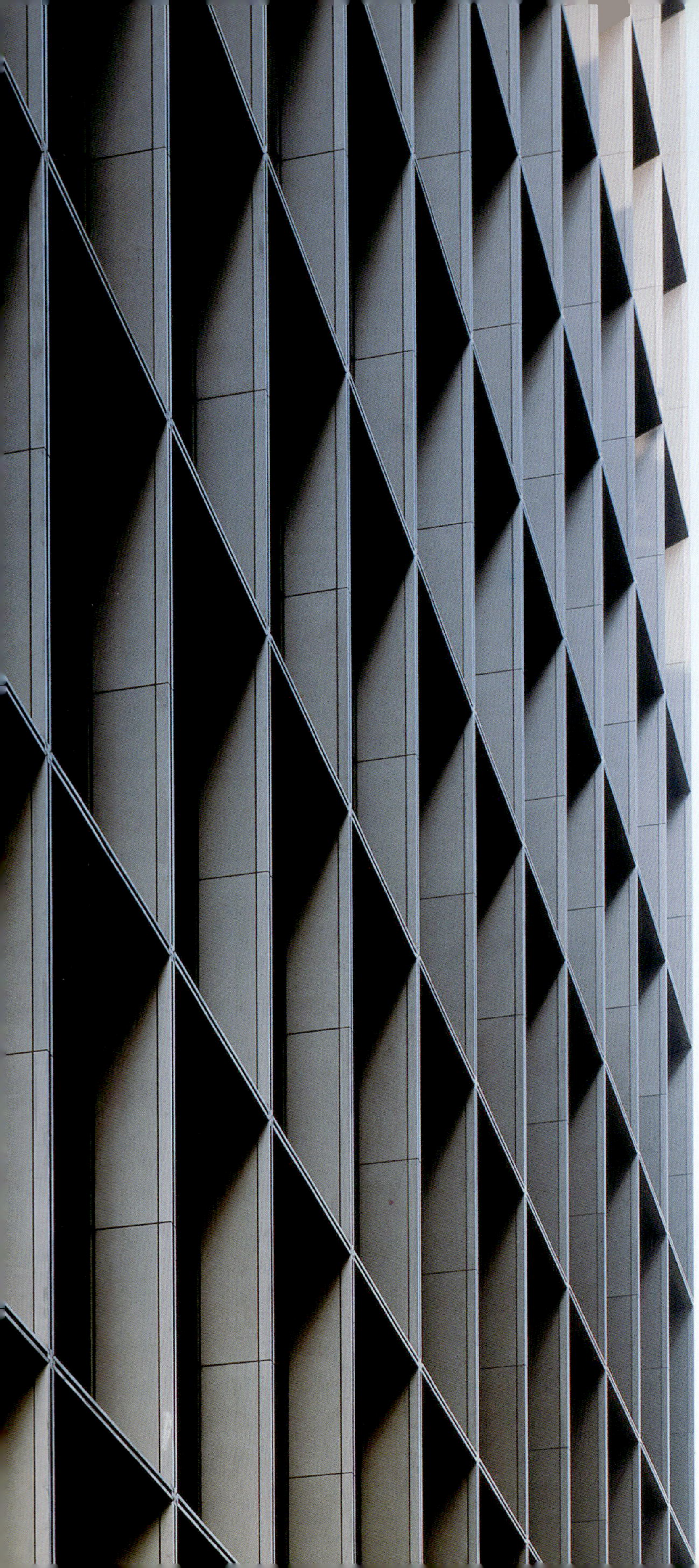

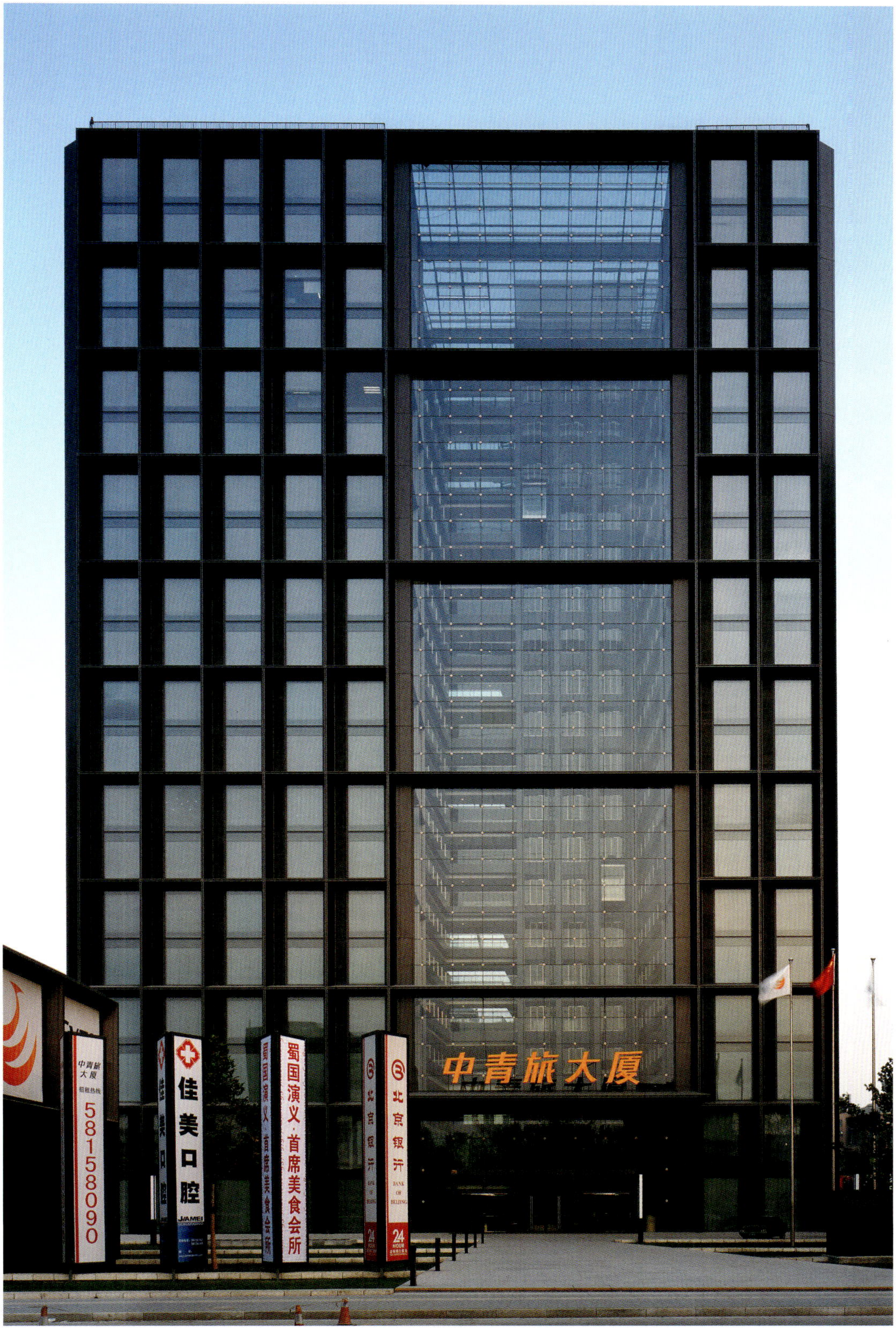

中青旅大厦　北京

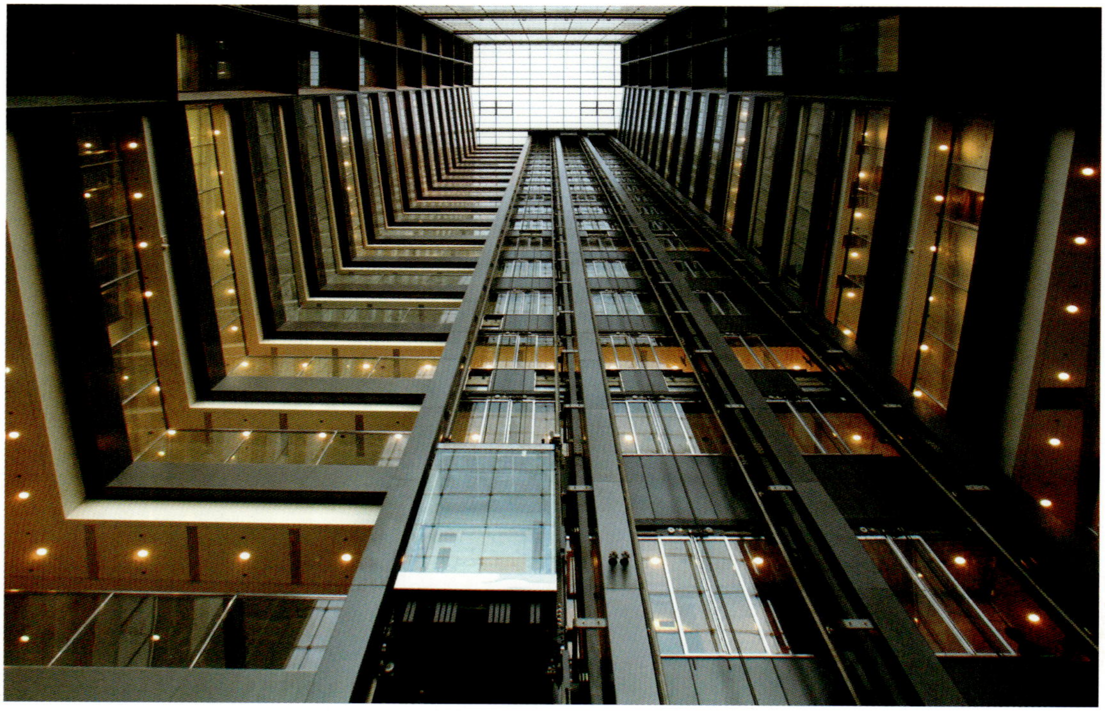

CYTS Plaza Beijing

中青旅大厦　北京

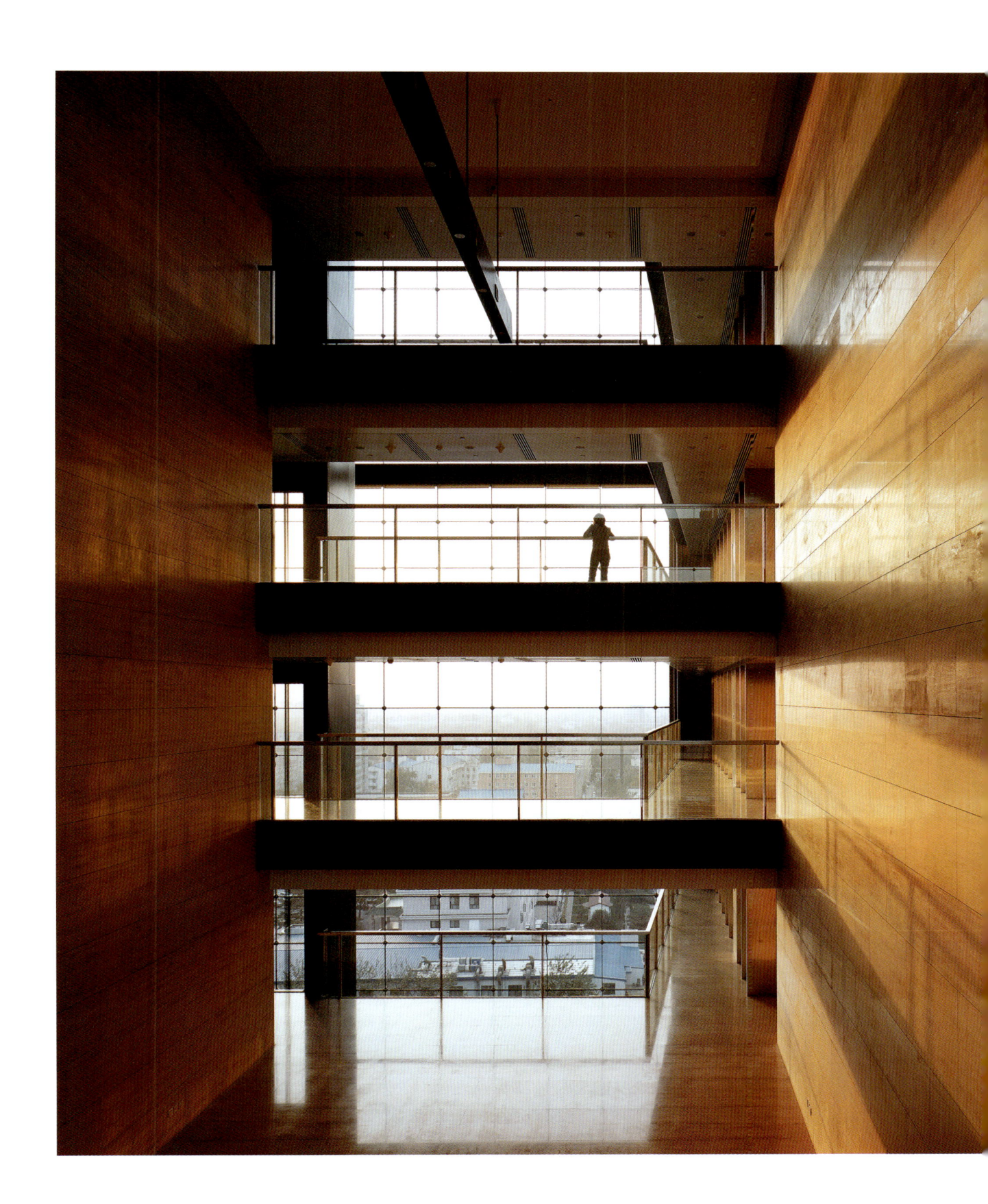

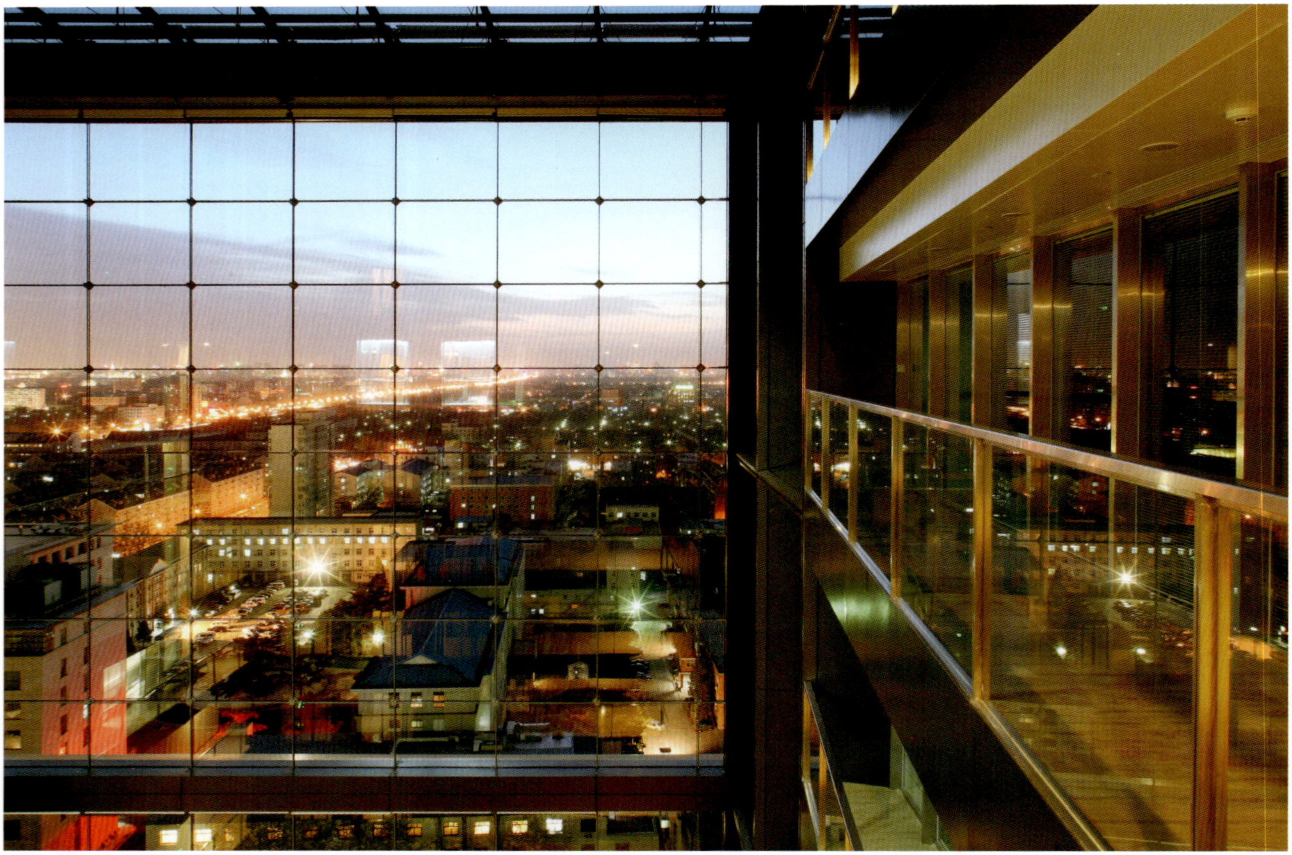

CYTS Plaza Beijing

54 ^{12} ↑

期货广场双子大厦
大连，中国

Twin Towers, Commodity Exchange Plaza
Dalian, China

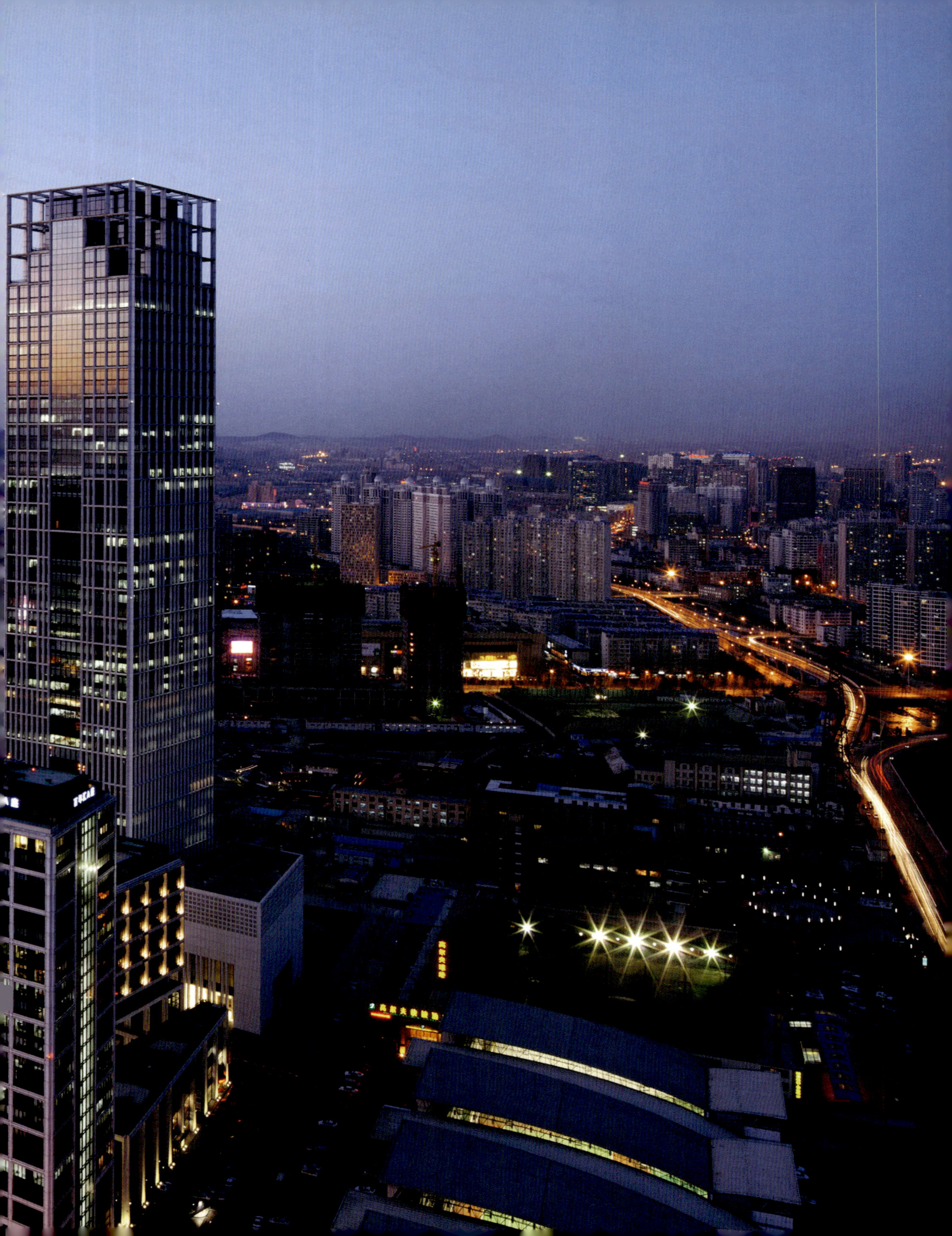

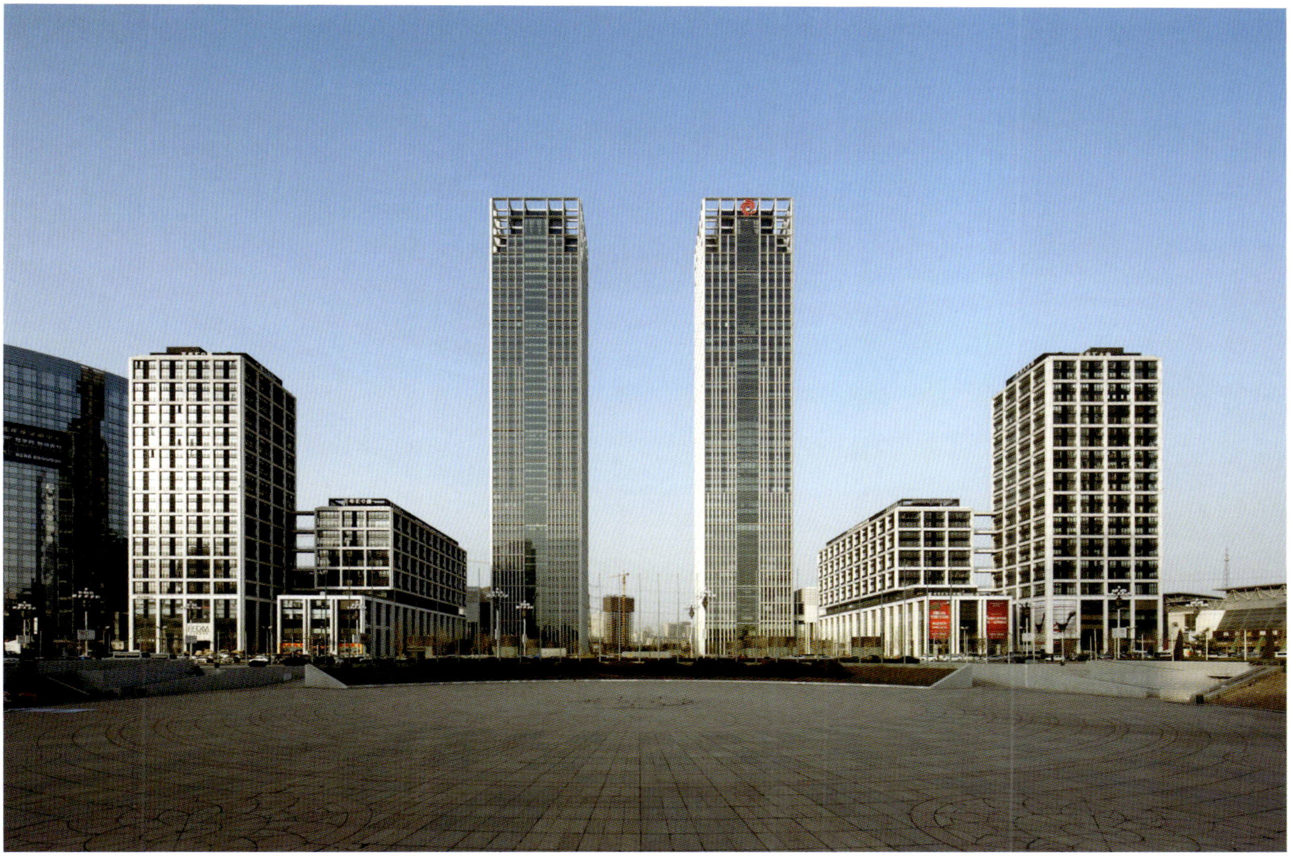

期货广场双子大厦　大连

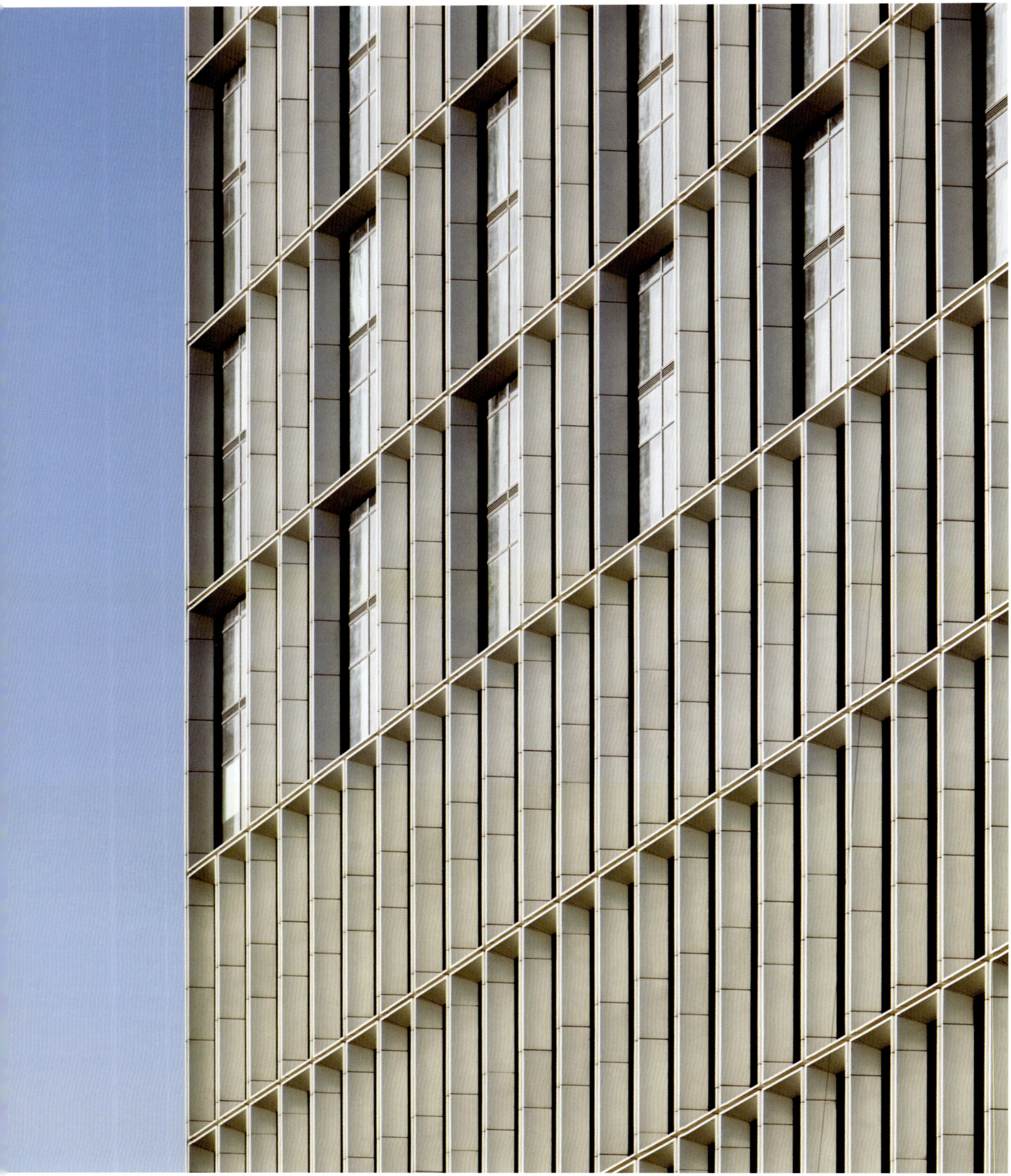

Twin Towers, Commodity Exchange Plaza Dalian

58　期货广场双子大厦　大连

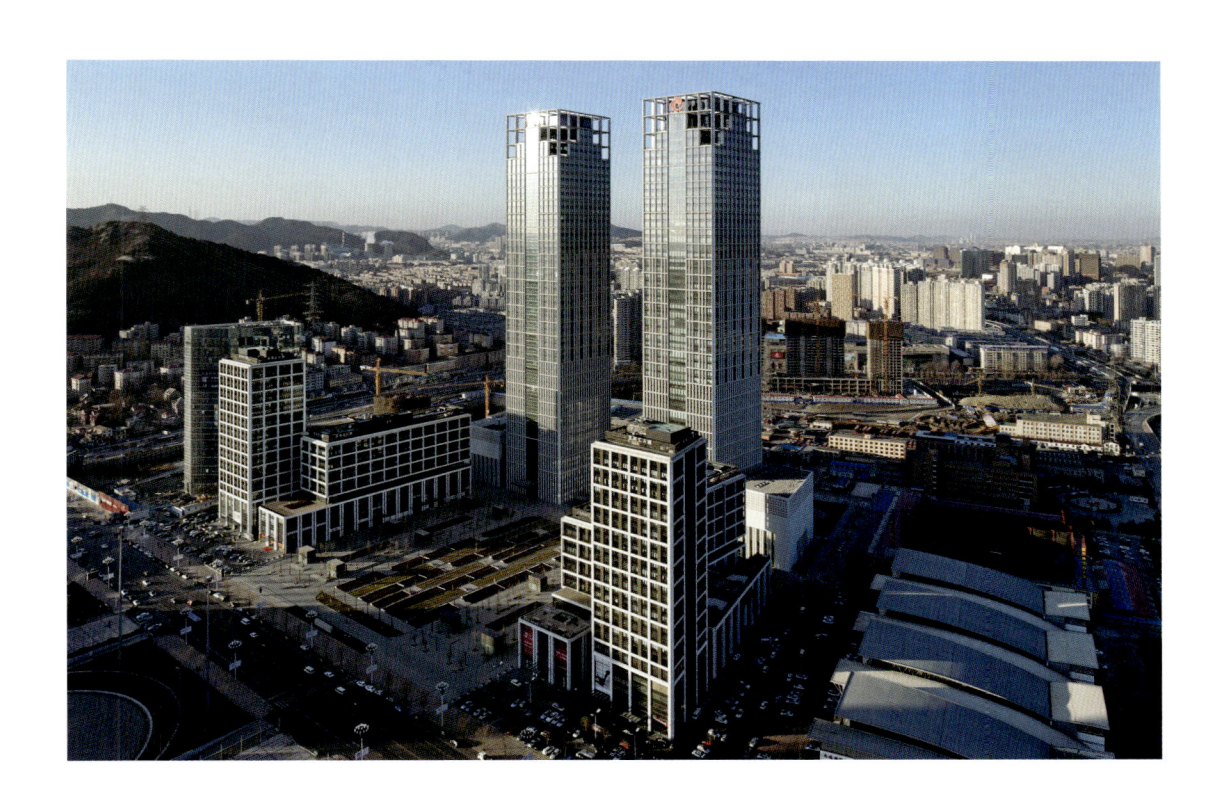

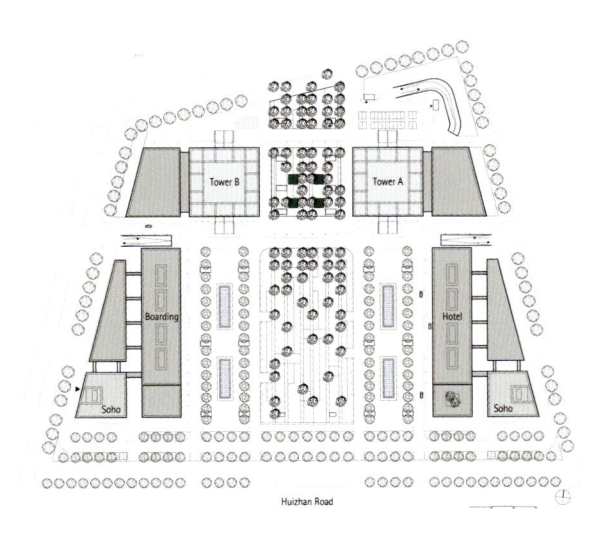

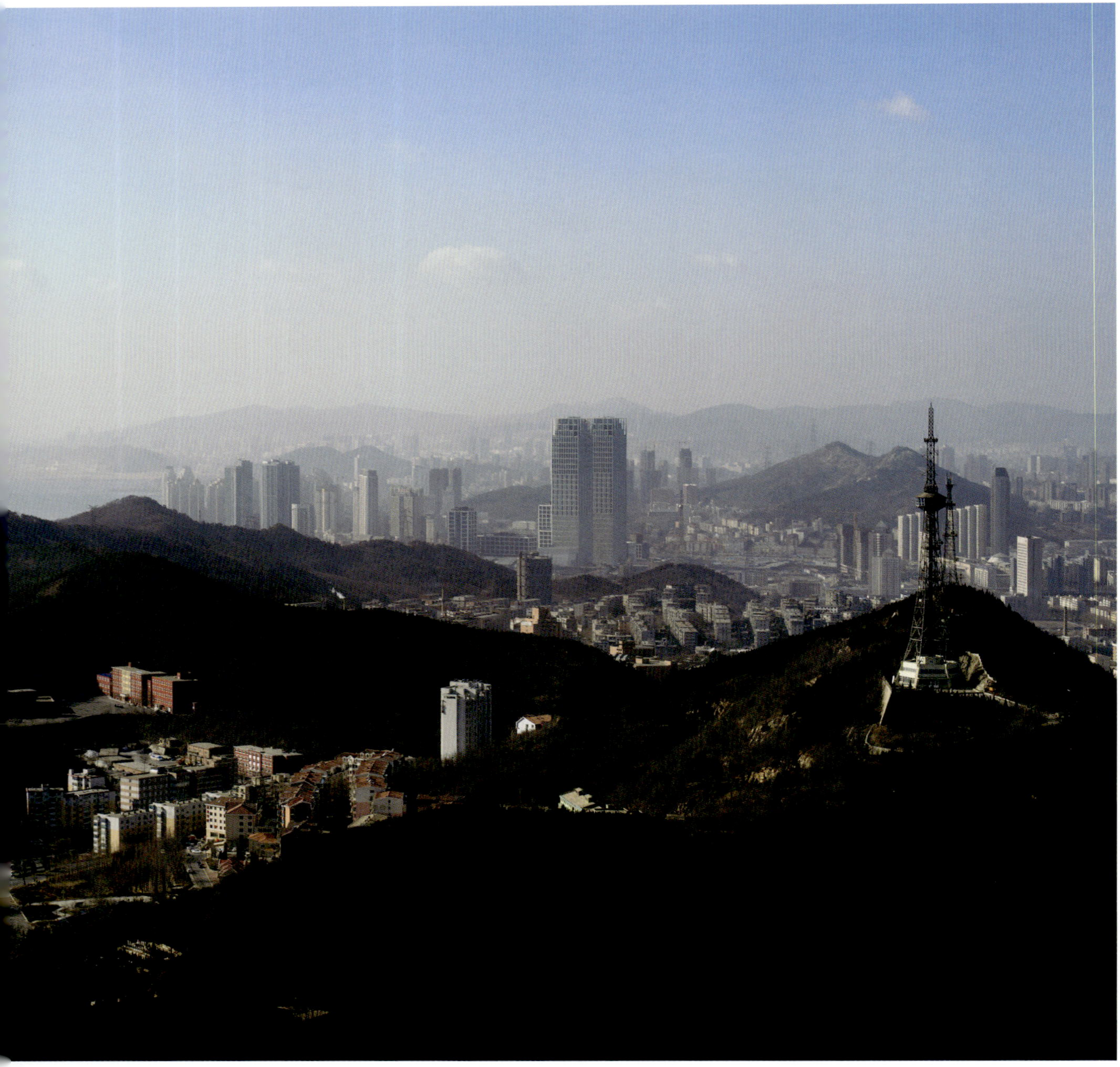

Twin Towers, Commodity Exchange Plaza Dalian

60 ¹²↑

重庆大剧院
重庆，中国

Chongqing Grand Theater
Chongqing, China

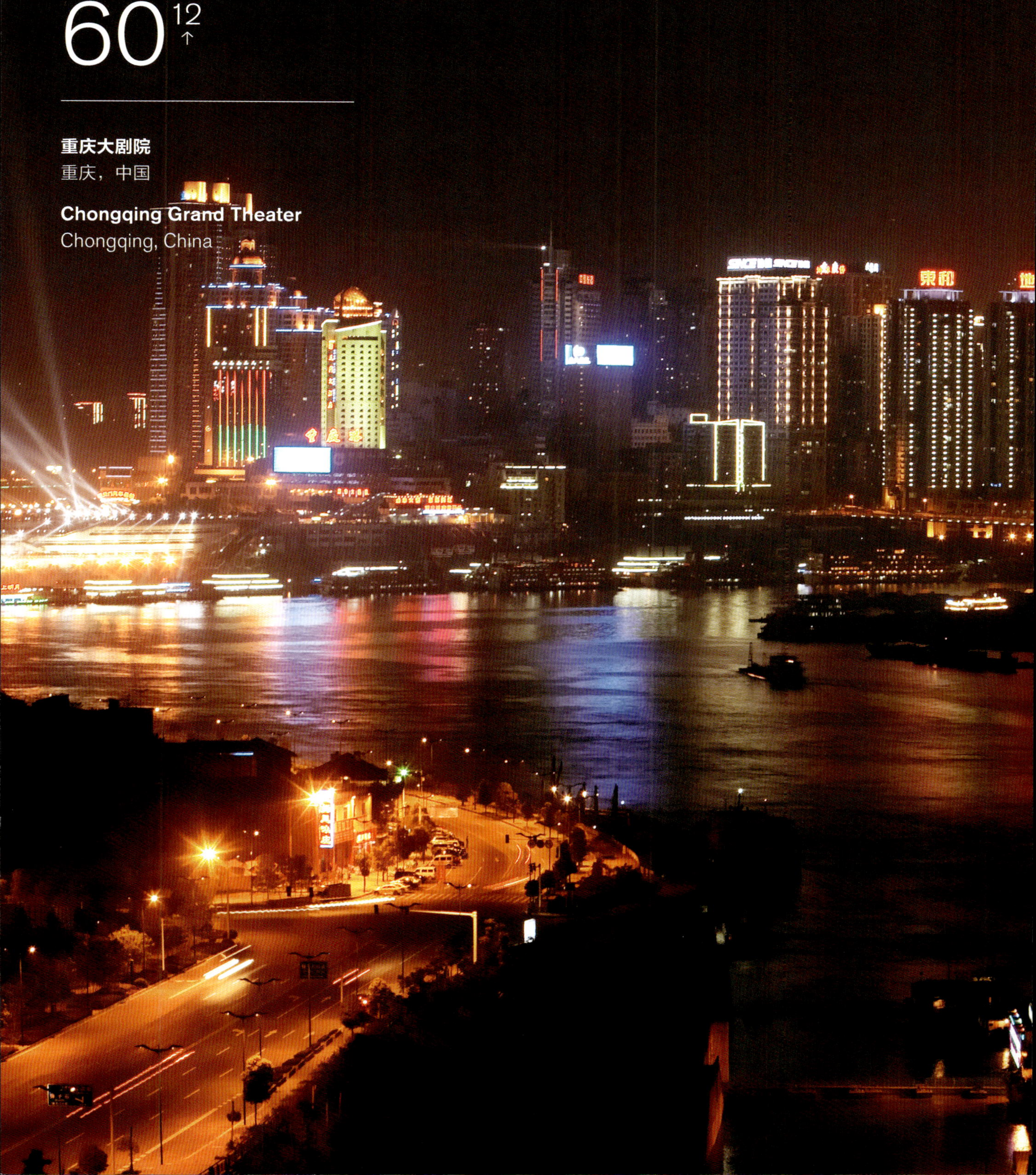

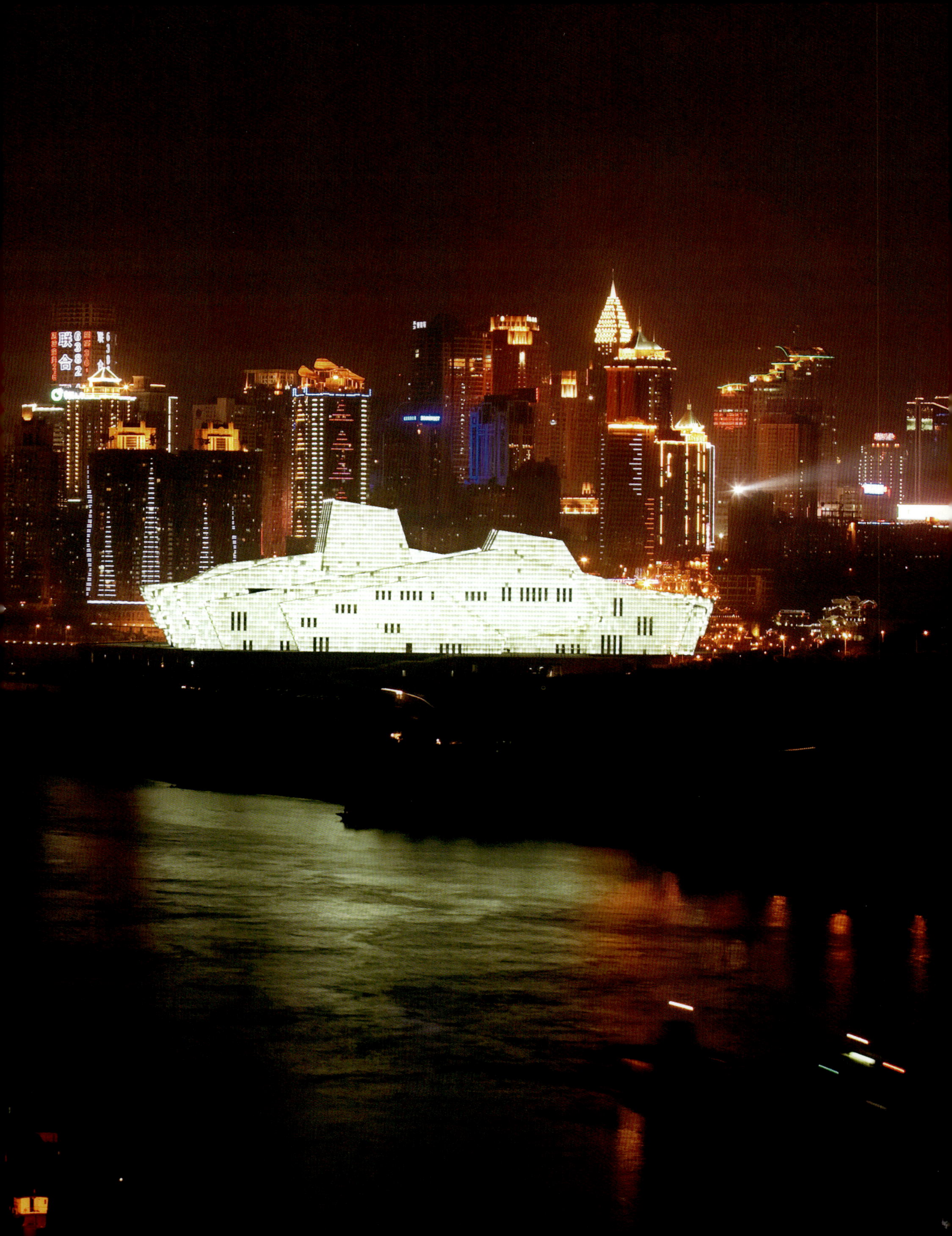
联合

重庆大剧院　重庆

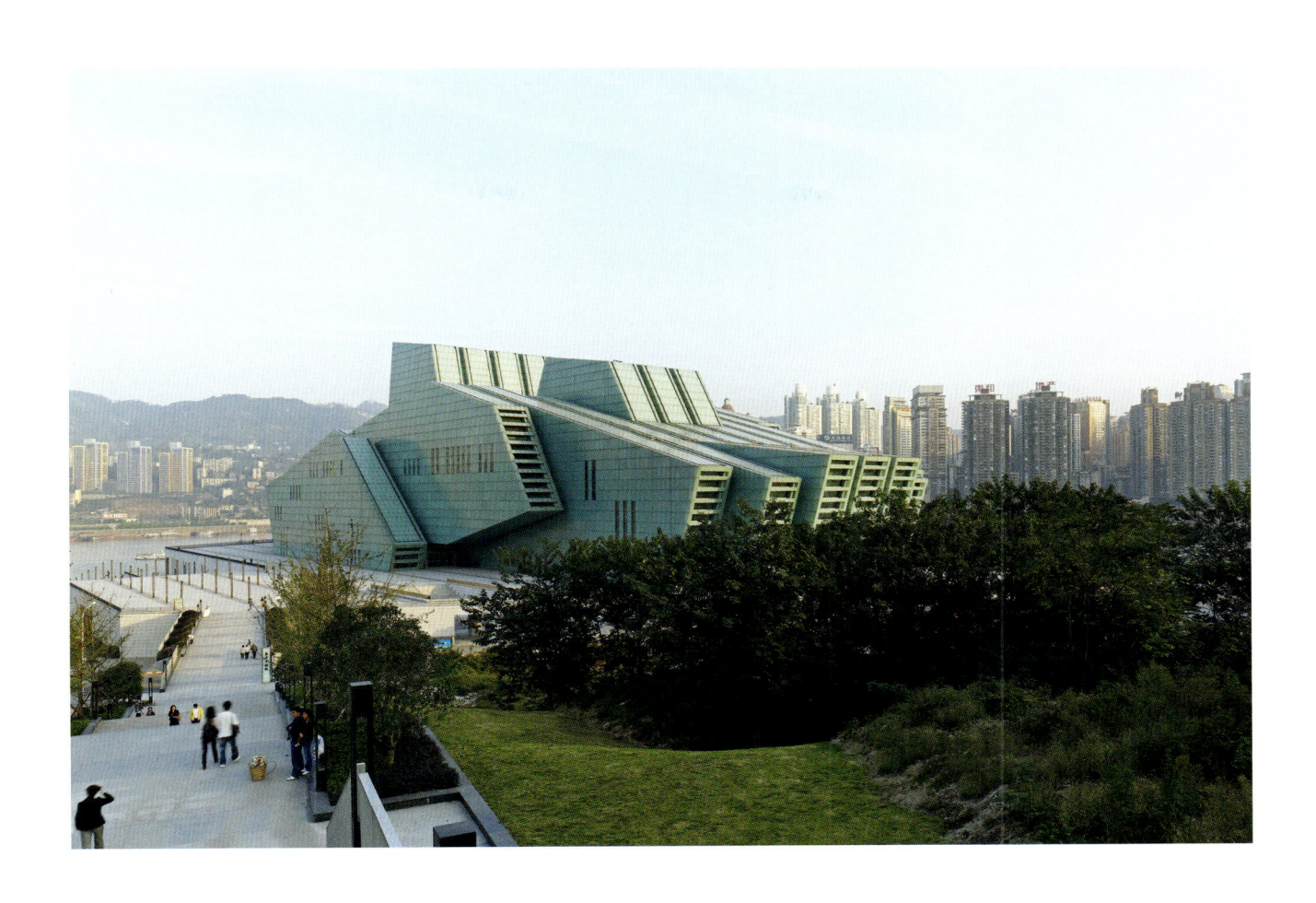

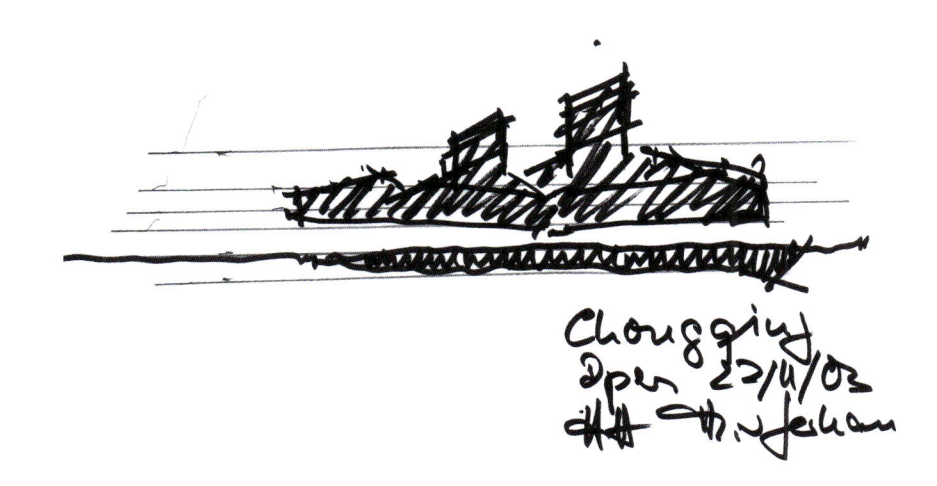

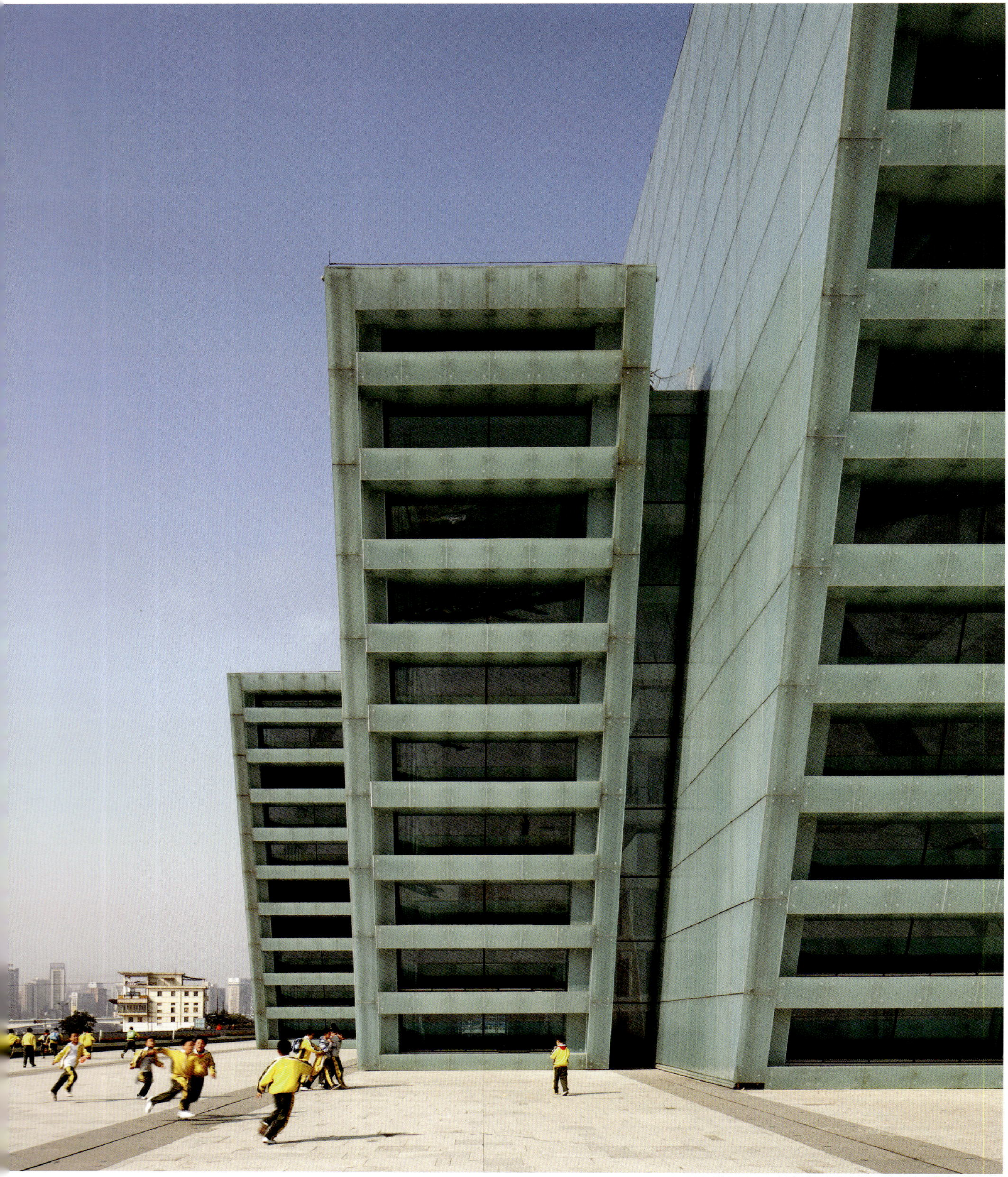

Chongqing Grand Theater Chongqing

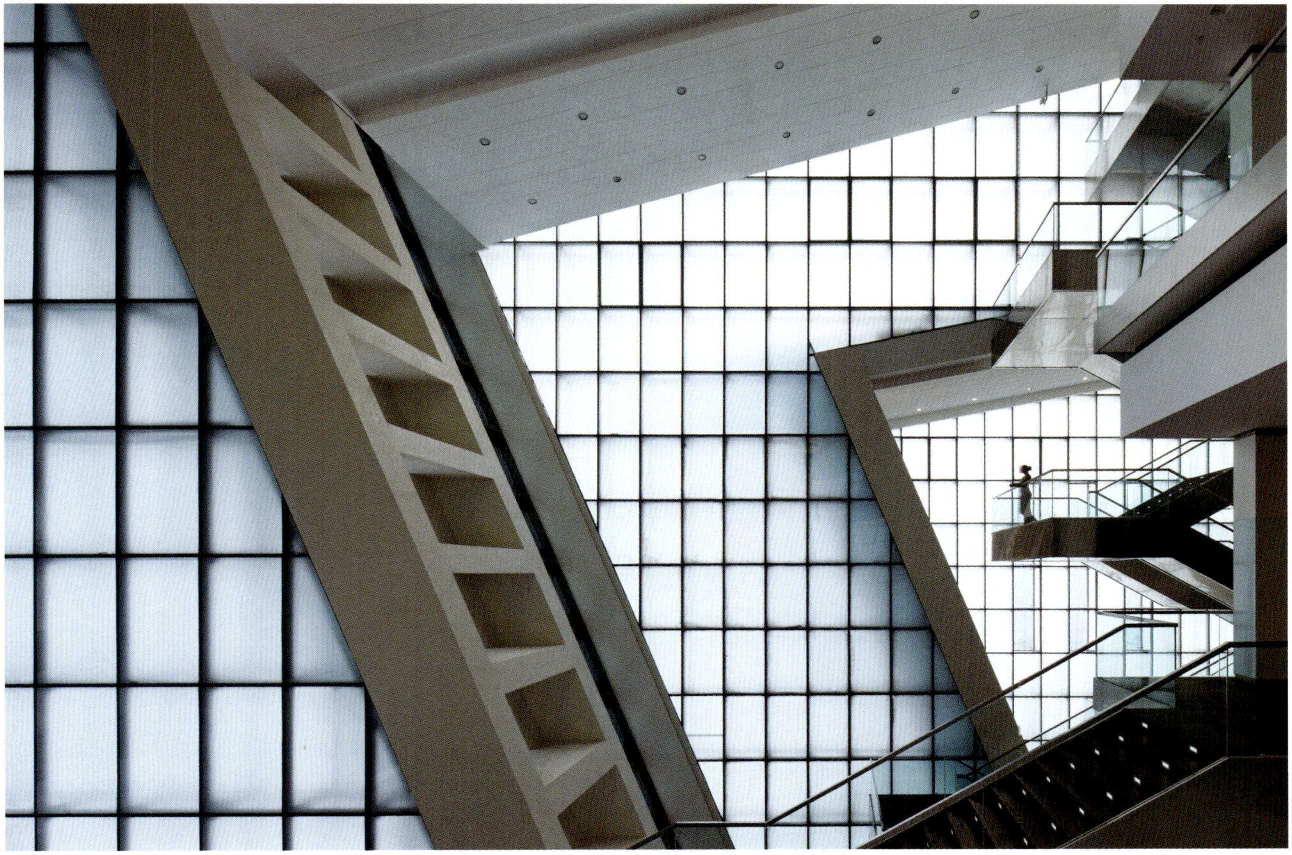

重庆大剧院　重庆

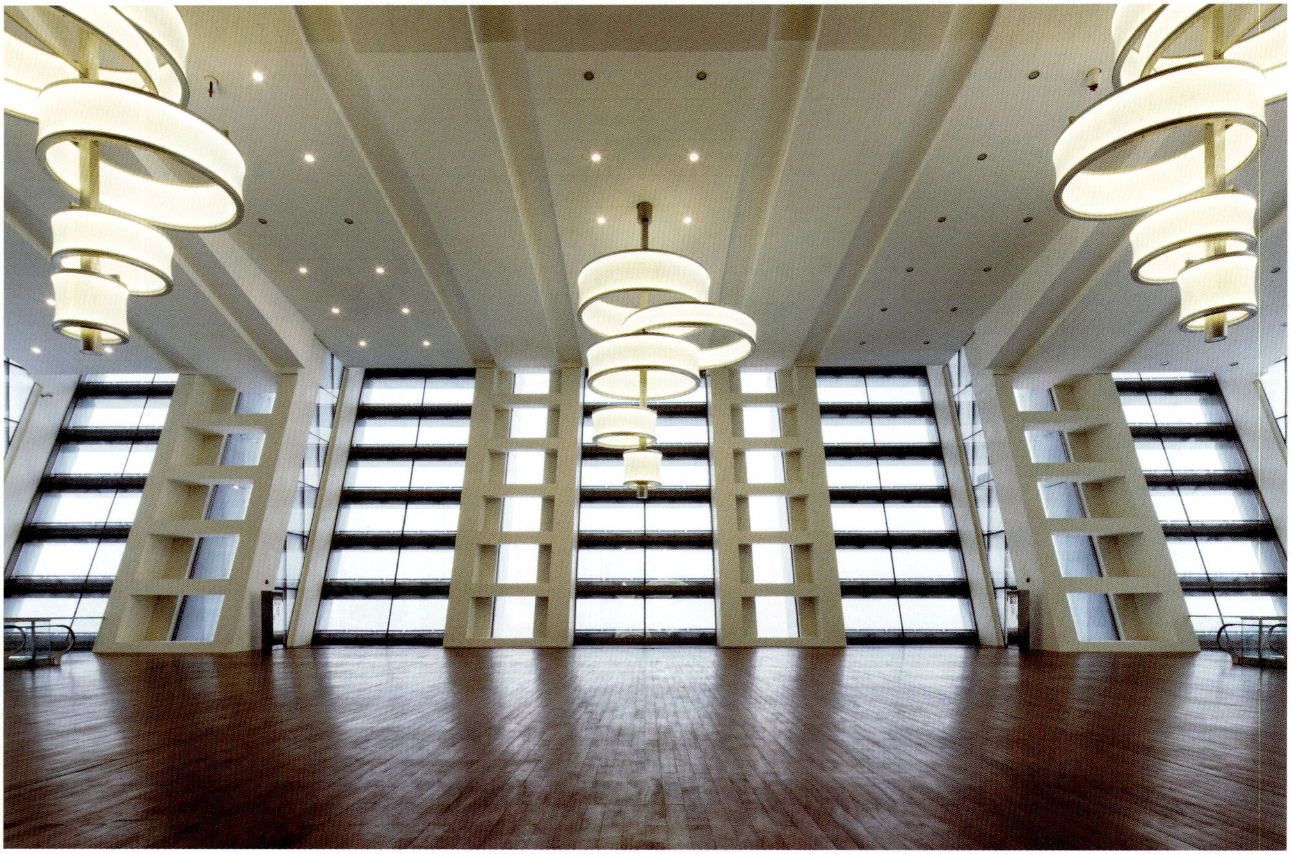

Chongqing Grand Theater Chongqing

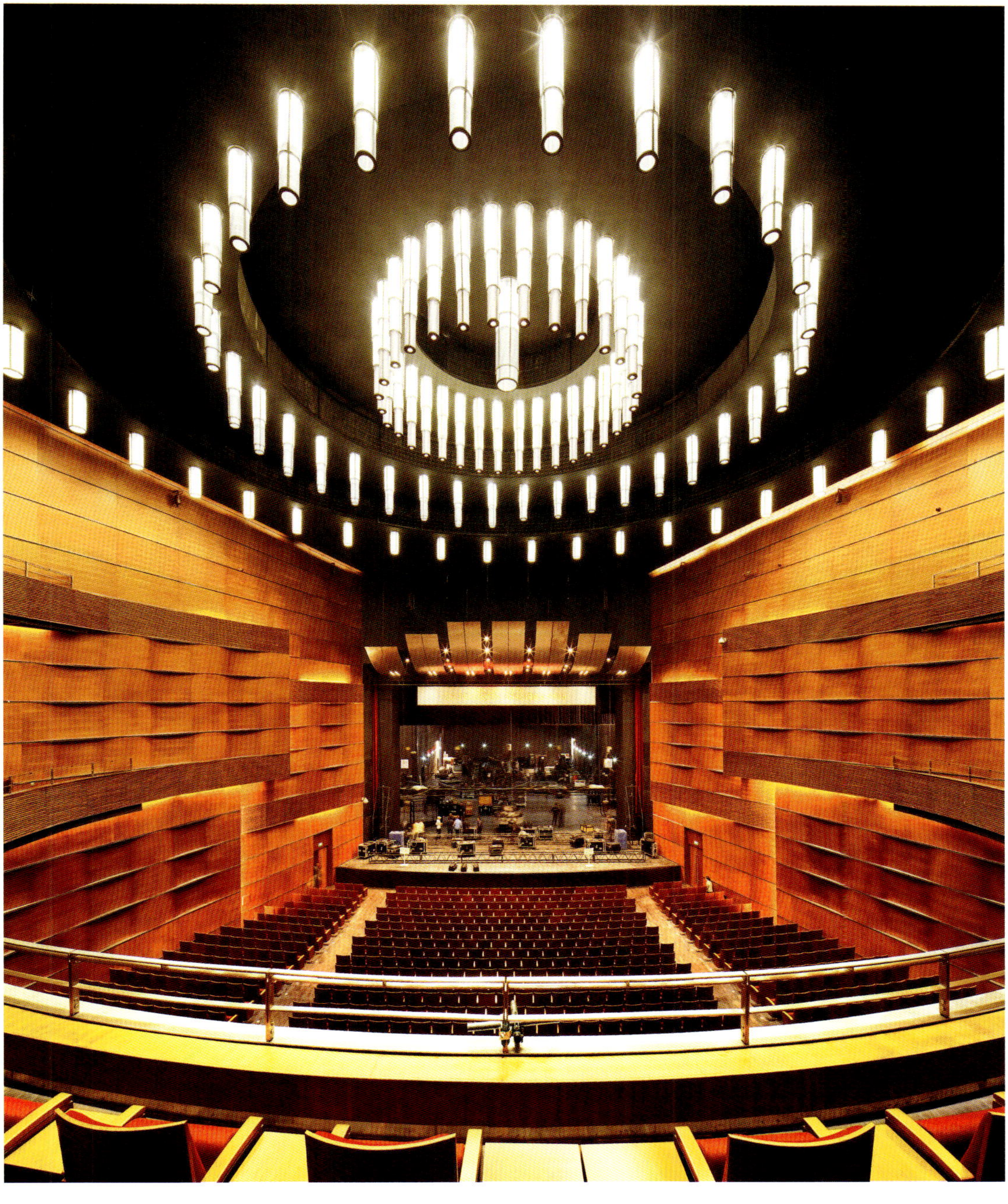

重庆大剧院　重庆

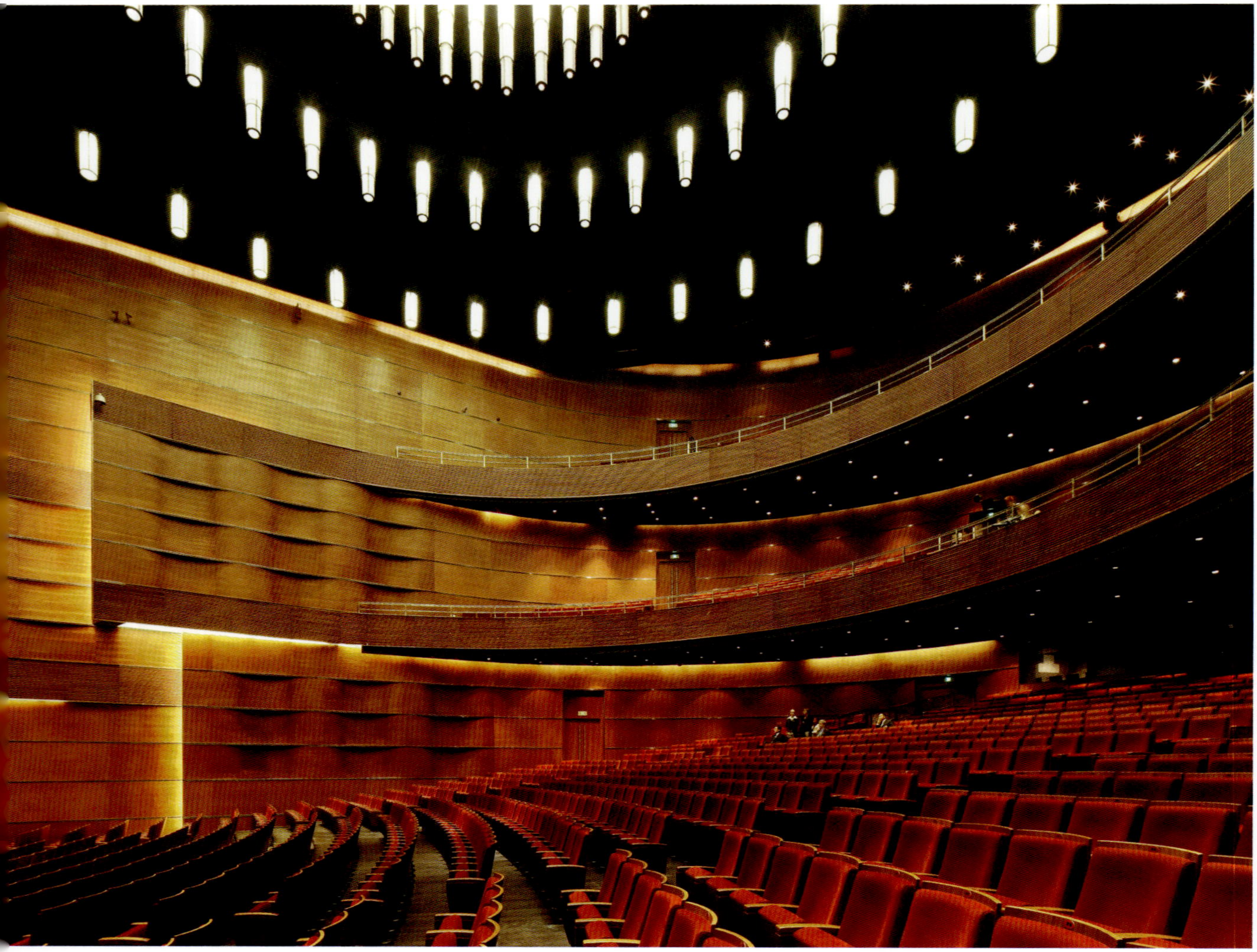

Chongqing Grand Theater Chongqing

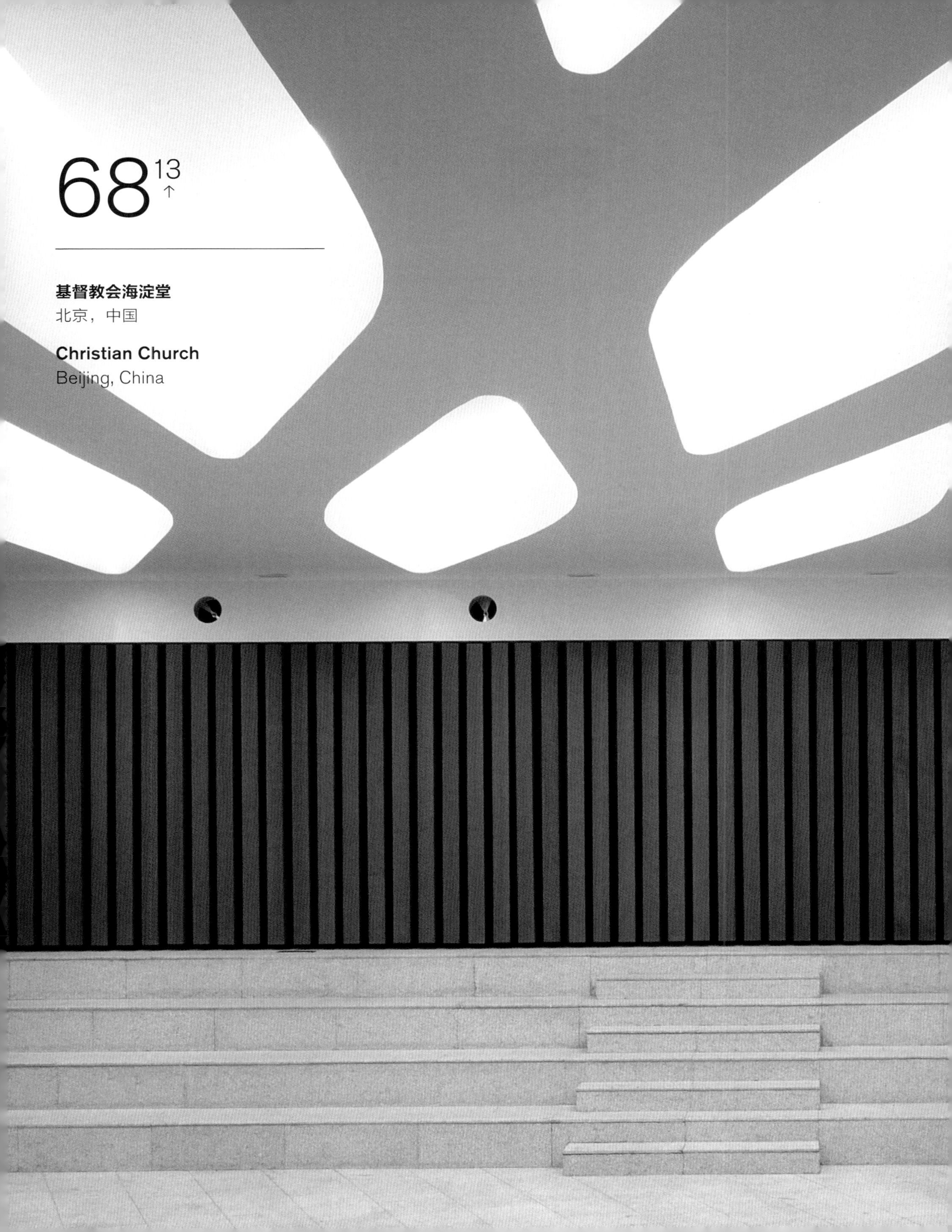

68 ¹³
↑

基督教会海淀堂
北京，中国

Christian Church
Beijing, China

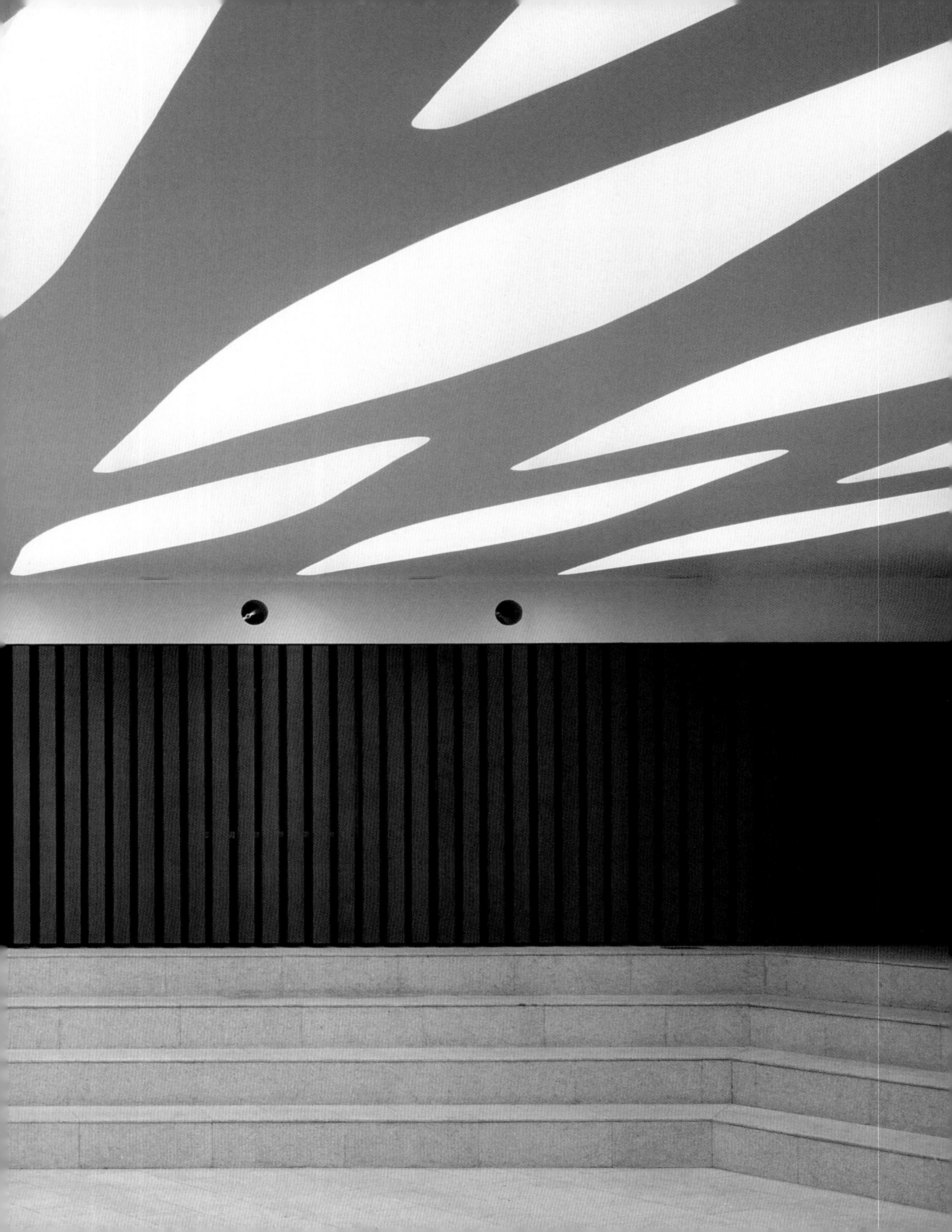

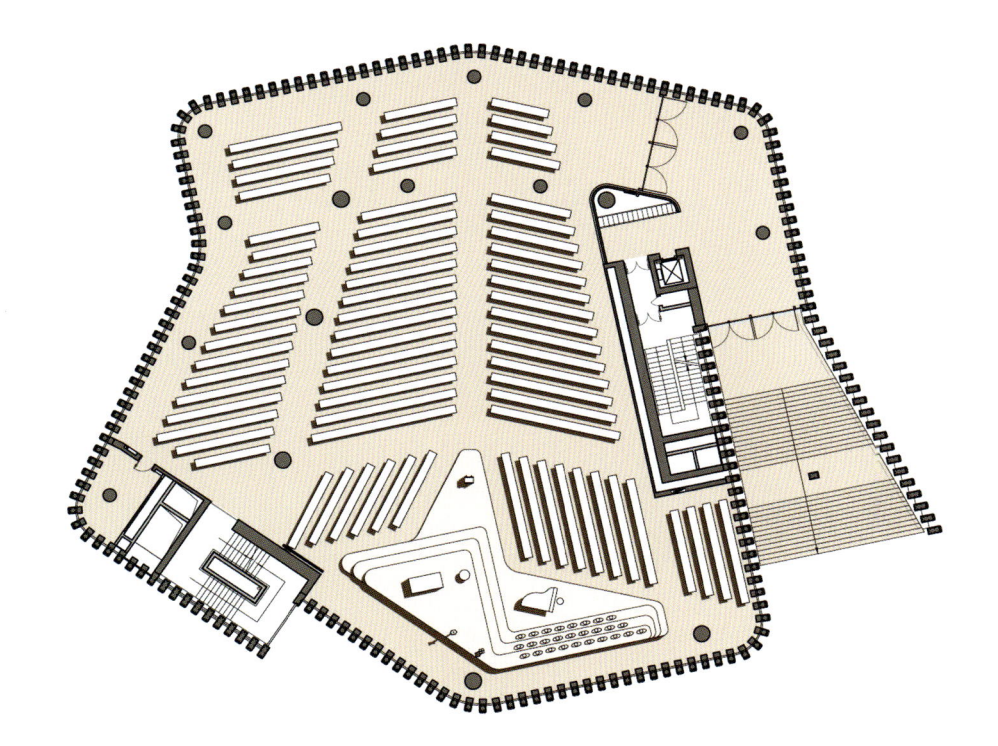

基督教会海淀堂 北京

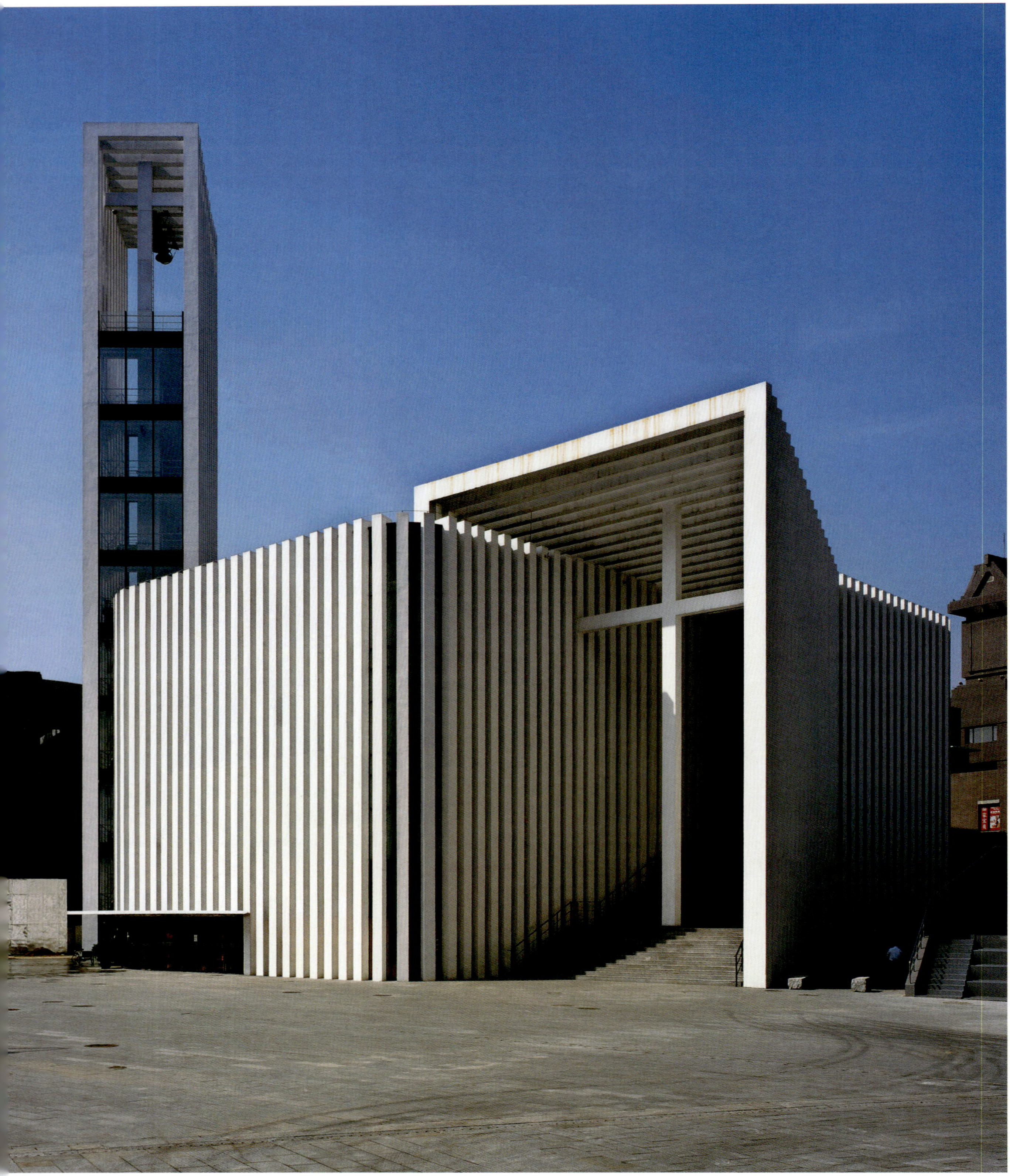

Christian Church Beijing

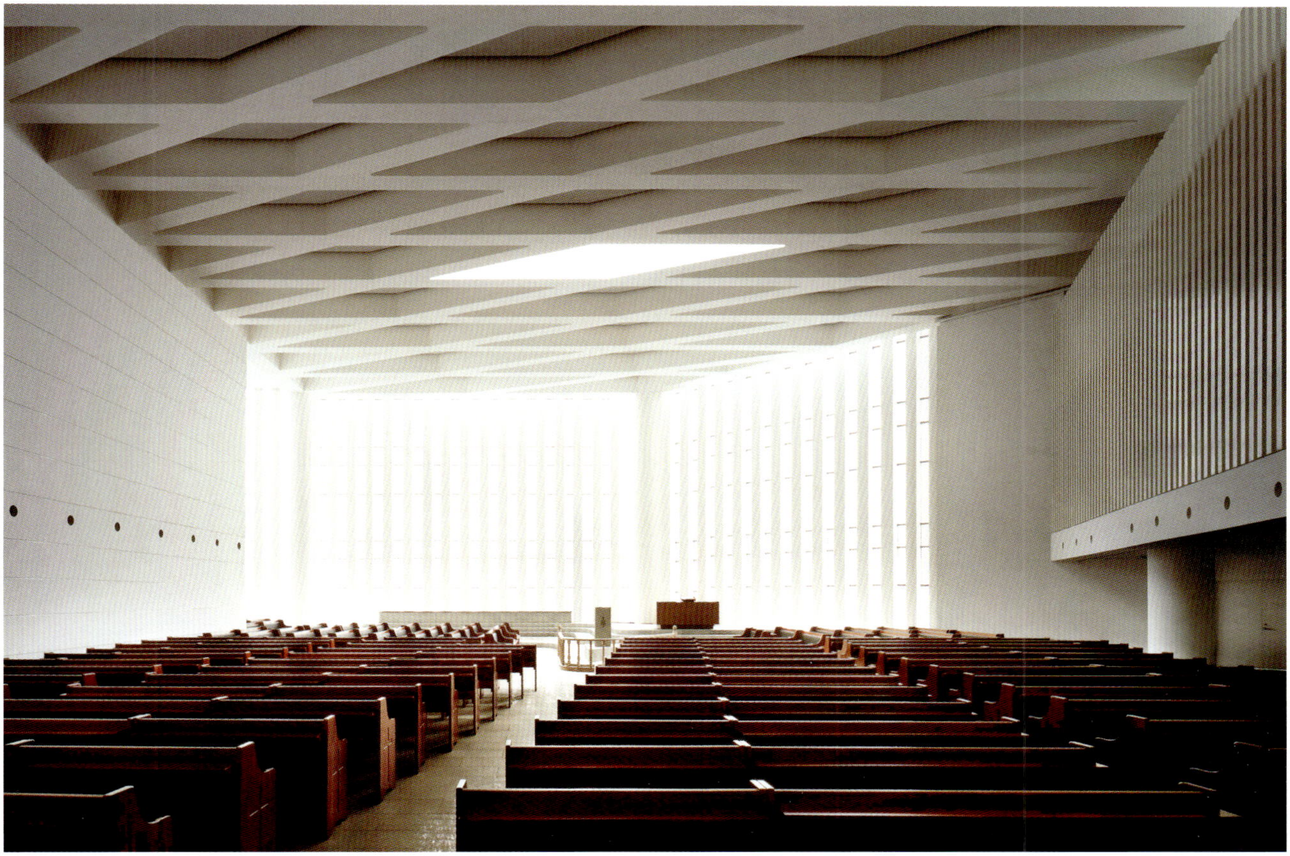

基督教会海淀堂　北京

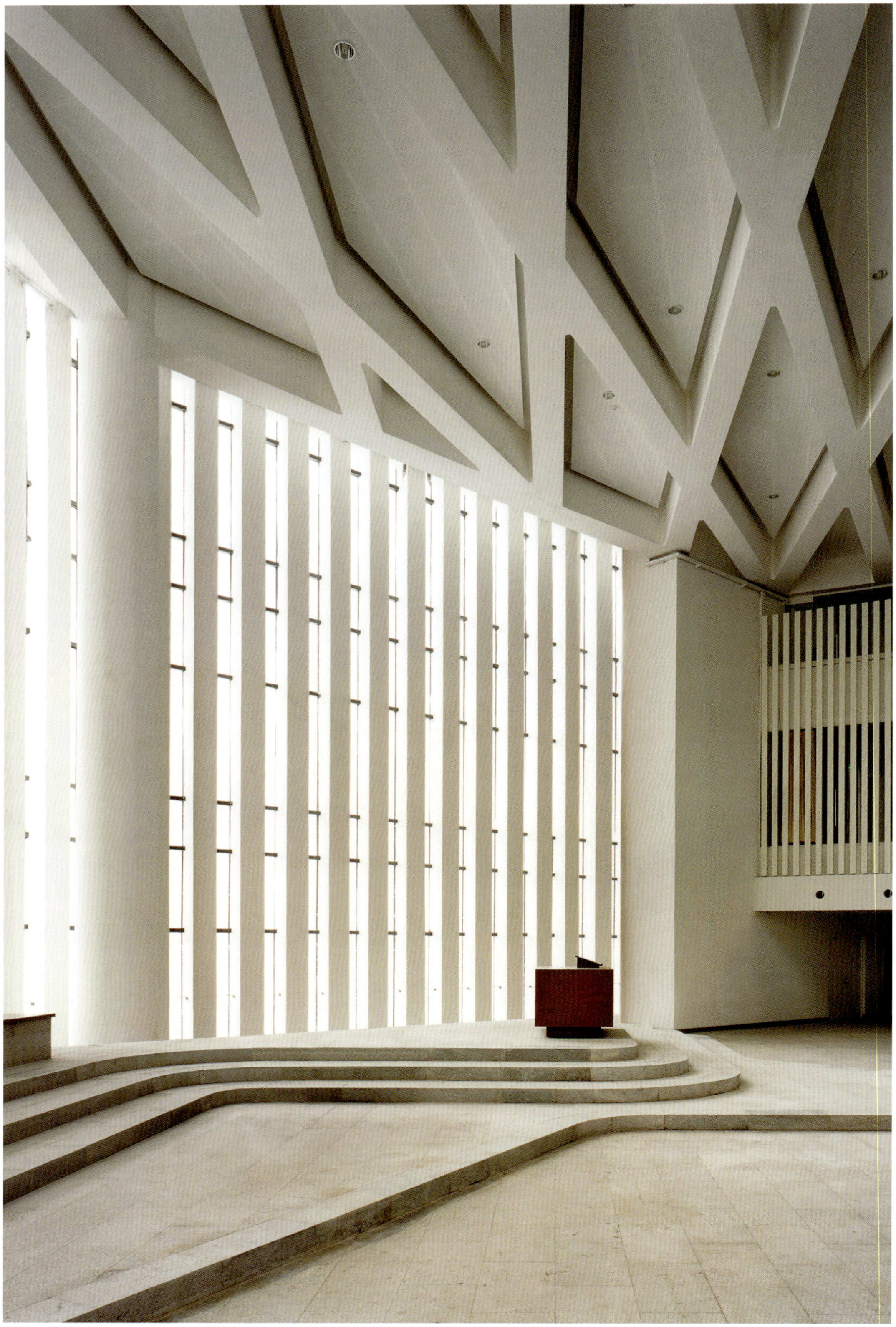

74 ¹³ ↑

国家会议中心
河内，越南

National Conference Center
Hanoi, Vietnam

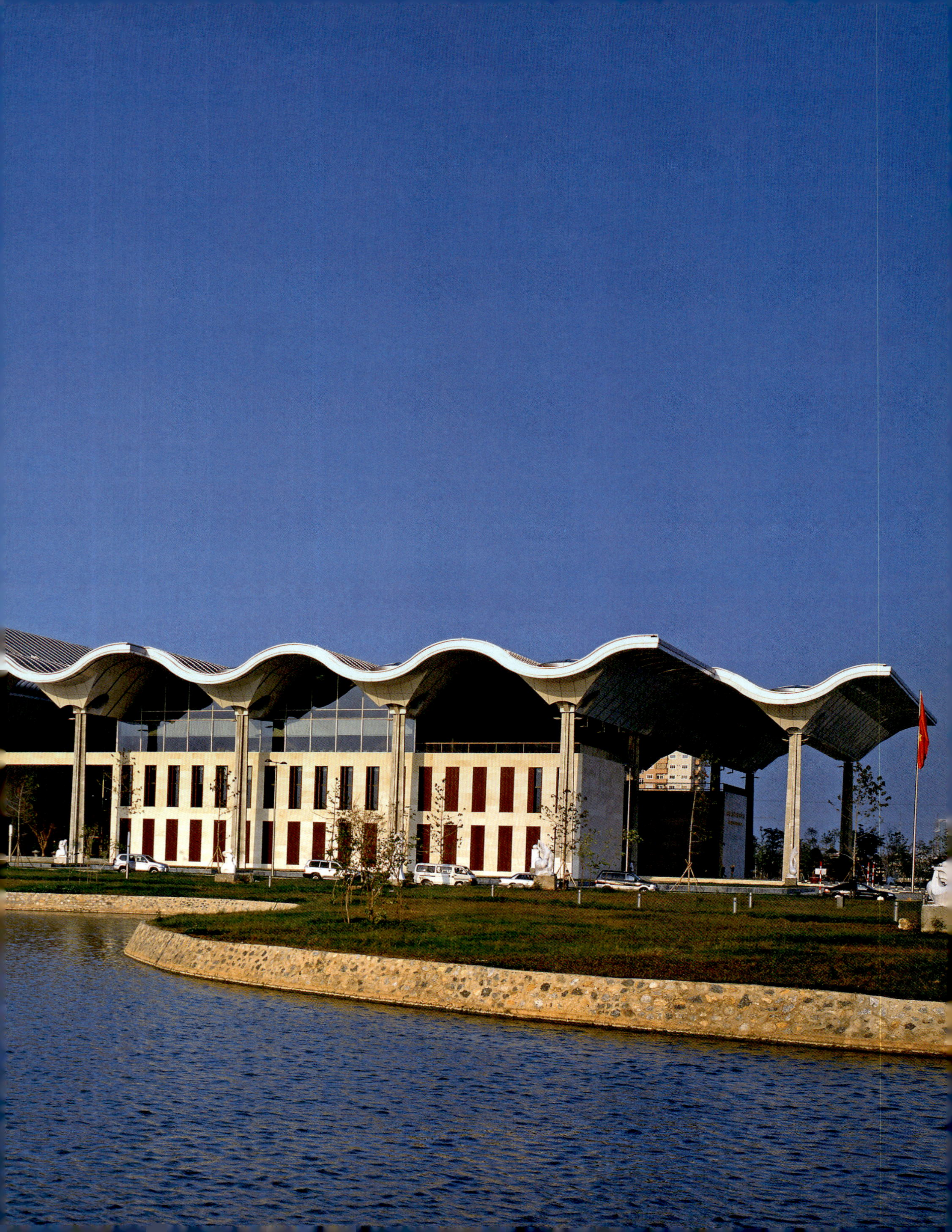

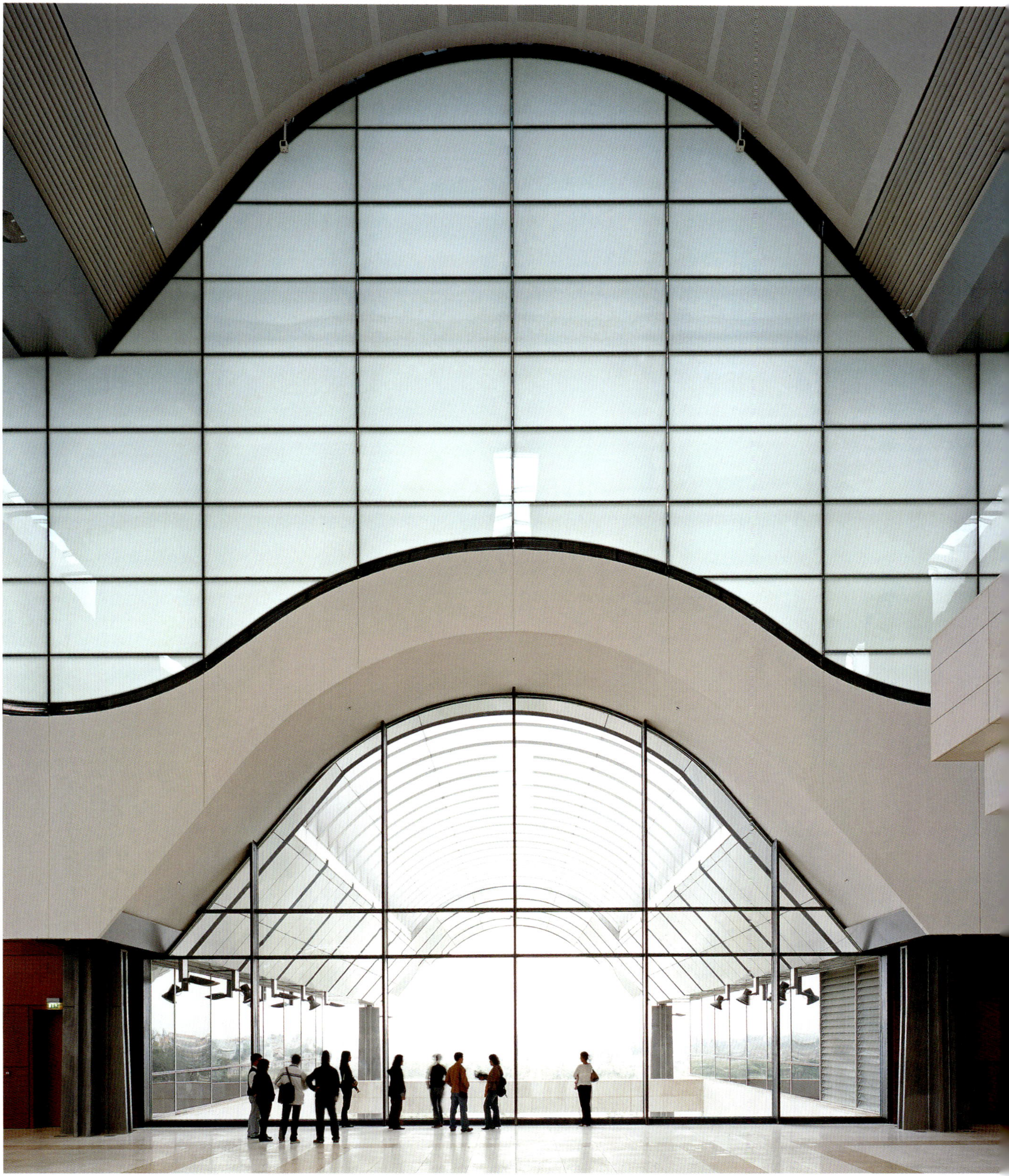

国家会议中心　河内

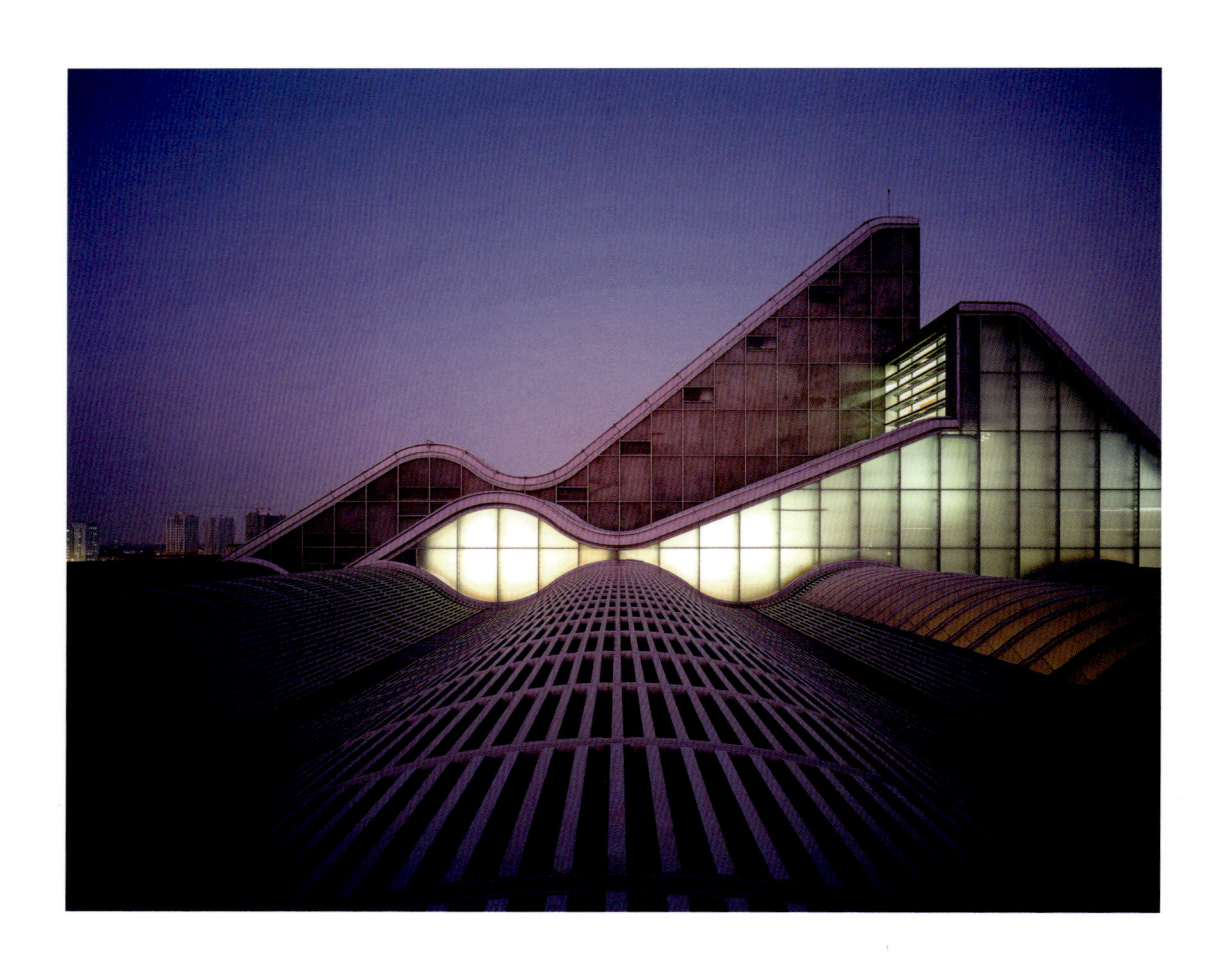

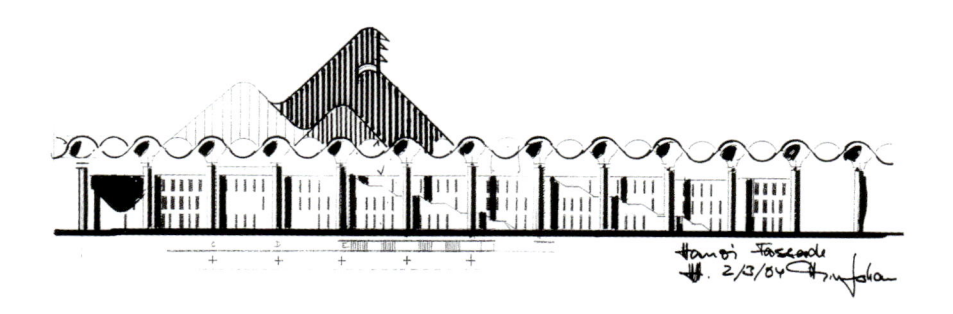

National Conference Center Hanoi   77

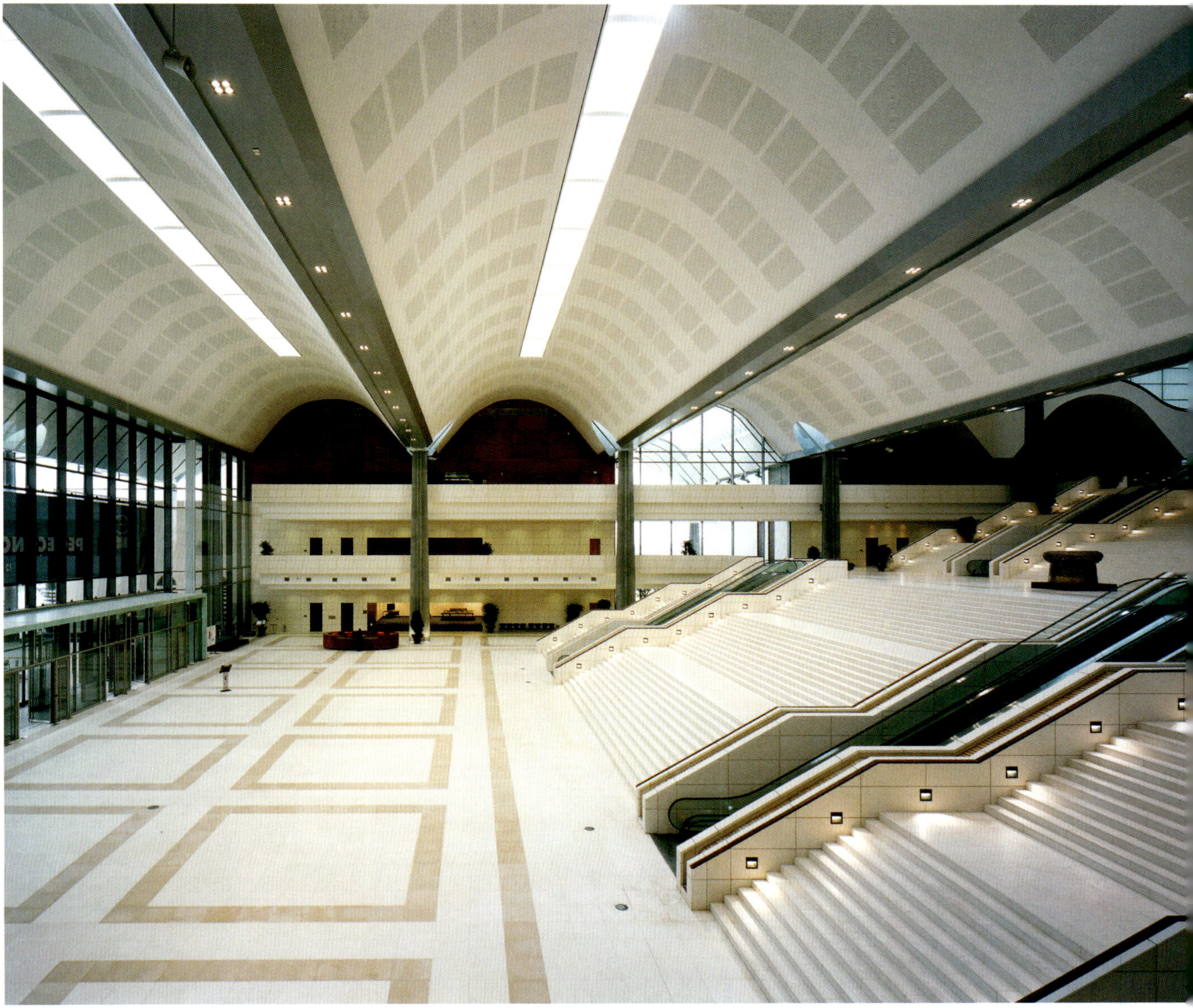

国家会议中心　河内

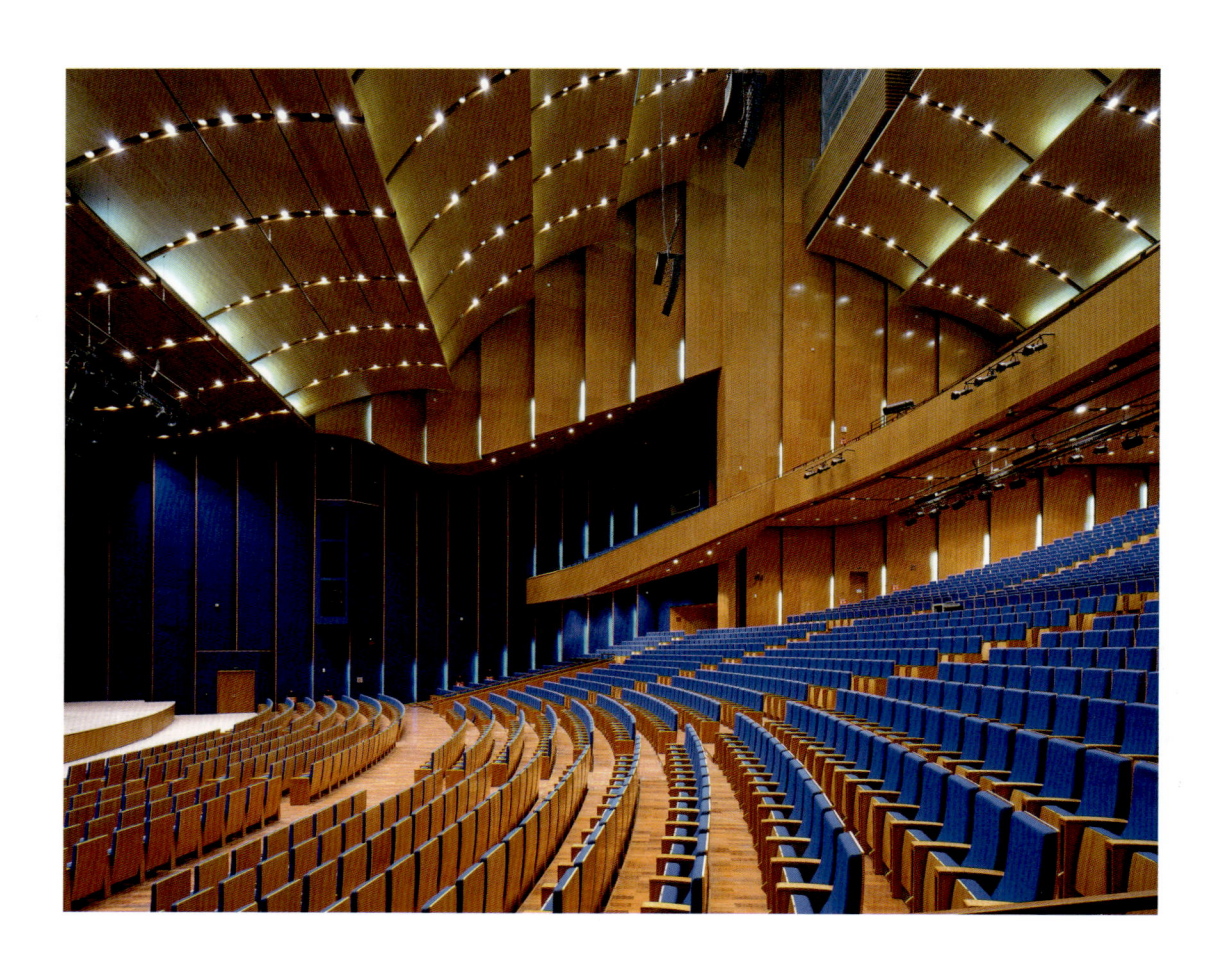

National Conference Center Hanoi

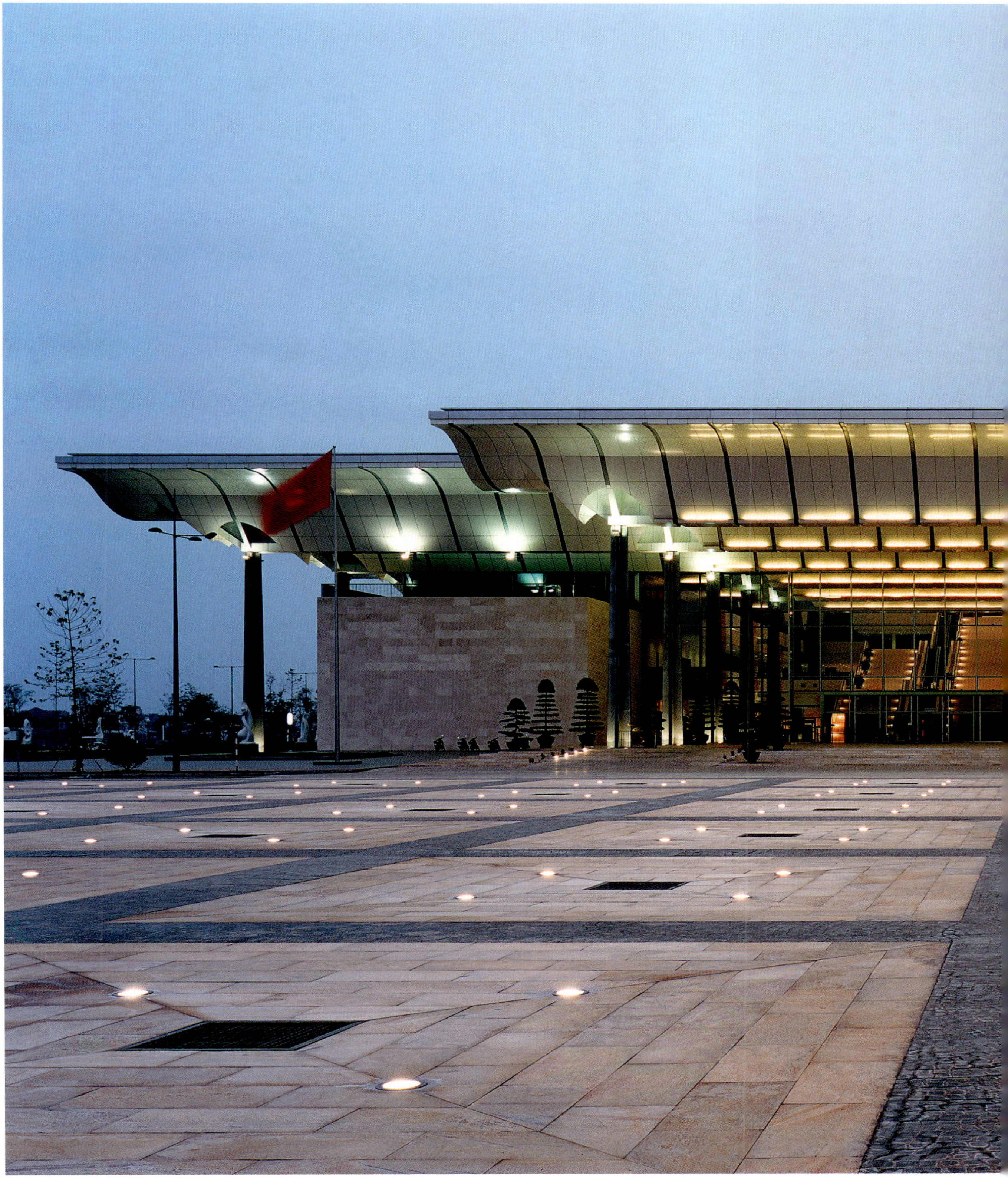

国家会议中心 河内

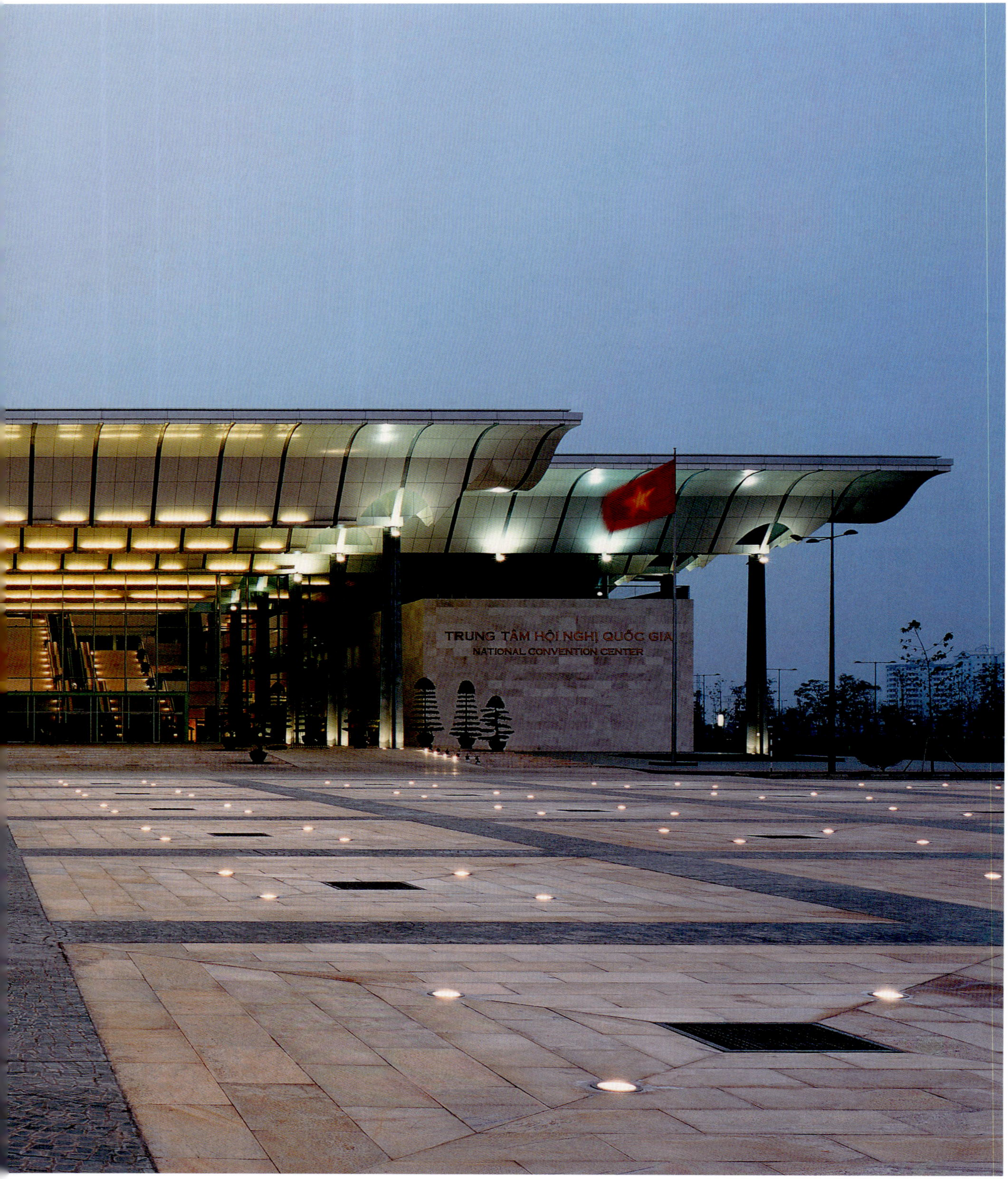
TRUNG TÂM HỘI NGHỊ QUỐC GIA
NATIONAL CONVENTION CENTER

82 ¹⁴
↑

中国国家博物馆
北京，中国

National Museum of China
Beijing, China

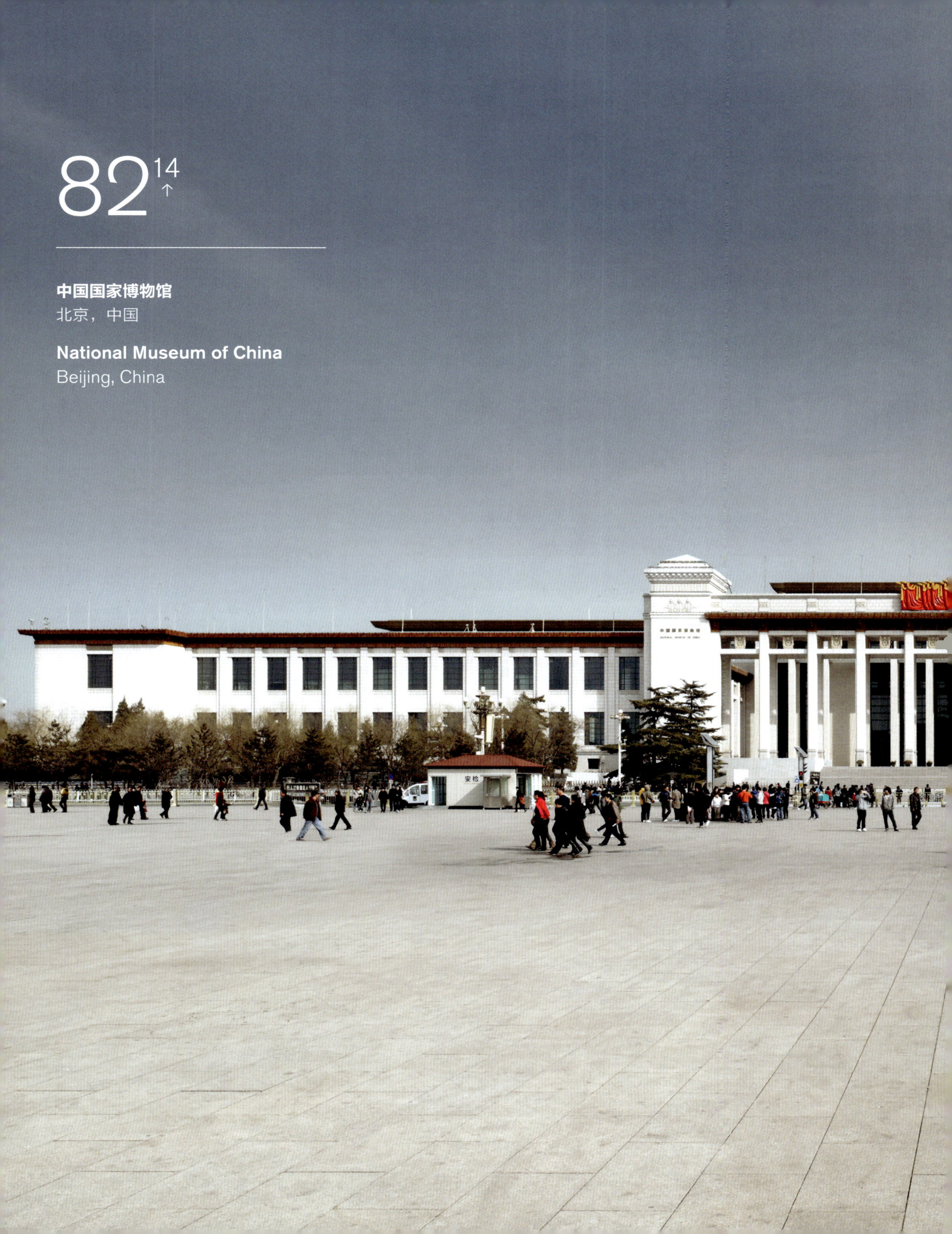

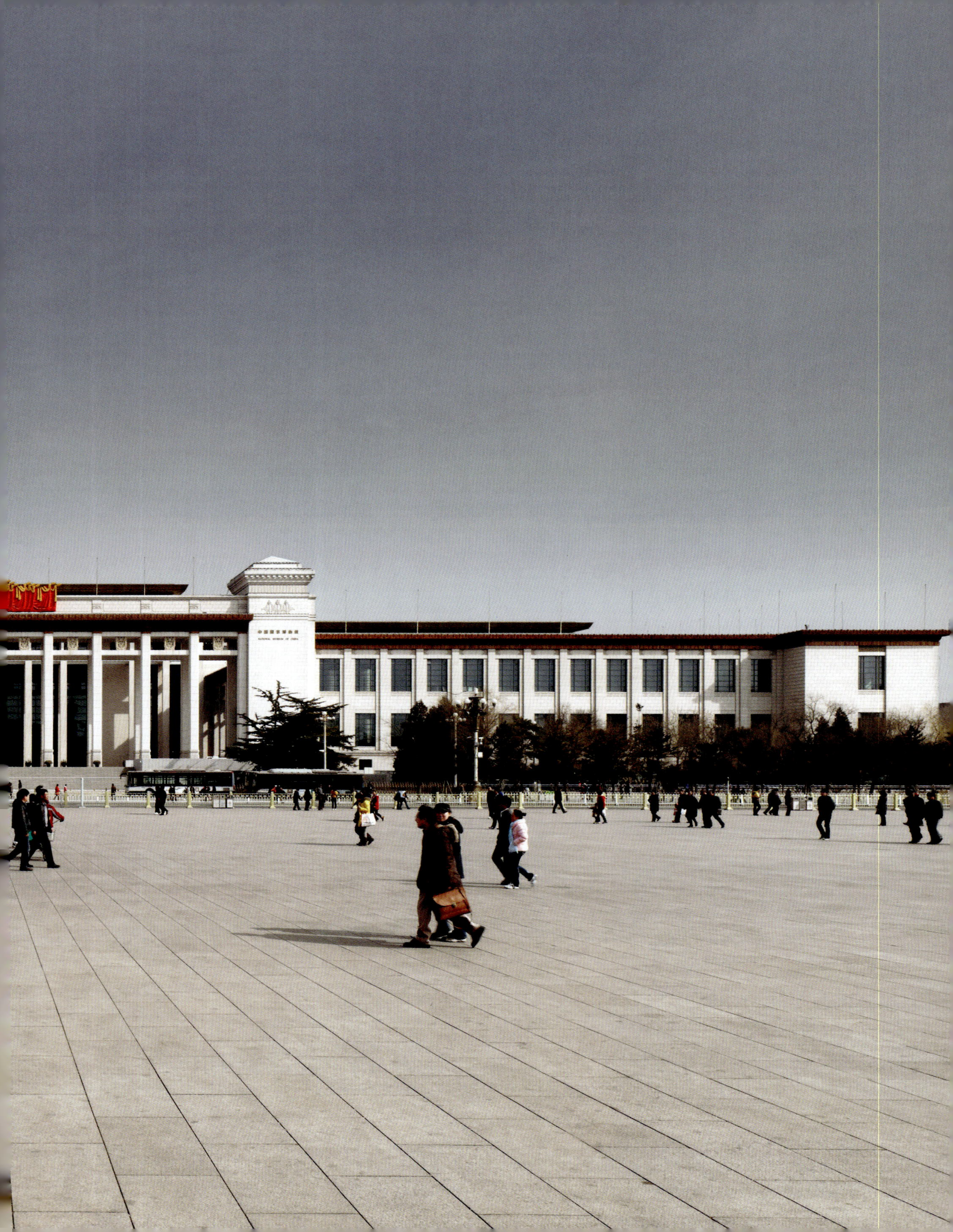

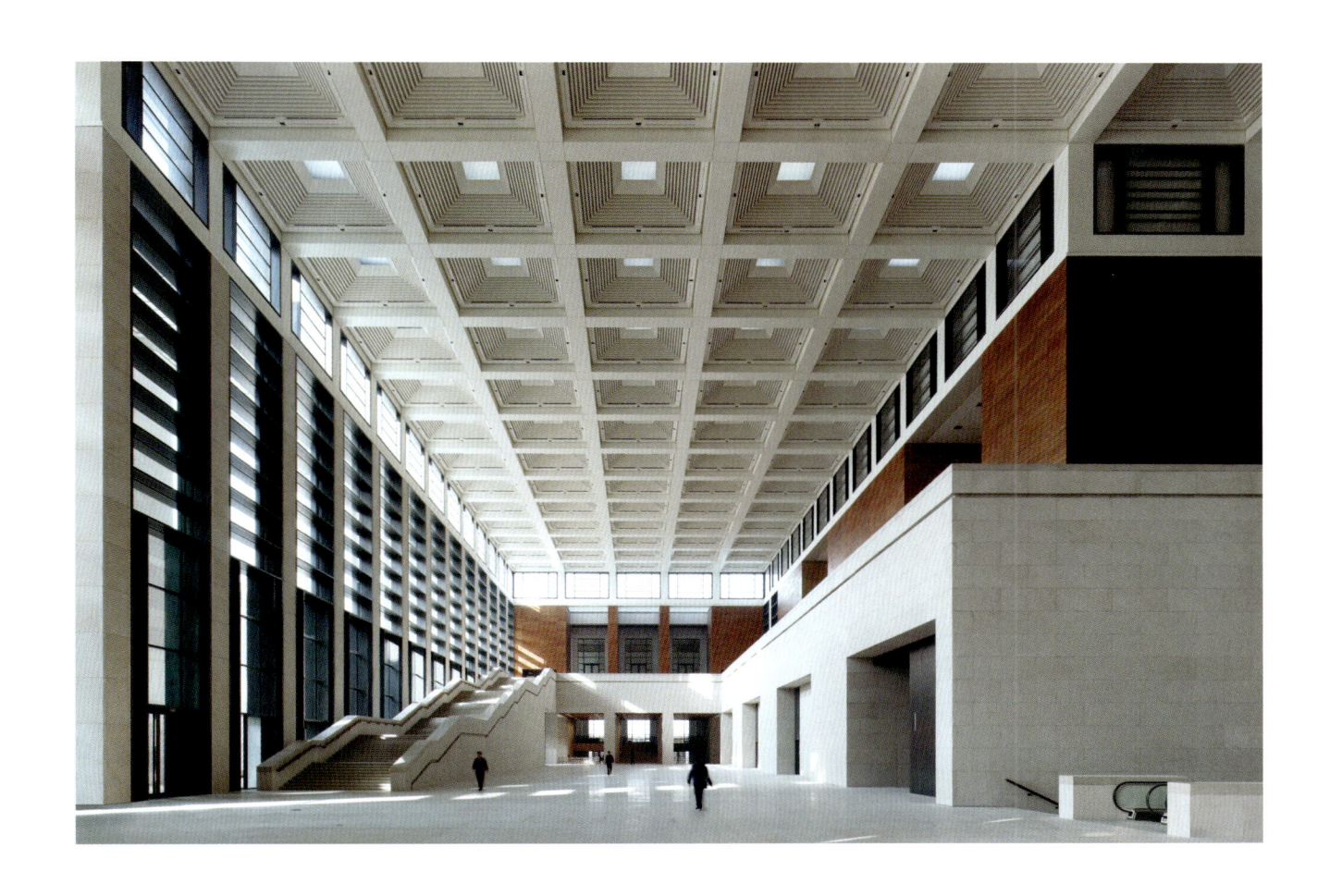

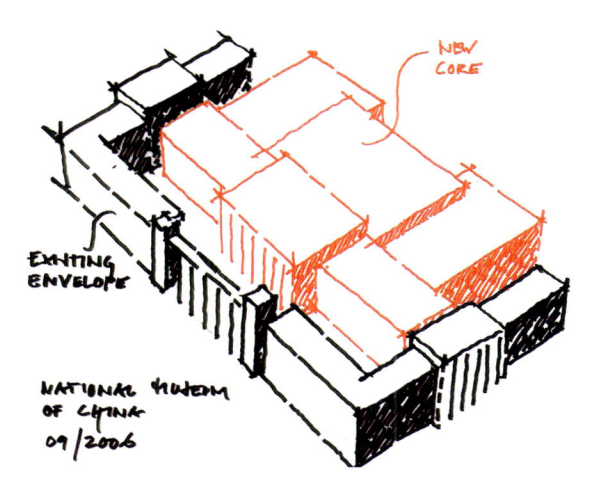

中国国家博物馆　北京

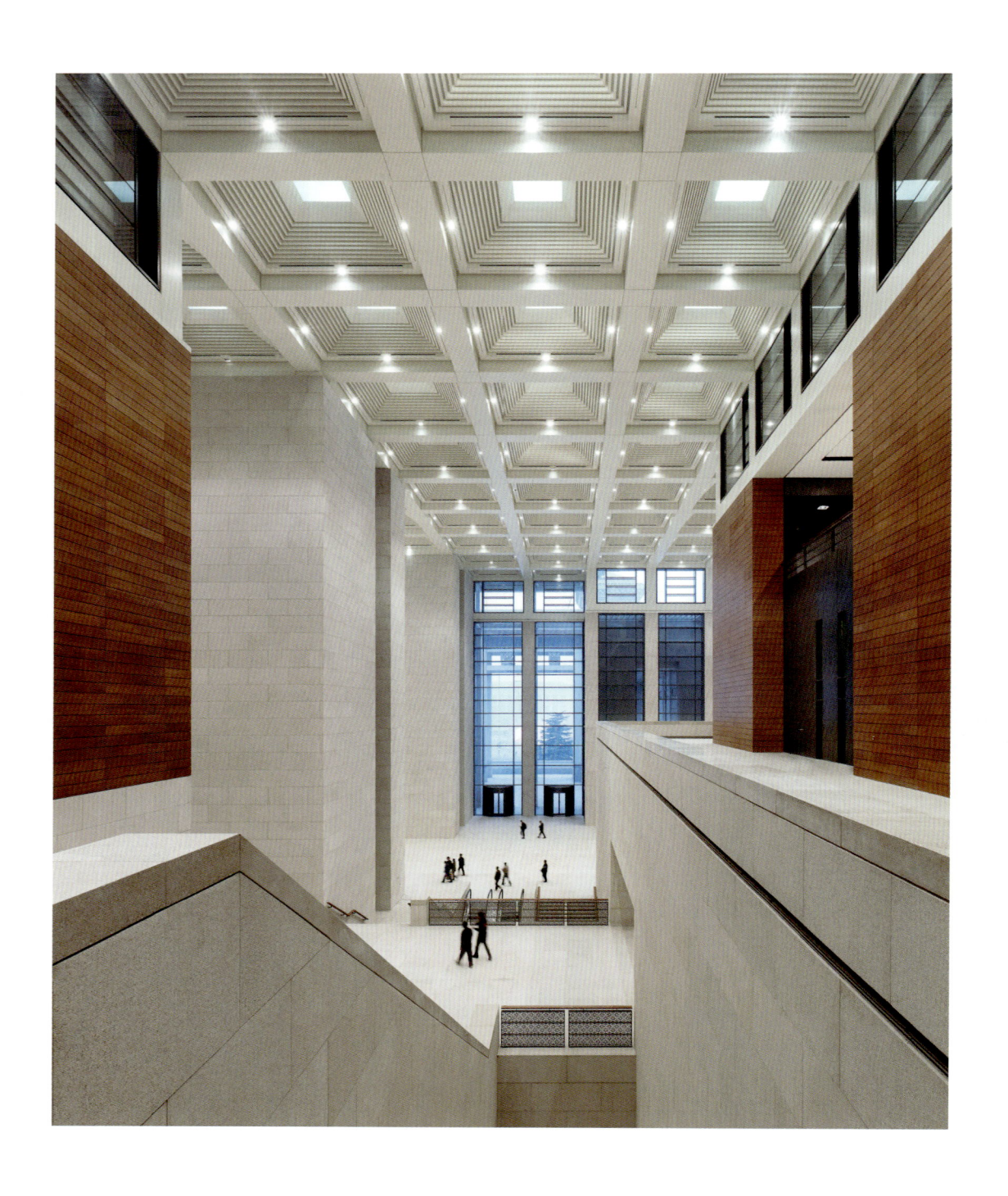

National Museum of China Beijing

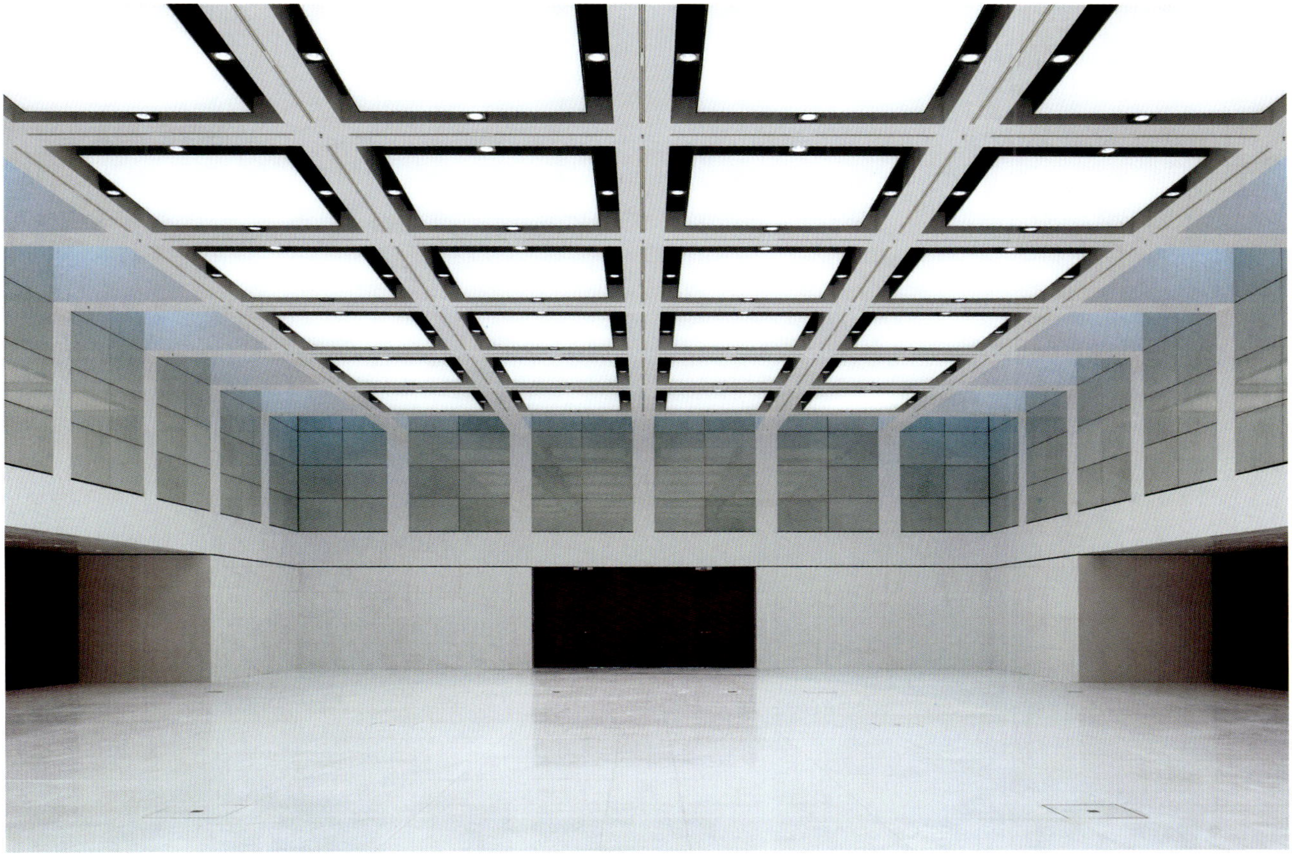

中国国家博物馆　北京

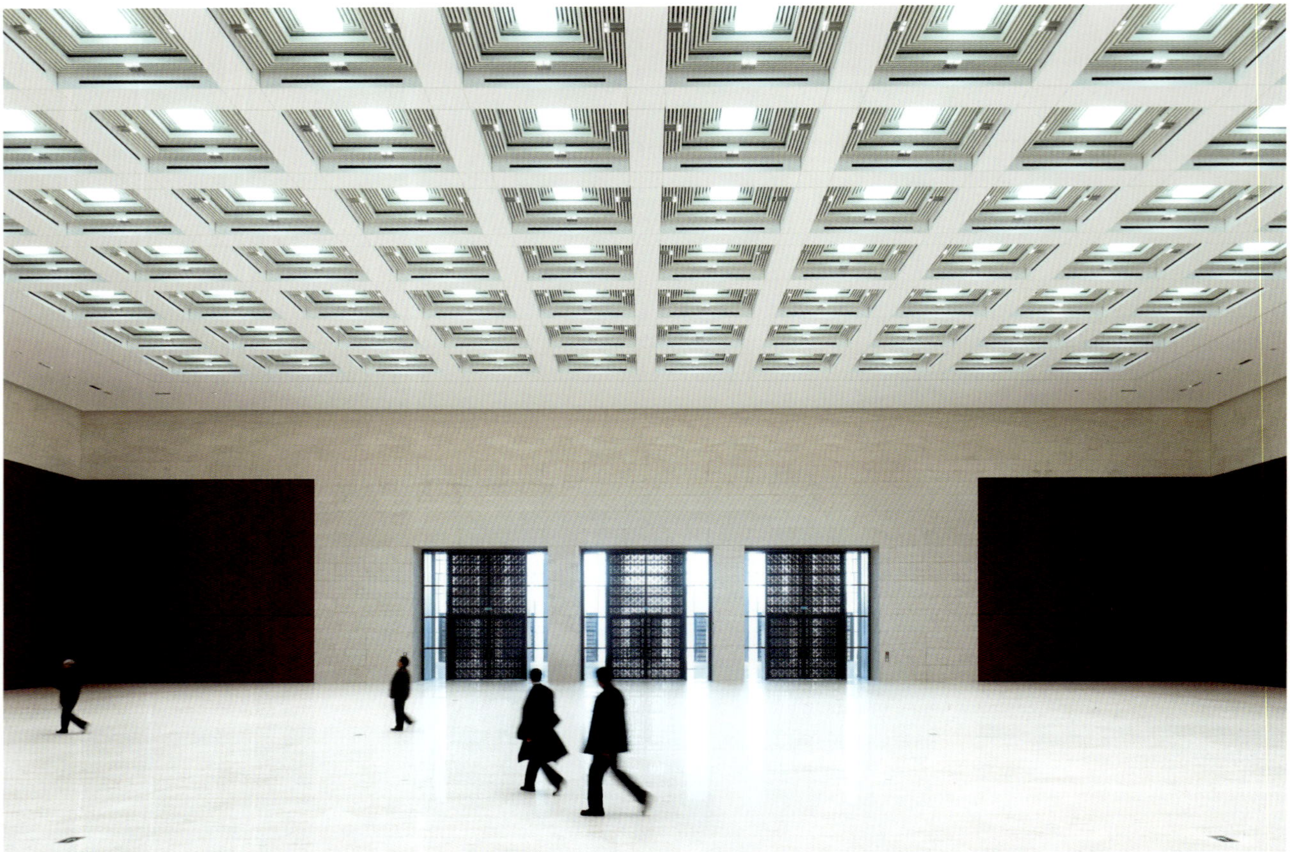

National Museum of China Beijing

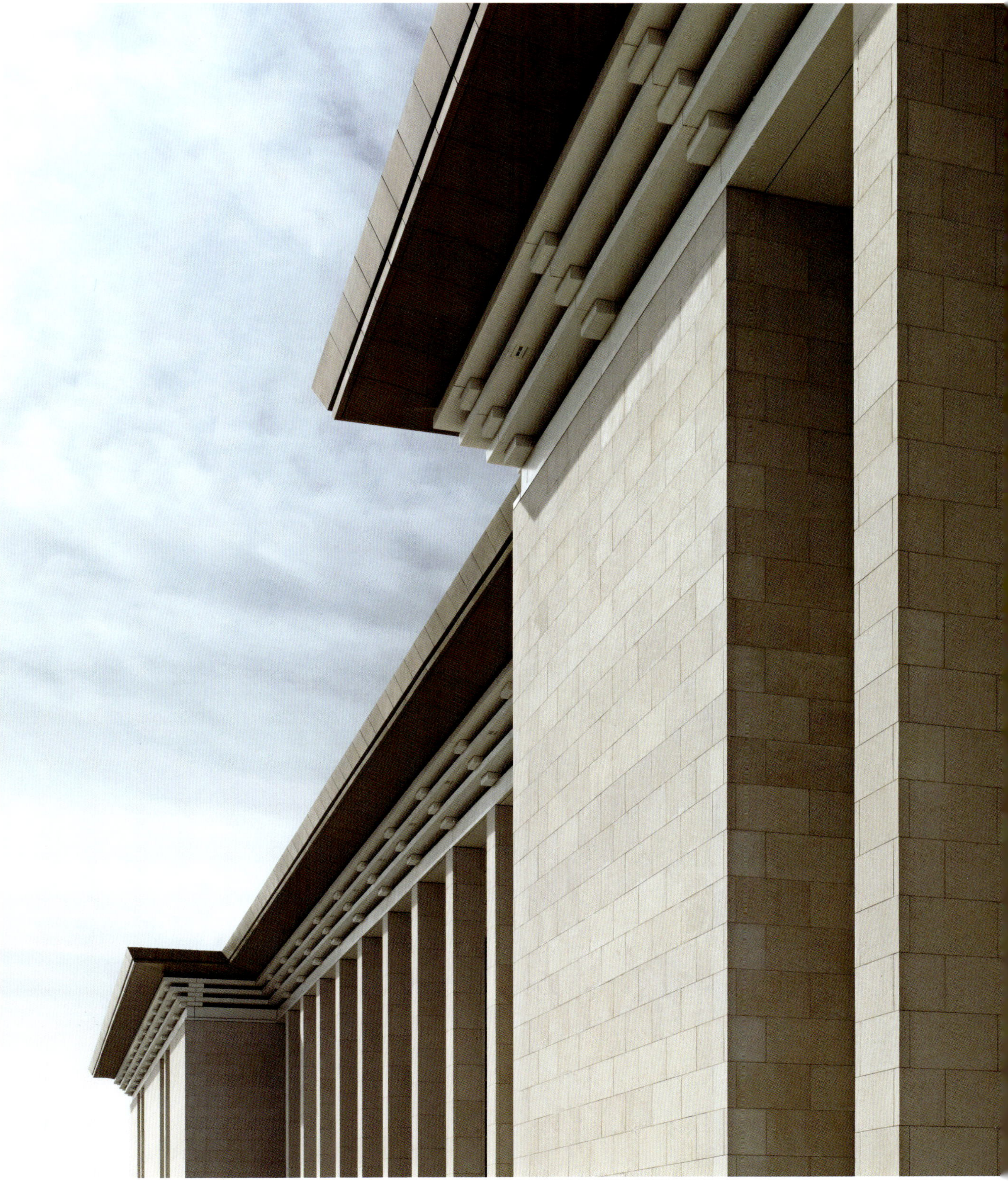

中国国家博物馆　北京

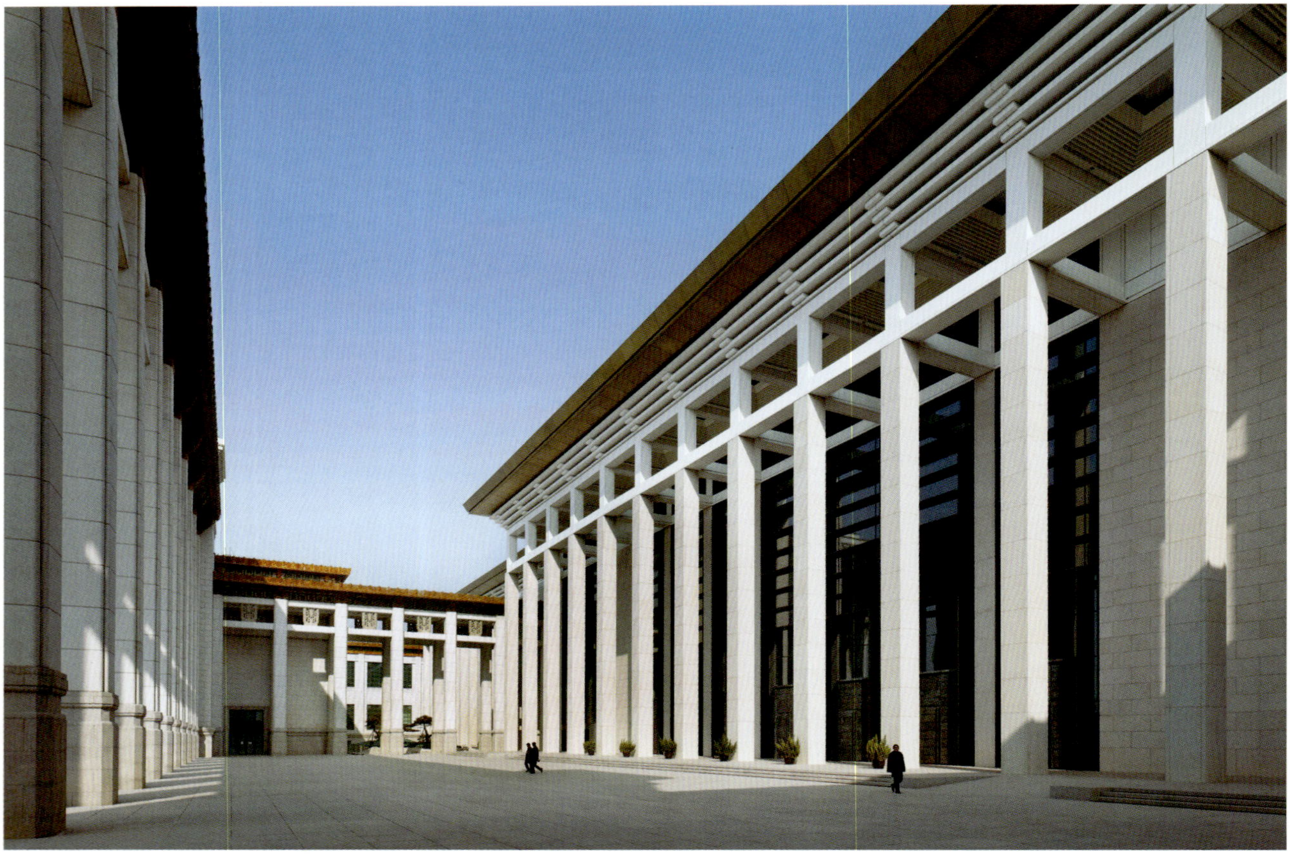

National Museum of China Beijing

90 ¹⁴
↑

青岛大剧院
青岛，中国

Qingdao Grand Theater
Qingdao, China

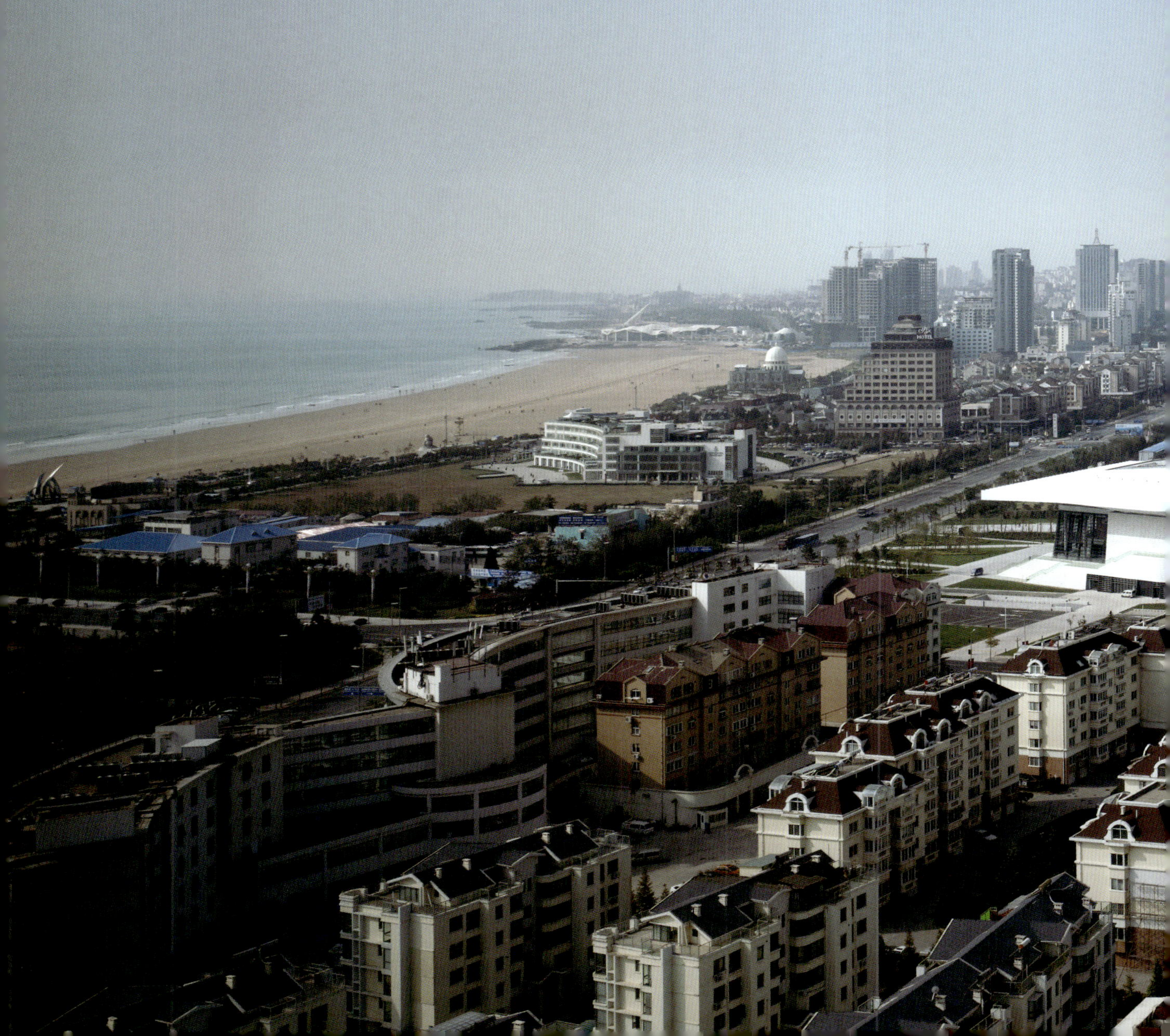

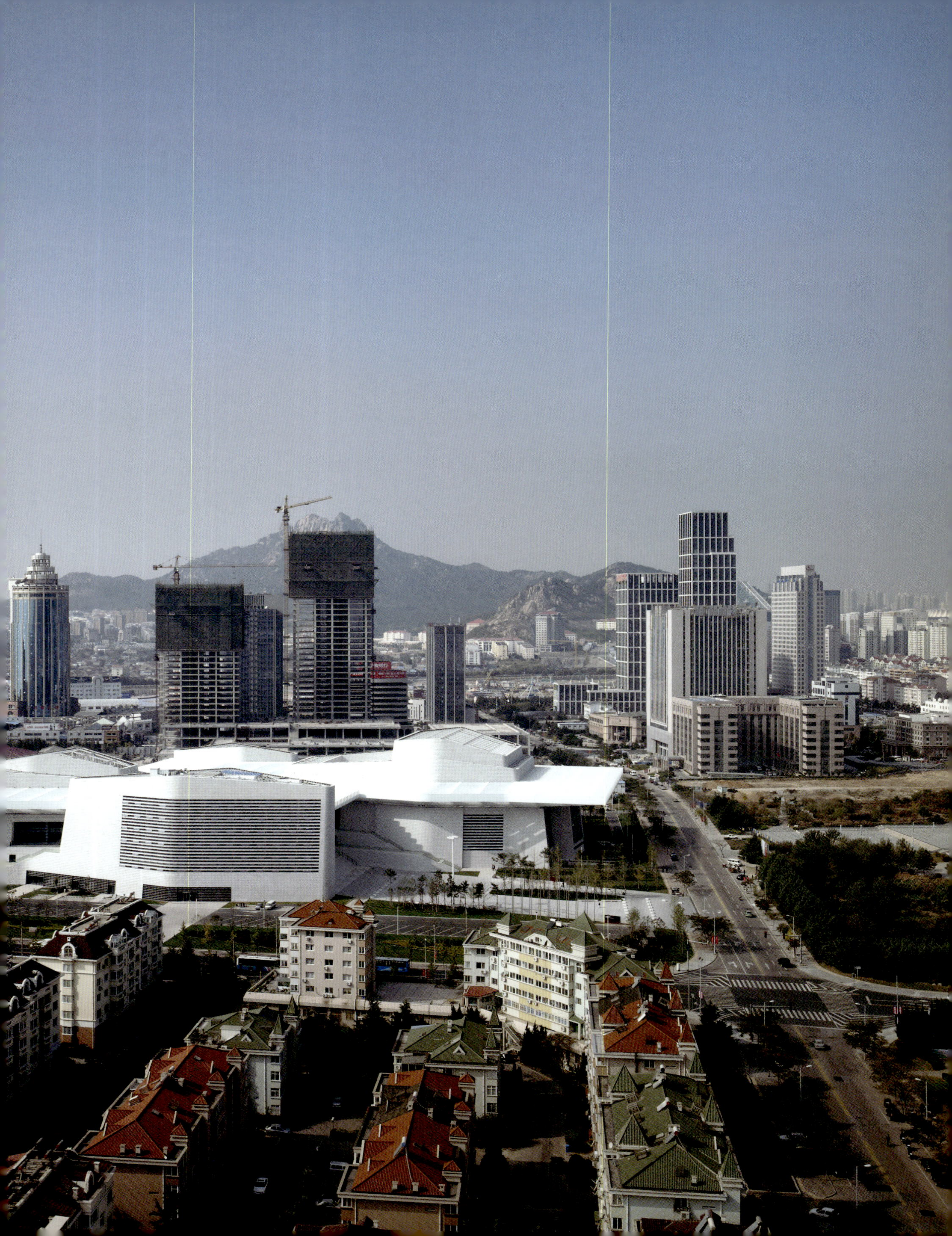

青岛大剧院　青岛

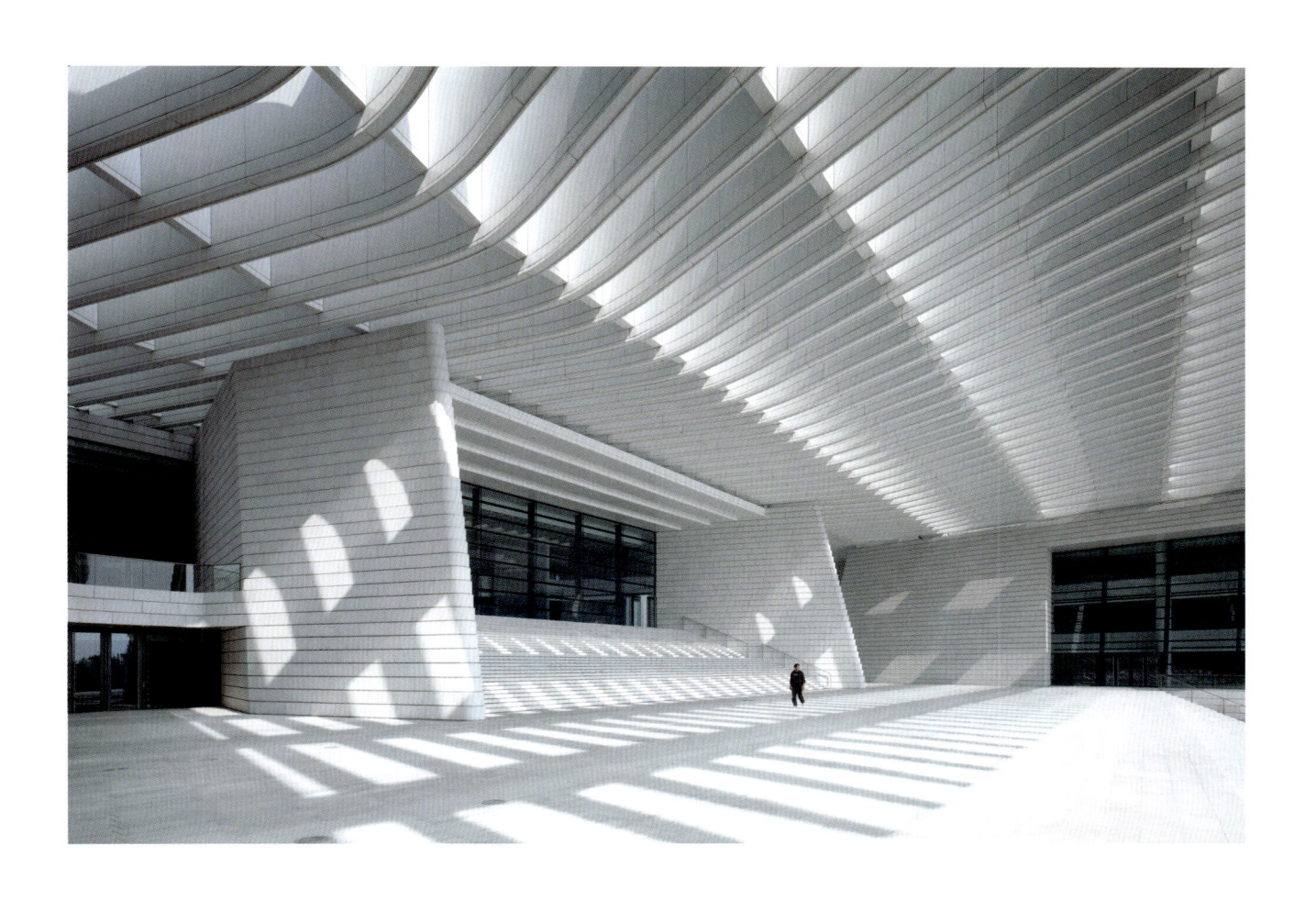

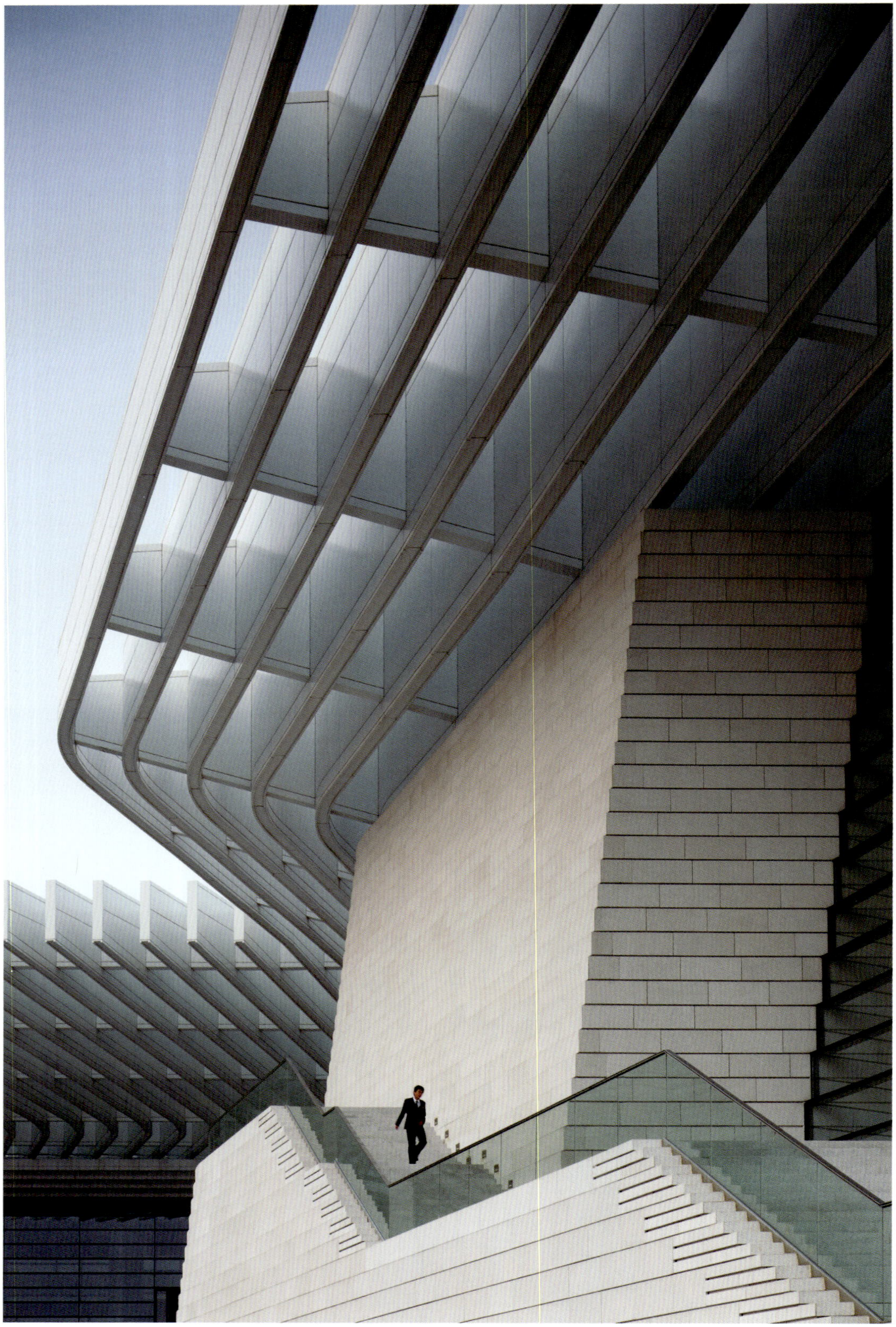

Qingdao Grand Theater Qingdao

青岛大剧院　青岛

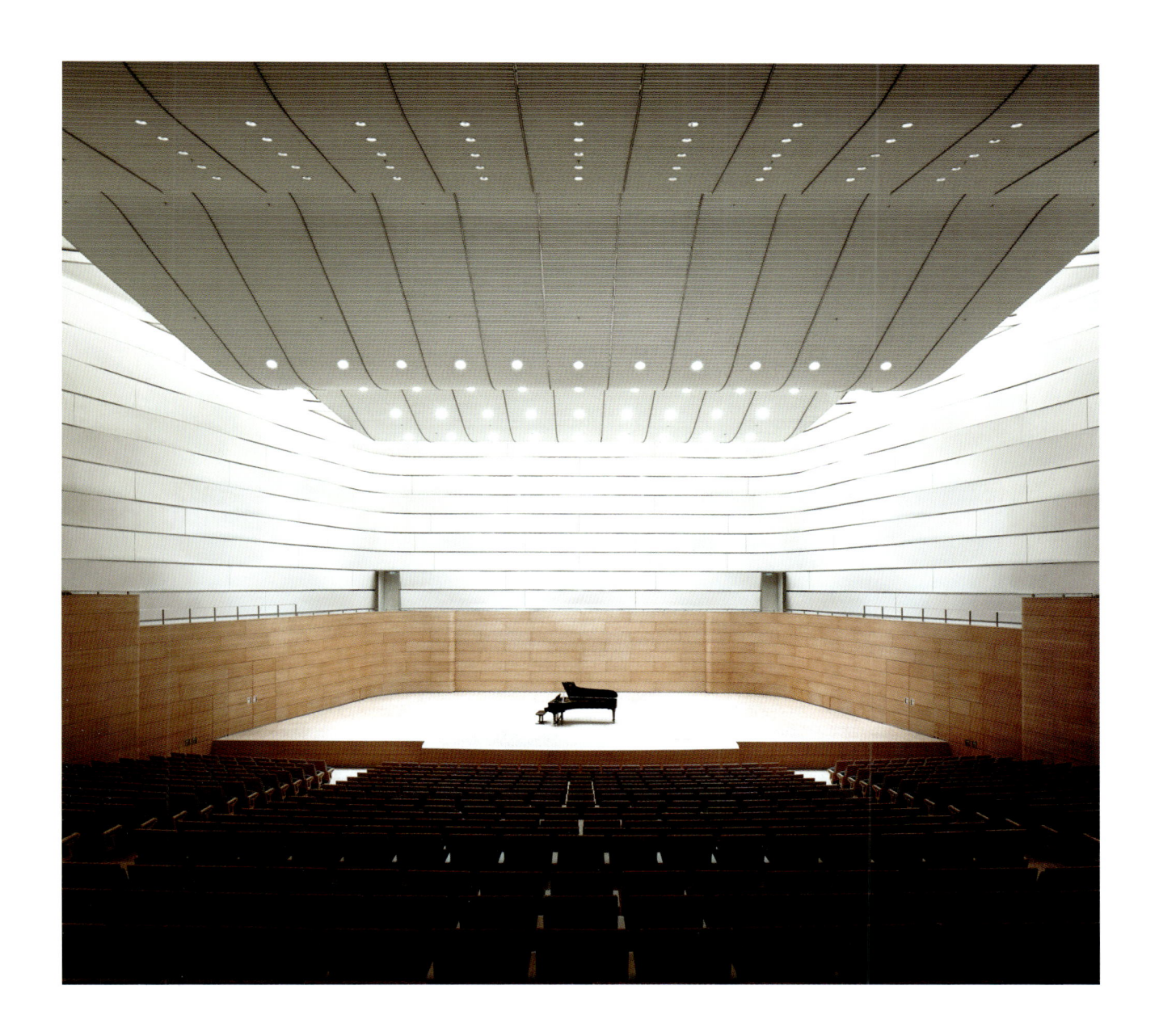

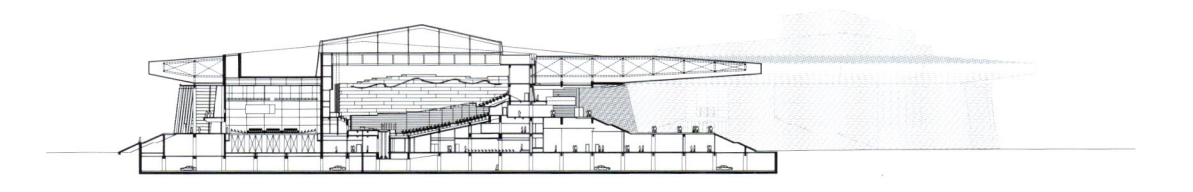

Qingdao Grand Theater Qingdao 95

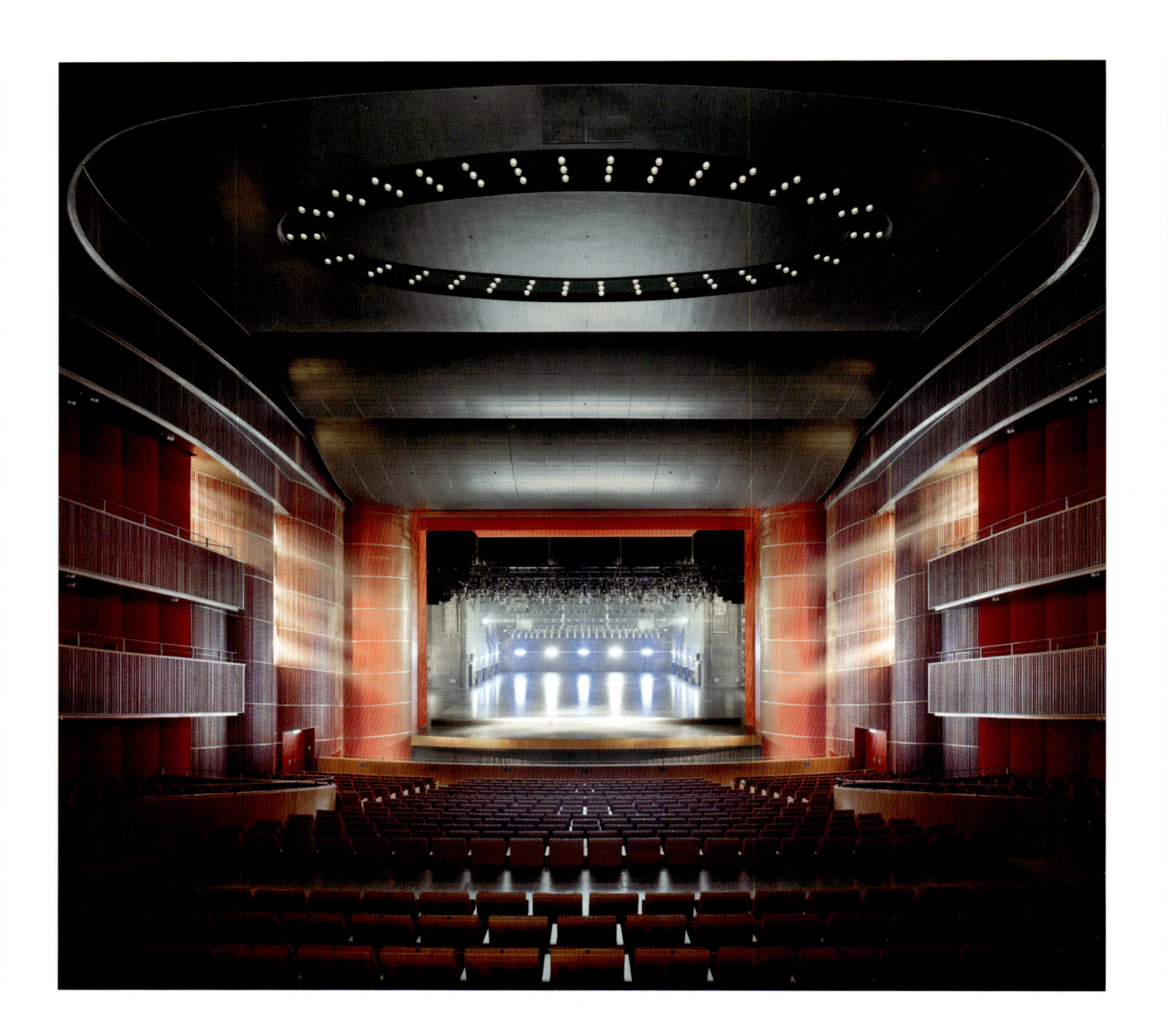

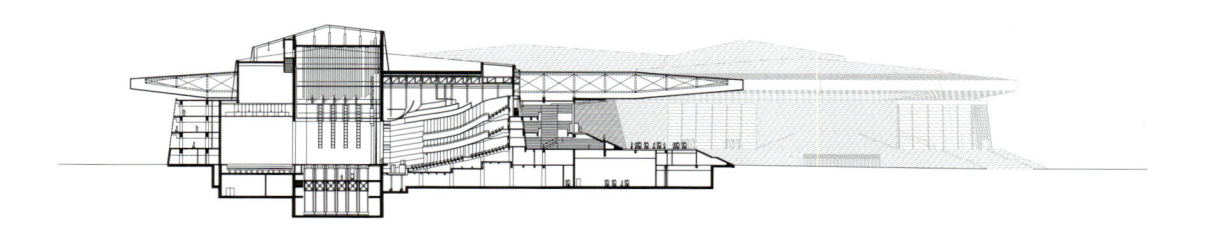

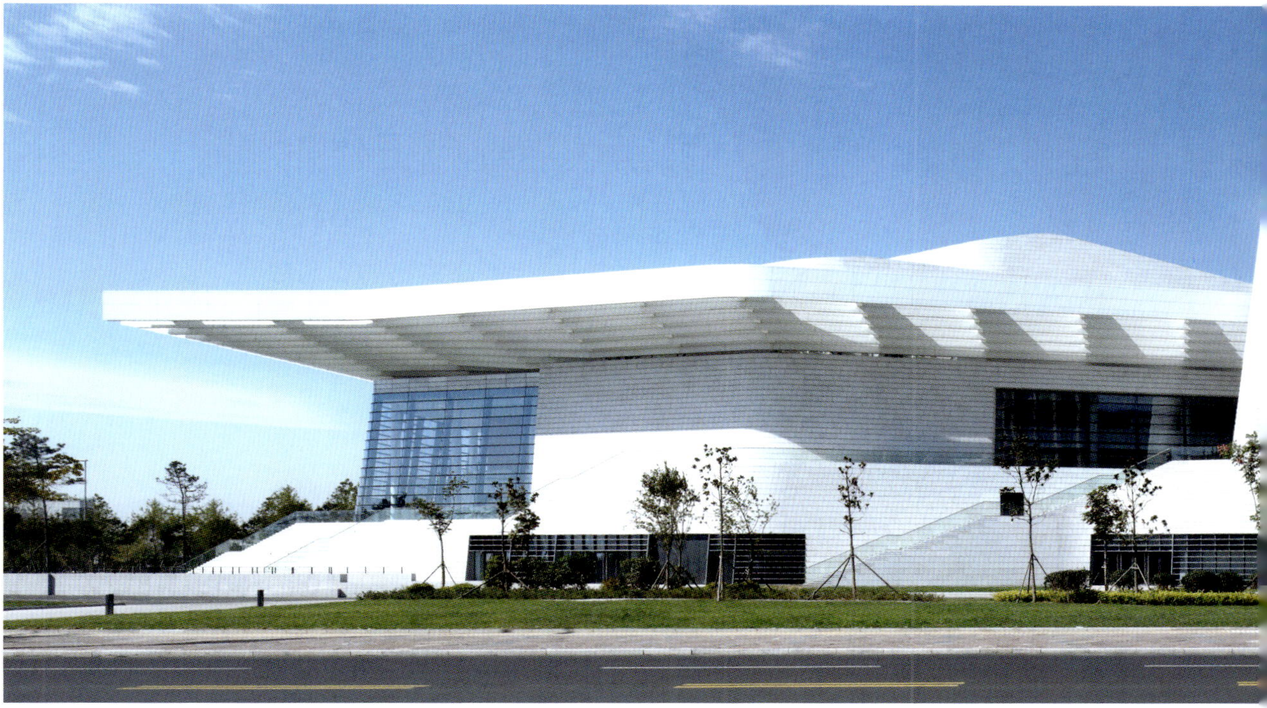

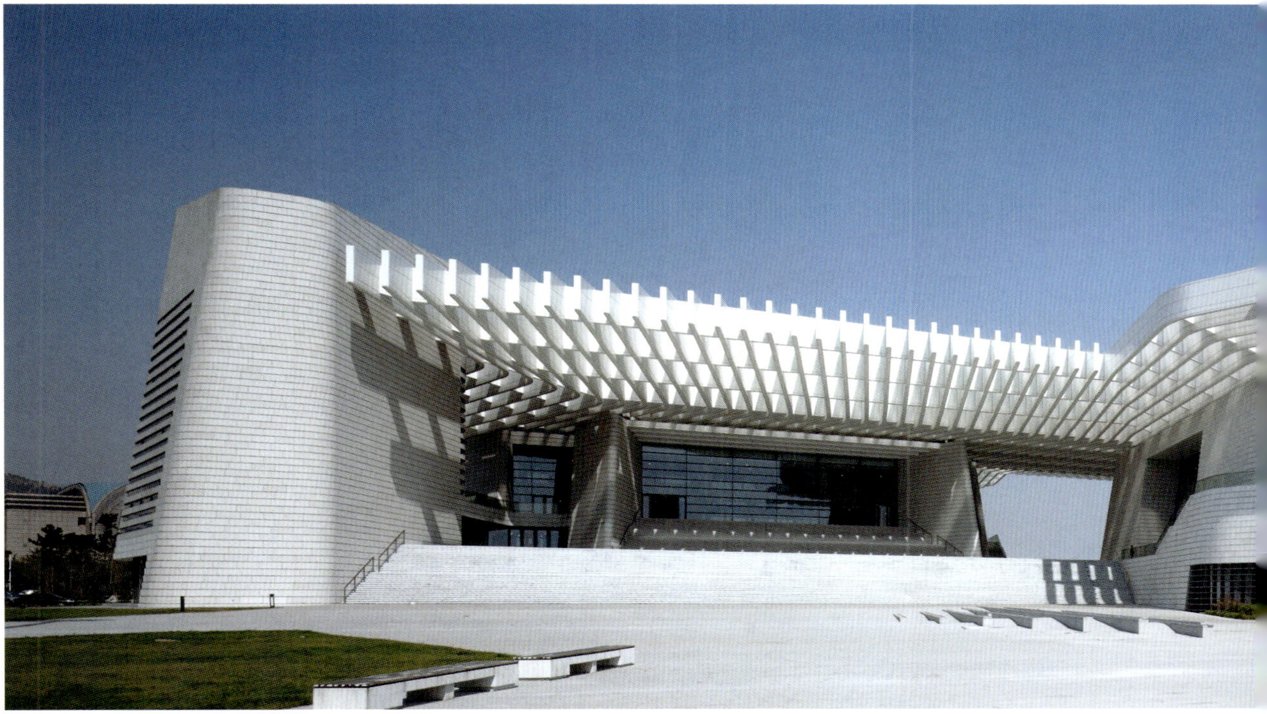

青岛大剧院　青岛

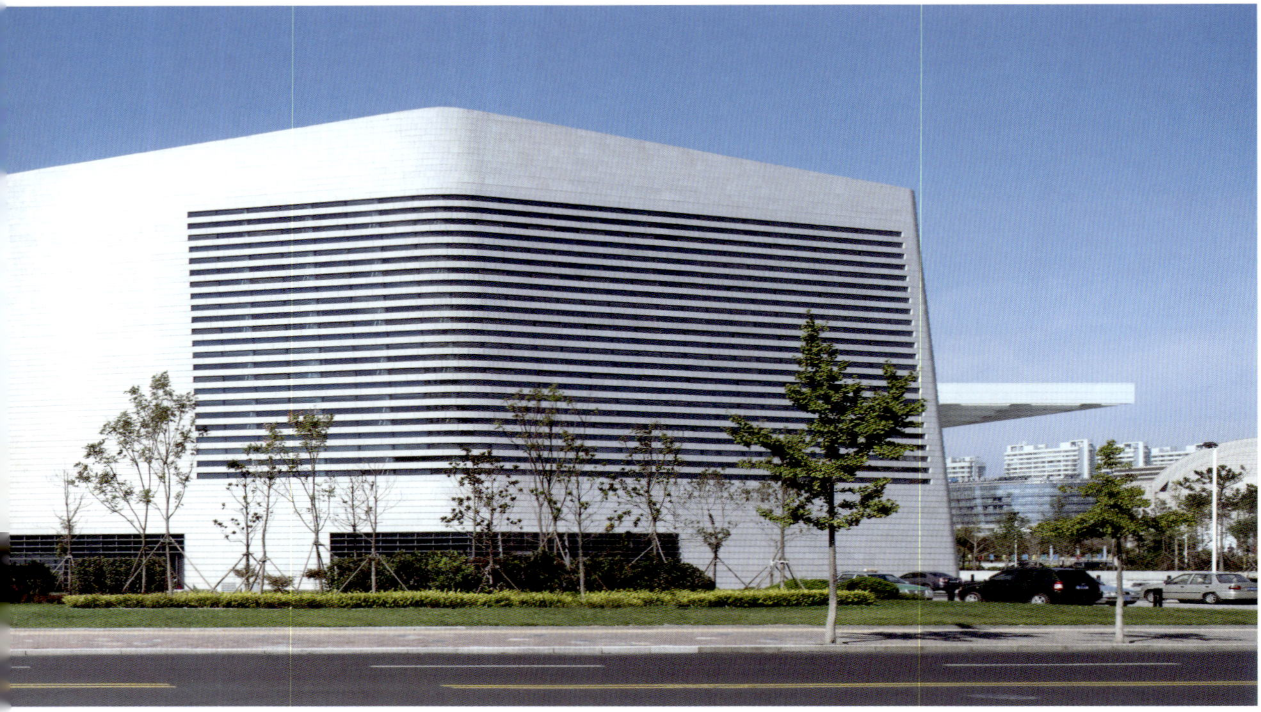

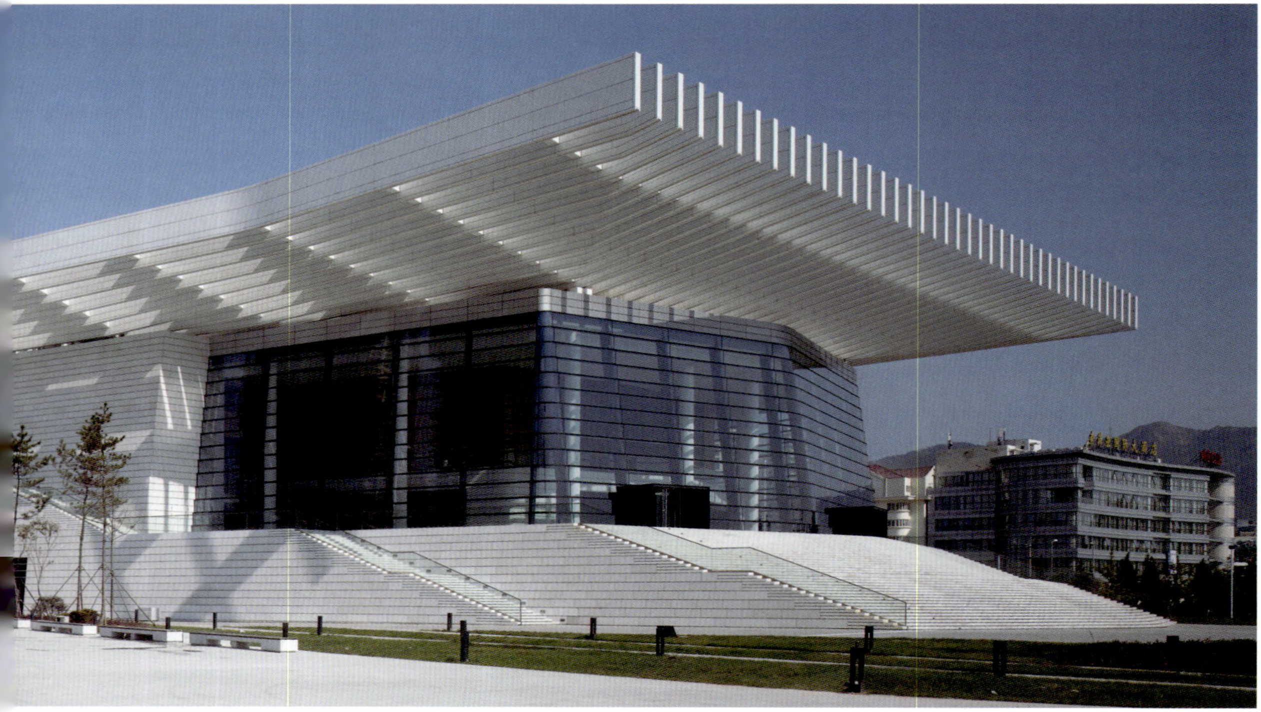

Qingdao Grand Theater Qingdao

98 ¹⁵
↑
──────────────────

中国航海博物馆
临港新城，上海，中国
China Maritime Museum
Lingang New City, Shanghai, China

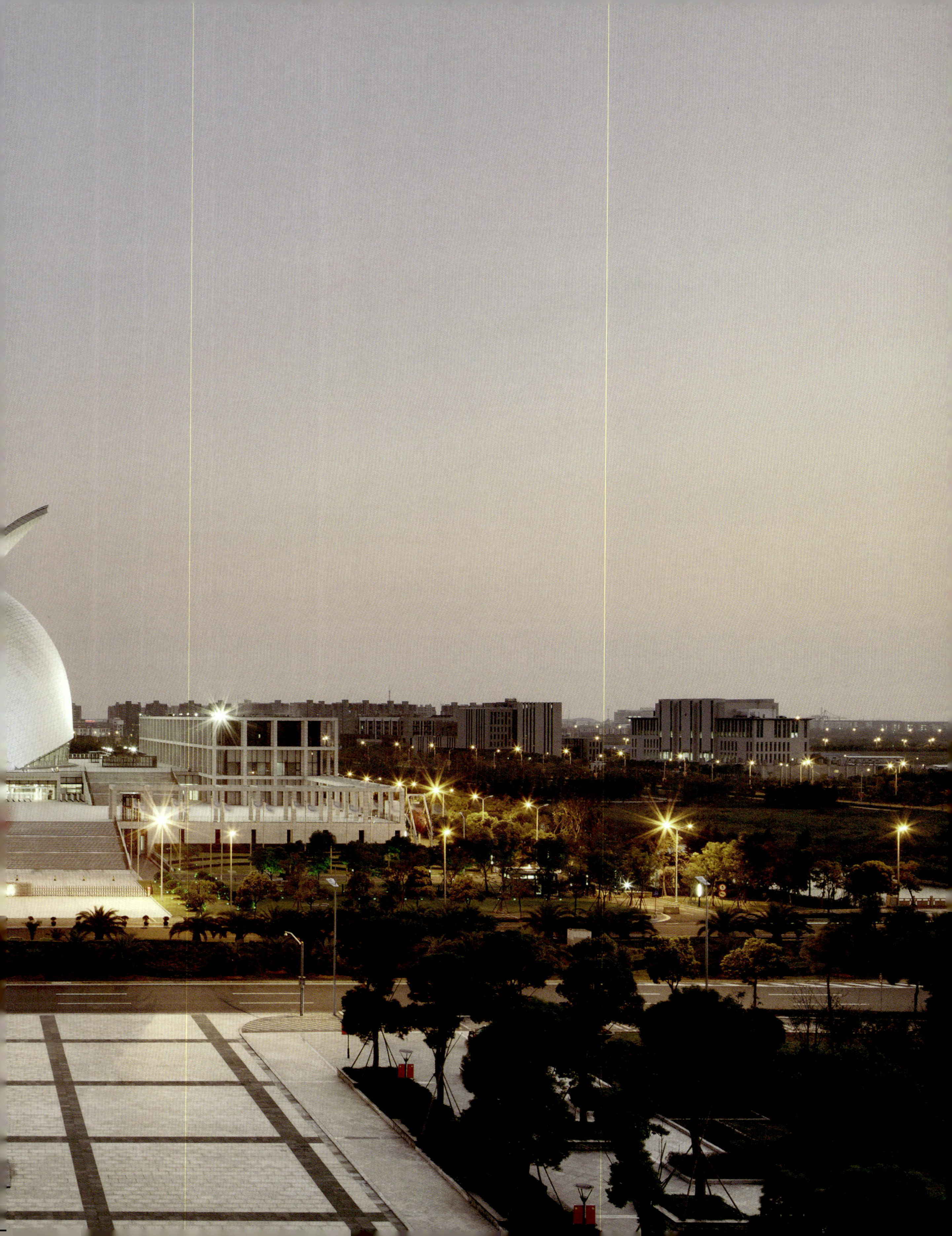

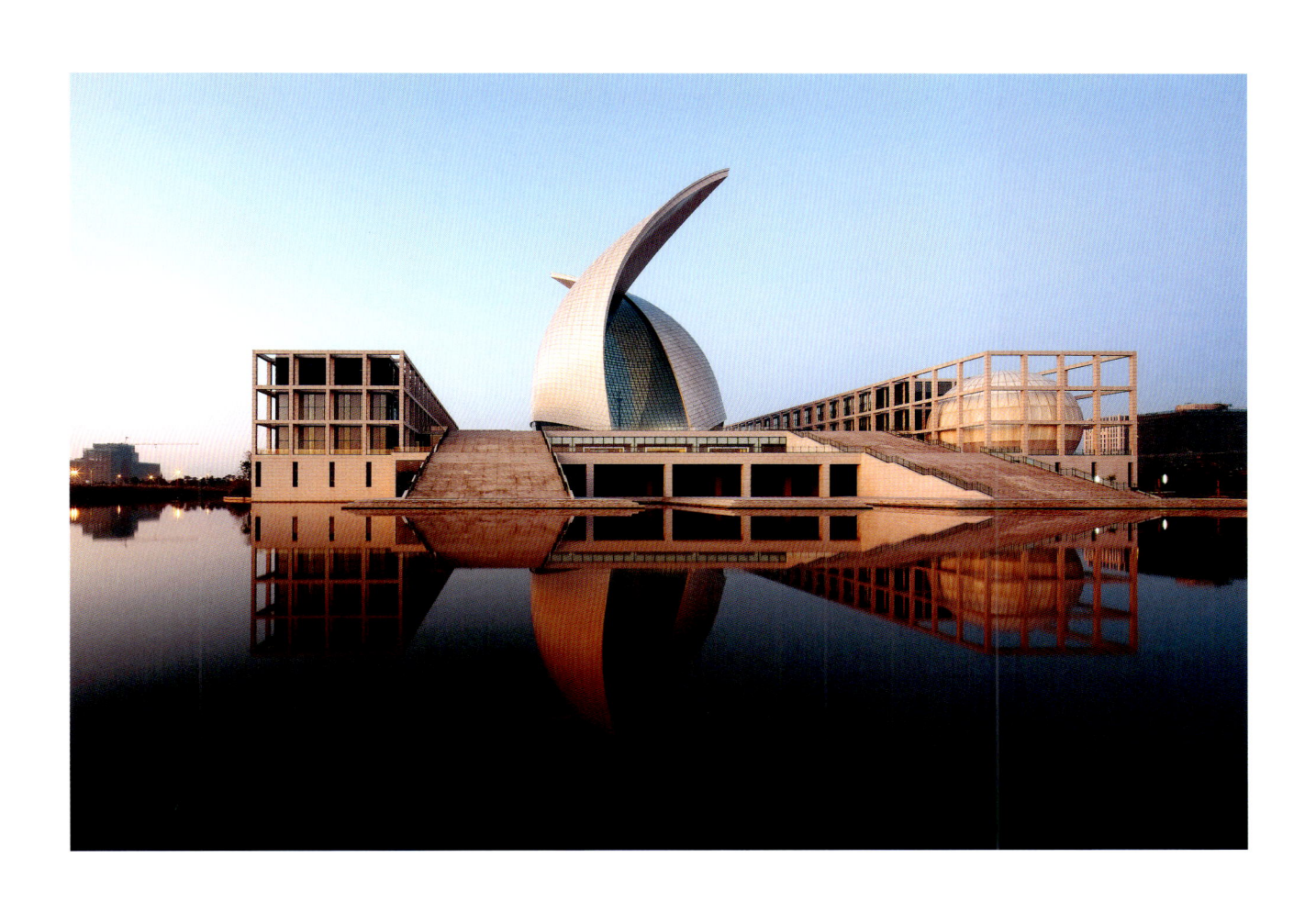

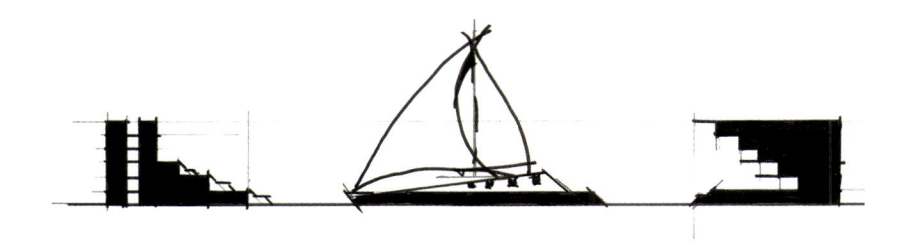

中国航海博物馆　临港新城，上海

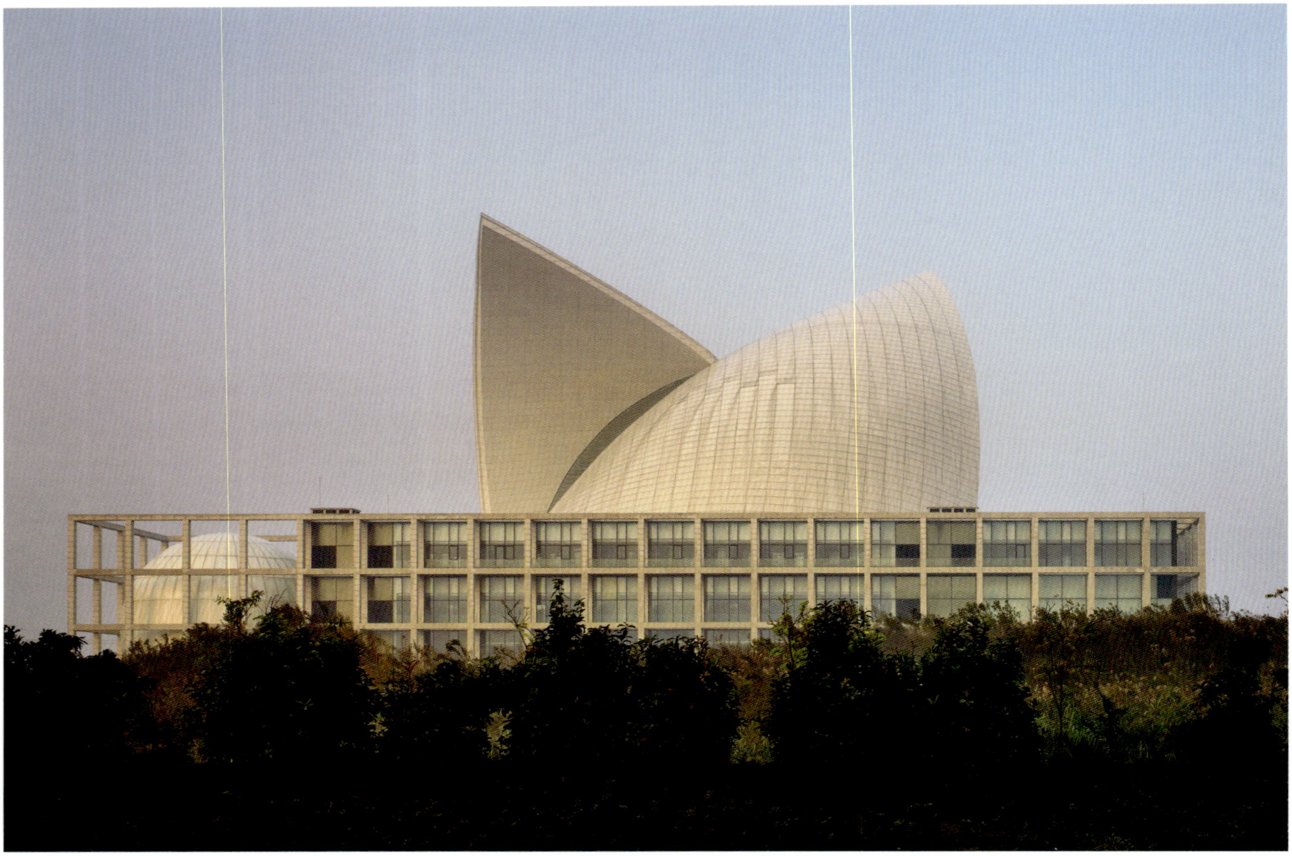

China Maritime Museum Lingang New City, Shanghai

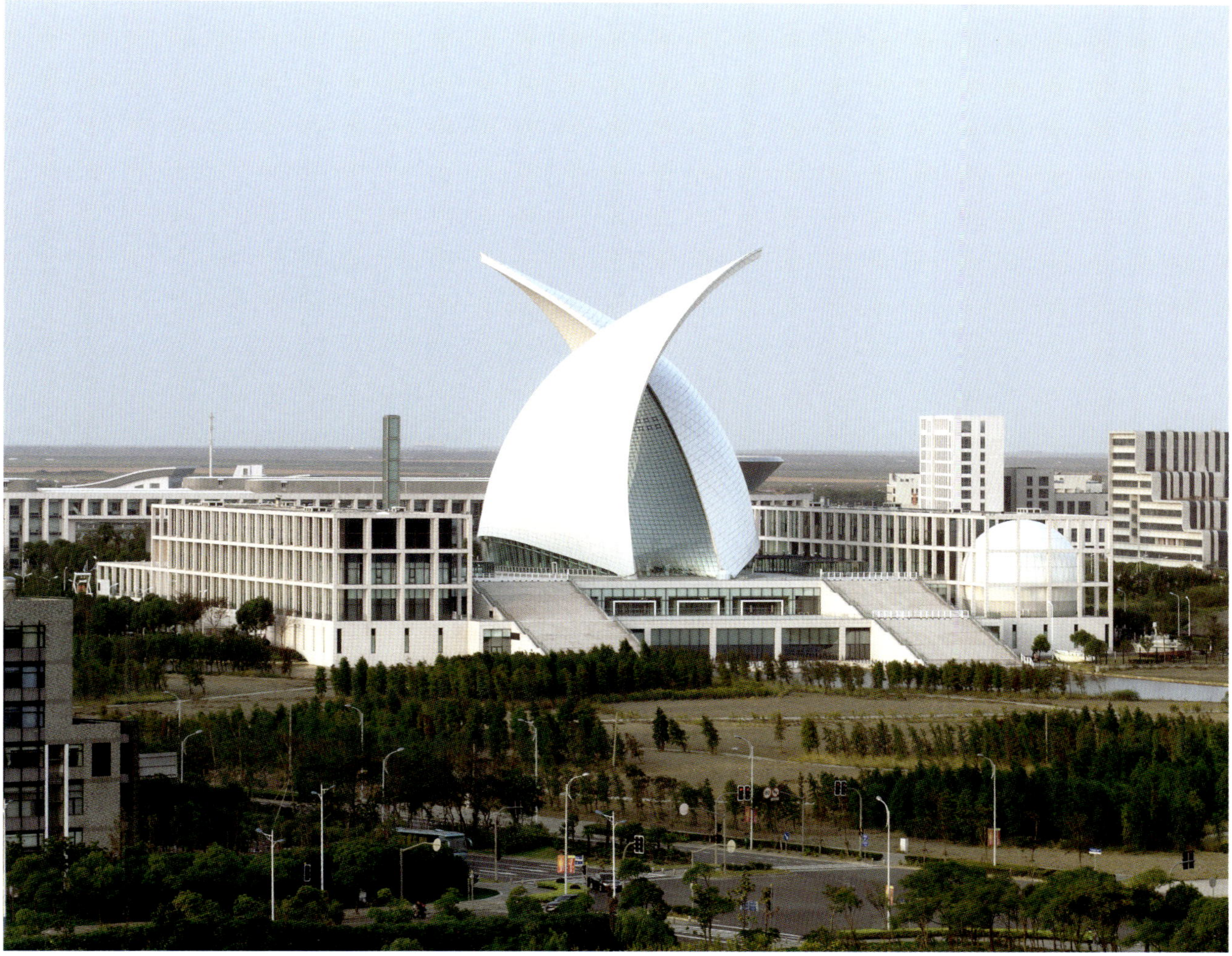

中国航海博物馆　临港新城，上海

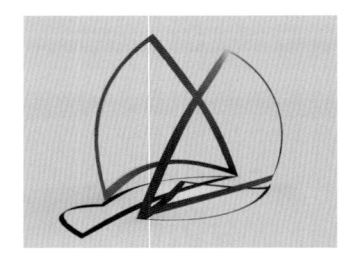

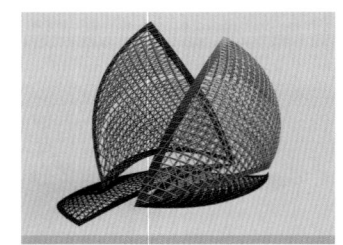

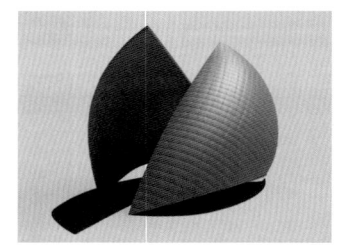

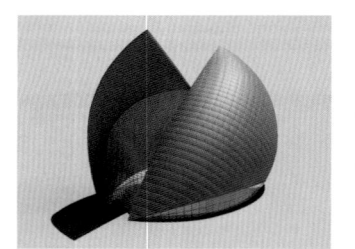

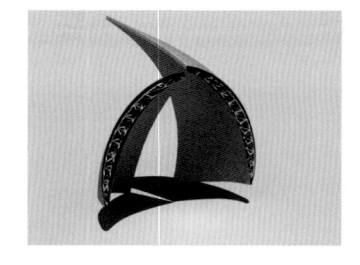

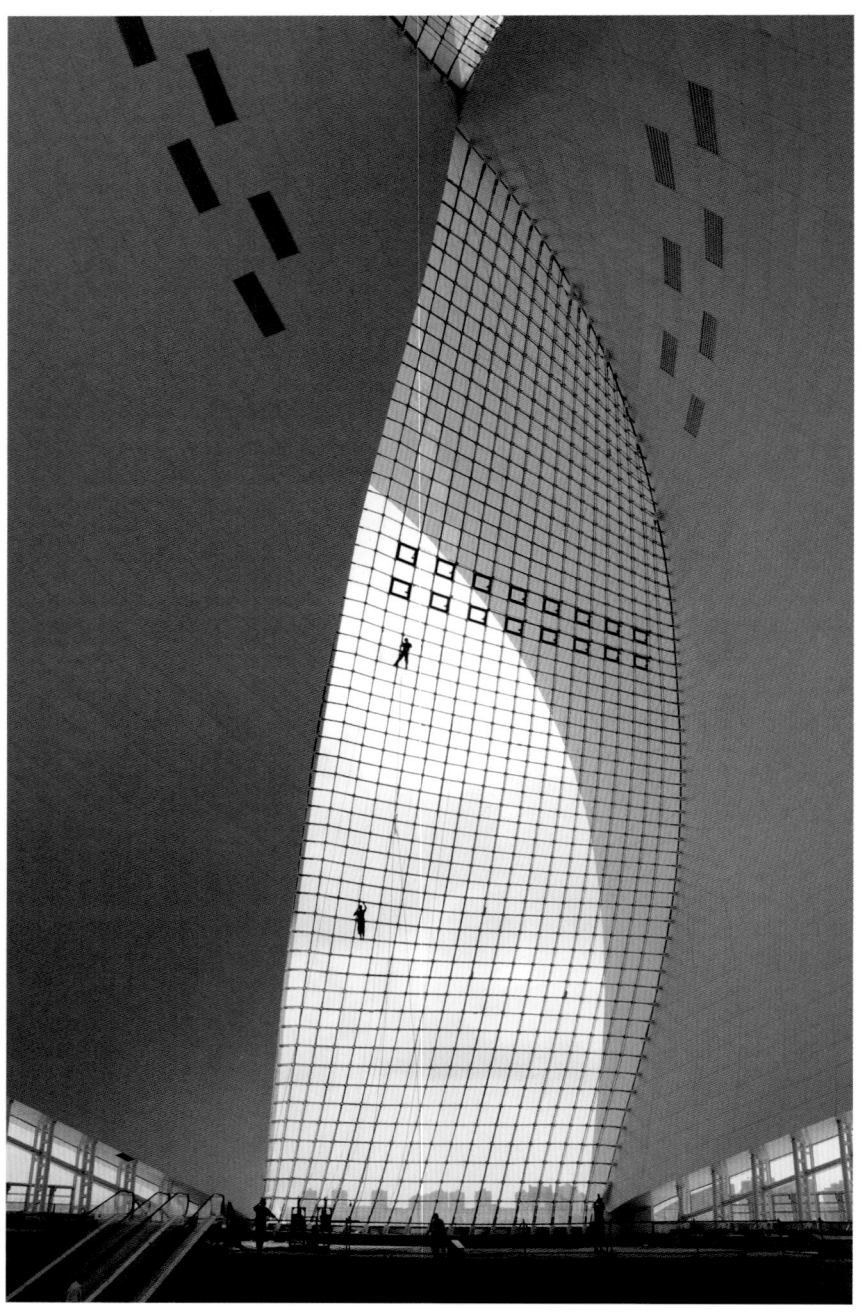

China Maritime Museum Lingang New City, Shanghai

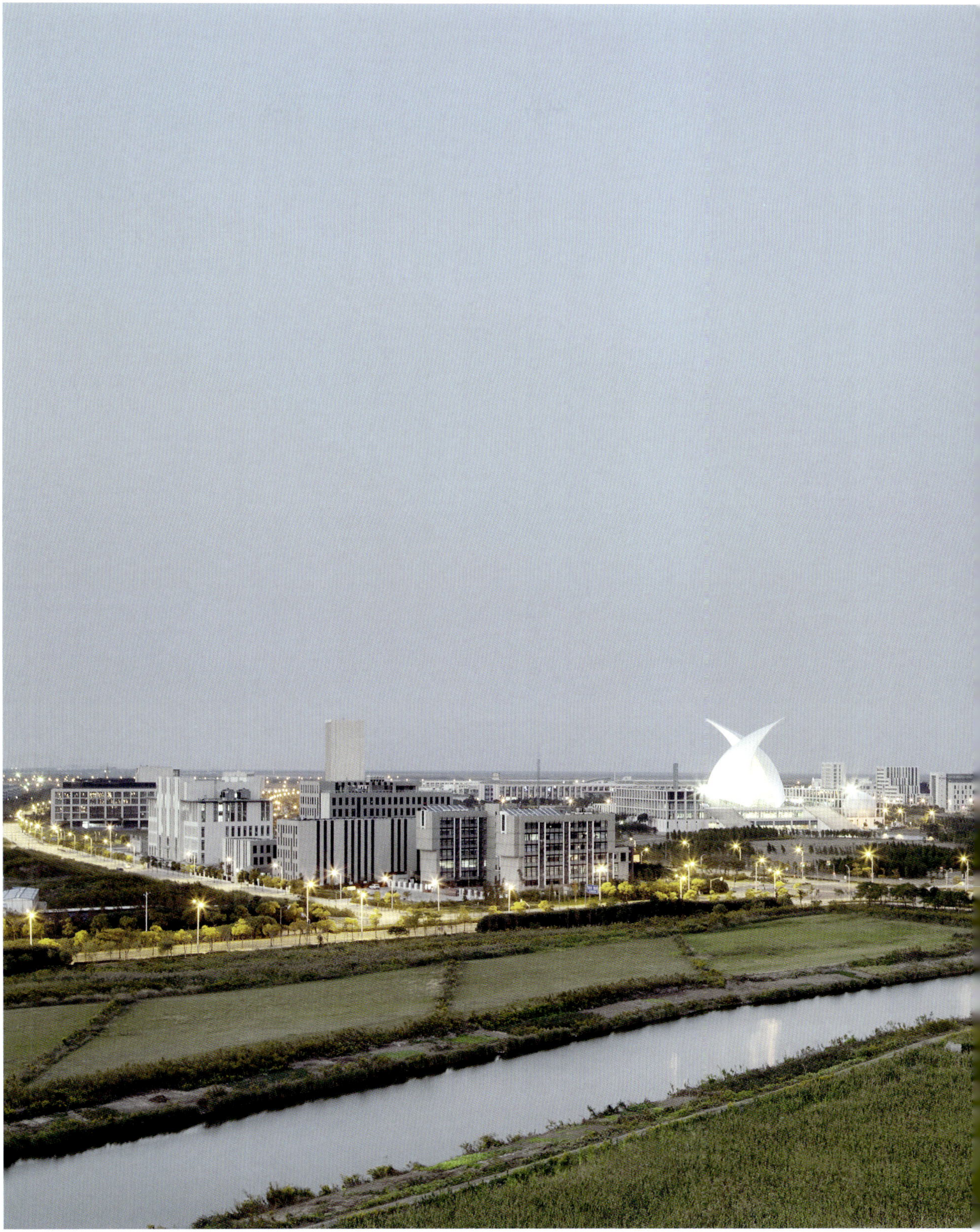

104　**中国航海博物馆**　临港新城，上海

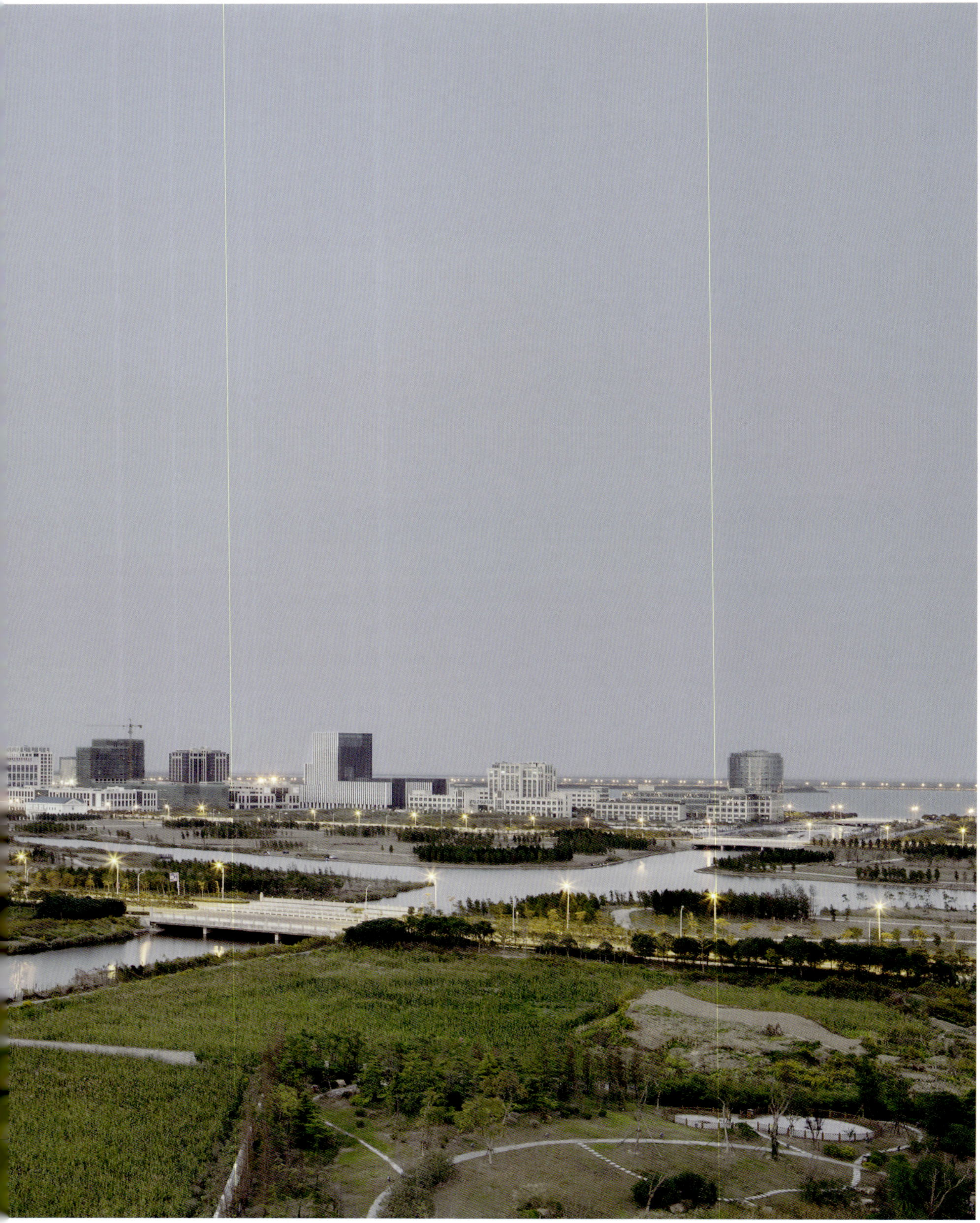

China Maritime Museum Lingang New City, Shanghai

106 ↑¹⁵

河内博物馆
河内，越南

Hanoi Museum
Hanoi, Vietnam

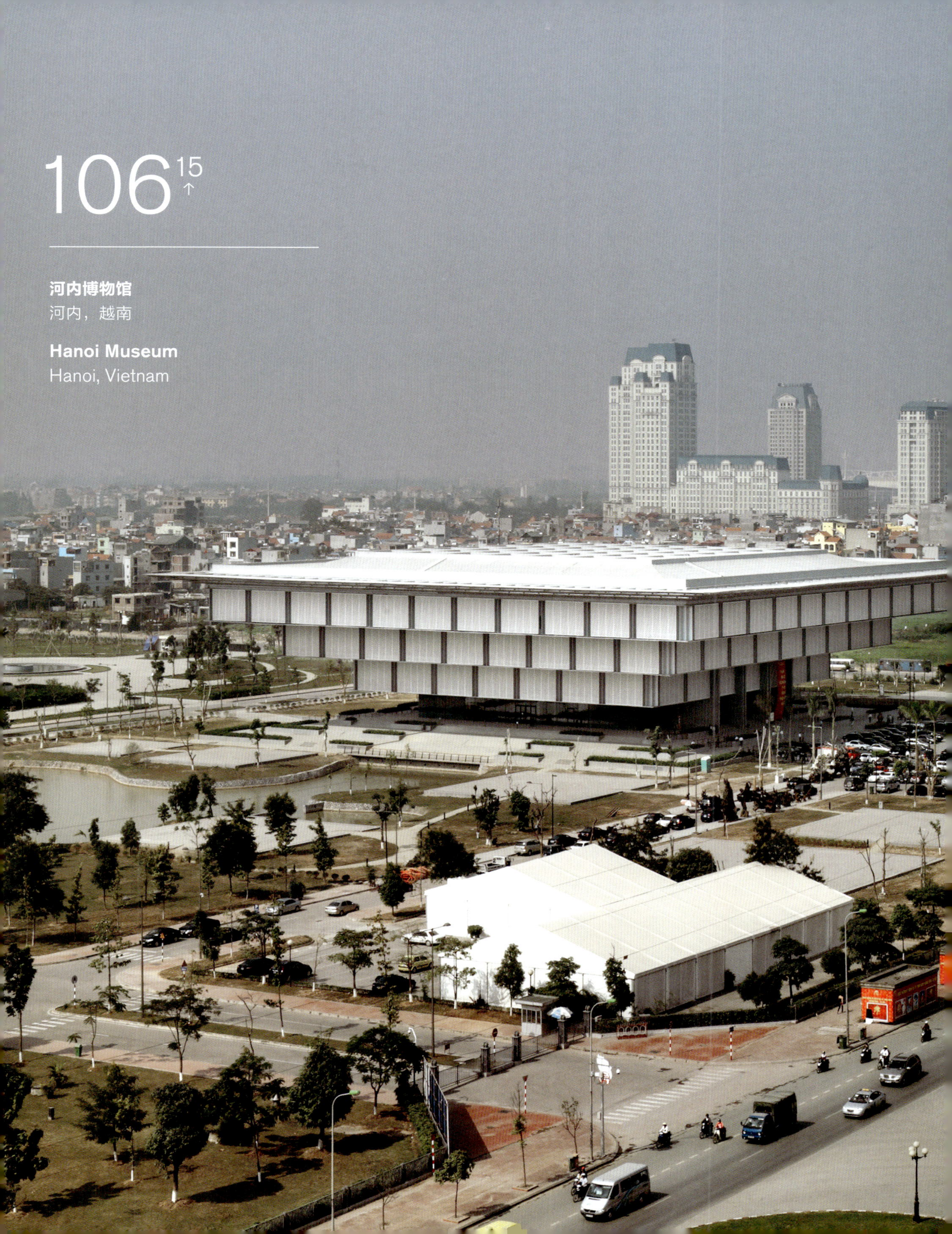

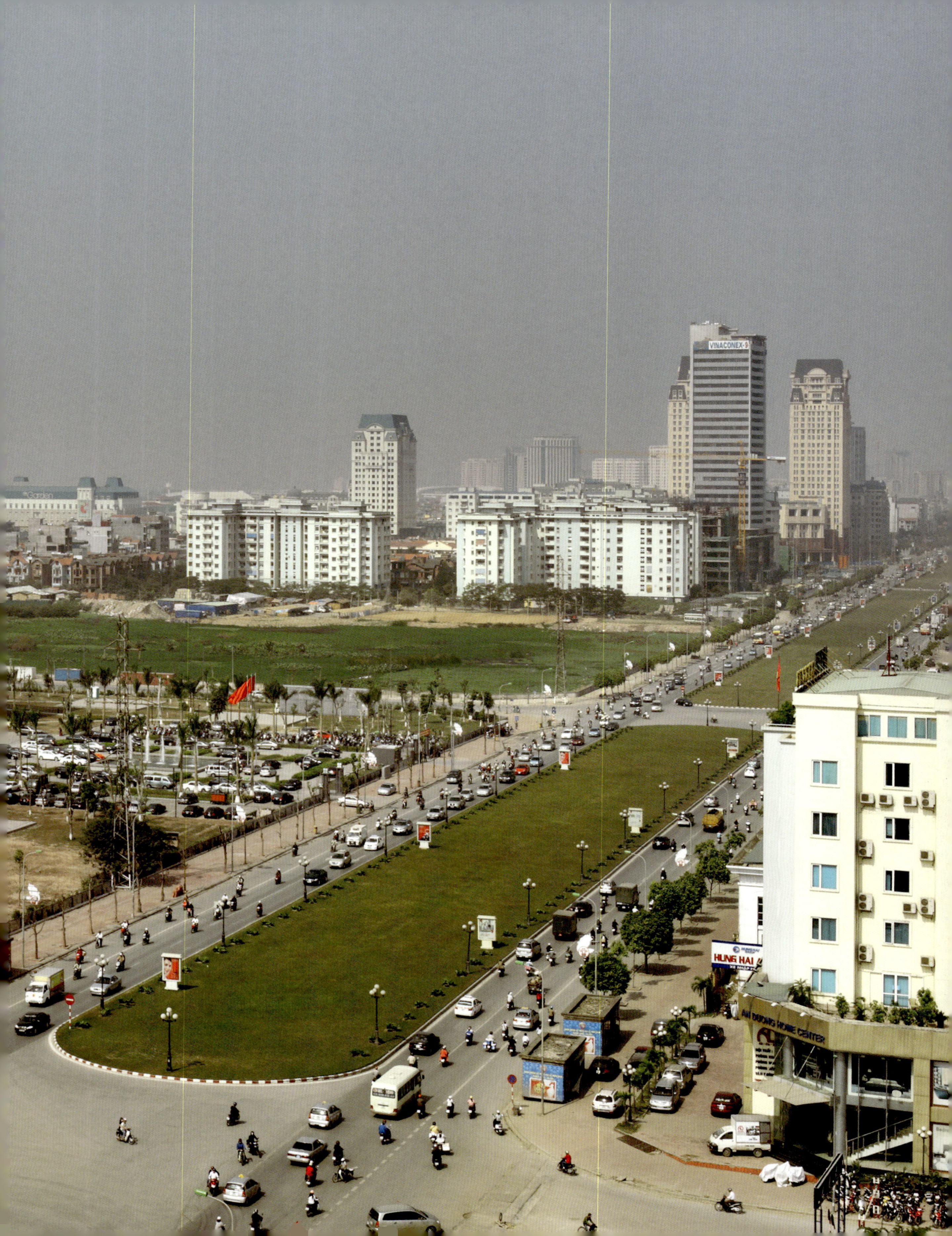
VINACONEX-9
HUNG HAI

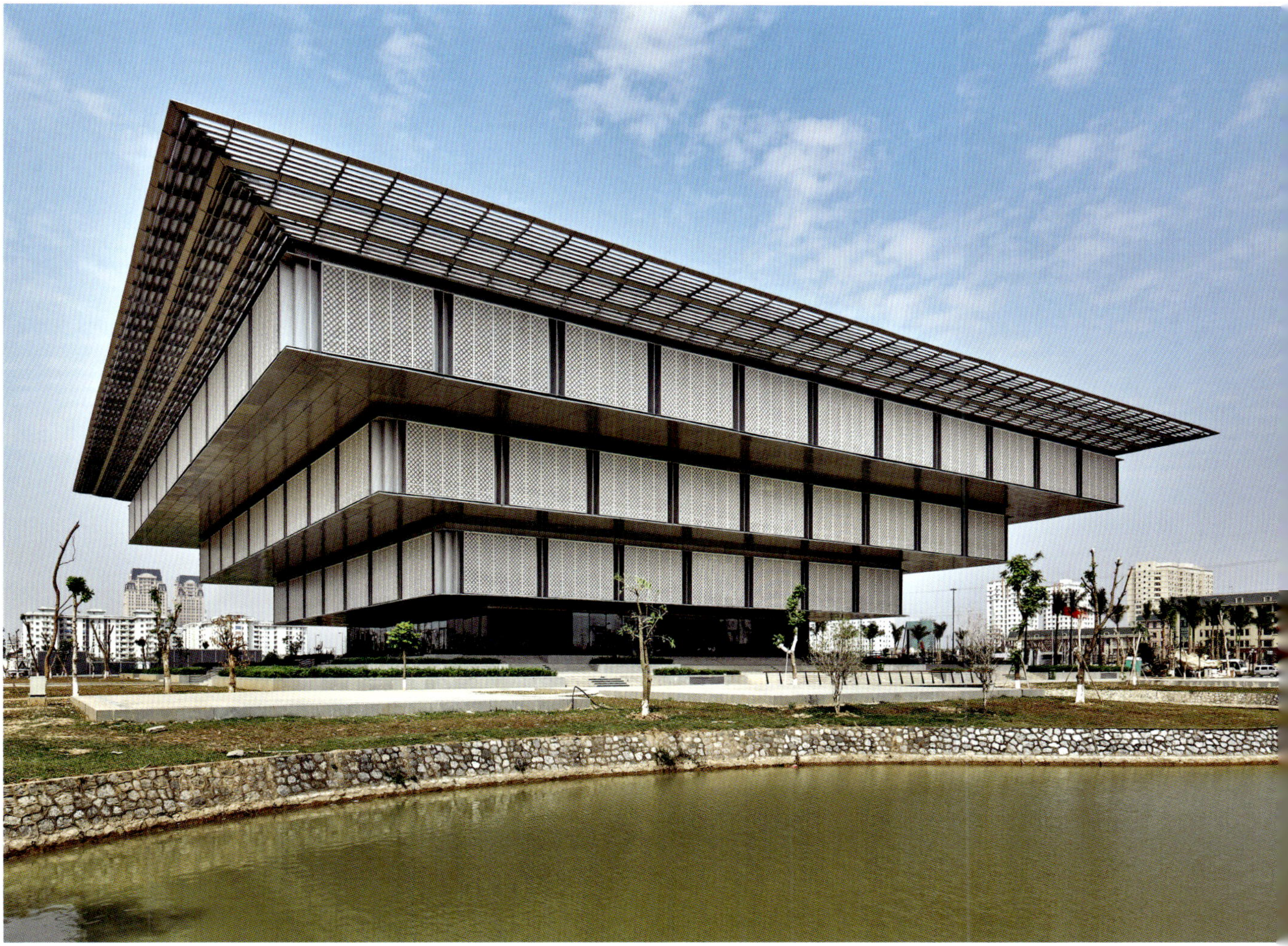

河内博物馆　河内

Hanoi Museum Hanoi

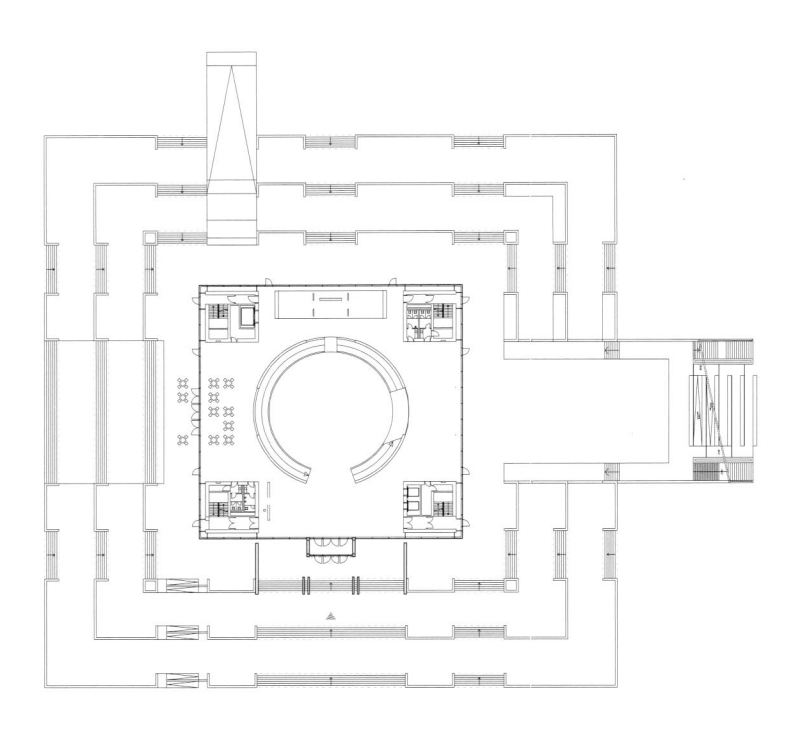

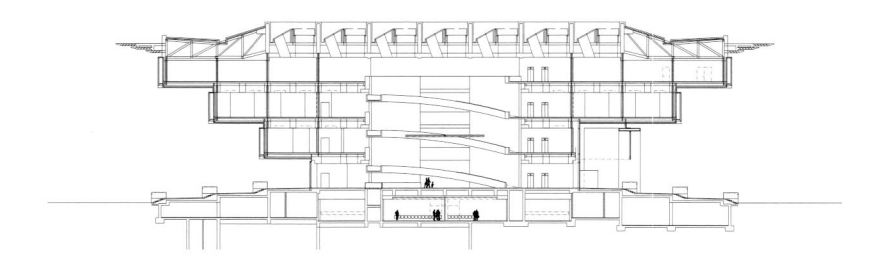

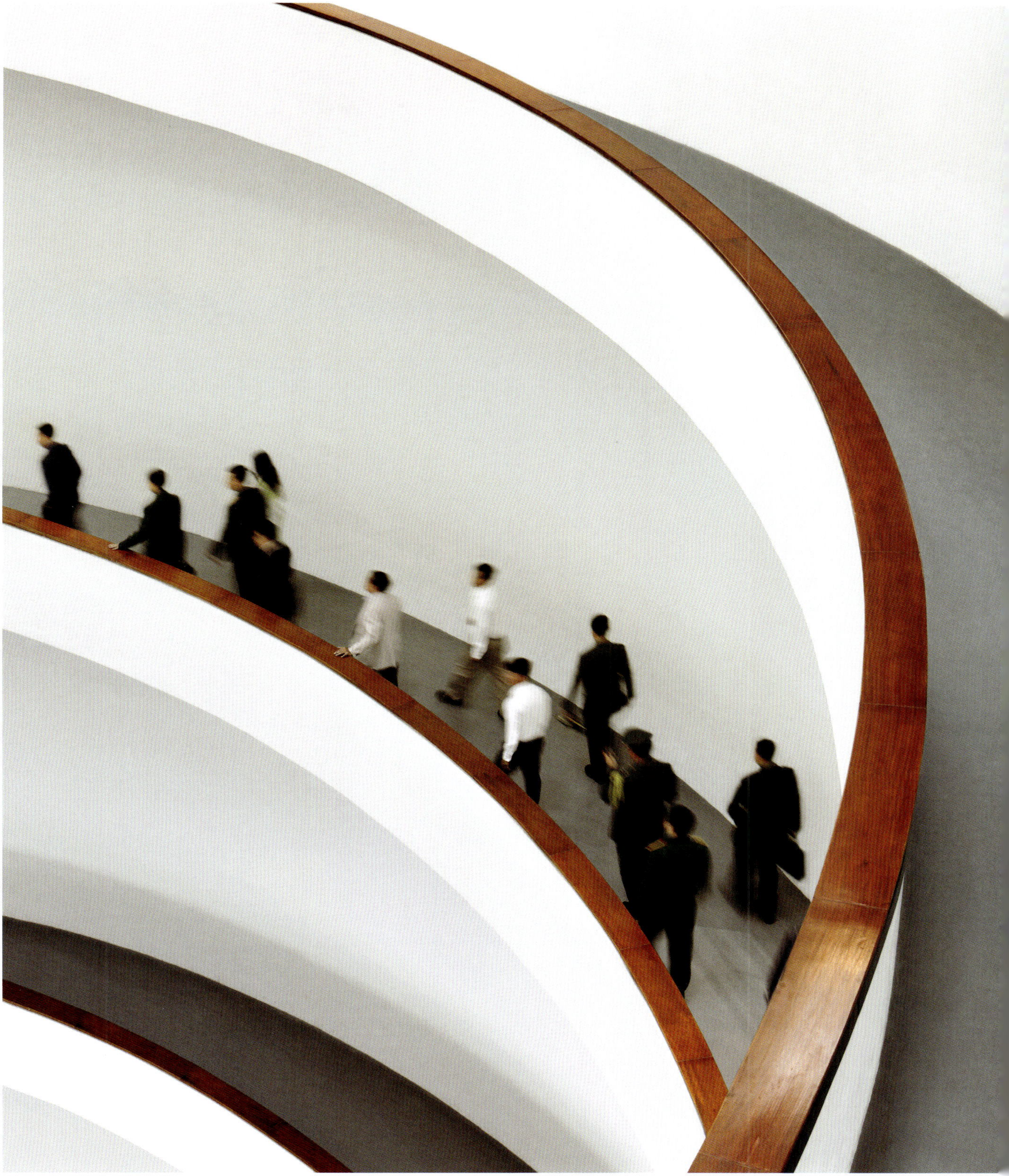

河内博物馆　河内

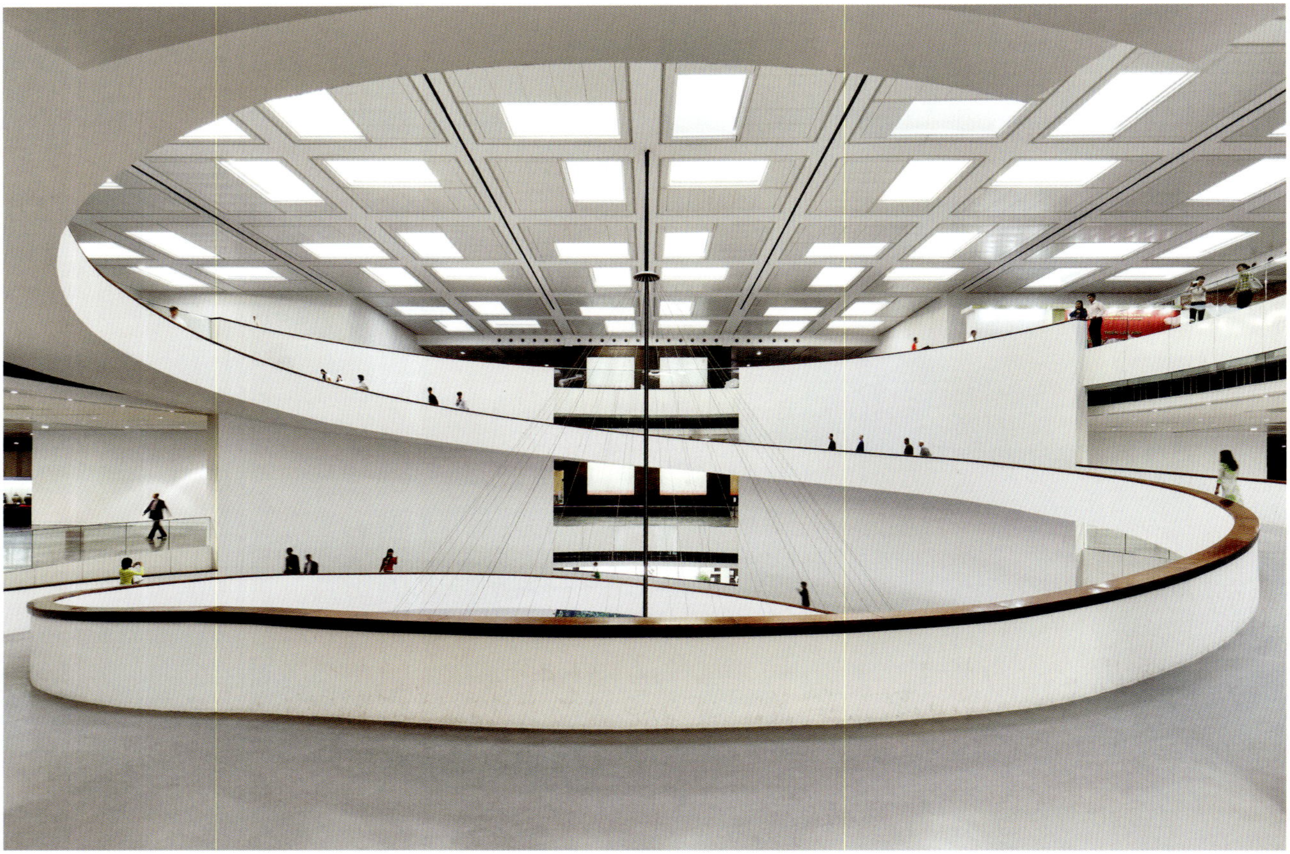

Hanoi Museum Hanoi

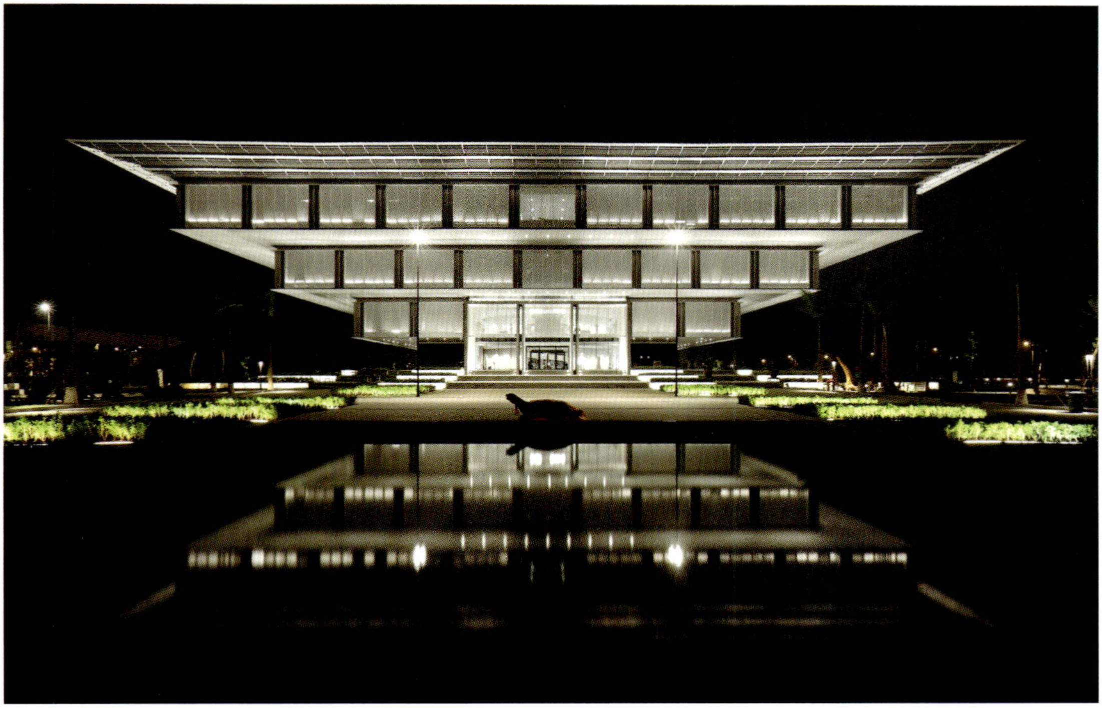

河内博物馆　河内

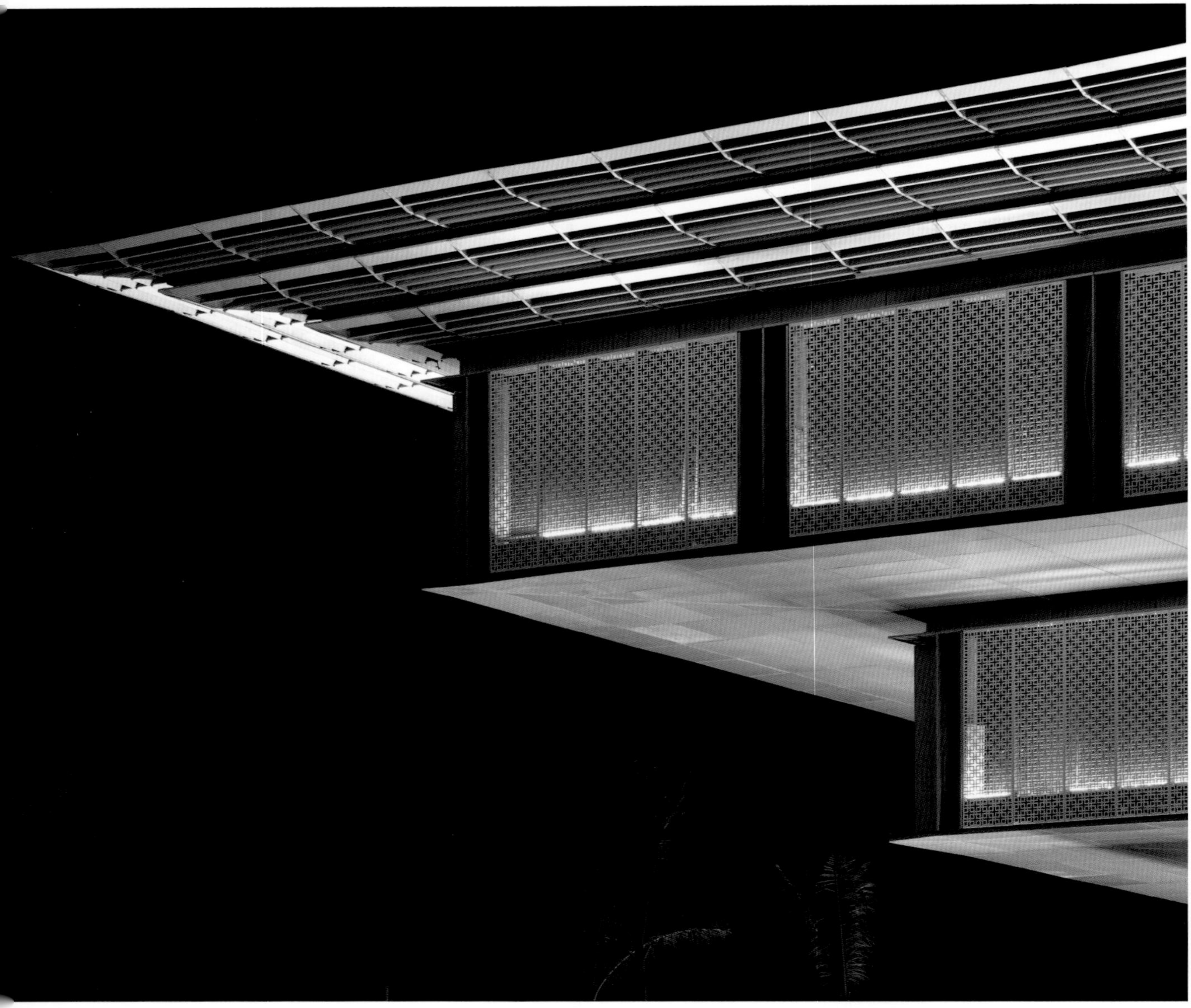

Hanoi Museum Hanoi

114 ¹⁶ ↑

南汇行政中心
临港新城，上海，中国

Nanhui Administration Center
Lingang New City, Shanghai, China

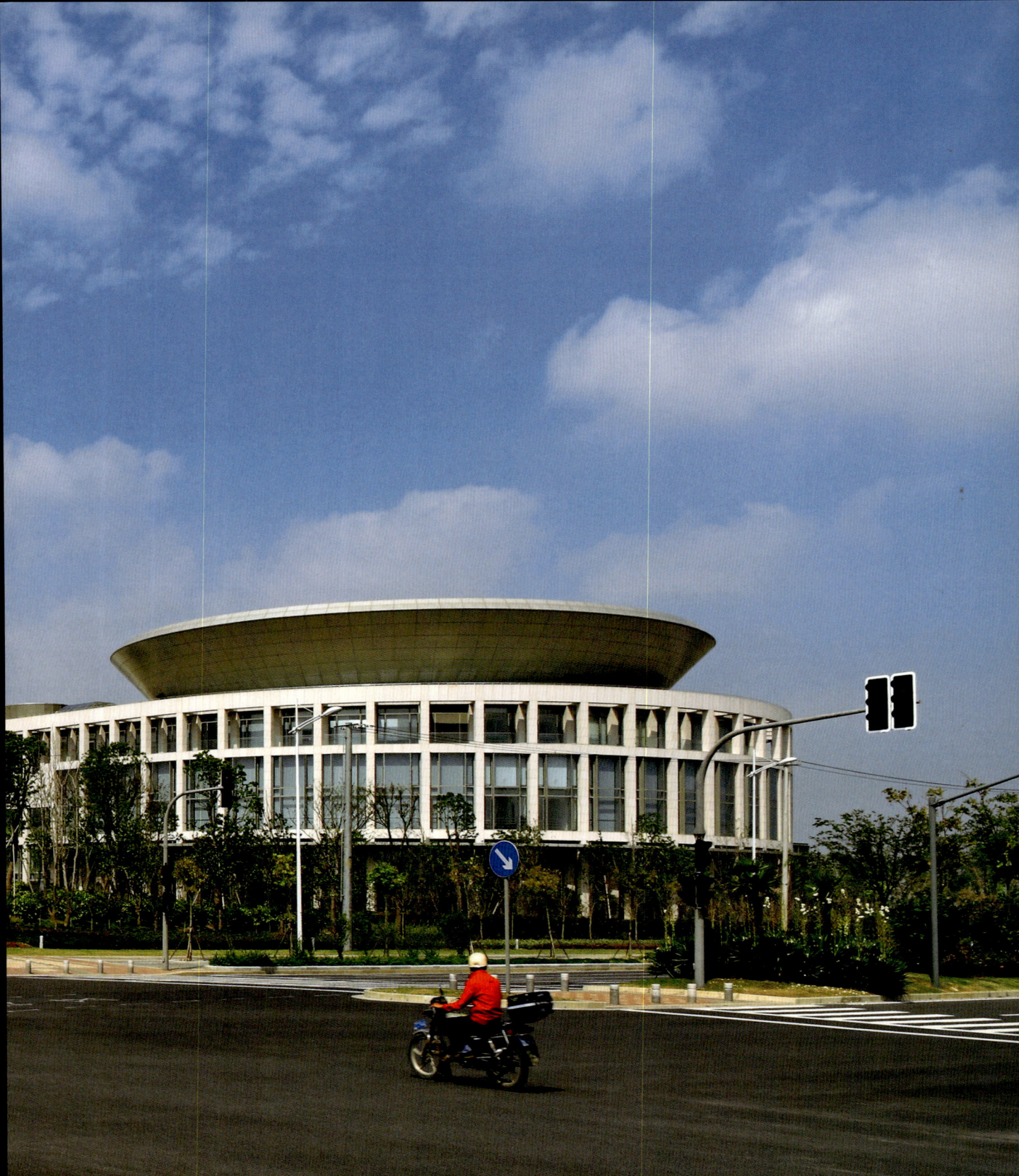

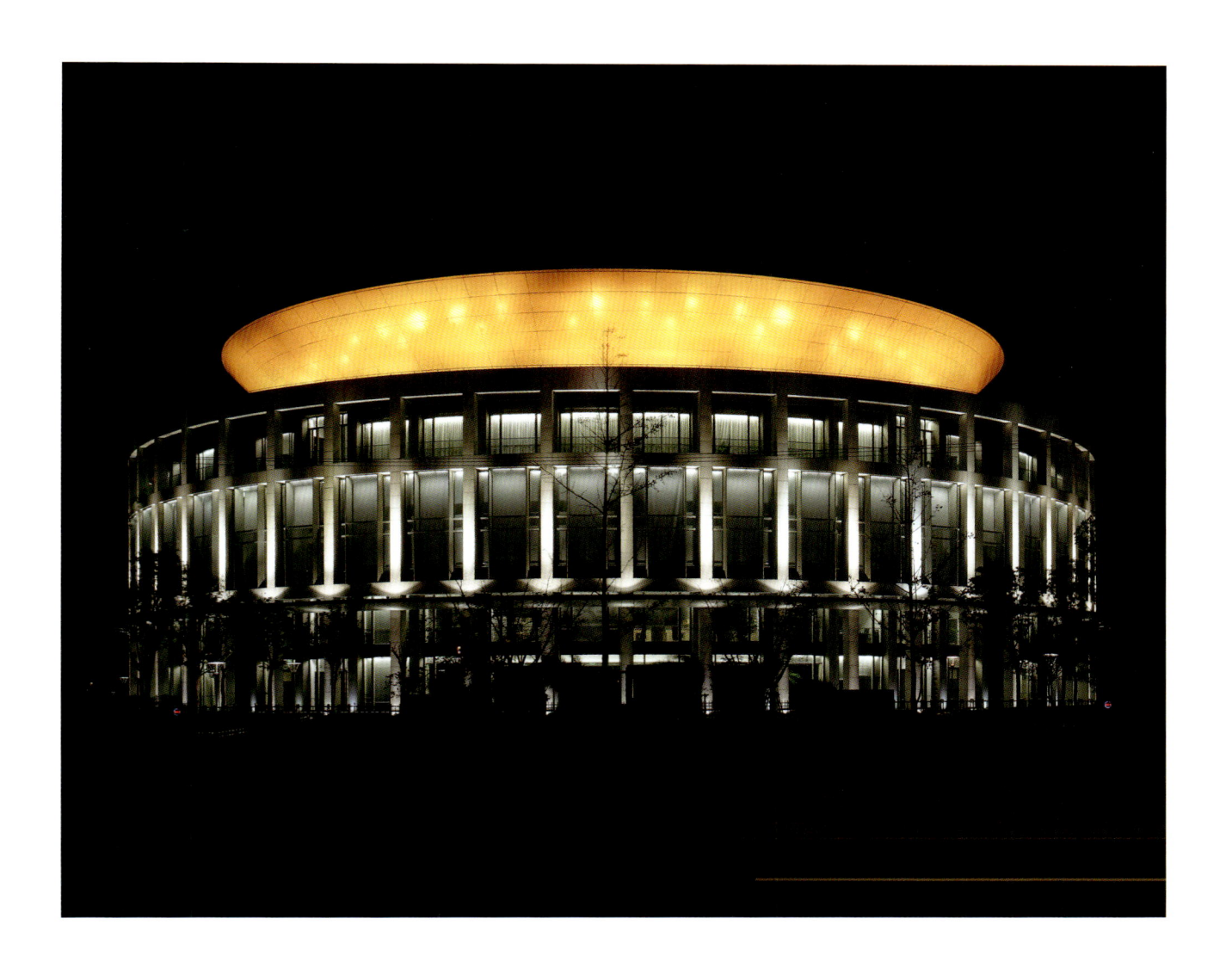

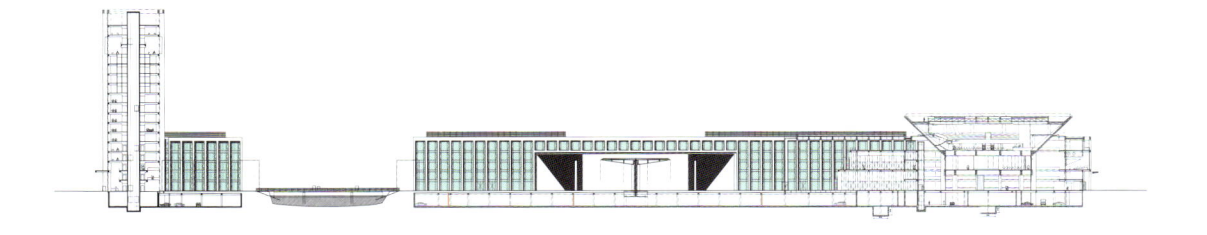

南汇行政中心 临港新城，上海

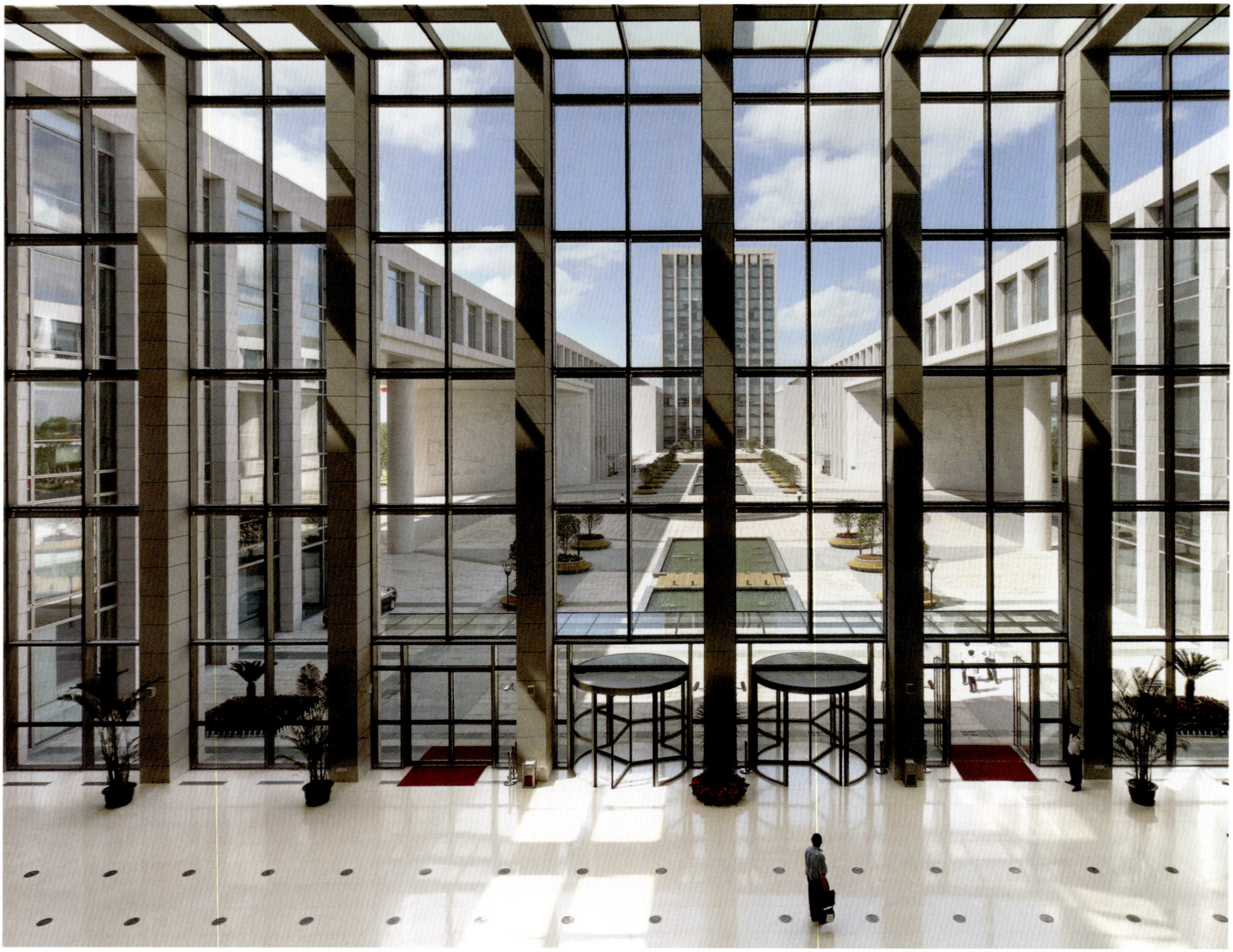

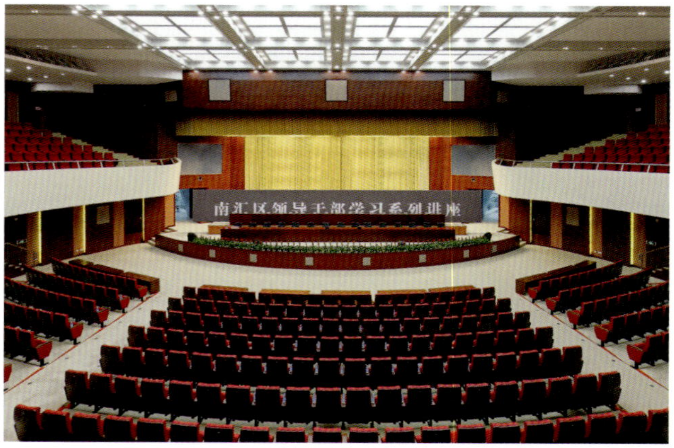

Nanhui Administration Center Lingang New City, Shanghai

118 16
↑

万向大厦
上海，中国

Wanxiang Plaza
Shanghai, China

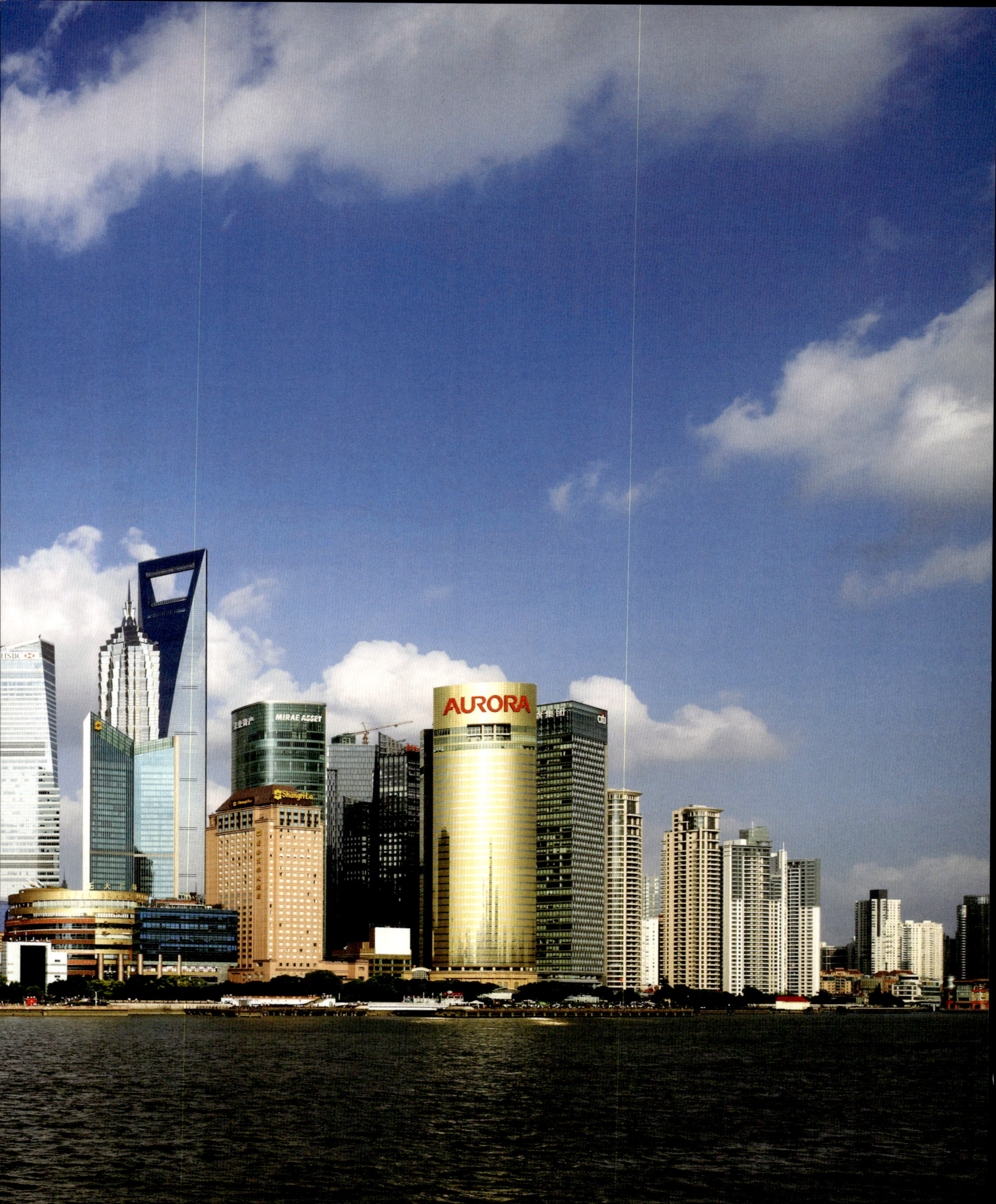
MIRAE ASSET
AURORA

万向大厦 上海

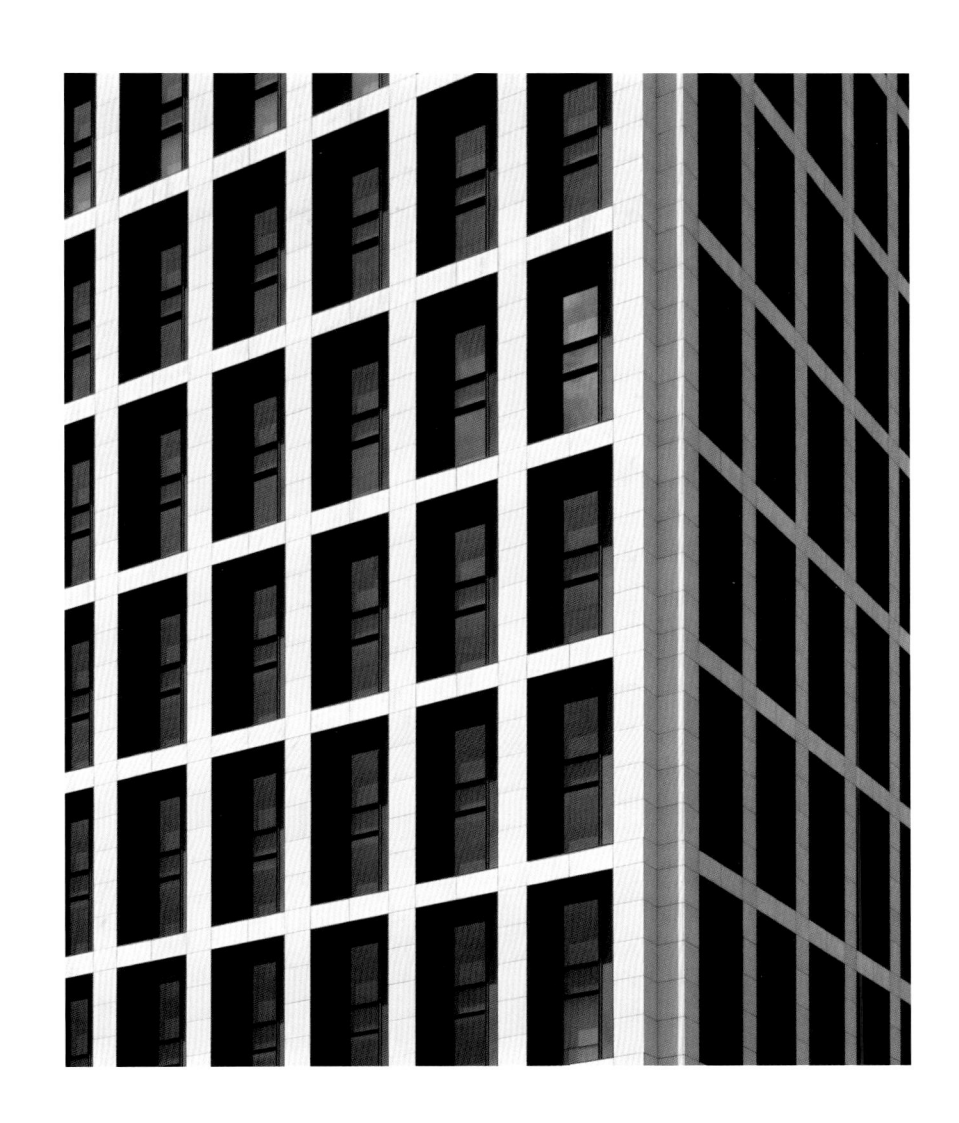

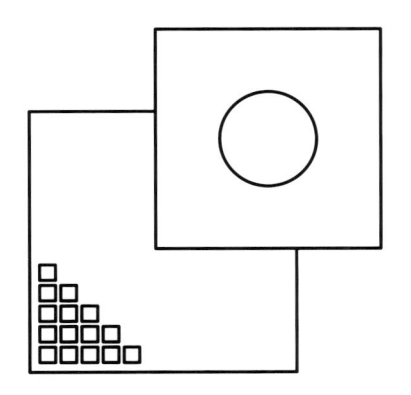

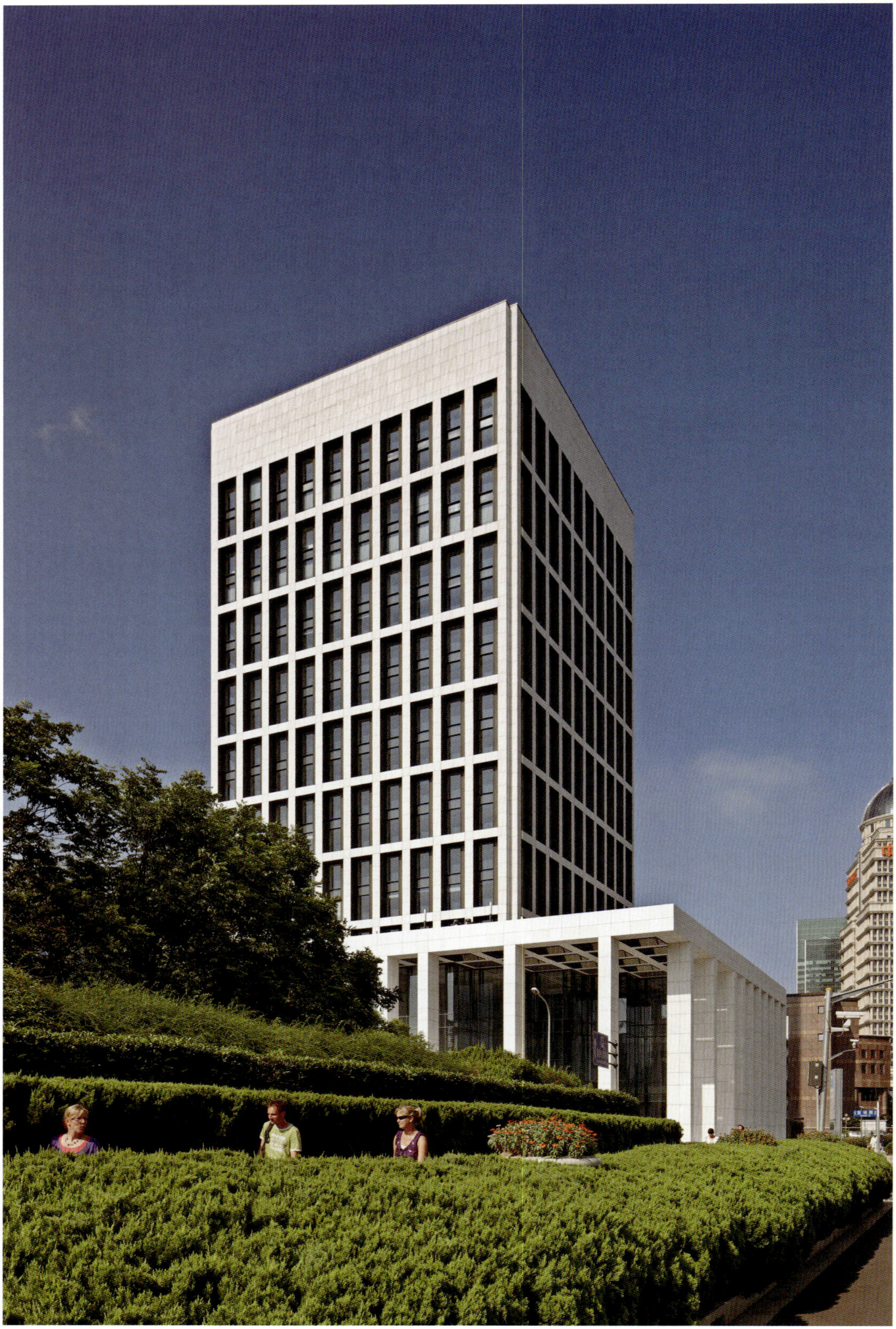

Wanxiang Plaza Shanghai

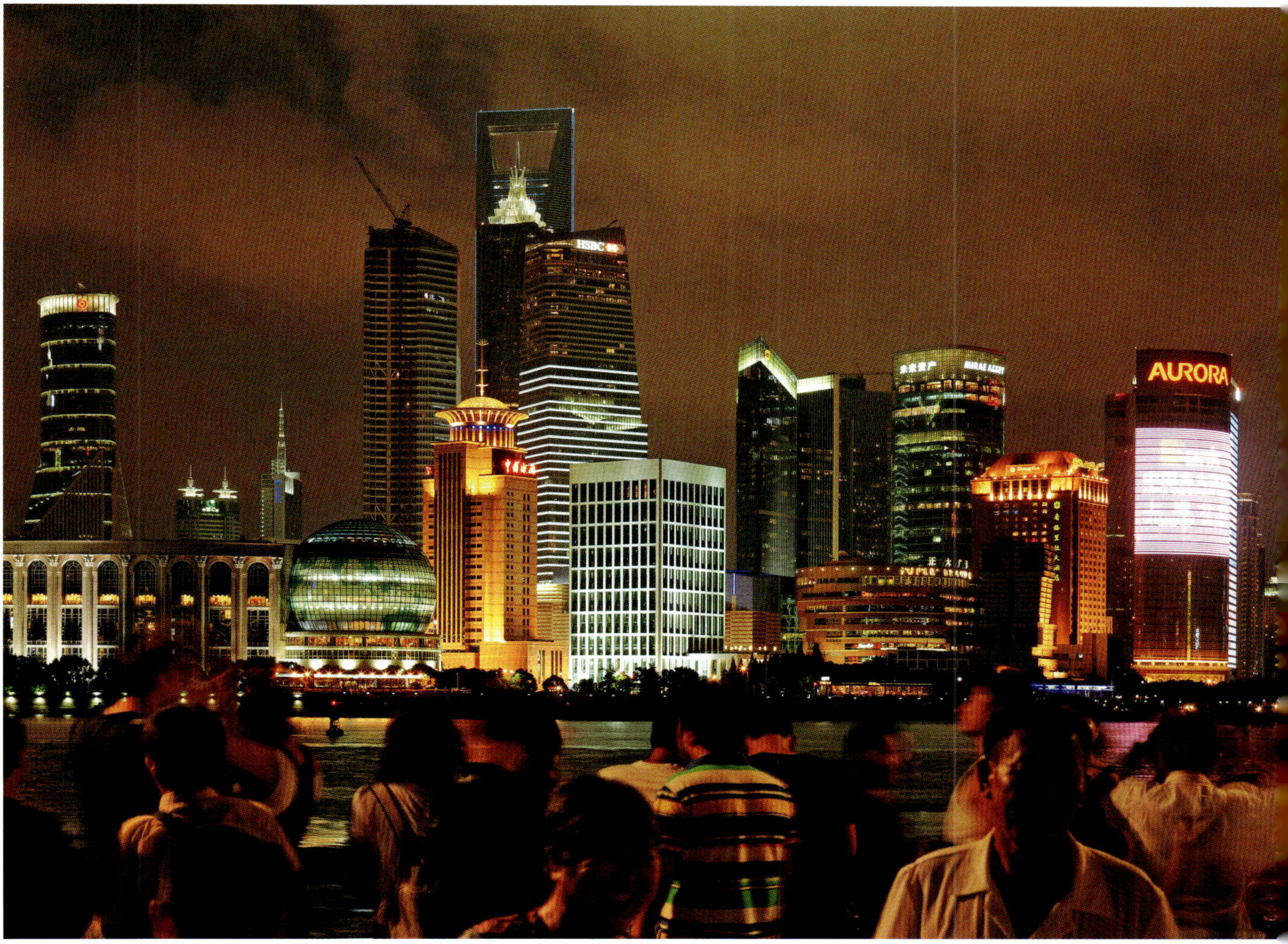

万向大厦　上海

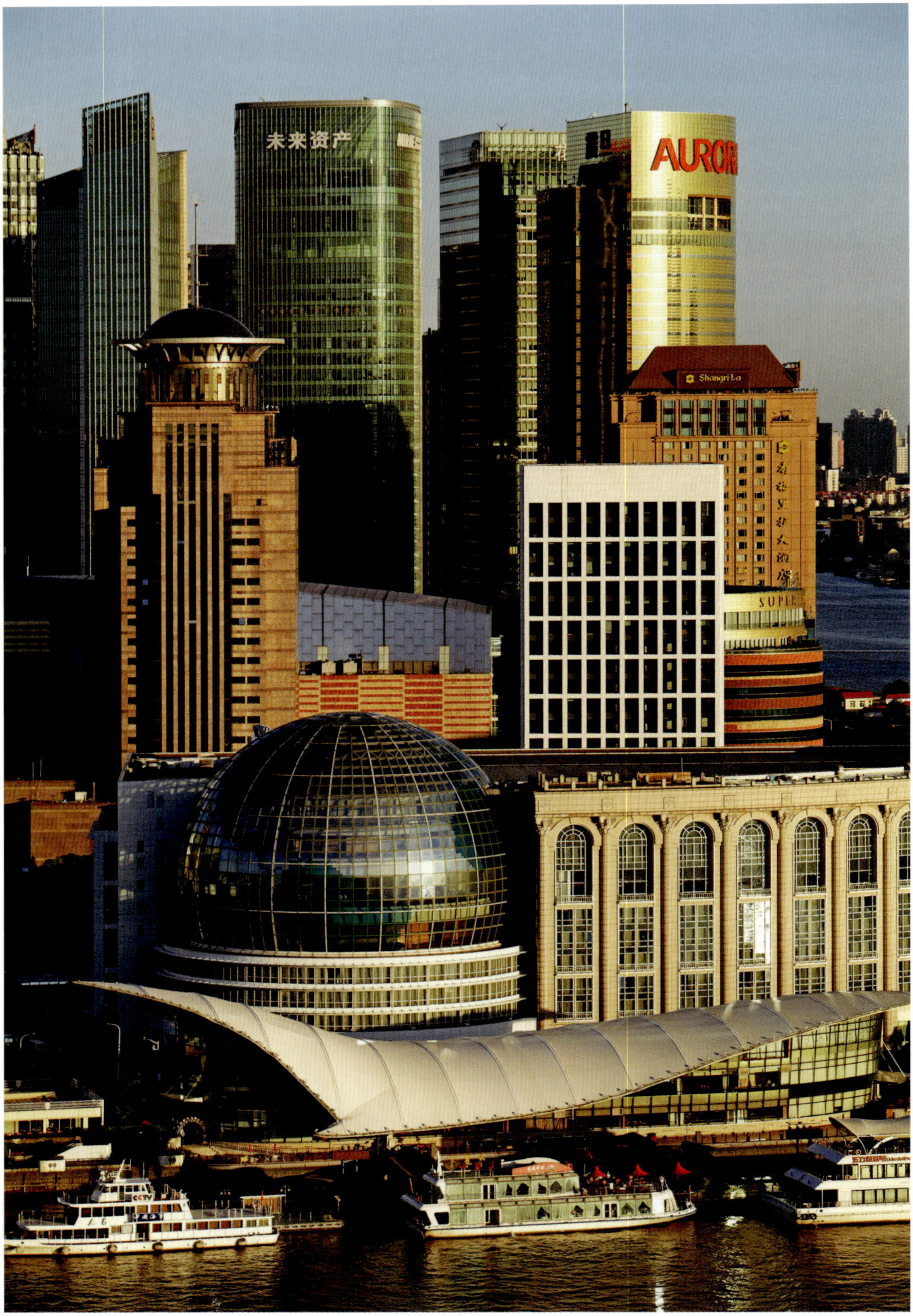

Wanxiang Plaza Shanghai

124 ↑ 17

内政部大厦
河内，越南

**Headquarters of the
Ministry of the Interior**
Hanoi, Vietnam

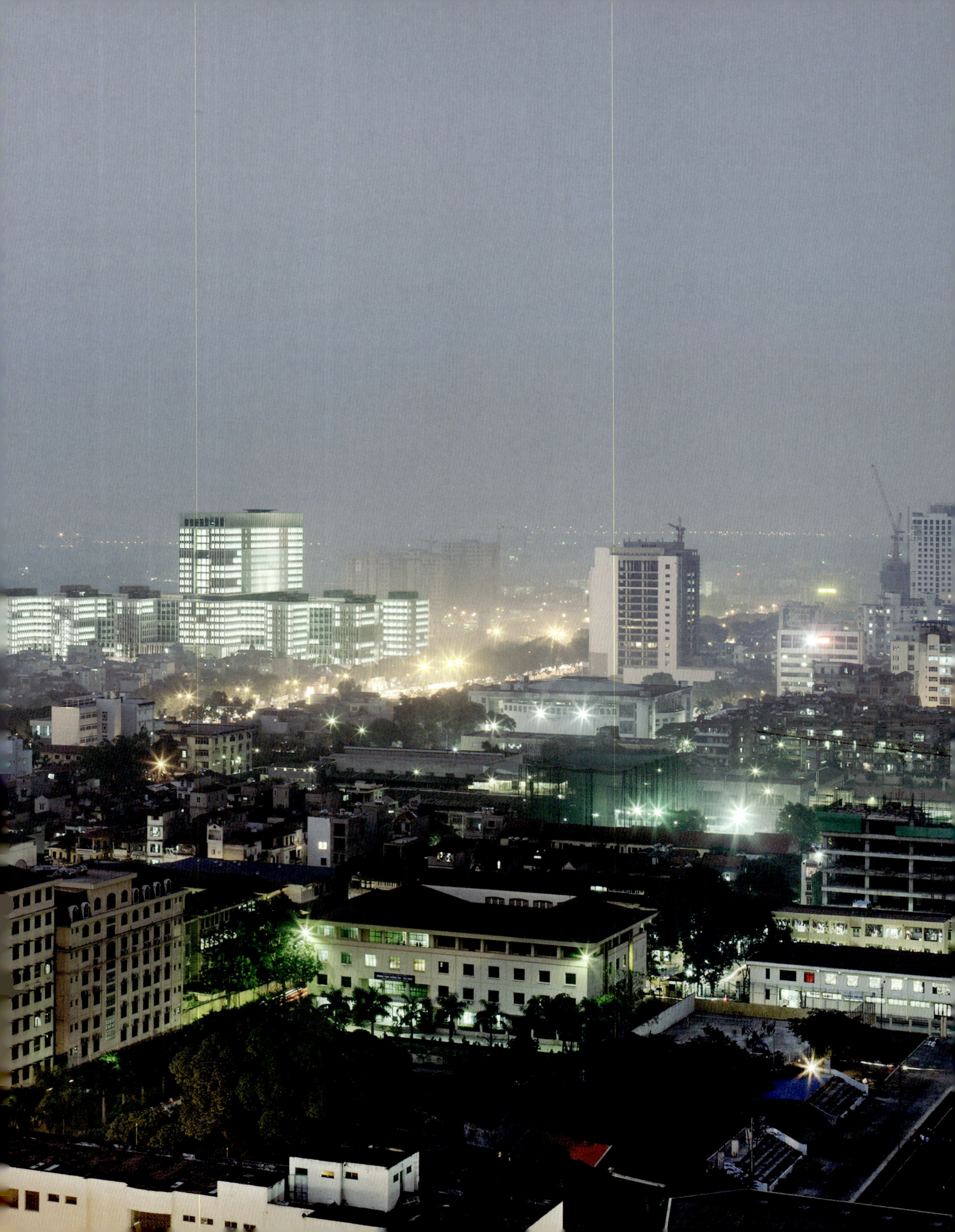

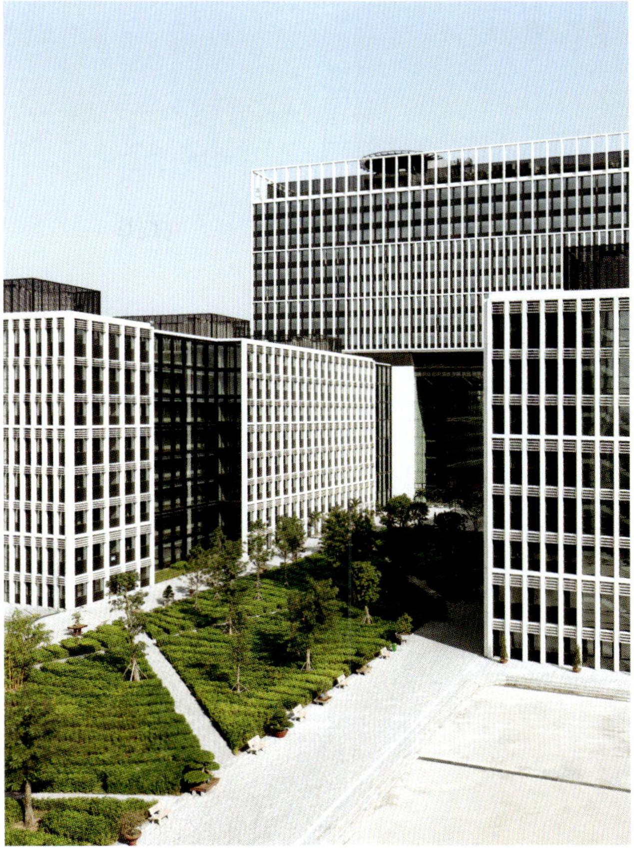

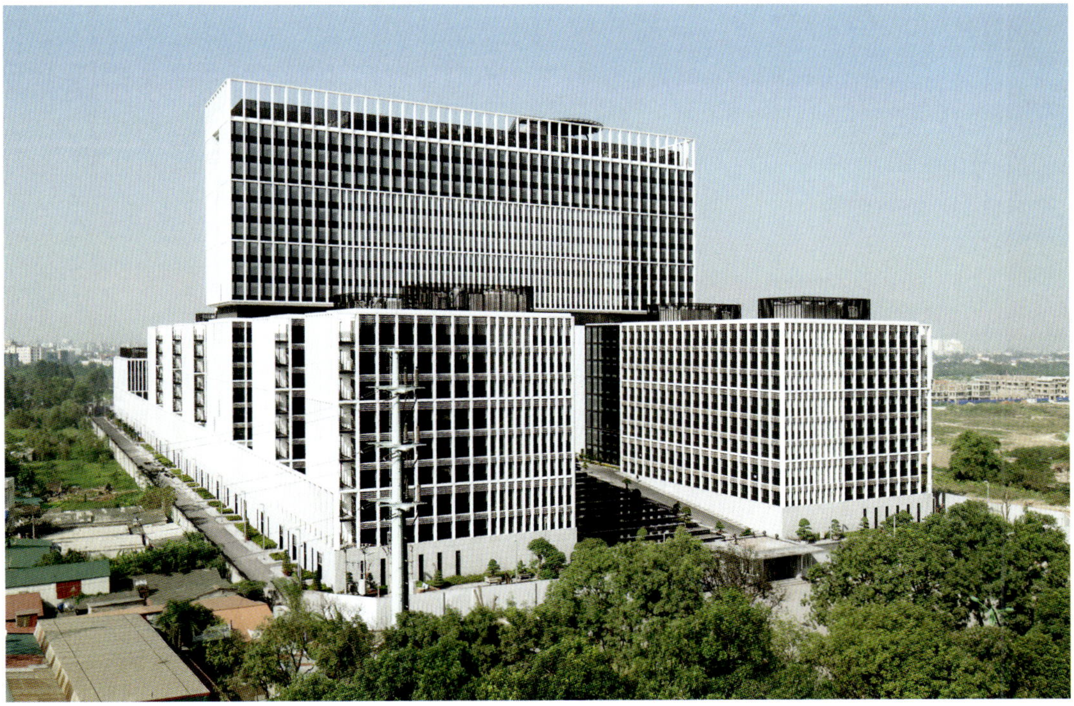

内政部大厦　河内

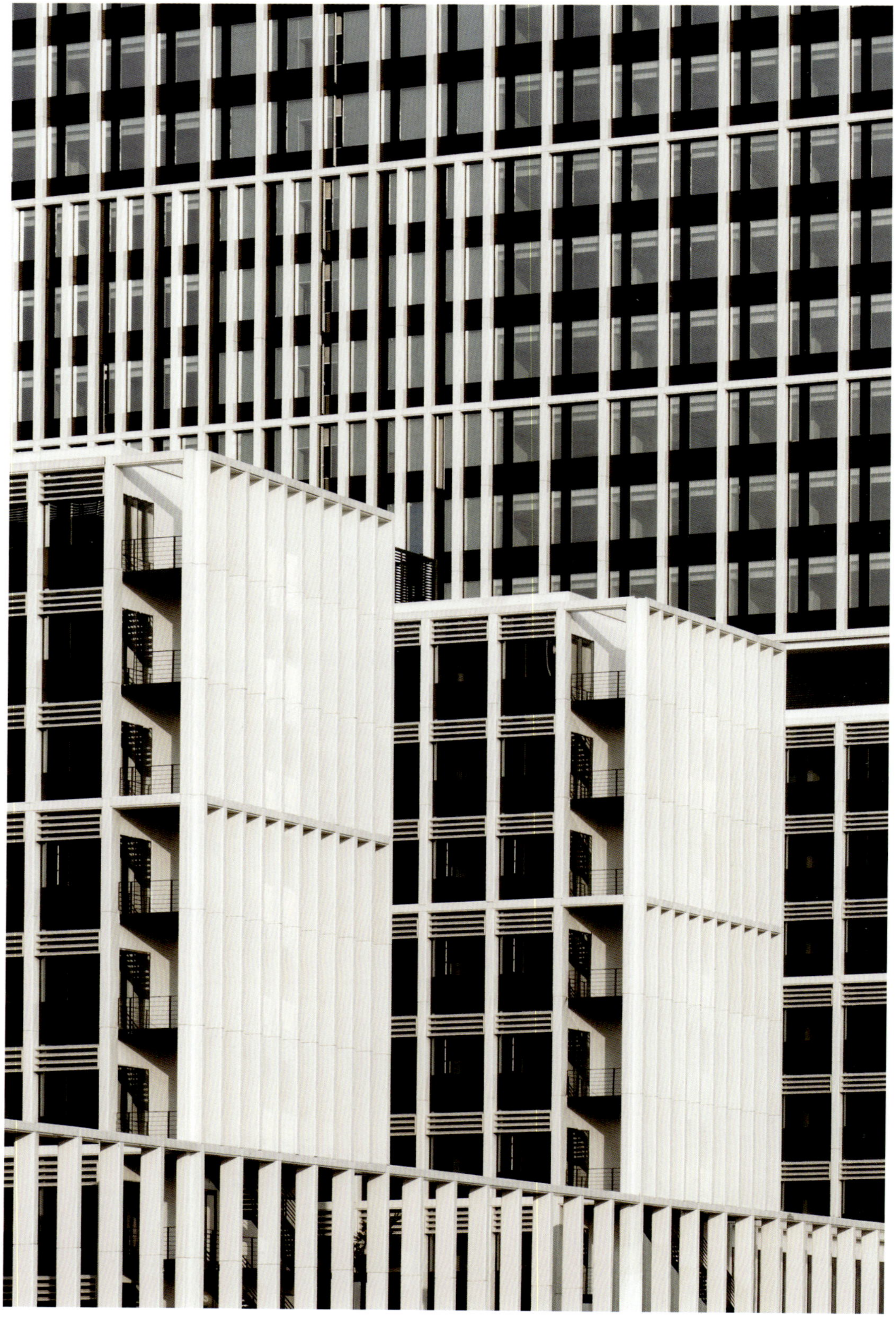

Headquarters of the Ministry of the Interior Hanoi

128 ¹⁷
↑

会议展览中心
淮安，中国

Convention & Exhibition Center
Huai'an, China

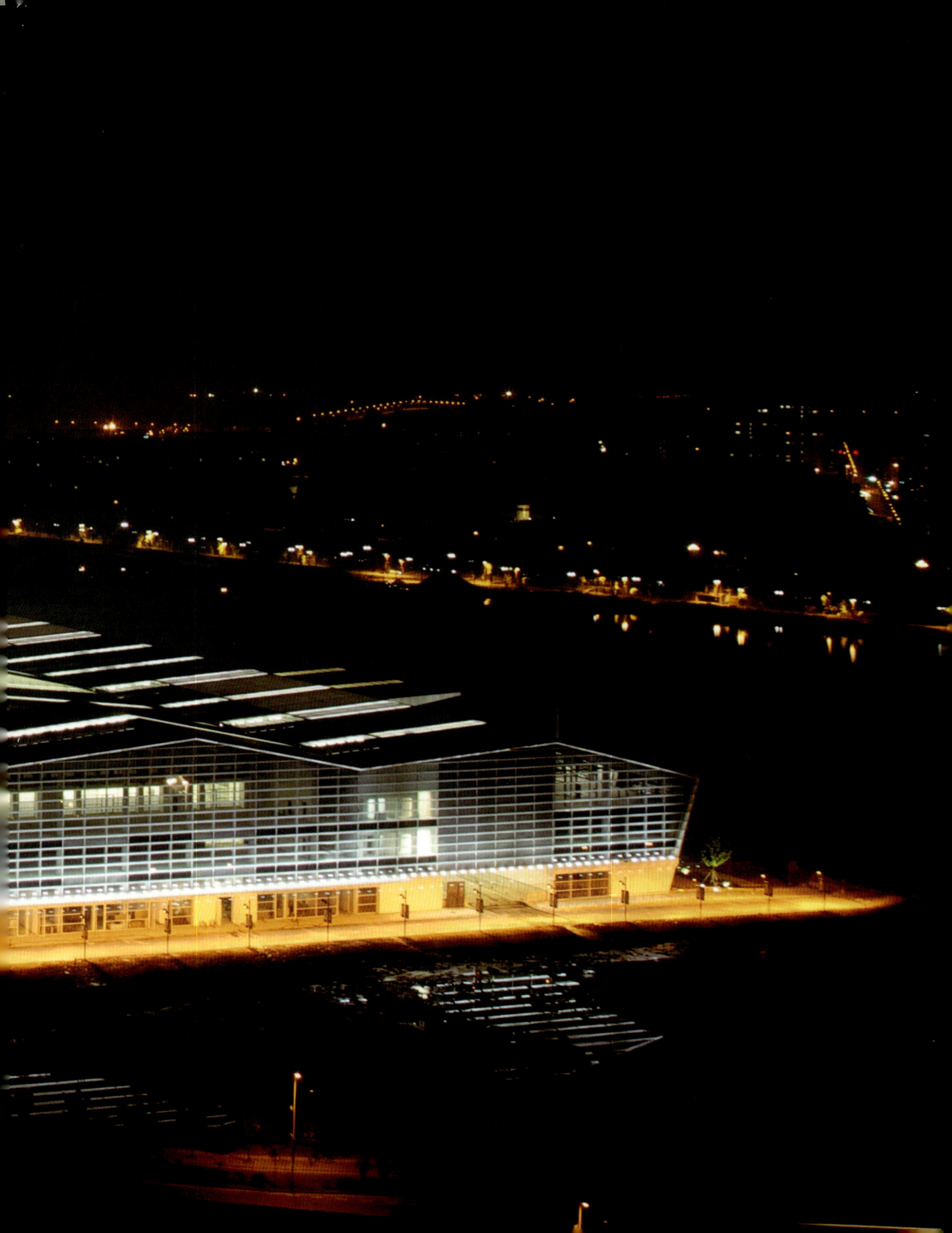

会议展览中心 淮安

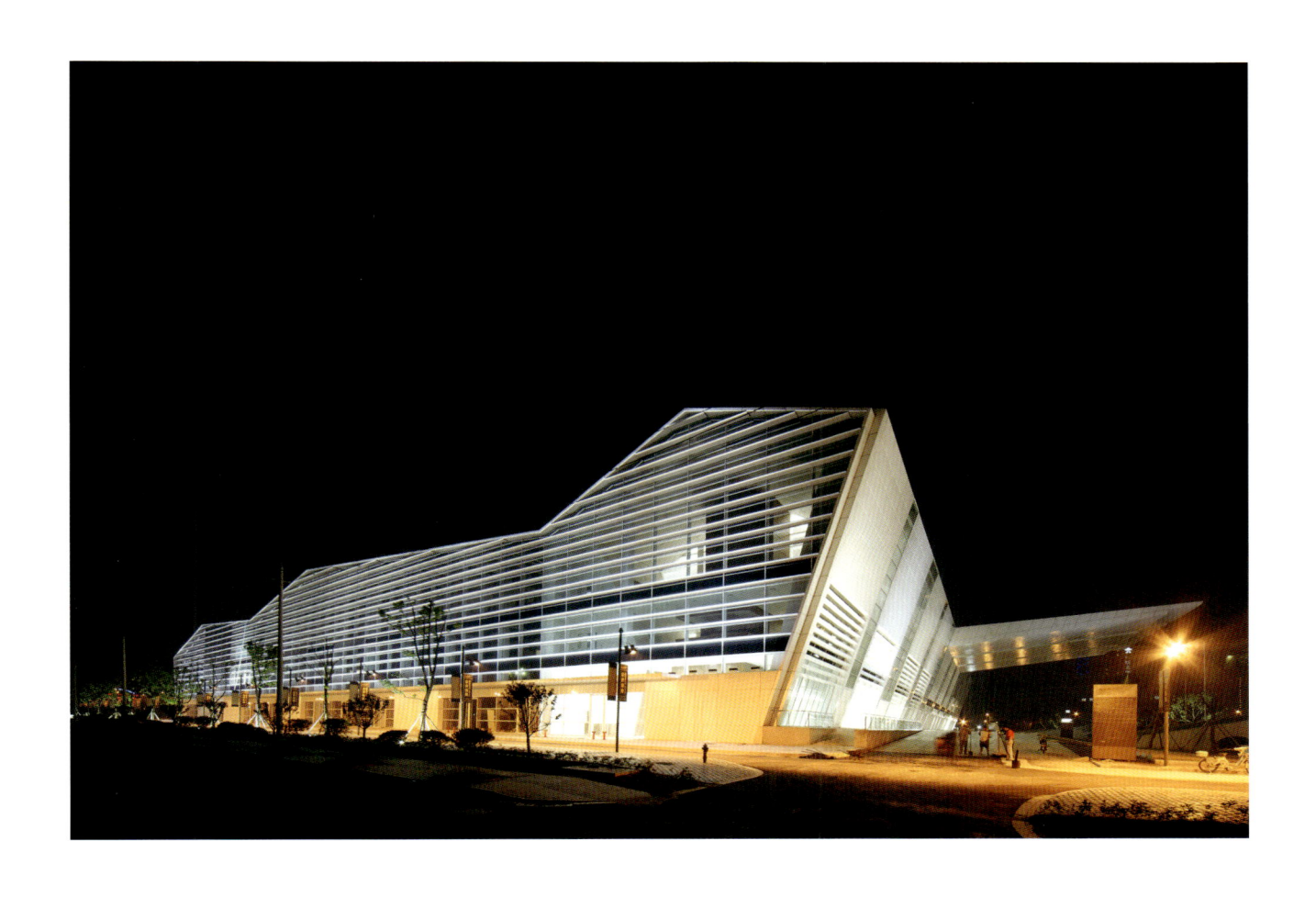

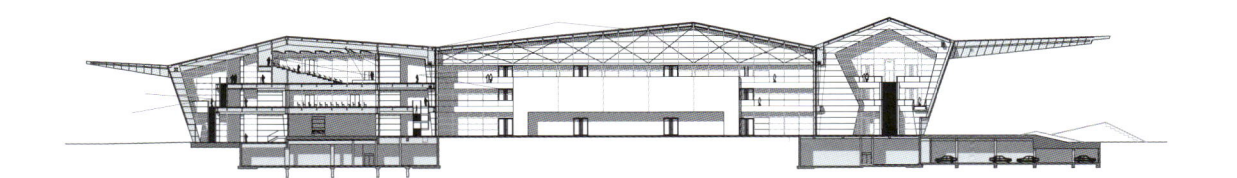

Convention & Exhibition Center Huai'an   131

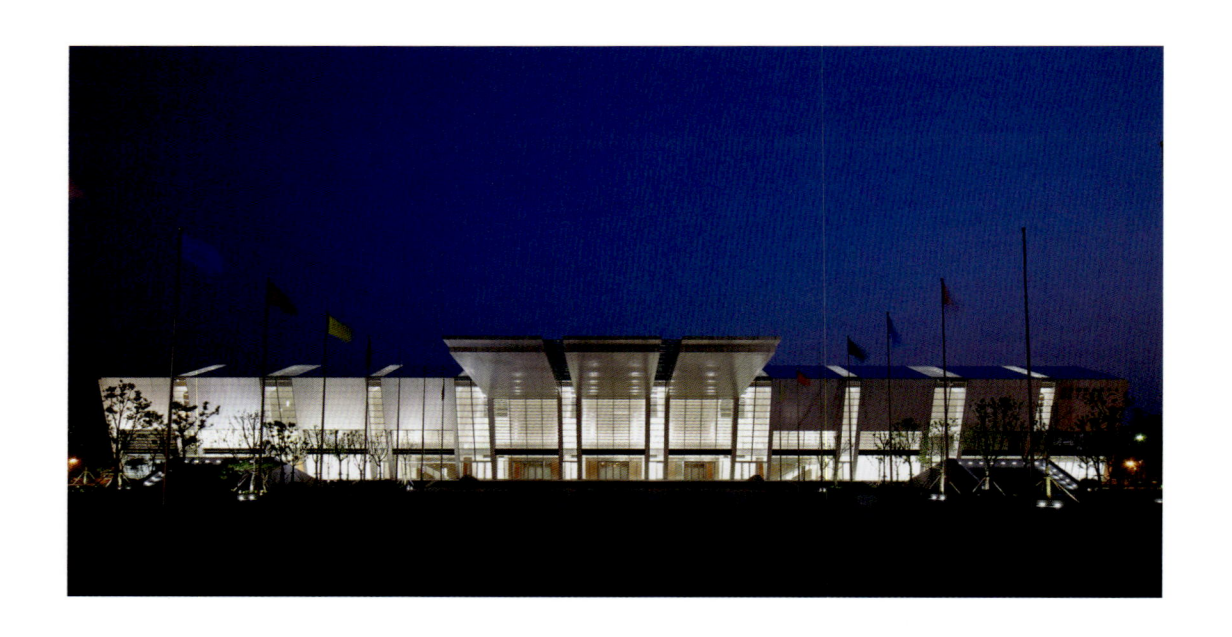

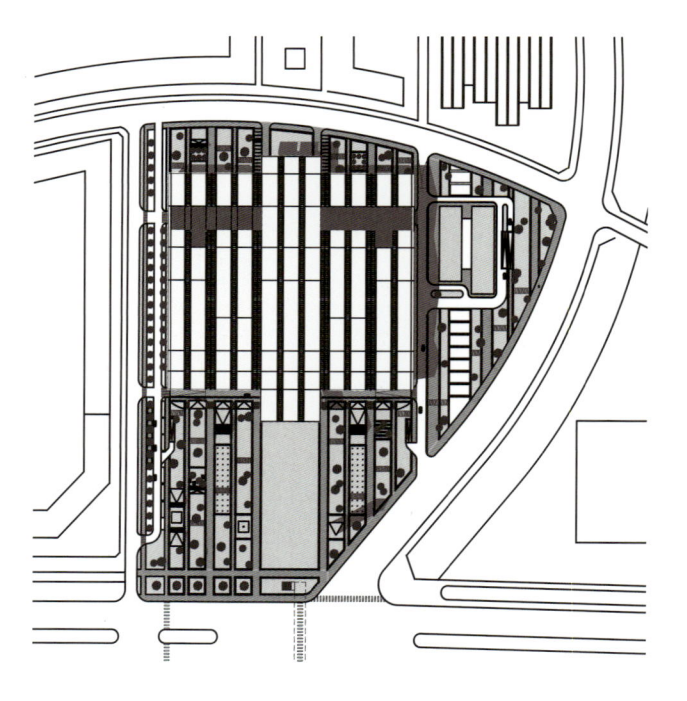

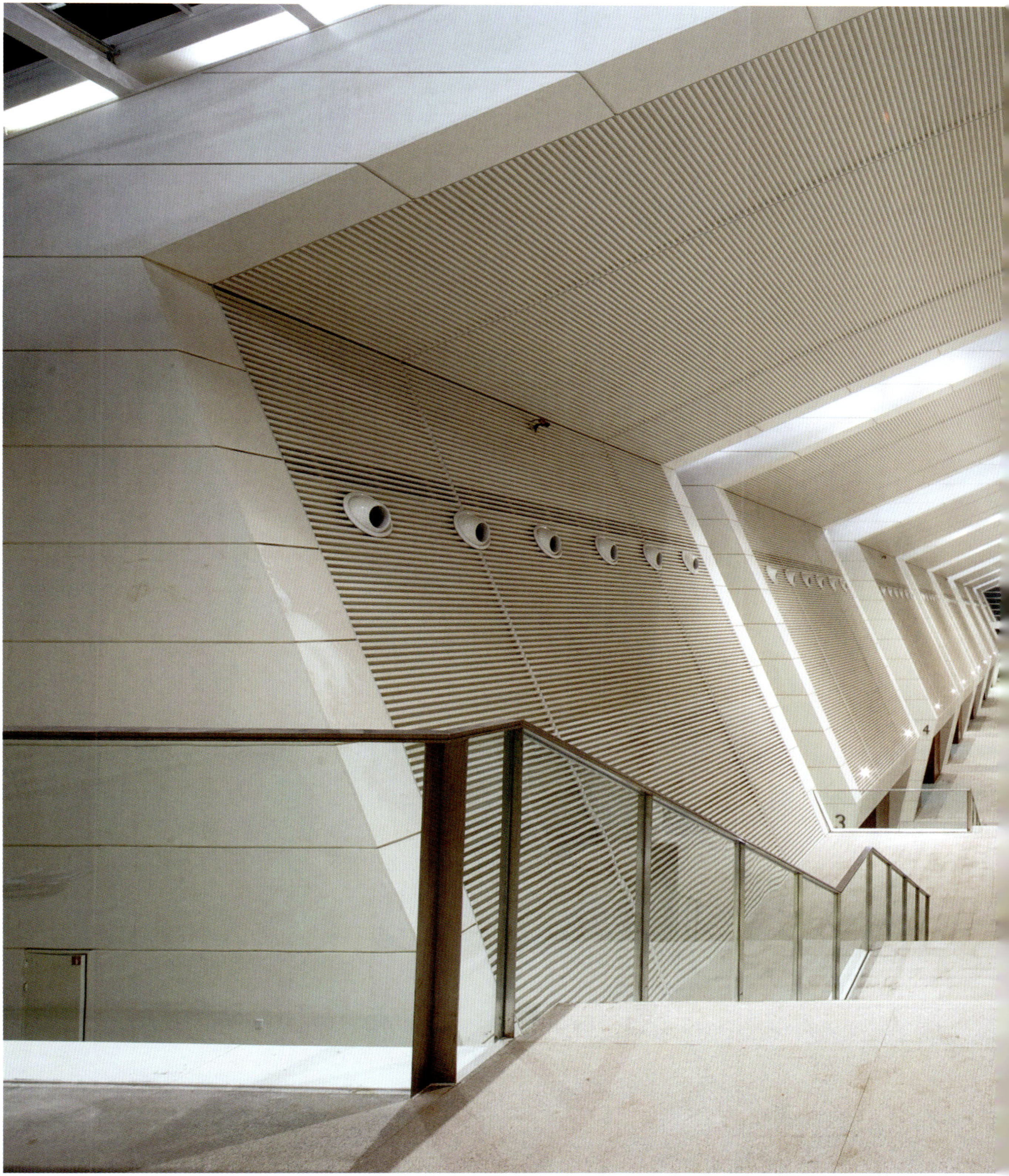

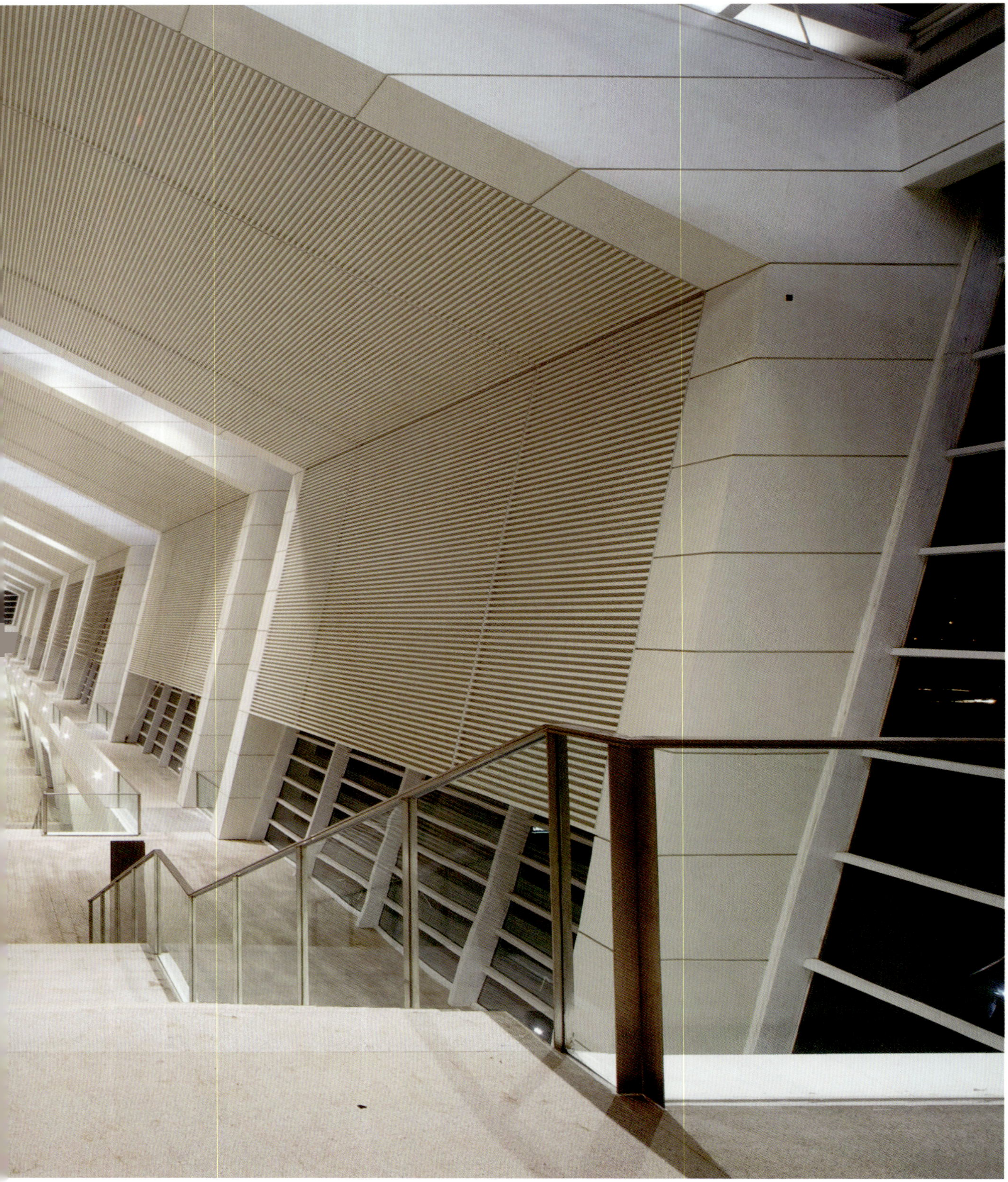

134 ¹⁸
↑

贾瓦哈拉尔·尼赫鲁体育场
新德里，印度

Jawaharlal Nehru Stadium,
Commonwealth Games 2010
New Delhi, India

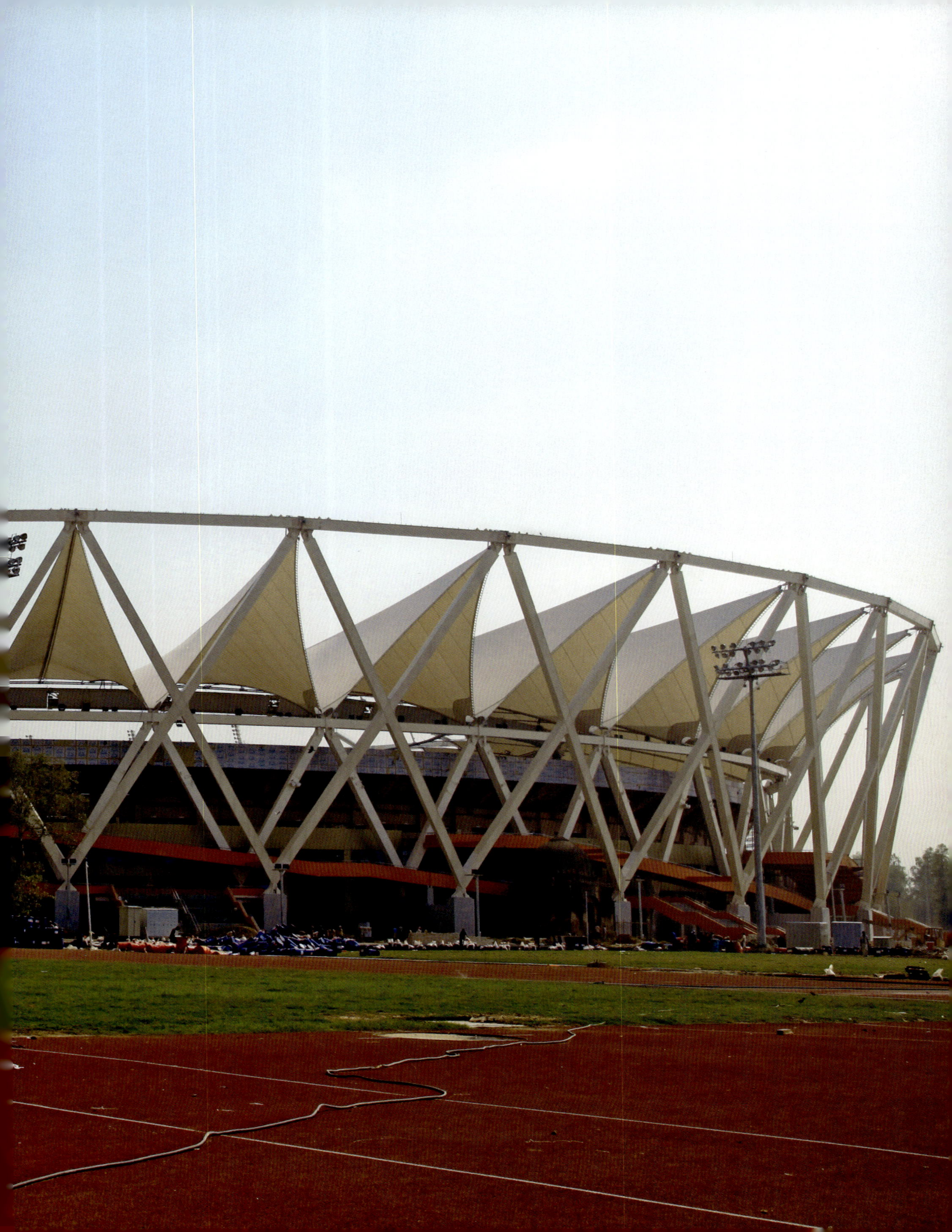

136　贾瓦哈拉尔·尼赫鲁体育场　新德里

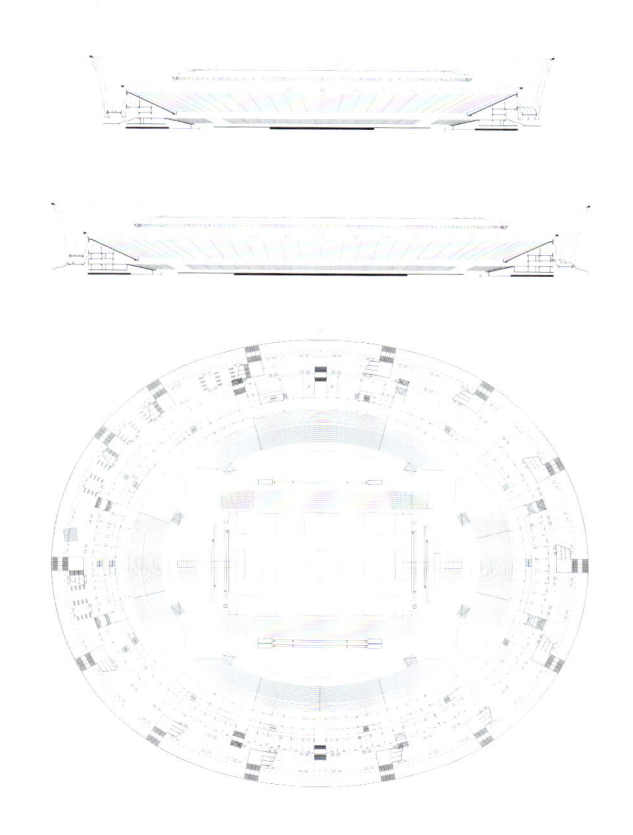

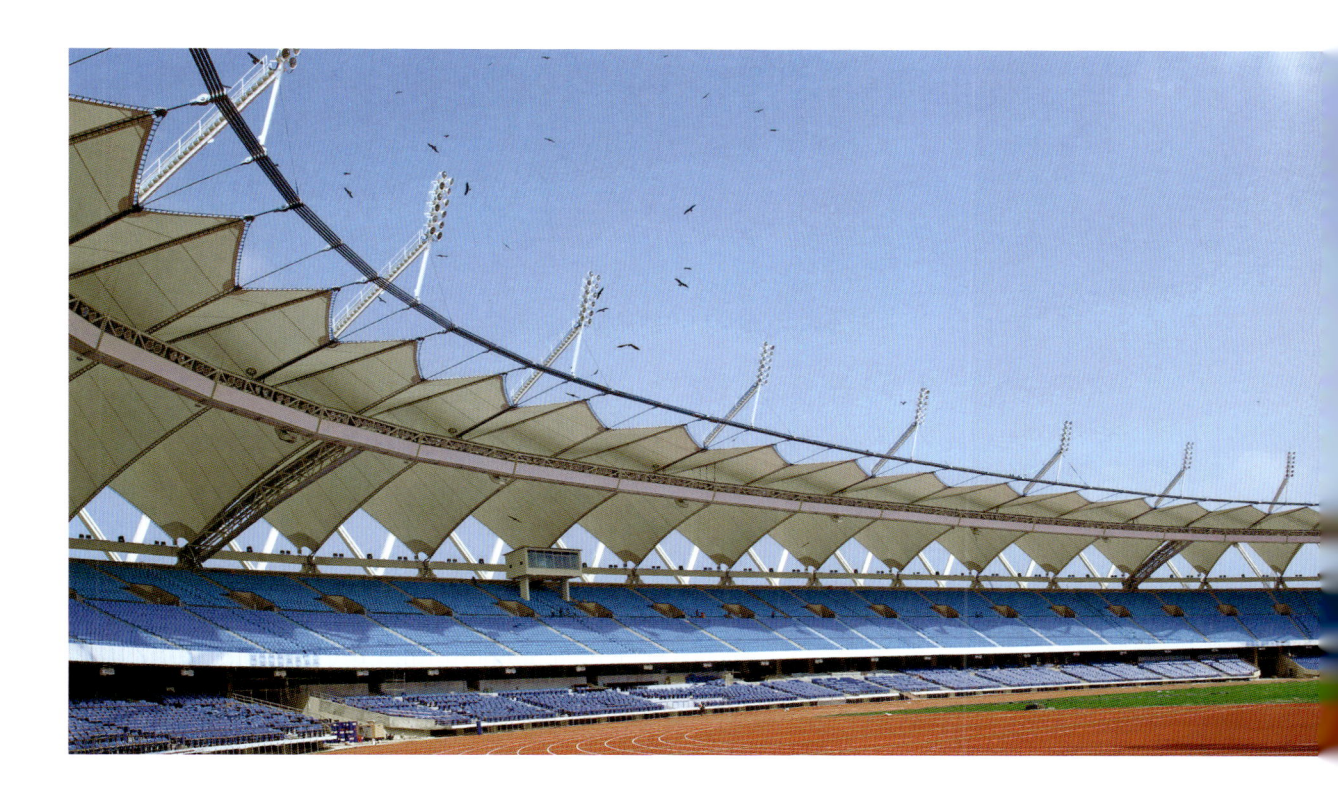

Jawaharlal Nehru Stadium, Commonwealth Games 2010 New Delhi

138 ¹⁸ ↑

嘉铭中心
北京，中国

Jiaming Center
Beijing, China

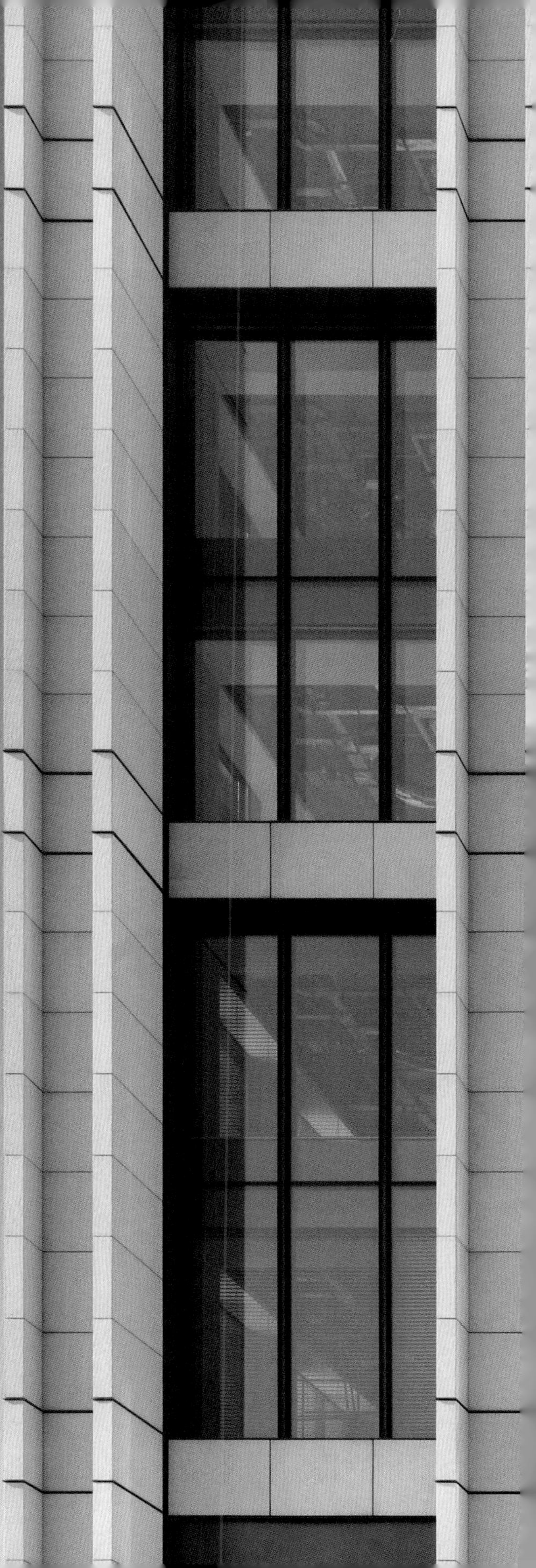

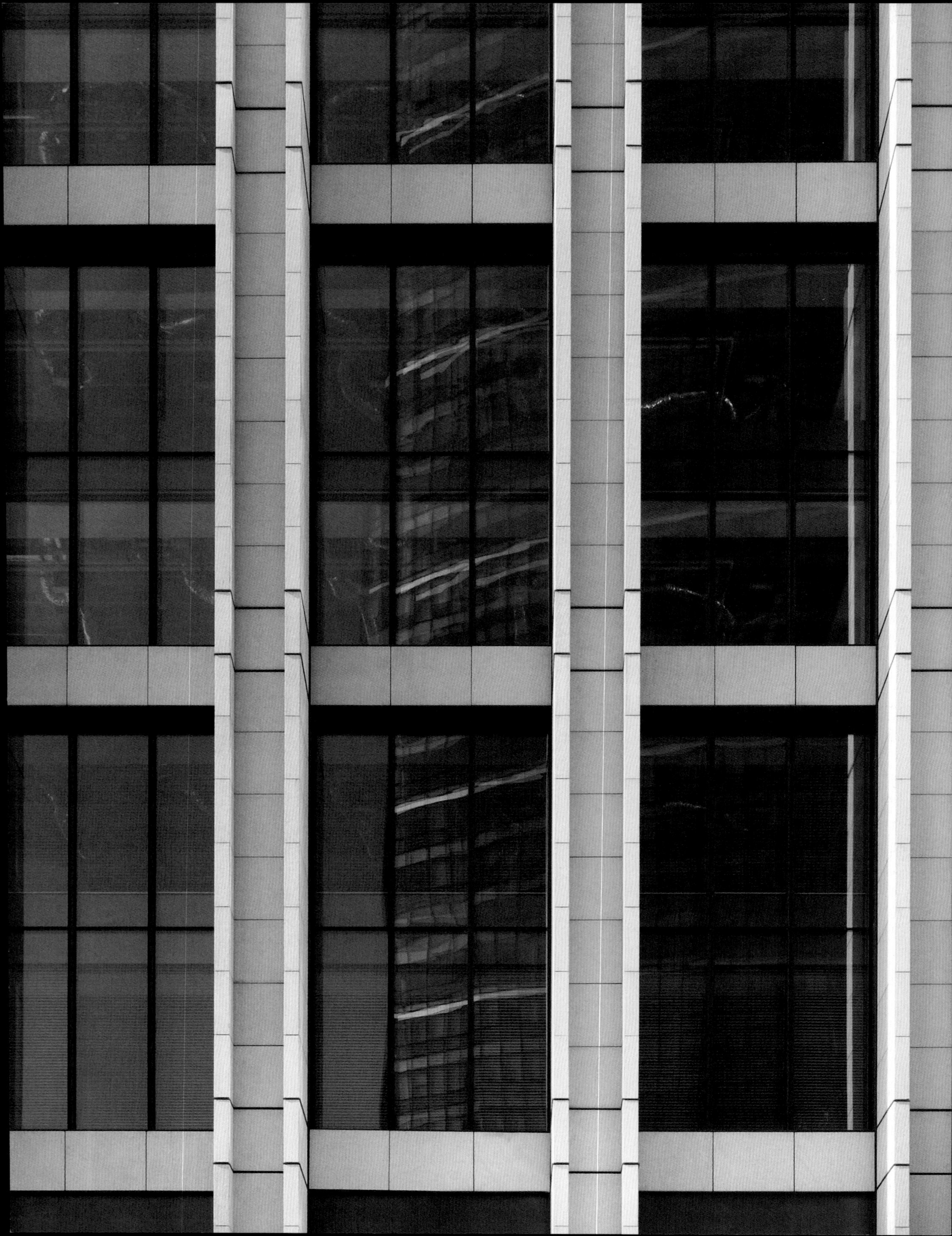

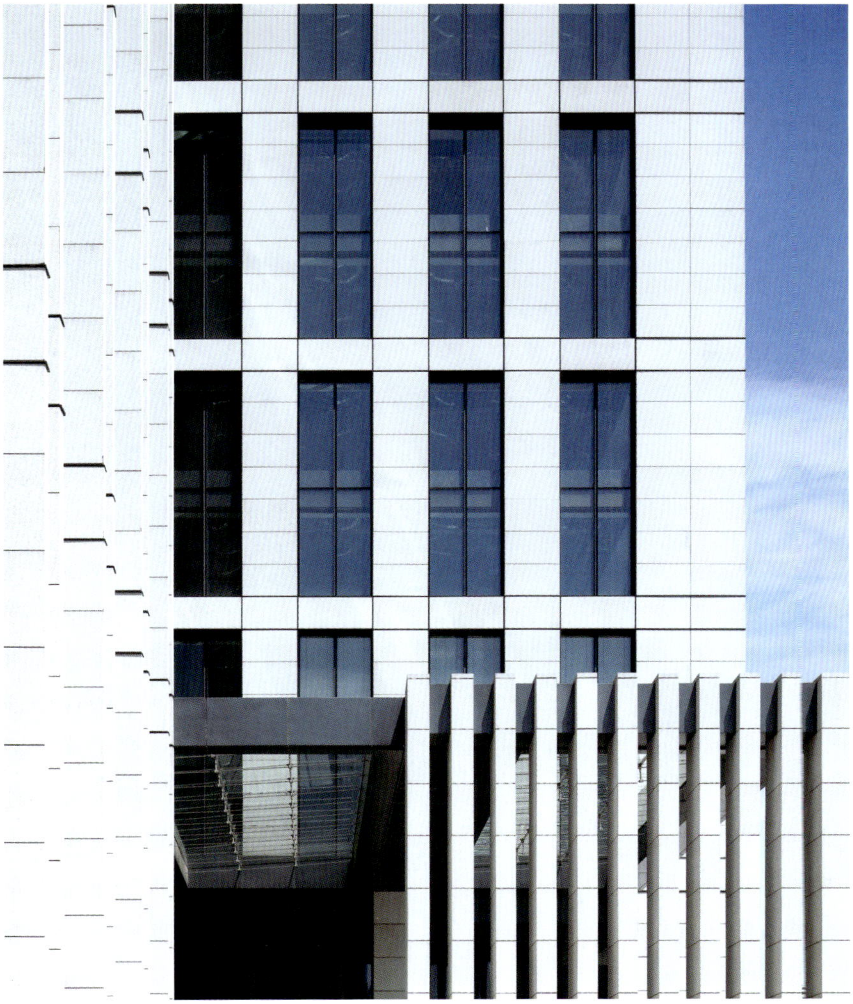

嘉铭中心　北京

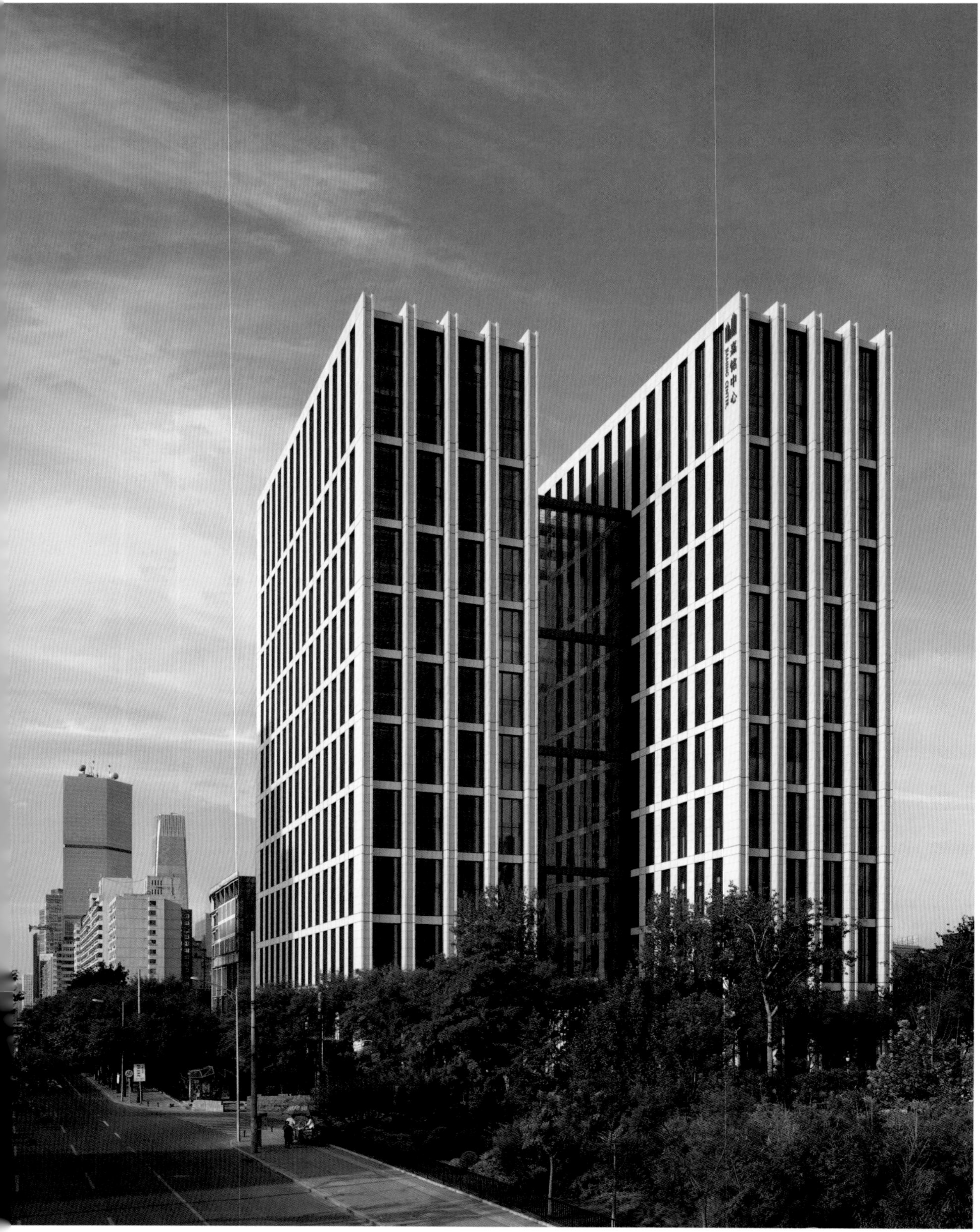

Jiaming Center Beijing

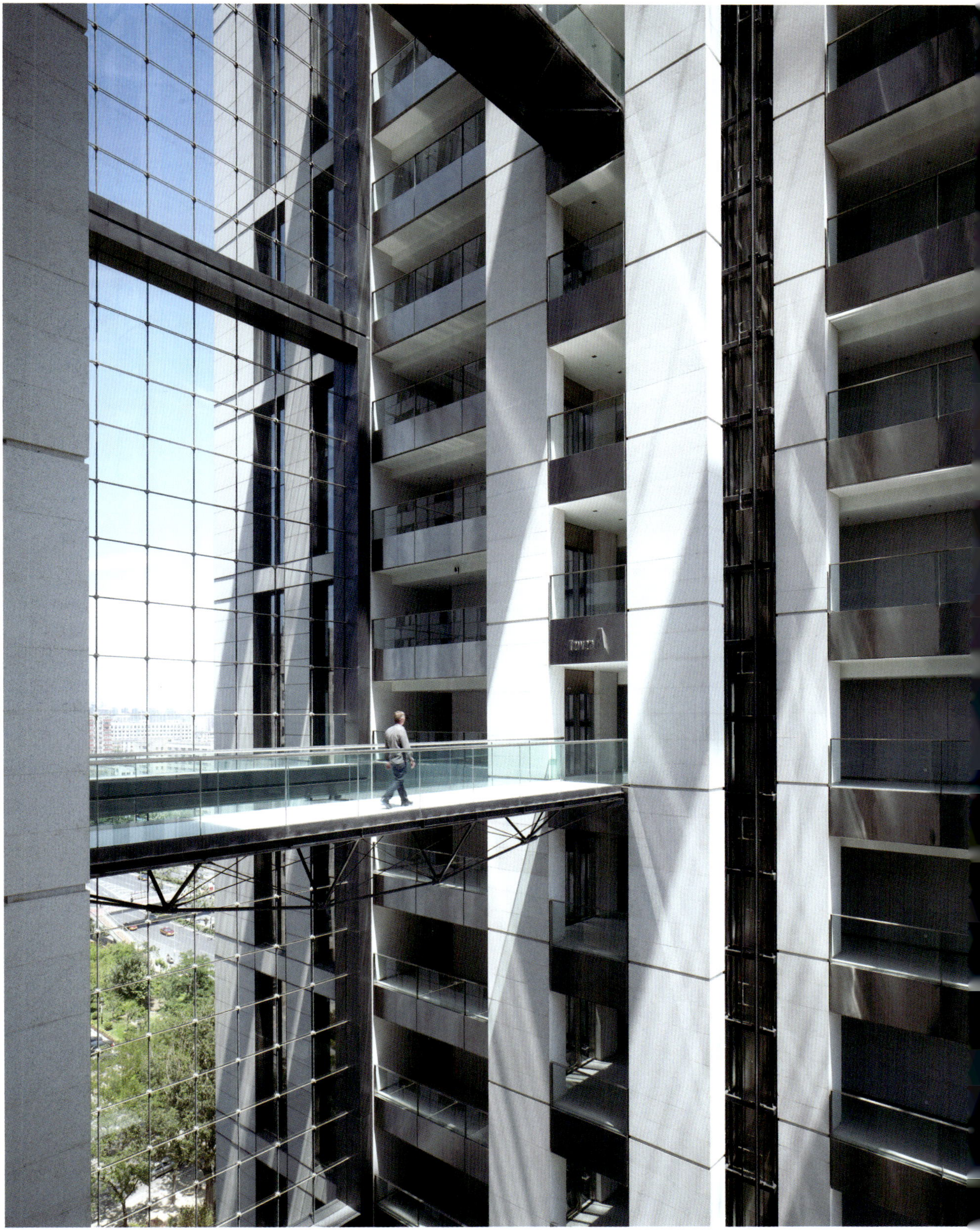

嘉铭中心　北京

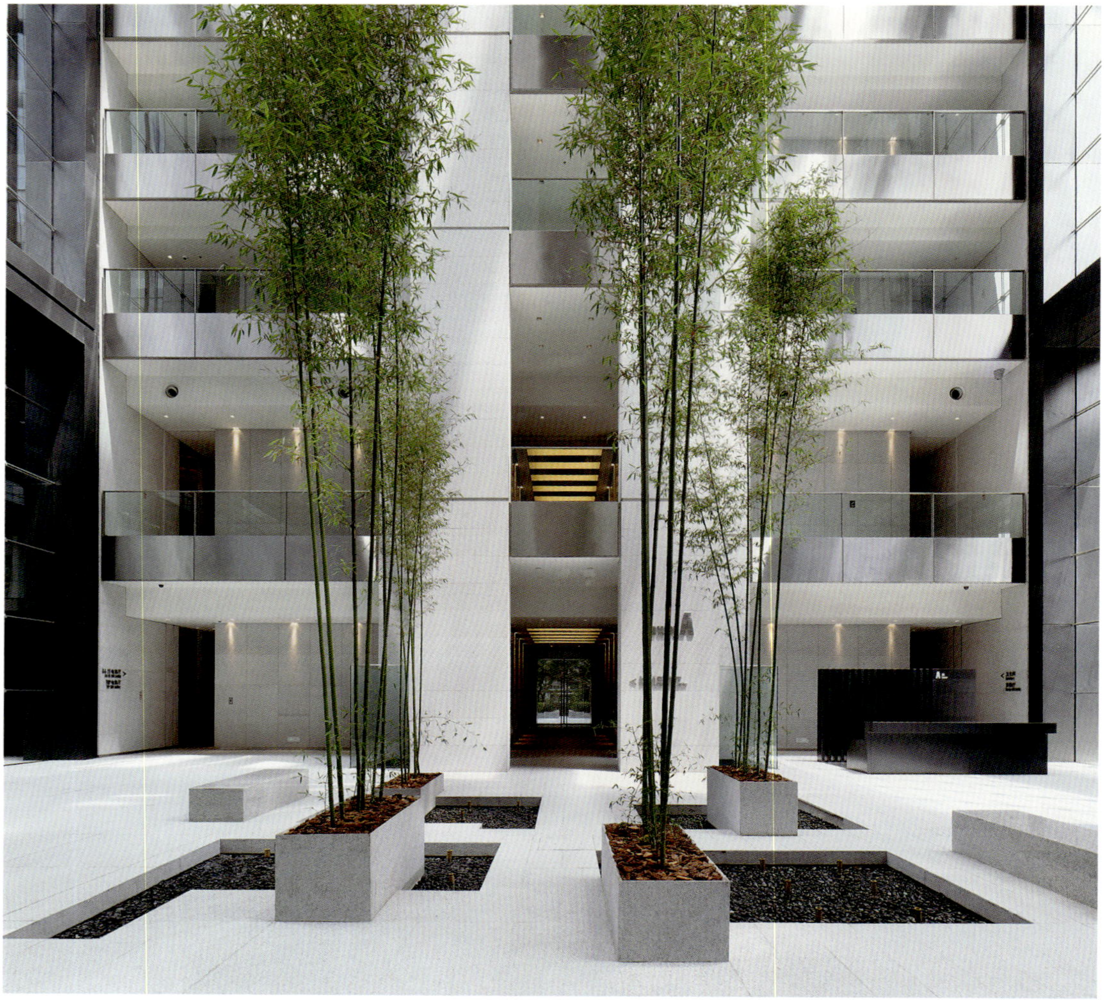

Jiaming Center Beijing

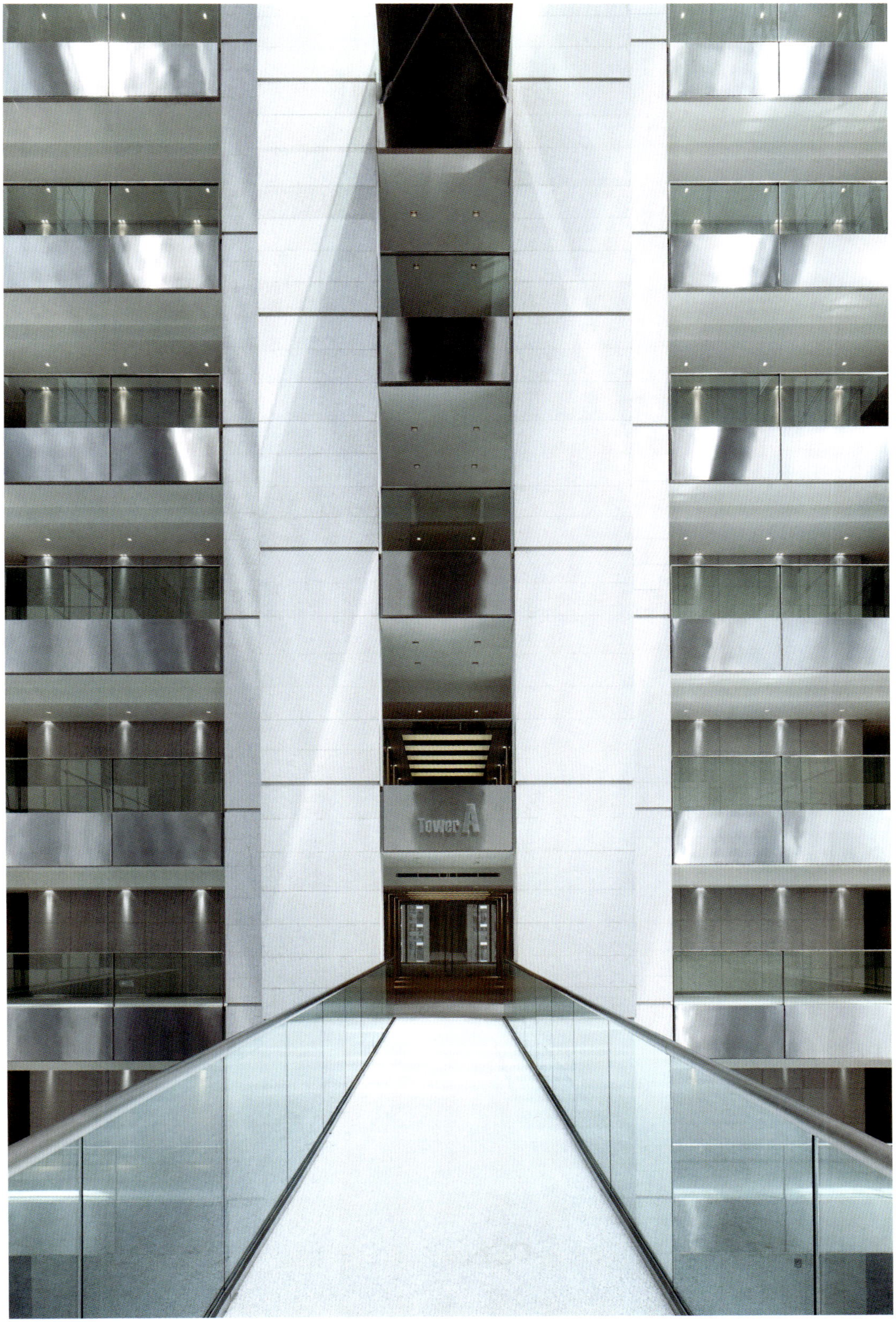

嘉铭中心 北京

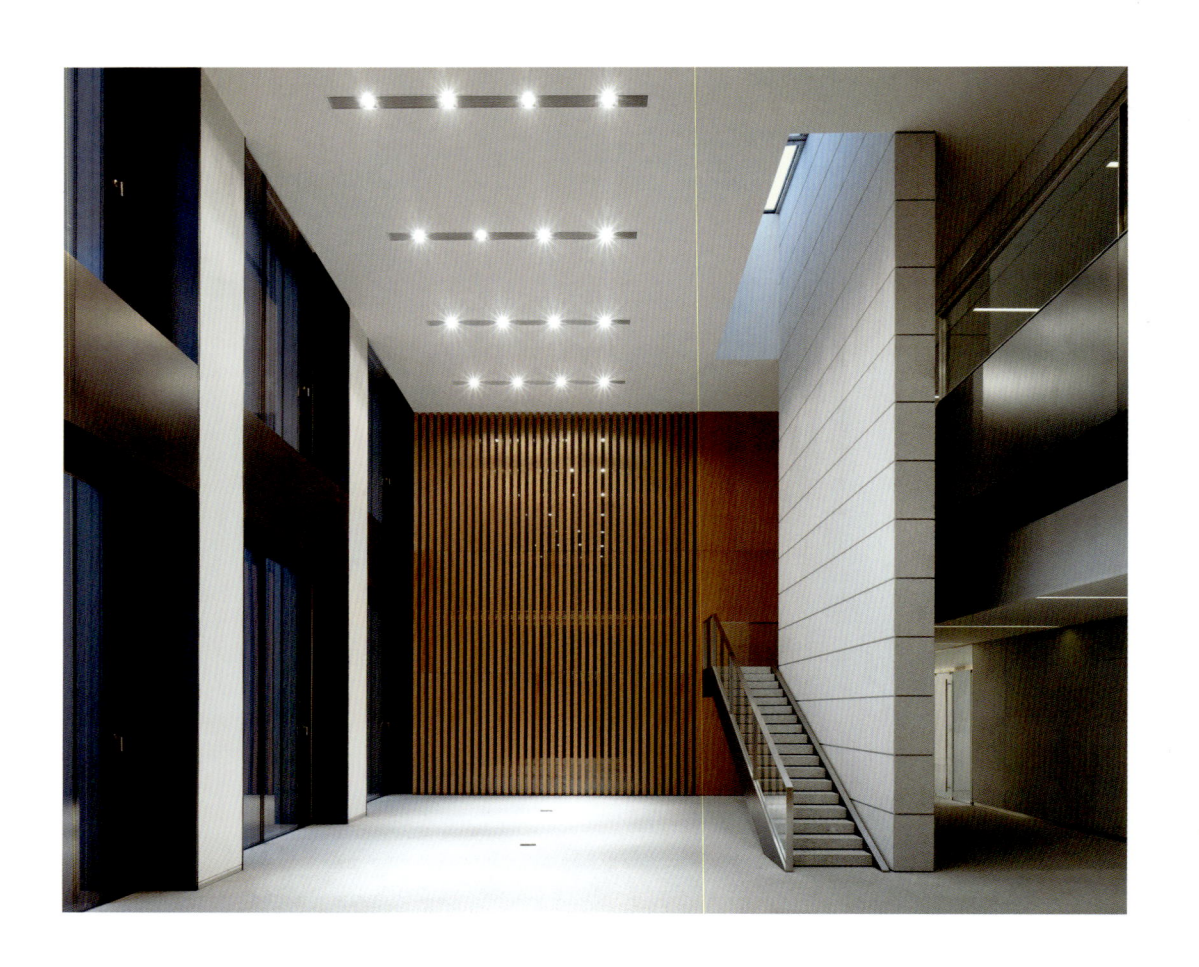

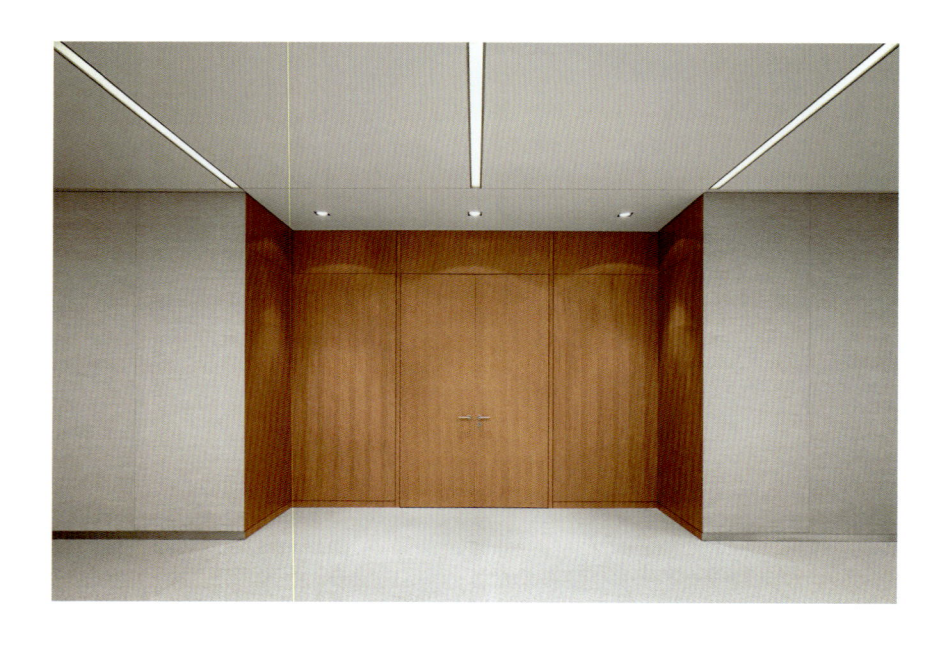

Jiaming Center Beijing

146 19 ↑

科技文化综合中心
长春，中国

Museum for Culture, Fine Arts and Science
Changchun, China

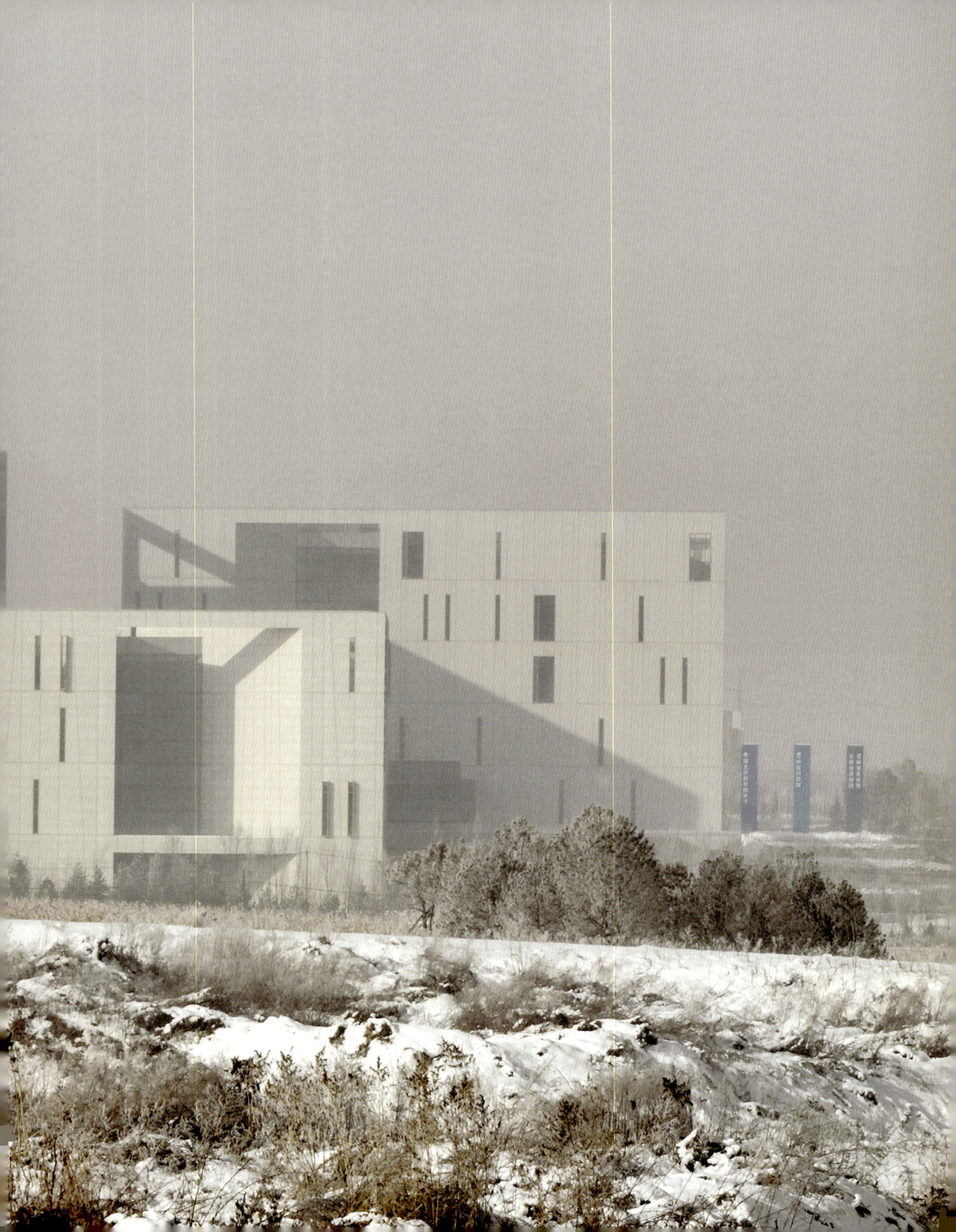

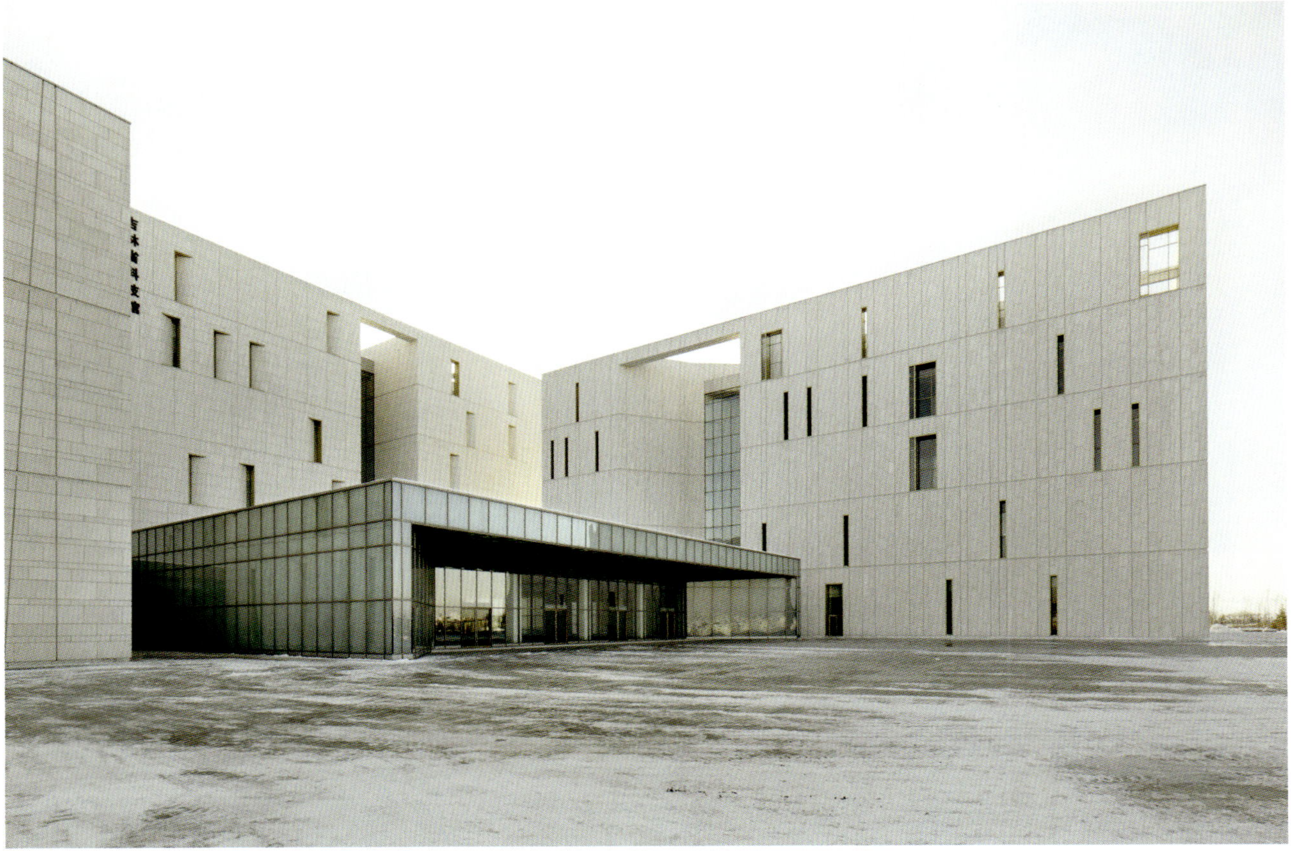

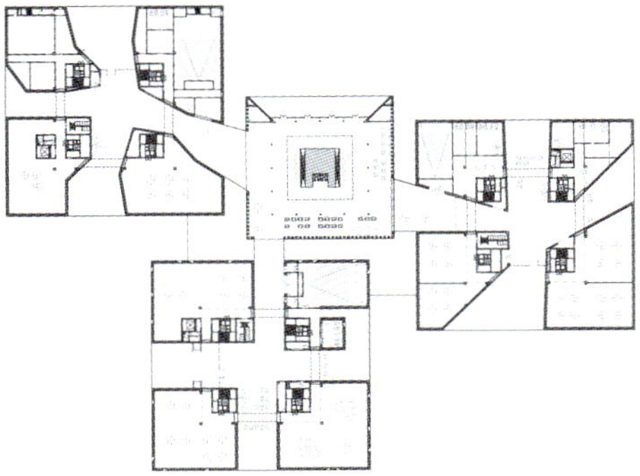

148　科技文化综合中心　长春

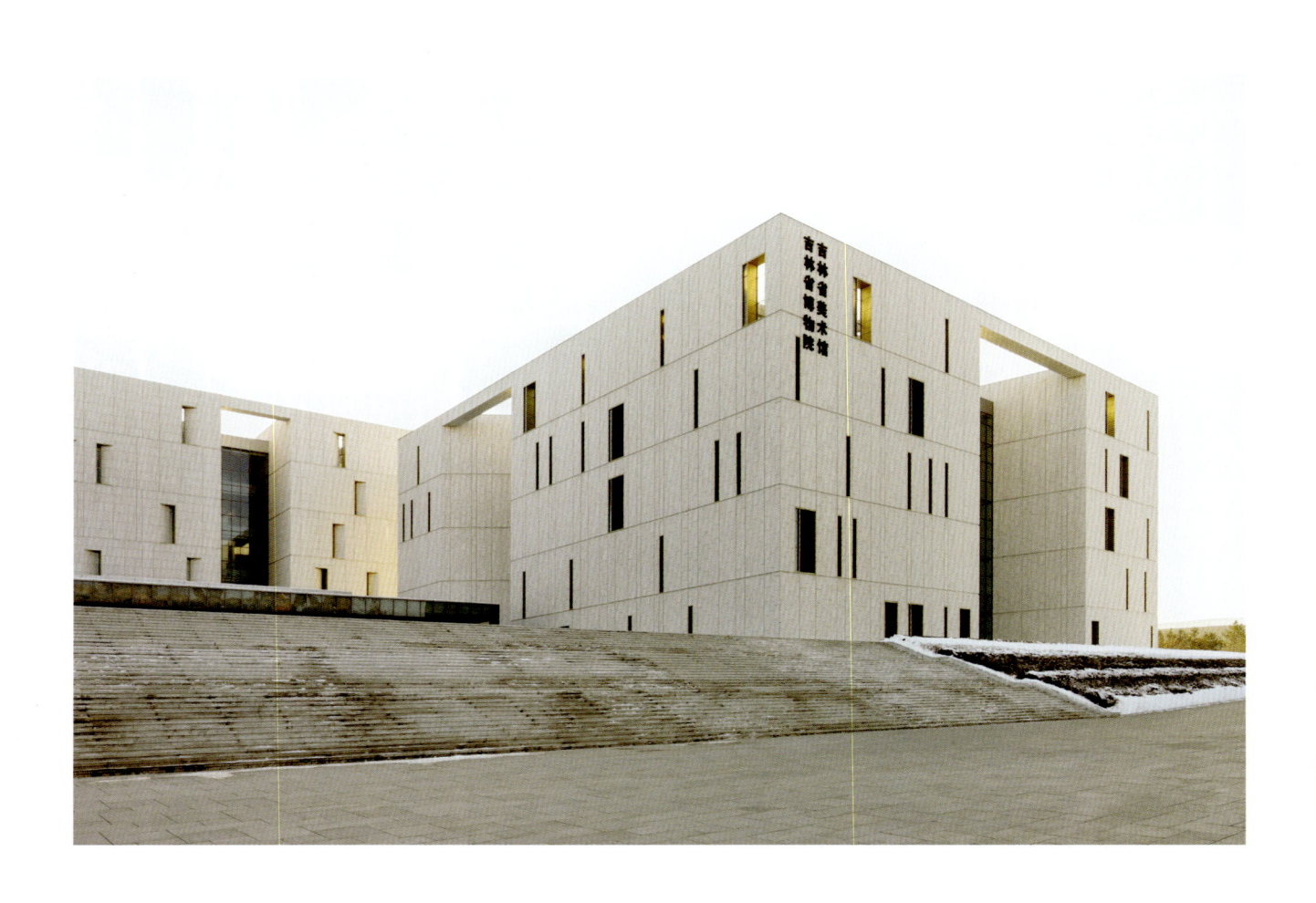

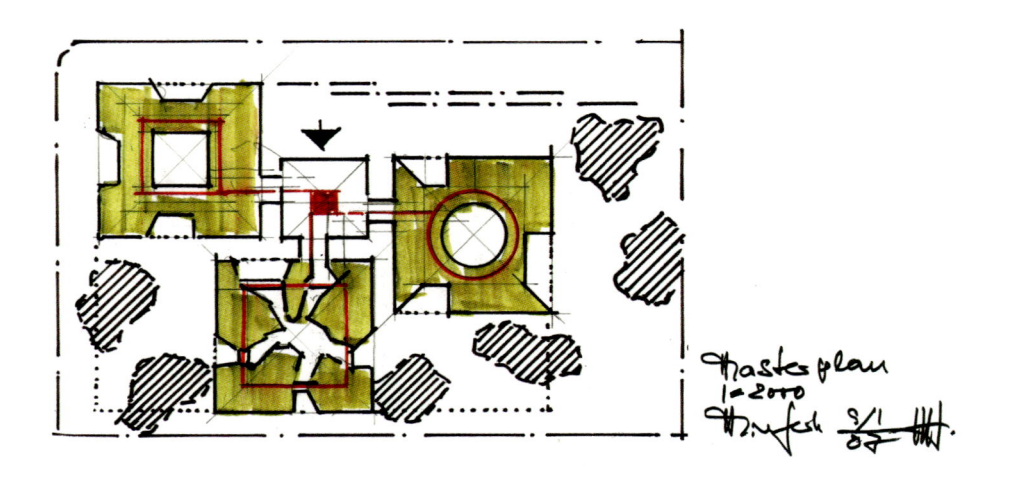

Museum for Culture, Fine Arts and Science Changchun

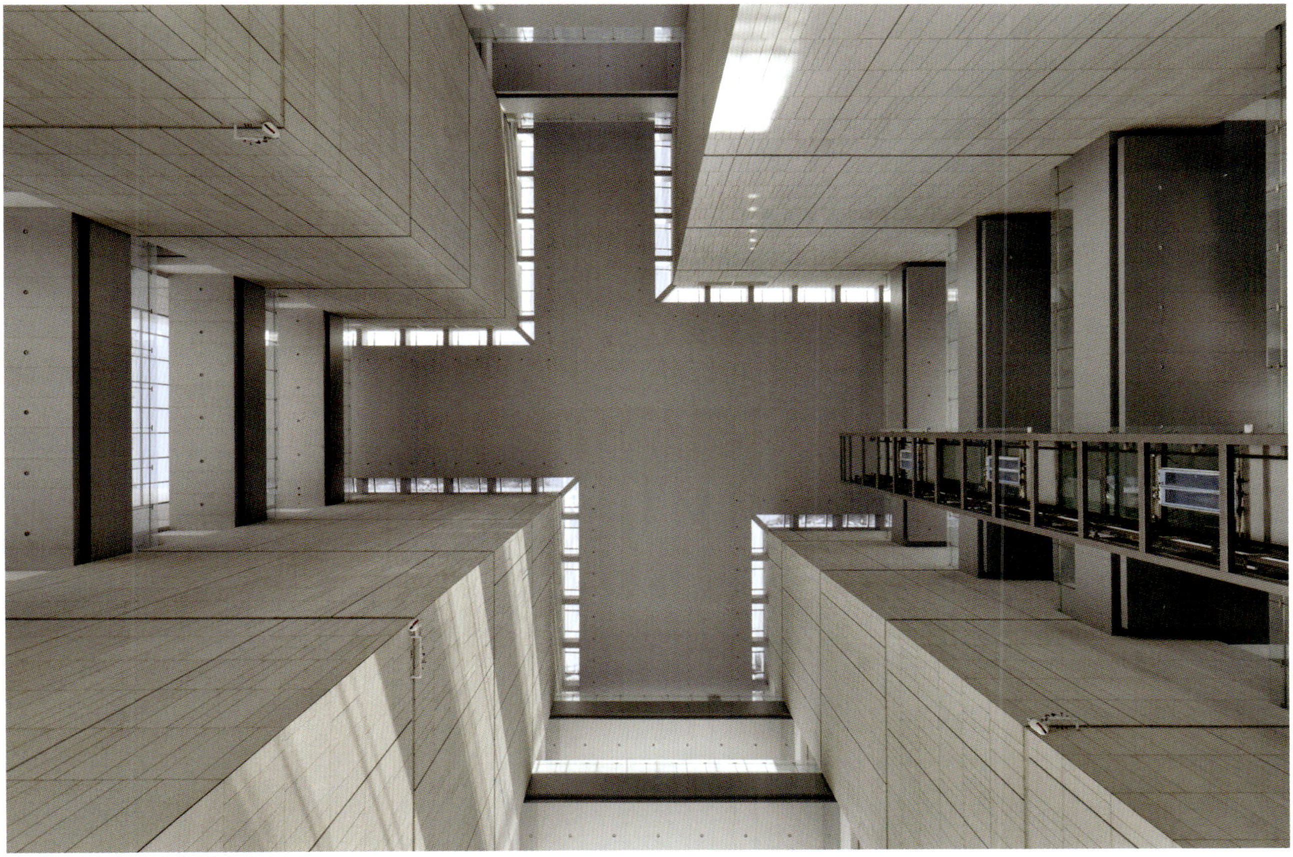

科技文化综合中心　长春

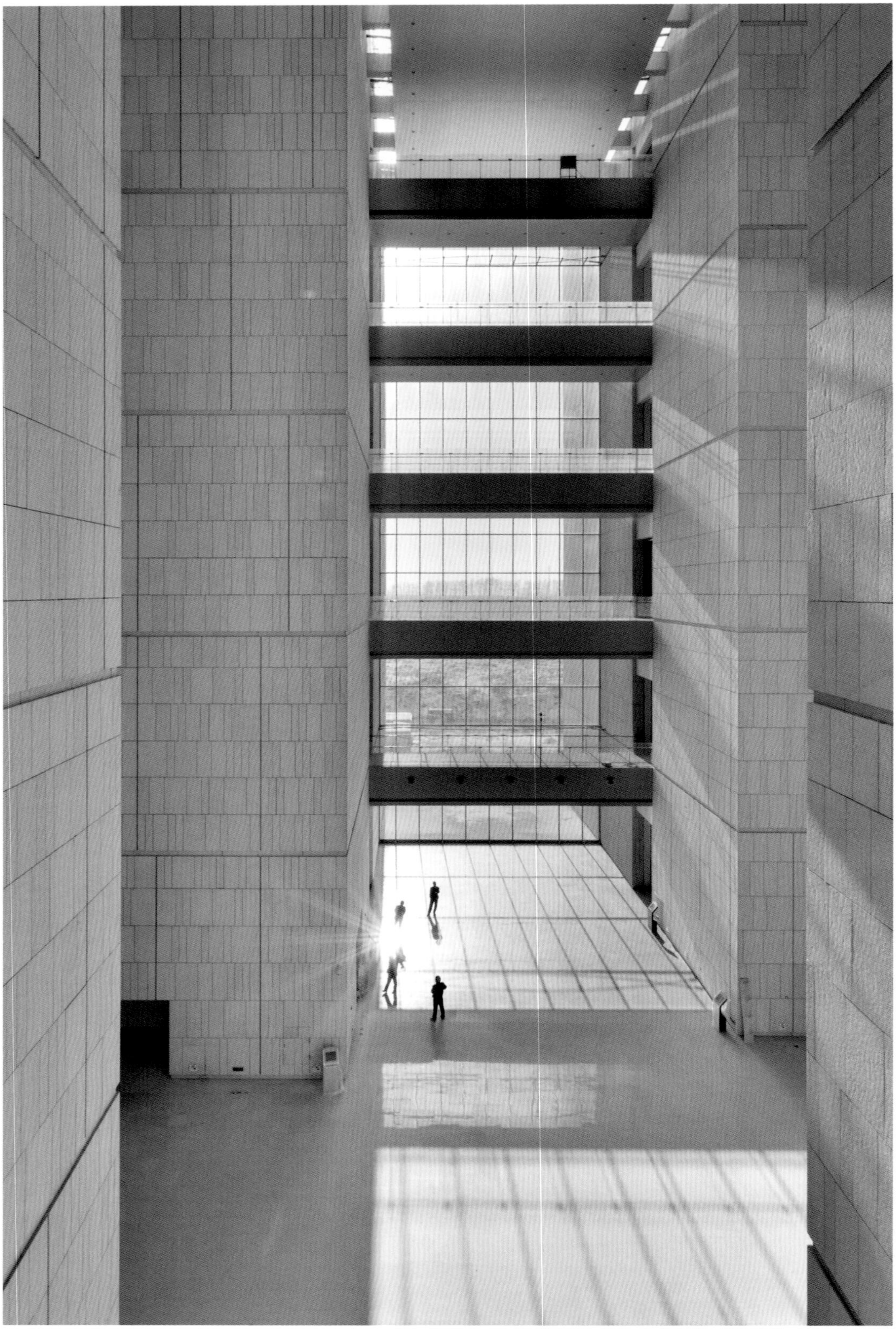

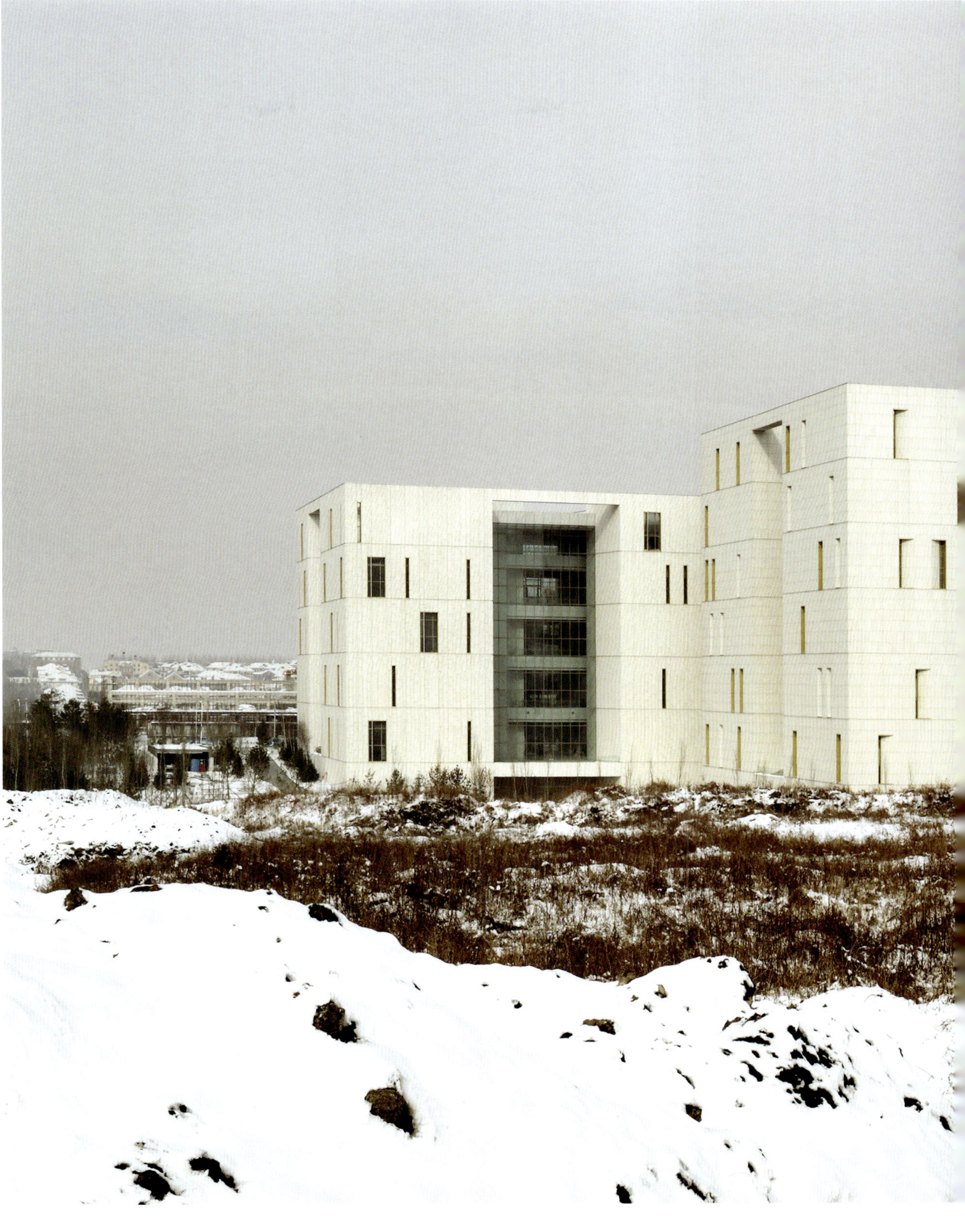

科技文化综合中心　长春

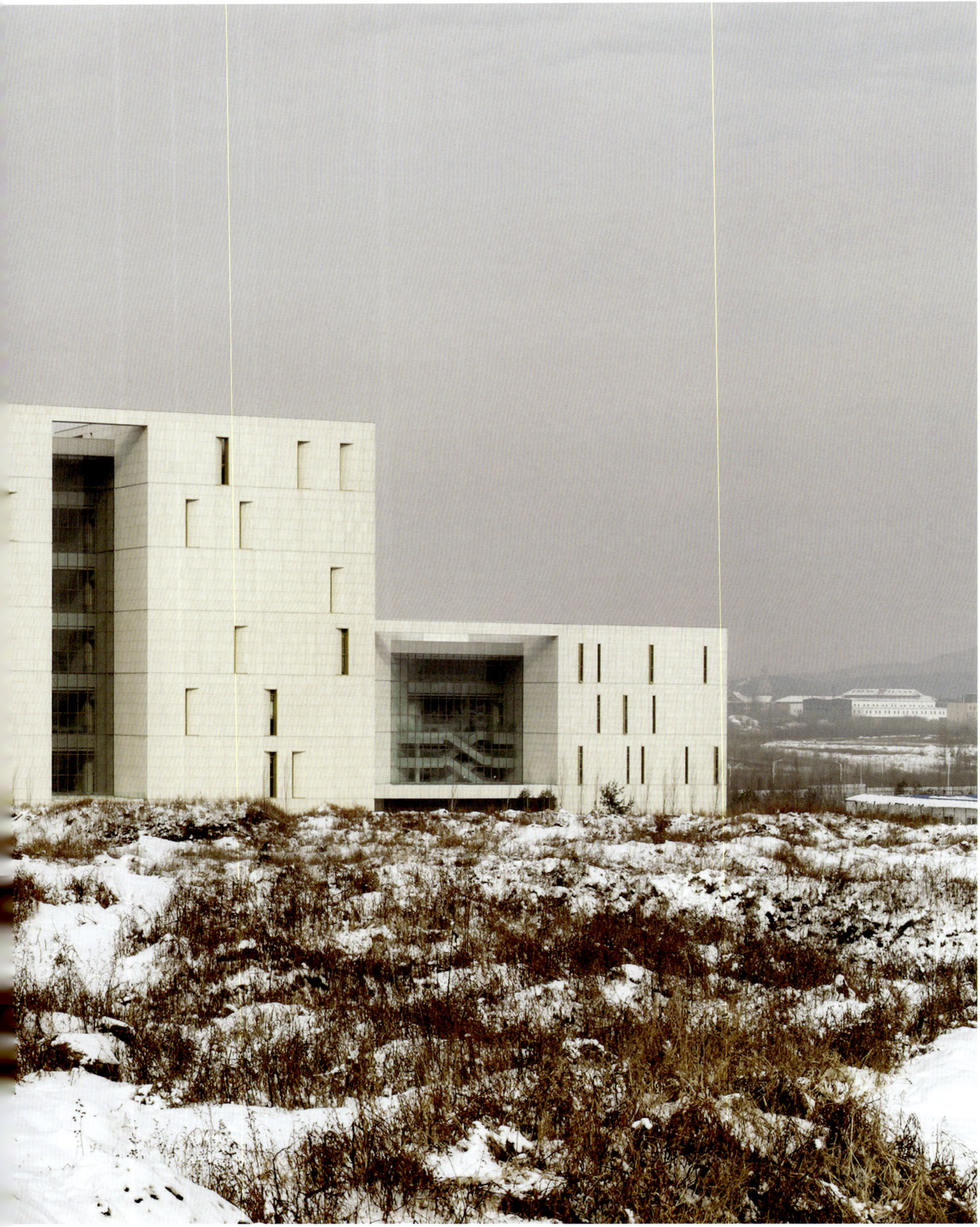

Museum for Culture, Fine Arts and Science Changchun

154 ¹⁹
↑

保利大厦
上海，中国

Poly Plaza
Shanghai, China

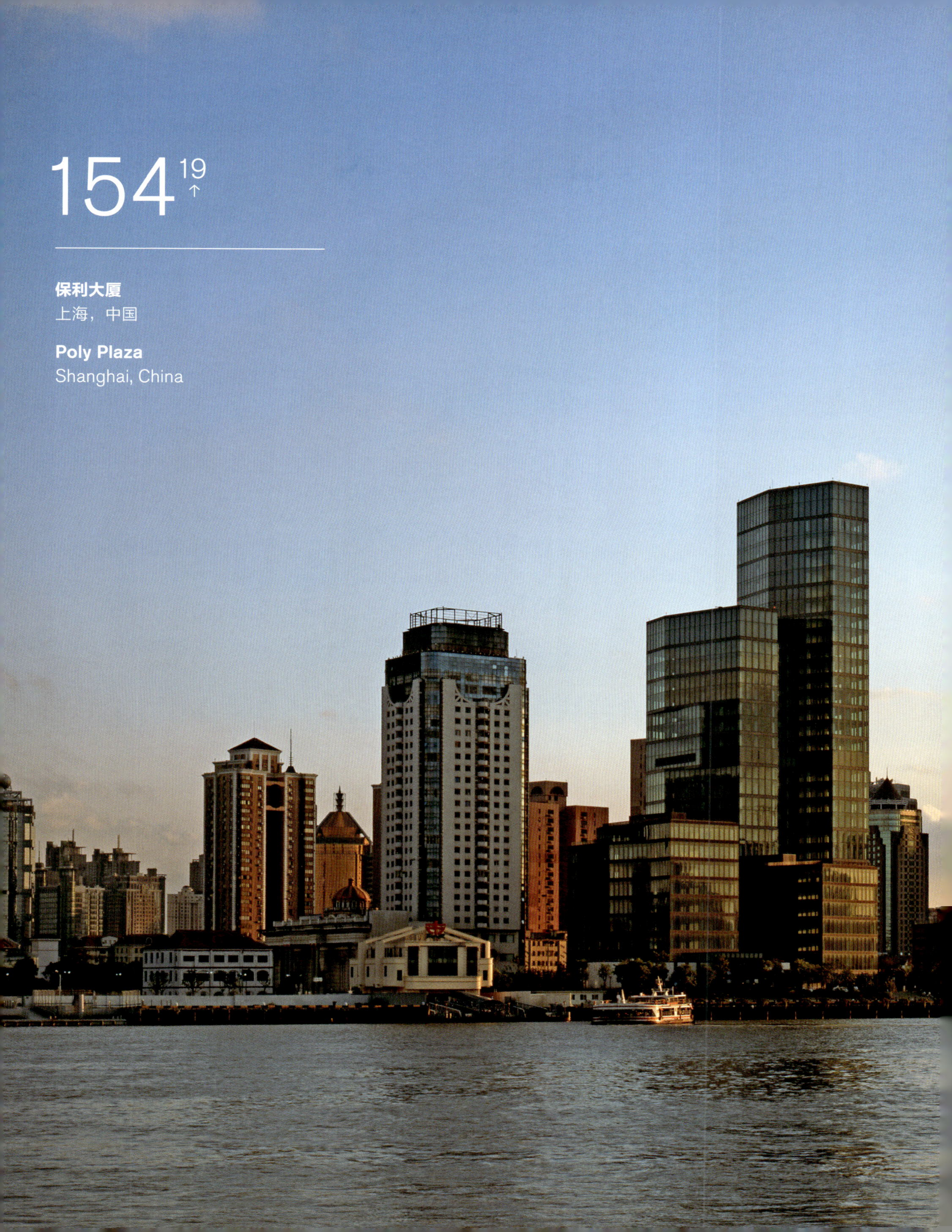

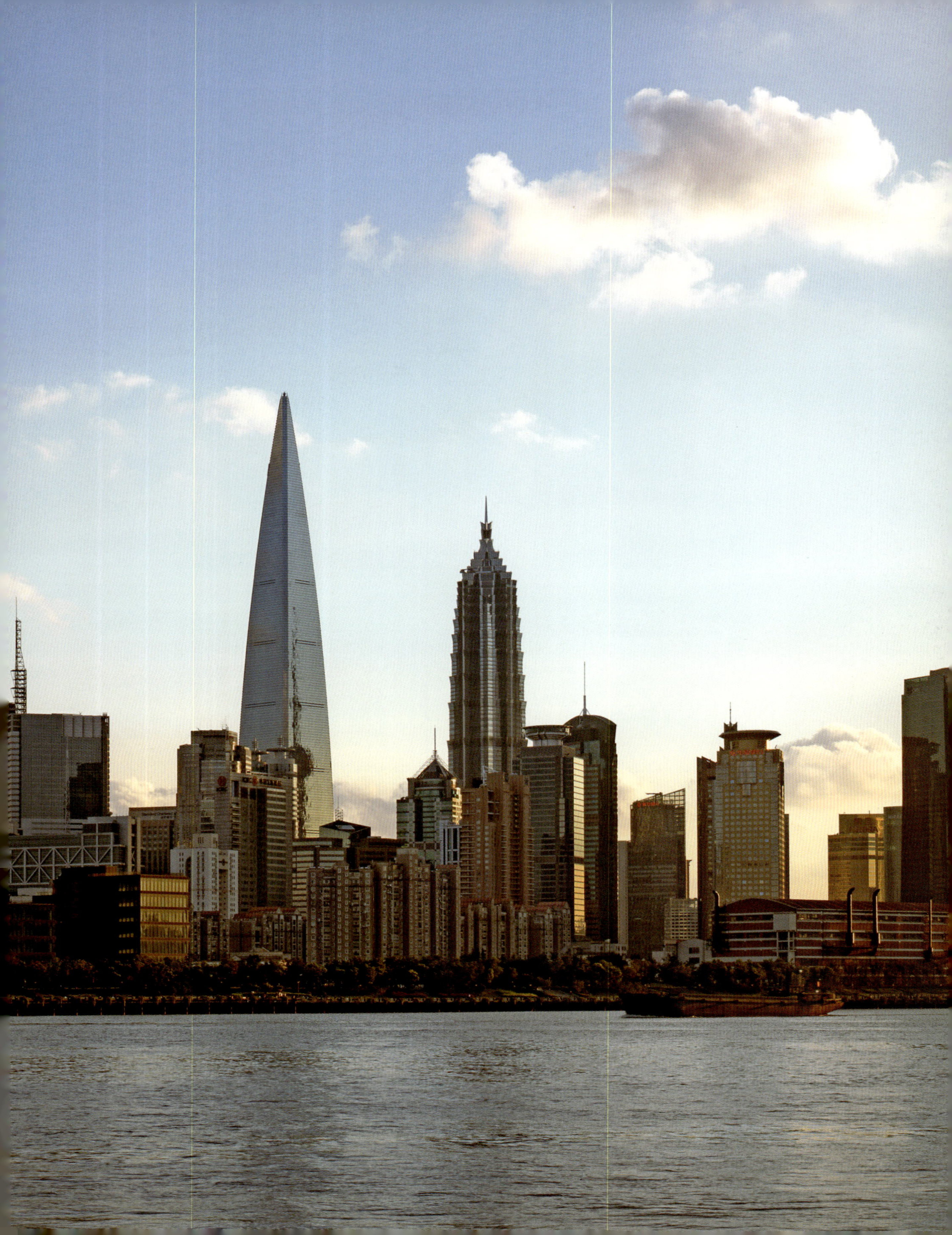

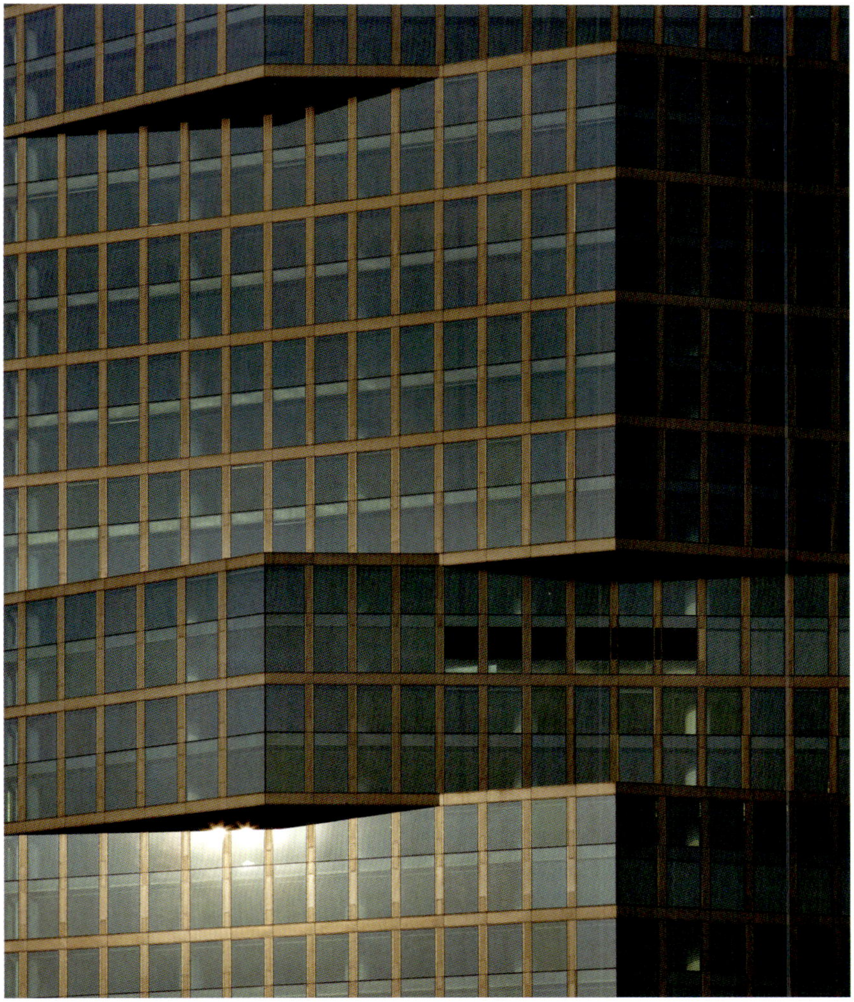

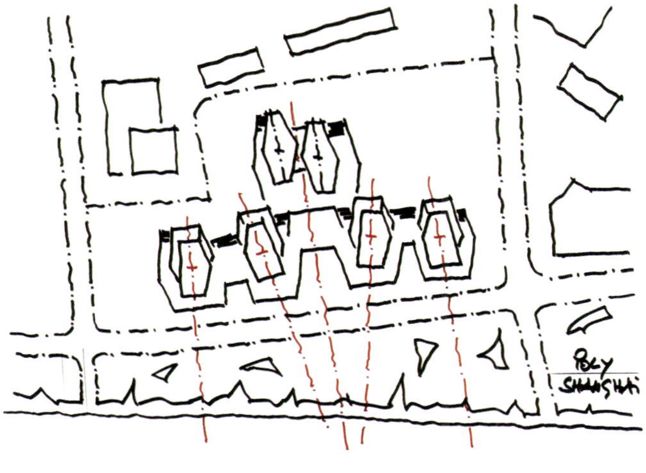

156　保利大廈　上海

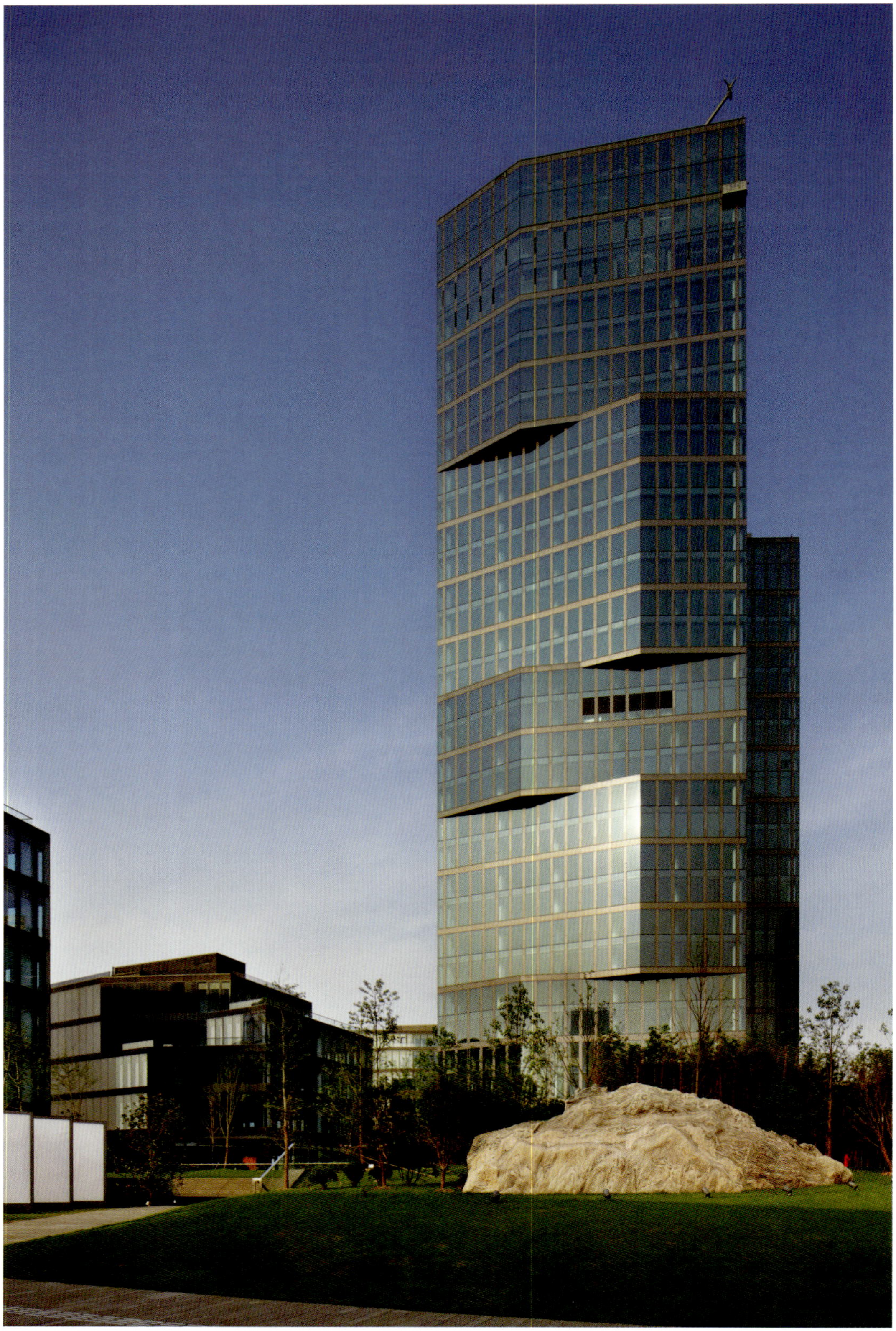

Poly Plaza Shanghai

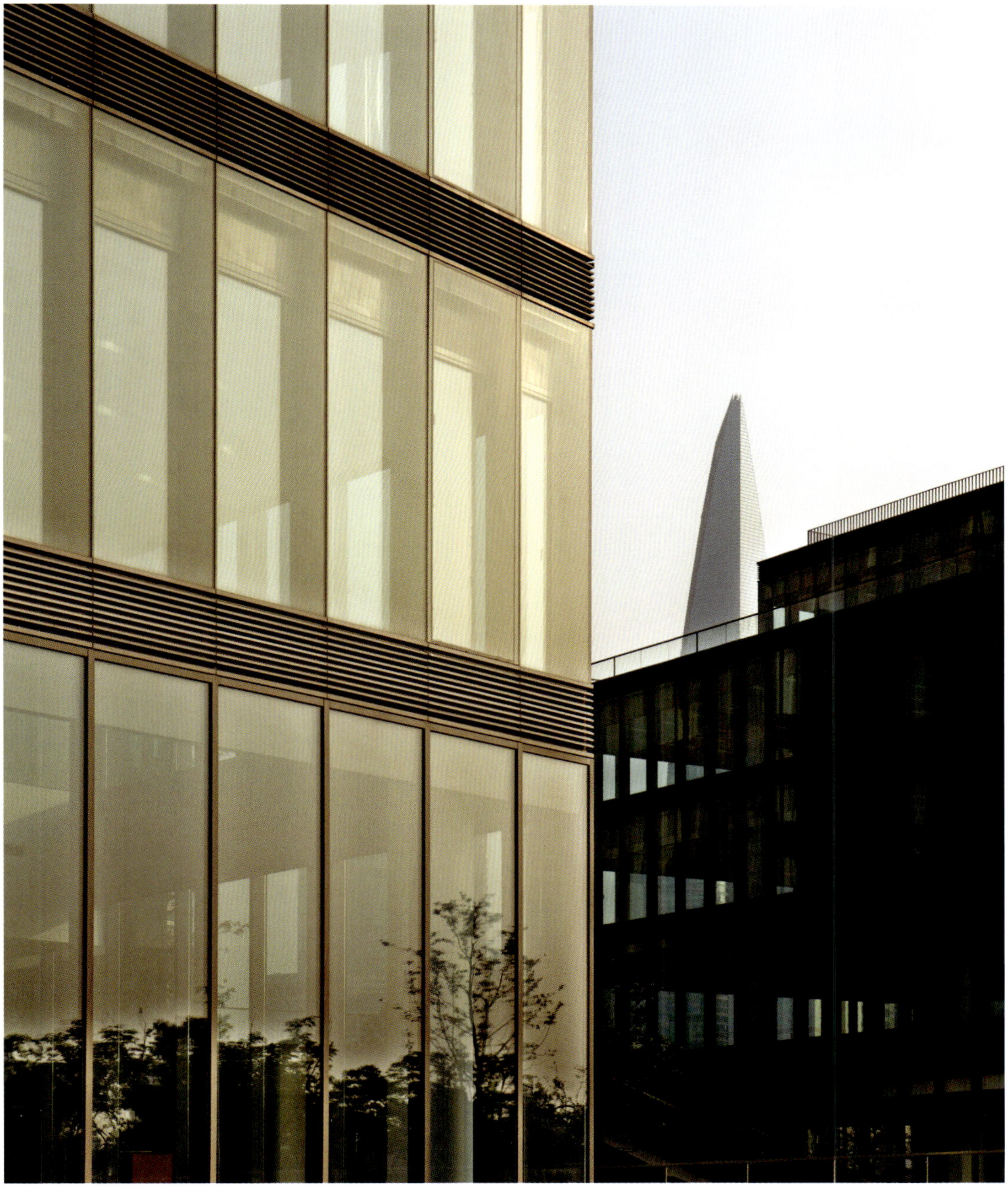

保利大廈　上海

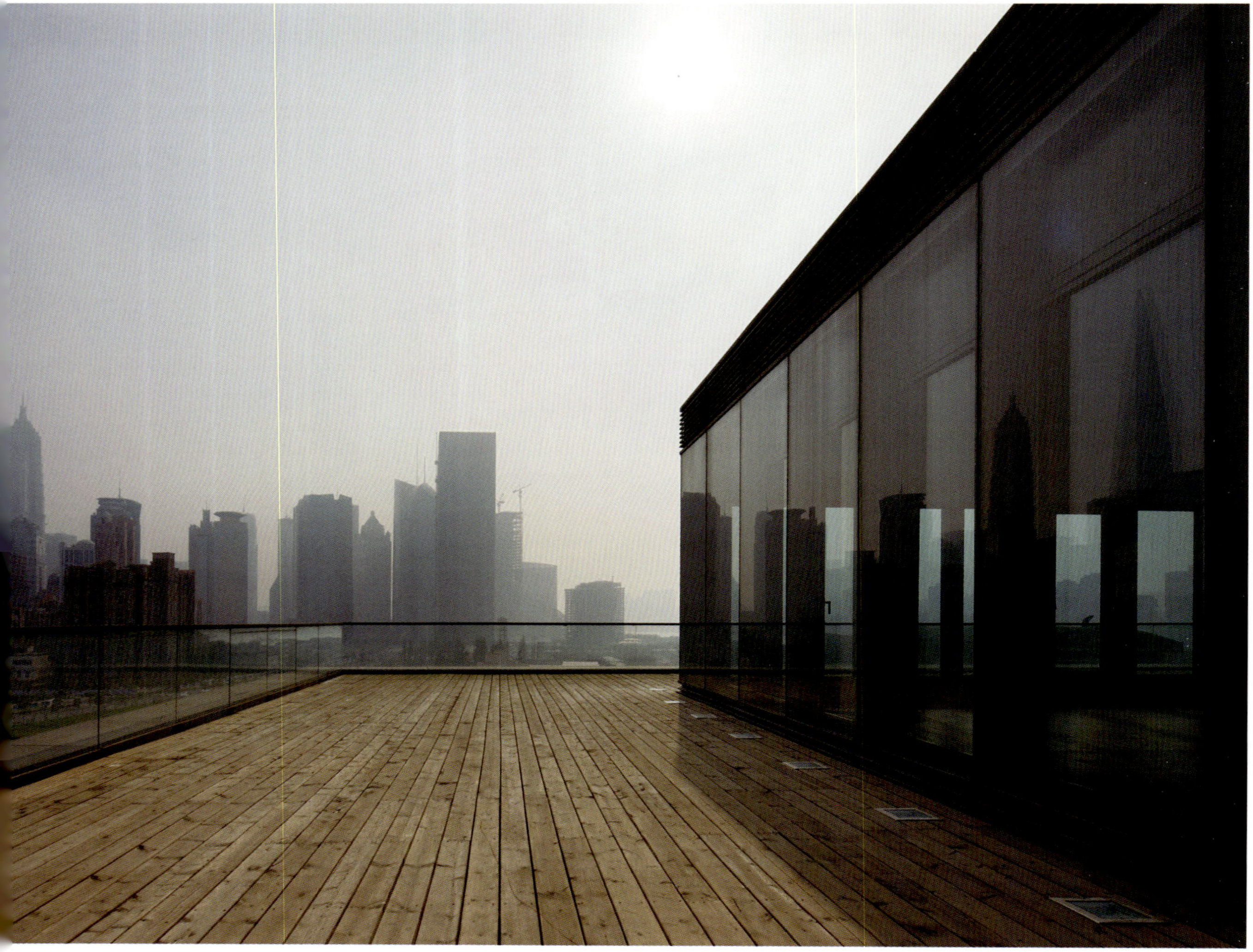

Poly Plaza Shanghai

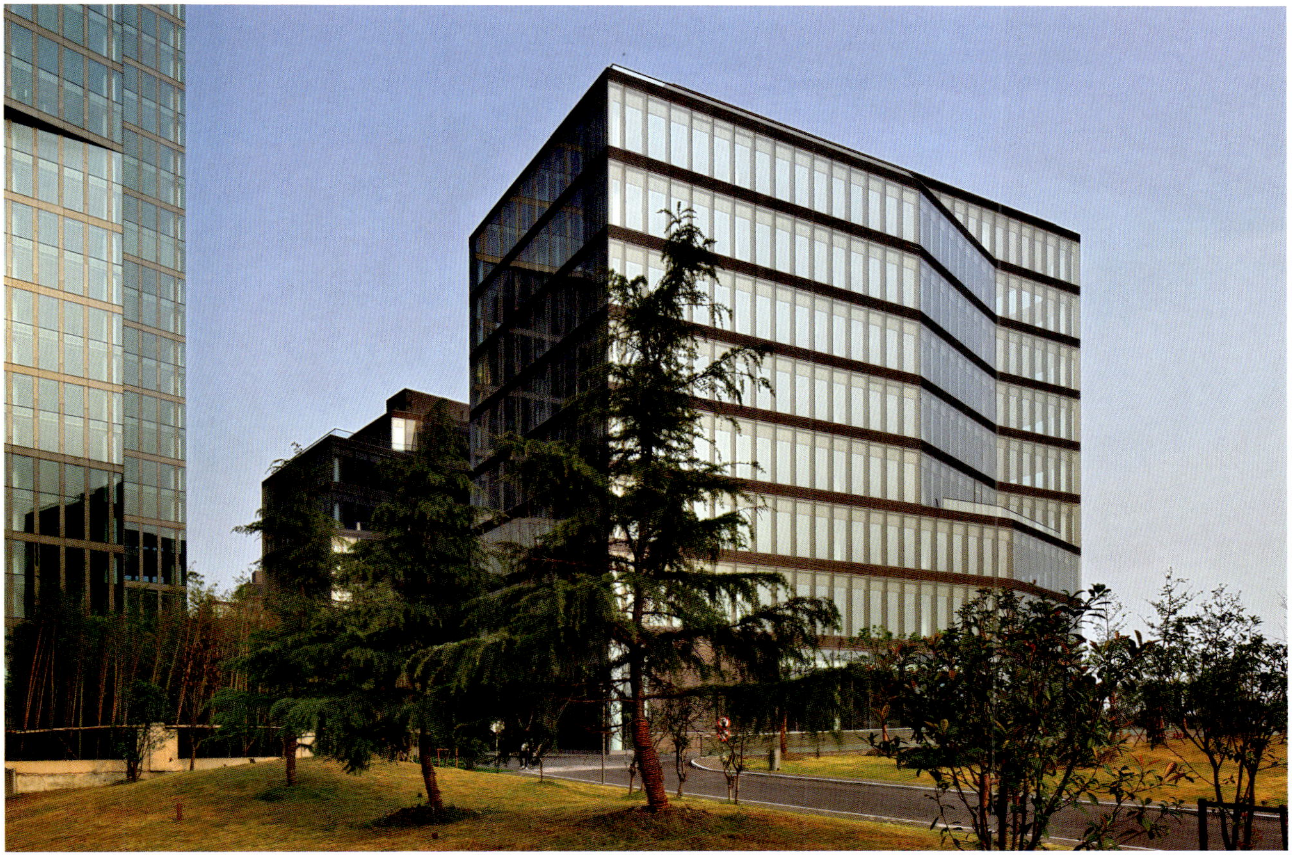

保利大廈　上海

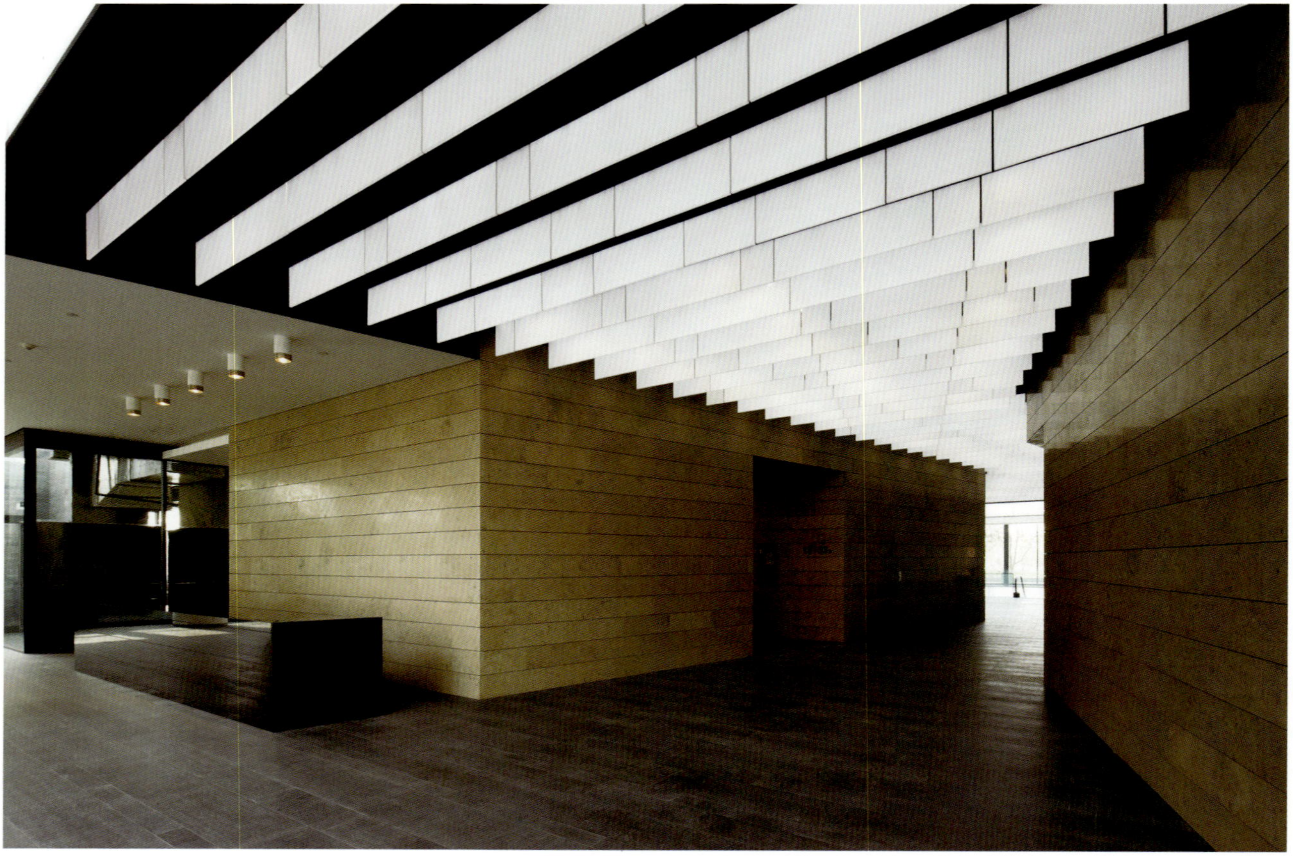

Poly Plaza Shanghai

162 ²⁰↑

2011年世界大学生运动会体育中心
深圳，中国
Universiade 2011 Sports Center
Shenzhen, China

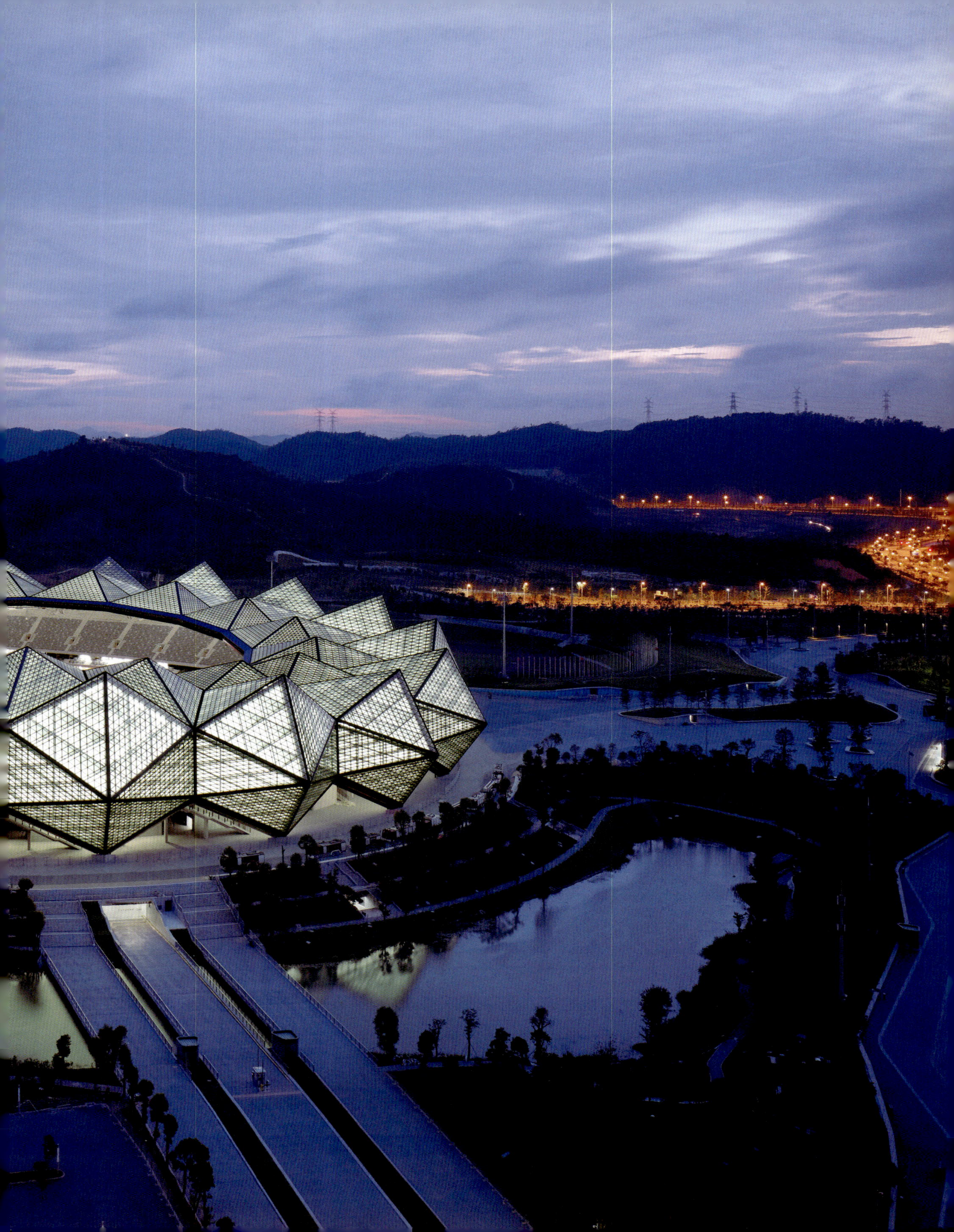

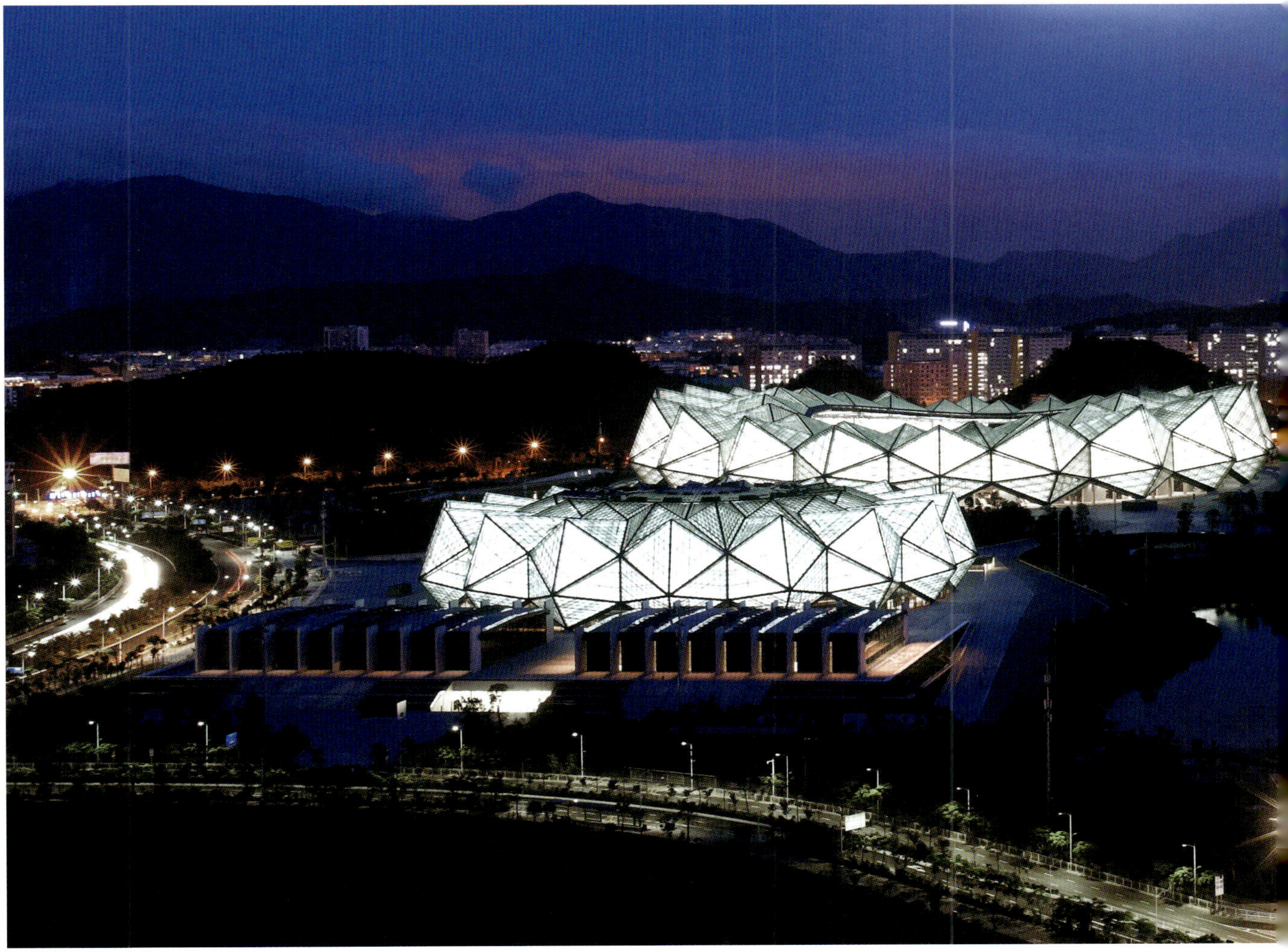

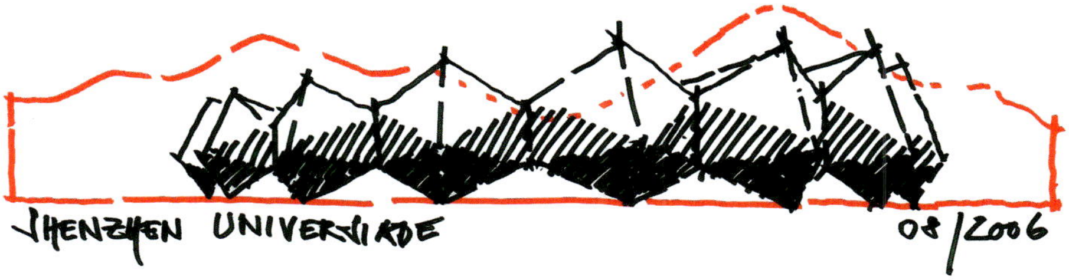

SHENZHEN UNIVERSIADE   08/2006

2011年世界大学生运动会体育中心　深圳

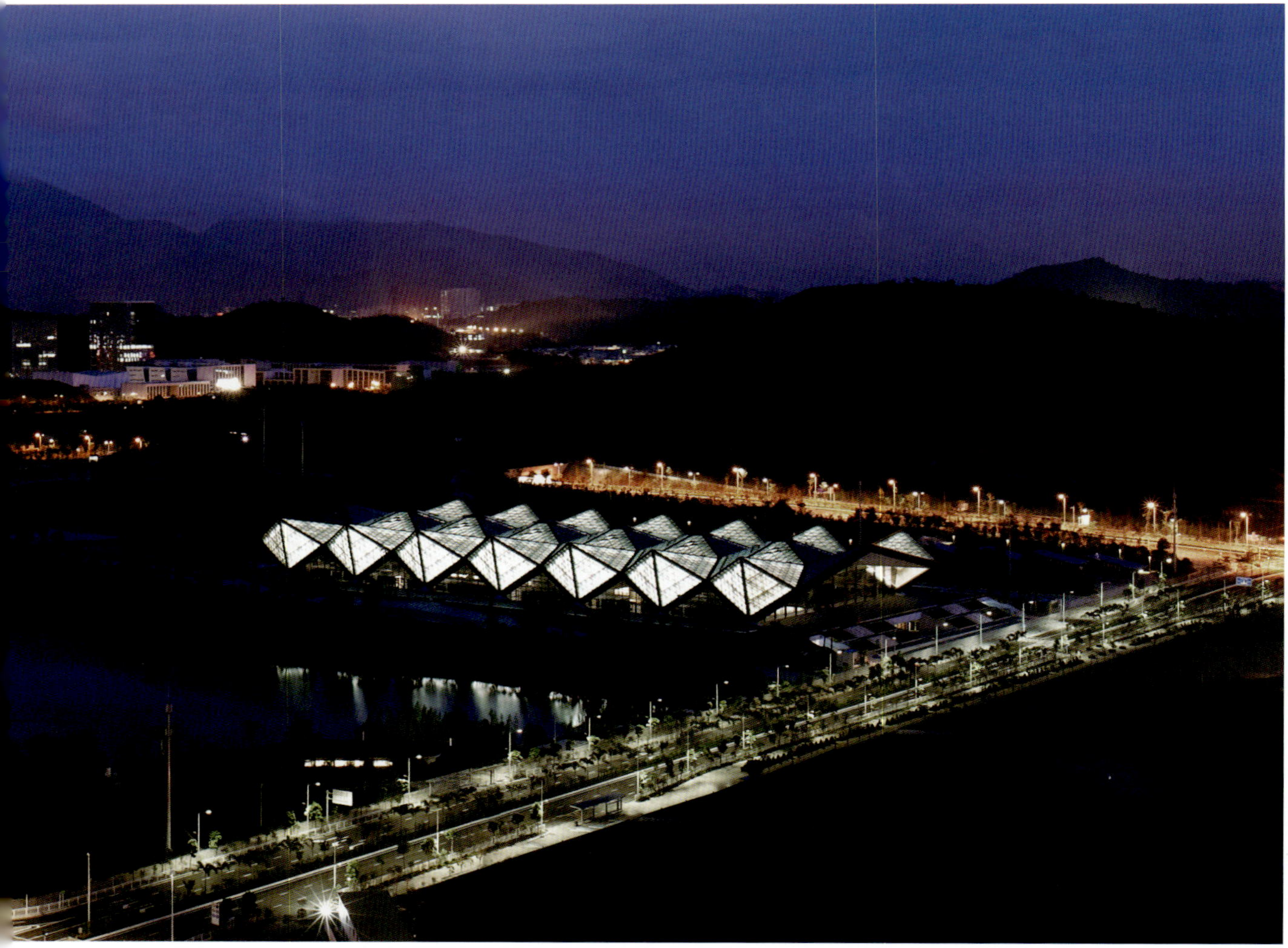

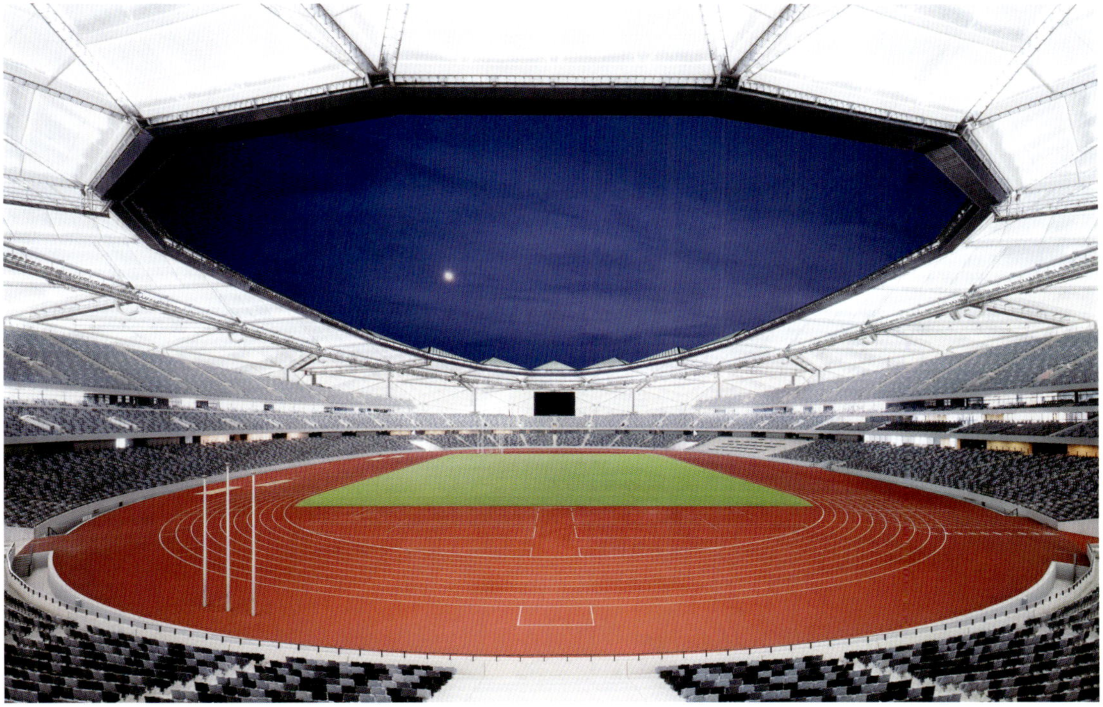

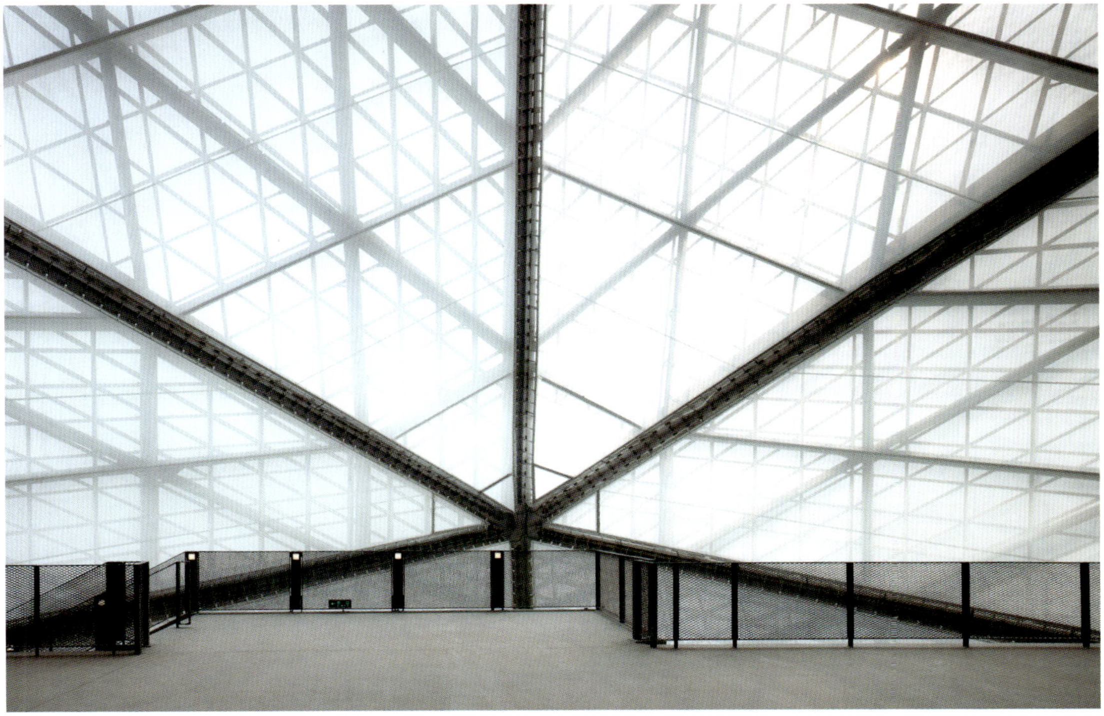

2011年世界大学生运动会体育中心　深圳

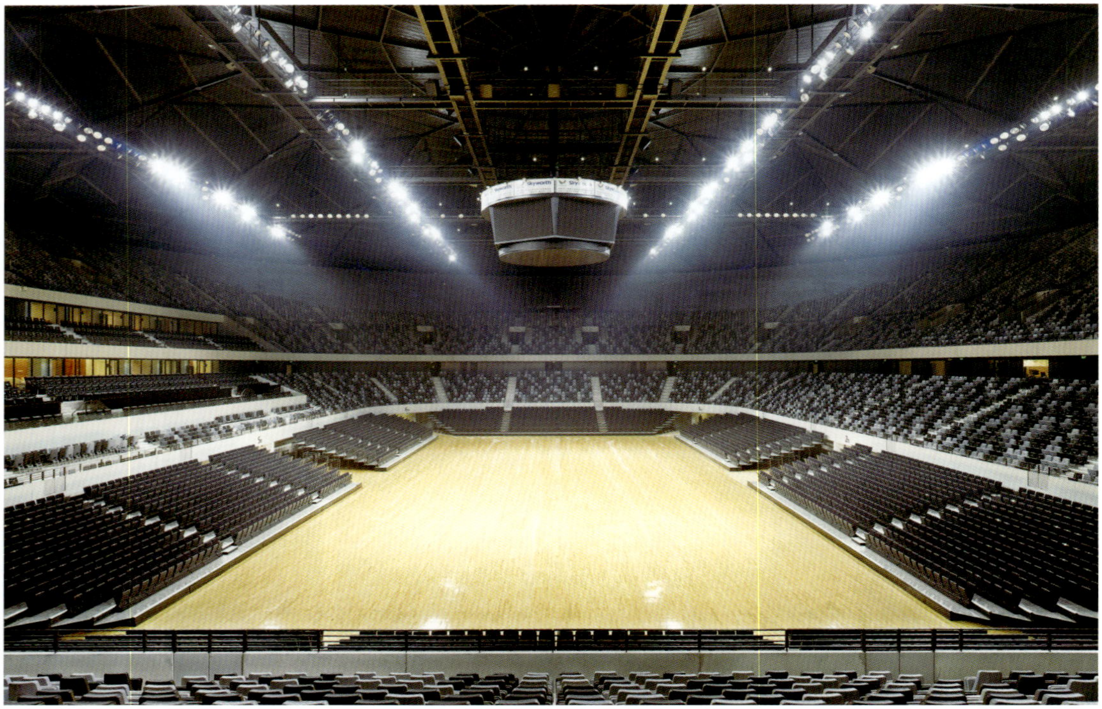

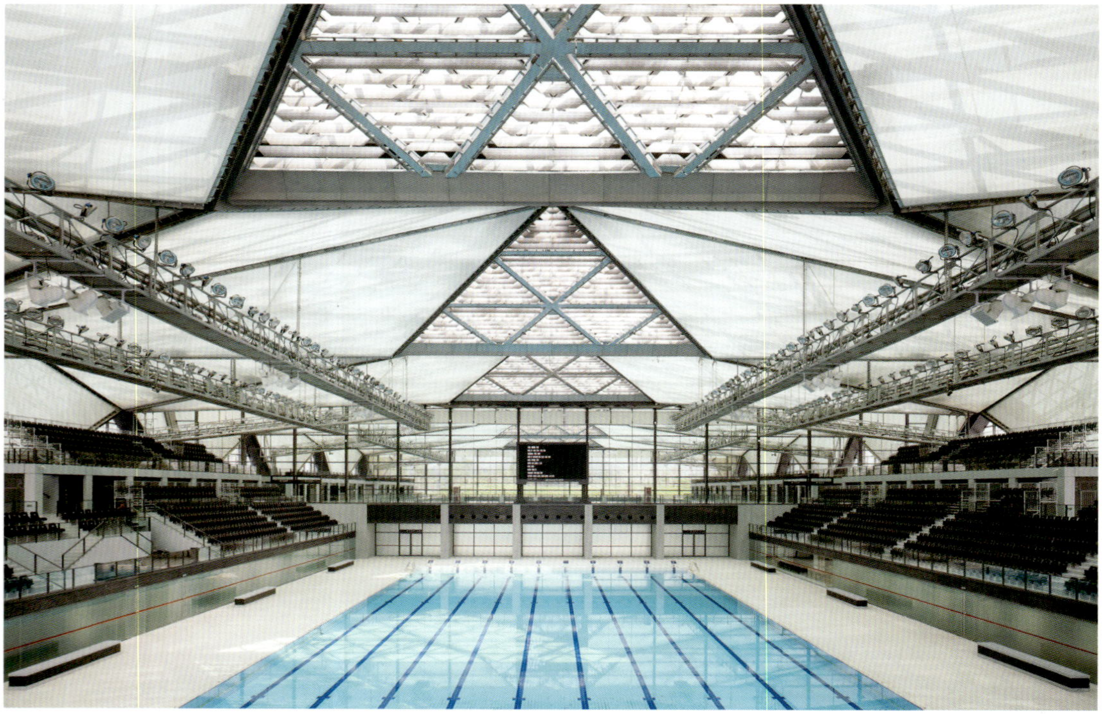

Universiade 2011 Sports Center ShenZhen

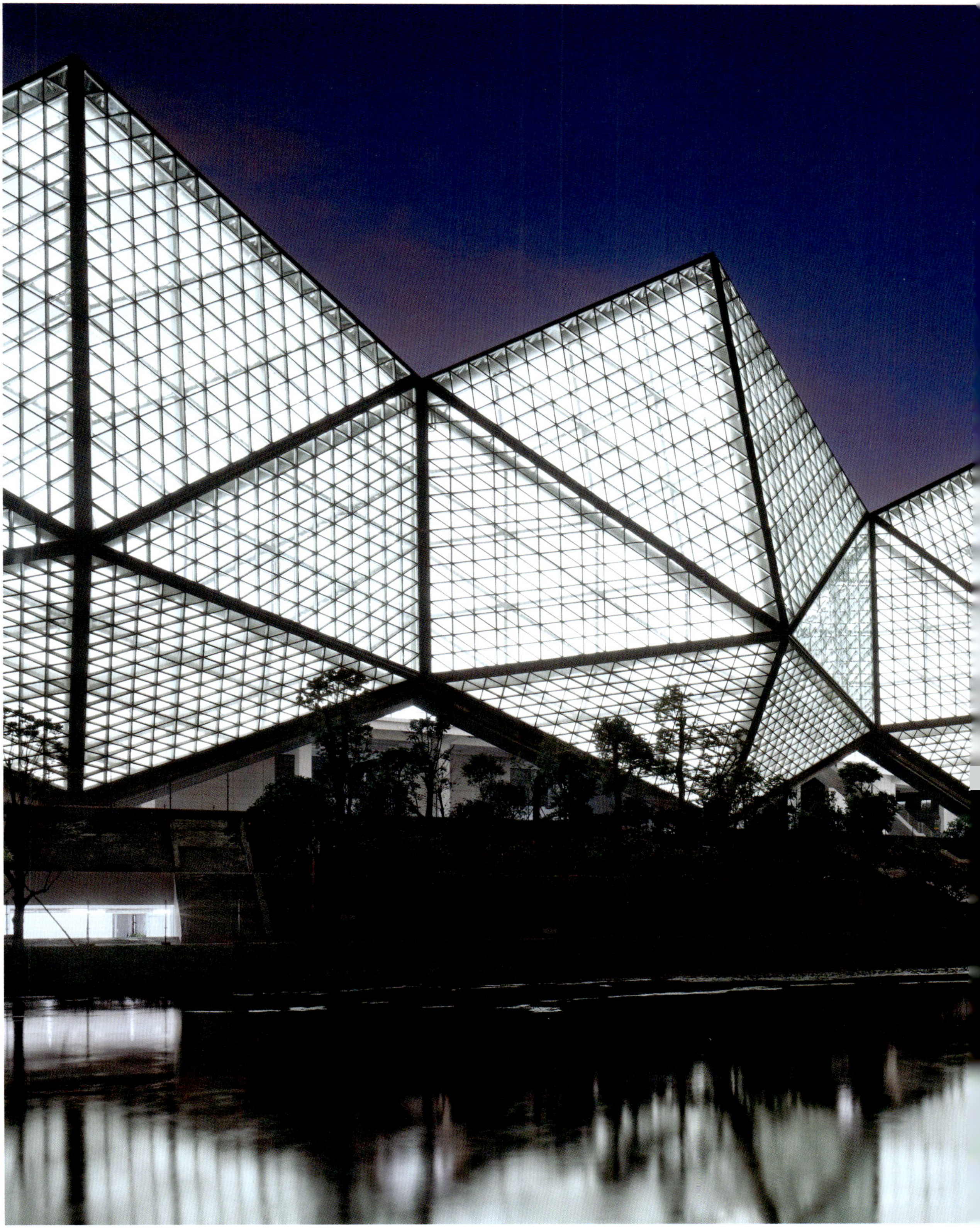

2011年世界大学生运动会体育中心　深圳

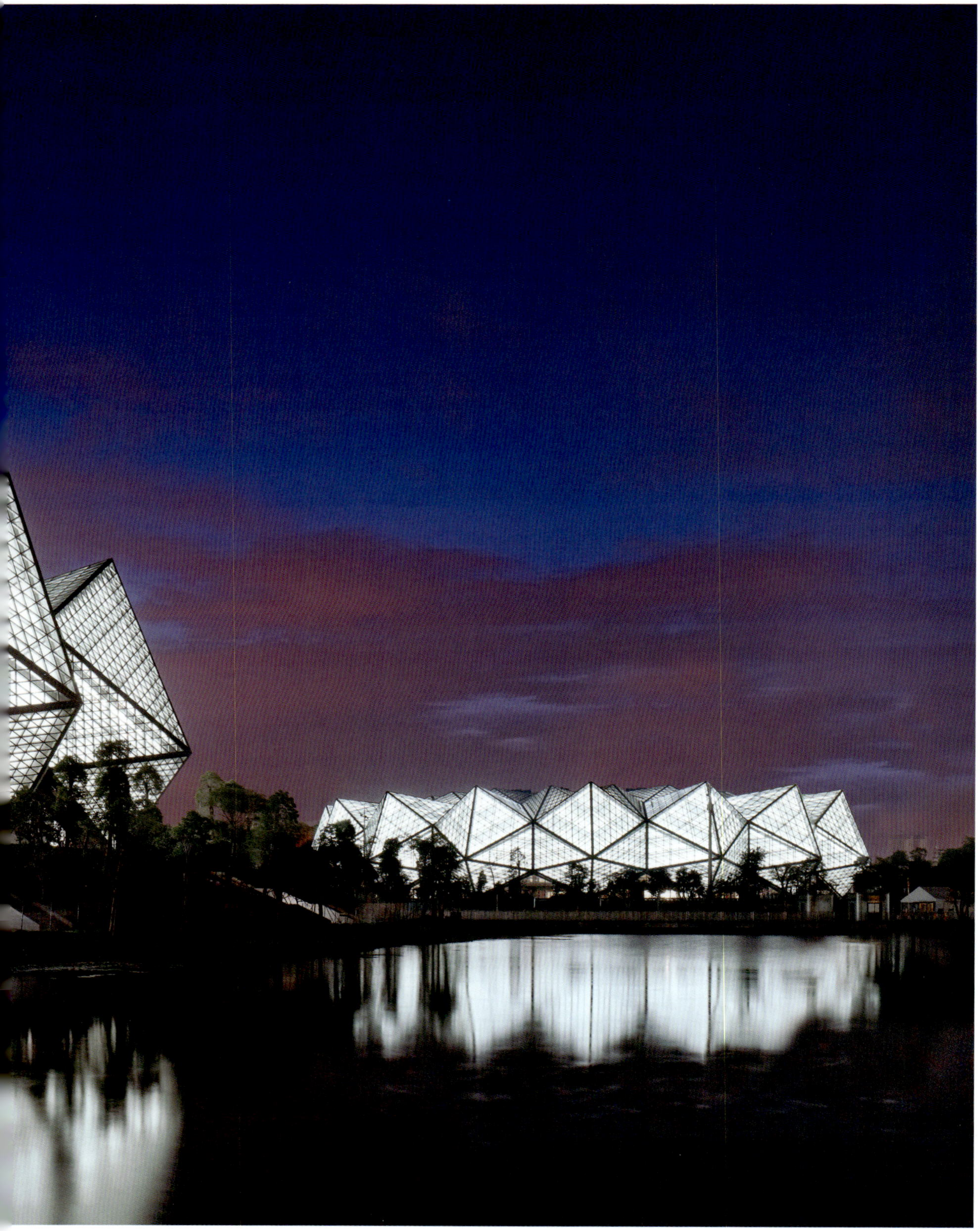

Universiade 2011 Sports Center ShenZhen

170 ²⁰ ↑

宝安体育场
深圳，中国

Bao'an Stadium
Shenzhen, China

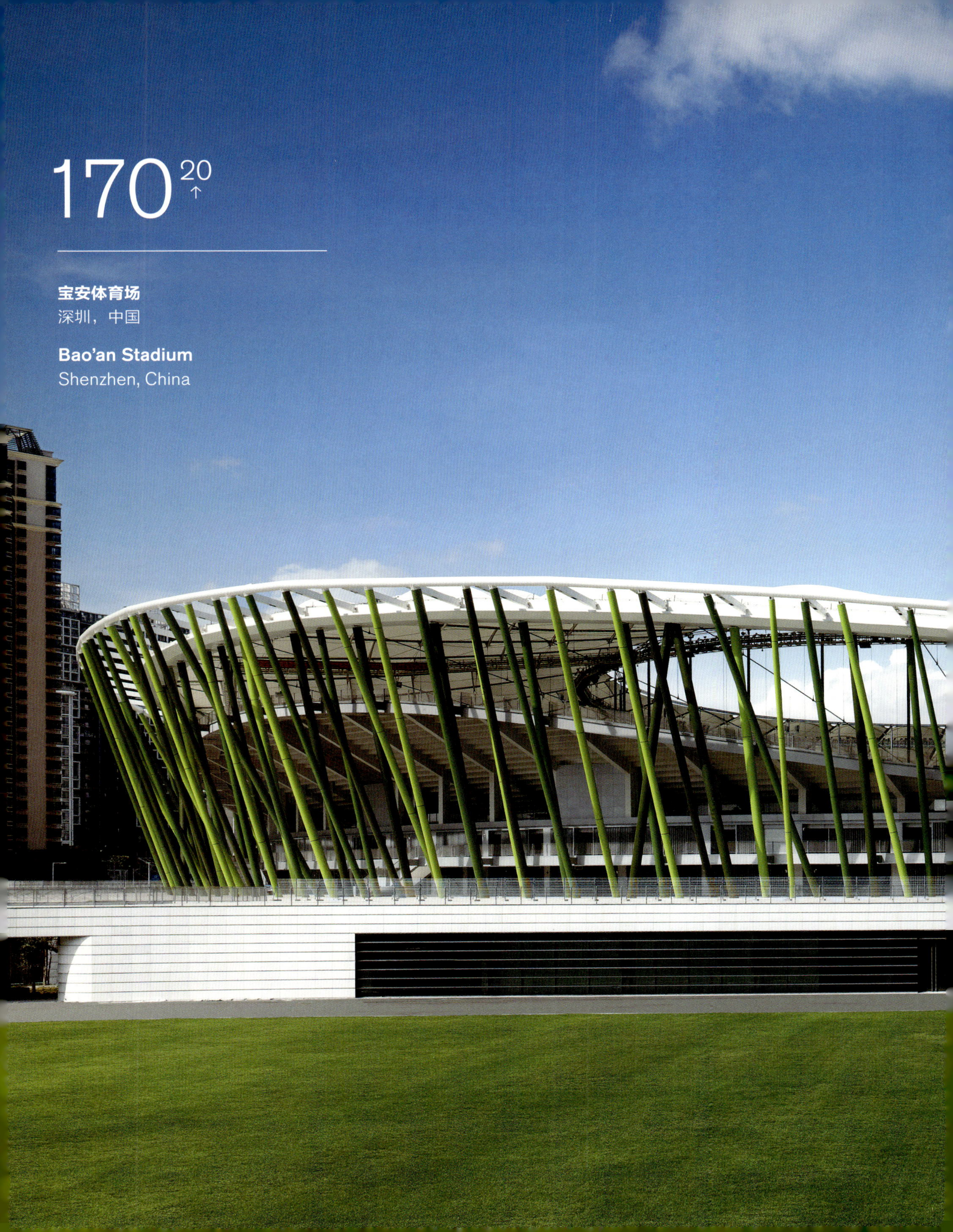

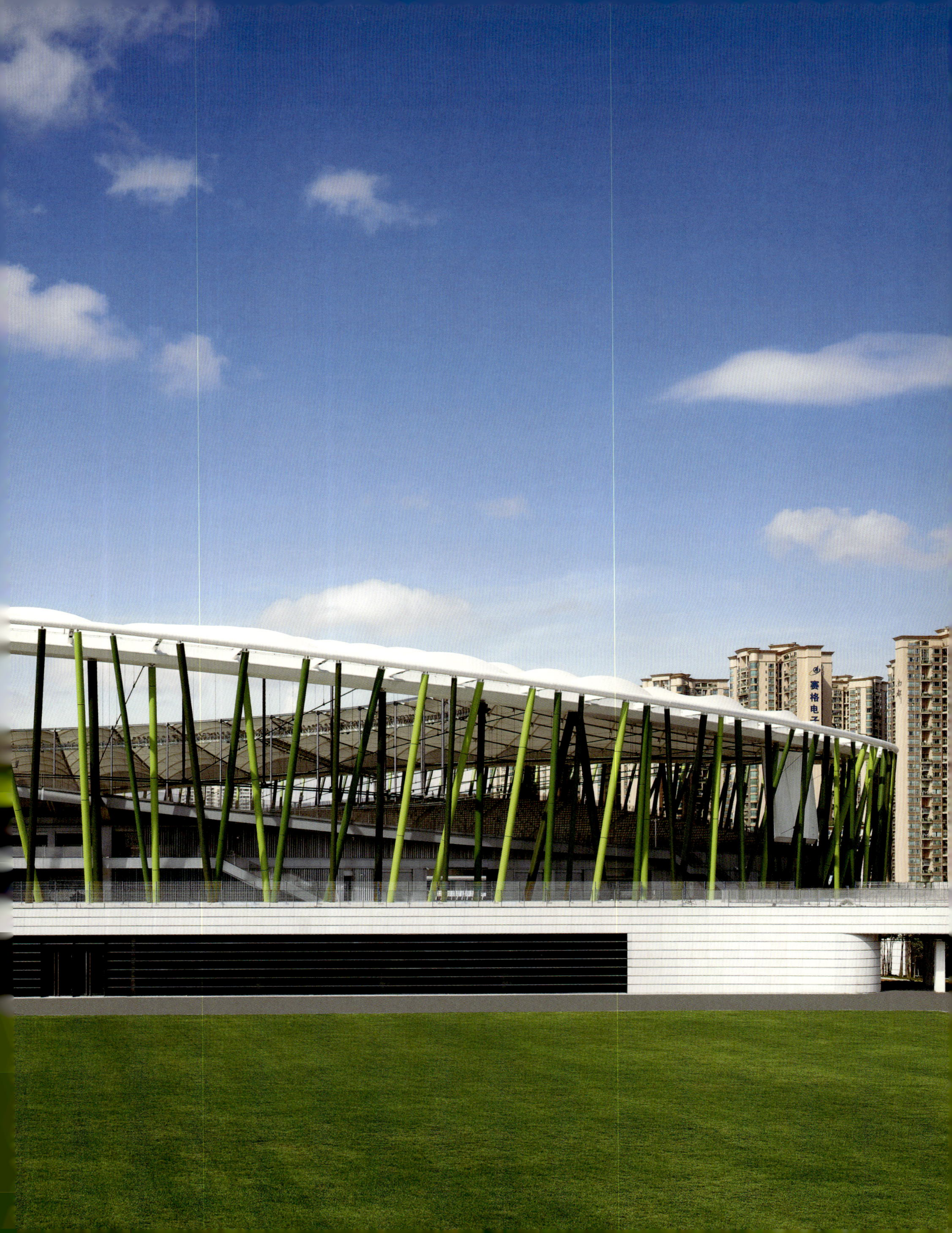
赛格电

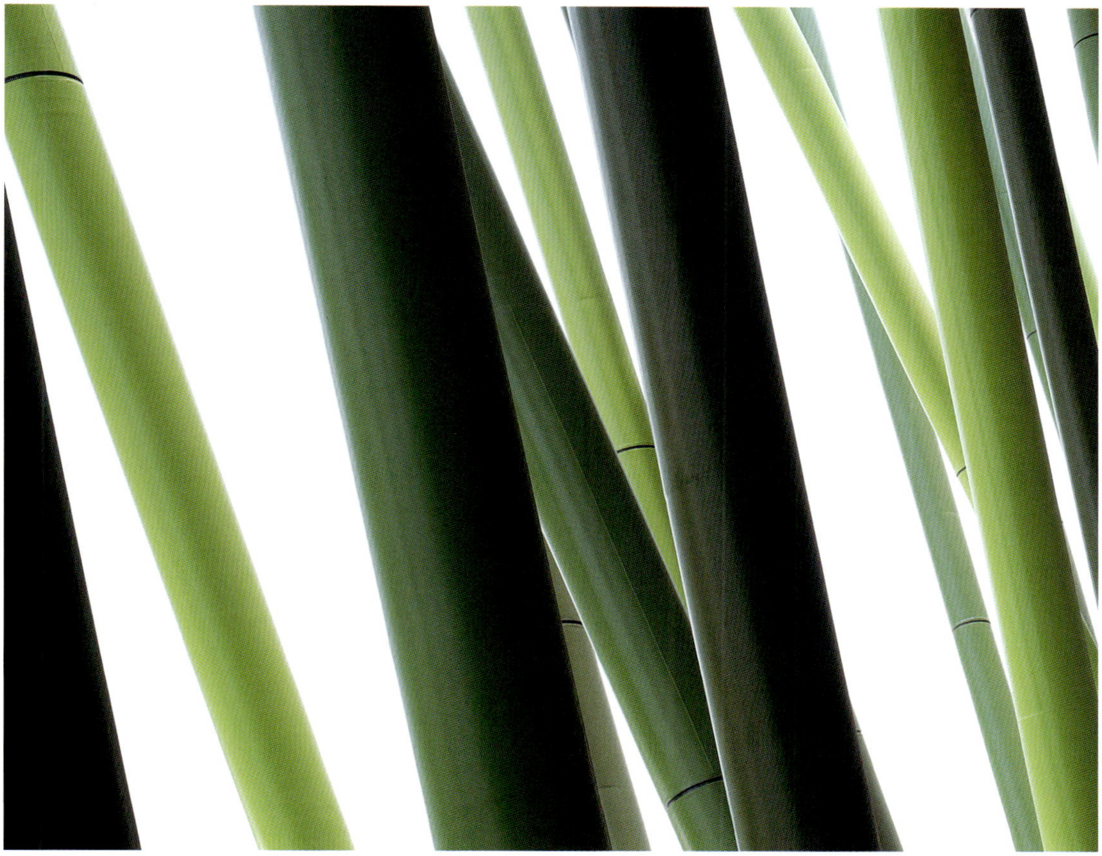

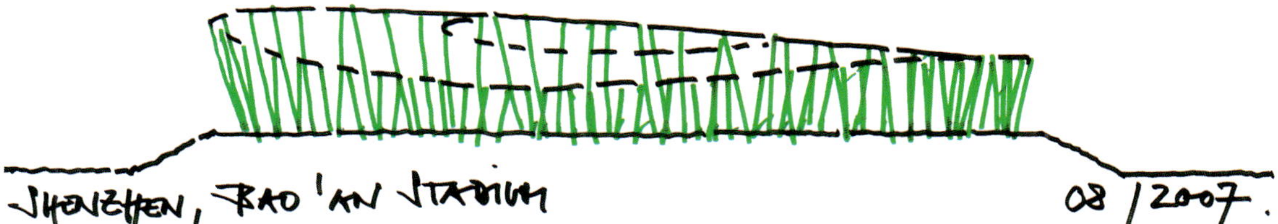

SHENZHEN, BAO'AN STADIUM   08/2007.

宝安体育场　深圳

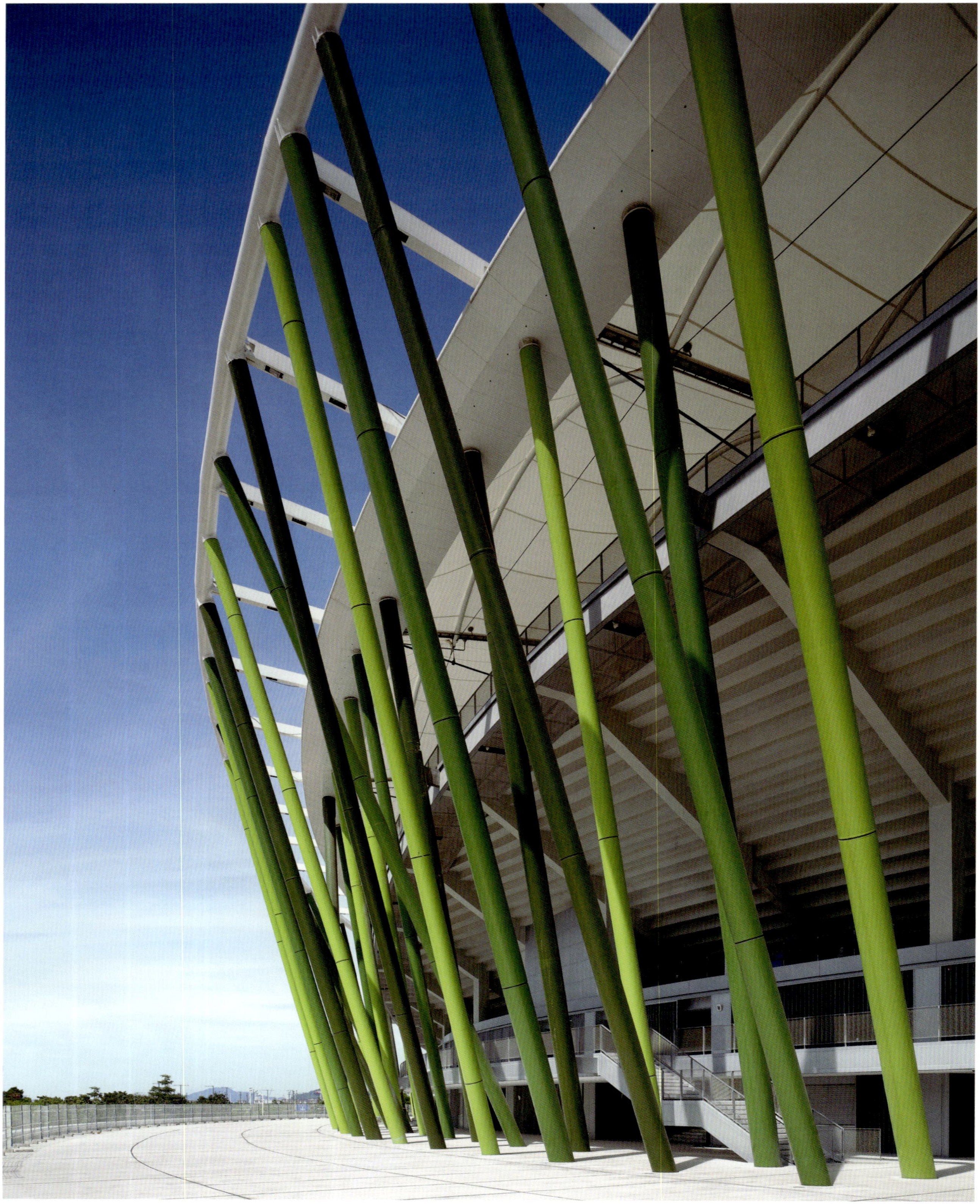

Bao'an Stadium Shenzhen

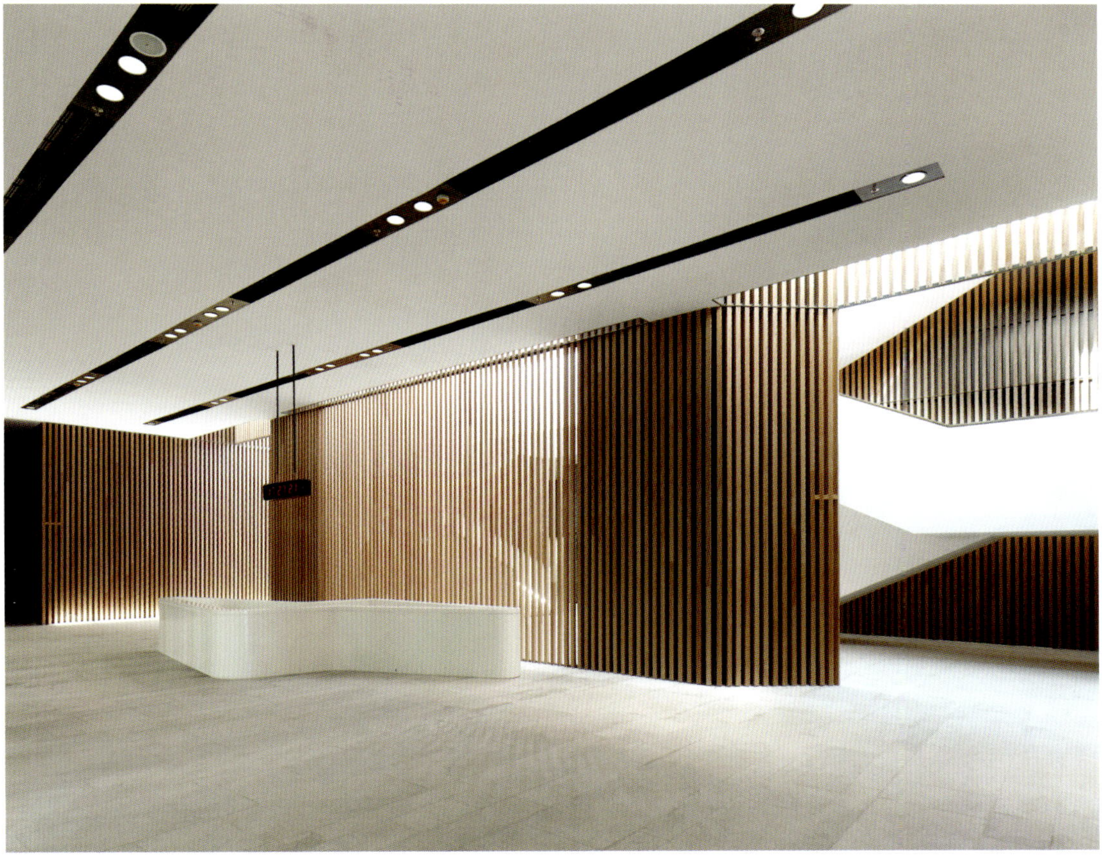

宝安体育场　深圳

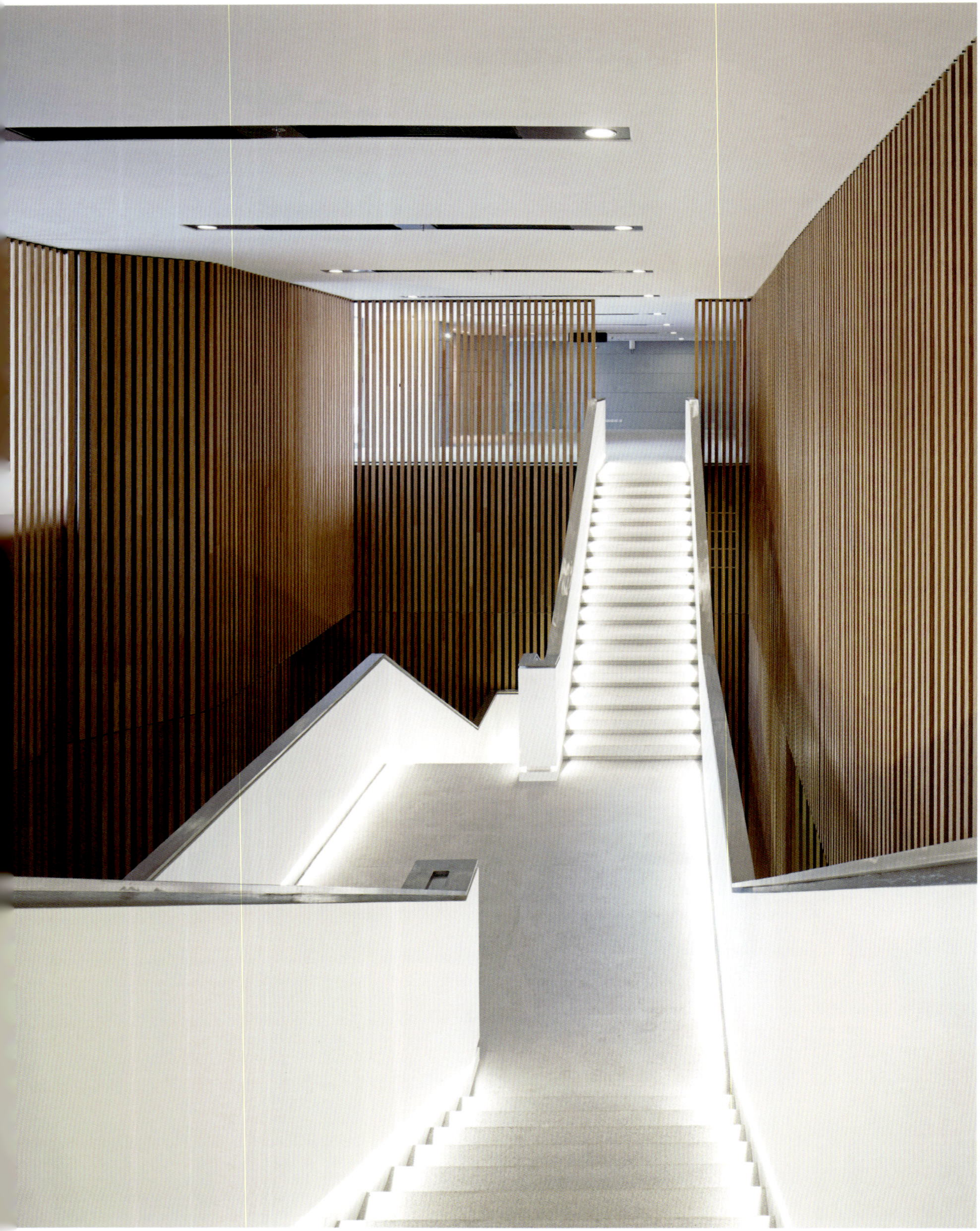

Bao'an Stadium Shenzhen

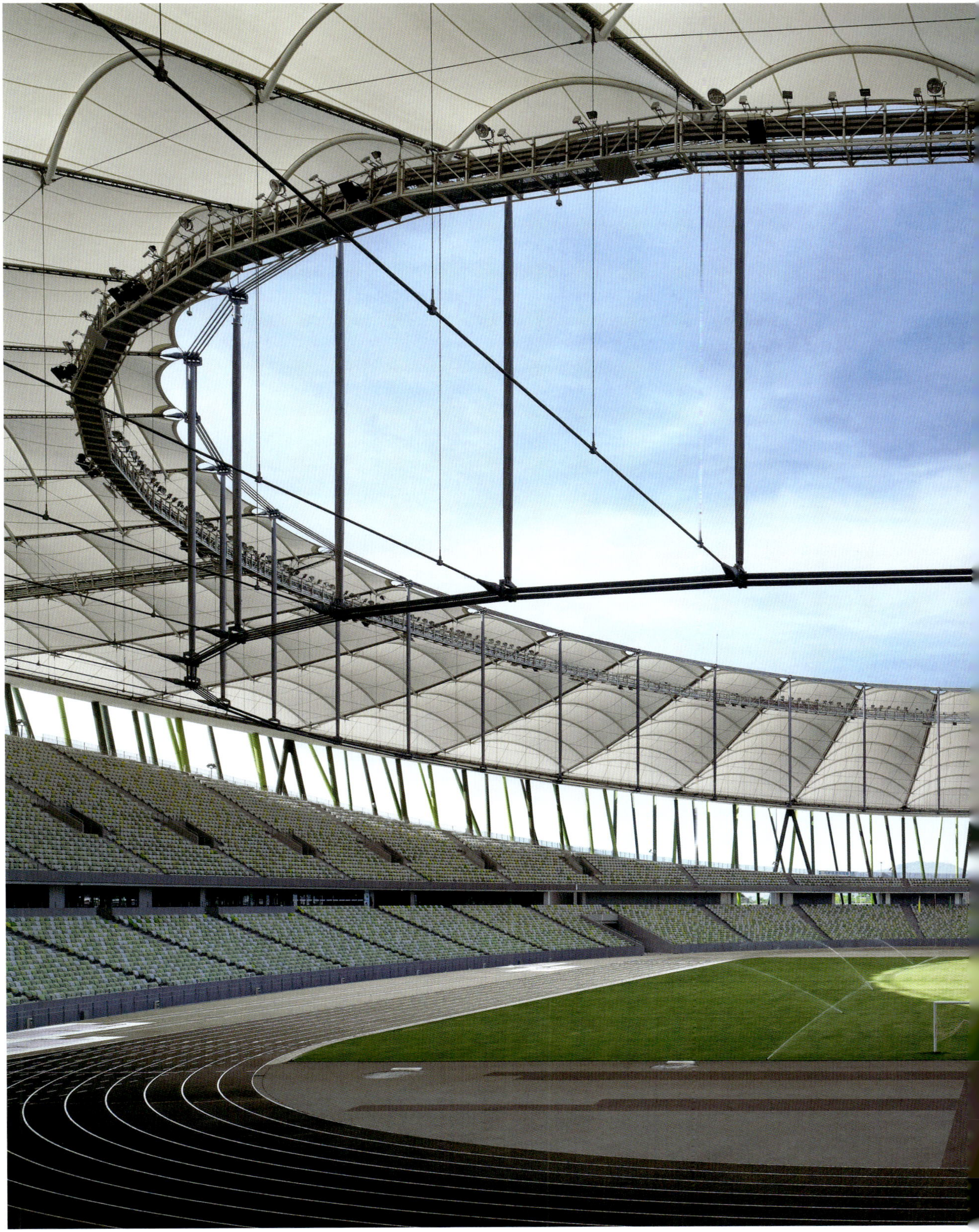

宝安体育场　深圳

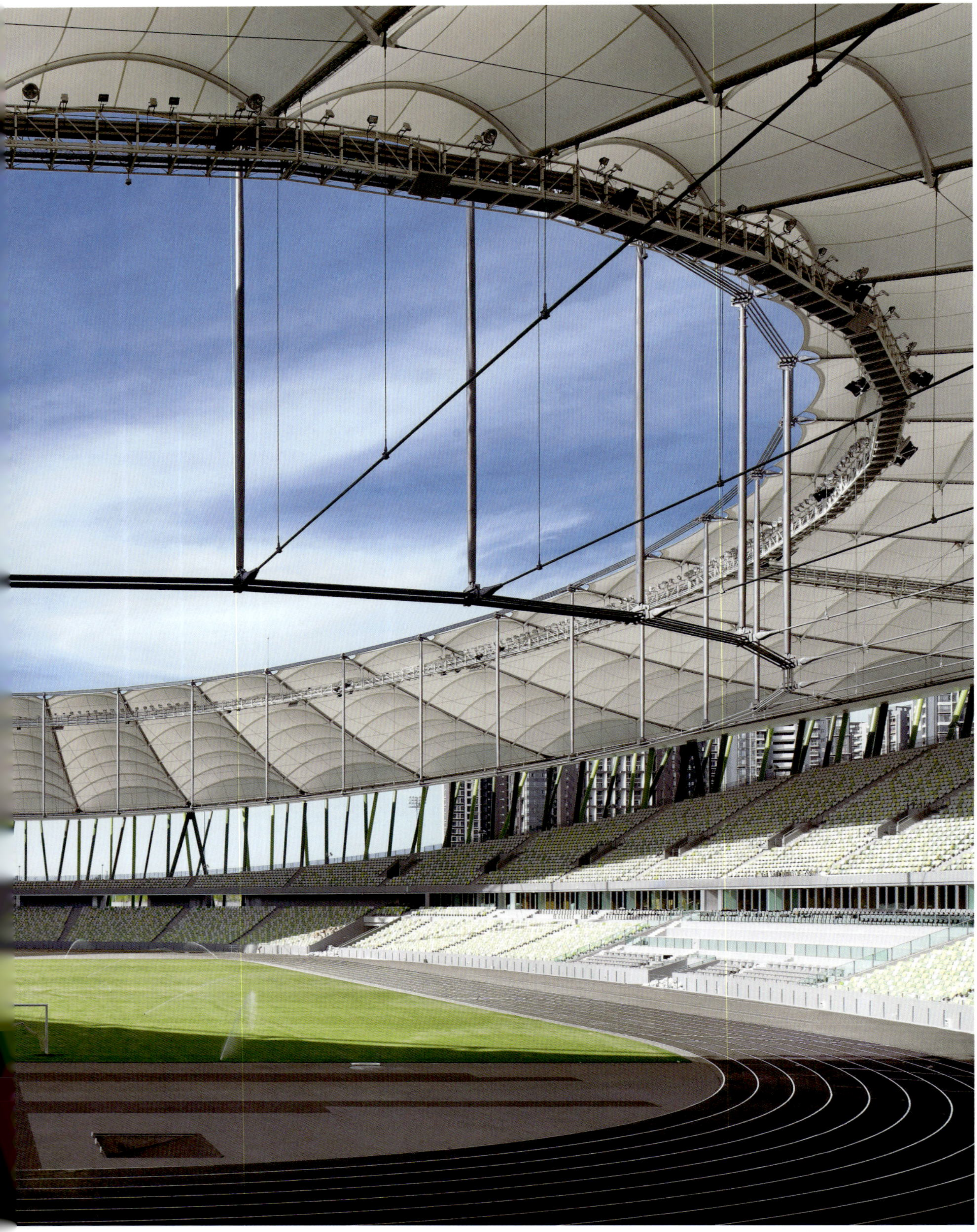

178 21/1

华为科研中心办公楼
深圳，中国

Huawei Development & Research Office Buildings
Shenzhen, China

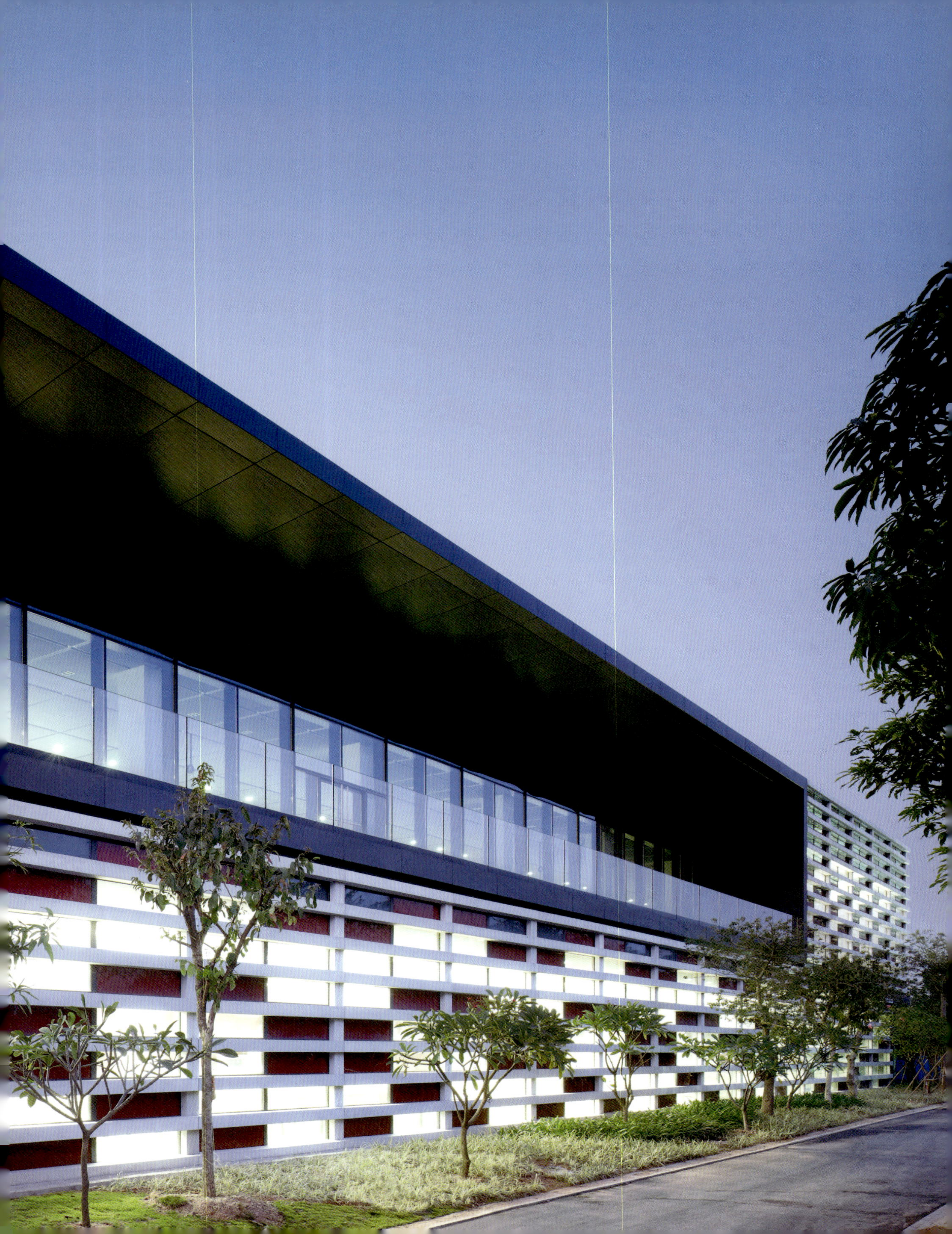

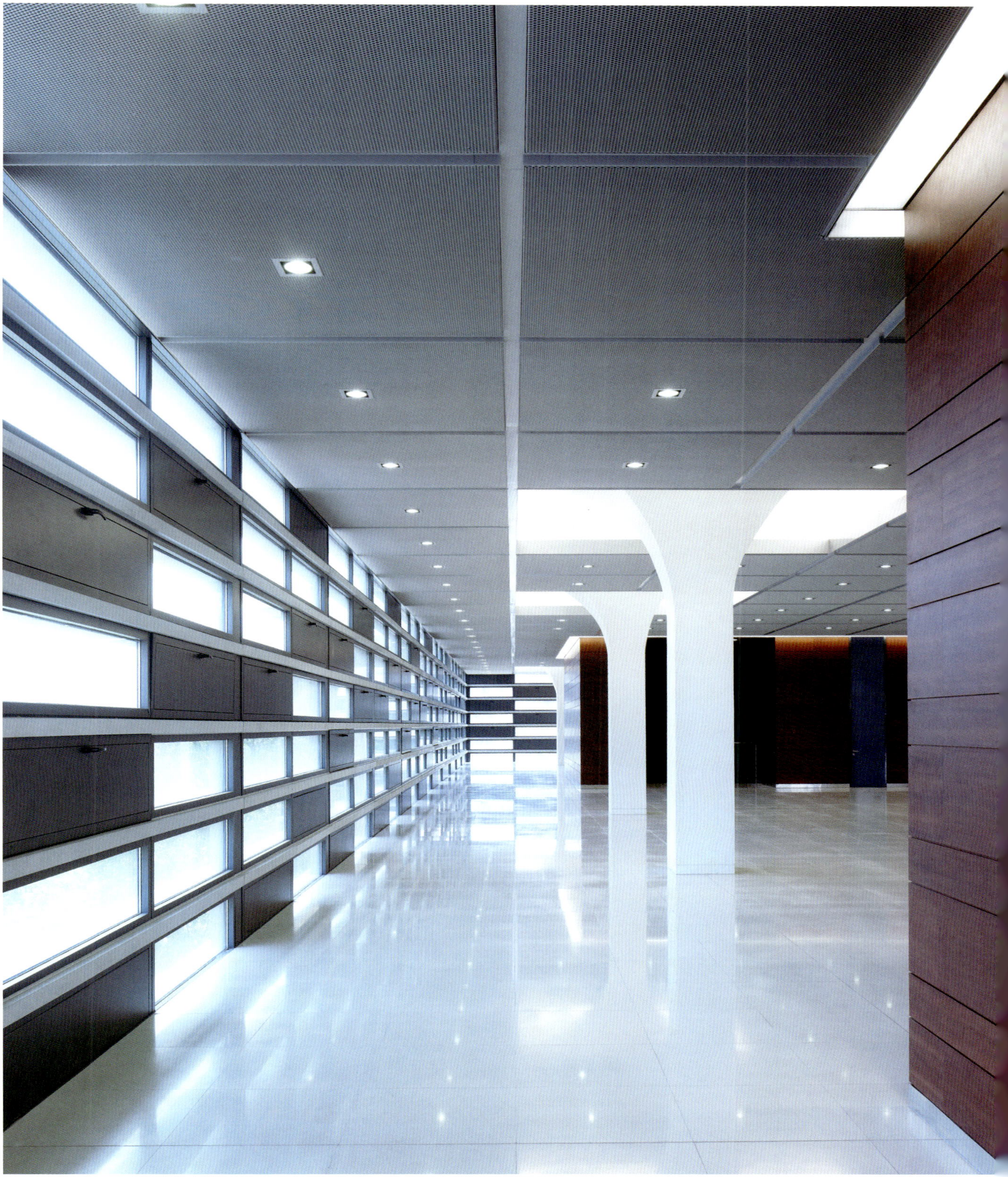

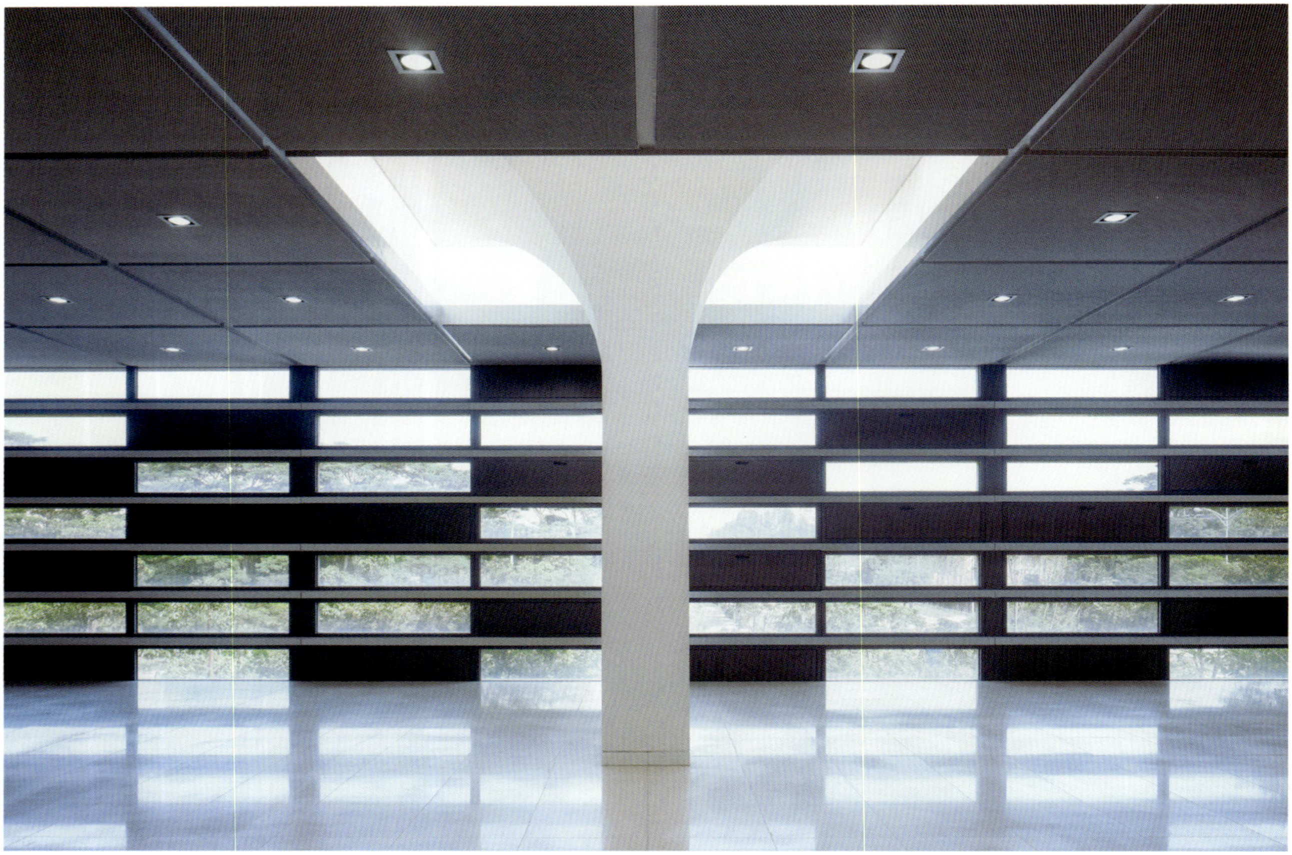

Huawei Development & Research Office Buildings Shenzhen

182　华为科研中心办公楼　深圳

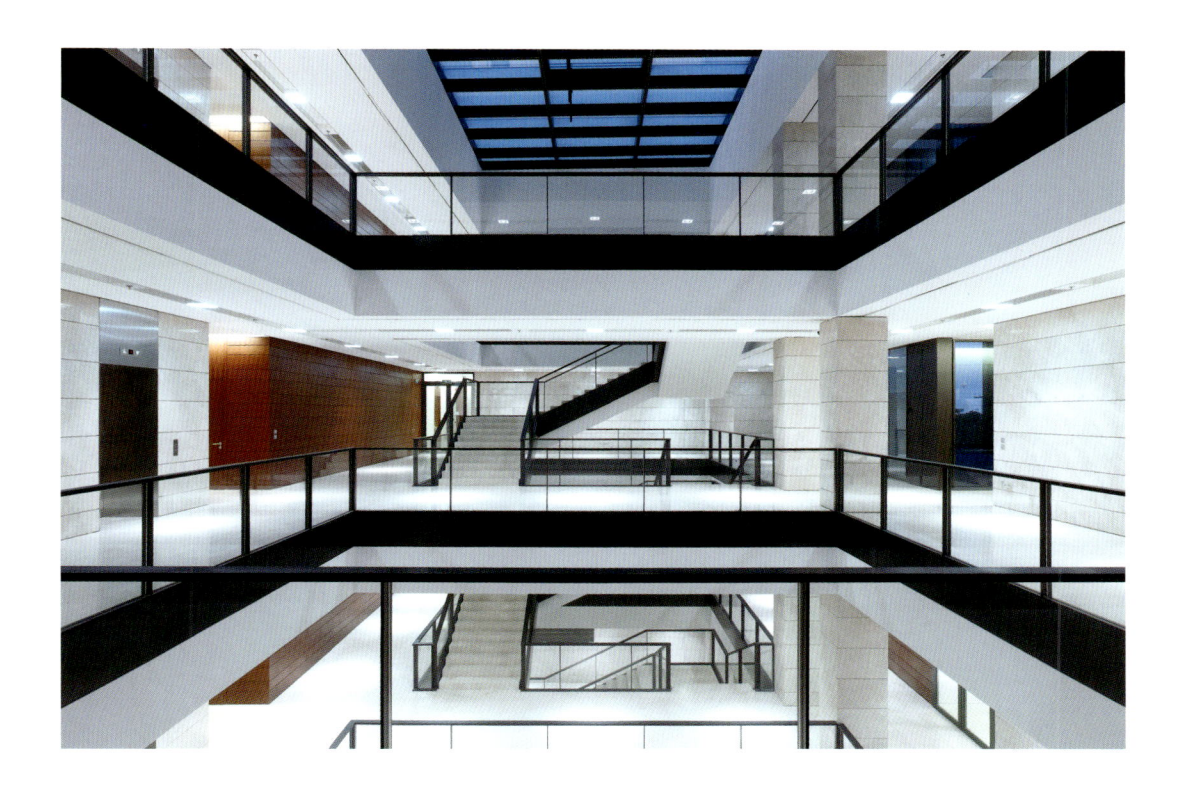

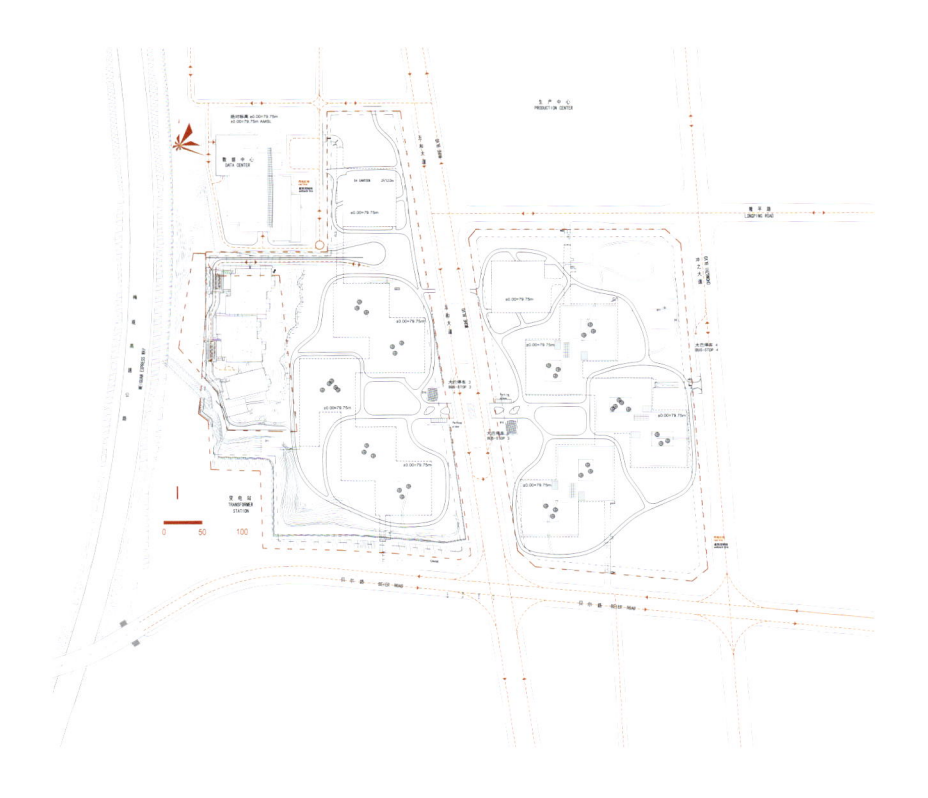

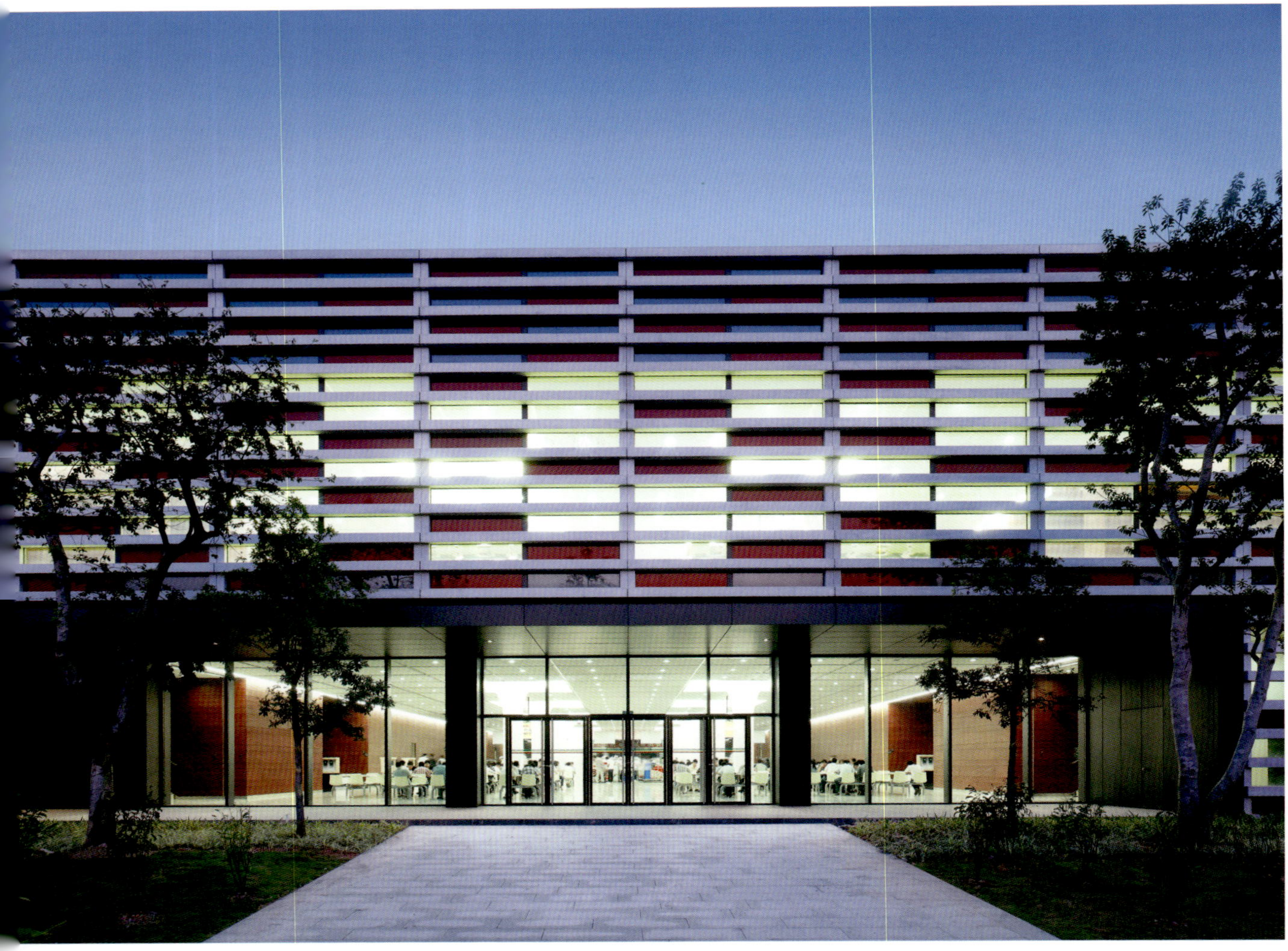

Huawei Development & Research Office Buildings Shenzhen

184 ^{21}
↑

国家议会大厦
河内，越南

Parliament House Hanoi
Hanoi, Vietnam

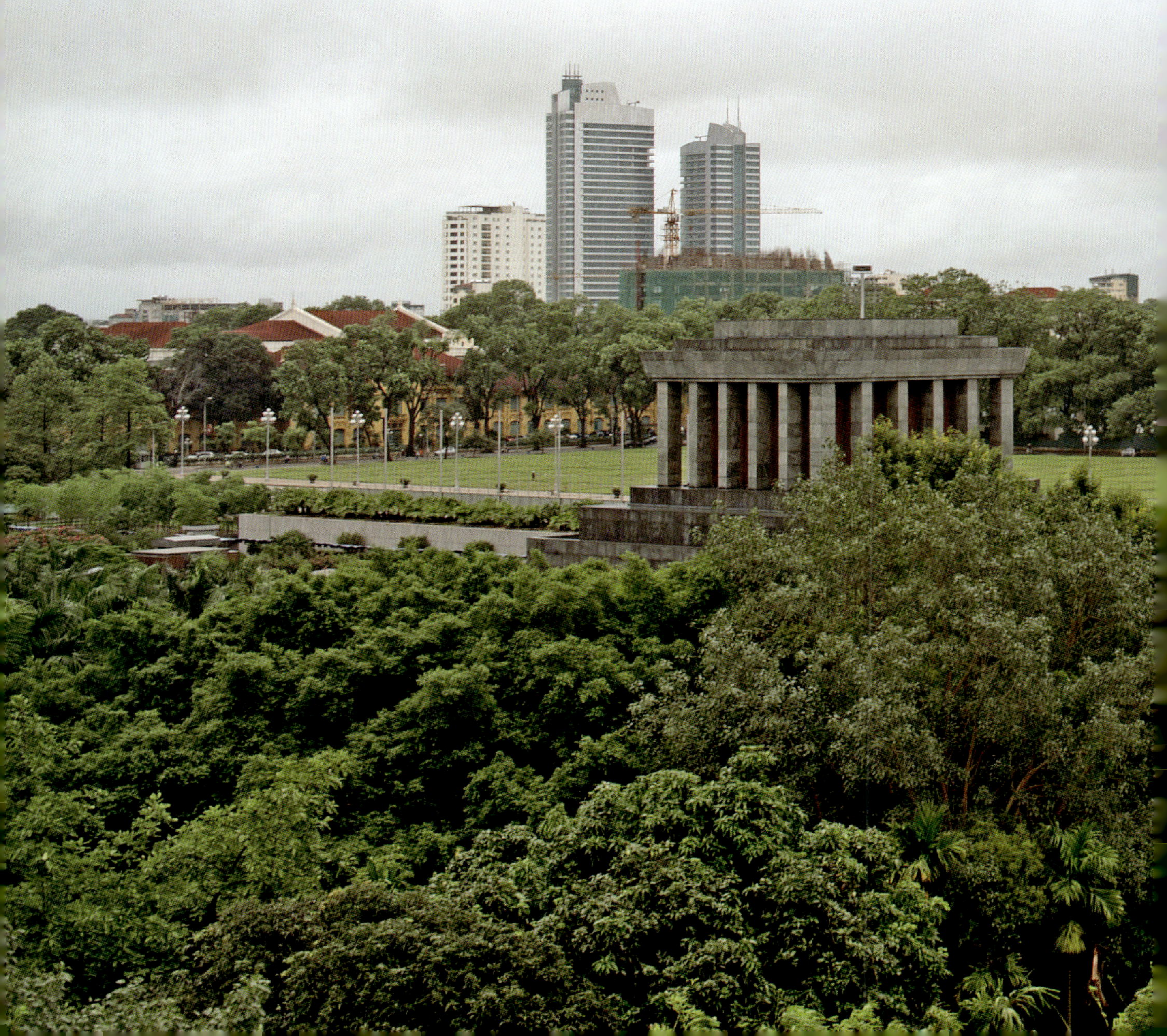

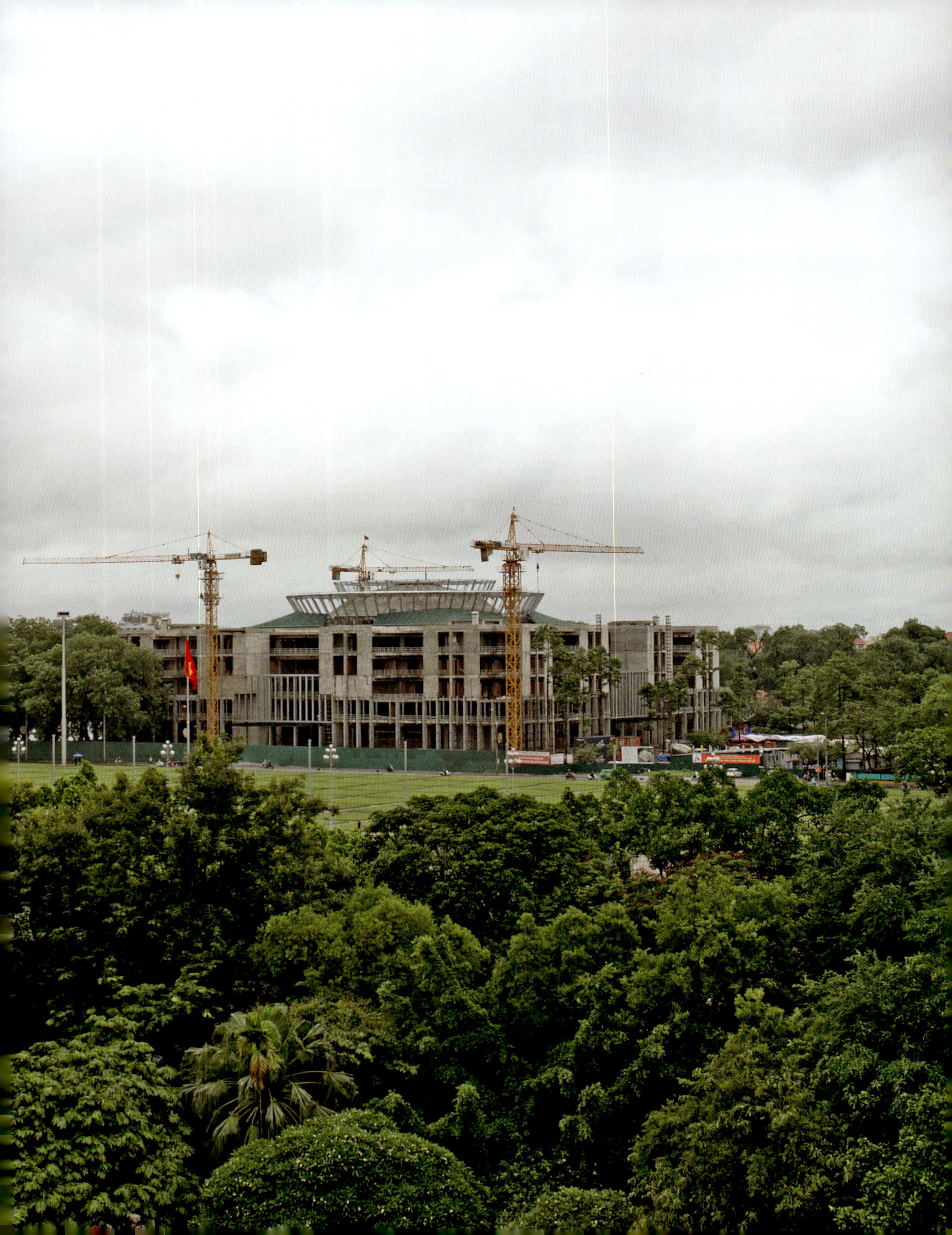

国家议会大厦　河内

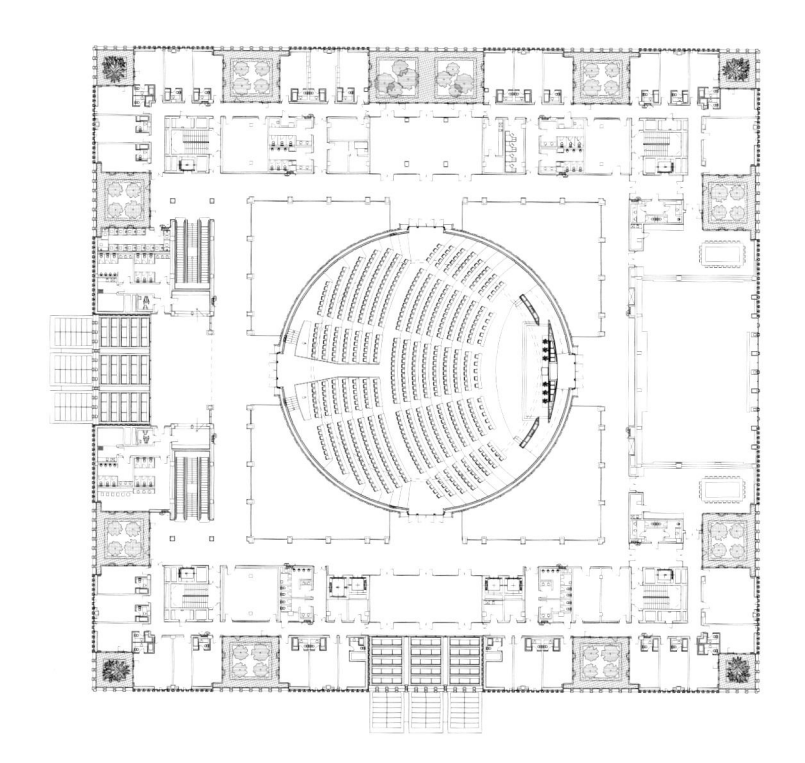

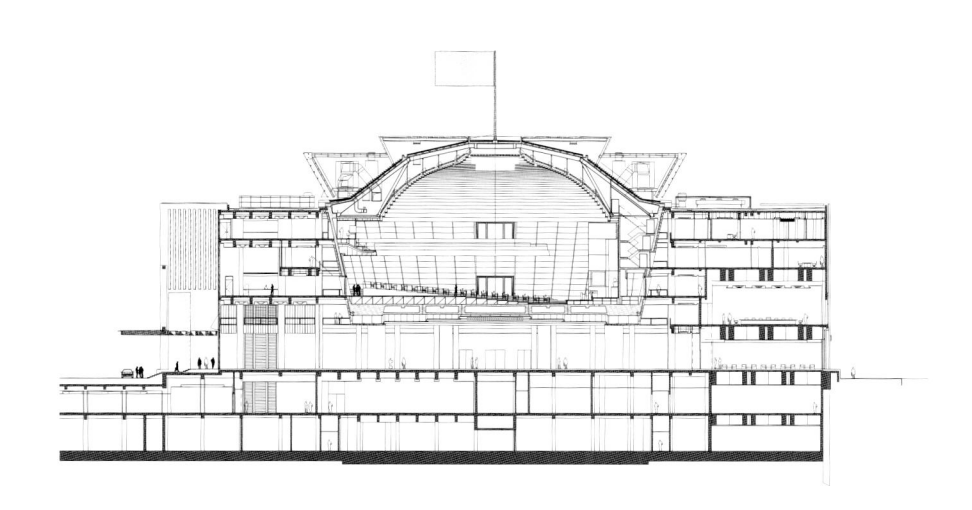

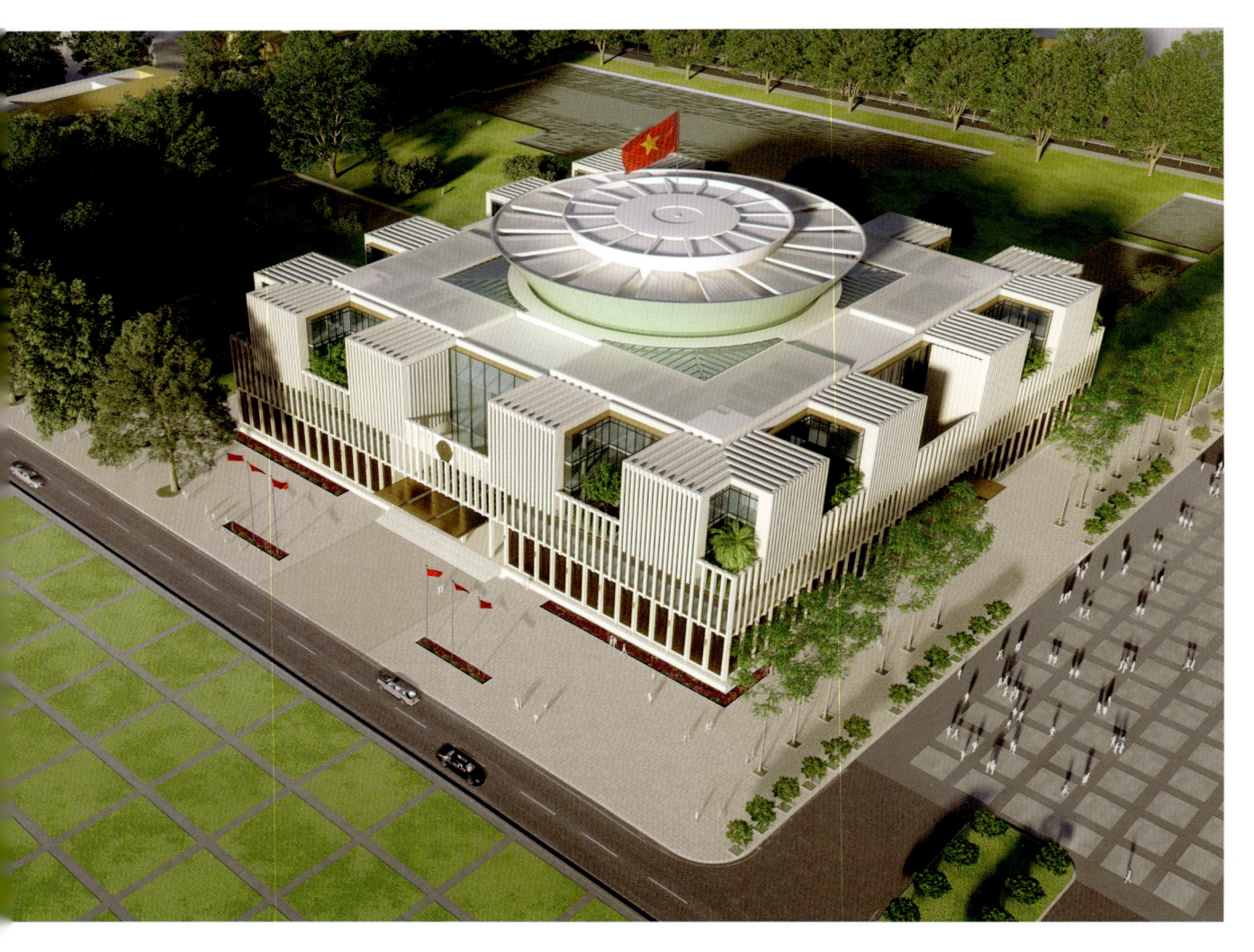

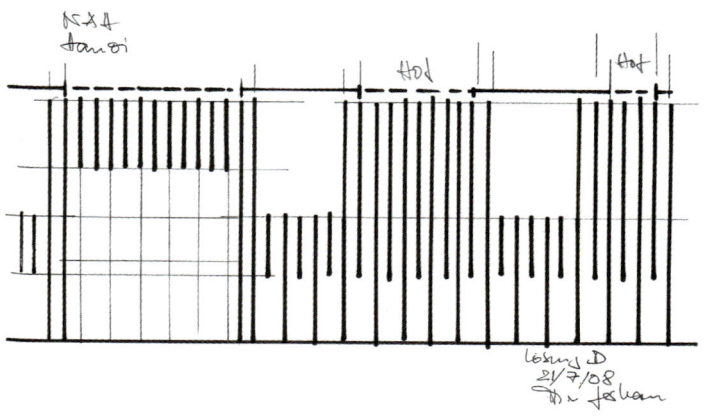

Parliament House Hanoi Hanoi

188 ↑²²

天津西站
天津，中国

Tianjin West Railway Station
Tianjin, China

天津西站　天津

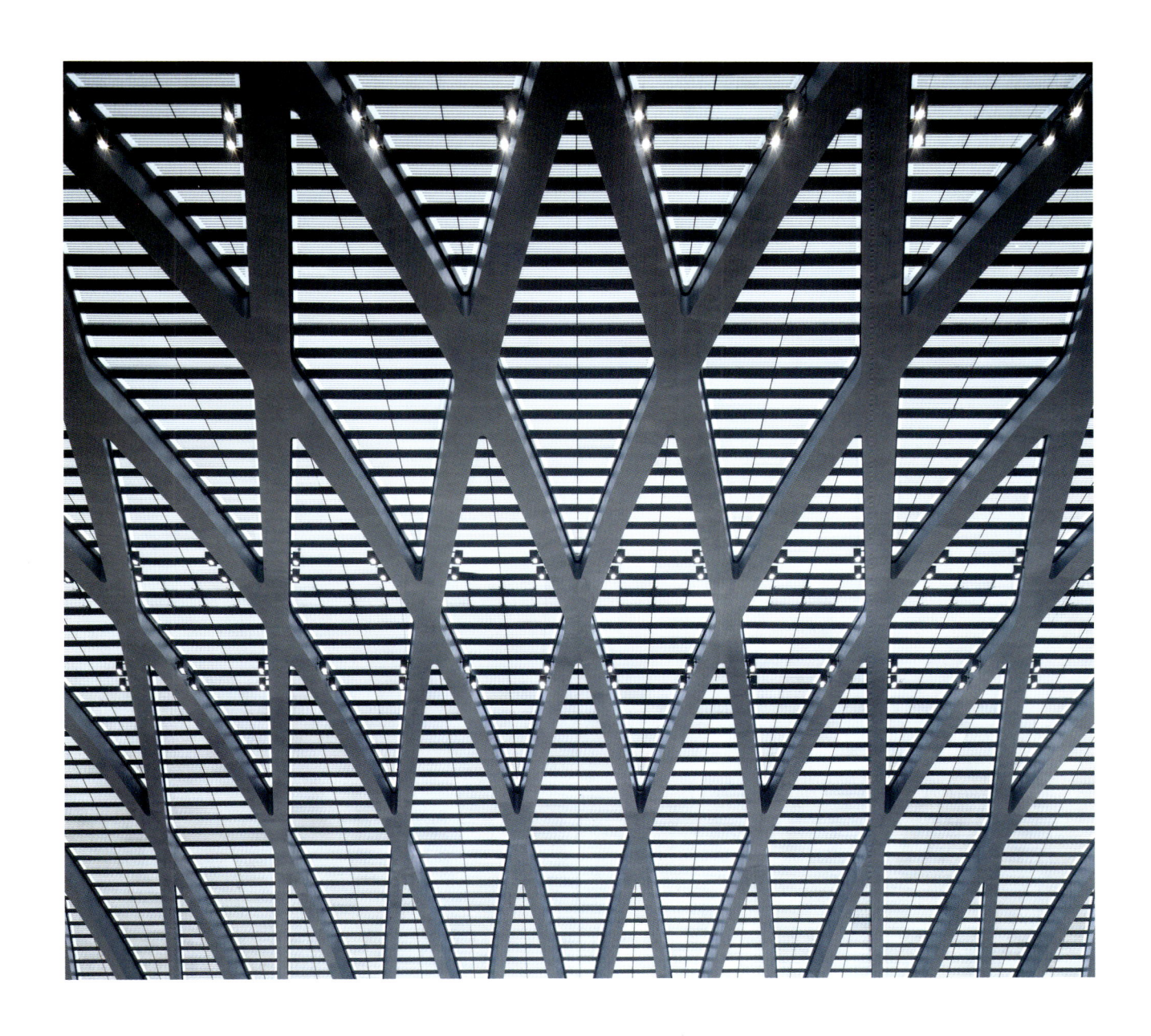

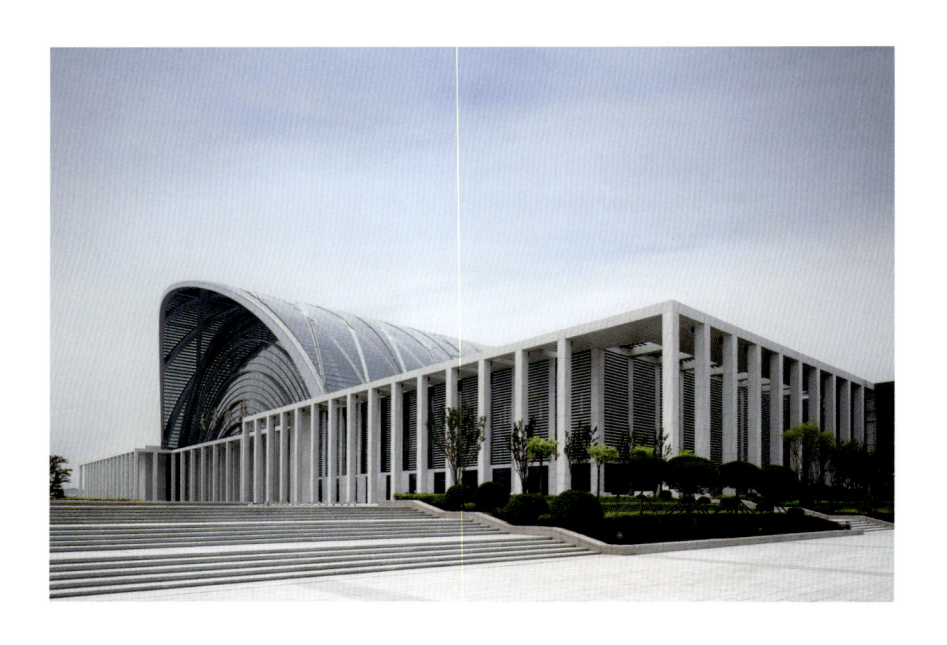

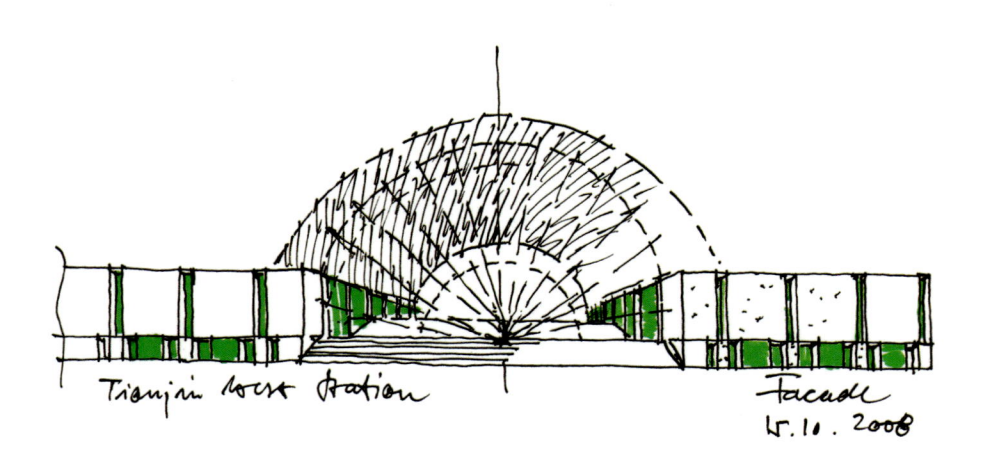

Tianjin West Railway Station Tianjin

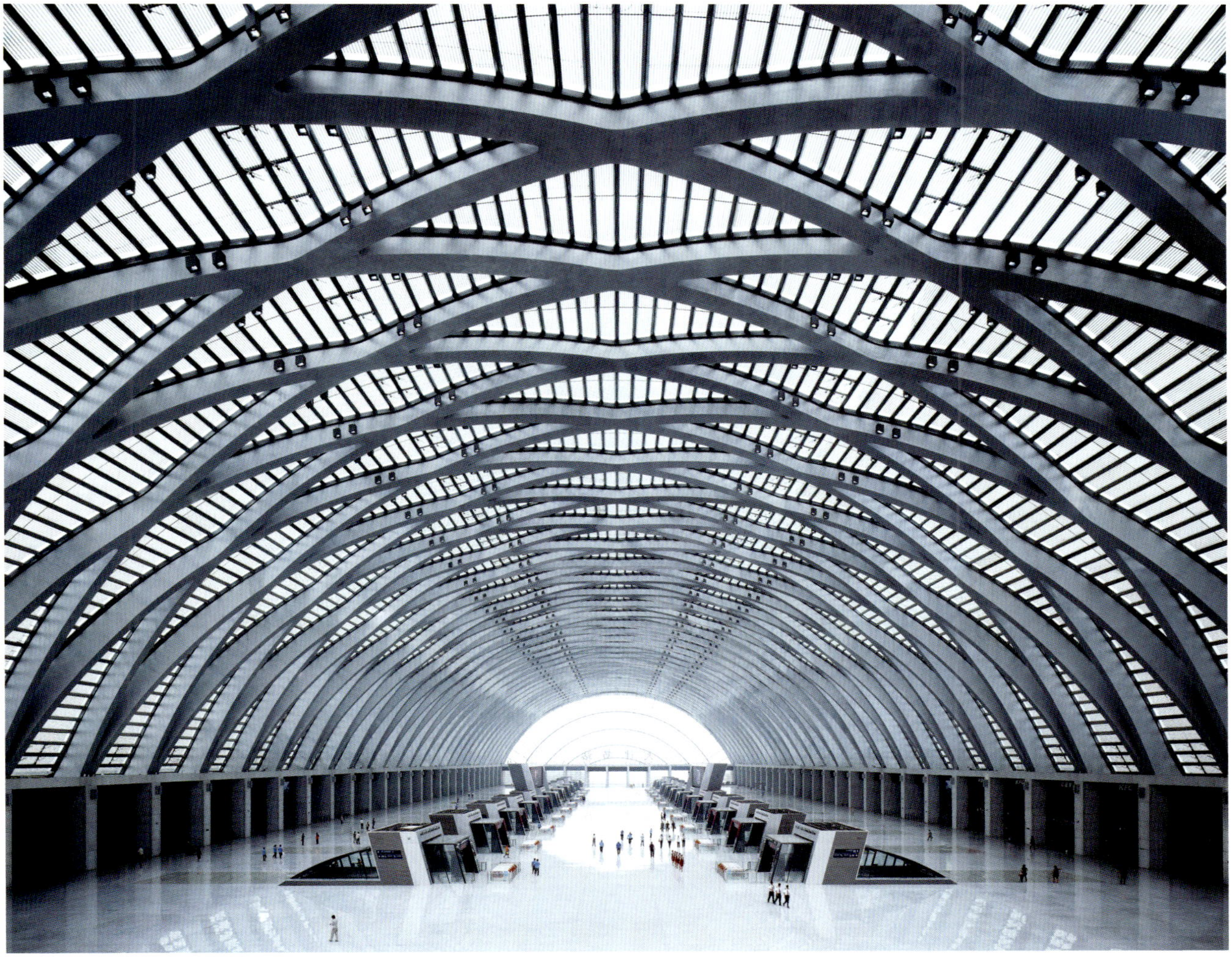

天津西站　天津

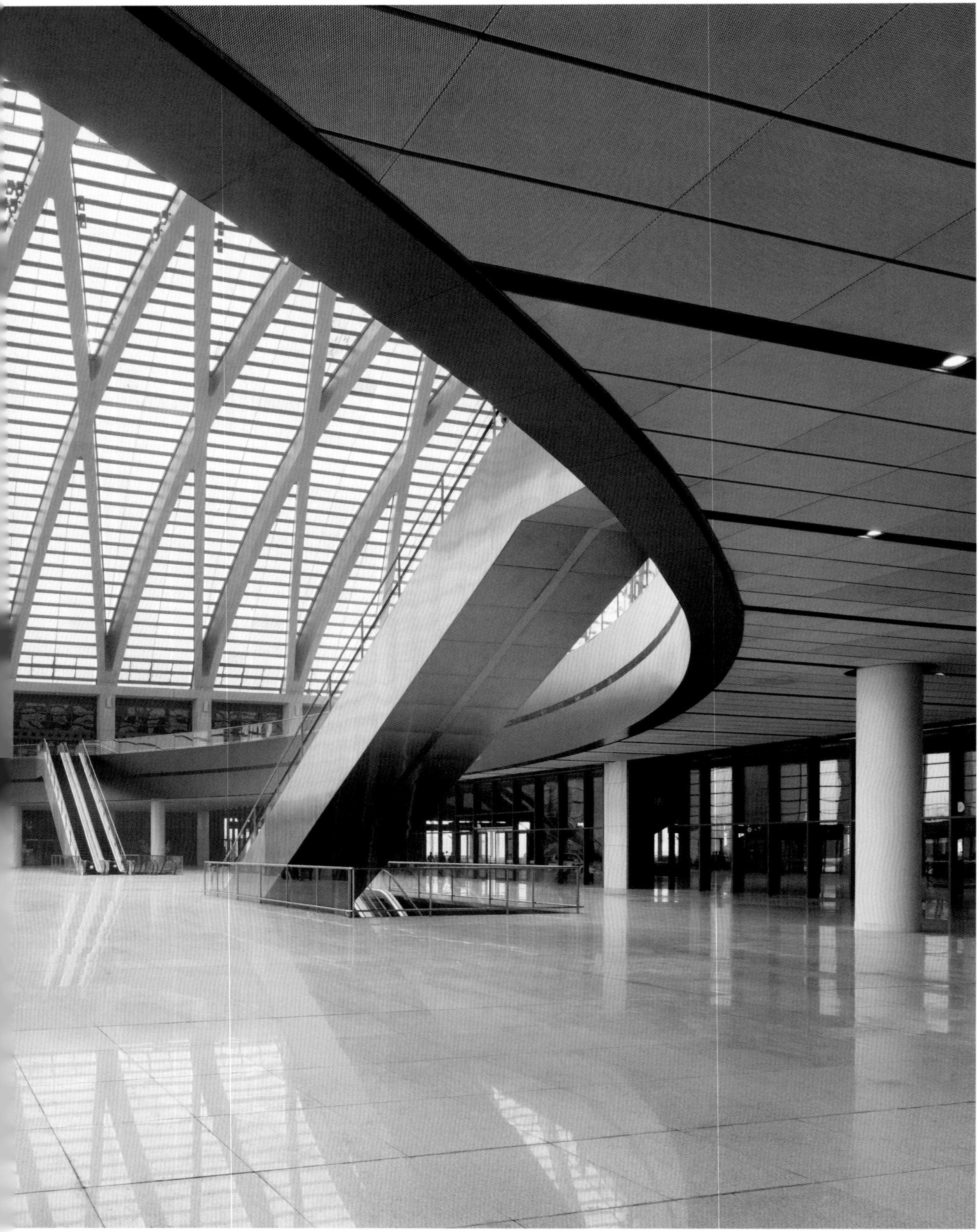

Tianjin West Railway Station Tianjin

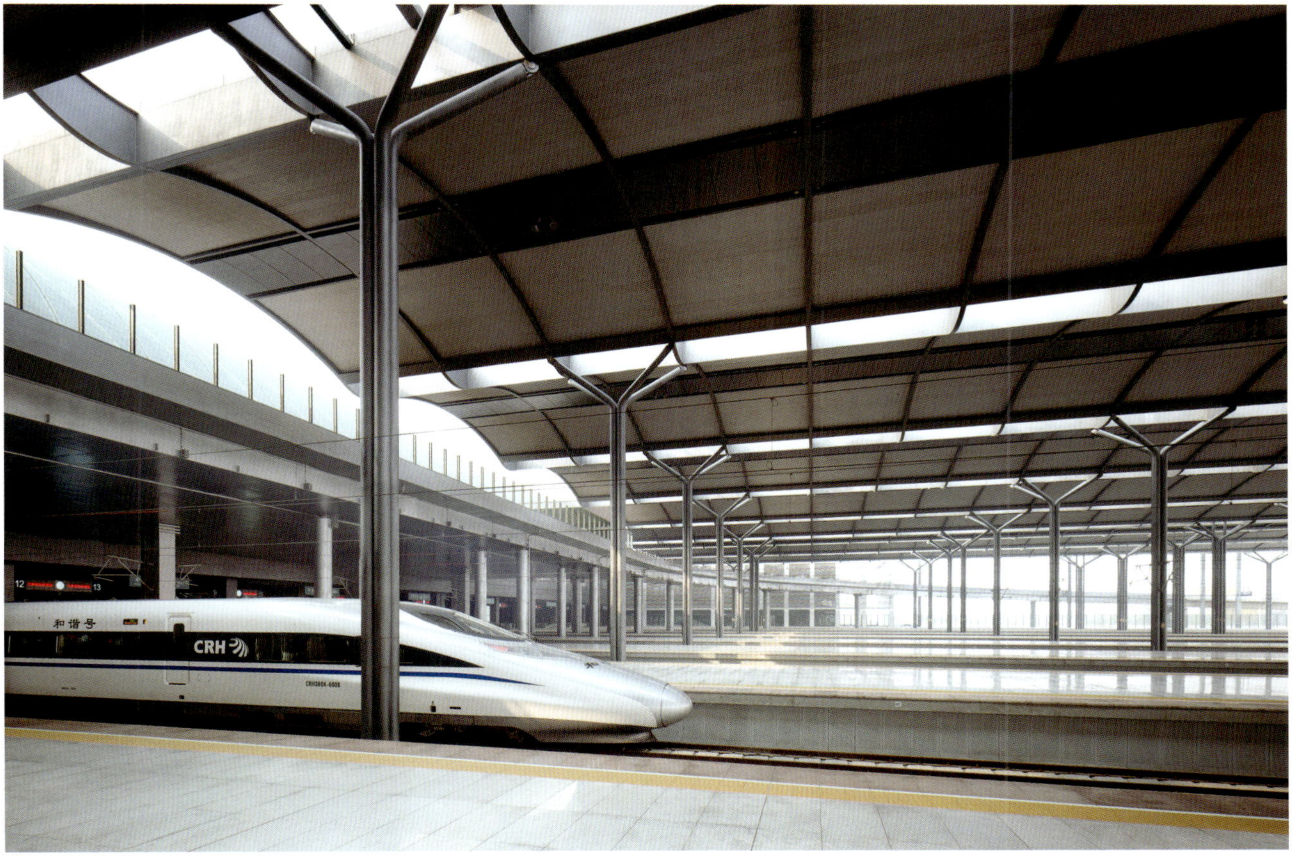

天津西站　天津

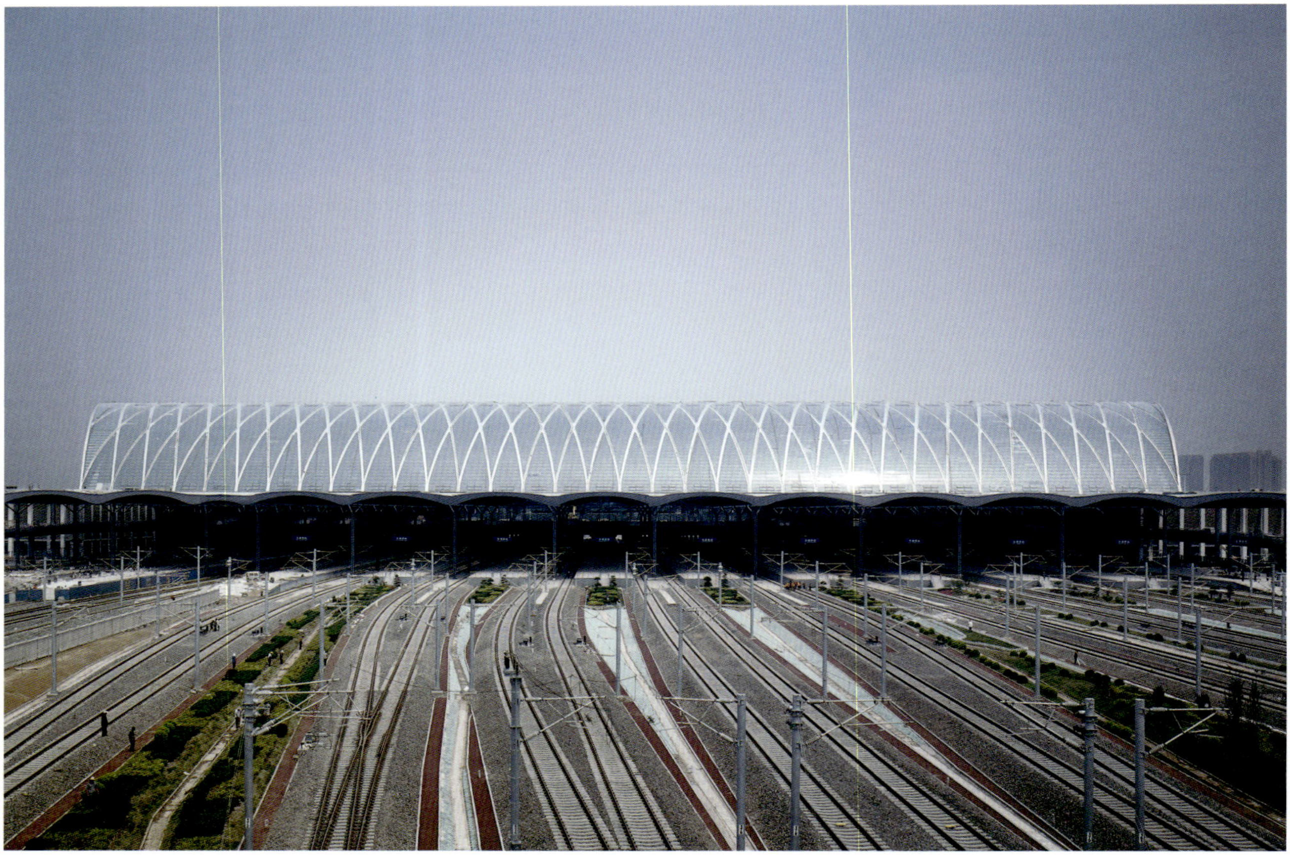

Tianjin West Railway Station Tianjin

196 ²² ↑

临港投资公司标准厂房"条码"外立面
临港新城重工业区，上海，中国

**"Barcode" Halls,
Standard Facades
for Manufacturing Buildings**
Heavy Industry Zone of
Lingang New City,
Shanghai, China

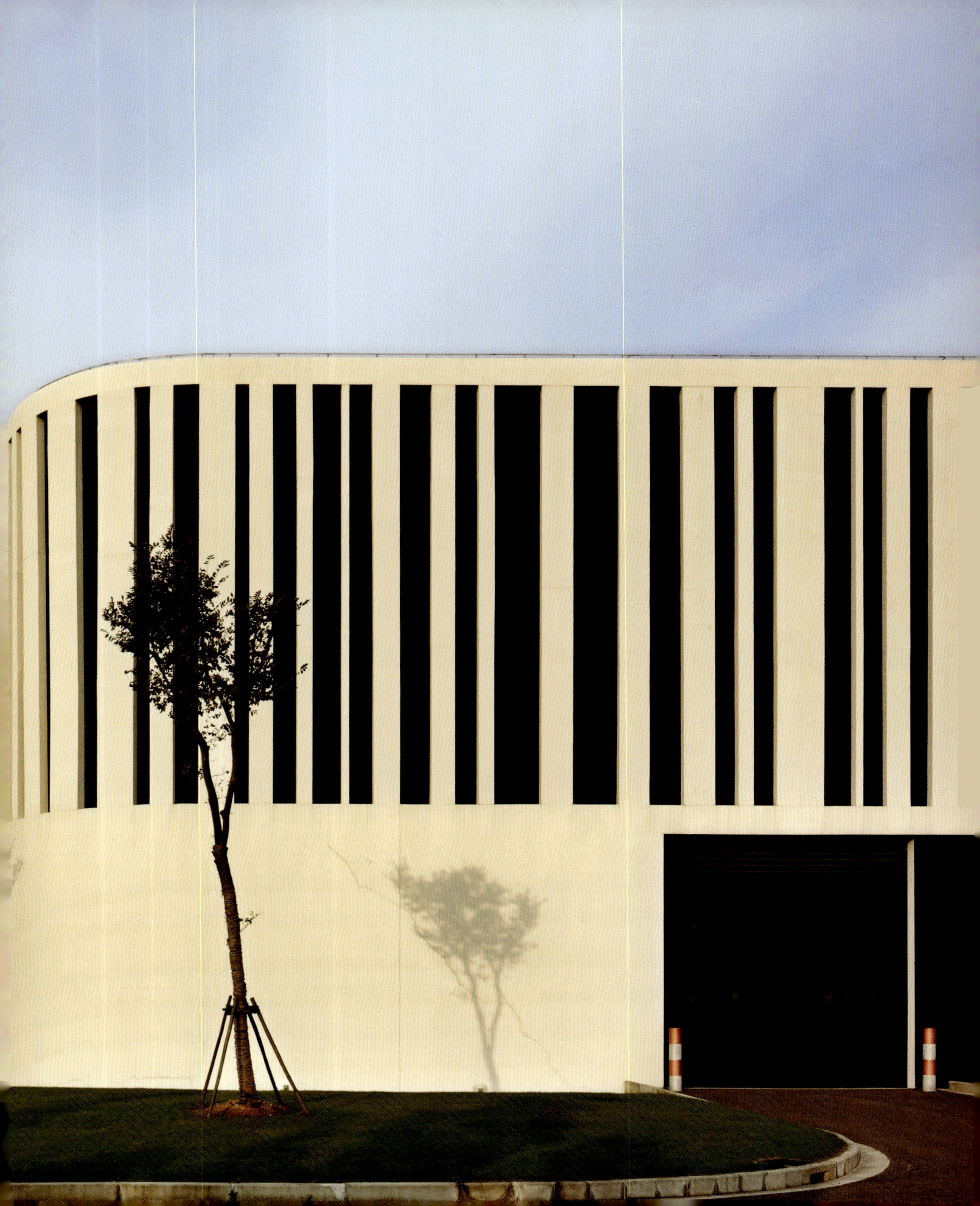

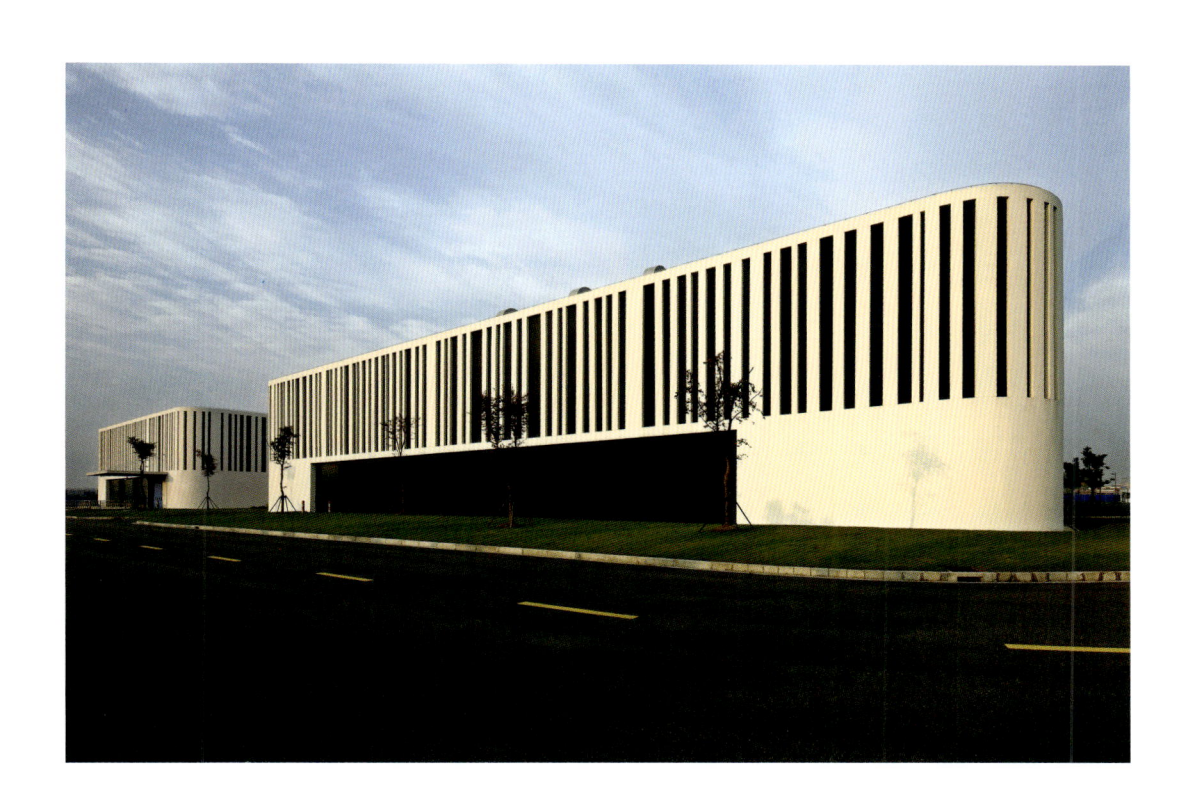

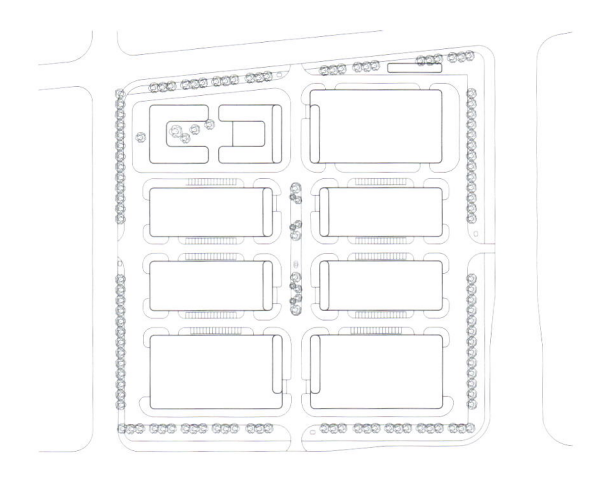

198　临港投资公司标准厂房"条码"外立面　临港新城重工业区，上海

"Barcode" Halls, Standard Facades for Manufacturing Buildings Heavy Industry Zone of Lingang New City, Shanghai

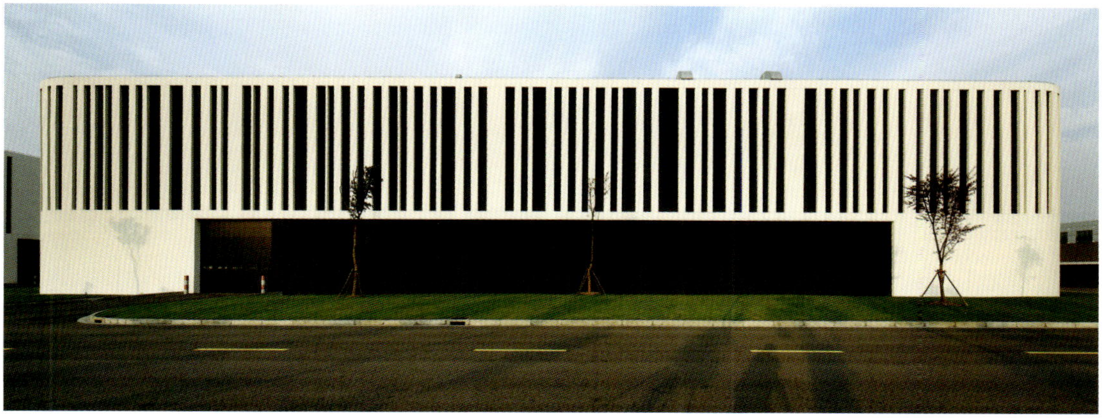

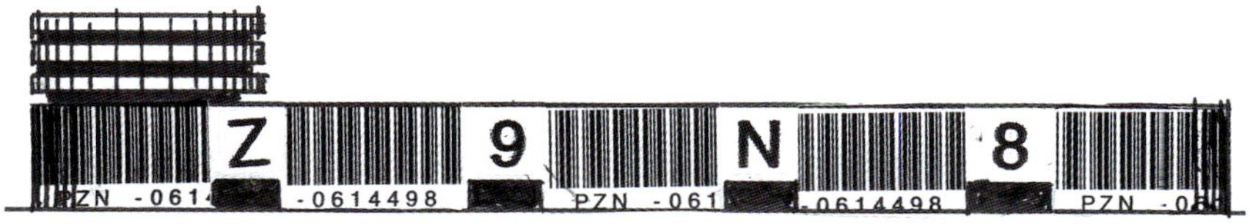

临港投资公司标准厂房"条码"外立面　临港新城重工业区，上海

"Barcode" Halls, Standard Facades for Manufacturing Buildings Heavy Industry Zone, Lingang New City, Shanghai

202 ²³ ↑

上海东方体育中心
上海，中国

Shanghai Oriental Sports Center
Shanghai, China

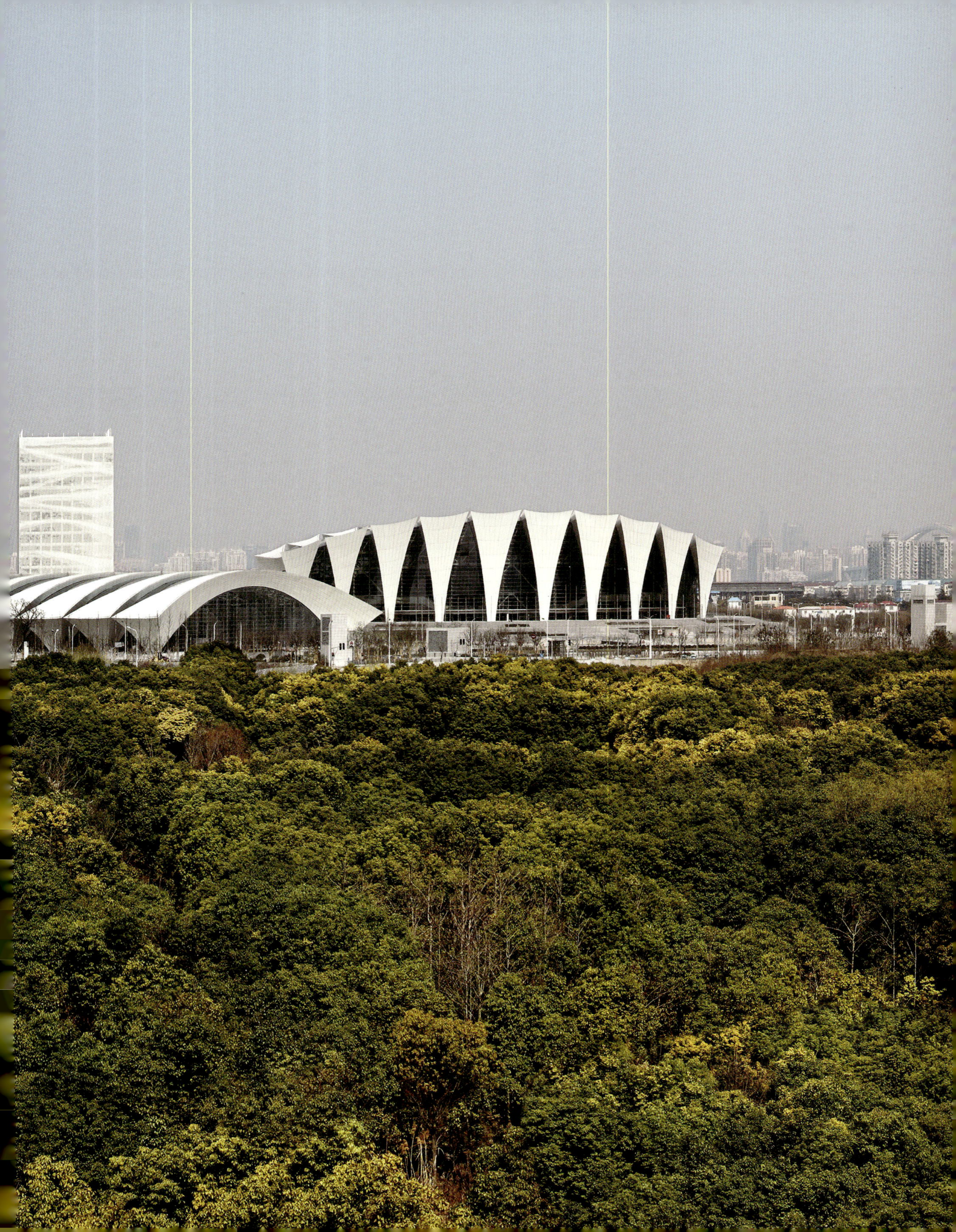

204　**上海东方体育中心**　上海

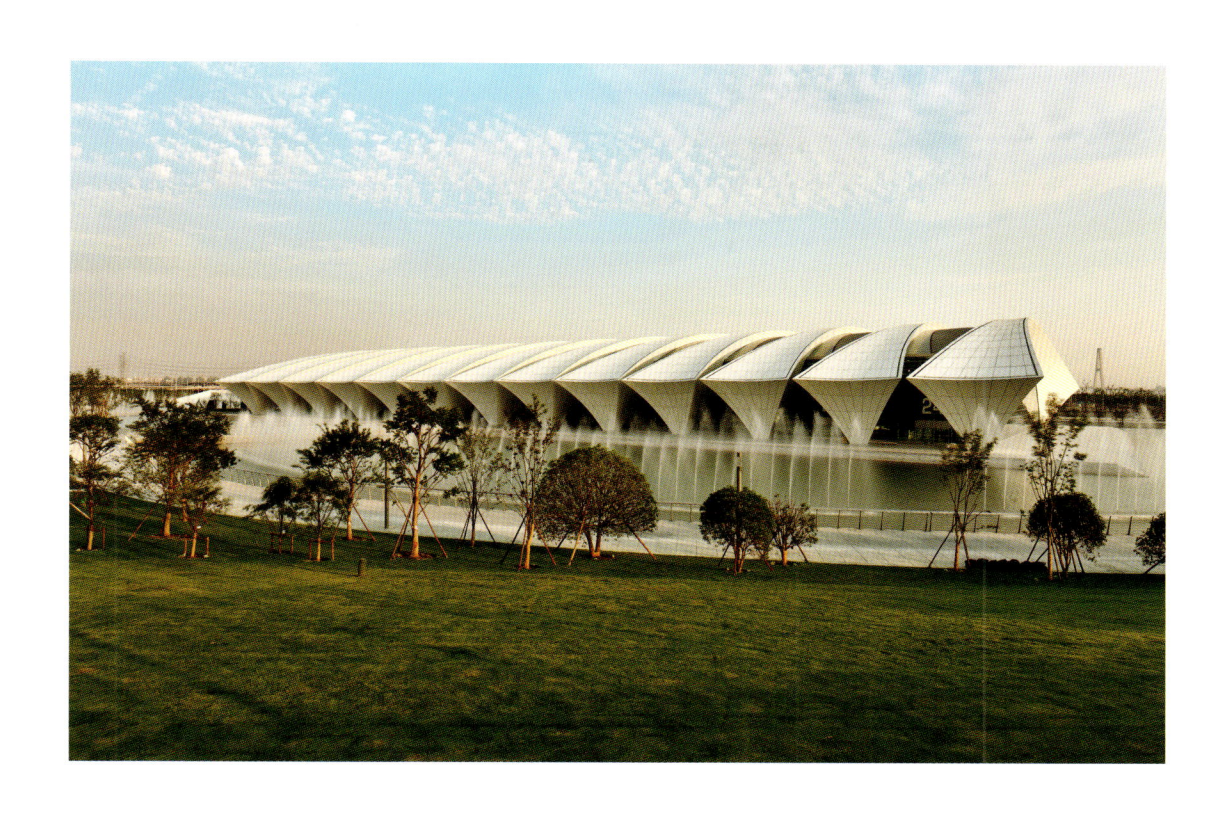

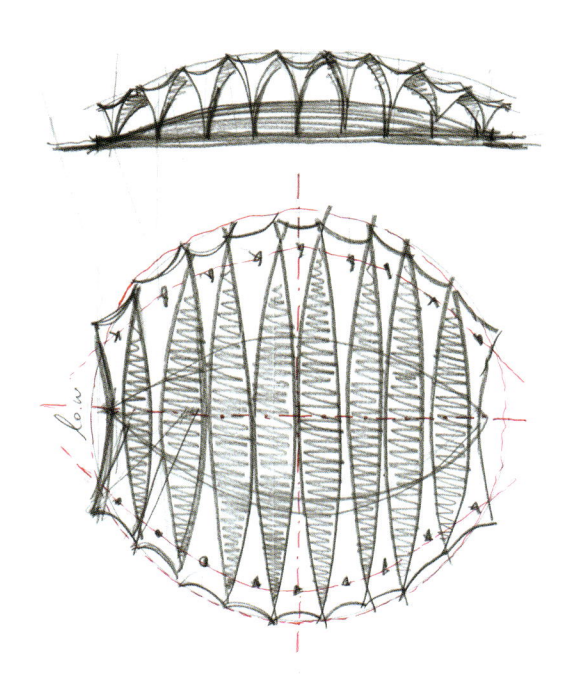

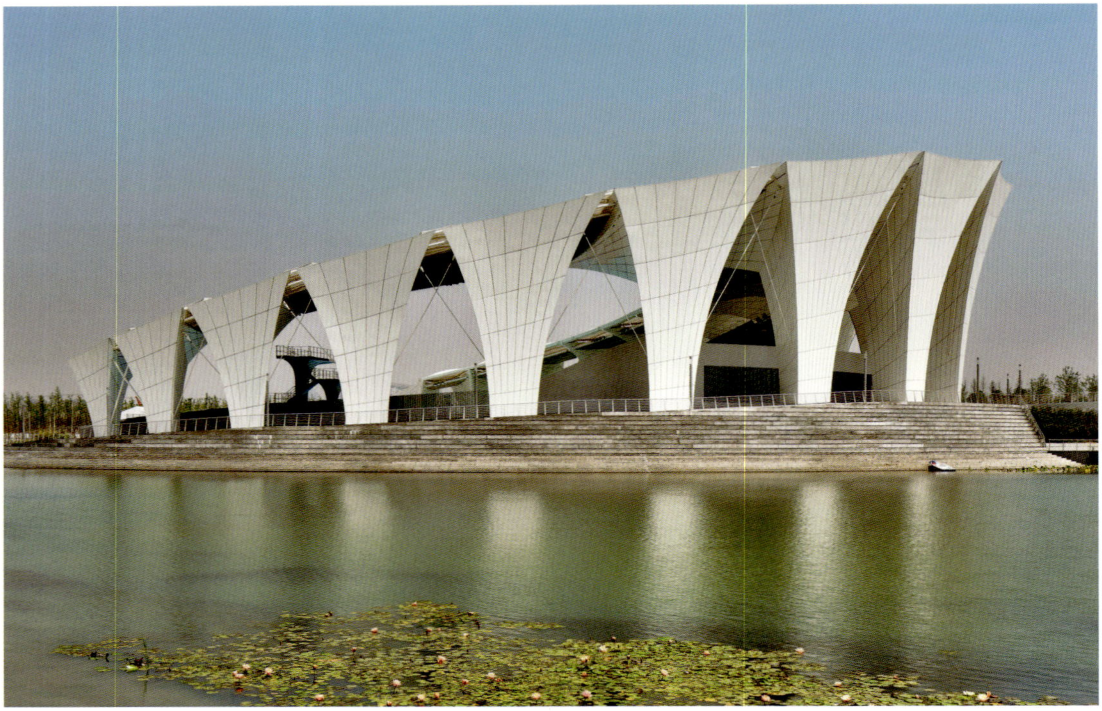

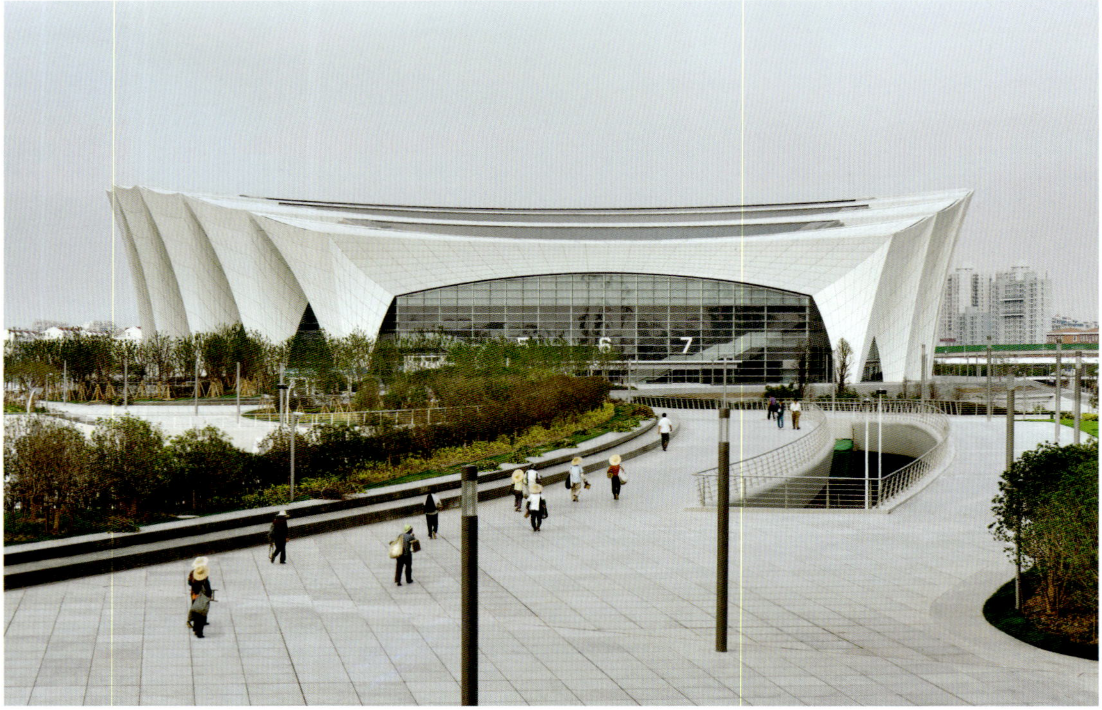

Shanghai Oriental Sports Center Shanghai

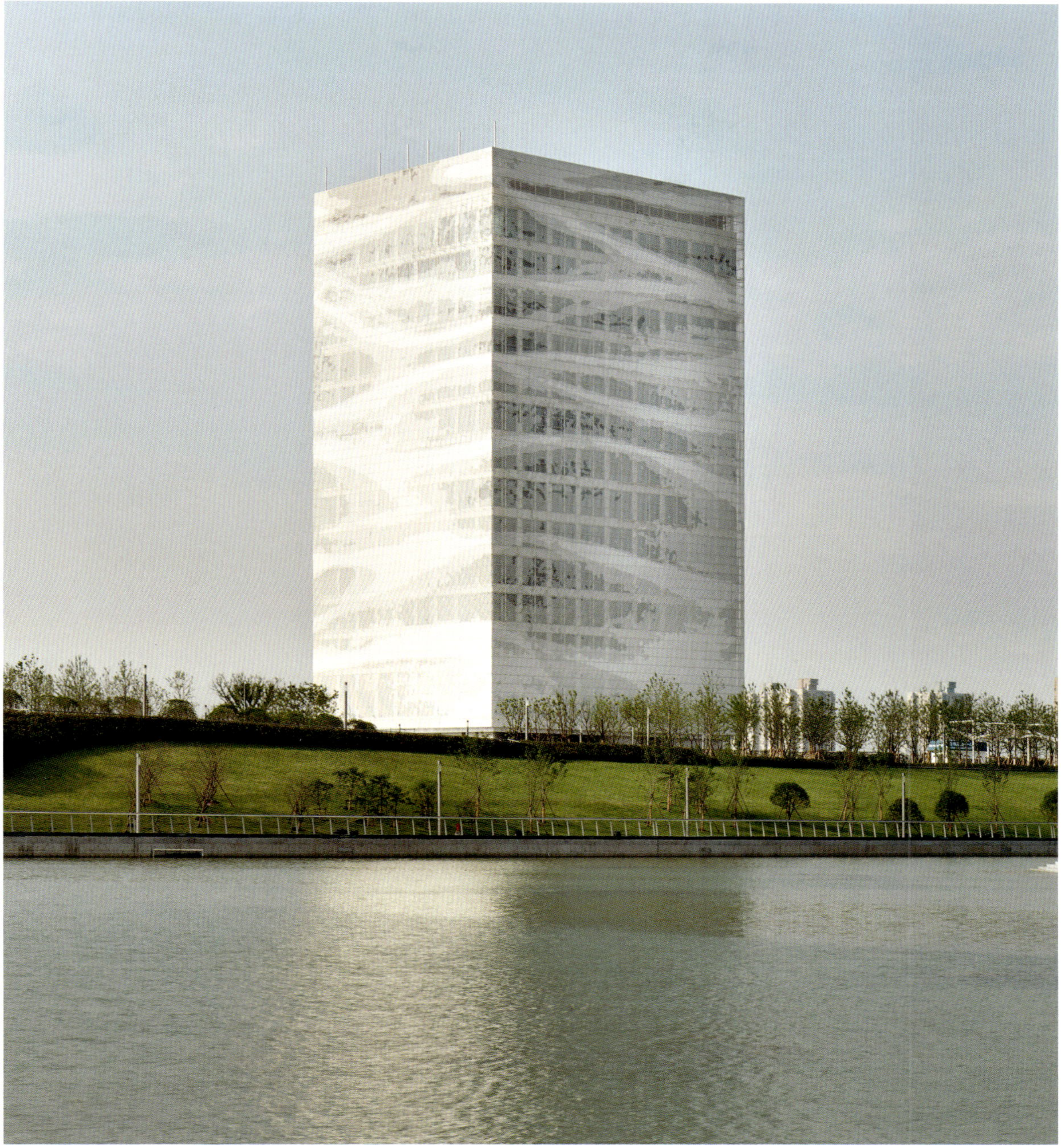

上海东方体育中心　上海

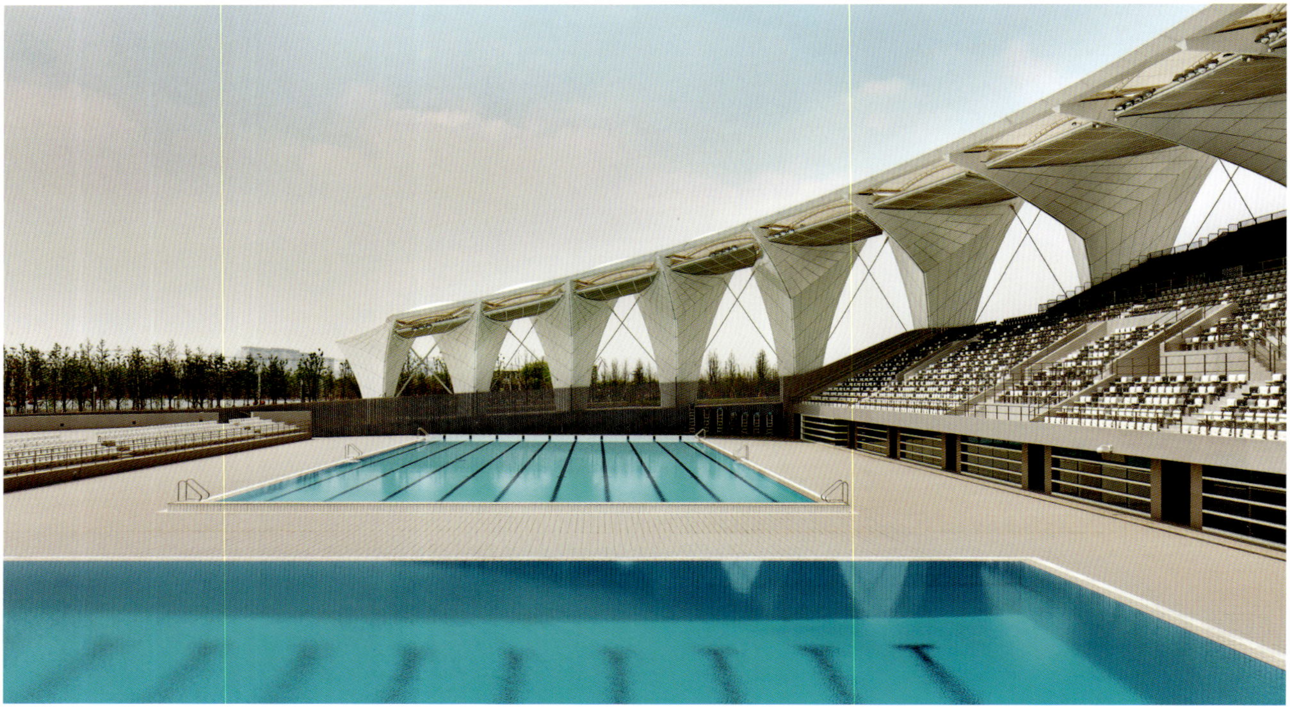

Shanghai Oriental Sports Center Shanghai

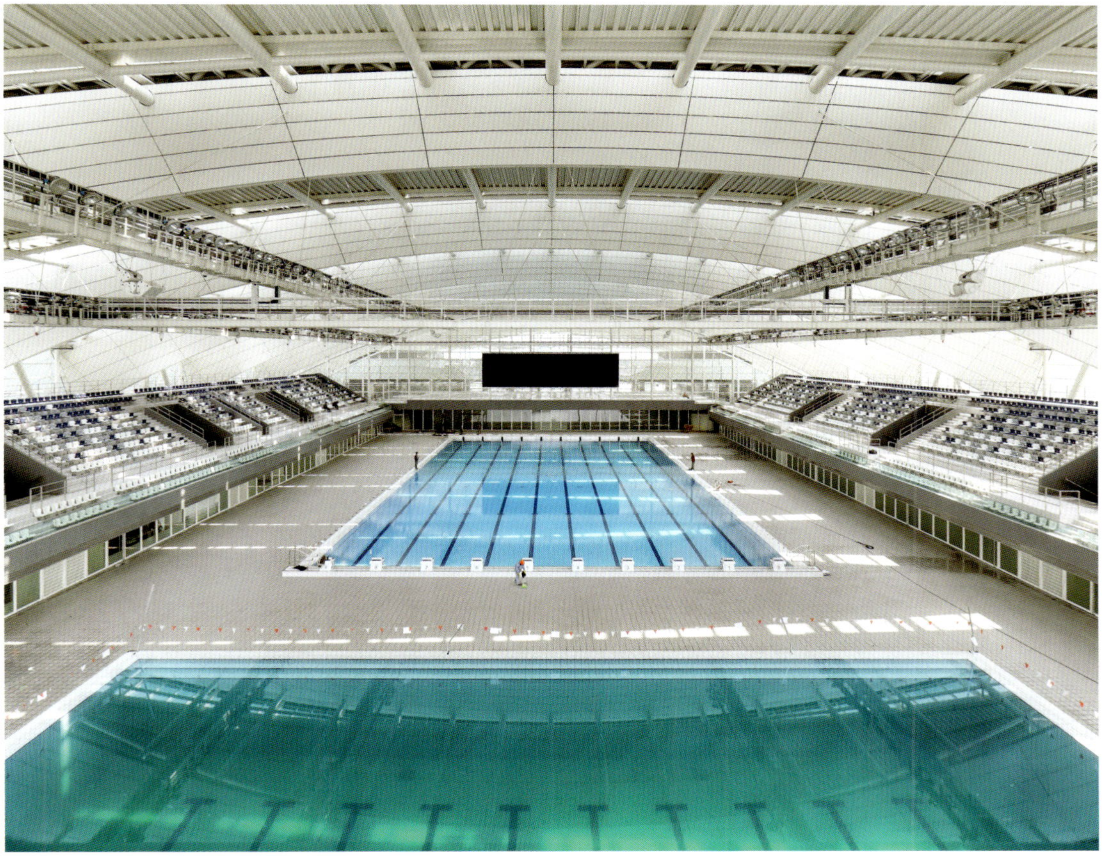

上海东方体育中心　上海

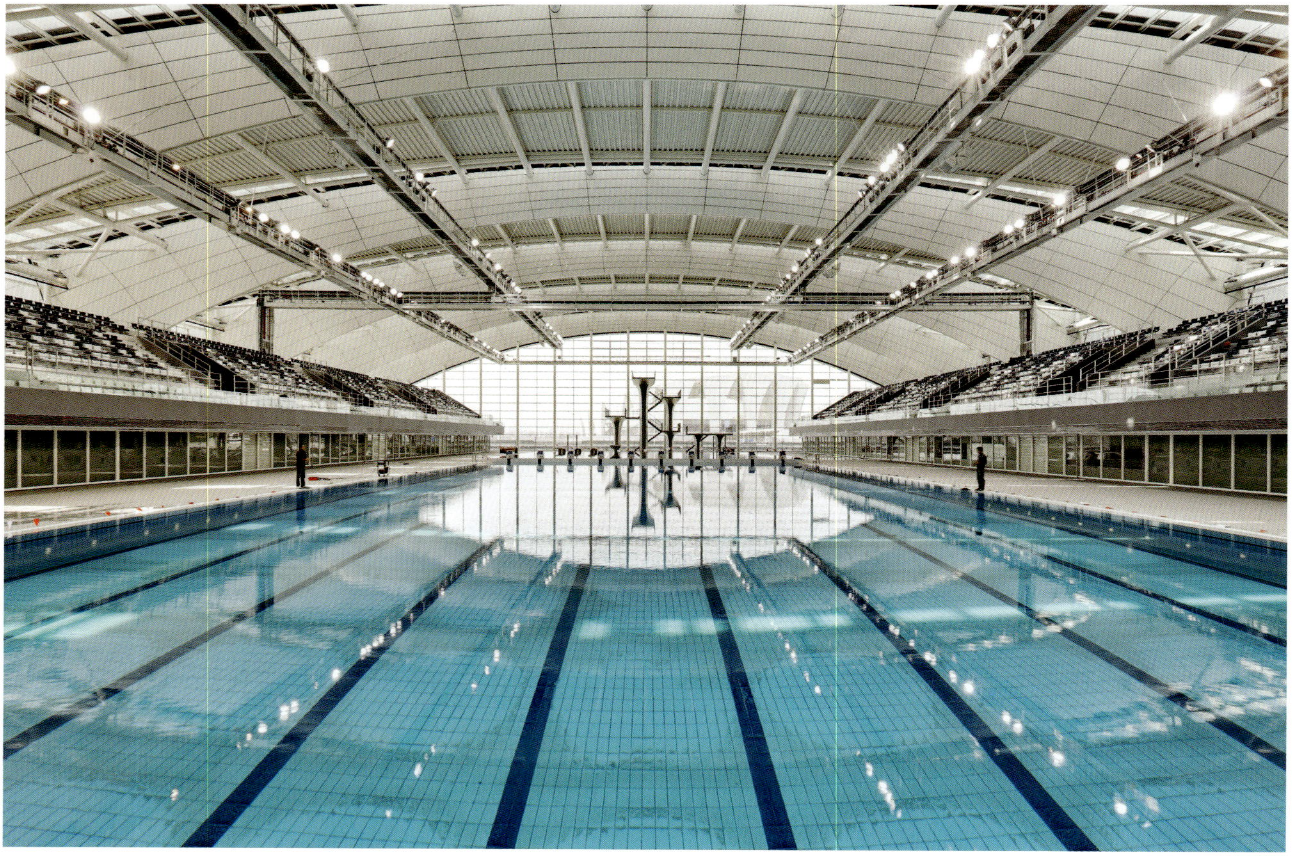

Shanghai Oriental Sports Center Shanghai

210 ²³
↑

三一重工奉贤产业中心概念规划
上海，中国

Sany Fengxian Master Plan
Shanghai, China

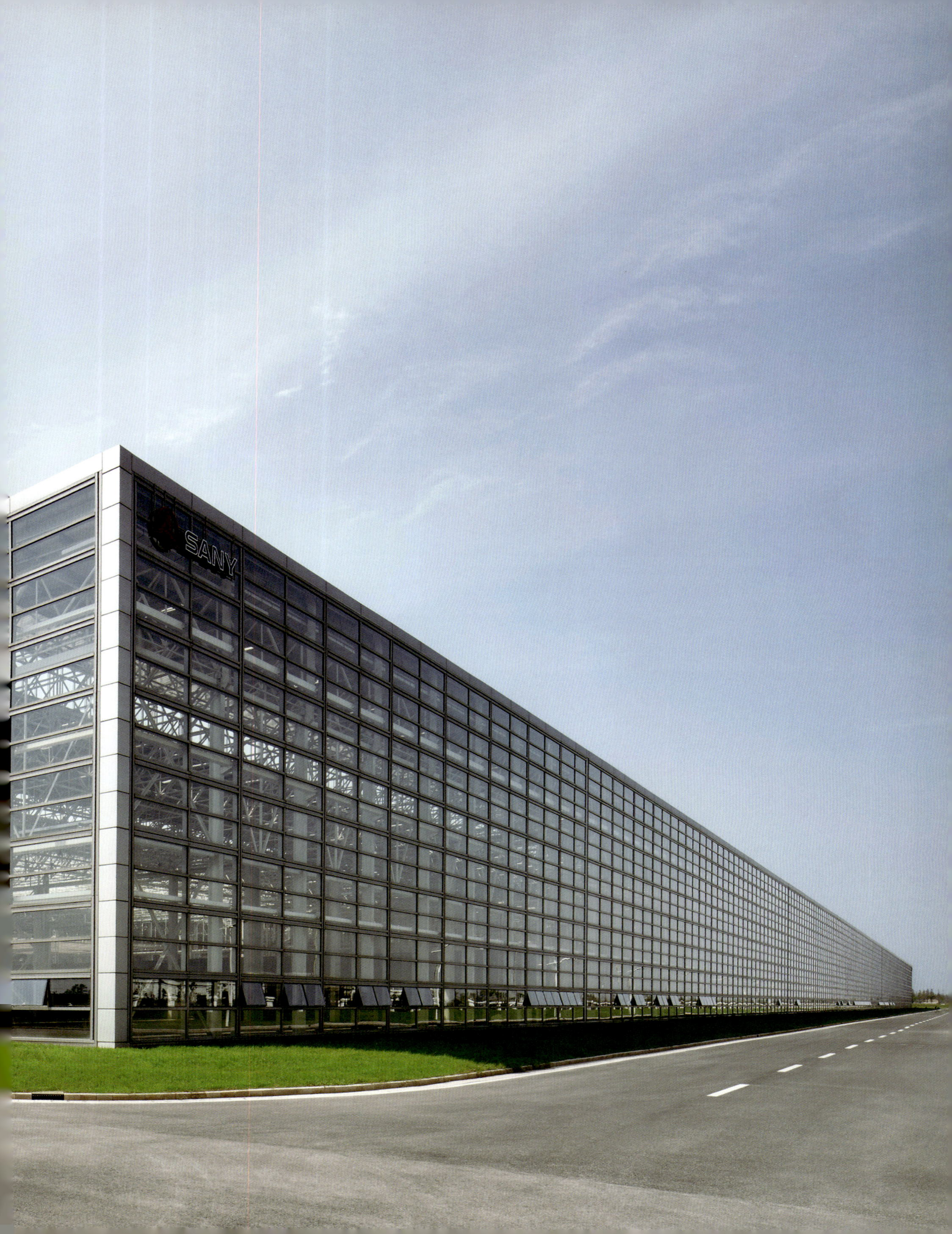
SANY

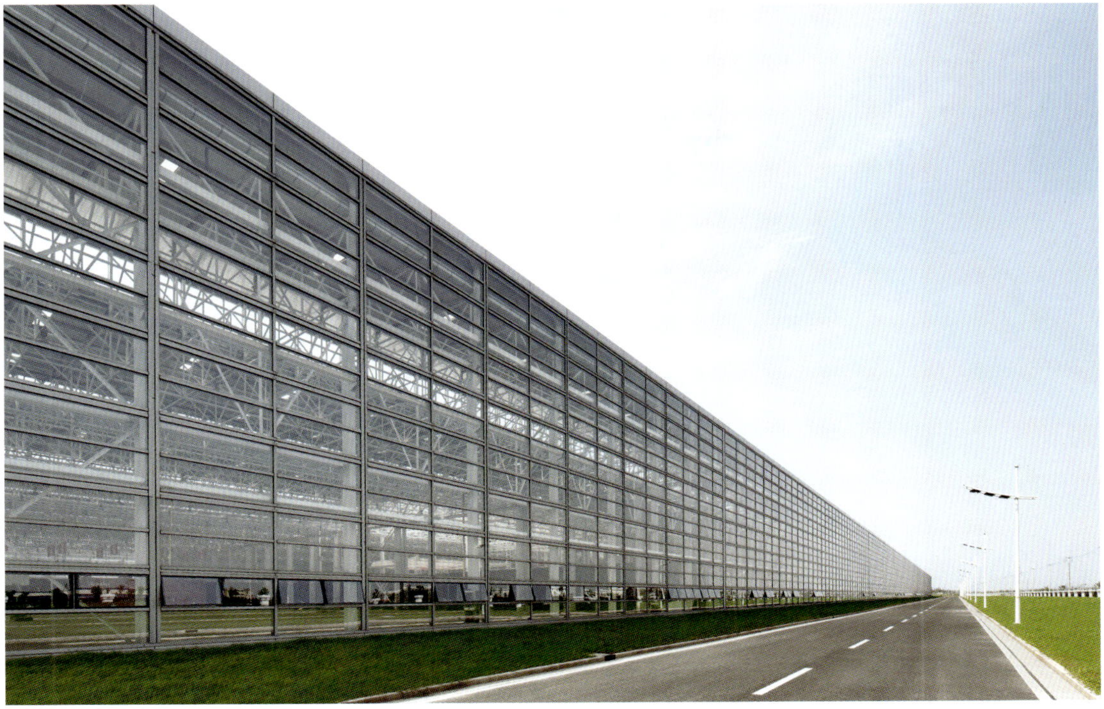

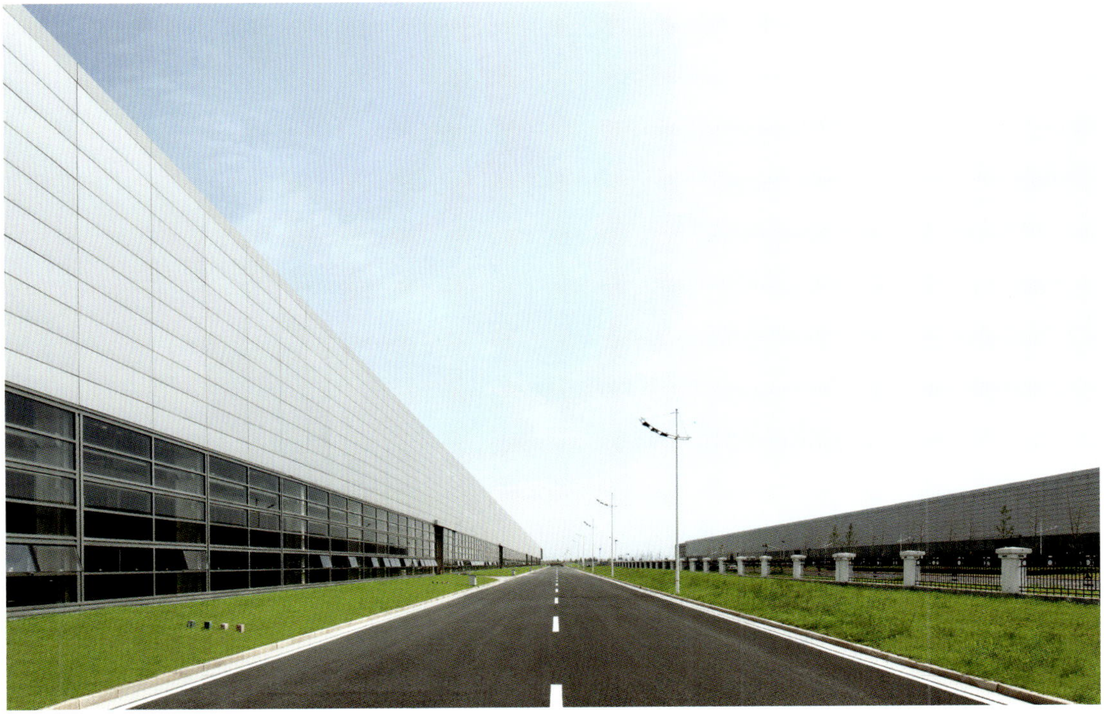

三一重工奉贤产业中心概念规划　上海

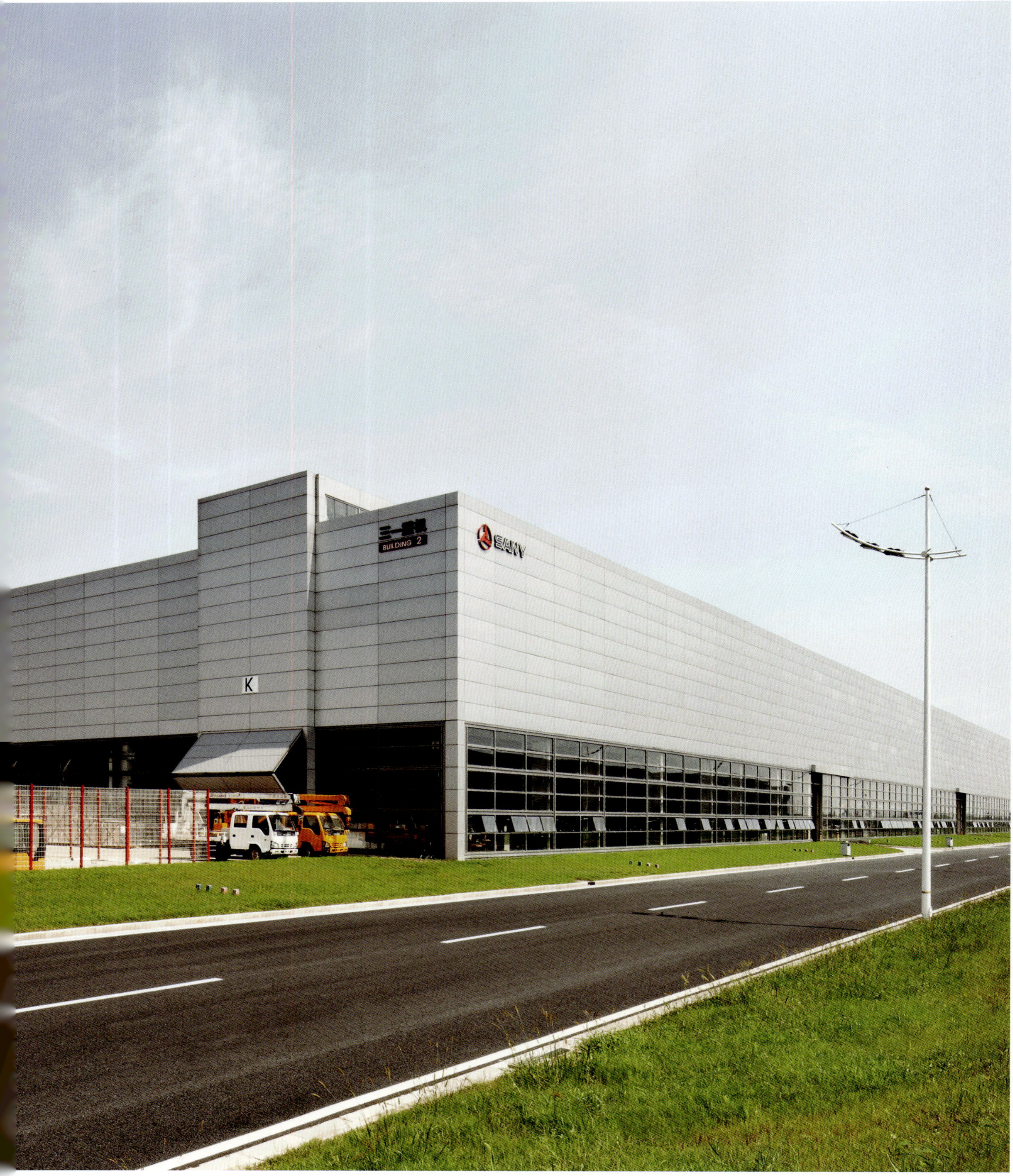

Sany Fengxian Master Plan Shanghai

214 ²⁴ ↑

天津大剧院
天津，中国

Tianjin Grand Theater
Tianjin, China

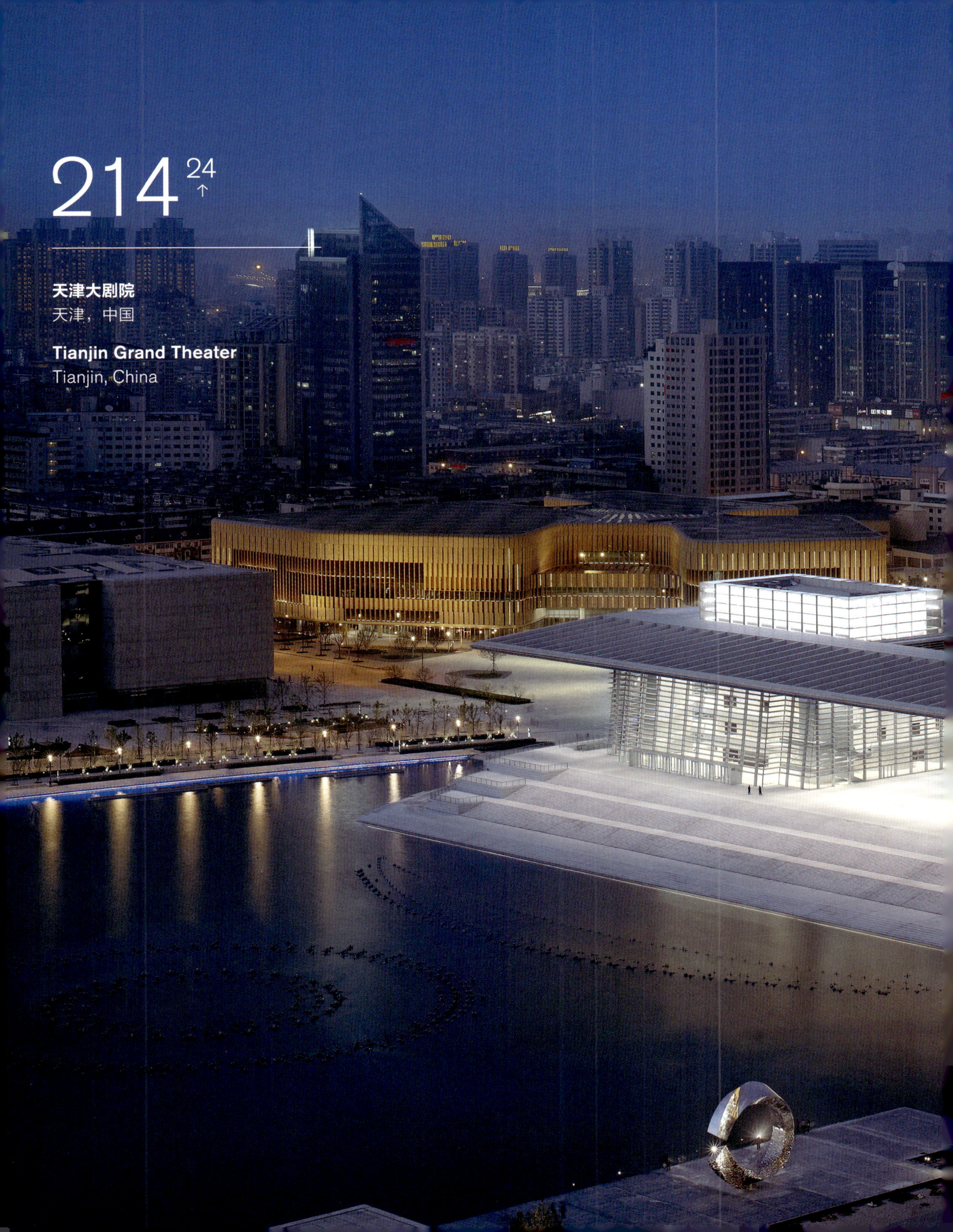

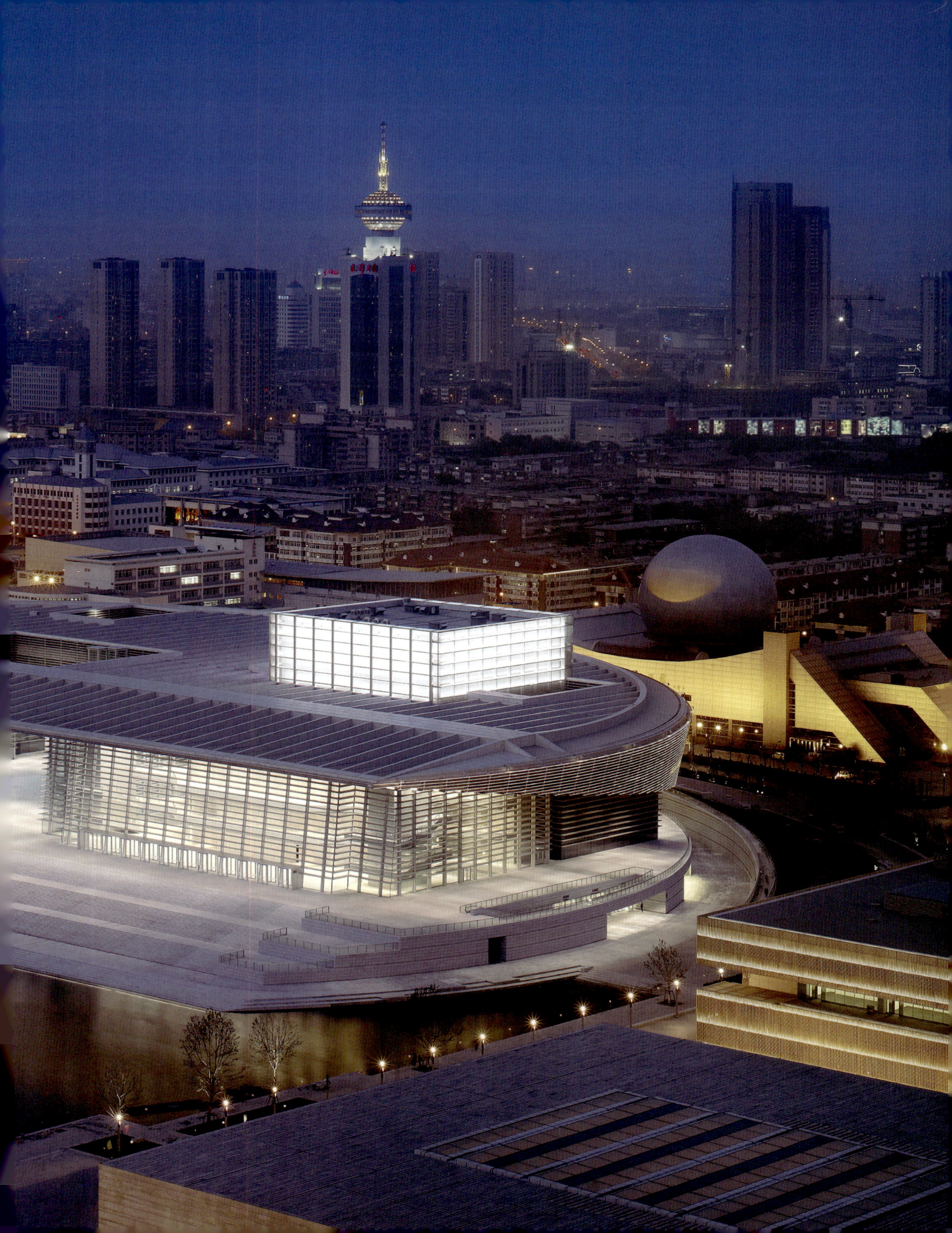

EXISTING THEATRE
"MOUND LIKE SHAPE"

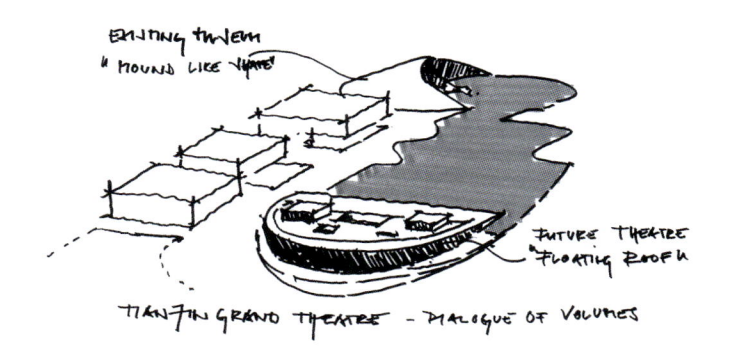

FUTURE THEATRE
"FLOATING ROOF"

TIANJIN GRAND THEATRE - DIALOGUE OF VOLUMES

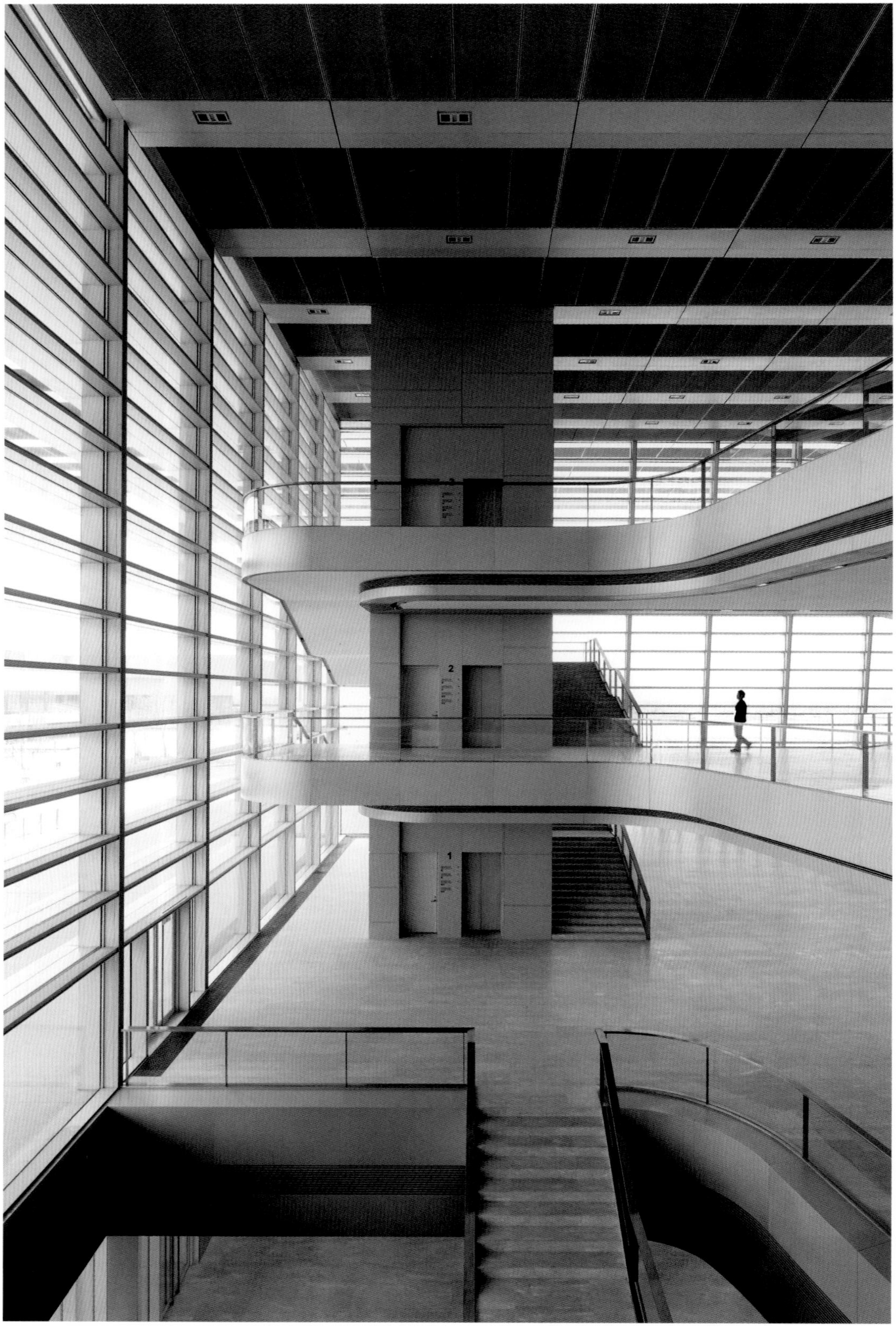

Tianjin Grand Theater Tianjin

218　天津大剧院　天津

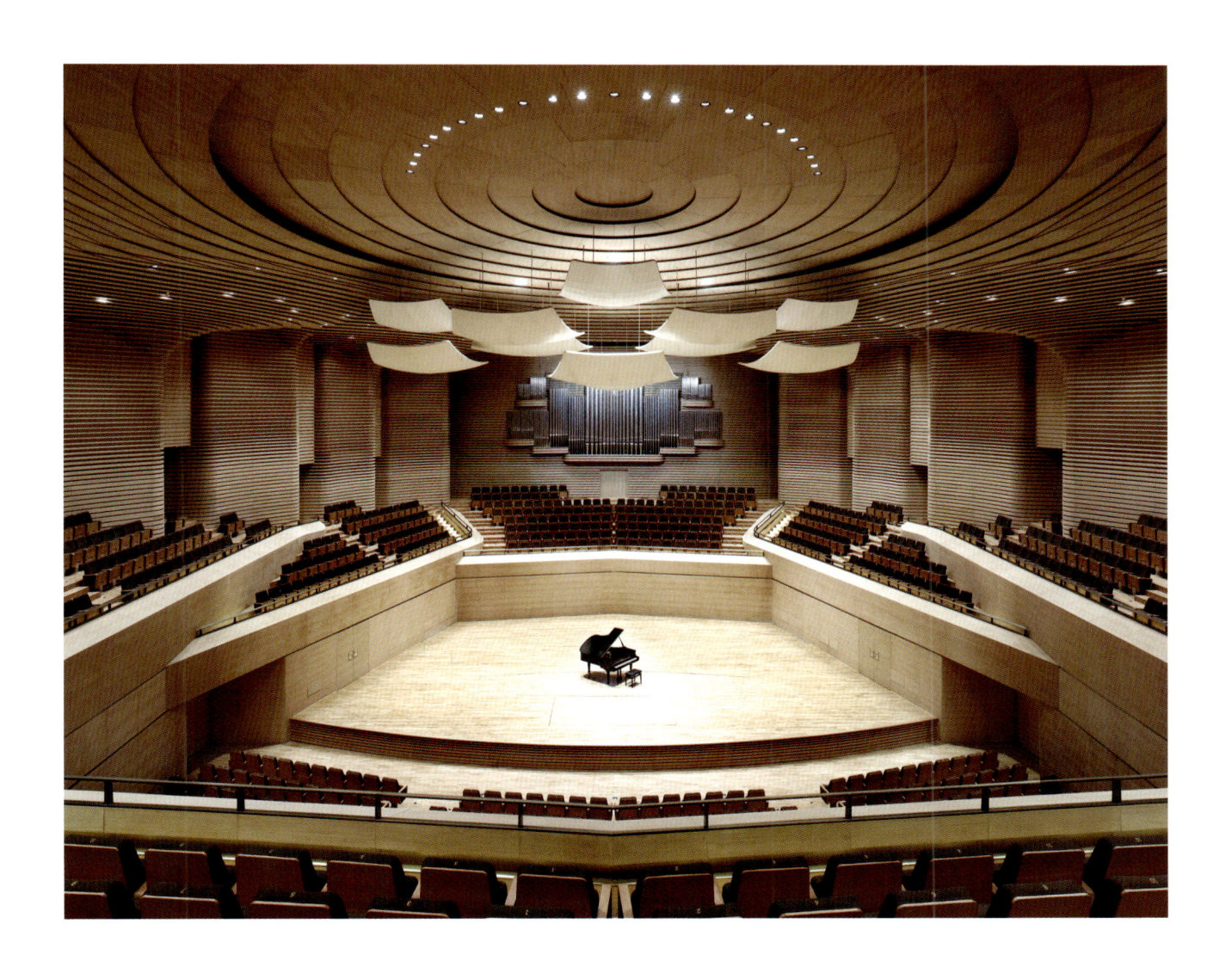

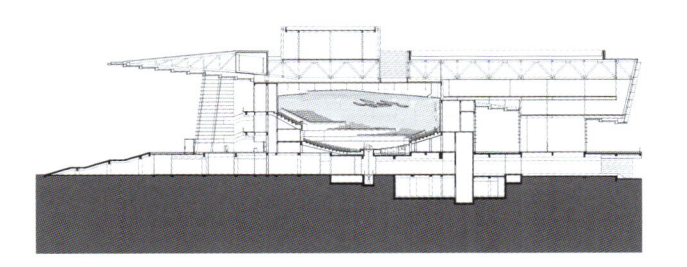

Tianjin Grand Theater Tianjin

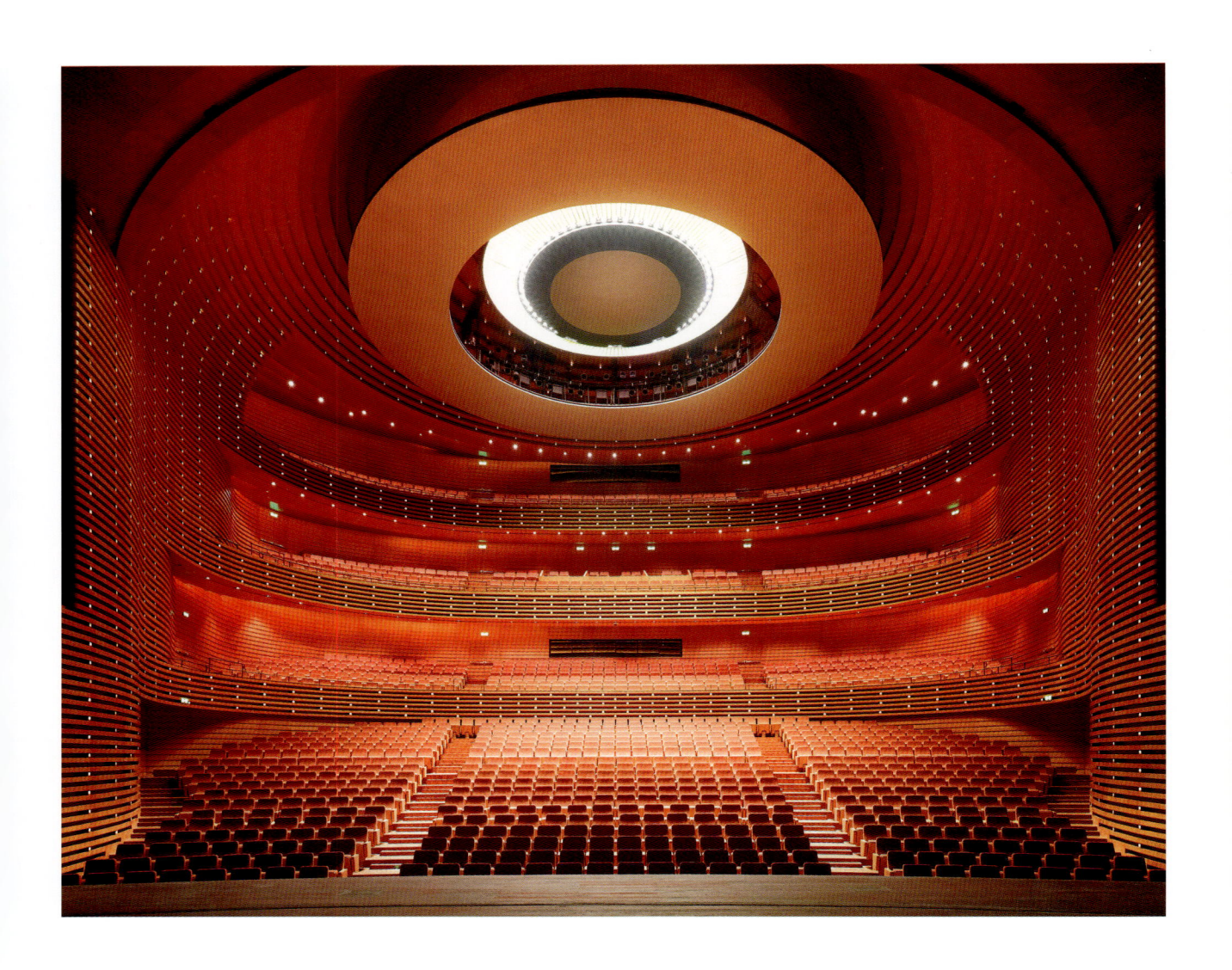

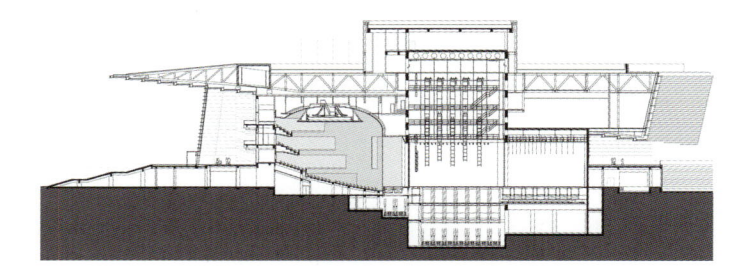

天津大剧院　天津

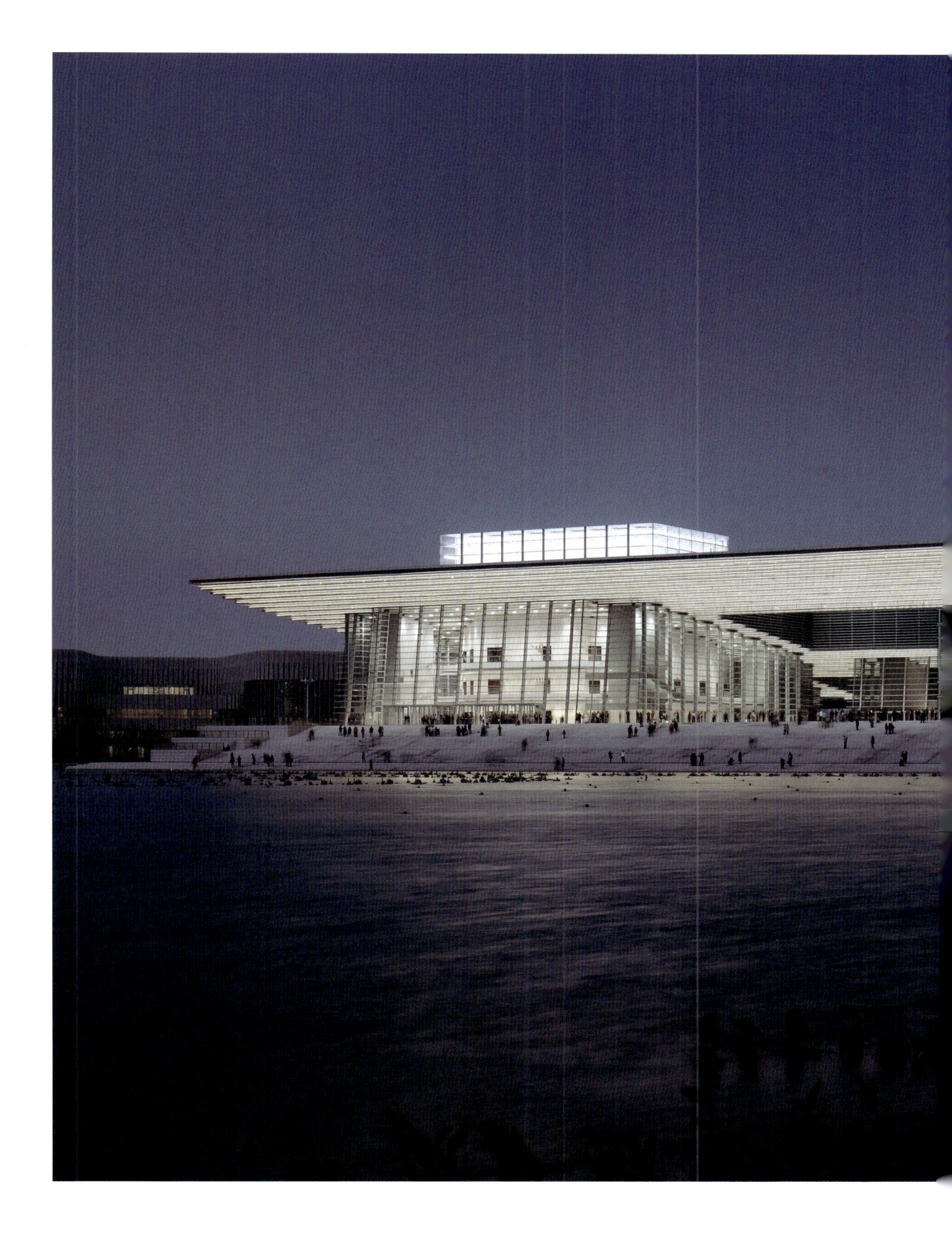

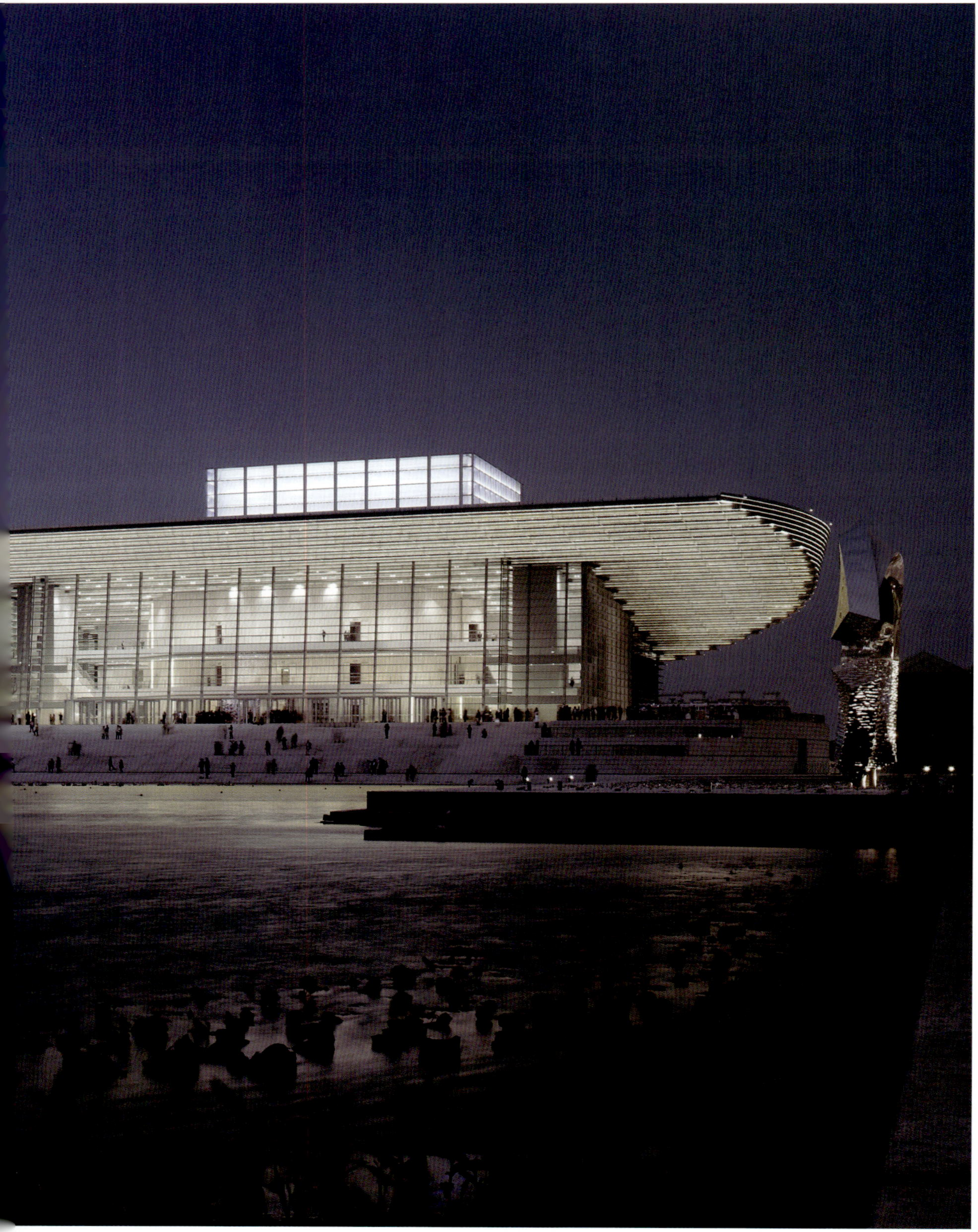

Tianjin Grand Theater Tianjin

222 ²⁴ ↑

郑东绿地中心
郑州，中国

Greenland Central Plaza
Zhengzhou, China

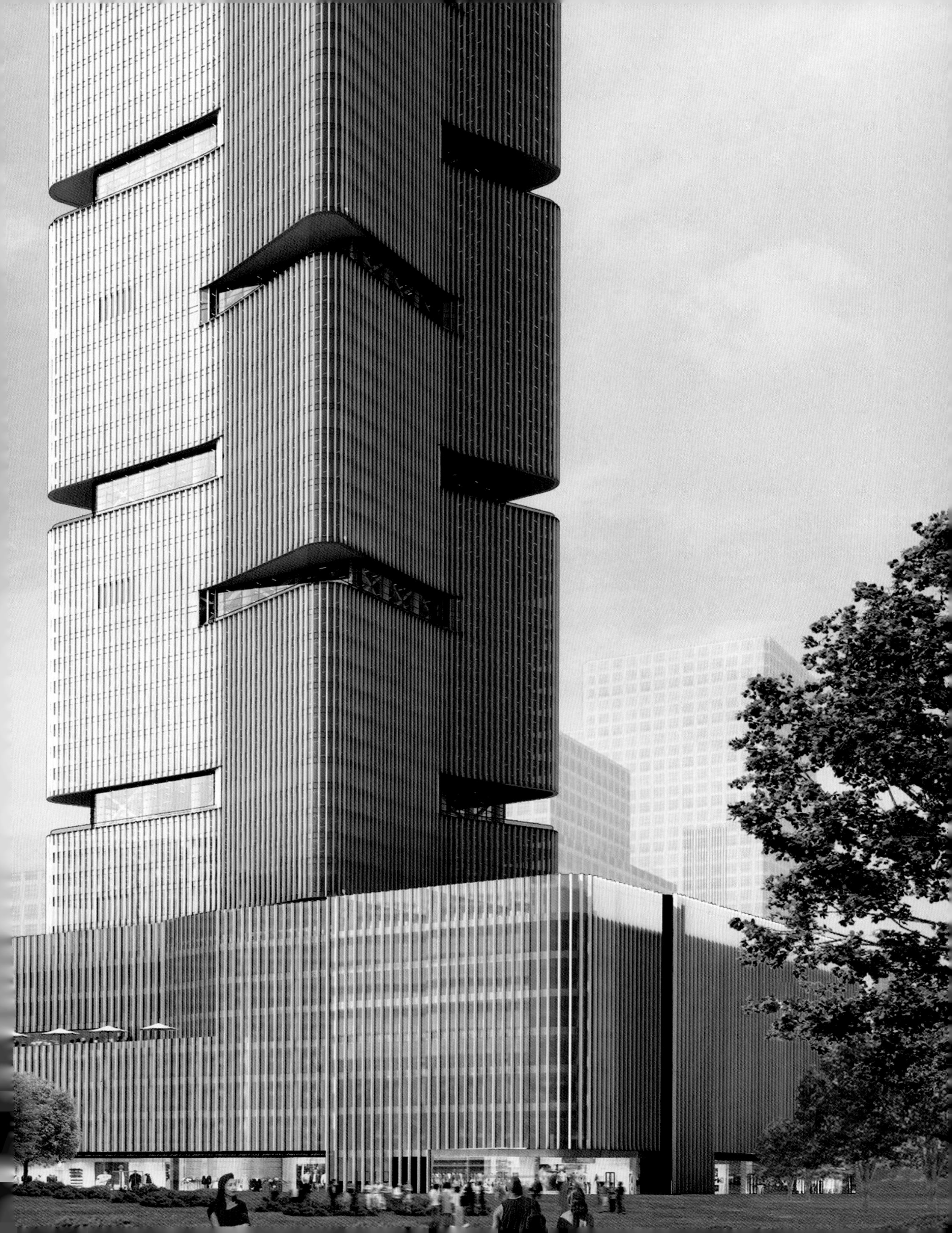

郑东绿地中心　郑州

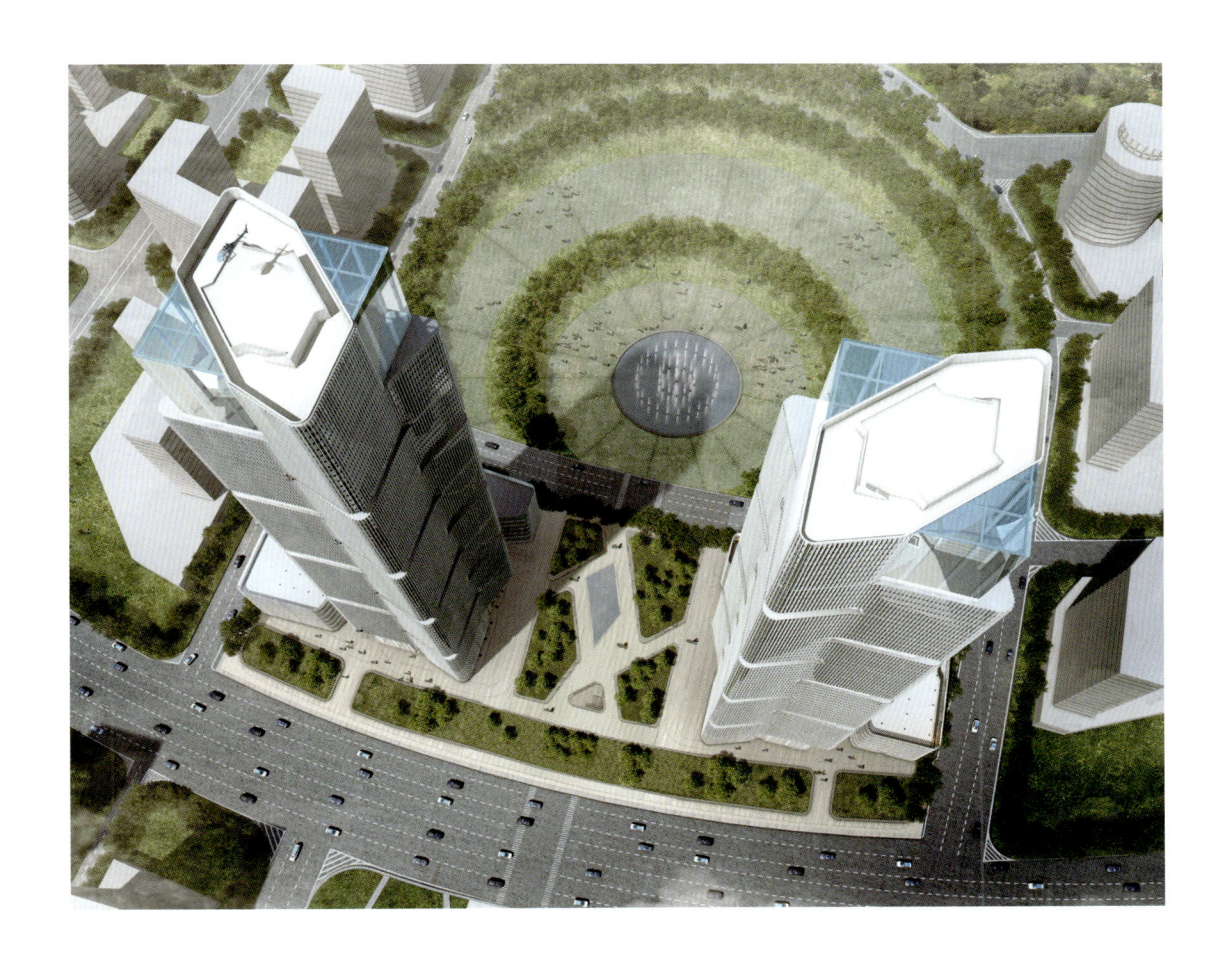

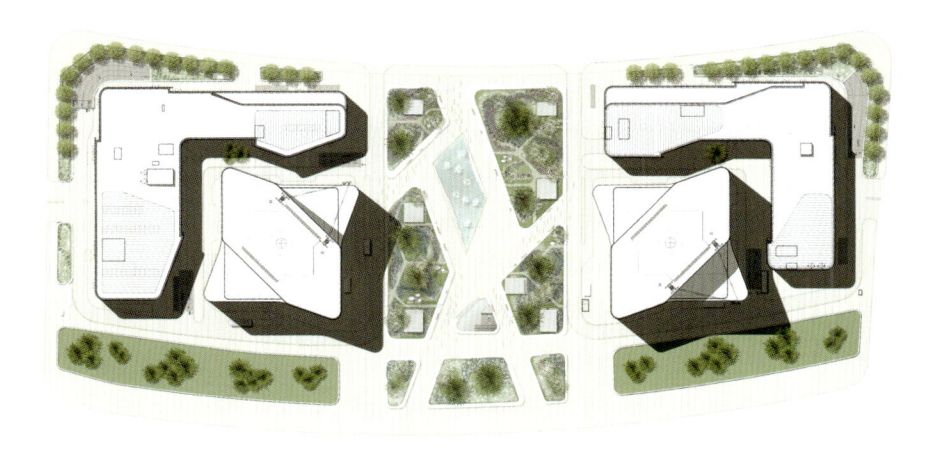

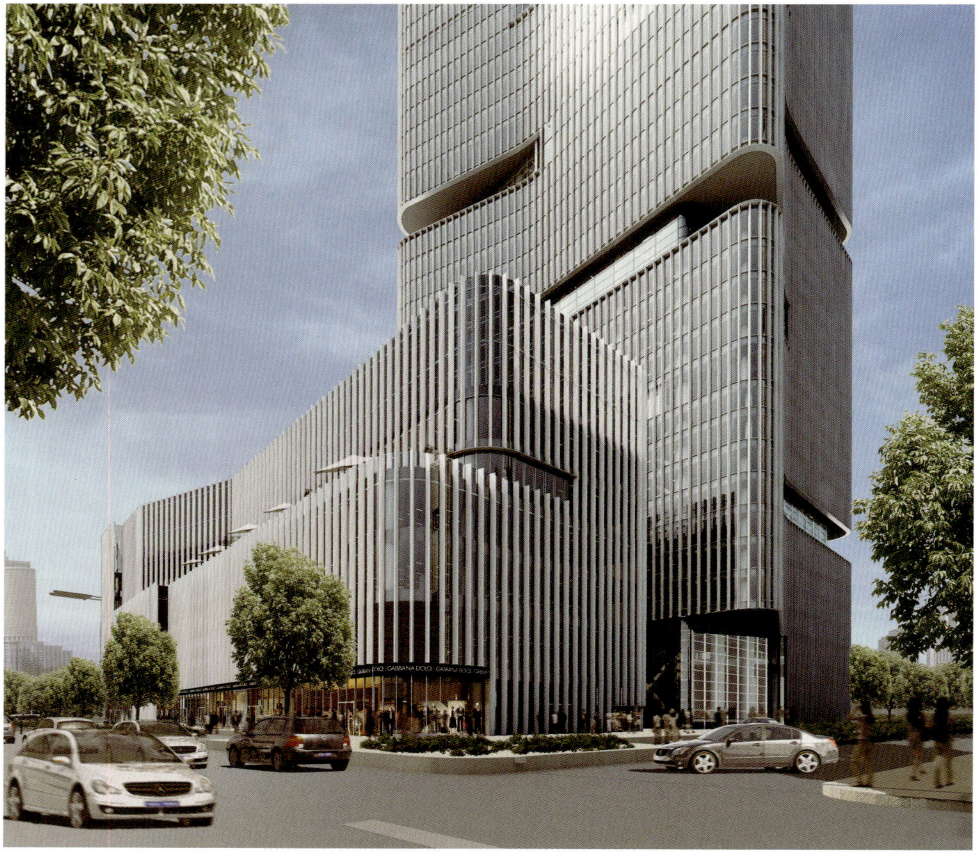

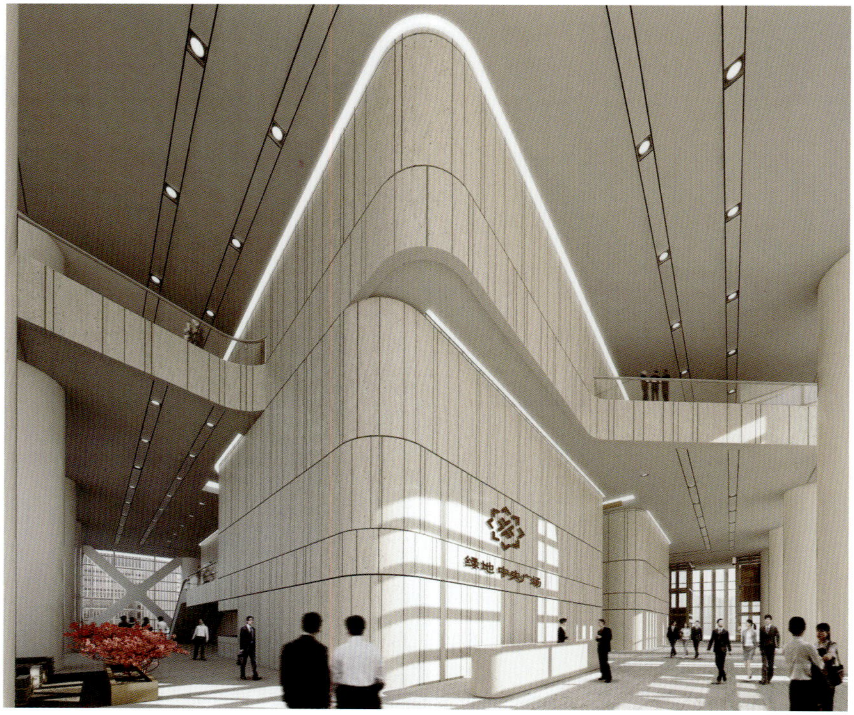

Greenland Central Plaza Zhengzhou

226 ²⁵
↑

印度理工学院
海得拉巴，印度

Indian Institute of Technology
Hyderabad, India

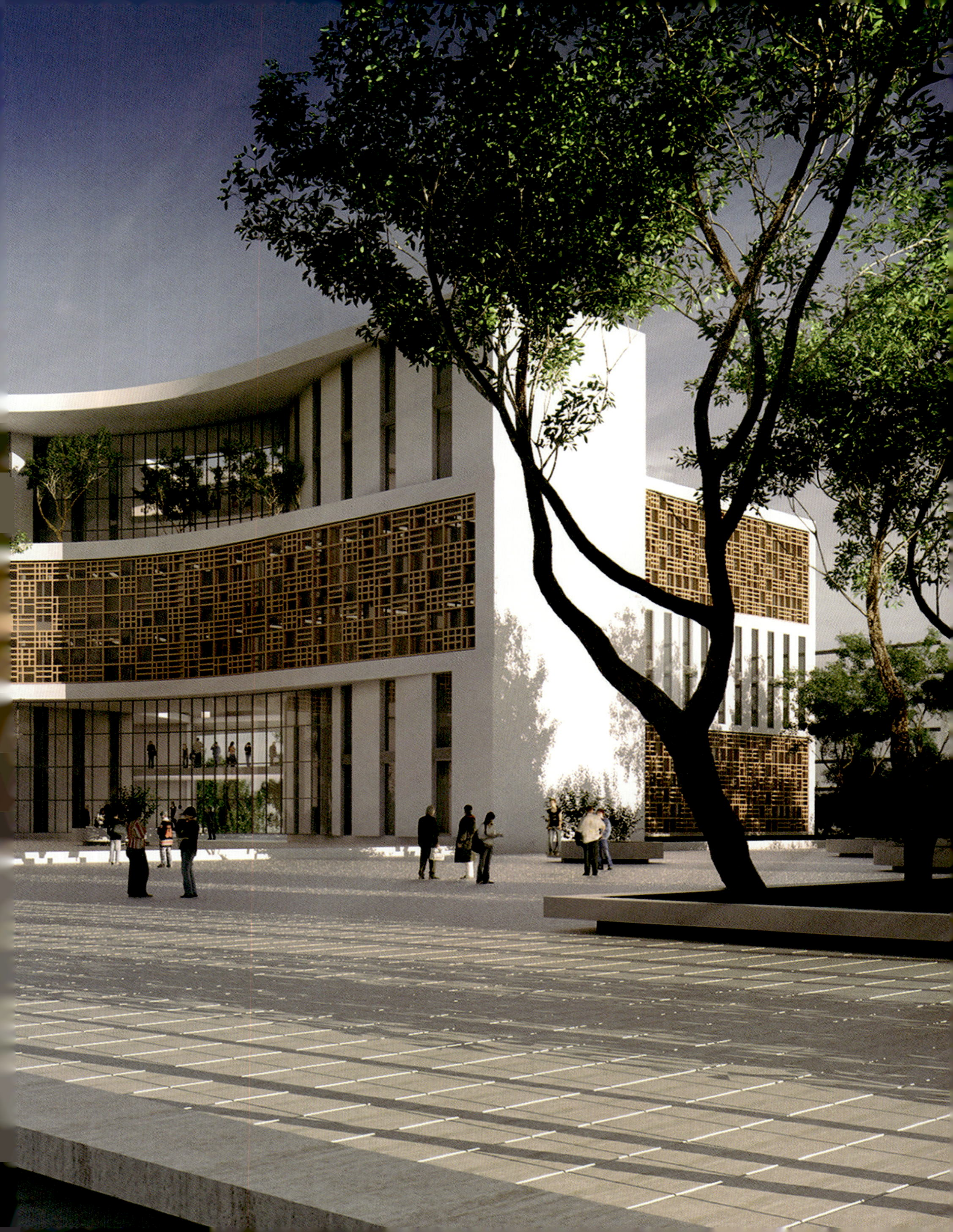

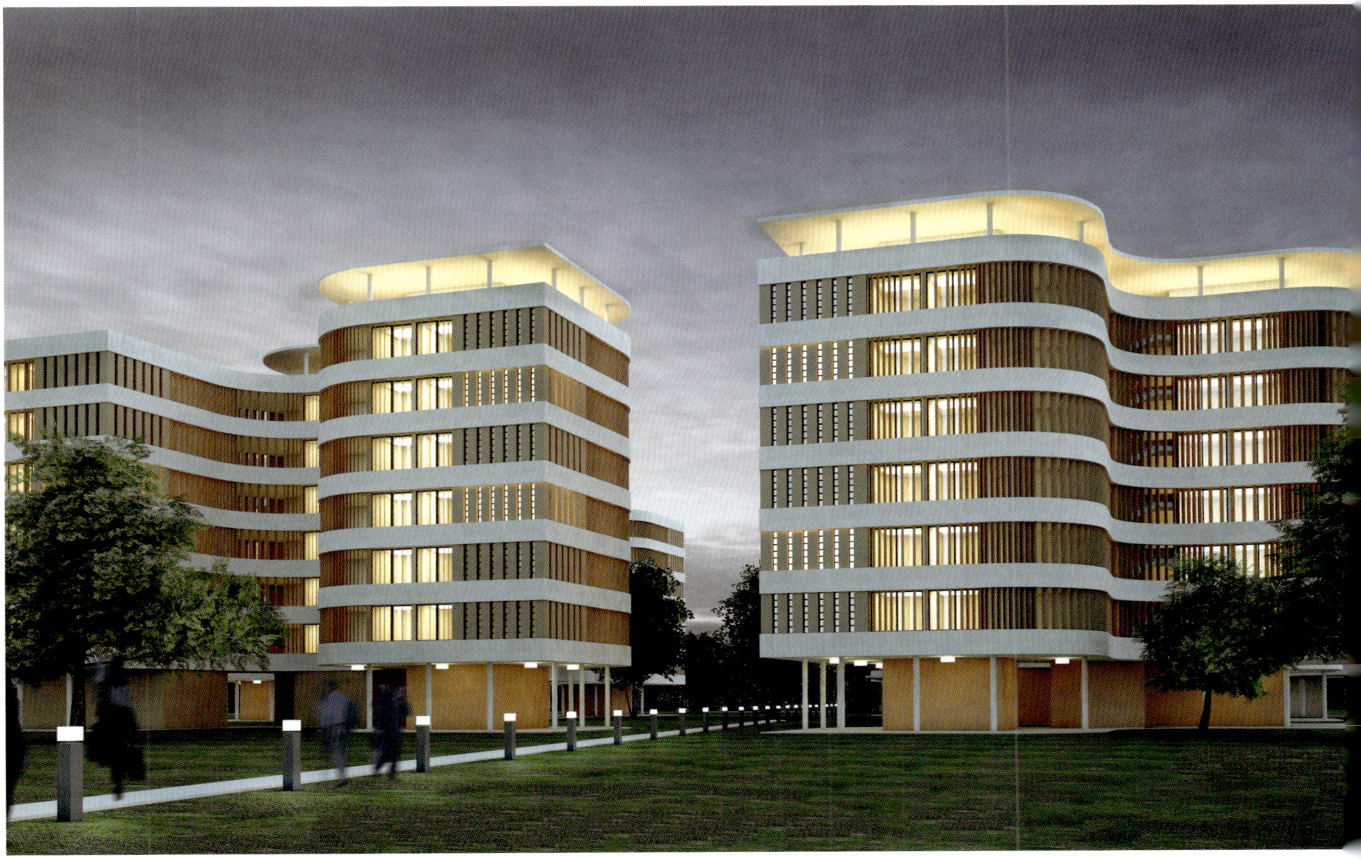

印度理工学院　海得拉巴

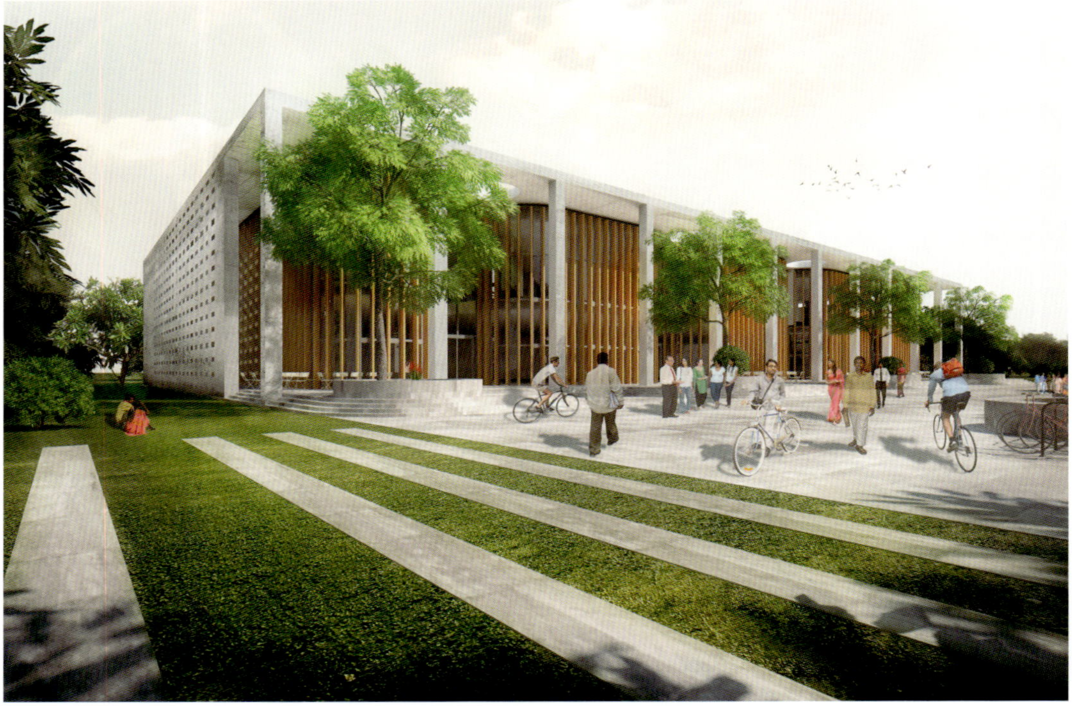

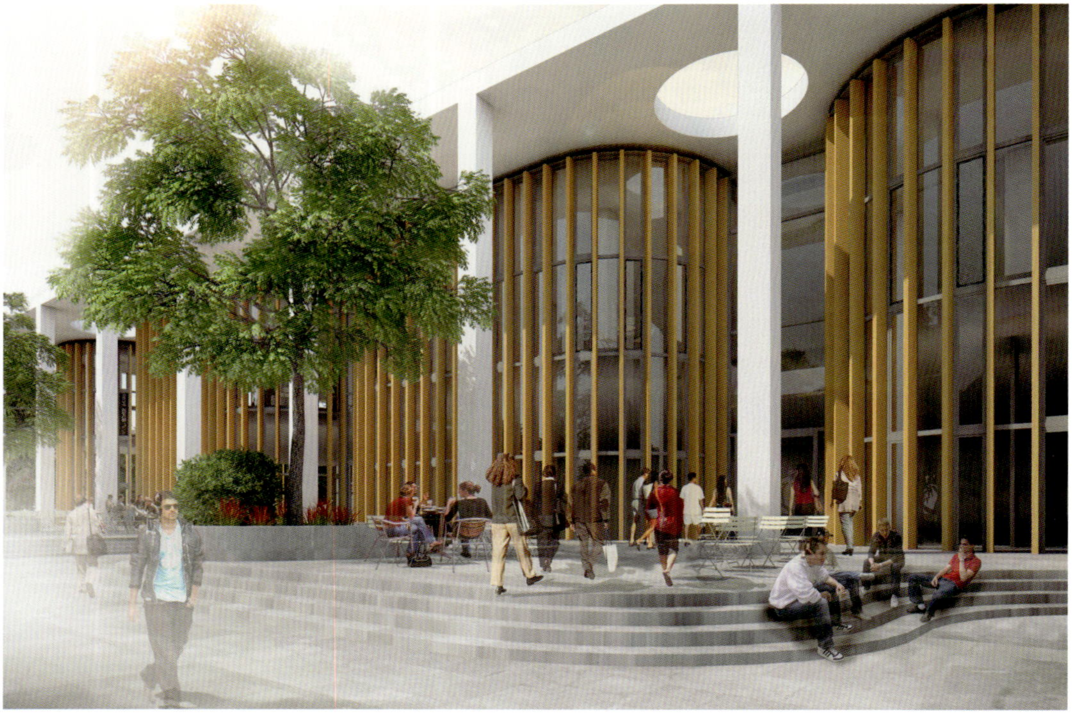

Indian Institute of Technology Hyderabad

230 $^{25}_\uparrow$

国家会展中心
天津，中国

**National Convention
and Exhibition Center**
Tianjin, China

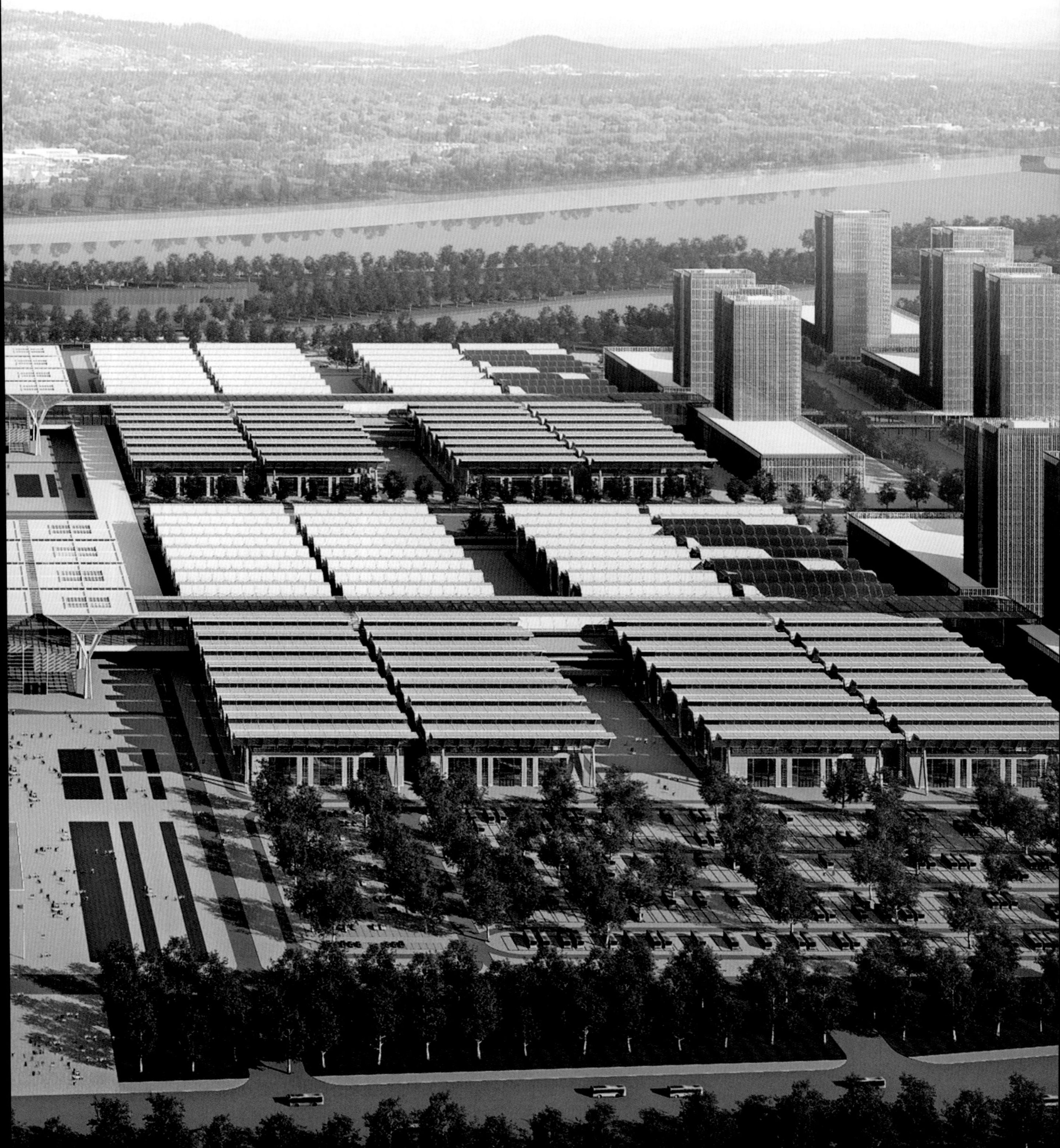

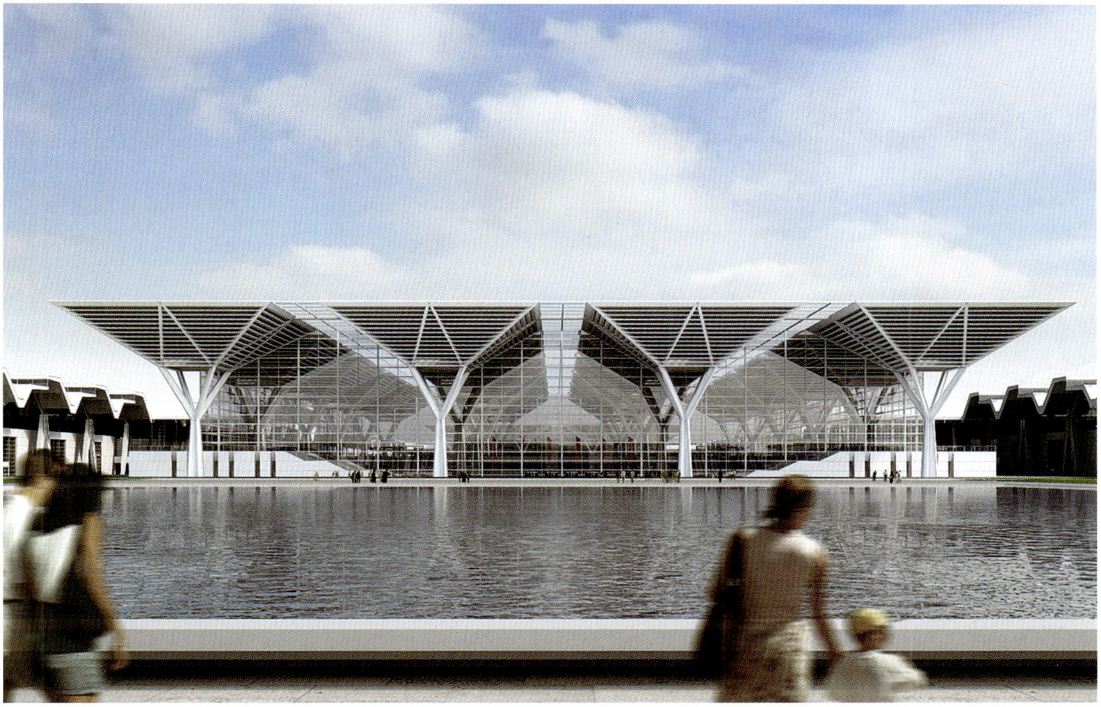

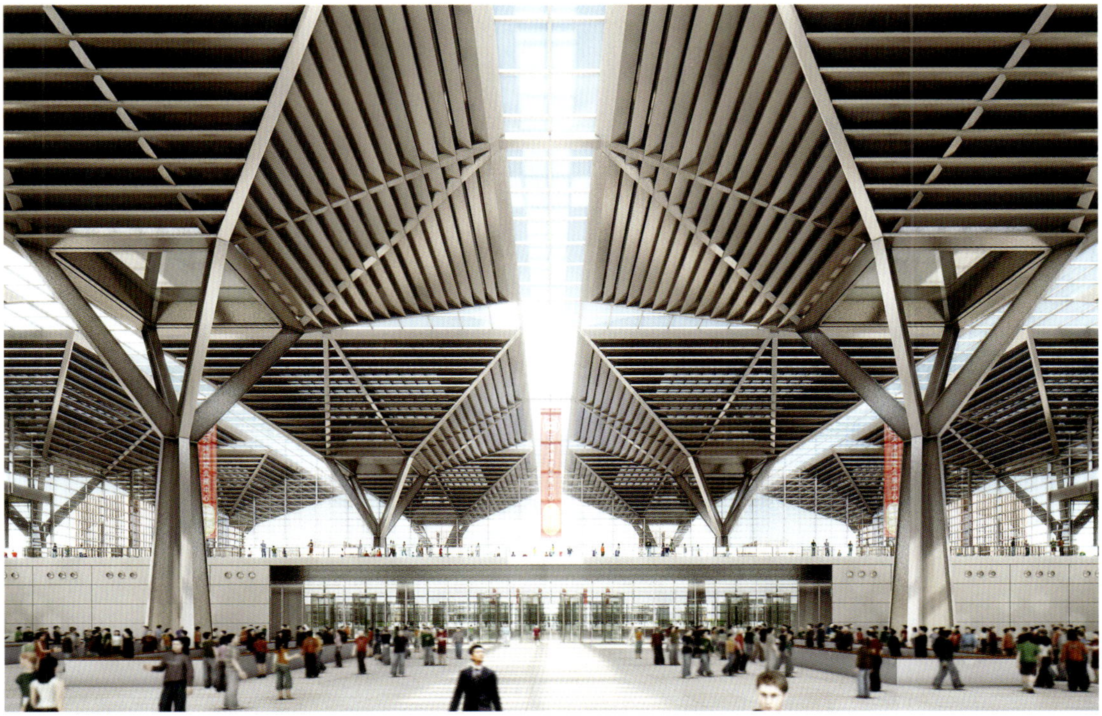

国家会展中心　天津

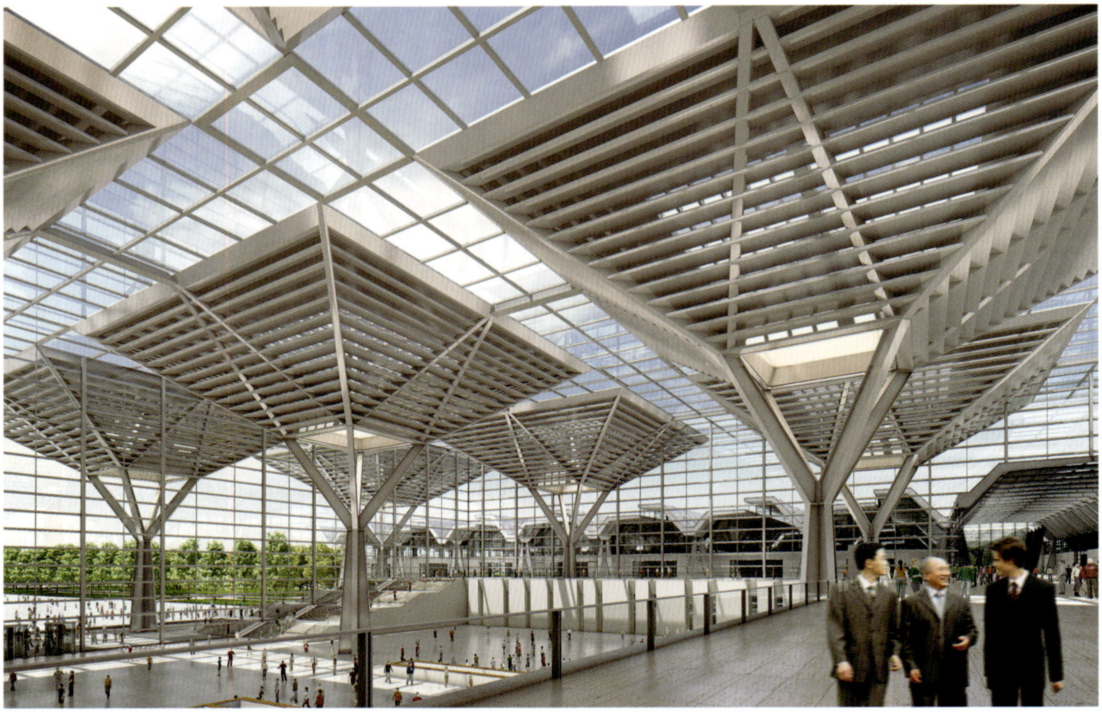

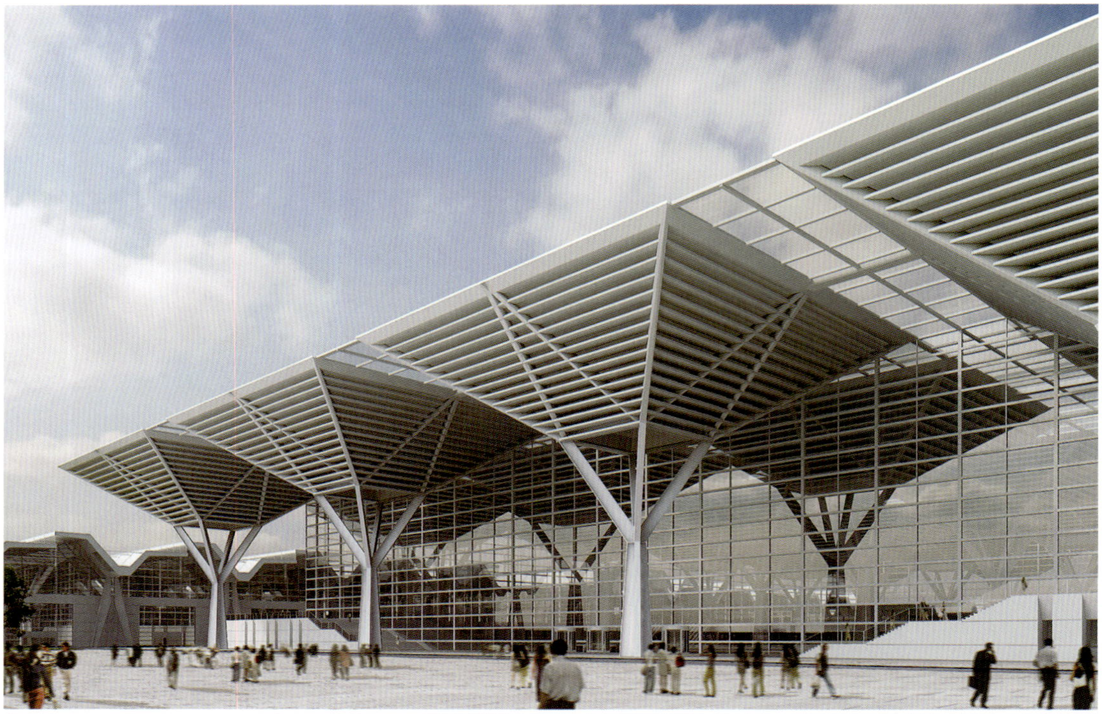

National Convention and Exhibition Center Tianjin

非洲
Africa

南非 South Africa
开普敦 Cape Town
德班 Durban
伊丽莎白港 Port Elizabeth

238

纳尔逊·曼德拉湾体育场
伊丽莎白港，南非

设计竞赛：2005年，一等奖　**方案设计**：福尔克温·玛格、胡贝特·尼恩霍夫以及霍格·贝兹　**项目负责人**：霍格·贝兹，Silke Flaßnöcker　**合作设计单位**：DBA 建筑事务所，波特·伊莎贝兹；ADA, Johannesburg; GAPP 建筑事务所，Cape Town; NOH 建筑事务所，波特·伊莎贝兹　**业主**：纳尔逊·曼德拉湾区政府，伊丽莎白港　**建设周期**：2007—2009年　**座席数**：46 000个

纳尔逊·曼德拉湾体育场位于起伏的山地上，毗邻湖面，围绕其四周建有阶梯平台。建筑的整体轮廓简洁，结构清晰。整座体育场被一座环形柱廊包围。玻璃休息厅在水平方向上定义了柱廊的终点。屋面呈花瓣状，其顶端从休息厅地面处伸出，向上弯曲成环形，悬浮于半空中。屋面结构设计充分考虑了当地的特殊情况，不但可以遮蔽阳光，还可阻挡当地常见的猛烈海风。屋面结构由三弦杆桁架结构托起的铝制屋面板构成，空隙处覆盖有白色PTFE膜。不透明和半透明模块的交替在体育场内部创造出独特的光影氛围。

Nelson Mandela Bay Stadium
Port Elizabeth, South Africa

Competition 2005 – 1st Prize　**Design** Volkwin Marg and Hubert Nienhoff with Holger Betz　**Project leaders** Holger Betz, Silke Flaßnöcker　**Co-operation with** DBA Architects, Port Elizabeth; ADA, Johannesburg; GAPP Architects, Cape Town; NOH Architects, Port Elizabeth　**Client** Nelson Mandela Bay Municipality, Port Elizabeth　**Construction period** 2007–2009　**Seats** 46,000

The stadium stands on a raised platform, in close proximity to the lake. Its silhouette is dominated by the curved shape of the roof girders and the structure of the stands, which includes a two-story colonnaded circulation area. The glazed box-level marks the top of the horizontal colonnades, from where the very wide girders of the cantilevered roof unfold like flowers towards the middle of the stadium. The roof gains its distinctive shape from the varying arrangement of triple chord girders clad in metal sheeting and the membrane fields between them. This matches the alternation of light and shade in the interior produced by the opaque and translucent roof covering.

244

开普敦体育场
开普敦，南非

咨询设计：2006年，一等奖　**方案设计**：福尔克温·玛格和胡贝特·尼恩霍夫及罗伯特·霍尔姆斯　**项目负责人**：罗伯特·霍尔姆斯，马丁·格兰斯　**项目经理**：米歇·罗格联合设计单位：路易斯·卡罗尔建筑事务所，尖端建筑事务所，开普敦业主：开普敦市，spv 2010　**建设周期**：2007—2010年　**座位数**：68 000个

开普敦体育场作为独立建筑，如同一颗宝石镶嵌在信号山脚下的绿点公园中，与周围的自然环境优雅地融为一体。体育场外壳由抽象的线条划分的薄膜结构组成，赋予建筑体强烈的雕塑感，加强了其个体与周围风景的联系。顶棚结构是悬吊式顶棚和放射状龙骨结构。起伏的外立面采用强化复合玻璃，内壁由透明薄膜覆盖。

Cape Town Stadium
Cape Town, South Africa

Consultancy 2006 – 1st Prize　**Design** Volkwin Marg and Hubert Nienhoff with Robert Hormes　**Project leaders** Robert Hormes, Martin Glass　**Project management** Michèle Rüegg　**Co-operation with** Louis Karol architects, Point architects, Cape Town　**Client** City of Cape Town, spv 2010　**Construction period** 2007–2010　**Seats** 68,000

Cape Town Stadium is situated as a solitary body, embedded in Green Point Common park at the foot of Signal Hill and is ordered into the landscaped complex. The shell of the stadium was designed as an abstract, linearly arranged membrane construction, which transforms the stadium into a sculpture and intensifies its integration in the existing landscape. The roof construction is a combination of a suspended roof with radial truss structure. It is outfitted with laminated safety glass elements and its interior is clad with a diaphanous membrane.

摩西·马布海达体育场
德班，南非

设计竞赛： 2006年，一等奖 **方案设计：** 福尔克温·玛格，胡贝特·尼思霍夫以及霍格·贝兹 **项目负责人：** 霍格·贝兹，贝兹和伊莎贝拉·曼妮以及伯克哈德·皮克 **合作设计单位：** IBHOLA LETHU CONSORTIUM, Theunissen Jankowitz 建筑事务所，Ambro Afrique 建筑事务所，Osmond Lange 建筑事务所，NSM 设计，Mthulusi Msimang 建筑事务所，SA **业主：** Municipality of Durban (eThekwini Municipality), Stategic Projects Unit **建设周期：** 2006—2009年 **座席数：** 70 000个

摩西·马布海达体育场坐落于印度洋岸边的中央体育公园内一个被抬起的平台上，其通向城市的一面为一座宽大的阶梯。一座高105米的拱结构极富标志性，令体育馆成为城市天际线上一道宏伟的景观，此外其还承担了膜状顶棚的全部荷载。碗状看台造型由圆形屋面构造结合体育馆几何形式发展而来。建筑外立面膜结构材质为带孔薄板，其在抵挡狂风暴雨冲击和阳光直射的同时可保证与外界的交流不受阻碍。

Moses Mabhida Stadium
Durban, South Africa

Competition 2006 – 1st Prize **Design** Volkwin Marg and Hubert Nienhoff with Holger Betz **Project leaders** Holger Betz, Elisabeth Menne, Burkhard Pick **Co-operation with** IBHOLA LETHU CONSORTIUM, Theunissen Jankowitz Architects, Ambro Afrique Architects, Osmond Lange Architects, NSM Designs, Mthulusi Msimang Architects, SA **Client** Municipality of Durban (eThekwini Municipality), Stategic Projects Unit **Construction period** 2006–2009 **Seats** 70,000

Moses Mabhida Stadium is situated on an elevated platform in the central sports park on the shore of the Indian Ocean. A 105-meter arch rises high over the stadium as a landmark visible from afar. It carries the weight of the inner membrane roof. The shape of the bowl results from the interaction of the circular roof structure with the triple-radius geometry of the arena. The facade membrane of perforated metal sheeting provides protection against driving rain, strong winds and direct sunlight without excluding the outside world.

238 ²³⁶ ↑

纳尔逊·曼德拉湾体育场
伊丽莎白港，南非

Nelson Mandela Bay Stadium
Port Elizabeth, South Africa

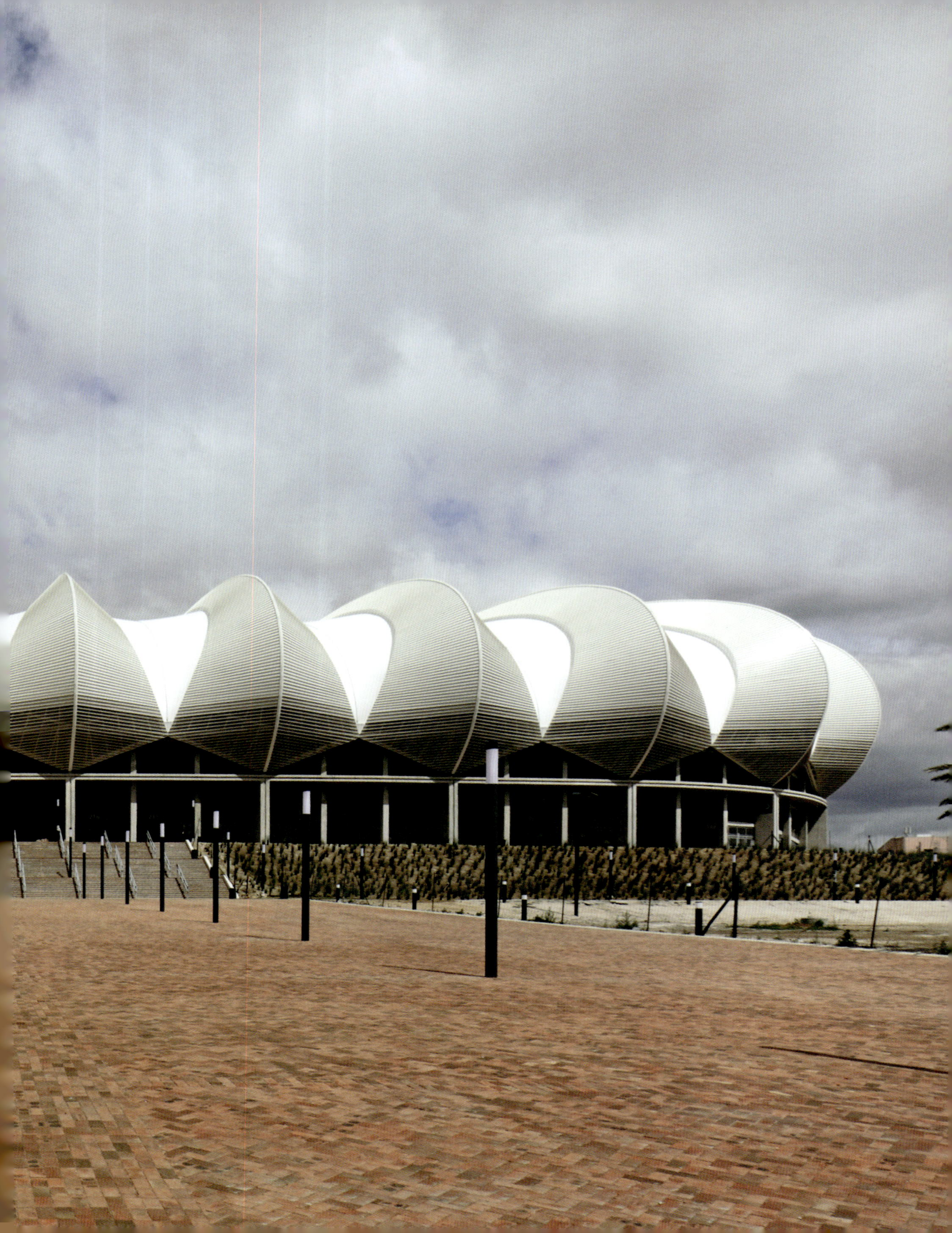

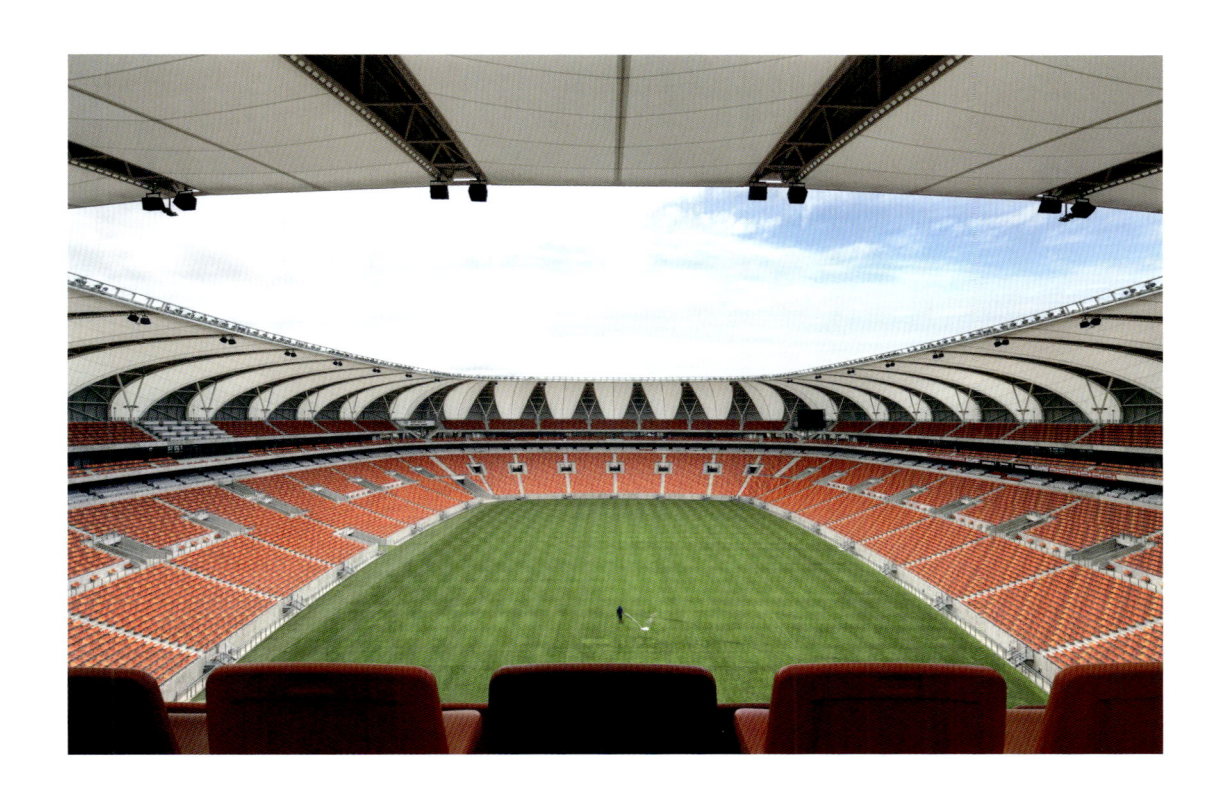

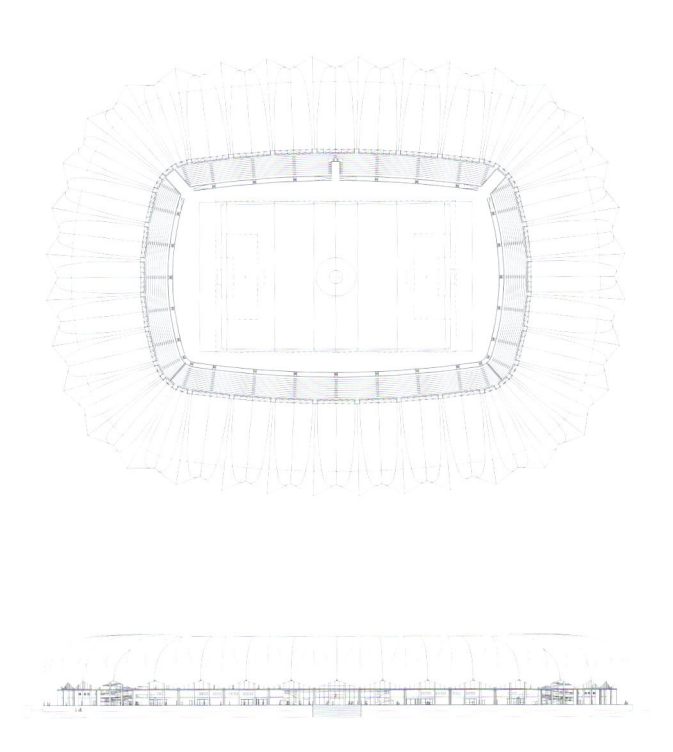

纳尔逊·曼德拉湾体育场　伊丽莎白港

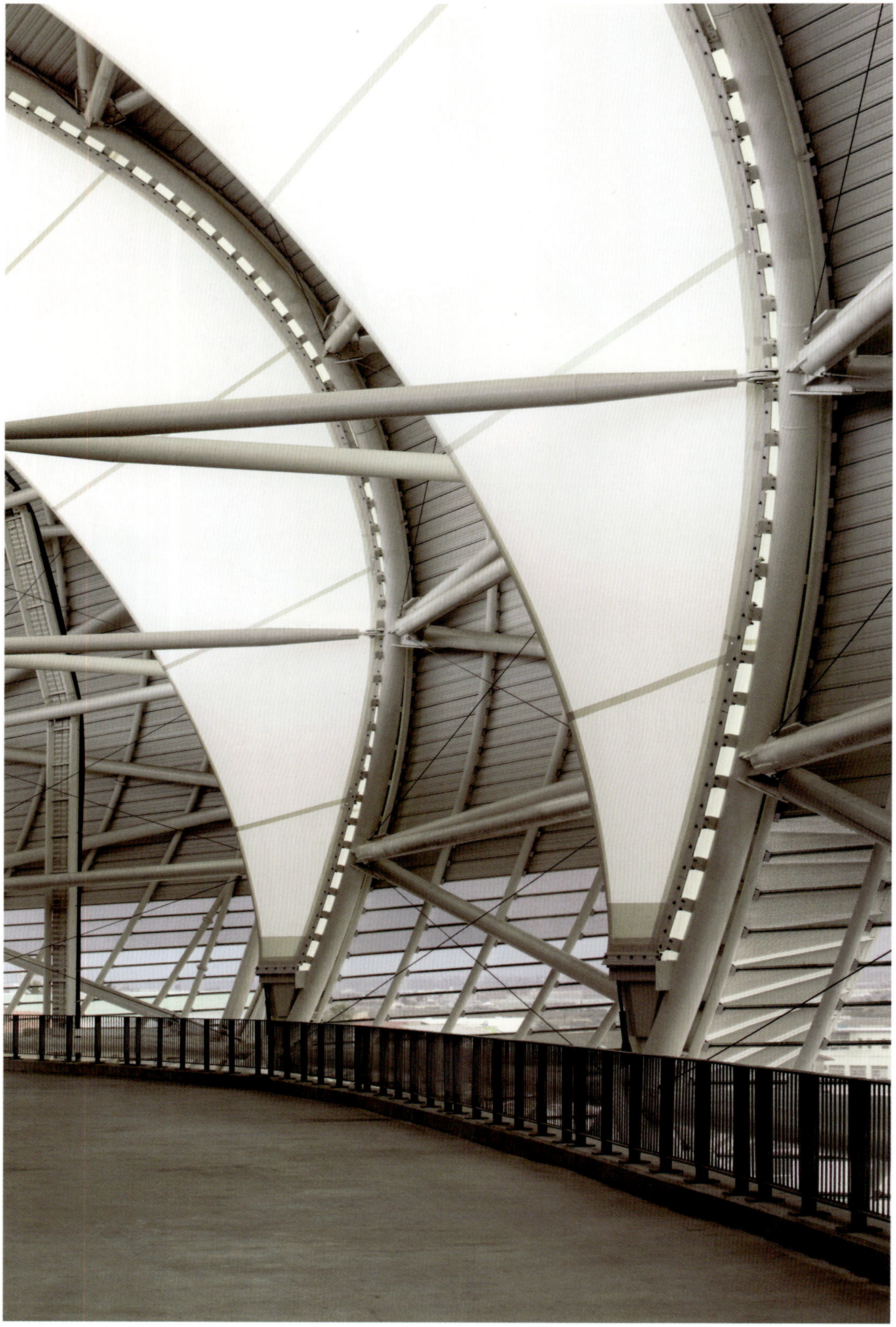

Nelson Mandela Bay Stadium Port Elizabeth

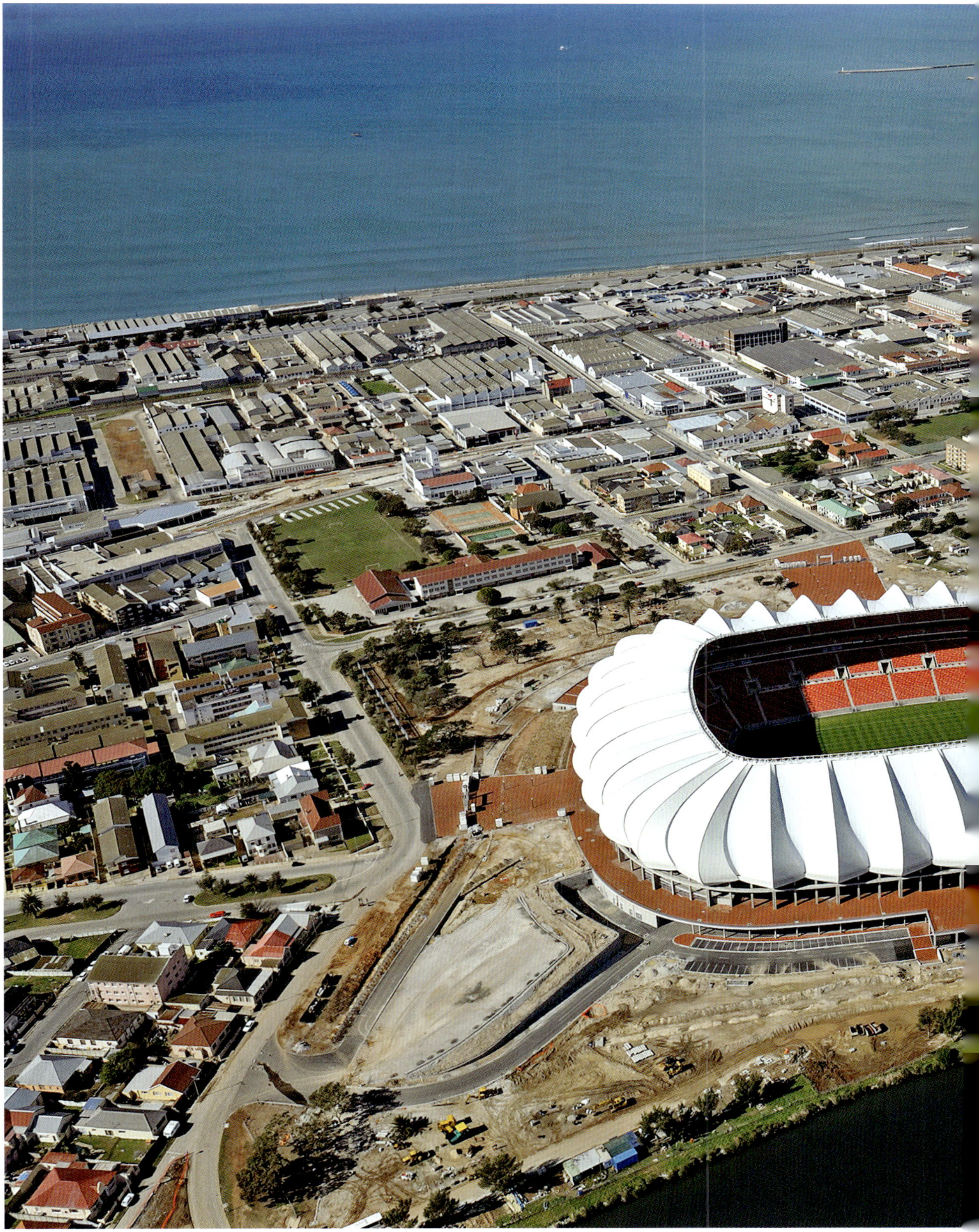

纳尔逊·曼德拉湾体育场　伊丽莎白港

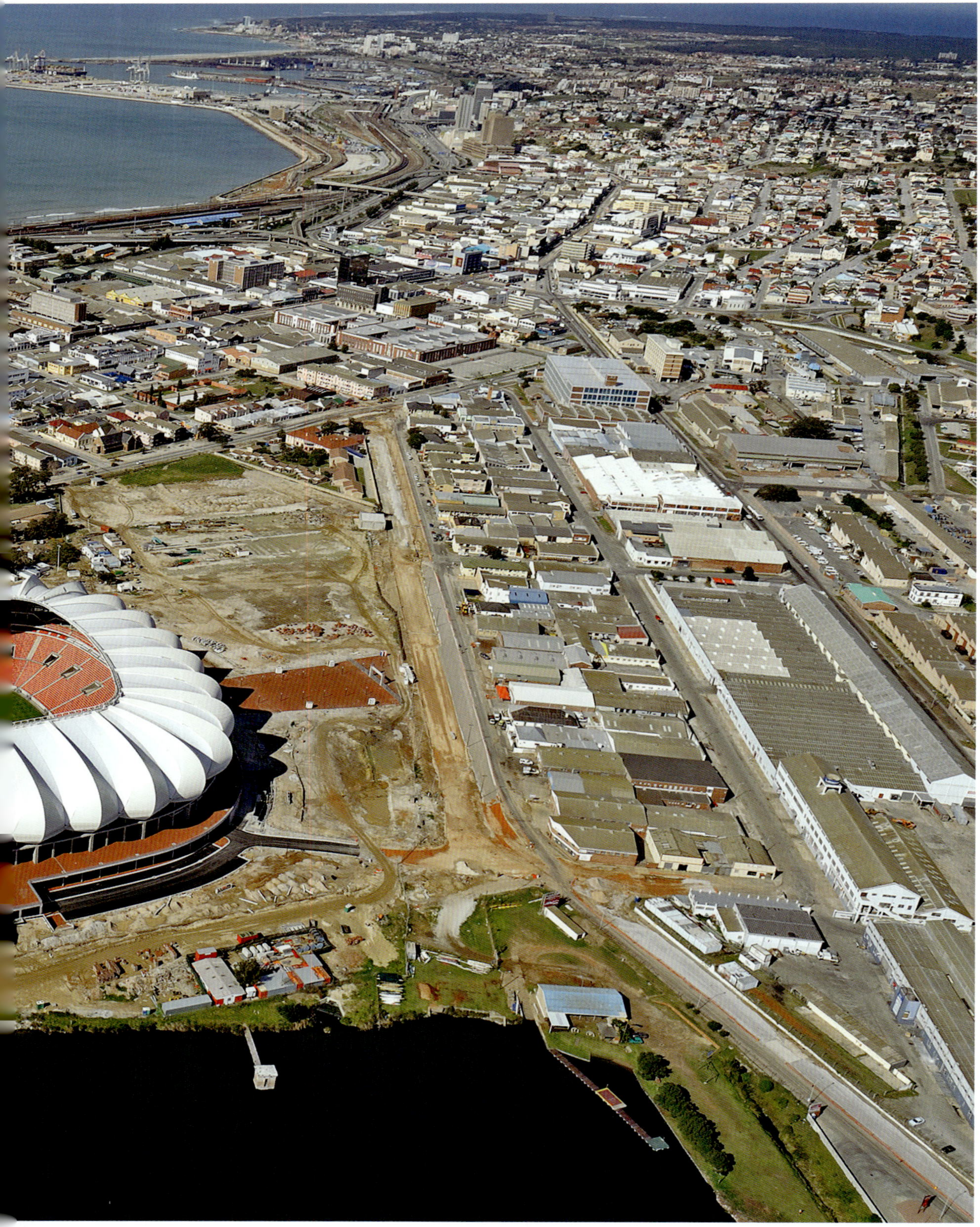

Nelson Mandela Bay Stadium Port Elizabeth

244 ²³⁶ ↑

开普敦体育场
开普敦，南非

Cape Town Stadium
Cape Town, South Africa

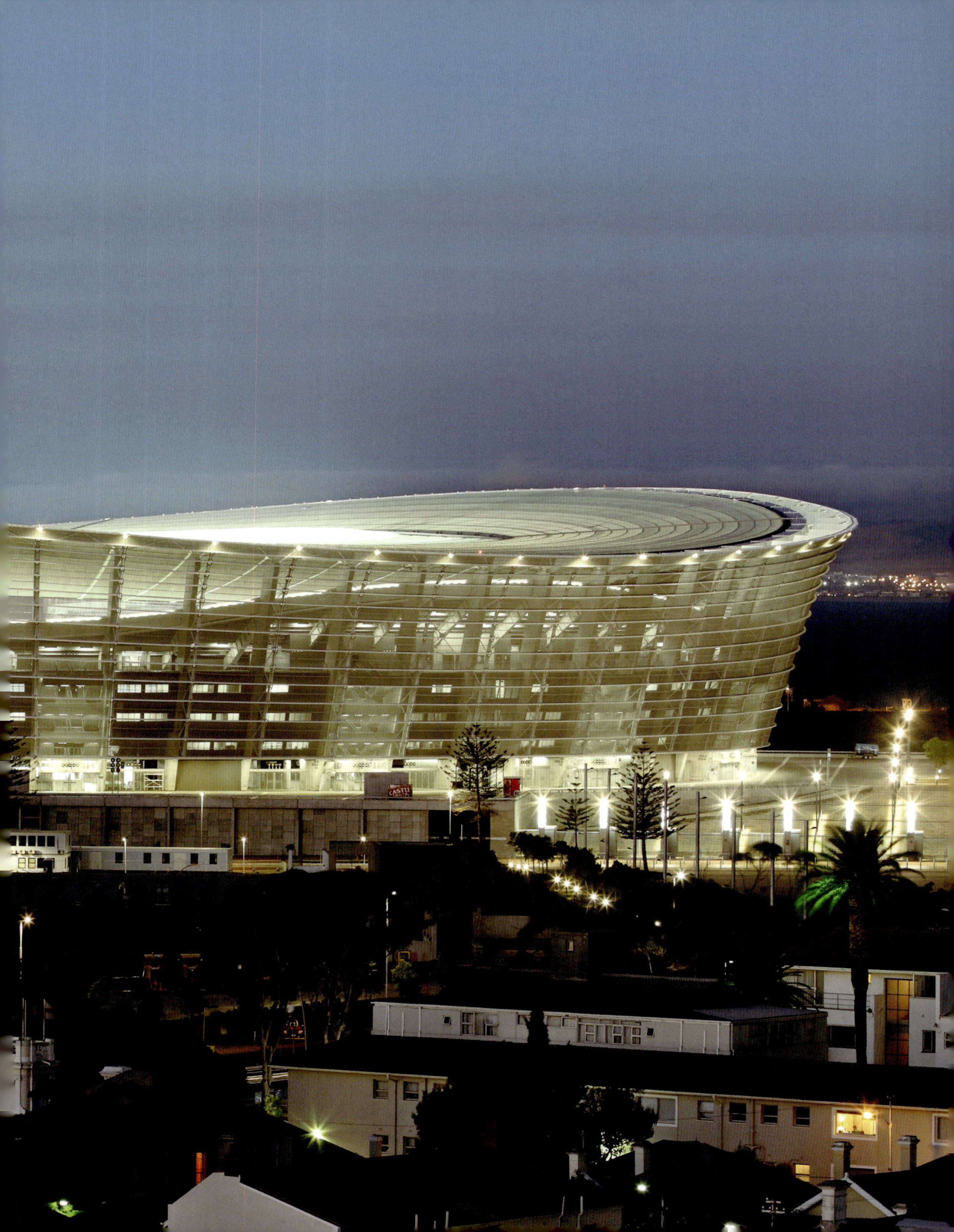

246　开普敦体育场　开普敦

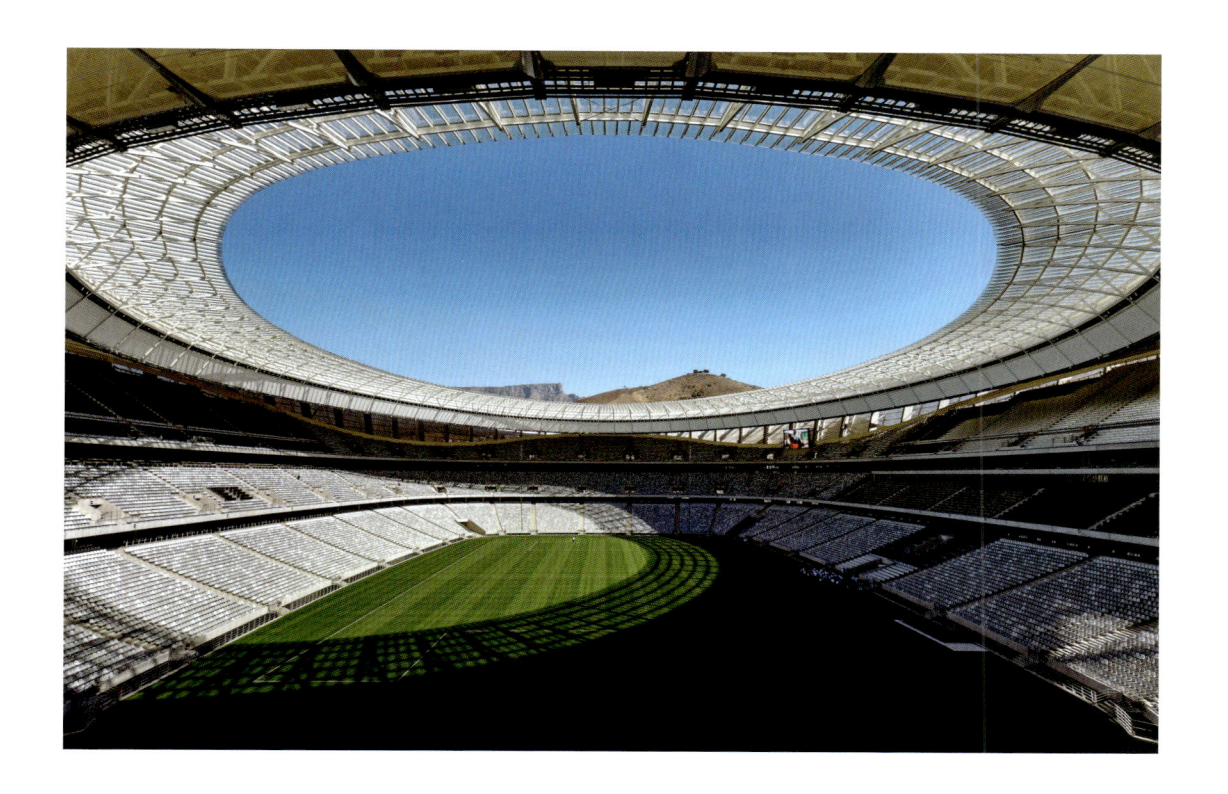

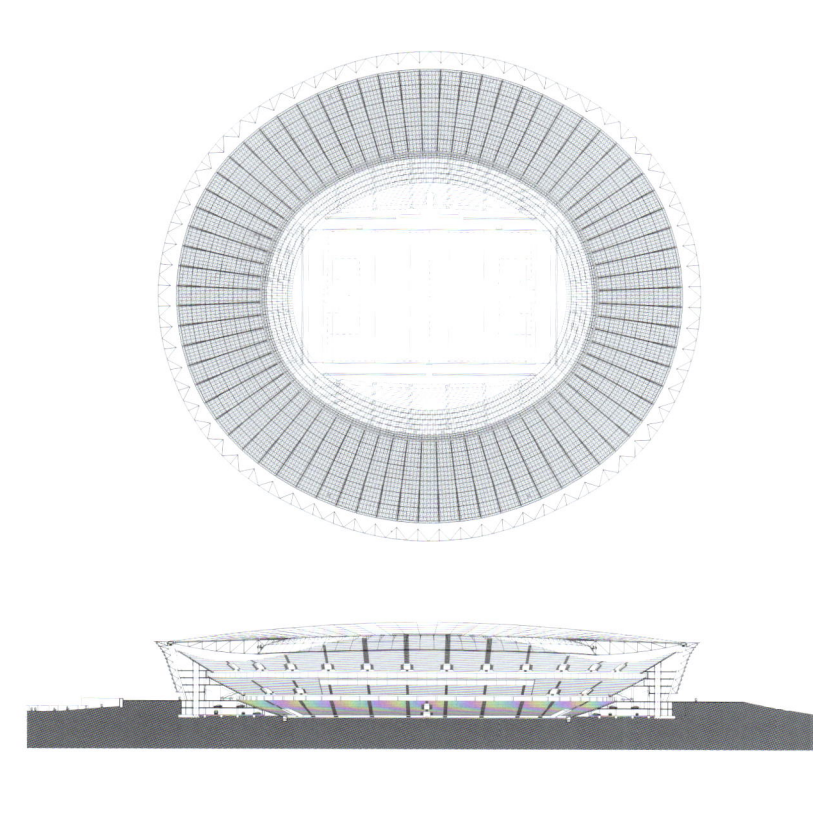

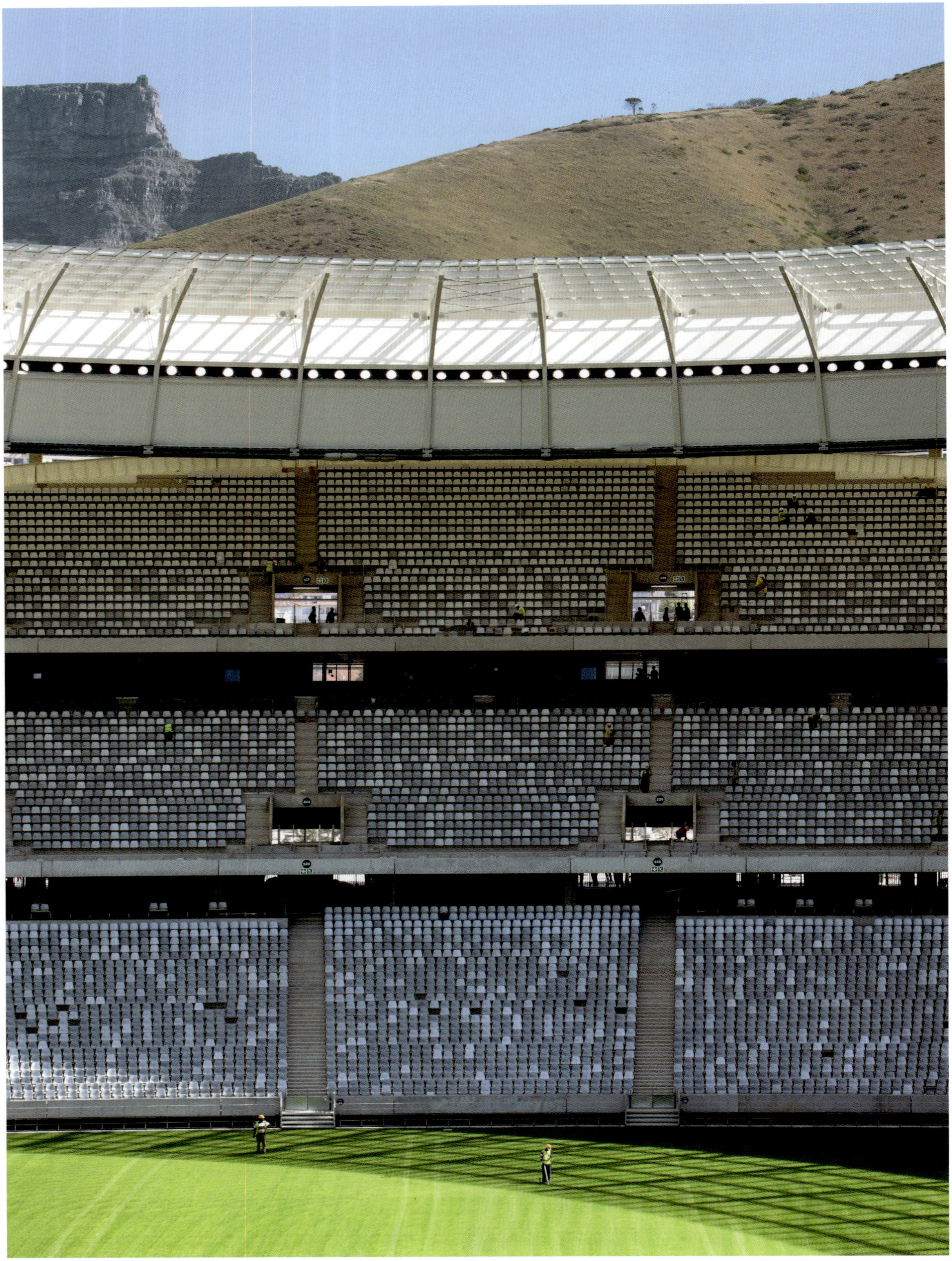

Cape Town Stadium Cape Town

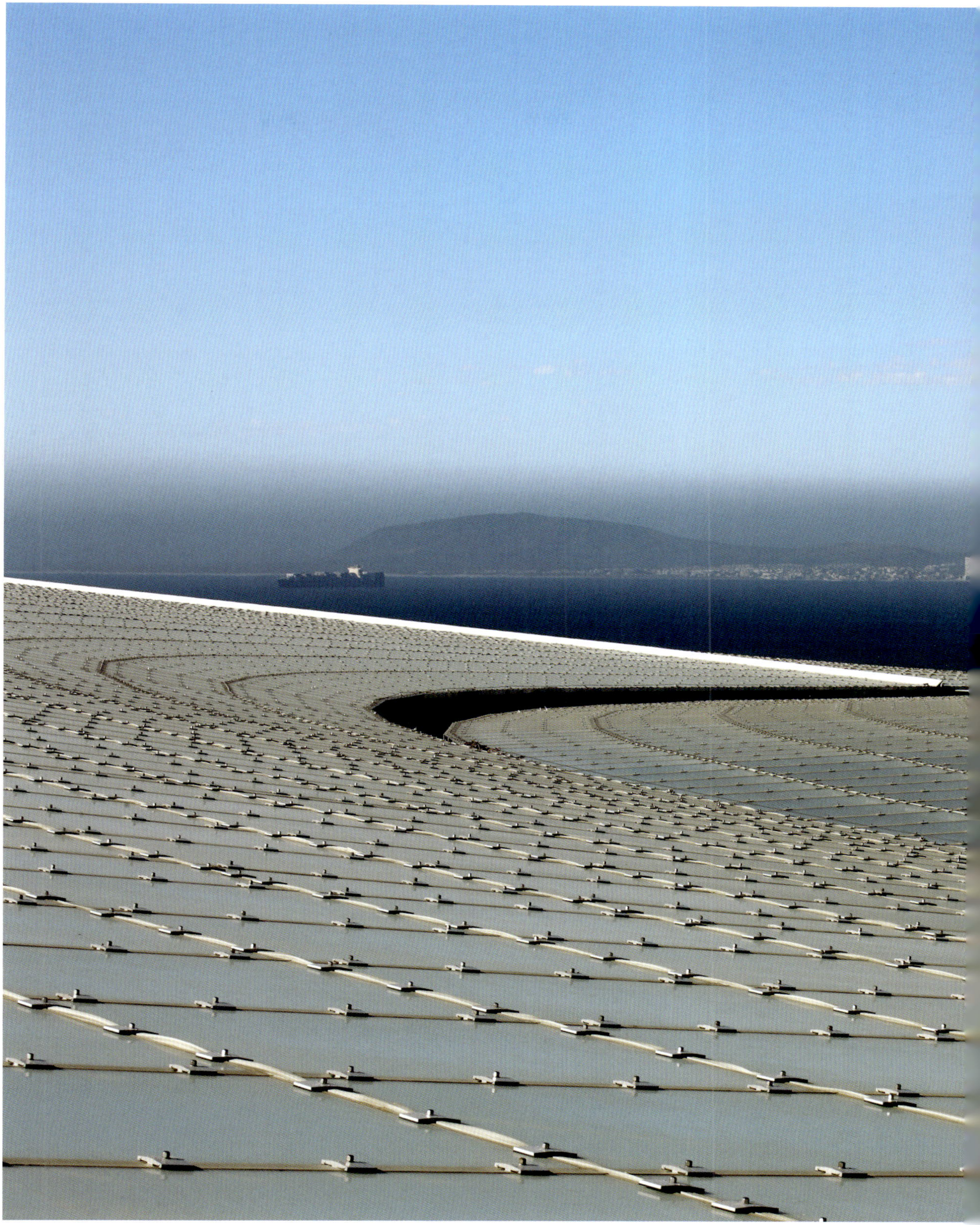

开普敦体育场　开普敦

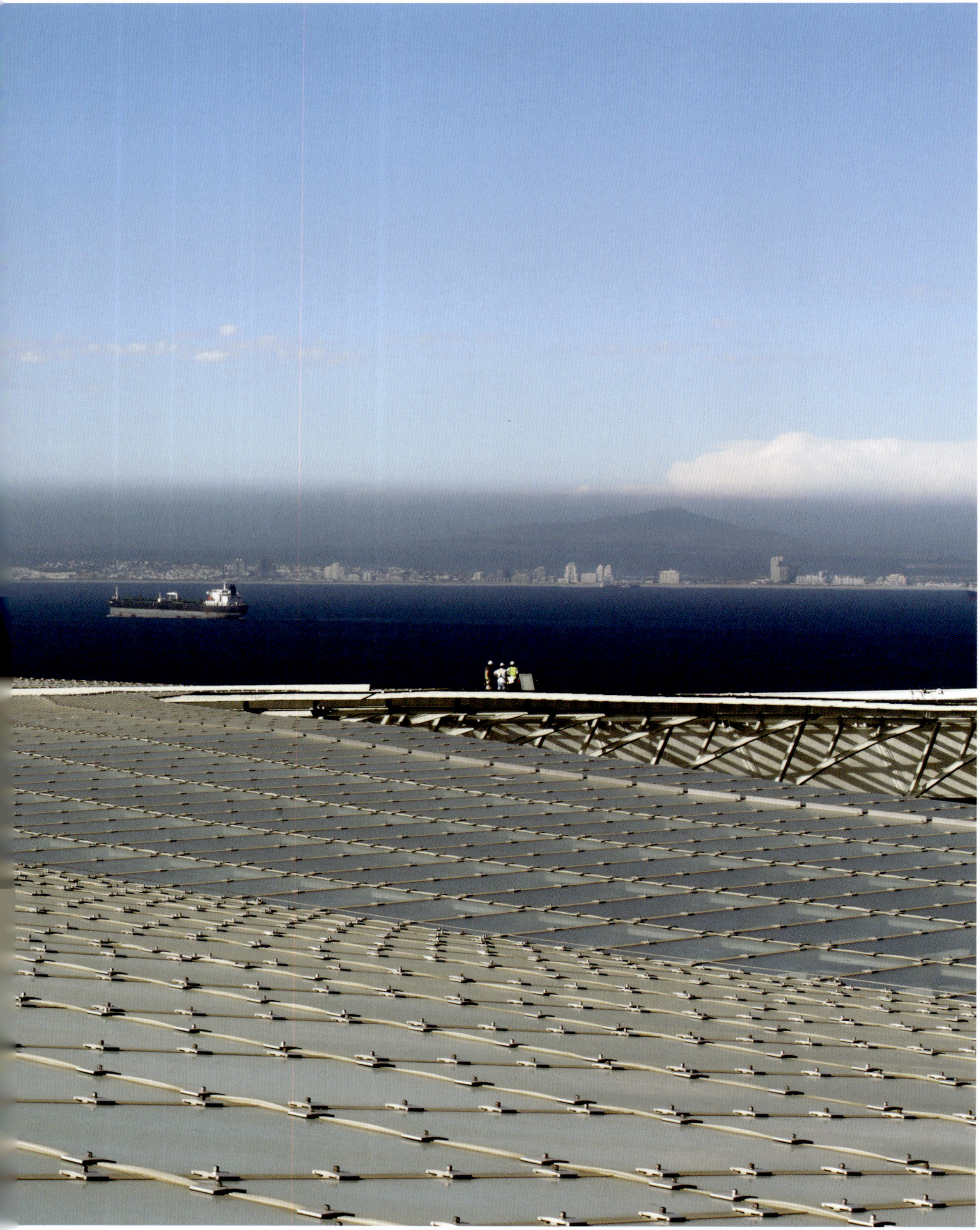

Cape Town Stadium Cape Town

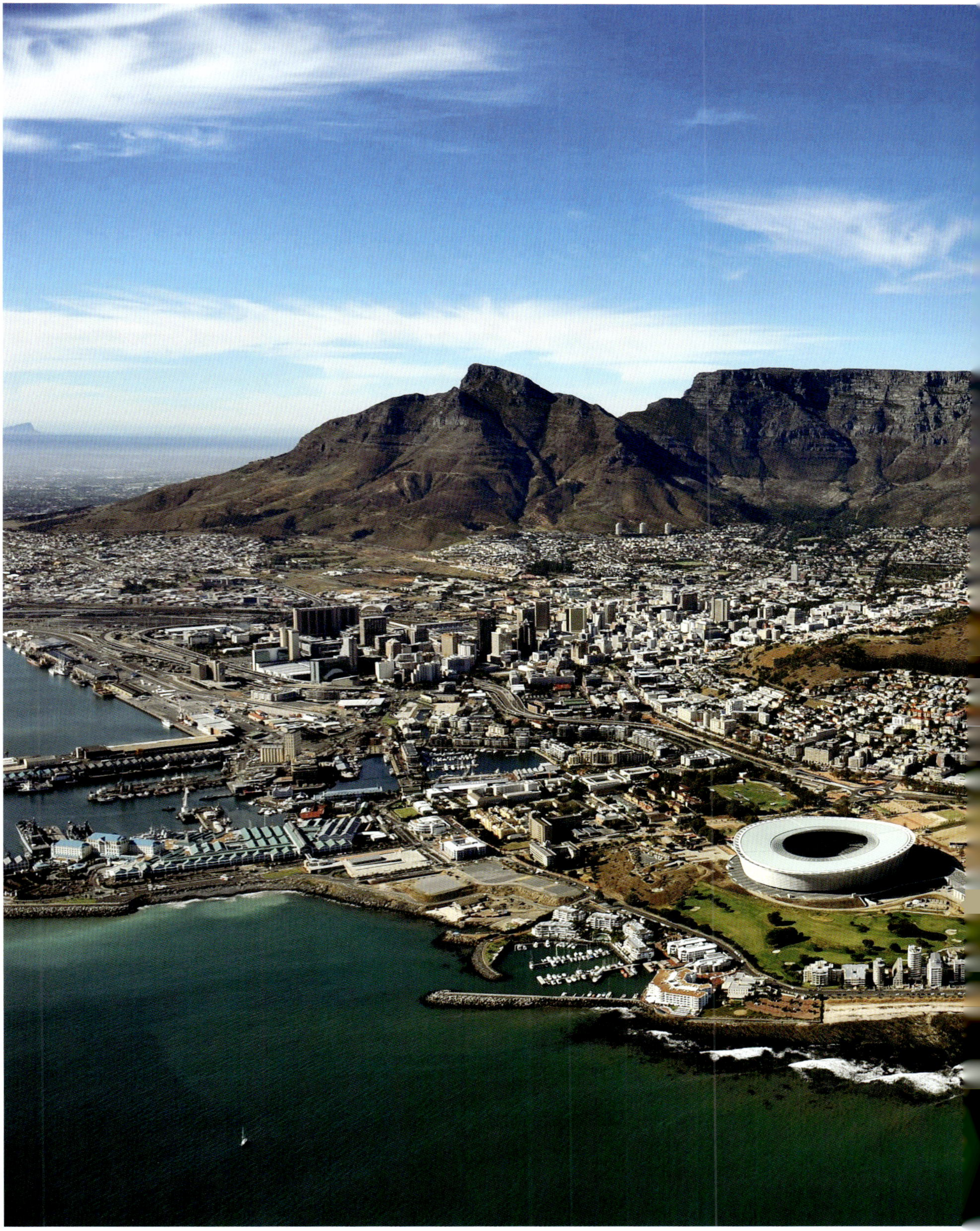

开普敦体育场　开普敦

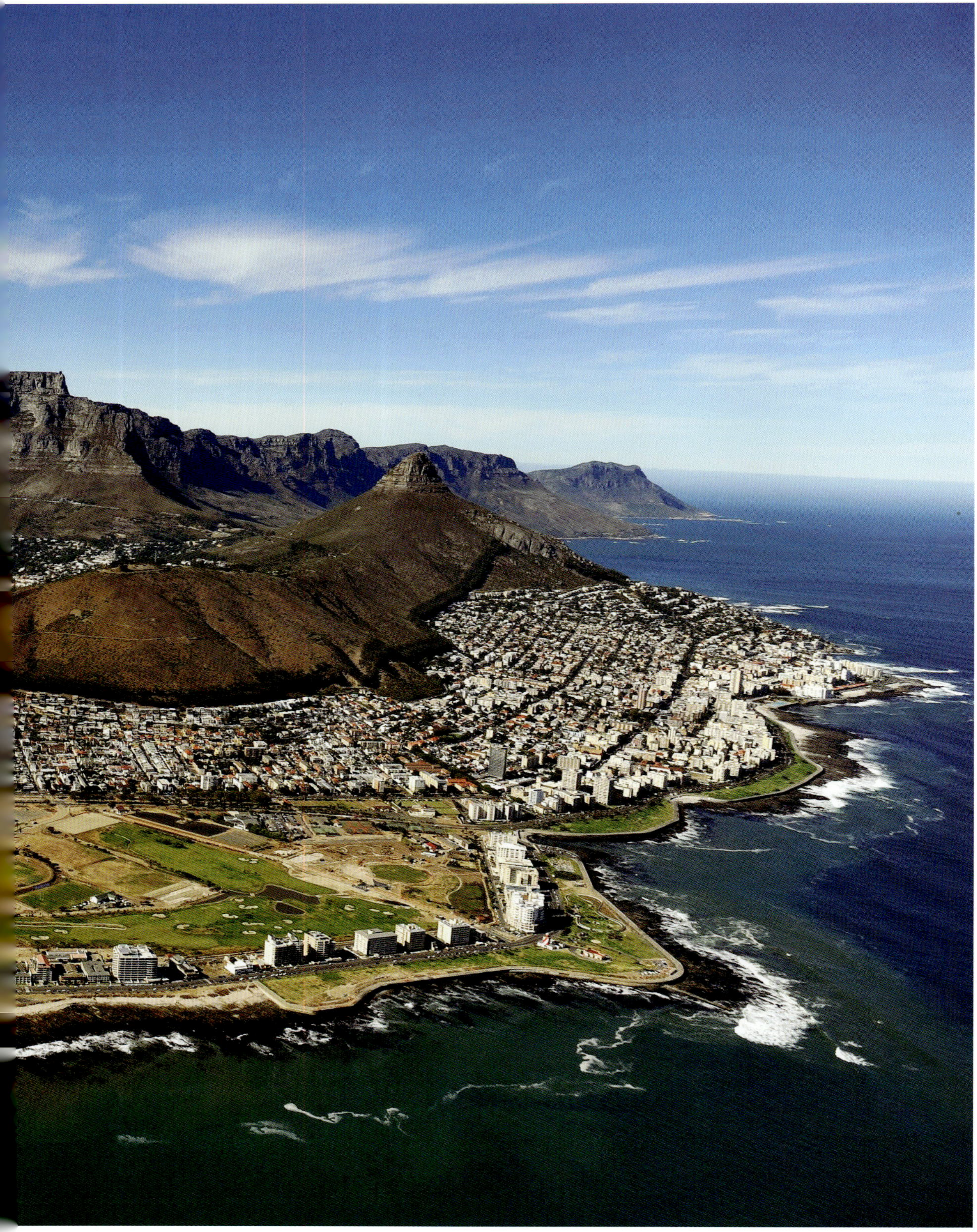

Cape Town Stadium Cape Town

252 ²³⁷ ↑

摩西·马布海达体育场
德班，南非

Moses Mabhida Stadium
Durban, South Africa

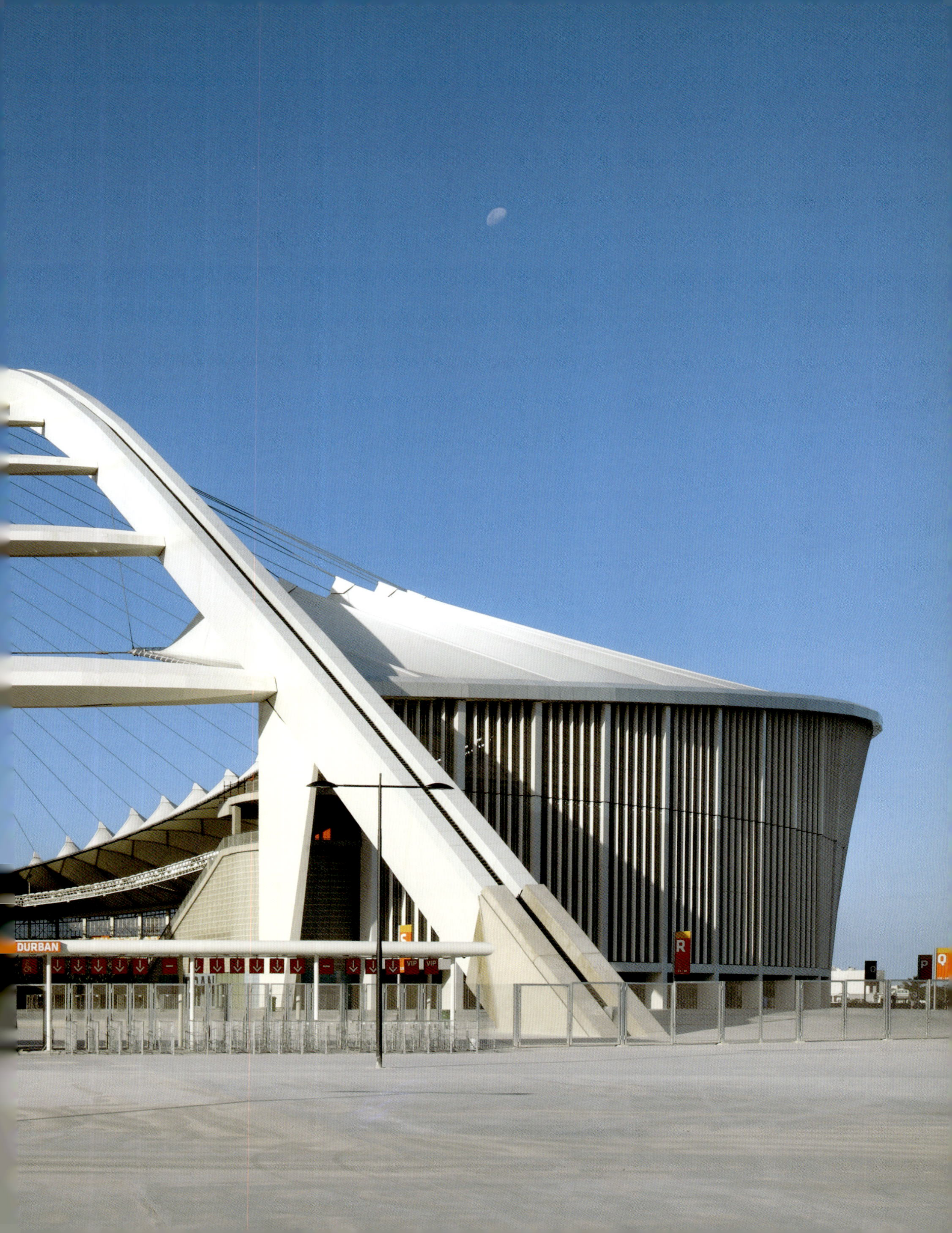
DURBAN
VIP
VIP
R
P
Q

254　摩西·马布海达体育场　德班

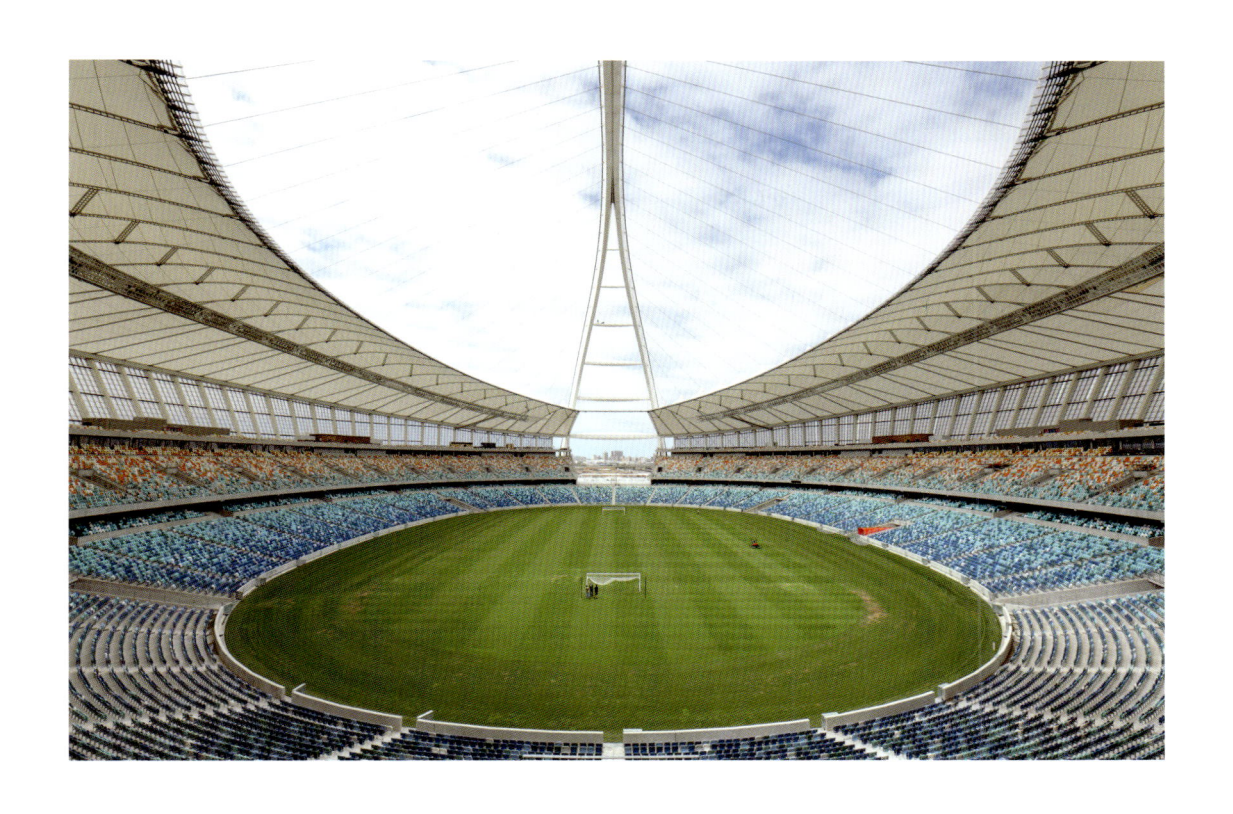

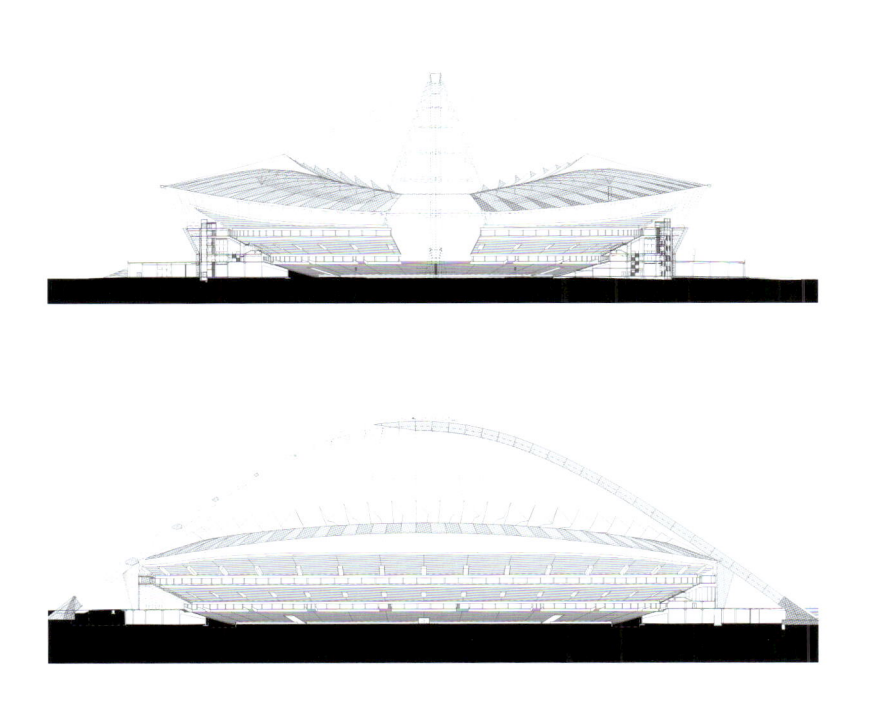

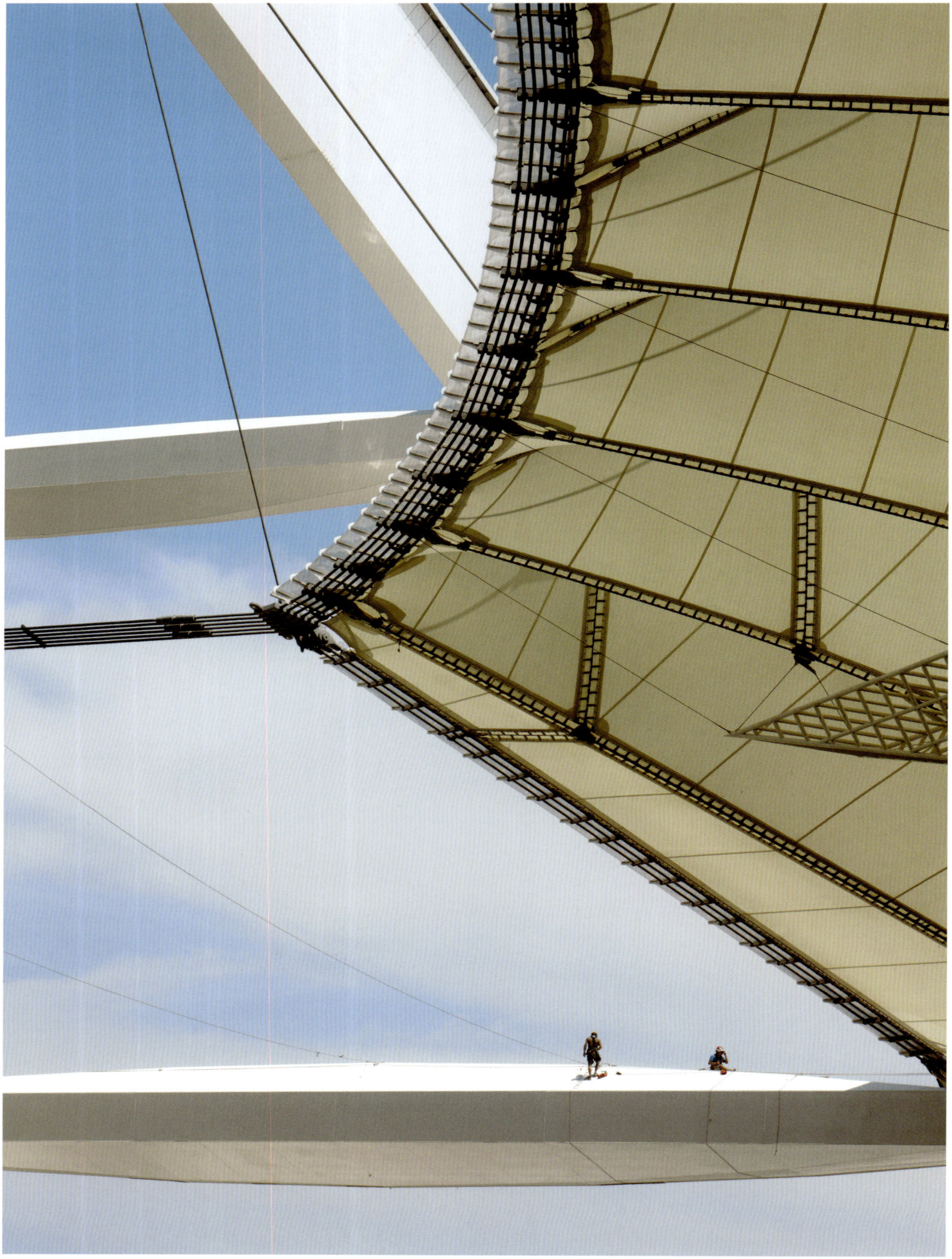

Moses Mabhida Stadium Durban   255

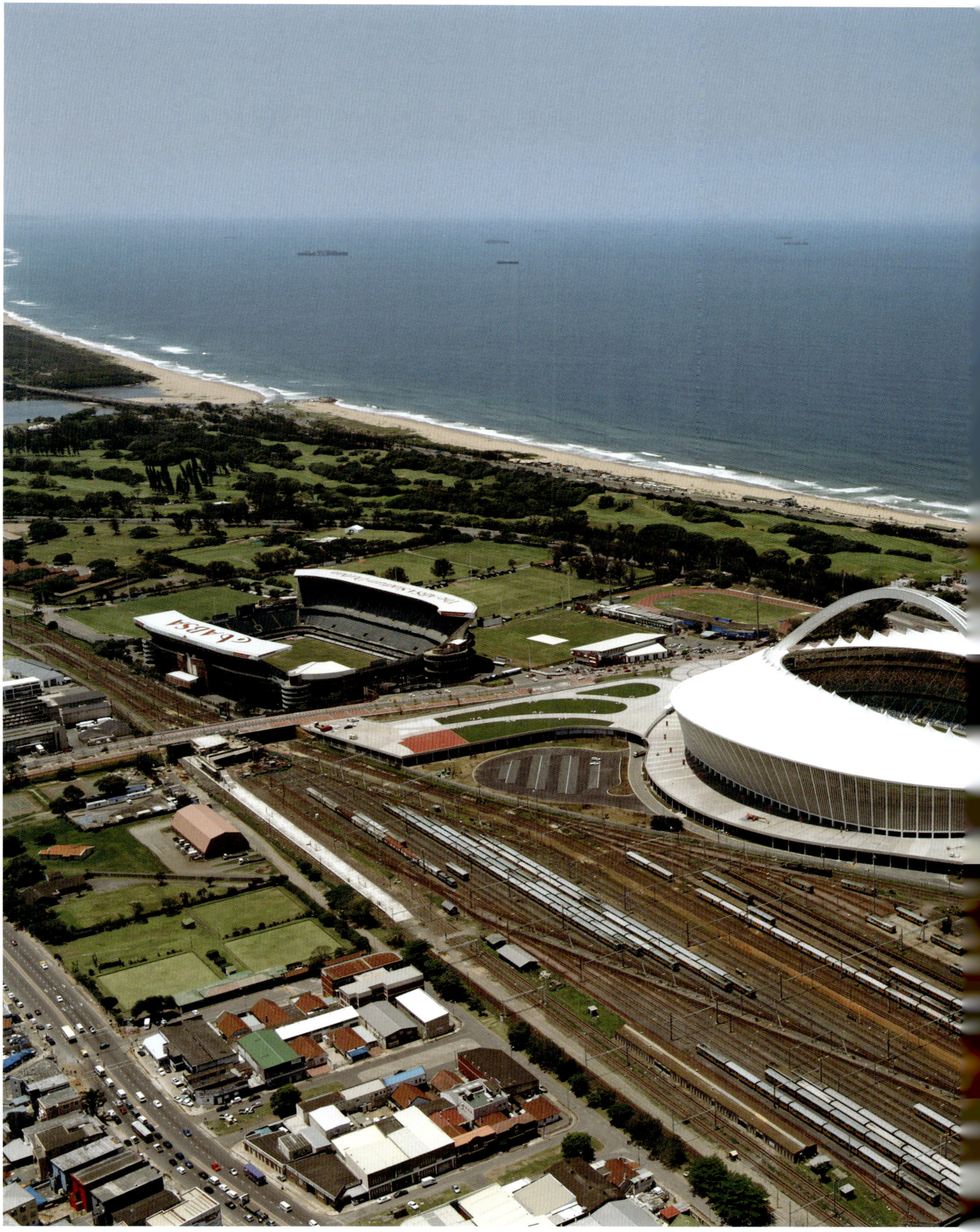

摩西·马布海达体育场 德班

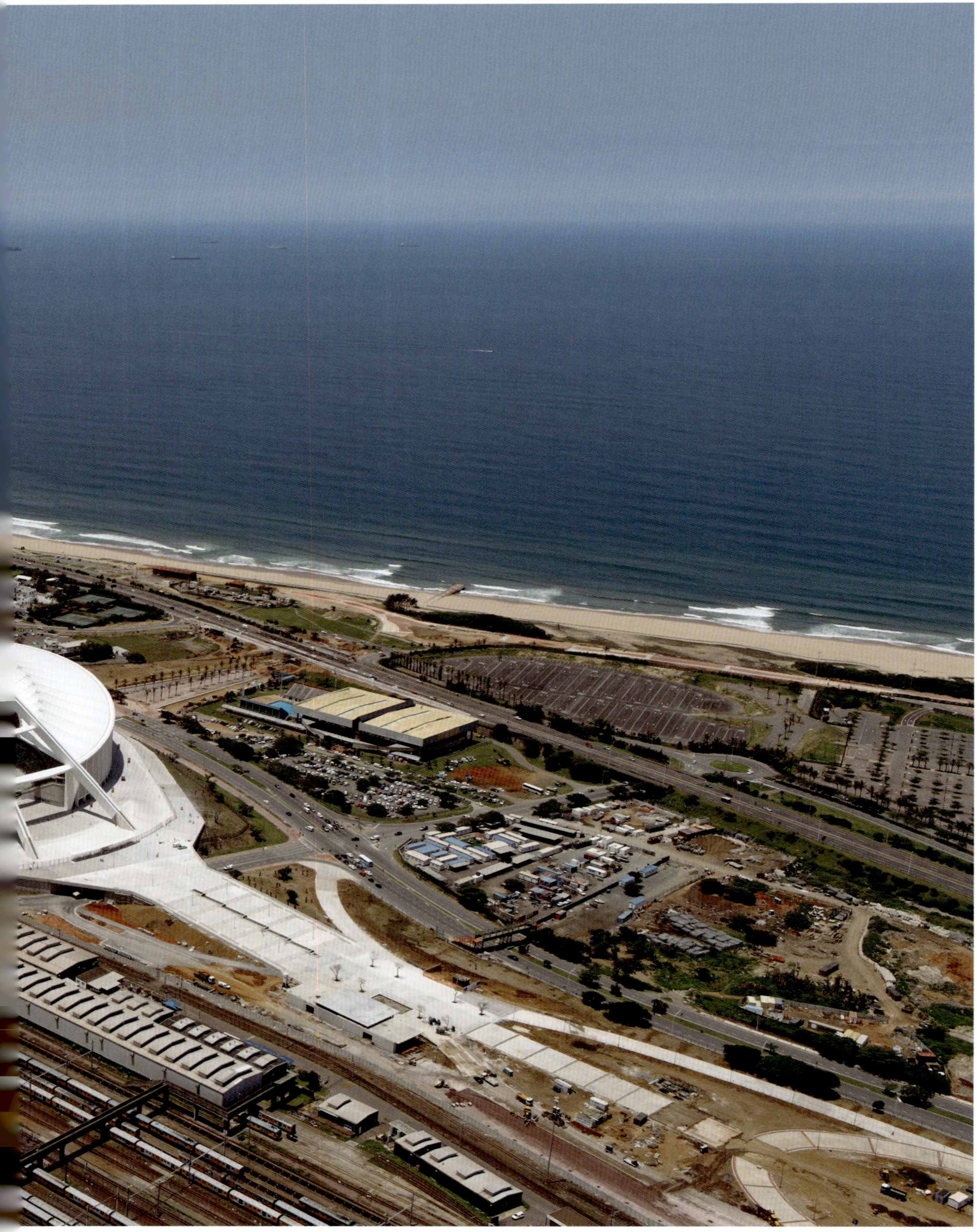

Moses Mabhida Stadium Durban

欧洲
Europe

德国 Germany
柏林 Berlin
科隆 Cologne
德累斯顿 Dresden
汉堡 Hamburg
法兰克福 Frankfurt
海利根港 Heiligenhafen
基尔 Kiel
莱比锡 Leipzig
曼海姆 Mannheim
斯图加特 Stuttgart
沃尔肯罗达 Volkenroda

意大利 Italy
里米尼 Rimini
维罗纳 Verona

拉脱维亚 Latvia
丘马拉 Jurmala

波兰 Poland
华沙 Warsaw

乌克兰 Ukraine
基辅 Kiev

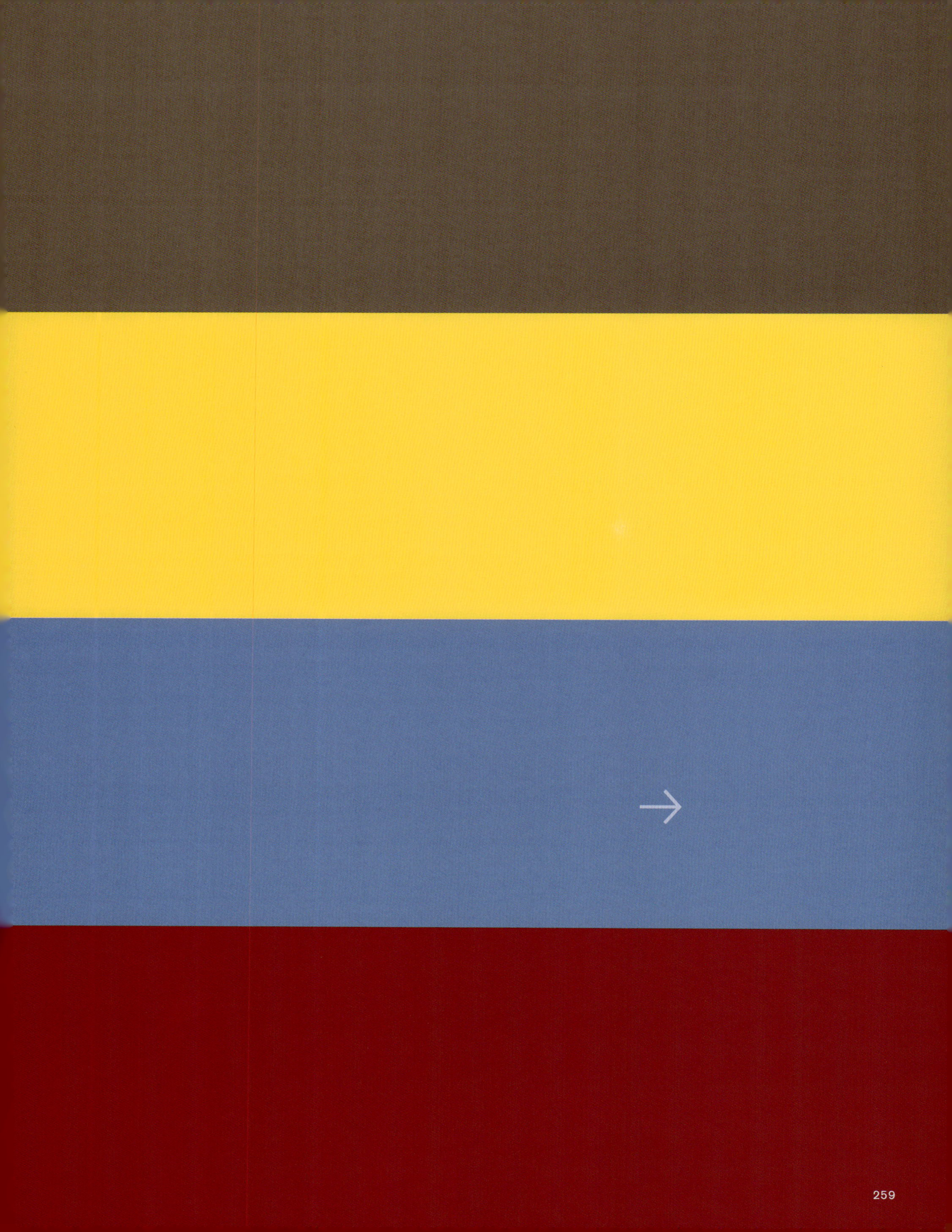

272

柏林泰格尔机场
柏林，德国

设计竞赛：1965年，一等奖　**方案设计**：曼哈德·冯·格康，福尔克温·玛格，克劳斯·尼克斯　**合伙人**：罗弗·内博拉，克劳斯·斯塔斯克，卡斯滕·布劳尔　**业主**：柏林机场　**建设周期**：1970—1975年　**建筑面积**：131 600m²

环形航站楼为机场创造出更大的空侧空间 —— 14座停机坪，同时为陆侧乘客缩短了搭转机距离，以及前往中央功能主楼的和位于六角形建筑中央的开放式停车场之间的距离。

Berlin-Tegel Airport
Berlin, Germany

International competition 1965 – 1st Prize **Design** Meinhard von Gerkan, Volkwin Marg, Klaus Nickels **Partners** Rolf Niedballa, Klaus Staratzke, Karsten Brauer **Client** Berliner Flughafen-Gesellschaft mbH **Construction period** 1970–1975 **Gross floor area** 131,600 m²

The ring shape of this terminal generates more spaces for the positioning of aeroplanes on the apron side (at 14 protruding bays). On the street side this ring form simultaneously reduces the distances for transferring passengers, to the central area with super-ordinate functions as well as to the parking garage in the open center of the hexagon.

276

斯图加特机场，1和3号航站楼
斯图加特，德国

1号航站楼设计竞赛：1980年，一等奖　**方案设计**：曼哈德·冯·格康，卡斯滕·鲍尔　**合伙人**：克劳斯·施塔茨克　**业主**：斯图加特机场有限公司　**建设周期**：1986—1991年　**建筑面积**：38 000m²

3号航站楼设计竞赛：1998年，一等奖　**方案设计**：曼哈德·冯·格康以及克劳斯·伦茨　**合伙人**：克劳斯·施塔茨克和于尔根·希尔默　**业主**：斯图加特机场有限公司　**建设周期**：2000—2004年　**建筑面积**：57 000m²

纵向的长翼、三角形的横剖面和矩形的大厅空间构成了航站楼简洁至无以复加的基本形式。屋面之下是树冠状的支承系统，其如同伞形花序般的结构特点赋予机场建筑独特的个性，令人印象深刻。

Stuttgart Airport, Terminals 1+3
Stuttgart, Germany

Competition Terminal 1 1980 – 1st Prize **Design** Meinhard von Gerkan and Karsten Brauer **Partner** Klaus Staratzke **Client** Flughafen Stuttgart GmbH **Construction period** 1986–1991 **Gross floor area** 38,000 m²

Competition Terminal 3 1998 – 1st Prize **Design** Meinhard von Gerkan with Klaus Lenz **Partners** Klaus Staratzke, Jürgen Hillmer **Client** Flughafen Stuttgart GmbH **Construction period** 2000–2004 **Gross floor area** 57,000 m²

The terminal buildings are reduced to the basic forms of the longitudinal wing with triangular cross-section and the rectangular hall. The structural "trees" supporting the roof are the inimitable characteristic of the airport building. The skeleton corresponds to the structure of a compound umbel.

284

290

汉堡机场
汉堡，德国

设计竞赛：1986年，一等奖　方案设计：曼哈德·冯·格康和卡斯滕·布劳尔　合伙人：于尔根·希尔默，卡斯滕·布劳尔　项目负责人：尼克莱·皮克斯（1号航站楼），托尔斯腾·辛兹（购物广场）　业主：汉堡机场有限公司　建设周期：1990—2008年　建筑总面积：77 066m²/53 000m²/33 000m²

新建的1号航站楼和购物广场延续了已建成的2号航站楼的设计风格。大厅十分宽敞，室内日光充盈，屋顶的设计借鉴了机翼的弧线，将其覆盖之下的空间筑成一个连续性整体。所有的航站楼每年共可容纳约1 350万人的客流量。一座如"脊柱"般的指廊将所有航站楼相连接。

Hamburg Airport
Hamburg, Germany

Competition 1986 – 1st Prize **Design** Meinhard von Gerkan and Karsten Brauer **Partners** Jürgen Hillmer, Karsten Brauer **Project leaders** Nicolai Pix (T1), Torsten Hinz (SP) **Client** Flughafen Hamburg GmbH **Construction period** 1990–2008 **Gross floor area** 77,066 m² / 53,000 m² / 33,000 m²

The newer buildings of the airport – Terminal 1 and Shopping Plaza – continue the design line of the already completed Terminal 2, which as a spacious daylight-flooded hall forms a generous spatial continuum underneath a roof with its curvature taking reference from the wing of an airplane. All terminals together are dimensioned for a passenger volume of approximately 13.5 million per year in total. A pier positioned in front interlinks the terminals like a spine.

音乐会议中心
吕贝克，德国

设计竞赛：1990年，一等奖　方案设计：曼哈德·冯·格康，克里斯蒂安·魏曼　项目负责人：托马斯·林纳，沃尔夫冈·豪克斯　业主：自由汉莎城吕贝克建设局　建设周期：1992—1994年　建筑面积：18 400 m²

新建的音乐会议中心并没有刻意地迎合吕贝克老城尺度较小的特点。相反的，它却是一个当代语境、当代尺度和当代美学的展示。其面向公众的定位使其很好地融入城市功能中。

Music and Congress Hall
Lubeck, Germany

Competition 1990 – 1st Prize **Design** Meinhard von Gerkan with Christian Weinmann **Project leaders** Thomas Rinne, Wolfgang Haux **Client** Hansestadt Lübeck, Hochbauamt **Construction period** 1992–1994 **Gross floor area** 18,400 m²

The building is not conceived to fit into the small-scale atmosphere of the old town of Lübeck. It is much more a semantic, scale, and aesthetic statement of the present day. The orientation of the building with its public facilities is however integrated into the urban structure.

296

莱比锡新会展中心
莱比锡，德国

设计竞赛：1992年，一等奖　方案设计：福尔克温·玛格和胡贝特·尼恩霍夫　项目负责人：克玛尔·阿凯　业主：莱比锡博览会有限公司　建设周期：1993—1995年　建筑面积：273 000m²

在毗邻机场、高速公路的莱比锡会展中心基地上，一座崭新的展厅应运而生。它将城市规划、景观设计、建筑表现与工程技术完美结合，其艺术综合体的特征亦不受制约地展现出来。

New Leipzig Trade Fair
Leipzig, Germany

Competition 1992 – 1st Prize **Design** Volkwin Marg and Hubert Nienhoff **Project leader** Kemal Akay **Client** Leipziger Messegesellschaft mbH **Construction period** 1993–1995 **Gross floor area** 273,000 m²

At the new site of the Leipzig Trade Fair in close proximity to the airport and the motorway a new, artificial place has been developed, a "synthesis of the arts" of urban and landscape planning, architecture and engineering skills in a surrounding that is characterized by uncontrolled growth.

302

柏林中央火车站
柏林，德国

设计竞赛：1993年，一等奖　方案设计：曼哈德·冯·格康和于尔根·希尔默　项目负责人：汉斯·约阿希姆·格兰，克劳斯·霍尔，普利斯卡·马施奈尔，苏珊娜·温特　业主：德国铁路股份有限公司，由柏林铁路项目有限责任公司代理　建设周期：1996—2006年　建筑面积：180 000 m²

柏林中央火车站建于原莱尔特火车站的旧址之上，是目前欧洲最大的铁路枢纽站，东西向和南北向运行的城际高速列车线路在此交会。一座长度超过320m的巨大玻璃顶棚和两座桥型办公大楼作为重要的建筑语汇，强调了现有的铁道线路走向。在整体建筑的基座上，不同空间和不同方向上的交通线路在车站中央形成"十字穿插"，构成一个巨大的开放空间，从而使日光也能照进地下的站台。

Berlin Central Station
Berlin, Germany

Competition 1993 – 1st Rank **Design** Meinhard von Gerkan and Jürgen Hillmer **Project leaders** Hans-Joachim Glahn, Klaus Hoyer, Prisca Marschner, Susanne Winter **Client** Deutsche Bahn AG represented by the DB Projekt GmbH-Knoten Berlin **Construction period** 1996–2006 **Area** 180,000 m²

On the site of the historic Lehrter Bahnhof Europe's largest station was realized: This is where an east-west and a north-south InterCity Express railway line intersect. Large filigree glass roofs with a length of more than 320 meters as well as two bridging office buildings emphasize the existing railway tracks with architectural means. In the central area of the station cross, which rests on a building base, the ceilings of all levels are equipped with large openings, allowing daylight to penetrate as far as the underground platform levels.

310

霍尔河折叠桥
基尔，德国

咨询设计：1994年　方案设计：福尔克温·玛格以及瓦格·徐勒斯　业主：基尔市市政府　建设周期：1996—1997年
长度：116m，25m为可折叠桥面　宽度：6m

无论观静观动，这个三段式开合桥都因其在桥梁史上的独一无二成为引人瞩目的地标。其开合的过程，展现了极富吸引力的优美力学过程，同时也创造了一个亲水散步绝佳场所。

Folding Bridge over the River Hörn
Kiel, Germany

Study 1994　**Design** Volkwin Marg with Jörg Schlaich　**Client** Magistrate of the Town of Kiel　**Construction period** 1996–1997　**Length** 116 m, 25 m as folding bridge　**Width** 6 m

Whether moving or at rest, the sectional folding bridge presents a significant landmark, which is unique in bridge construction. During the opening and closing it offers a kinetic procedure providing an attraction, whilst simultaneously generating an optimal proximity to the water as a seaside footbridge.

314

2000年汉诺威世博会基督教馆
沃尔肯罗达，德国

设计竞赛：1997年，一等奖　方案设计：曼哈德·冯·格康和约阿西姆·蔡斯　项目负责人：约恩·奥尔特曼　项目委托方：2000年世博会基督教办公室　建设周期：1999—2000/2001年
建筑面积：2 004m²

为世界博览会而建的教堂，本身就是一项不同寻常的建筑任务。当这座教堂从举办盛会的繁华广场迁至宁静偏远的沃尔肯罗达乡村修道院中，便成就了一个独一无二的特殊氛围。

Christ Pavilion, Expo 2000
Volkenroda, Germany

Competition 1997 – 1st Prize　**Design** Meinhard von Gerkan and Joachim Zais　**Project leader** Jörn Ortmann　**Client** Evangelisches Büro für die Weltausstellung Expo 2000, Evangelisch-Lutherische Landeskirche, Hanover　**Construction period** 1999–2000/2001　**Gross floor area** 2,004 m²

The construction of a church has become a rare building task – especially a church for a world exhibition. When this church is transported from the fairground of world events to the calm seclusion of the Volkenroda Cloister, then this is a unique occurrence.

322

里米尼新会展中心
里米尼，意大利

设计竞赛：1997年，一等奖　方案设计：福尔克温·玛格　项目负责人：施特凡妮·约布施，克莱门斯·库什　业主：里米尼市政府　建设周期：1999—2001年　建筑面积：169 600m²

由16个展厅组成的里米尼会展中心提供了107 000m²的展览空间和63 000m²的服务空间。建筑设计理念以传统的艾米尼亚－罗马涅地区艺术风格为基础。该艺术风格在古典时期及文艺复兴时期对整个欧洲建筑史有过深远的影响。

New Trade Fair
Rimini, Italy

Competition 1997 – 1st Prize **Design** Volkwin Marg **Project leaders** Stephanie Joebsch, Clemens Kusch **Client** Rimini Fiera S.p.A **Construction period** 1999–2001, extension up until 2005 **Gross floor area** 169,600 m²

The "Nuova Fiera di Rimini" with 16 exhibition halls offers approx. 107,000 m² of exhibition and 63,000 m² of service area. The architectural concept is orientated around the Emilia Romagna tradition, which has characterized European architectural history through the ancient world and the Renaissance.

330

柏林勃兰登堡机场
柏林，德国

设计竞赛：1998年，一等奖　方案设计：曼哈德·冯·格尔康和胡贝特·尼恩霍夫以及汉斯·约阿希姆·帕普　项目总负责人：汉斯·约阿希姆·帕普　合作设计：JSK国际建筑和工程设计有限公司　业主：柏林Schönefeld机场有限公司　建设周期：2008—2015年　建筑面积：600 000m²

机场主体建筑坐落在与东西向的飞机起降跑道系统平行的中央轴线上，构成整个基地的"脊柱"，并且连接了主要的交通干道。新建旅客航站楼的主要组成元素为主航站楼和位于其前端的指廊。旅客候机大厅分布在两个层面上，由此分隔了陆侧到港和离港旅客人流。离港层为一座巨大的日光大厅，坐落于主平面上，大厅屋面的跨度通过一个精致的，富有金属编织感的钢架-玻璃结构实现。航站楼的外立面采用了简洁的几何建筑元素，重拾了从辛克尔到包豪思的建筑风格元素。

Berlin Brandenburg Airport
Berlin, Germany

Competition 1998 – 1st Prize **Design** Meinhard von Gerkan and Hubert Nienhoff with Hans-Joachim Paap **Co-operation with** JSK International **Client** Flughafen Berlin-Schönefeld GmbH **Construction period** 2008–2015 **Gross floor area** 600,000 m²

The spine of the new airport is a central axis of parallel takeoff and landing systems on an east-west alignment. The main access features are arranged accordingly. The new passenger terminal consists of a main hall and adjoining pier buildings. It is divided into two levels, separating arrivals and departures on the landside. The main level is Departures, designed as a spacious, light-filled hall spanned by a filigree steel-and-glass roof. With its articulated facades and clear, geometrical shapes, the terminal incorporates architectural features from Schinkel to the Bauhaus.

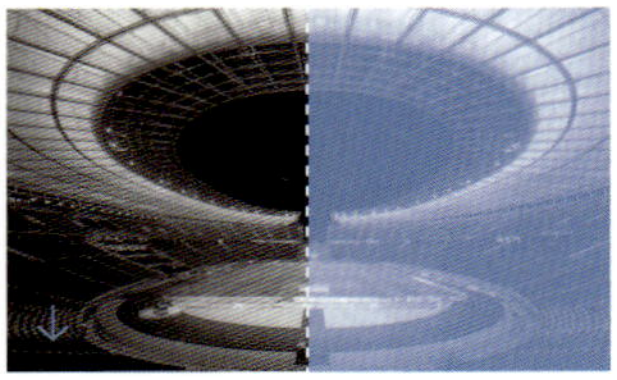

338

柏林奥林匹克体育场改建和屋顶加建工程
柏林，德国

设计竞赛：1998年，一等奖　**方案设计**：福尔克温·玛格，胡贝特·尼恩霍夫　**设计联合体负责人**：克玛尔·阿凯，乌韦·格拉尔　**项目总负责人**：约翰·科恩　**项目负责人**：马丁·格拉斯，伊万卡·佩库维奇，亚里山大·布赫豪夫　**业主**：柏林市政府　**建设周期**：2000—2004年　**座位数**：76 000个

柏林奥林匹克体育场的总体规划由建筑师维纳·马赫于1936年制定，并被列为文物保护建筑。新增建的部分位于体育场外围的地下。新建屋面结构简洁含蓄，保留了马拉松大门处的开放，但在材料的选择上有意识地与传统体育场建筑构造风格产生对比。悬挑的钢结构和张拉膜的使用，令屋面显得尤为轻盈。体育场内部由20根直径仅为25cm的钢柱支撑。

Olympic Stadium, Reconstruction and Roofing
Berlin, Germany

Competition 1998 – 1st Prize　**Design** Volkwin Marg and Hubert Nienhoff　**Managers of planning partnership** Kemal Akay, Uwe Grahl　**General project manager** Jochen Köhn　**Project leaders** Martin Glass, Ivanka Perkovic, Alexander Buchhofer　**Client** City of Berlin　**Construction period** 2000 – 2004　**Seats** 76,000

The master plan proposed by Werner March in 1936 remains under urban historic preservation. All additions have been placed underground, outside of the stadium. The new roof structure with its open-ended ring towards the Marathon Gate sets itself apart from stadium typology with its simple construction and choice of surface material. The roof is designed as a light cantilevering steel construction with an upper and lower membrane. From the interior, the roof rests on 20 steel columns, which each have a slim profile of 25 cm in diameter.

346

Borgo Trento医院
维罗纳，意大利

设计竞赛：2000年，一等奖　**方案设计**：福尔克温·玛格和Altieri工作室　**项目负责人**：罗伯特·弗兰德　**合作设计单位**：cfk工作室　**业主**：Azienda ospedaliera di Verona　**建设周期**：2005—2010年　**使用面积**：96 300m²

医院坐落于维罗纳南部，埃施河畔，紧邻城市中心，医院包括一个新建的综合建筑群，各医学学科部门以及日常功能单位被密集地安置于其内（包括外科、急救室、病房、手术室、急诊、夜间和日间诊所、放射科以及例如店铺、餐饮等公共设施区）。已有100年历史的医院基地内将建起一栋九层高的住院楼。西面的功能区为一座高两层并沉入地面的实验和分析楼，其日常采光通过下沉的中央庭院实现。通过这种设计手法，在集约紧密规划的高层建筑群中，一片绿化园林景观——"新庭园"应运而生。

Borgo Trento Hospital
Verona, Italy

Competition 2000 – 1st Prize　**Design** Volkwin Marg and Studio Altieri　**Project leader** Robert Friedrichs　**Partner** firm studio cfk　**Client** Azienda ospedaliera di Verona　**Construction period** 2005 – 2010　**Gross floor area** 96,300 m²

The Borgo Trento Hospital near the city center got a new but compact multifunctional building complex, in which various medical and general functions are accommodated (including the surgical ward, intensive care units, wards, operating theaters, A&E ward department, polyclinic, day-unit, radiology, plus public areas with shops, catering etc.). Overall, the new complex has nine floors, and occupies the center of the 100-year-old hospital site. The arrangement of putting a part of the site underground in combination with the compactness of the above-ground structures opens up a large landscaped park-like area as an extended garden.

352

莱茵能量体育场

科隆，德国

设计竞赛：2001 年，一等奖　**方案设计**：福尔克温·玛格，约阿希姆·林特，马莱克·诺瓦克，施特凡·尼克斯多夫　**业主**：科隆体育场有限公司　**总承包商**：Max Bögl　**建设周期**：2002—2004年　**座席数**：46 200个

钢制屋面结构的展开如同吊桥般横跨在70m高的照明灯柱之间，并承载着四座看台之上的无支撑屋面，看台是紧密环绕赛场布置的。屋面中轴线将悬浮的顶棚分成两个部分，内环透光，外环封闭。看台主体为立方体，混凝土预制构件形成其开放的框架，外立面为悬挂式轻质玻璃幕墙。

RheinEnergie Stadium
Cologne, Germany

Competition 2001 – 1st Prize　**Design** Volkwin Marg with Joachim Rind, Marek Nowak, Stefan Nixdorf　**Client** Kölner Sportstätten GmbH　**General contractor** Max Bögl　**Construction period** 2002–2004　**Seats** 46,200

The steel roof structure spans like suspension bridges between the 70 meters high illuminated masts and allows for the column-free roofing of the four stands, which directly adjoin the playing field. On both sides of the central axis the hovering roof element is divided into an inner ring, transparent for ultraviolet light, and an outer, covered ring. The stand structure is designed as a cubic, open framework from precast concrete components and added to with a lightweight glass facade.

358

科隆大学医院心脏中心

科隆，德国

设计竞赛：2002年，一等奖　**方案设计**：福尔克温·玛格　**项目负责人**：马丁·布莱克曼　**业主**：科隆大学医院，由医疗管理处代表　**建设周期**：2004—2007年　**建筑面积**：29 700m²

心脏中心具备先进的诊断和医疗设施，进入大楼后，12m高的大厅是接待病患和探望者的空间。接待大厅和整体建筑等高，光线充足，使人不禁产生身在酒店大堂而并非医院的错觉。病房的外观采用了明亮的、令人愉悦的配色方案。护理站位于建筑四层，通过其通高的玻璃外墙以及木材饰面突显出来。这里每两间双人病房共享一个拥有内阳台的休息室。建筑体格局呈H形，框架式外立面采用了色彩明亮的壳灰岩饰面。暗红色闪光的铝制遮阳构件安装于大面积玻璃幕墙之前，赋予古典端庄的立面以额外的肌理，令人印象深刻。

Cardiac Center University Clinic of Cologne
Cologne, Germany

Competition 2002 – 1st Prize　**Design** Volkwin Marg　**Project leader** Martin Bleckmann　**Client** University Hospital Cologne, represented by Medfacilities　**Construction period** 2004–2007　**Gross floor area** 29,700 m²

Equipped with the latest medical technology, the Cardiac Center welcomes patients and visitors with a glazed 12 meters high entrance and light filled reception lobby as high as the building, its atmosphere resembling more a hotel than a clinic. The wards are decorated in light, friendly colors. The nursing wards on the 3rd floor are notable for their storey-high glazing and wood paneling. Each pair of double rooms has a day room with a loggia outside. The column beam facade of the new H-shaped building is clad in light shell limestone. Reddish-tinted aluminum shades in front of the large glazed surfaces lend the classical facade additional structure, giving the building a distinctive look.

364

易北大道别墅

汉堡，德国

方案设计：曼哈德·冯·格康，2002年　项目负责人：福克玛·西弗斯　建设周期：2007—2009年　建筑面积：1 600m²

新建的住宅位于山地斜坡上，其居住空间为五口之家设计，拥有两个完整楼层、一个半地下层以及一个由露台环抱的退进式顶层。建筑平面为正交直角式布置，拥有流线型立面的建筑体坐落其上。别墅北面面向街道的大部分立面完全封闭，只有在中轴处透过玻璃幕墙以及中庭才可一窥易北河的壮观景致。别墅面向南面一侧拥有与室内空间通高的开窗和向外伸出的宽敞阳台。外立面由大块的白色金属板覆盖，横向的型材刻画出了楼层的分割秩序。

Villa at Elbchaussee
Hamburg, Germany

Design Meinhard von Gerkan, 2002　**Project leader** Volkmar Sievers　**Construction period** 2007–2009　**Gross floor area** 1,600 m²

The new home constructed on the sloping site is for a five-member family. It has two full stories, a basement and a floor on the slope, and a staggered floor with a terrace running round it. The orthogonal ground plan structure has curved shapes superimposed on it. On the north side facing the street, the villa is largely closed, with only the glazed central axis offering a view of the Elbe River through the atrium. Southwards, the building opens up through room-high windows and capacious balconies. The facades are clad with large-format white metallic panels, while horizontal profiles characterize the floor slabs.

370

古纳别墅

丘马拉，拉脱维亚

方案设计：曼哈德·冯·格康(2003年)　施工单位：文森特公司，里加　建设周期：2006—2007年　总建筑面积：410m²

古纳别墅的设计特色不在于建筑本身的功能性，而在于它所创造的空间体验：与周围自然环境的对话，及穿越松林眺望波罗的海的开阔视野。这座现代主义风格的建筑为一座错层住宅，内部层面通过中央的一个多向坡道相连接，它也成为该建筑的中心元素。

Guna Villa
Jurmala, Latvia

Design Meinhard von Gerkan, 2003　**Construction company** Vincents, Riga　**Construction period** 2006–2007　**Gross floor area** 410 m²

The primary feature of the villa's design is not the actual functionality, but the spatial experience, characterized by the dialog with the surrounding nature and the view over the dunes towards the Baltic Sea. Formally based on the tradition of modernism, the whole villa is organized as a split-level house with staggered floors, which are linked by a broad ramp as the central element.

378

鸟类观察站
海利根港的格拉斯瓦尔德，德国

方案设计：曼哈德·冯·格康，2004年　**项目负责人**：福克玛·西弗斯　**业主**：德国自然保护联盟，海利根港　**建设周期**：2004—2005年　**建筑面积**：48m²　**高度**：12.5m

木结构的排列使建筑仿佛一座金属编织的雕塑——一只形态生动的小鸟，矗立在这个鸟类自然保护区中。由对角线结构支撑的瞭望塔设有一个双向的楼梯，它连接了地面到空中的15m高度，装有玻璃幕墙的空中的观察站可以提供足够的空间供来访者使用。

Bird-Watching Tower
Graswarder in Heiligenhafen, Germany

Design Meinhard von Gerkan, 2004　**Project leader** Volkmar Sievers　**Client** NABU Heiligenhafen　**Construction period** 2004–2005　**Gross floor area** 48 m²　**Height** 12.5 m

The timber structure integrates into the bird sanctuary as a filigree sculpture resembling a stylized sitting bird. The 15 meters high tower, which is stiffened with diagonal braces, is accessible via a platform stair. The glazed viewing pulpit offers space even for larger groups of visitors.

384

国家芭蕾舞学校
柏林，德国

设计竞赛：2006年，一等奖　**方案设计**：福尔克温·玛格和胡贝特·尼恩霍夫，以及克里斯汀·斯潘　**项目负责人**：克里斯汀·斯潘，米歇尔·斯克兹　**业主**：联邦州柏林，城市发展部　**建设周期**：2008—2010年　**建筑面积**：8 800m²

柏林国家芭蕾舞学校设计构思的灵感源于学校的特殊性质：在此就读的学生需不断地在充满创造性的舞蹈世界和典型的全日制学校管理中实现自身角色的转换。一个流线型的多层大厅贯穿于整个新建建筑，舞蹈大厅建筑和四层高的学校教学楼分立于其两侧。这座大厅将建筑综合体内的各个功能区域连成网络，其在二层上通过空中联廊相连接。建筑立面上的大面积开窗实现了室内外视线的交流，在舞者享有良好的视野的同时，路人也可一窥教室内的舞蹈教学。

State Ballet School
Berlin, Germany

Competition 2006 – 1st Prize　**Design** Volkwin Marg and Hubert Nienhoff with Kristian Spencker　**Project leaders** Kristian Spencker, Michael Scholz　**Client** Senate Administration for Urban Development, State of Berlin　**Construction period** 2008–2010　**Gross floor area** 8,900 m²

The overall architectural concept for the State School of Ballet and Artistry focuses on the special nature of the school, with its constant ebb and flow of pupils between the creative world of dance and the classic functions of full-time schooling. A curved multi-story hall runs through the new building, with the adjacent four-story school and ballet rooms facing each other. The various areas of the ensemble are related to each other above this linking space, and accessed on the second floor via a bridge. Large display-window openings in the facade provide transparency and a view of the outside world for the dancers and give passers-by a glimpse of the ballet rooms and dance training.

390

德意志银行双塔
法兰克福，德国

方案设计： 马里奥·博里尼建筑事务所　**项目负责人：** 格里奥·卡斯特尼　**技术设计：** gmp建筑师事务所，福尔克温·玛格和胡贝特·尼恩霍夫　**项目负责人：** 巴博特·科瓦斯基，伯恩德·高斯曼尼，博德·阿道夫　**业主：** 德意志银行　**建设周期：** 2007—2011年　**建筑面积：** 120 000m²　**高度：** 155m

德意志银行两栋具有标志性双塔建成于1984年，是法兰克福天际线上的重要地标。对其120 000m²建筑面积的翻修工程历时三年，是欧洲最大的翻修改建项目。经过现代化改造后的业主中心在2011年重新交付使用，建筑满足了目前领先的生态建筑标准，并且获得了"美国能源与设计先锋"LEED铂金级认证以及德国DGNB可持续建筑评估金级认证。建筑的耗能仅为一般建筑的一半，对水的消耗以及二氧化碳的排放量将较原先减少将近百分之九十。一座极富建筑感的雕塑"天球"刻画出德意志银行大厦的入口，充斥整个空间的金属编织造型象征了德意志银行遍布全球的商业触角。

Deutsche Bank Twin Towers
Frankfurt, Germany

Principle architects Mario Bellini Architects　**Project leader** Giulio Castegini　**Technical architects** gmp · von Gerkan, Marg and Partners, Volkwin Marg and Hubert Nienhoff　**Project leaders** Babette Kowalsky, Bernd Gossmann, Bernd Adolf　**Client** Deutsche Bank　**Construction period** 2007–2011　**Gross floor area** 120,000 m²　**Height** 155 m

The striking double towers of Deutsche Bank have become an urban-planning icon on the Frankfurt skyline since their completion in 1984. After a three-year program of refurbishment – the largest such program in Europe, involving a total floor area of 120,000 m² – the modernized company headquarters was reopened in 2011, and now sets exemplary ecological standards, as witness American LEED Platinum certification and German DGNB Gold certification. The energy consumption was halved, water consumption cut by 70% and CO_2 emissions were reduced by nearly 90%. The entrance to the new Deutsche Bank features the architectural sculpture of the 'Sphere', a filigree but large entity that symbolizes the global links of Deutsche Bank.

394

国家体育场
华沙，波兰

设计竞赛： 2007年，一等奖　**方案设计：** 福尔克温·玛格，胡贝特·尼恩霍夫和马库斯·费斯特勒　**项目负责人：** 马库斯·费斯特勒，马丁·哈基尔　**合作设计单位：** J.S.K. Architekci Sp. z o.o. 建筑设计事务所和施莱希工程设计公司　**业主：** Narodowe Centrum Sportu Sp. z o.o.　**建设周期：** 2008—2011年　**座席数：** 55 000个

这座足球场可容纳55 000名观众，历史遗留下来的坚实天然石材基座与钢材、玻璃和PTFE膜建成的新体育场呈现出形象上的二元化，令人印象深刻。外立面金属薄板采用了代表波兰民族的红白两色，其编织篮的外观使其成为独一无二的城市地标。这一半透明的表皮覆盖了体育场内部不同的功能区域，促成一个形式统一的整体。穿插交织的立面金属构件在柔和的光线条件下即可产生富有戏剧性的光影效果。夜间集中的灯光照射更将凸现立面的斑斓的色彩以及形象上的别具一格。

National Stadium
Warsaw, Poland

Competition 2007 – 1st Prize　**Design** Volkwin Marg and Hubert Nienhoff with Markus Pfisterer　**Project leaders** Markus Pfisterer, Martin Hakiel　**Co-operation with** J.S.K. Architekci Sp. z o.o. and schlaich bergermann und partner　**Client** Narodowe Centrum Sportu Sp. z o.o.　**Construction period** 2008–2011　**Seats** 55,000

The duality of a solid historic stone base and the new structure made of steel, glass and PTFE membrane gives the design of the football stadium with a 55,000 capacity its character. Also unmistakable as a feature visible from a distance is the facade, made up of expanded metal panels in the Polish national colors of red and white. This translucent layer unites the very diverse areas within the stadium into a single large-scale shape. Even with low incidental light, the crisscross elements of the facade set up a fascinating pattern of light and shadow. At night, the coloration and distinctiveness of this facade are reinforced by the integrated illumination.

402

奥林匹克体育场
基辅，乌克兰

咨询设计：2008年　**方案设计**：福尔克温·玛格以及克里斯蒂安·霍夫曼和 Marek Nowak　**项目负责人**：马丁·布莱克曼　**支承结构和屋面解构设计**：施莱希工程设计公司　**业主**：National Sport Complex "Olympiysky"　**建设周期**：2009—2011年　**座席数**：68 055个

对场馆的修复和重建设计尊重了其原有的历史构造，建于1968年，精巧且极具特色的预应力混凝土上层看台被保留了下来，新建的屋面支承结构与保留的碗装基座分离并且相互独立。极具代表性的结构将被一座崭新的玻璃外罩覆盖，在适当的照明条件下熠熠生辉。而拥有68 000个座席的体育场内部，由金银细工般空中钢柱和圆拱光井构成的膜结构屋面，赋予建筑令人难忘的独特形象。

Olympic Stadium
Kiev, Ukraine

Consultancy 2008　**Design** Volkwin Marg with Christian Hoffmann and Marek Nowak　**Project leader** Martin Bleckmann　**Structural concept and design, roof** schlaich bergermann und partner　**Client** National Sport Complex „Olympiysky"　**Construction period** 2009–2011　**Seats** 68,055

The design for the reconstruction of the stadium respects the historic fabric with its important filigree prestressed concrete upper tier, which was built in 1968, the frame of the new roof structure being detached and placed clear in front of the existing bowl. The new filigree glass facade acts almost as a kind of showcase. The interior of the stadium gains an unmistakable identity with a membrane roof structure incorporating air supports and domes of light.

408

德累斯顿文化宫修缮与重建
德累斯顿，德国

设计竞赛：2009年，一等奖　**方案设计**：曼哈德·冯·格康，斯特凡·胥茨以及尼古拉斯·博兰克　**项目负责人**：Christian Hellmund　**业主**：德累斯顿市政府　**建设周期**：2014—2017年　**建筑面积**：36 000m²

新方案中的文化宫集音乐厅与图书馆于一身，旨在使其重拾原有的重要地位，成为城市文化生活的中心，一个开放的"城市客厅"。建筑位于旧市集、宫殿区和新市集之间，地理位置得天独厚，从而要求建筑面向各个方向开放，这种空间构成的开放性将使这里成为地区市民聚集交流的场所。建筑的蝶形的阶梯以及前厅极富体量感，是修复城市肌理的重要元素。新文化宫内部的历史遗留空间和新建空间形成了一种富有时代感并且充满张力的对话。无色玻璃的大面积玻璃幕墙，促成了建筑与其外部旧城中心的交流。同时最大程度地实现了设计意向中所要表达的通透感和公共性。

Dresden Kulturpalast, Renovation and Reconstruction
Dresden, Germany

Competition 2009 – 1st Prize　**Design** Meinhard von Gerkan and Stephan Schütz with Nicolas Pomränke　**Project leader** Christian Hellmund　**Client** Town of Dresden　**Construction period** 2014–2017　**Gross floor area** 36,000 m²

With the new design for the concert hall and the integration of the Central Library, the intention is for the Kulturpalast ("Culture Palace") to revert to its original key role as a cultural meeting point – a kind of urban "open house". The unique central location necessitates a building oriented in every direction so as to meet the requirement for geographical and conceptual openness as a civic meeting place. The attractiveness of the internal area of the new Kulturpalast will be enhanced by the contrast between the historic and the new areas. The large glazed areas of the facade will be finished in color-neutral glass so as to produce the maximum possible communication with the external areas of the historic city center.

412

TXL⁺总体规划
柏林，德国

方案设计： 曼哈德·冯·格康，斯特凡·胥茨以及尼古拉斯·博兰克，2009年　**业主：** 柏林州政府，城市发展参议院

柏林勃兰登堡新机场的启用宣告了柏林泰戈尔机场至2011年完全关闭的进程已进入倒计时状态。为了赋予弃用后的机场基地以及该区域内极富价值的建筑面向未来视野，一个针对整个地区的全方位的战略发展规划呼之欲出。在机场的旧址上严格按照可持续性发展原则规划并建立一座面向未来的城市。而这座未来城市的核心为原机场航站楼，届时将被改建为德国环境工业现状的展示厅，并在未来较长的一段时期内作为节能城市的设计中心予以充分利用。

TXL⁺
Berlin, Germany

Design Meinhard von Gerkan and Stephan Schütz with Nicolas Pomränke, 2009
Client City of Berlin, Senatsverwaltung für Stadtentwicklung

With the opening of Berlin Brandenburg Airport (BER), which was also planned by gmp, Berlin's Tegel airport will be closed. To make the best possible use of the Tegel site and its valuable architectural assets for the future, a comprehensive strategy had been developed as an integral solution for the entire area. Therefore, a city of the future shall be built on the airport site, with construction and utilization following sustainable principles. The terminal building is to act as a nucleus for this future city, being put to immediate use as a showroom for Germany's environment industry and constituting long-term the planning center of an "energy-plus" city.

418

曼海姆美术馆
曼海姆，德国

设计竞赛： 2012年，一等奖　**方案设计：** 曼哈德·冯·格康和尼古劳斯·格茨以及福克玛·西弗斯　**项目负责人：** 苗笛，Liselotte Knall　**业主：** 曼海姆博物馆基金会　**建筑面积：** 15 600m²

博物馆空间结构从曼海姆棋盘状的城市布局中得到启发，一系列长方体体块交互错落，不同的高度、宽度以及穿插其间的扩展空间，打破了建筑形体的单一感。尺度各异的挑空空间为来访者带来充满张力的空间体验，同时为参观流线增添了丰富多变的视角。设计方案中百叶幕墙的构想，其色彩以及材料的选用均令美术馆从邻近建筑中鲜明地凸现出来。设计者力图寻找一种色调温和的金属材质，它一方面可以与当地特有的红色砂岩石材形成对比，另一方面在呈现出超越时代的品质的同时避免了予人冷漠的隔绝感。简洁凝练的建筑语言与其半透明的幕墙表皮赋予建筑独一无二的气质。

Kunsthalle Mannheim
Mannheim, Germany

Competition 2012 – 1st Prize　**Design** Meinhard von Gerkan and Nikolaus Goetze with Volkmar Sievers　**Project leader** Di Miao, Liselotte Knall　**Client** Stiftung Kunsthalle Mannheim　**Gross floor area** 15,600 m²

Similar to the checkerboard layout of Mannheim's city center, the design is composed of multiple cubes whose regular pattern is, however, interrupted by a staggered arrangement of heights and widths as well as extensions with courtyards and squares. Visitors touring the hall discover exciting rooms of different sizes and varying air spaces that generate multiple inward and outward views. A copper-colored, woven metal encases the facade, invoking the typical red sandstone of the region and emphasizing the careful adaptation to the historic Friedrichplatz. In addition, the simple contemporary architecture with its translucent facade shell positively glows with special significance.

272 ²⁶⁰ ↑

柏林泰格尔机场
柏林，德国

Berlin-Tegel Airport
Berlin, Germany

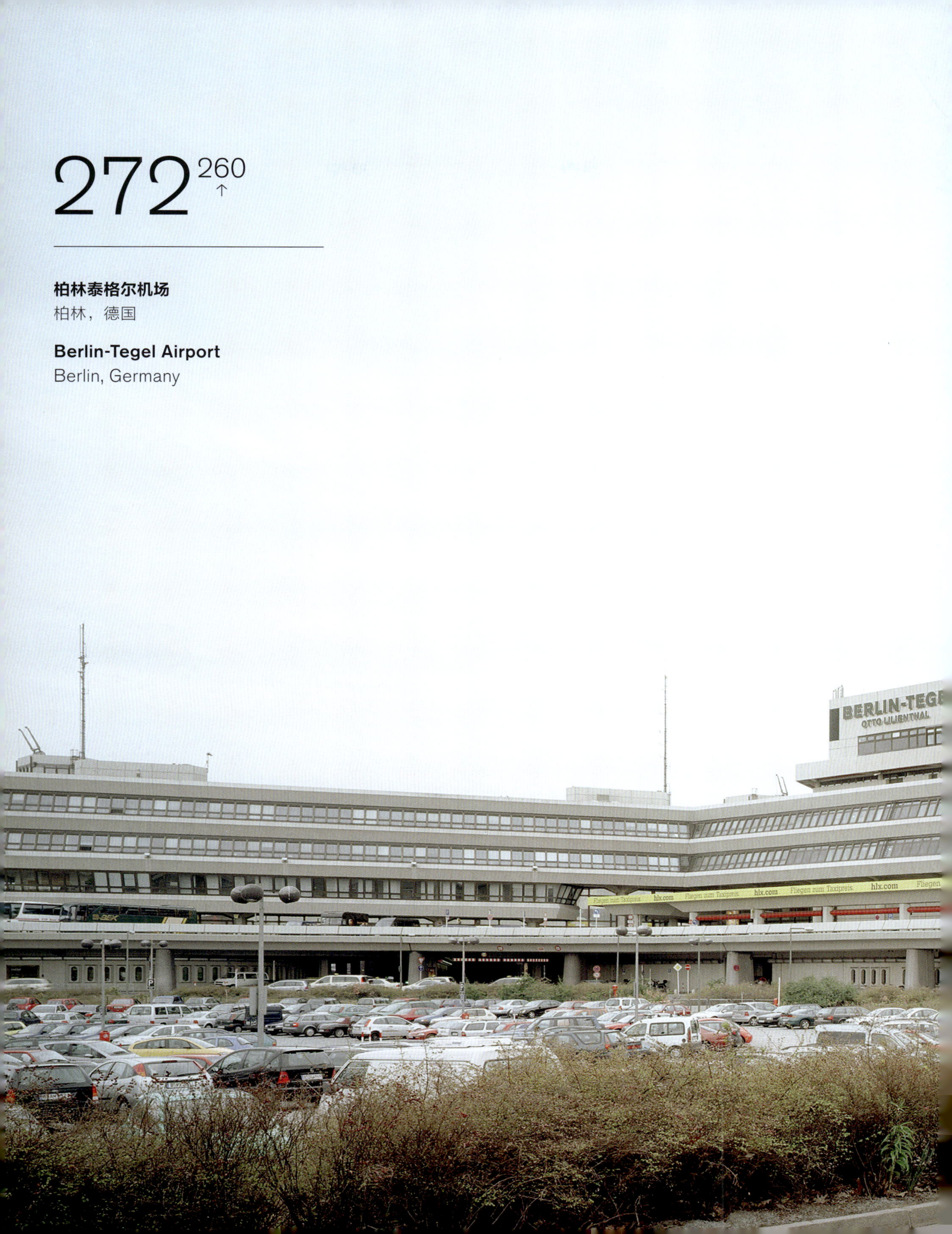

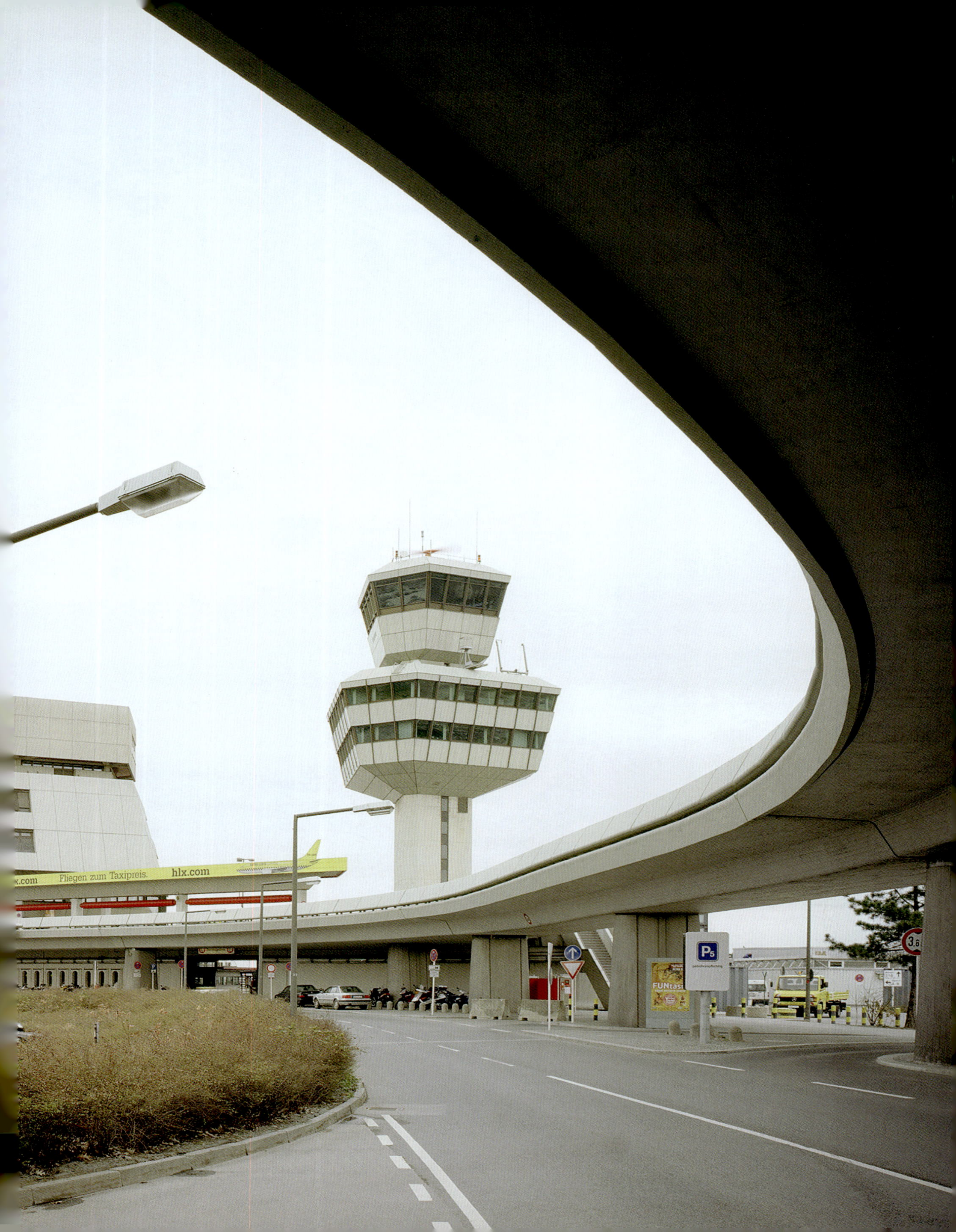
Fliegen zum Taxipreis.
hlx.com
P5

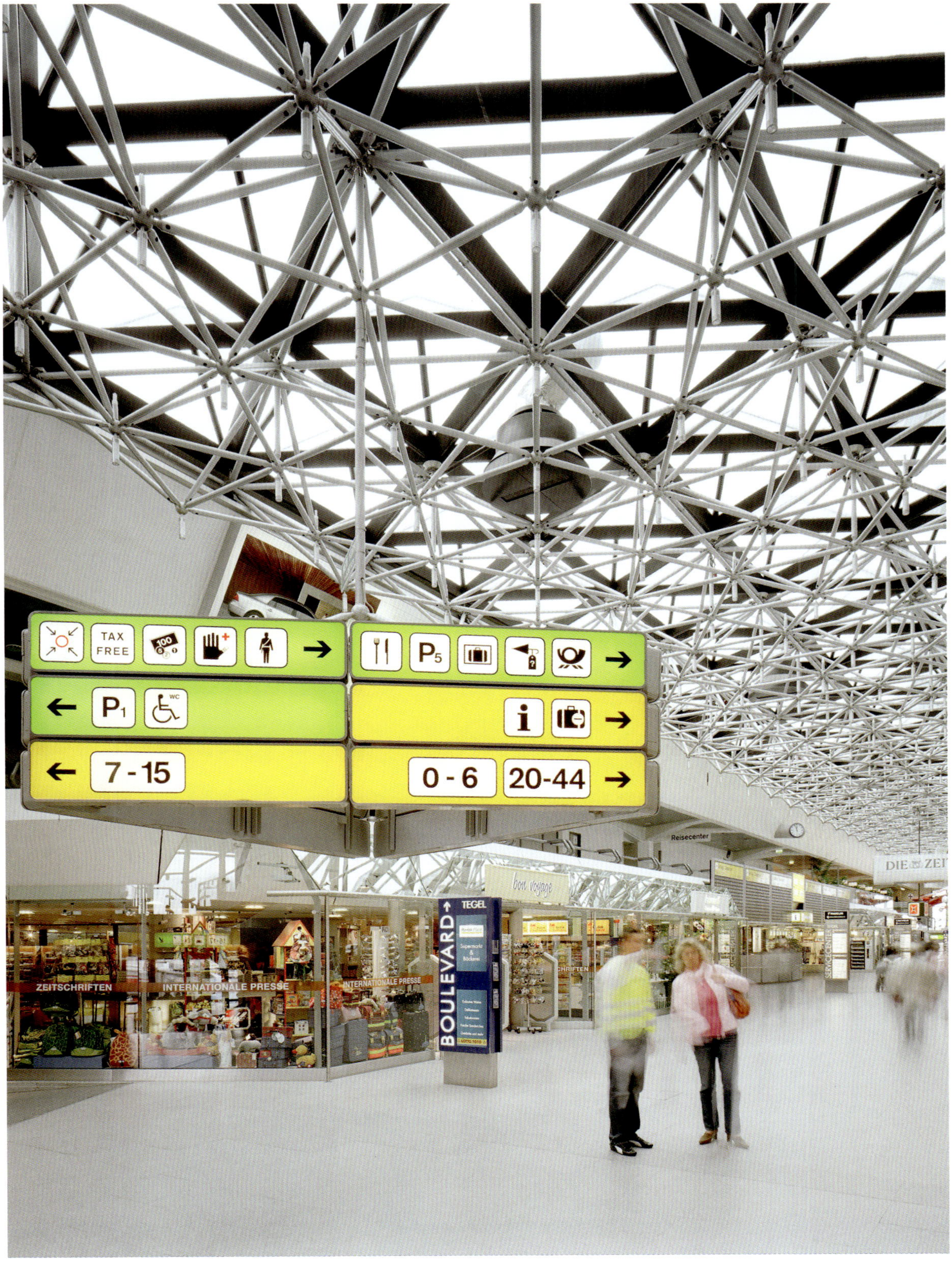

柏林泰格尔机场 柏林

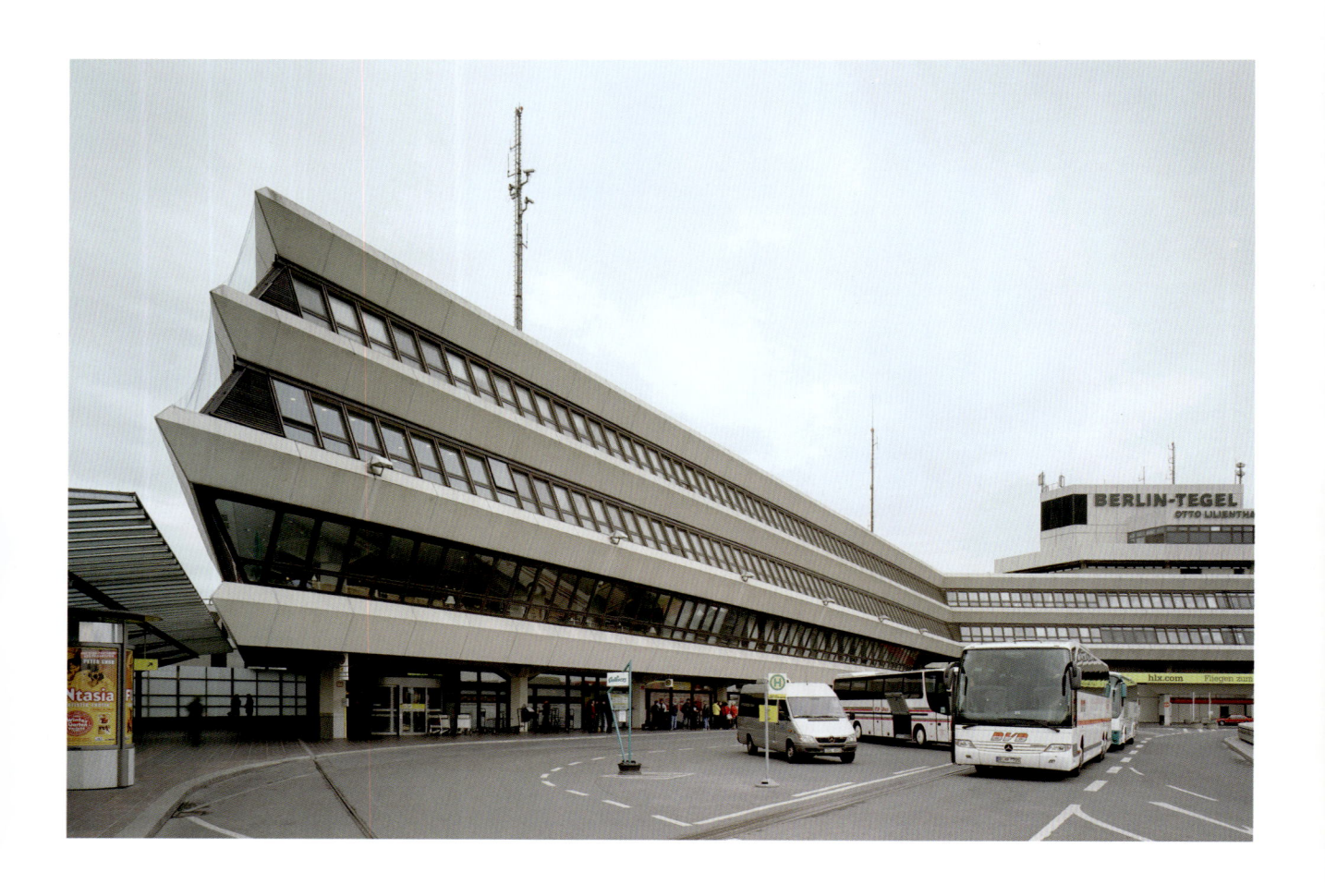

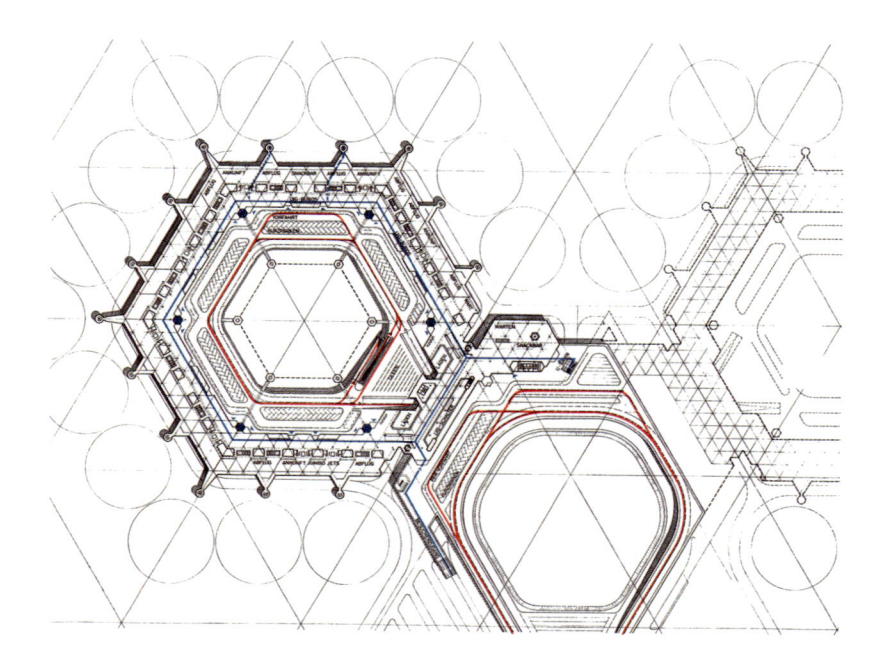

Berlin-Tegel Airport Berlin

276 ²⁶⁰ ↑

斯图加特机场，1和3号航站楼
斯图加特，德国

Stuttgart Airport, Terminals 1 + 3
Stuttgart, Germany

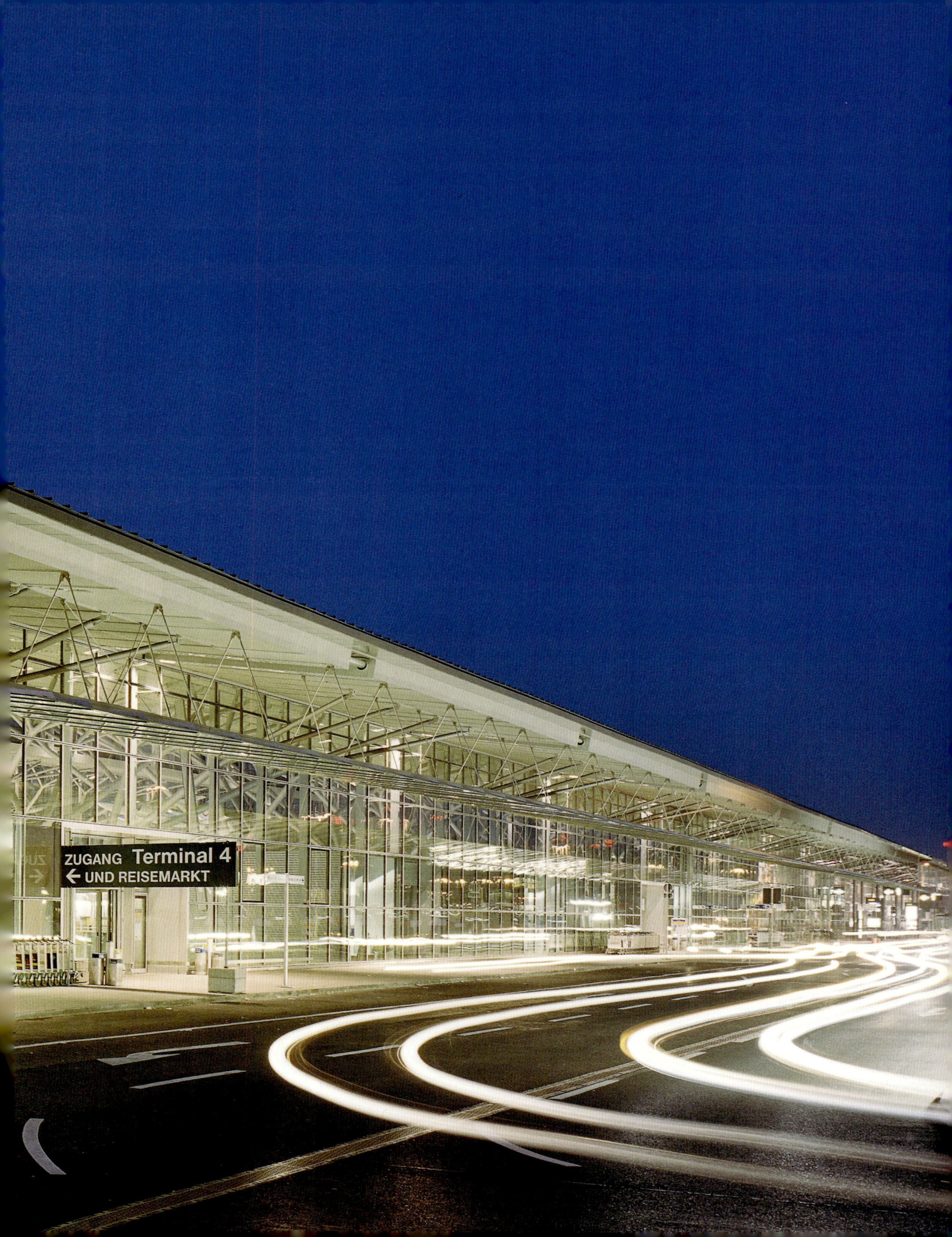
ZUGANG Terminal 4
UND REISEMARKT

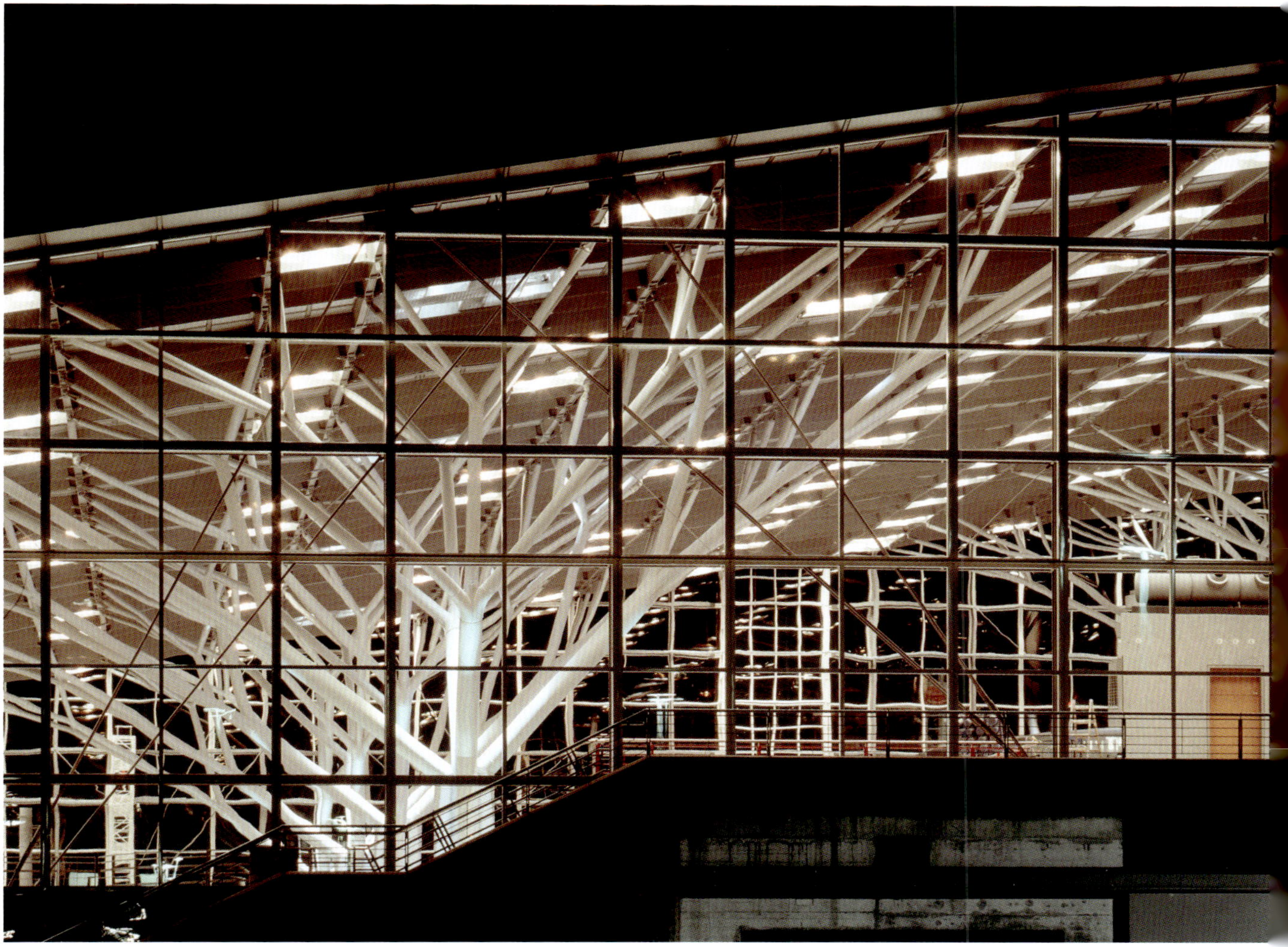

斯图加特机场，1和3号航站楼　斯图加特

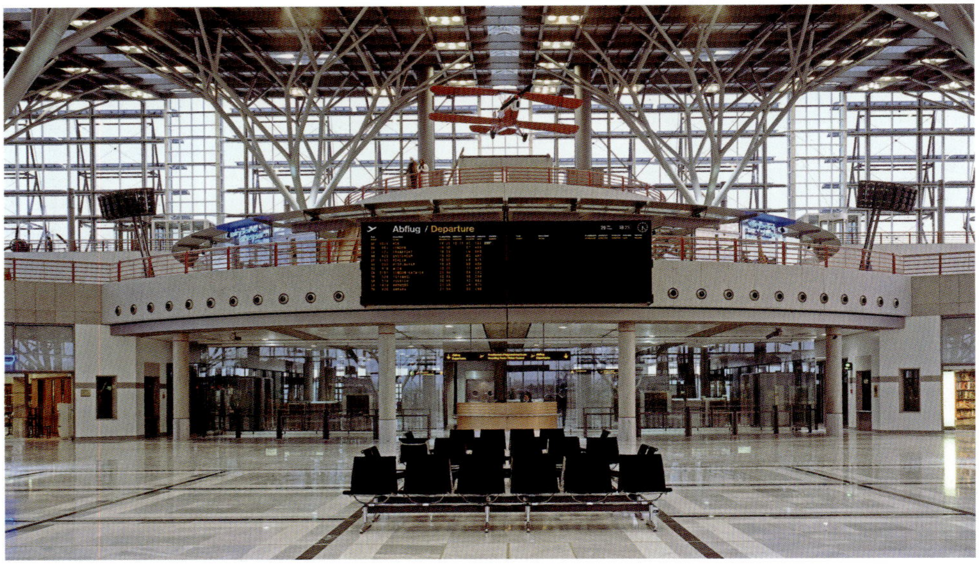

Stuttgart Airport, Terminals 1+3 Stuttgart

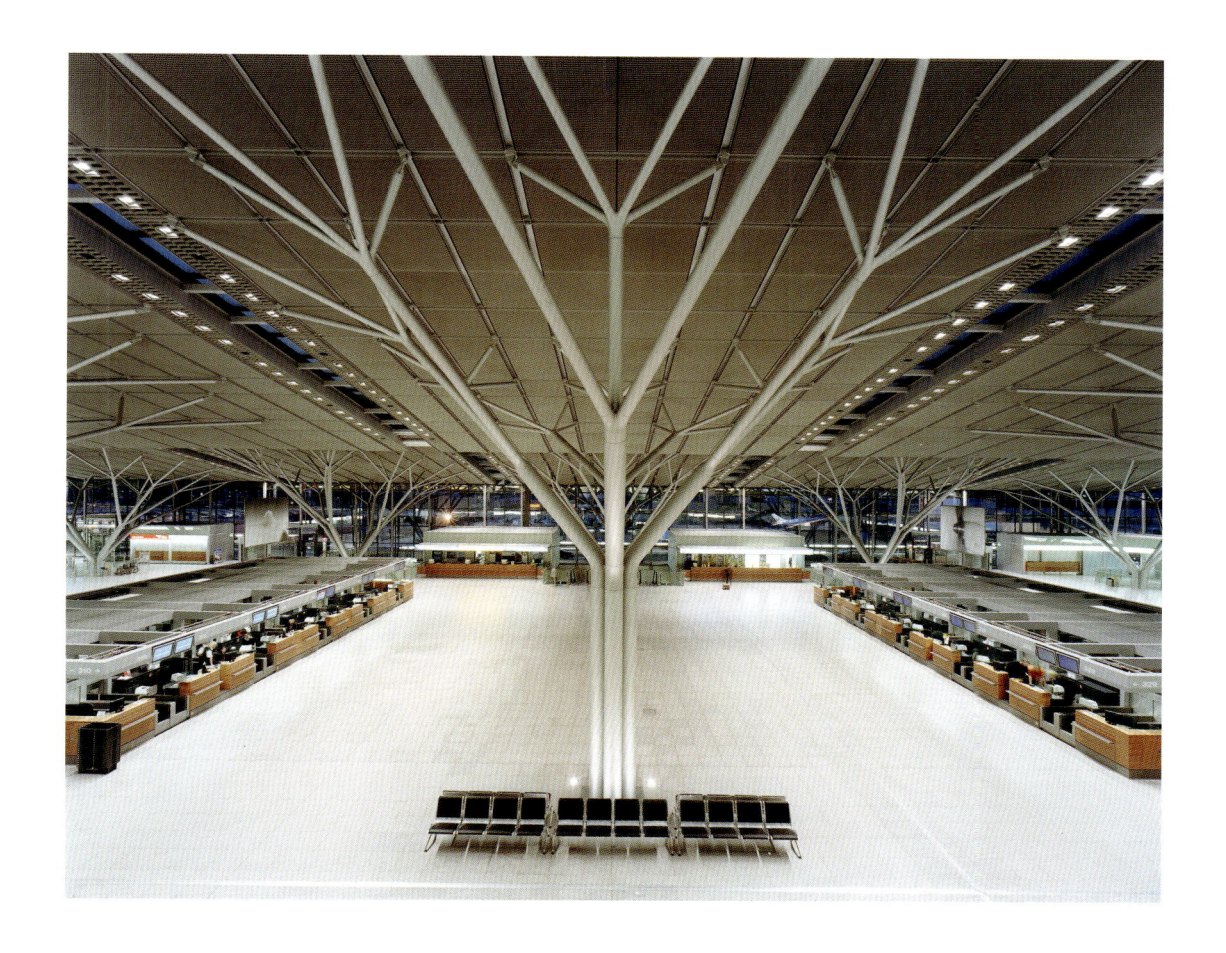

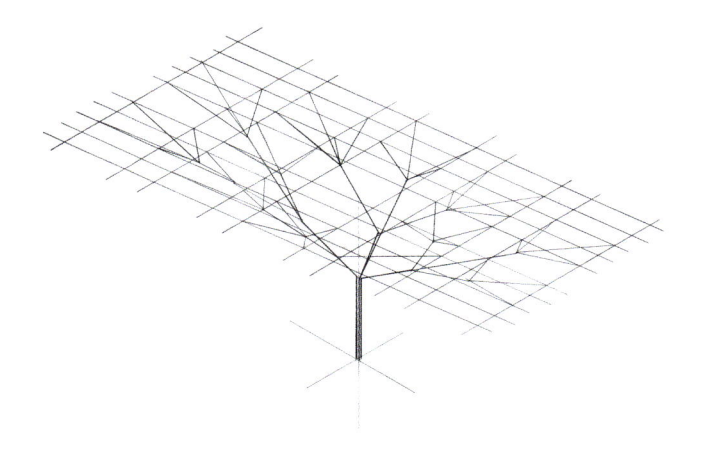

斯图加特机场，1和3号航站楼　斯图加特

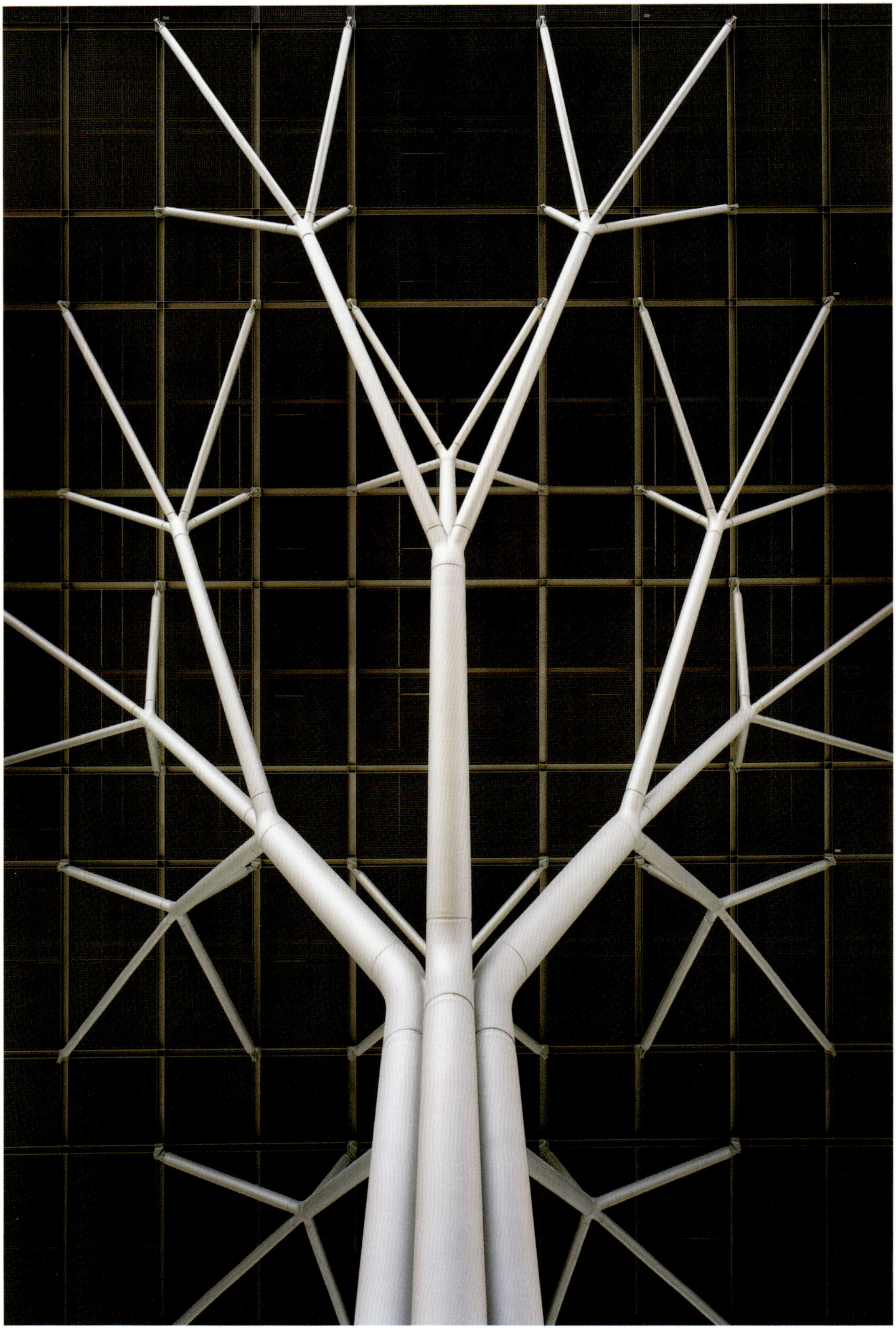

Stuttgart Airport, Terminals 1+3 Stuttgart

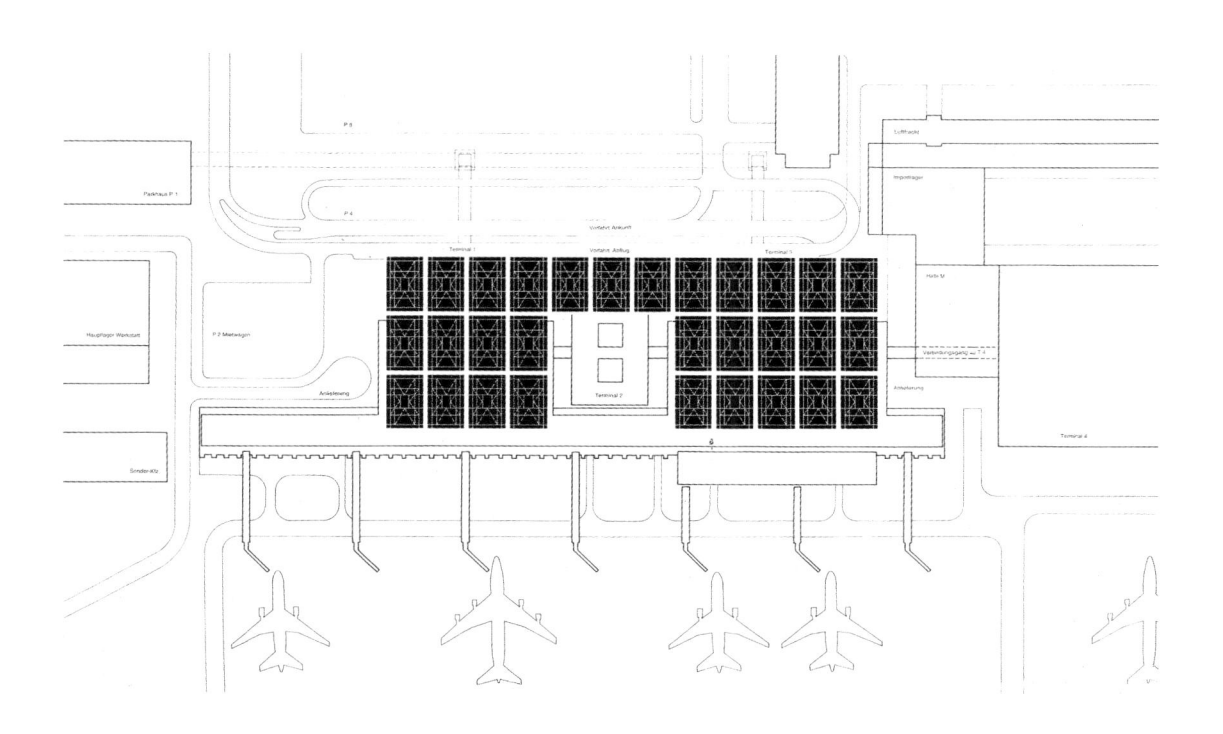

斯图加特机场，1和3号航站楼　斯图加特

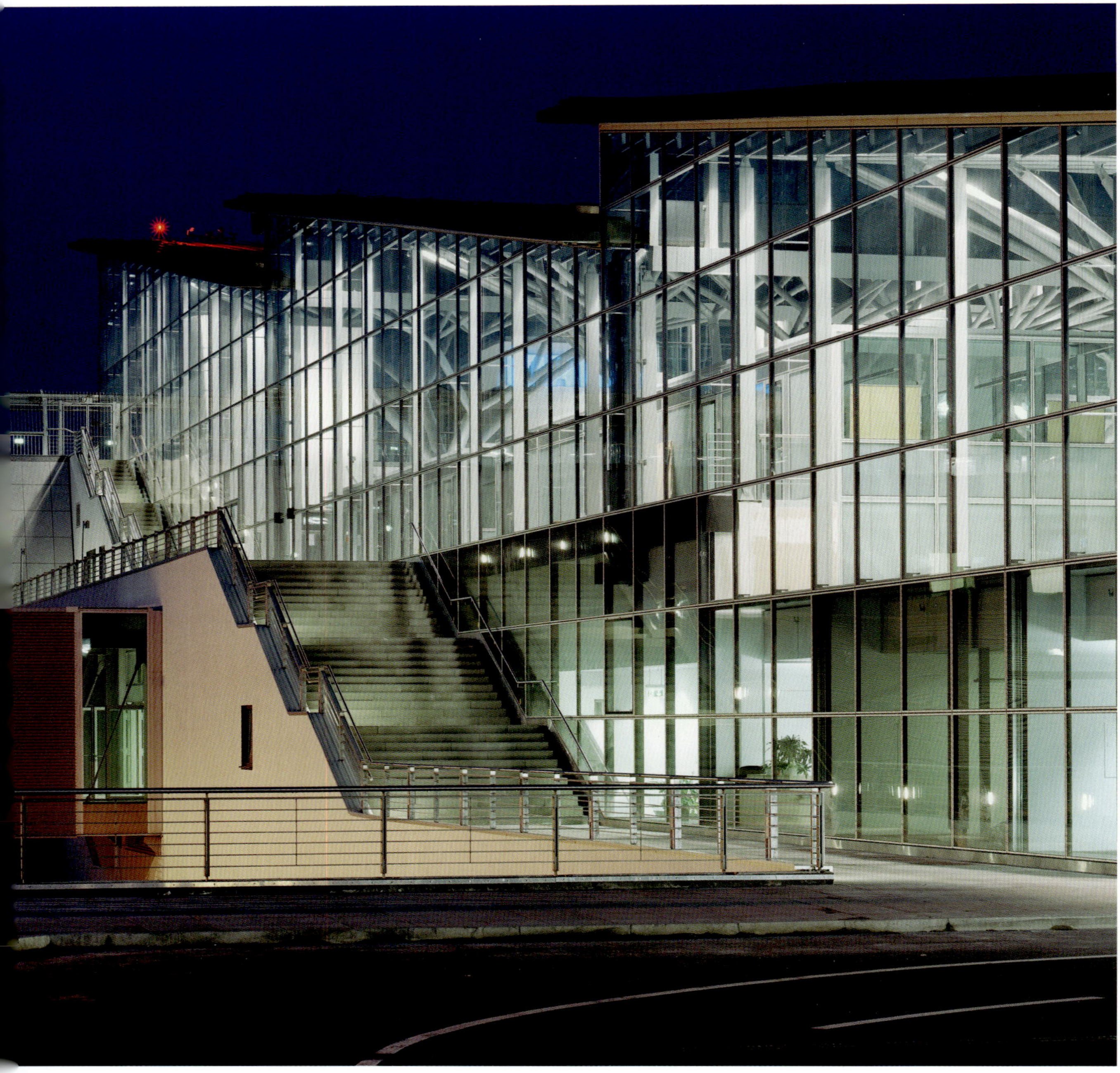

Stuttgart Airport, Terminals 1+3 Stuttgart

284 ²⁶¹ ↑

汉堡机场
汉堡，德国

Hamburg Airport
Hamburg, Germany

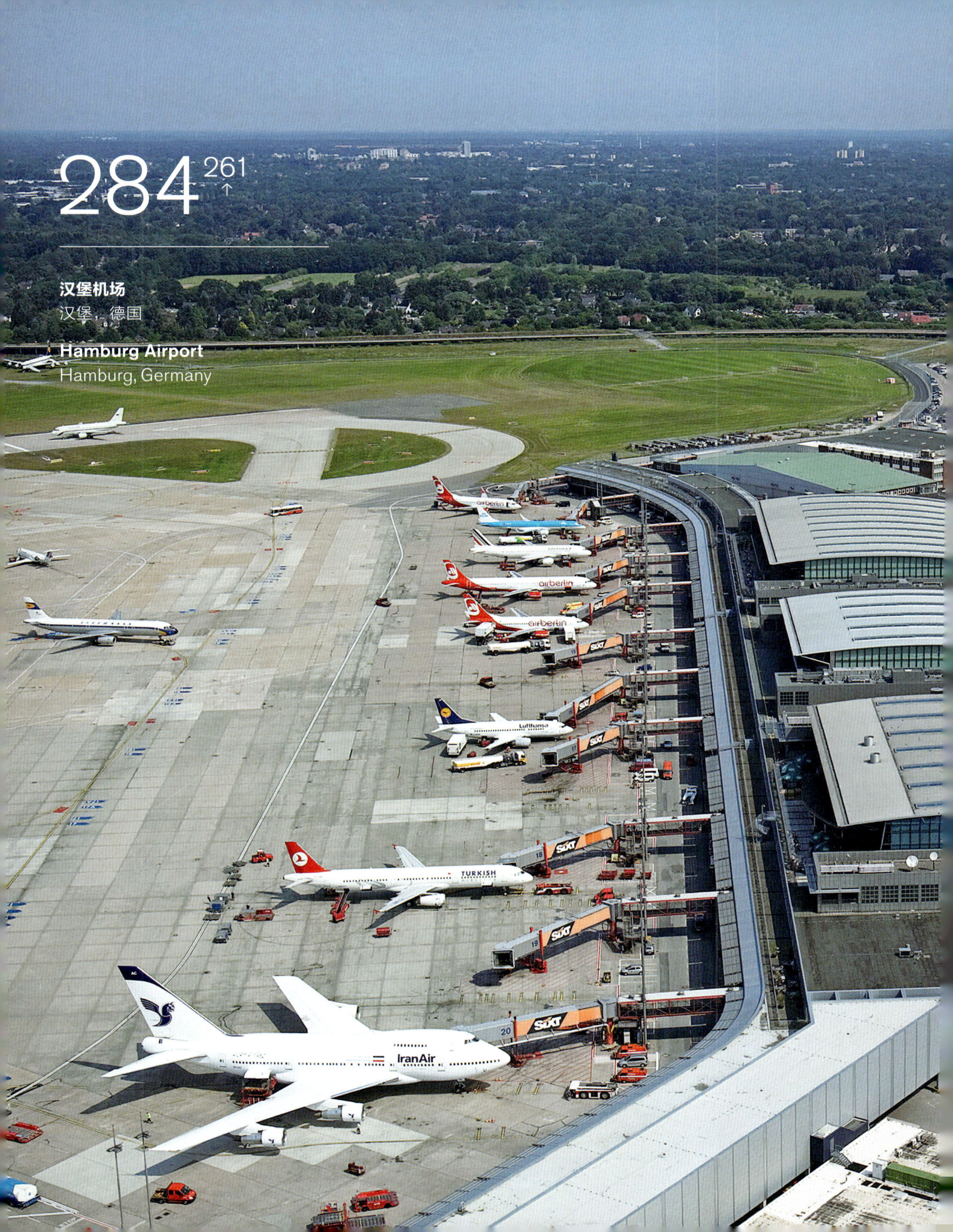

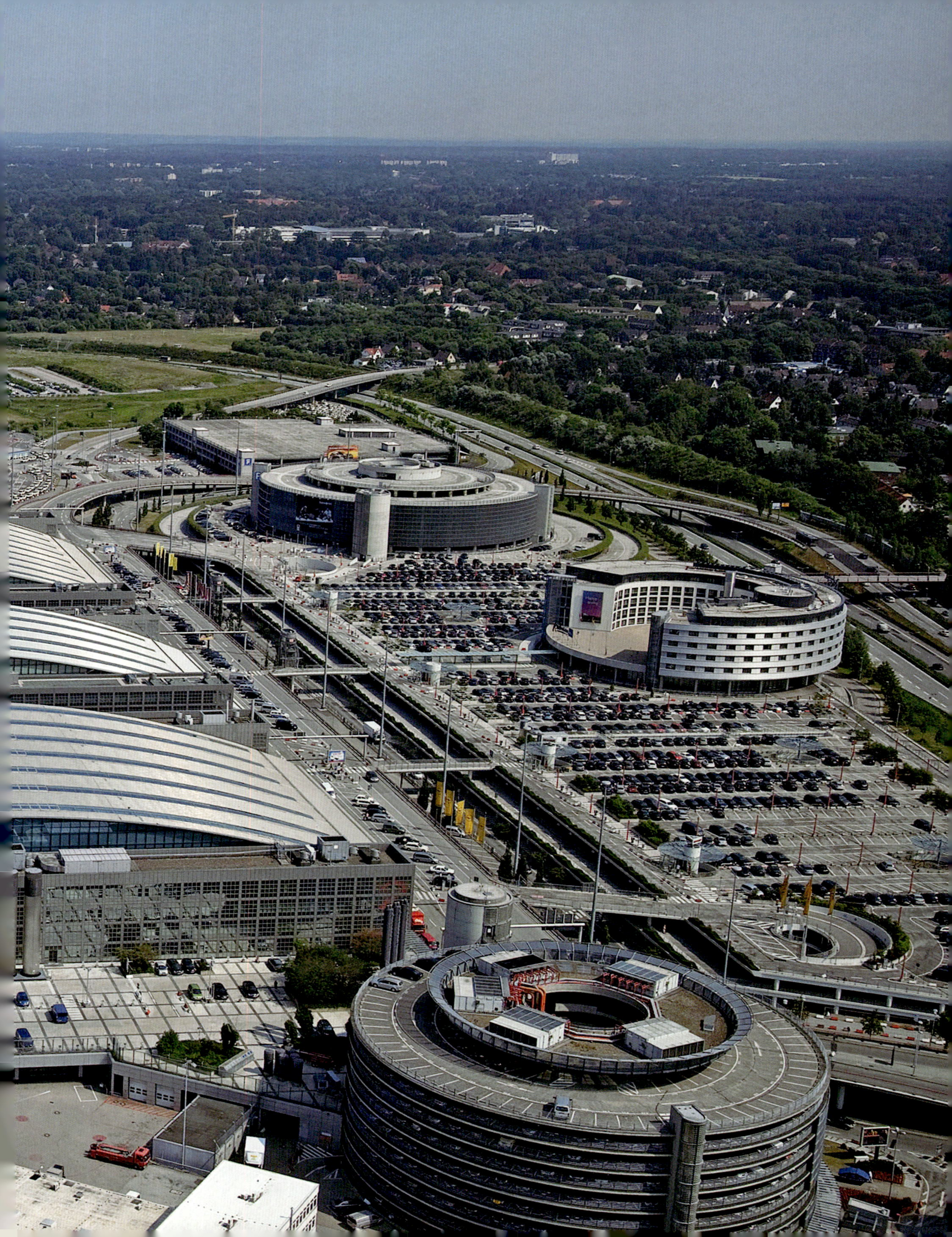

286　汉堡机场　汉堡

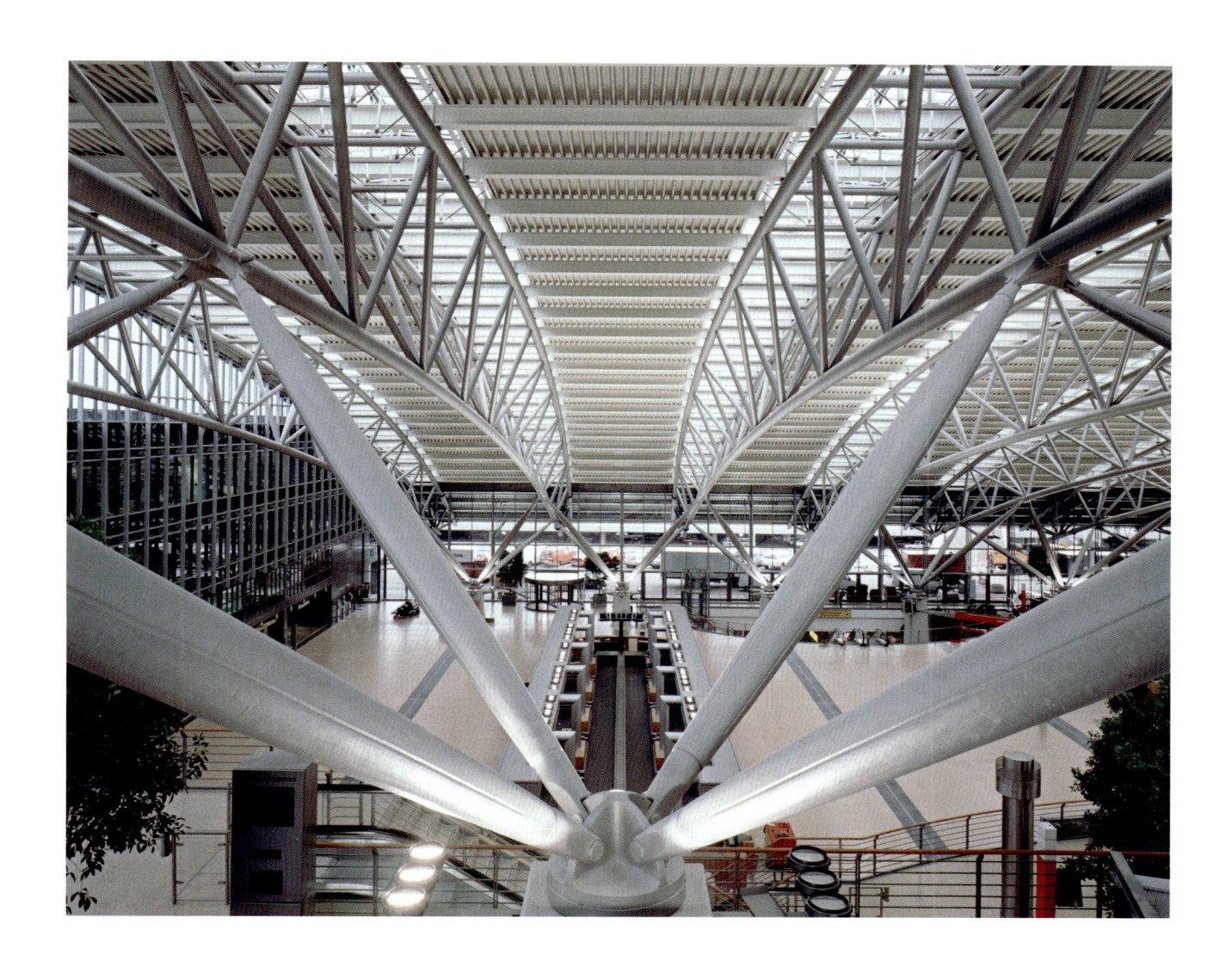

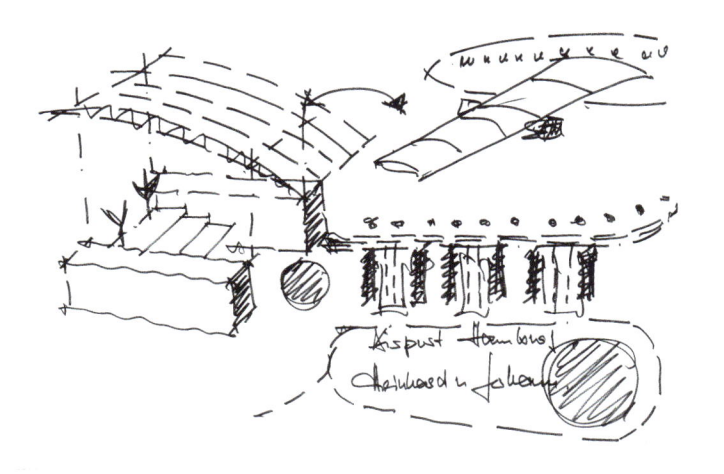

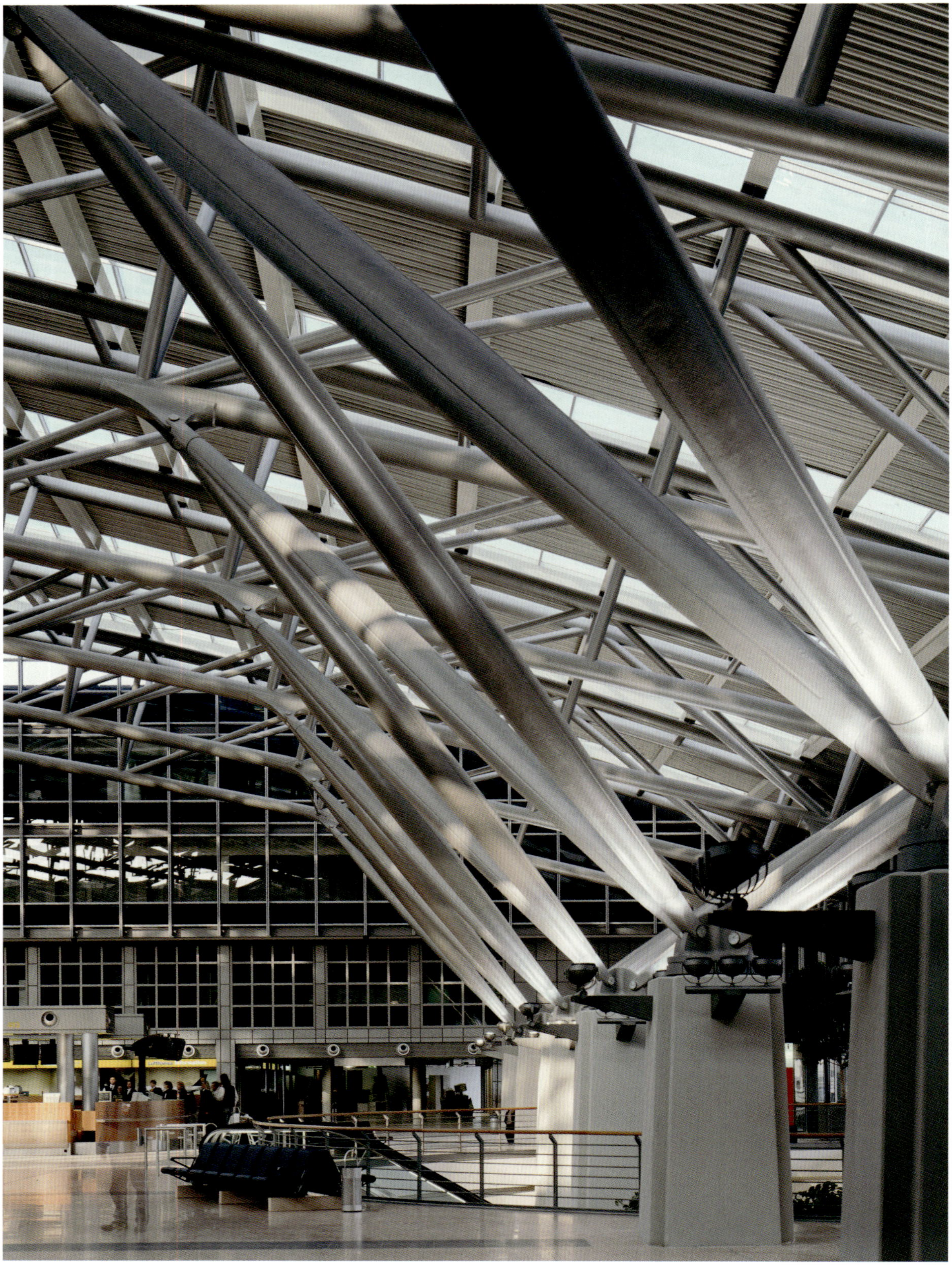

Hamburg Airport Hamburg

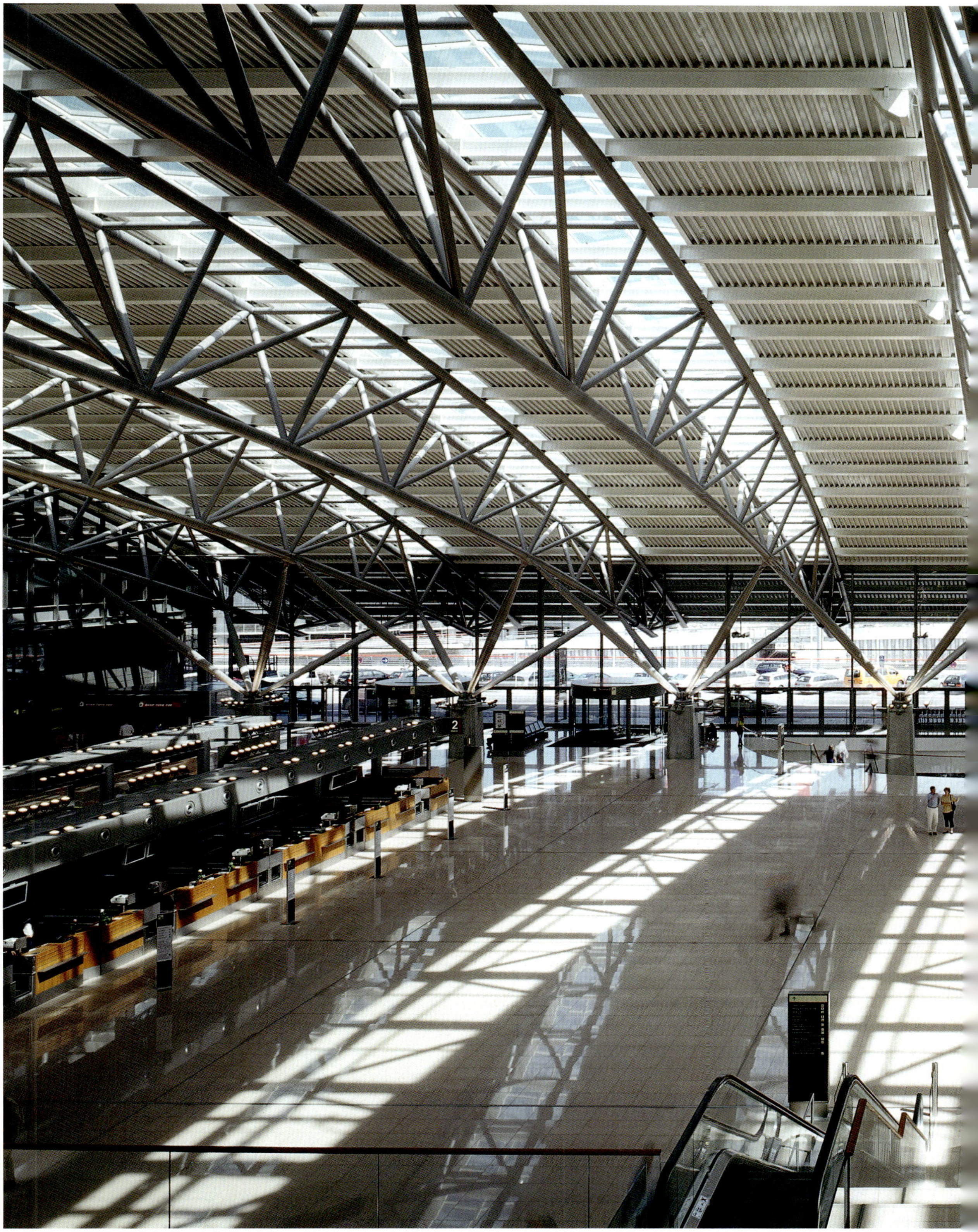

汉堡机场　汉堡

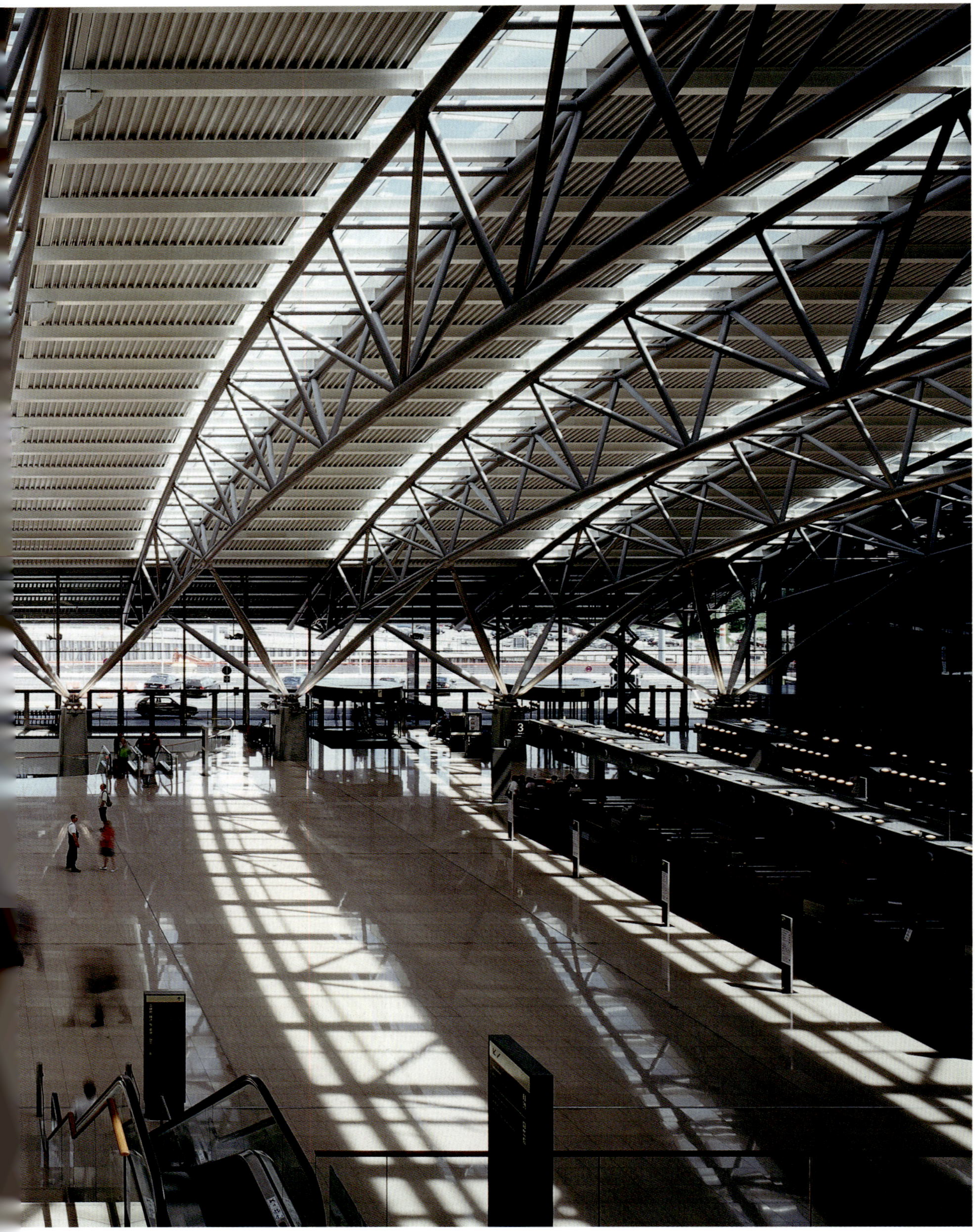

Hamburg Airport Hamburg

290 ²⁶¹ ↑

音乐会议中心
吕贝克，德国

Music and Congress Hall
Lubeck, Germany

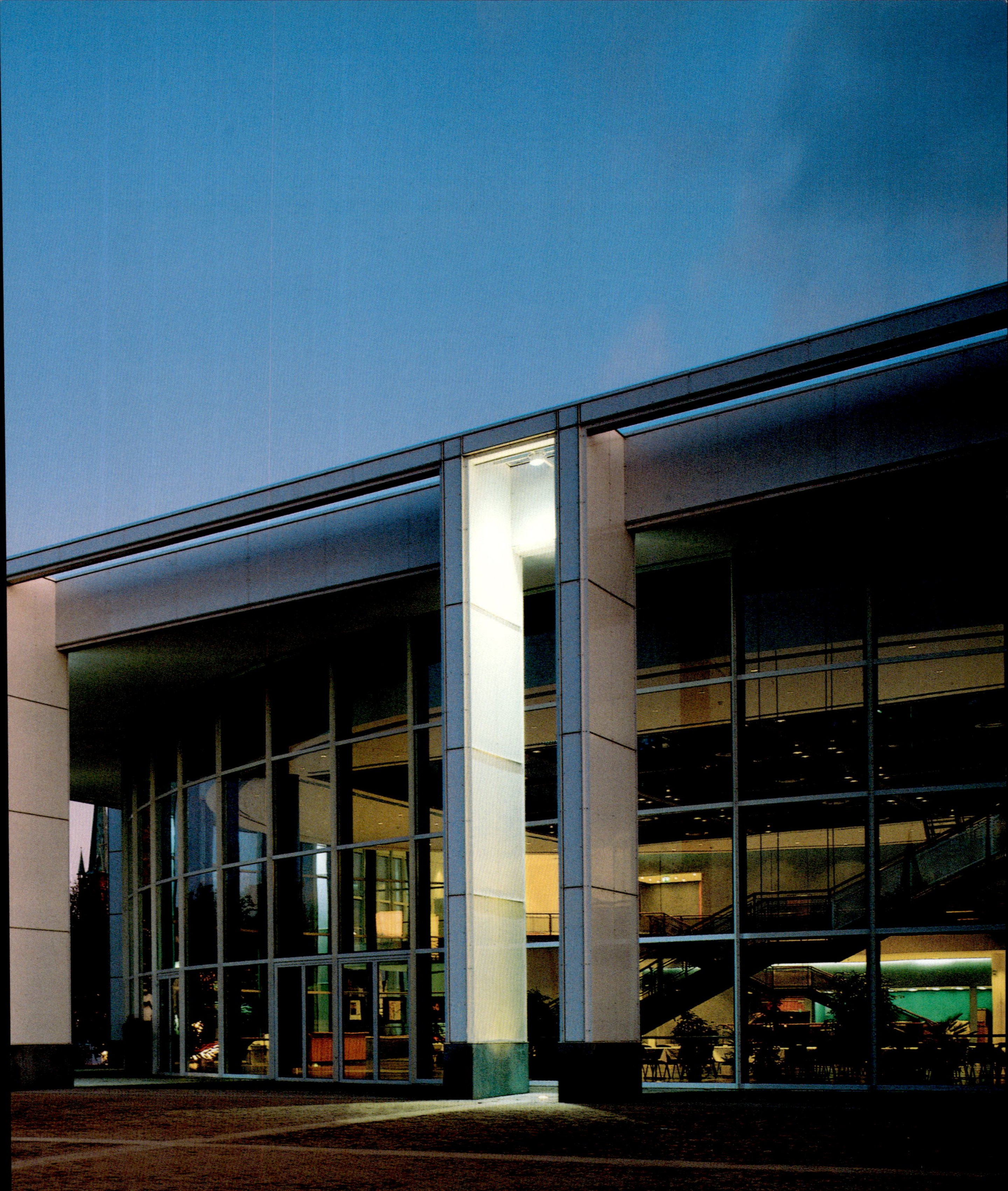

292　音乐会议中心　吕贝克

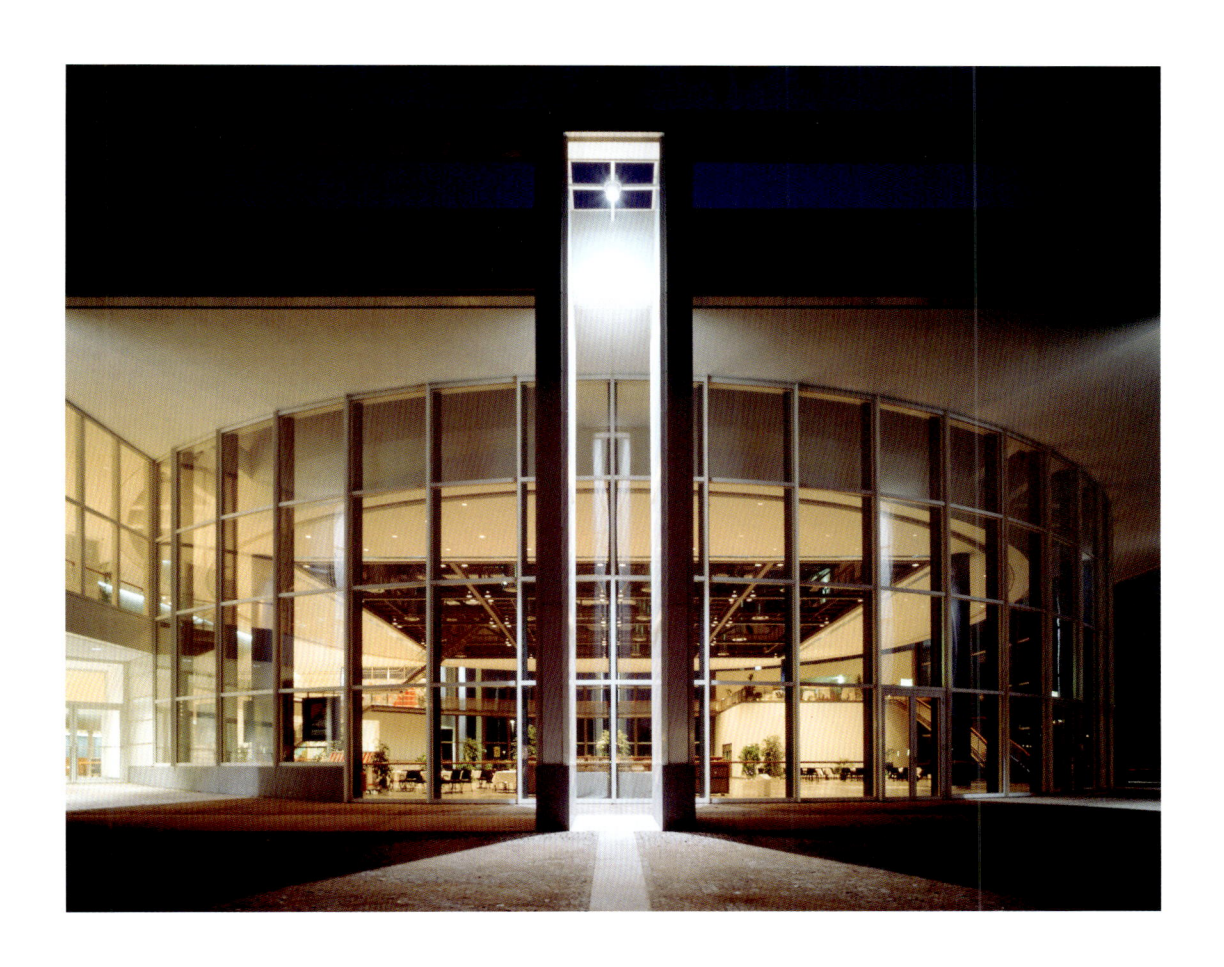

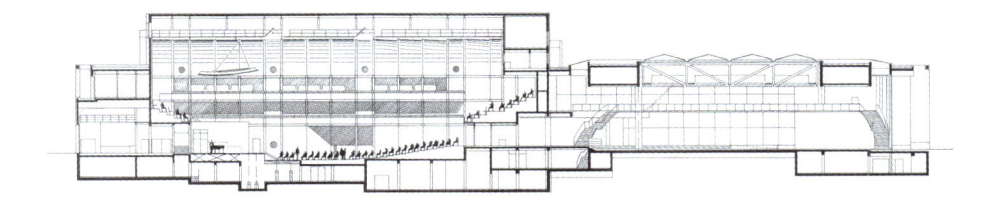

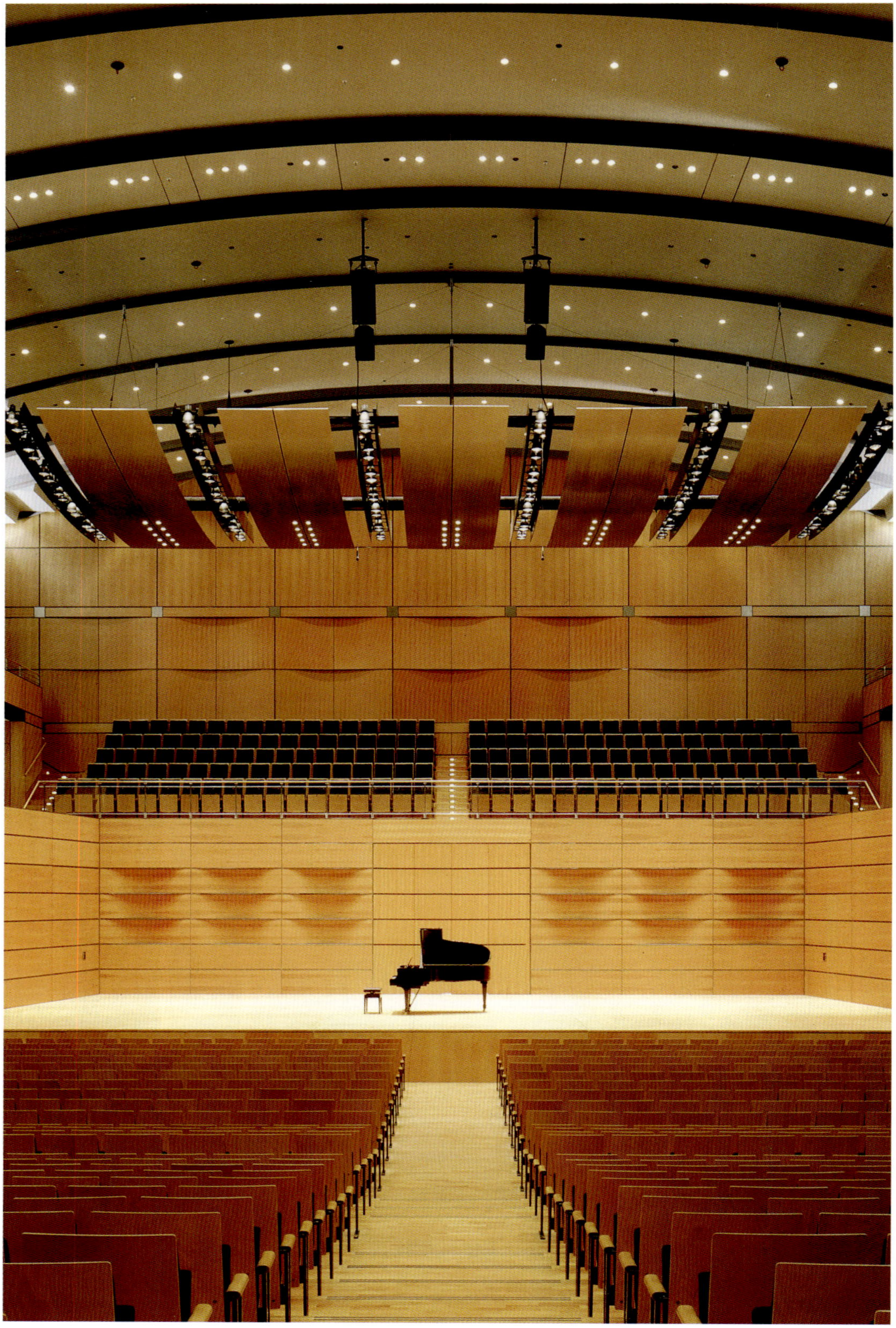

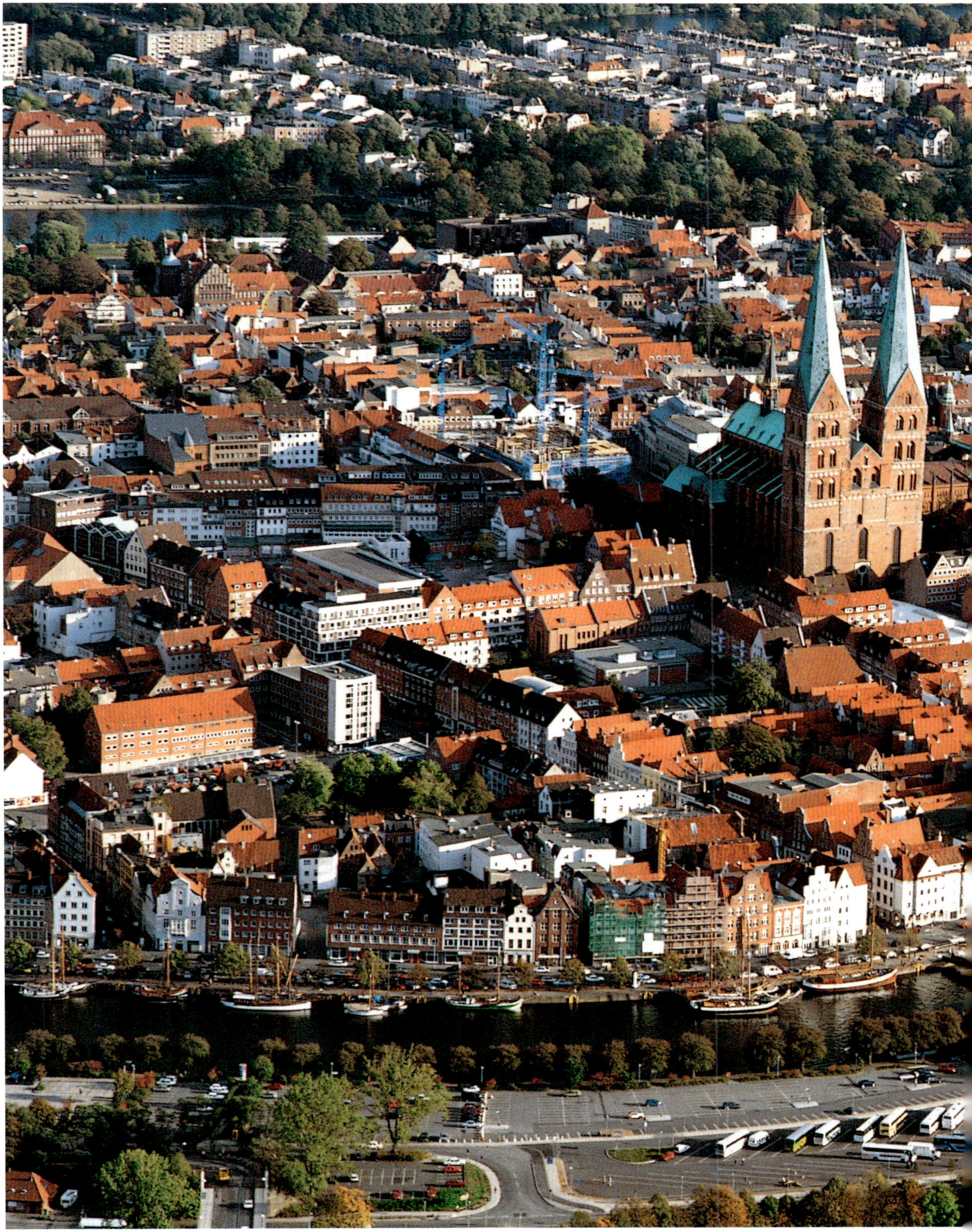

音乐会议中心　吕贝克

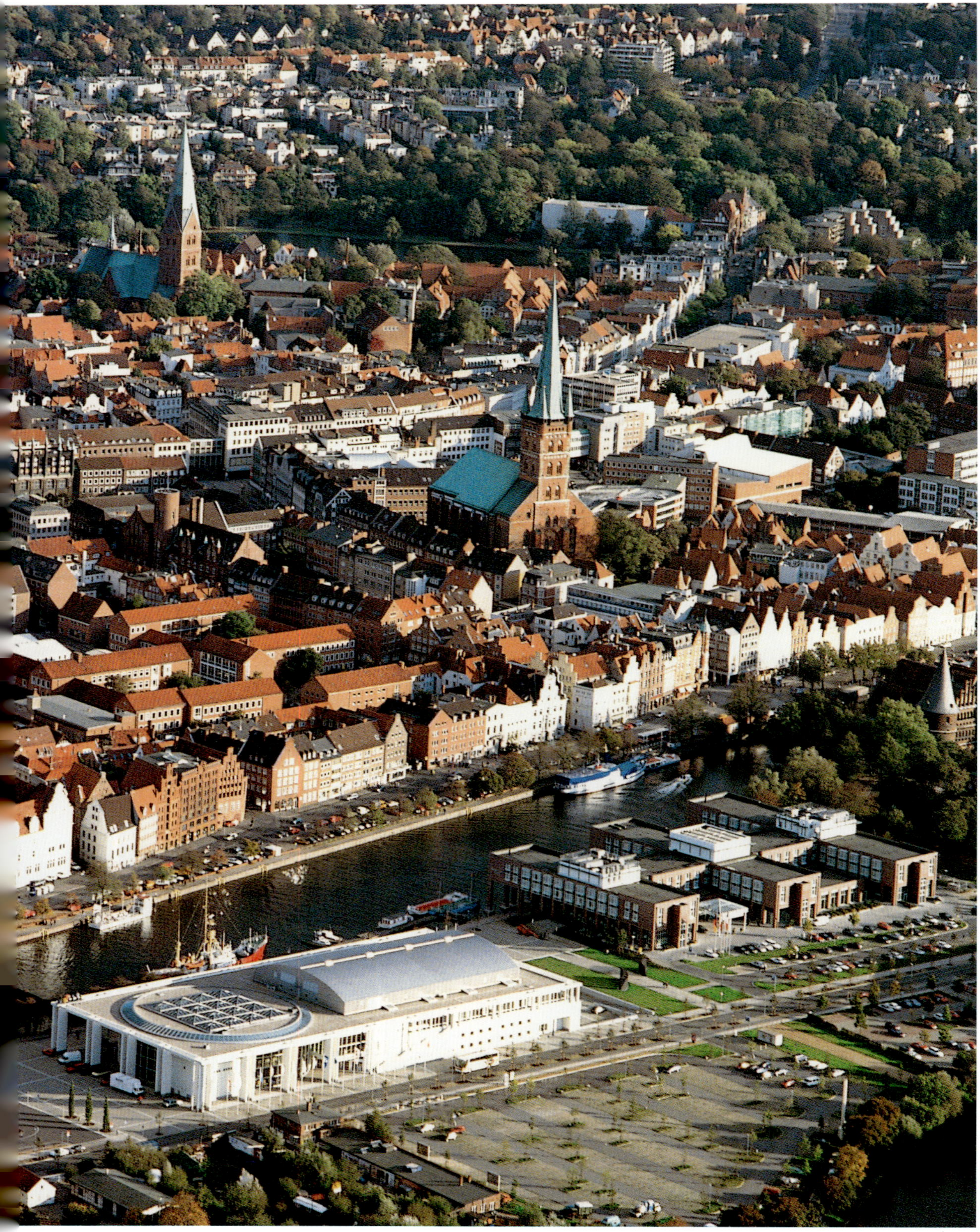

Music and Congress Hall Lubeck   295

296 ²⁶²

莱比锡新会展中心
莱比锡，德国

New Leipzig Trade Fair
Leipzig, Germany

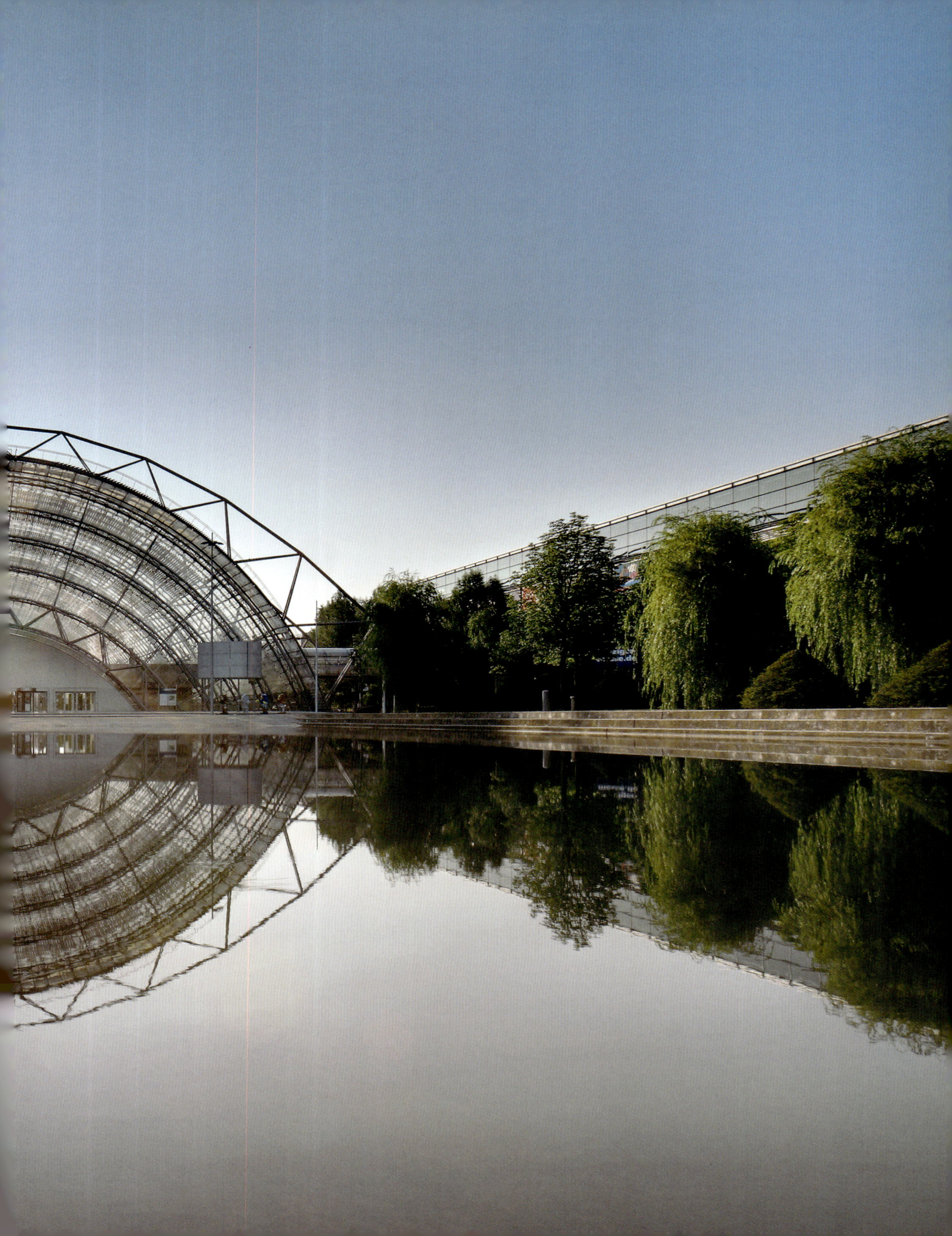

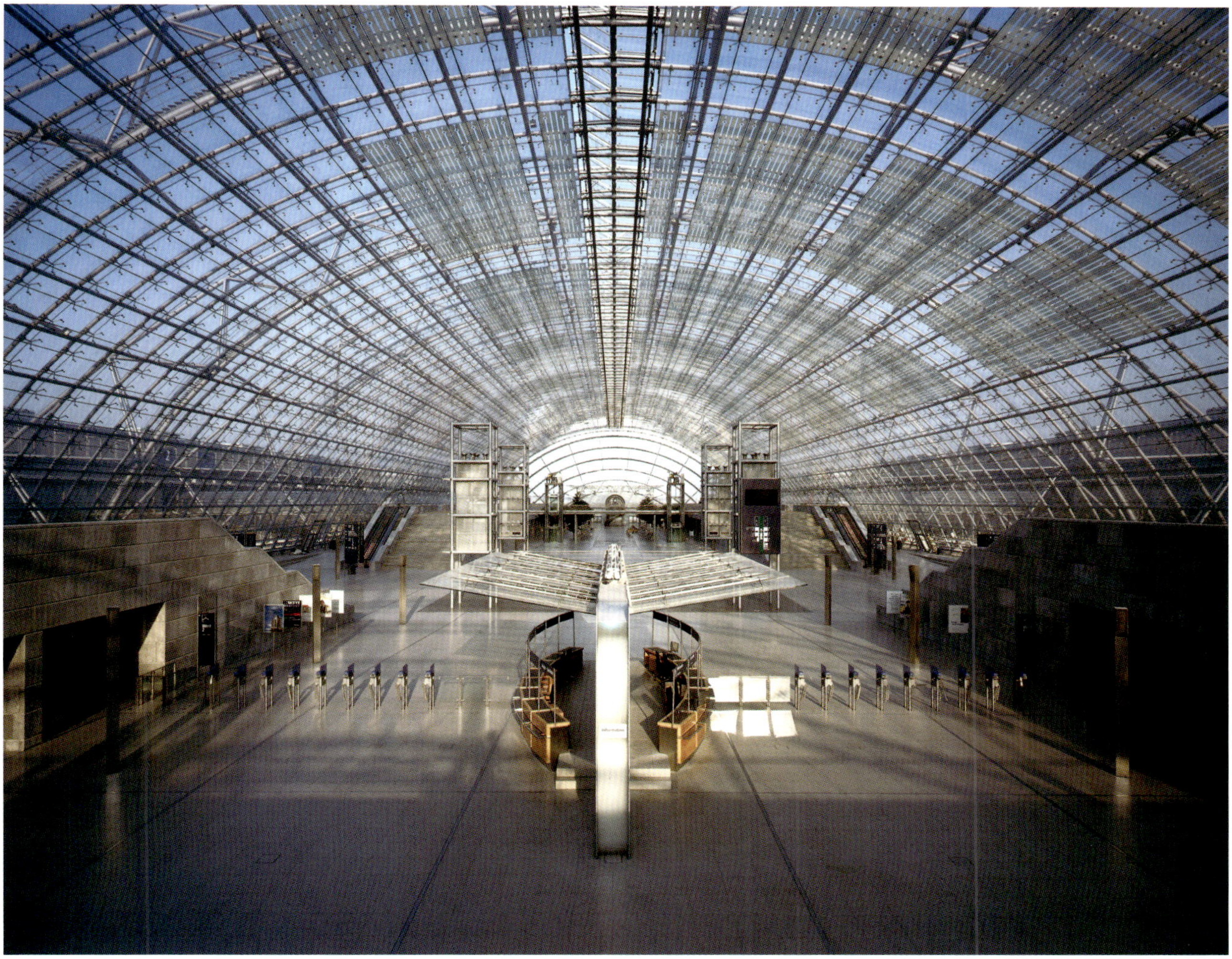

莱比锡新会展中心　莱比锡

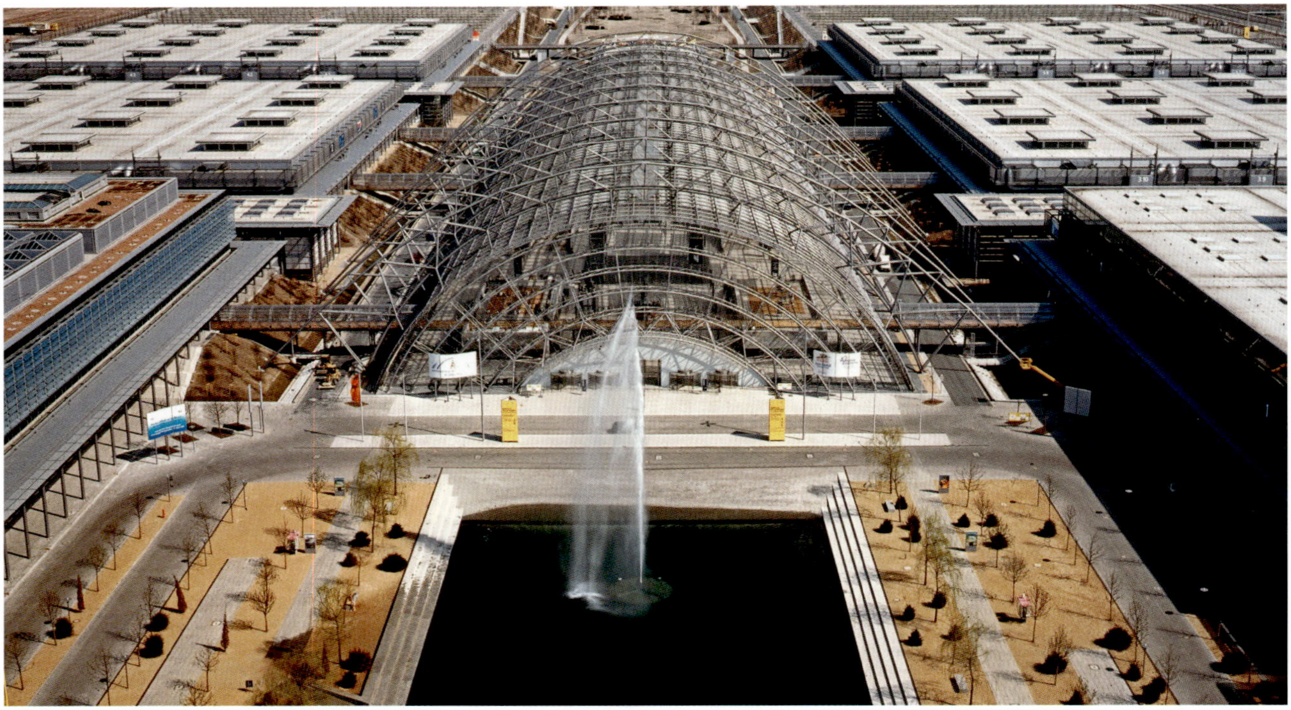

New Leipzig Trade Fair Leipzig

HERZLICH
WILLKOMMEN
zur Leipziger Messe
Glashalle
mit
Übergängen
zu den Hallen
2
4
und dem
Freigelände

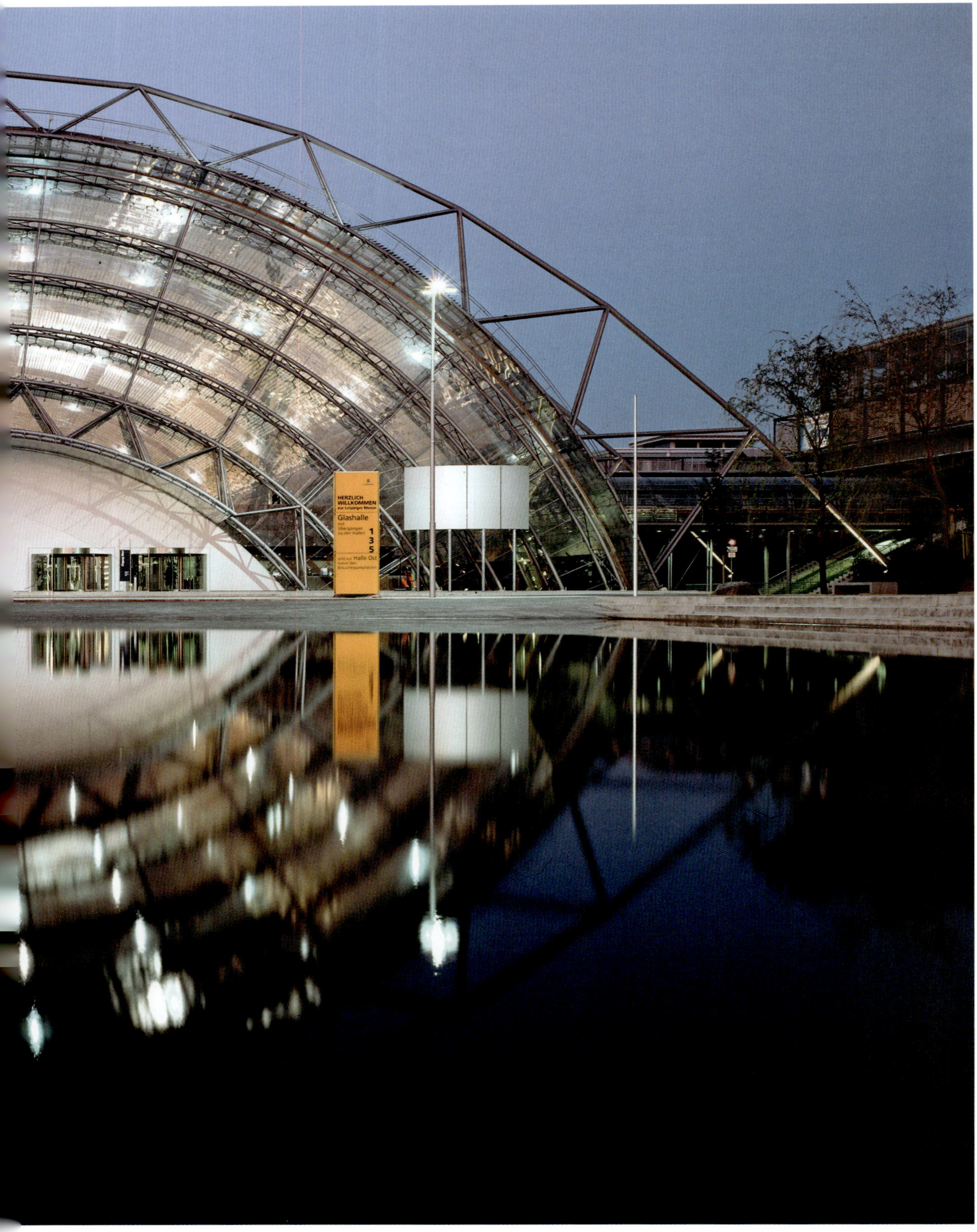

New Leipzig Trade Fair Leipzig

302 ²⁶²
↑

柏林中央火车站
柏林，德国

Berlin Central Station
Berlin, Germany

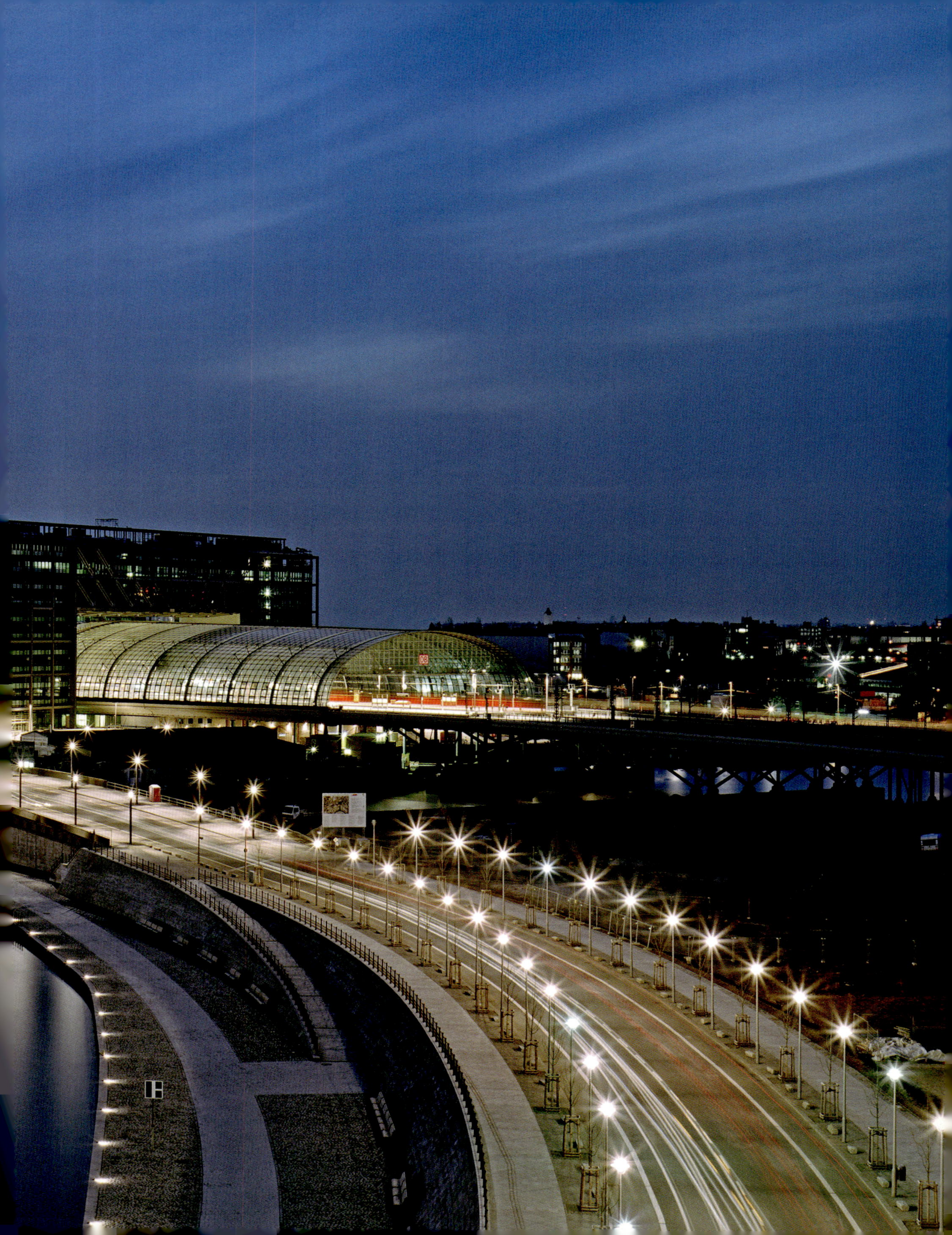

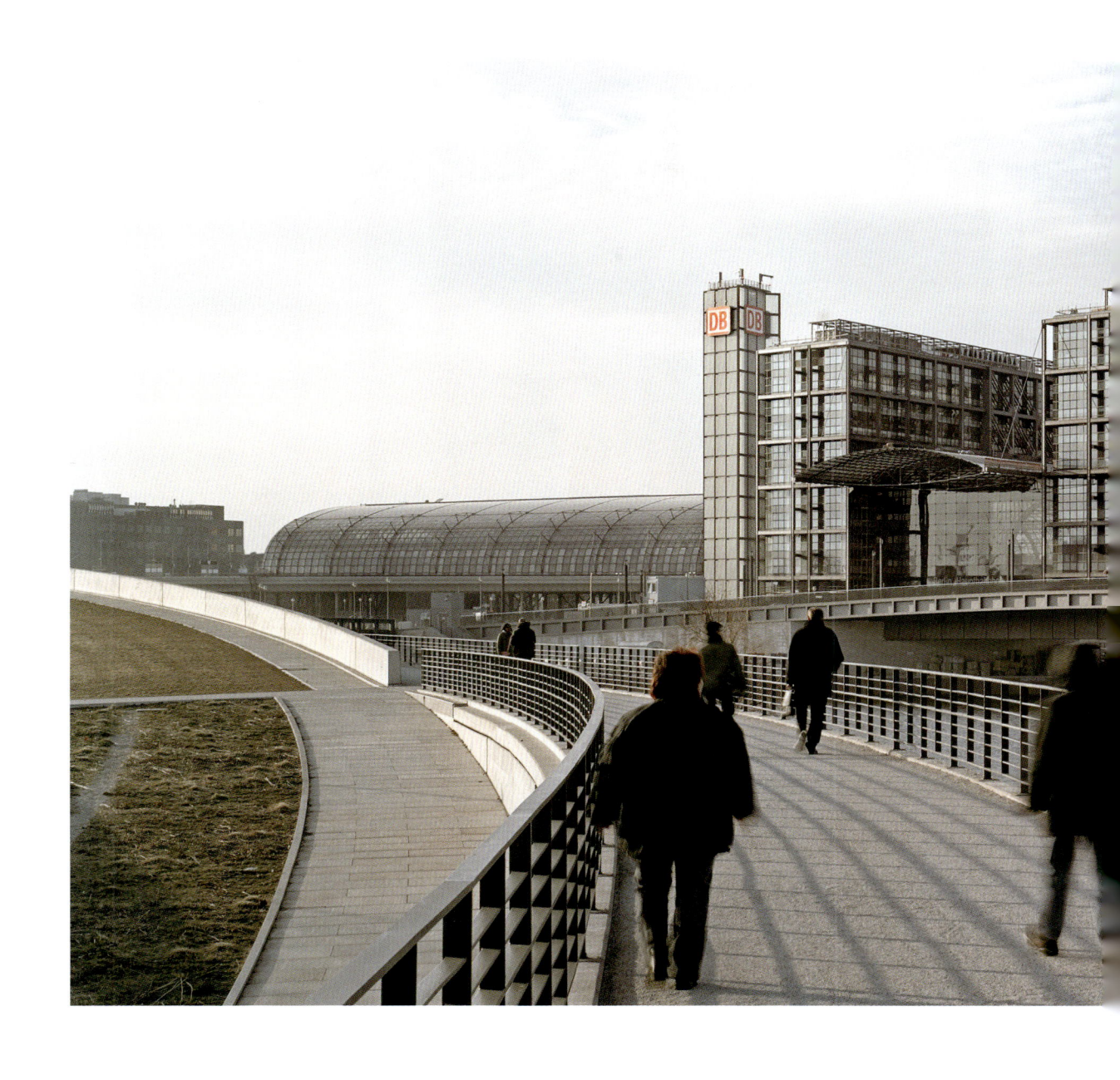

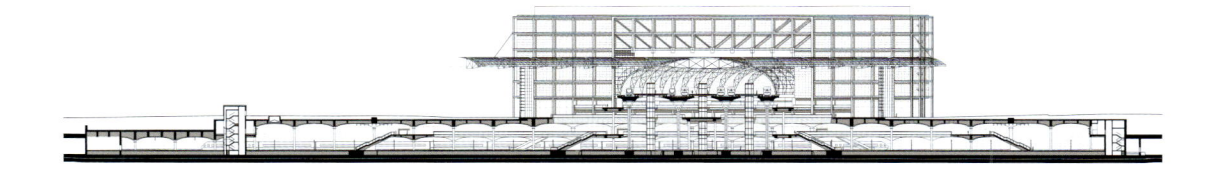

柏林中央火车站 柏林

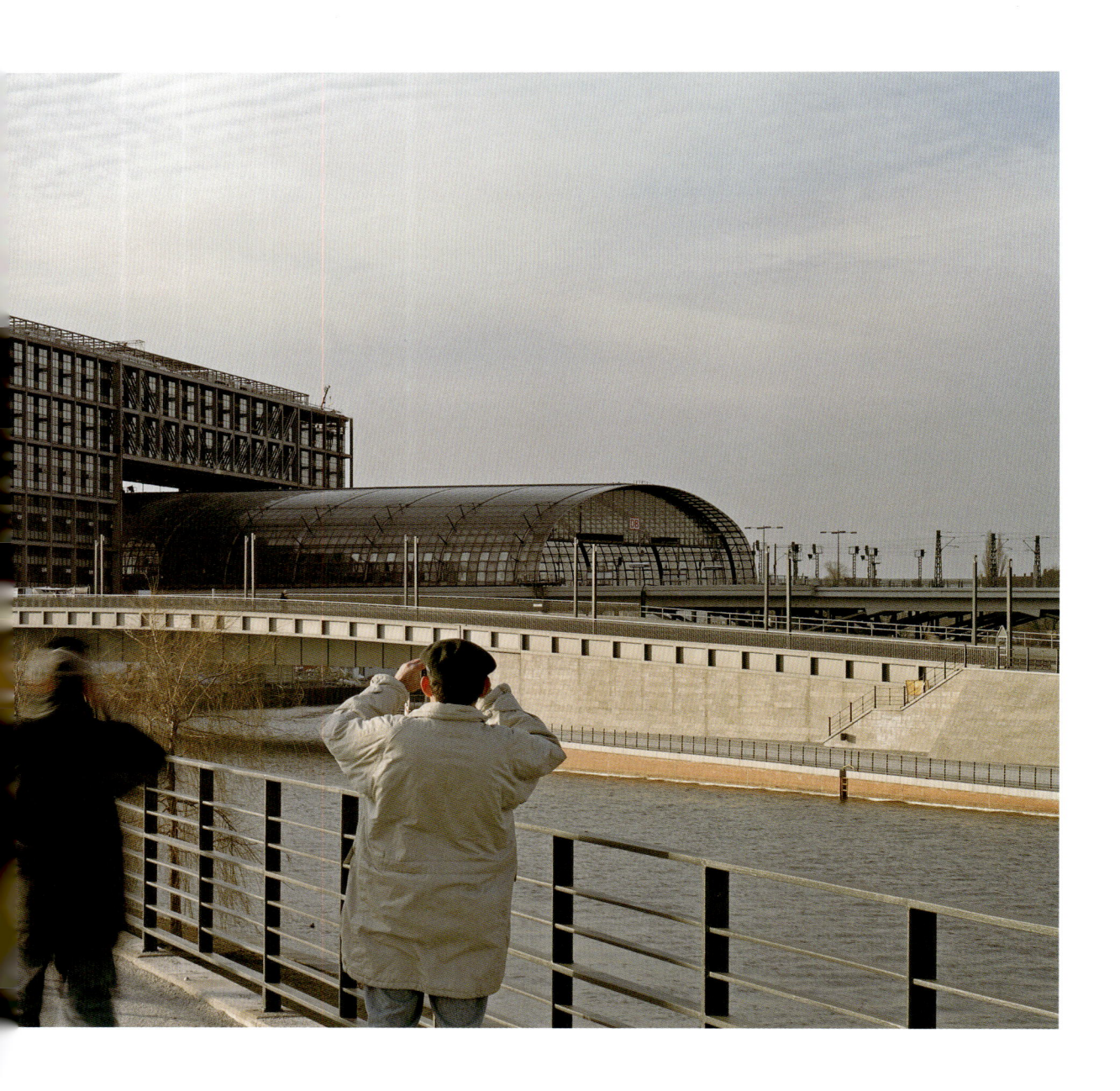

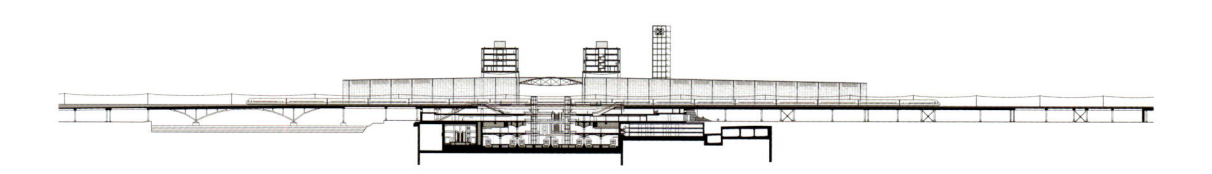

Berlin Central Station Berlin

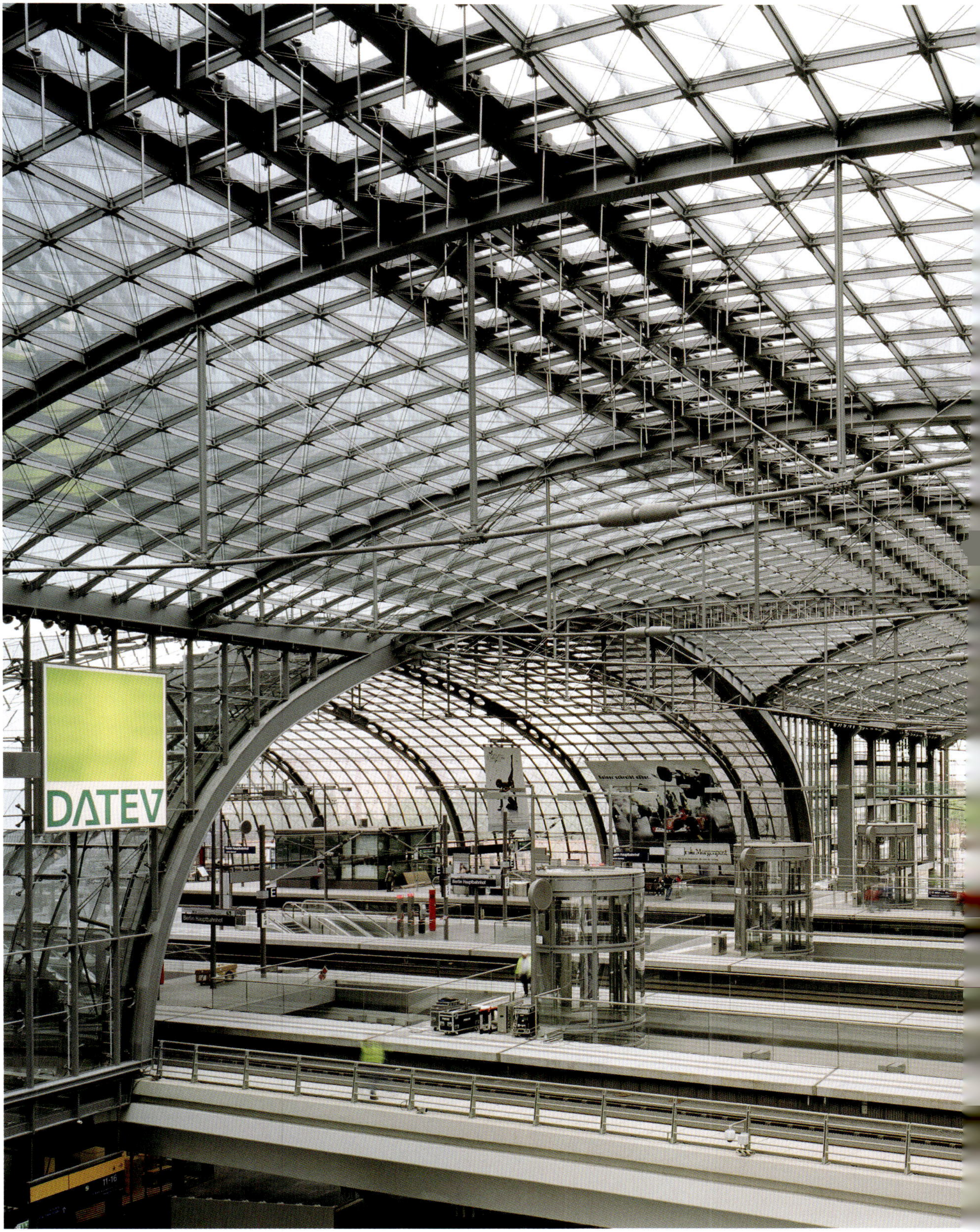

柏林中央火车站　柏林

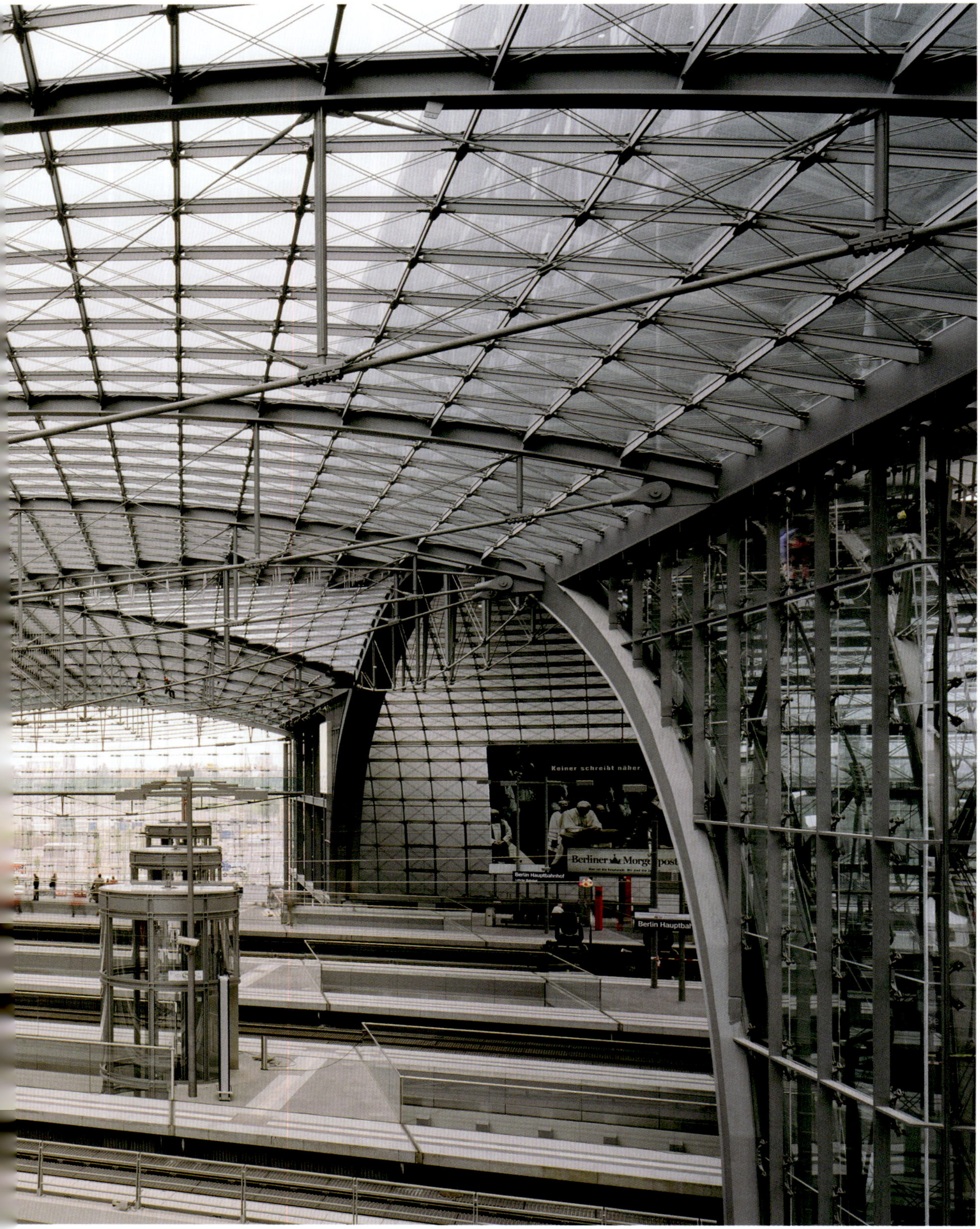

Berlin Central Station Berlin

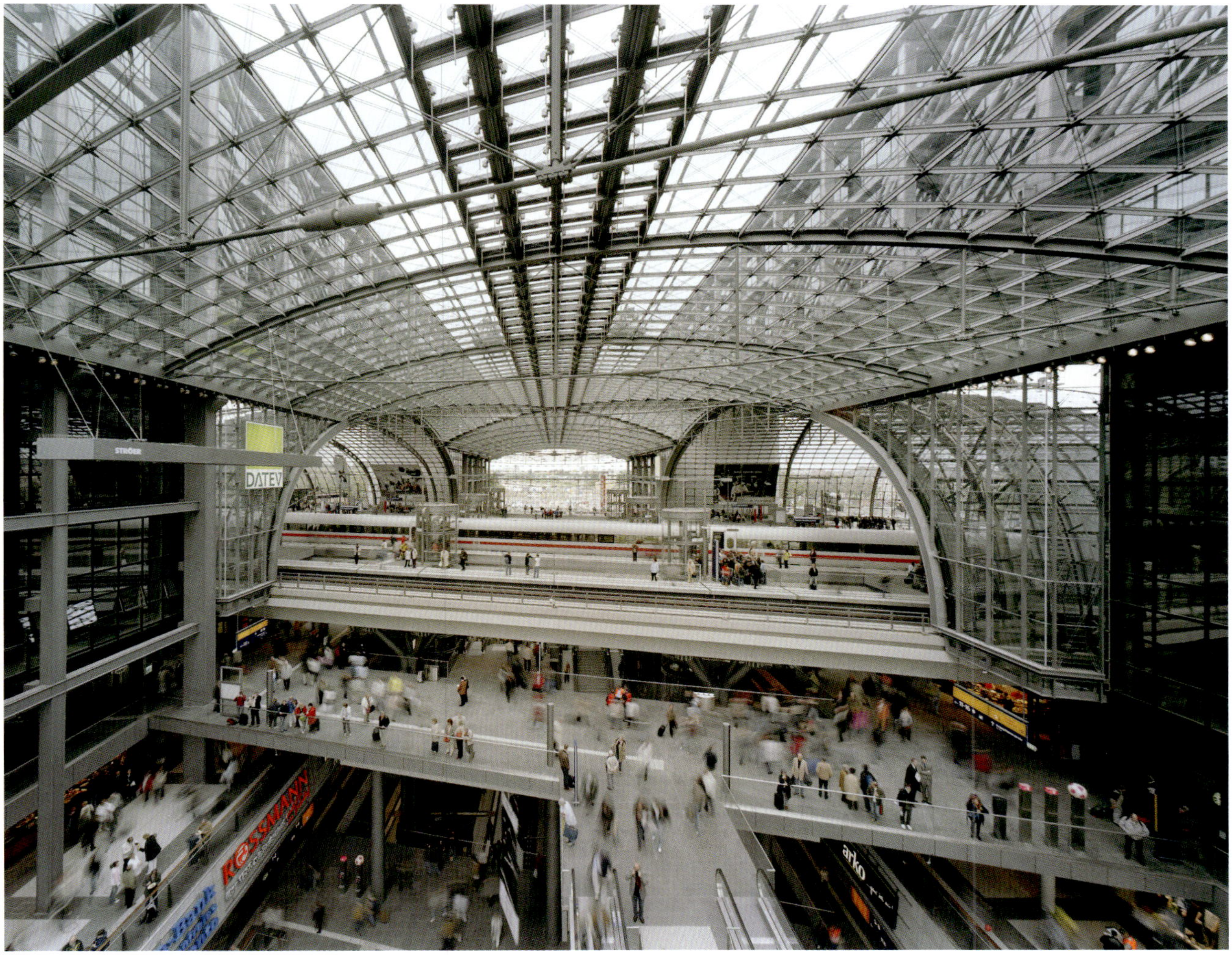

柏林中央火车站　柏林

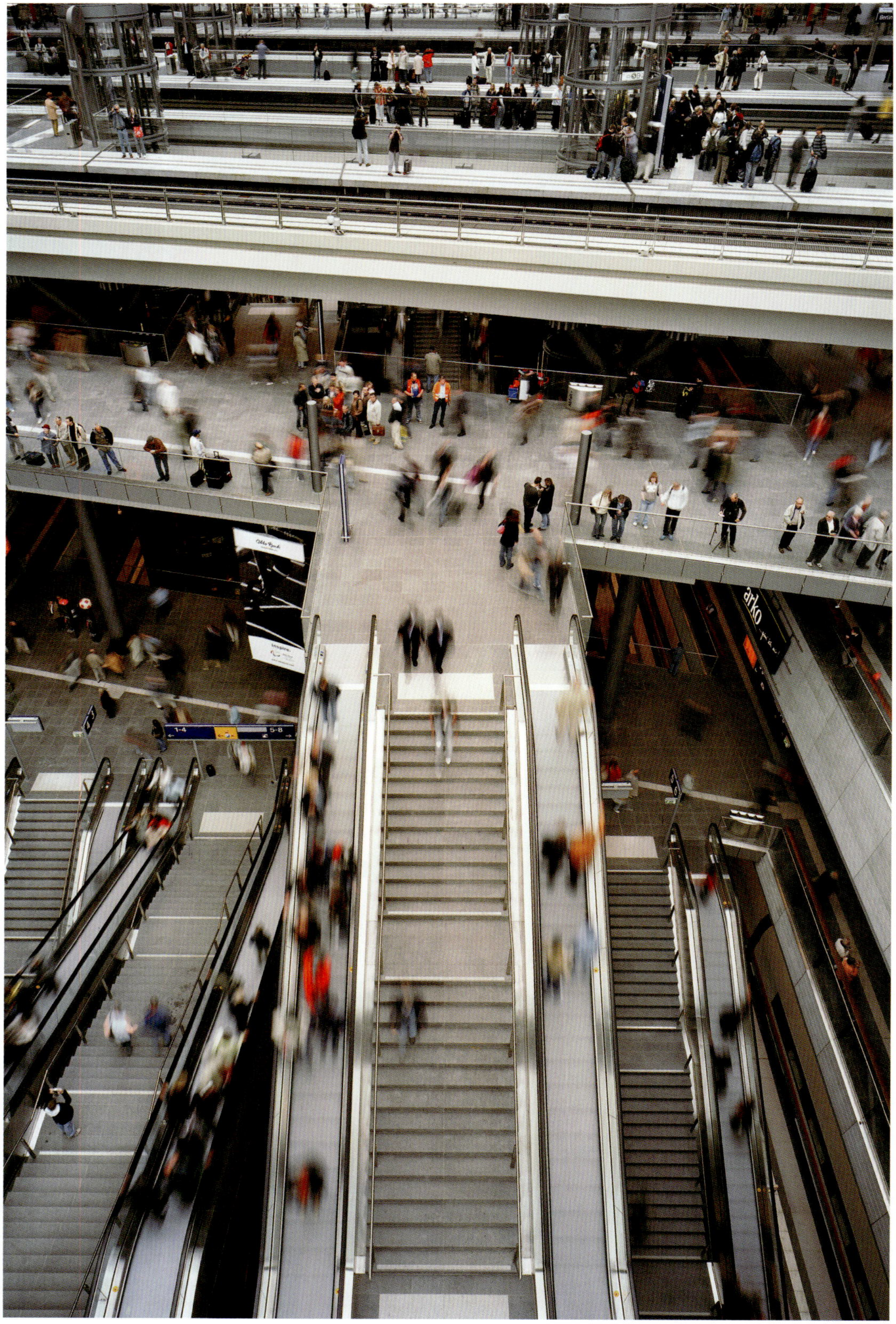

310 [263]

霍尔河折叠桥
基尔，德国

Folding Bridge over the River Hörn
Kiel, Germany

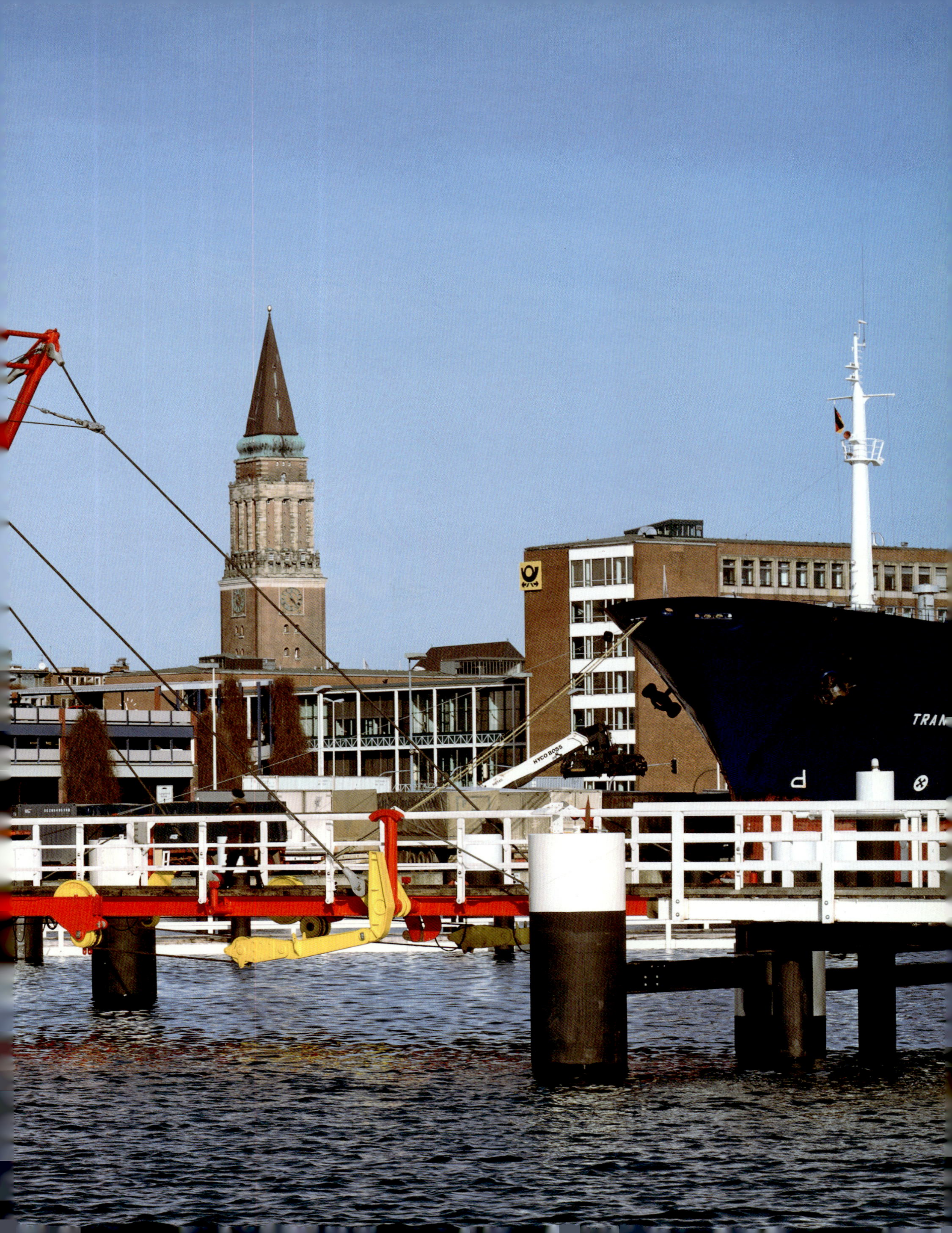
HYCO BOSS
TRAN

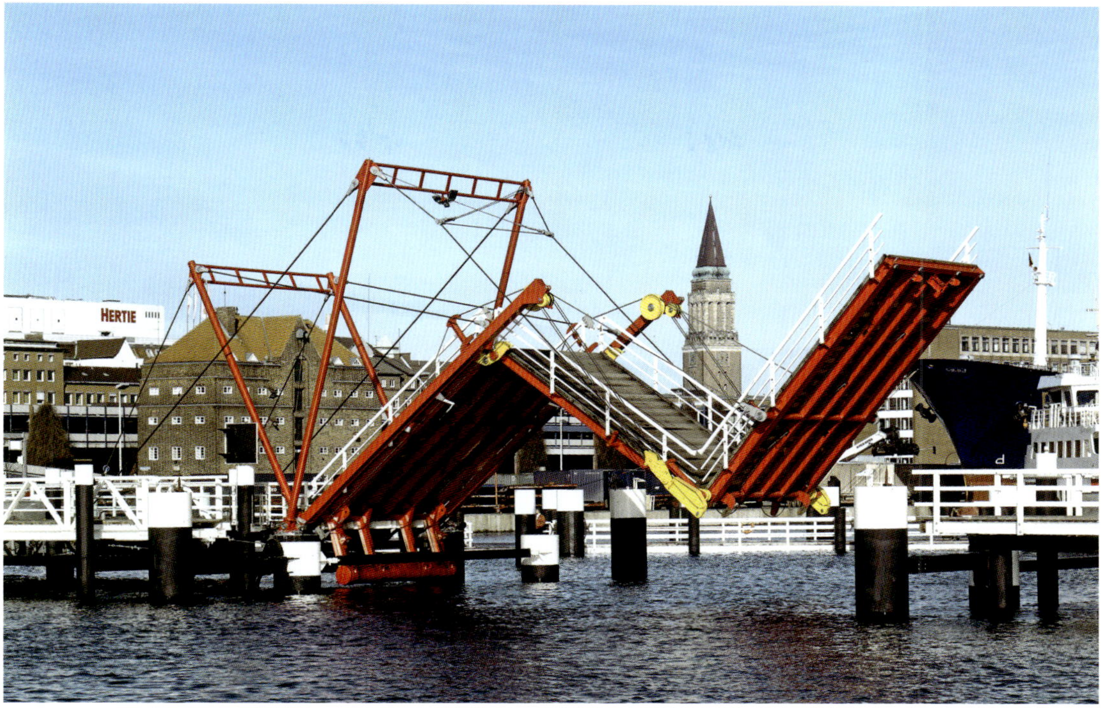

霍尔河折叠桥　基尔

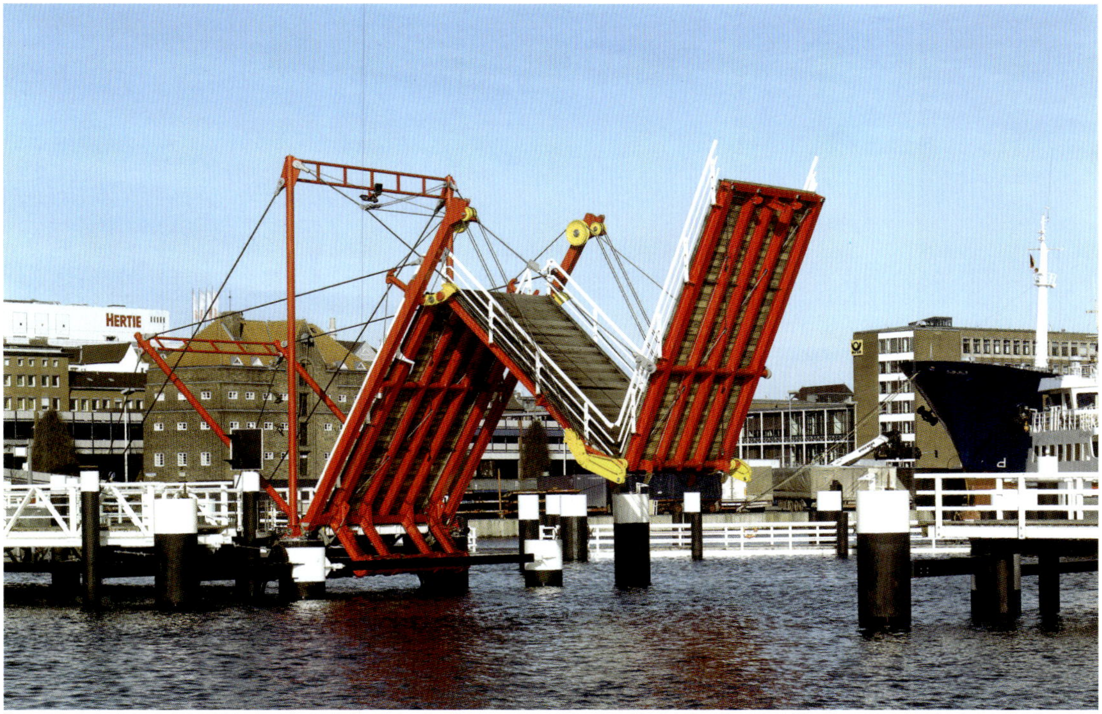

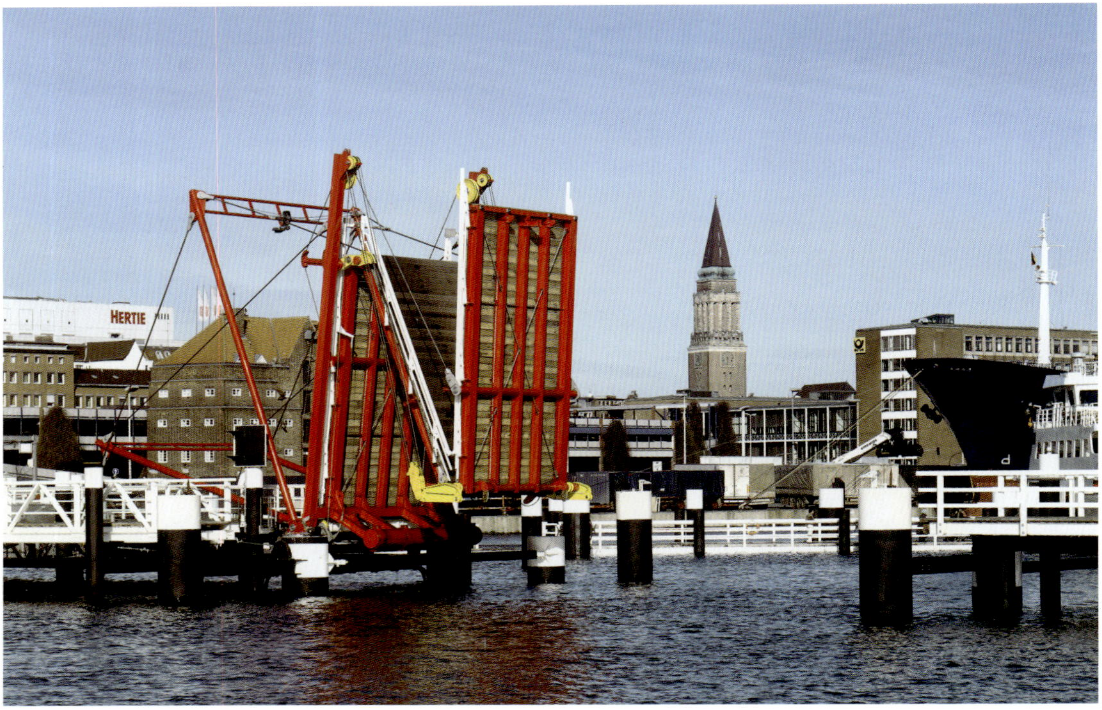

Folding Bridge over the River Hörn Kiel   313

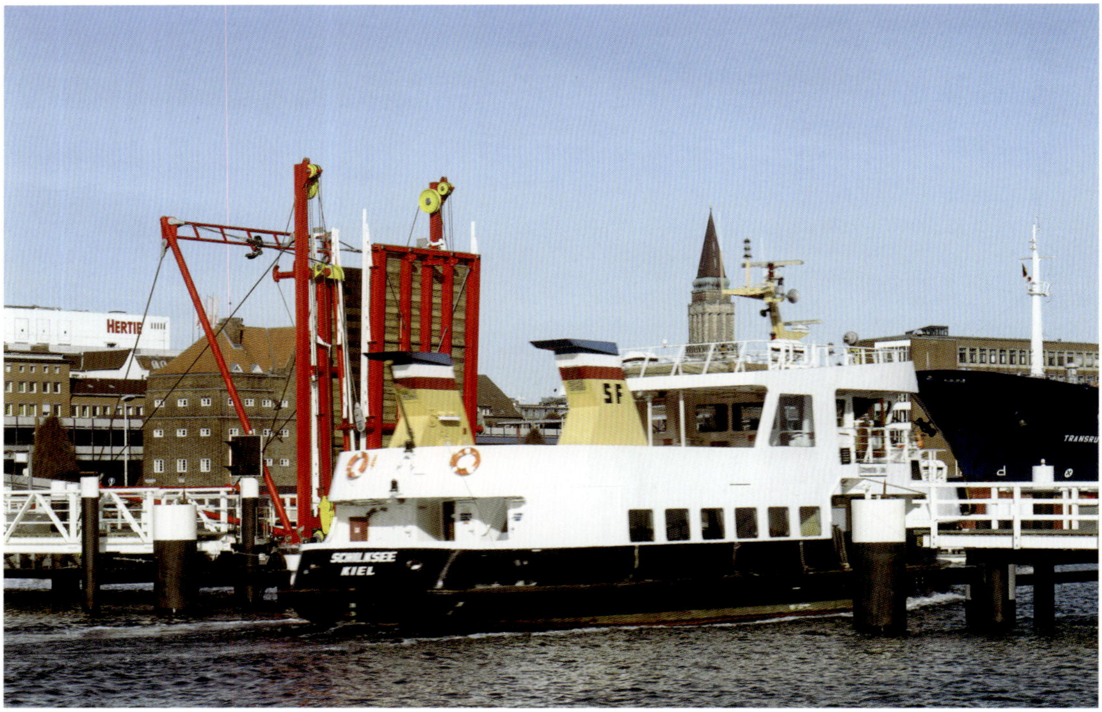

314 ²⁶³

2000年汉诺威世博会基督教馆
沃尔肯罗达,德国

Christ Pavilion, Expo 2000
Volkenroda, Germany

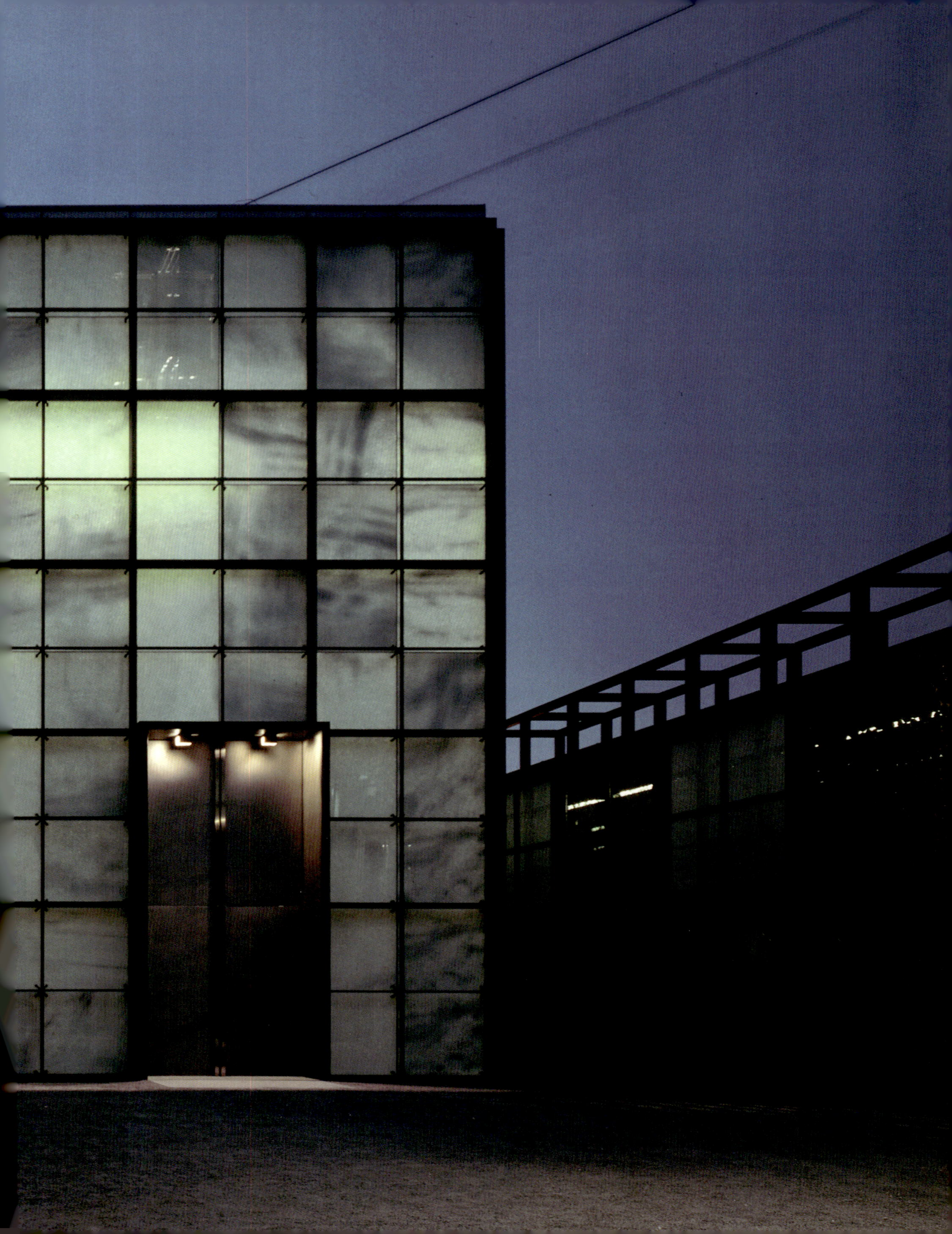

2000年汉诺威世博会基督教馆　沃尔肯罗达

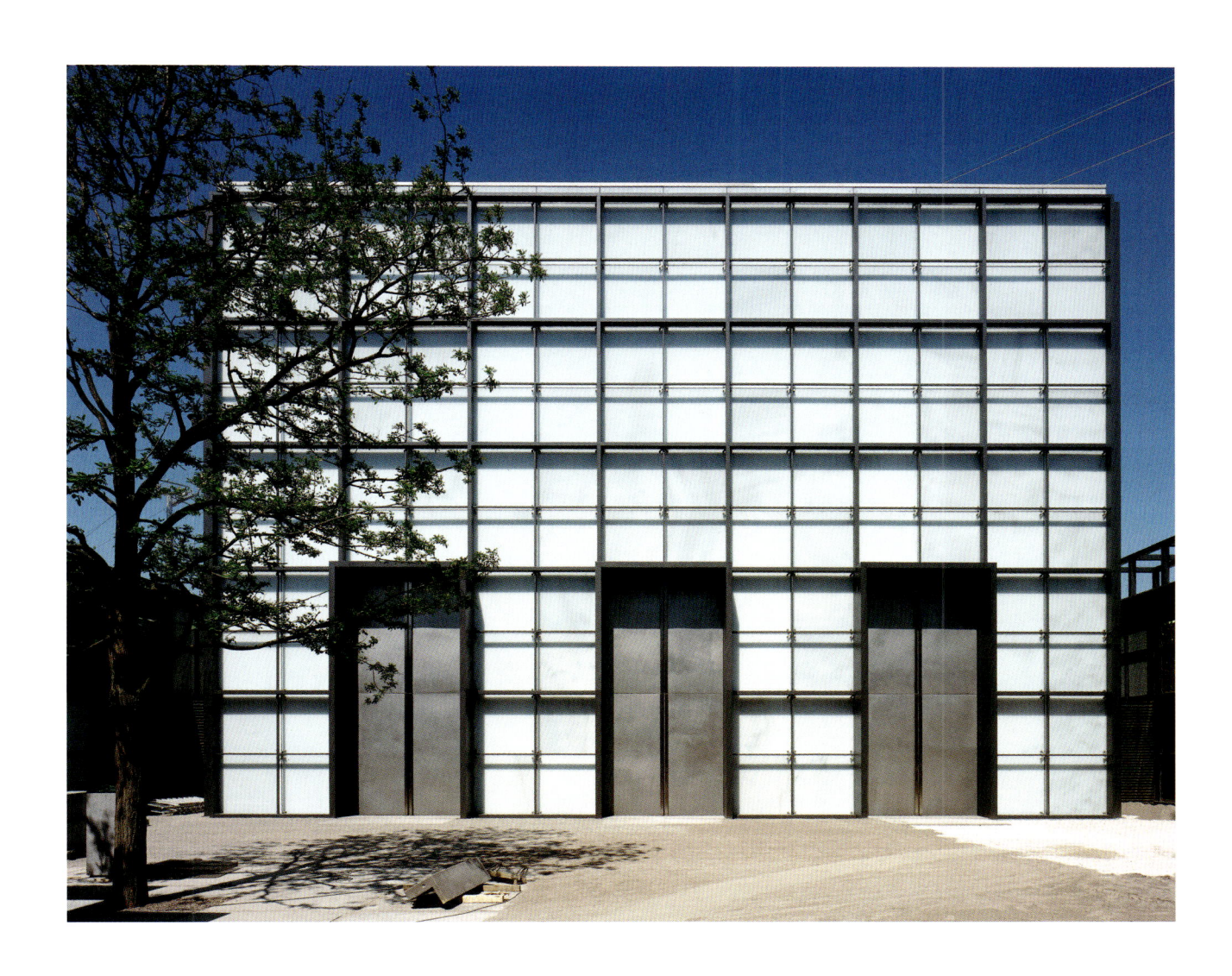

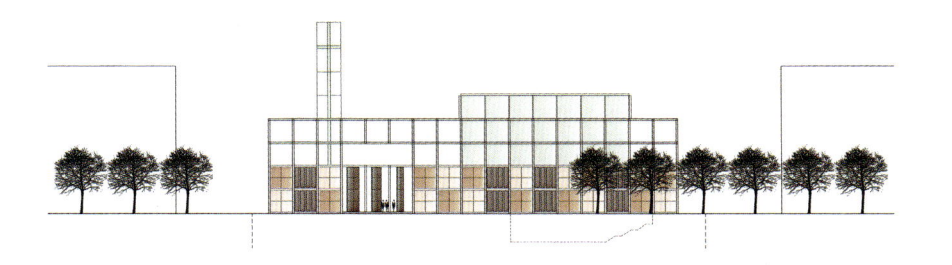

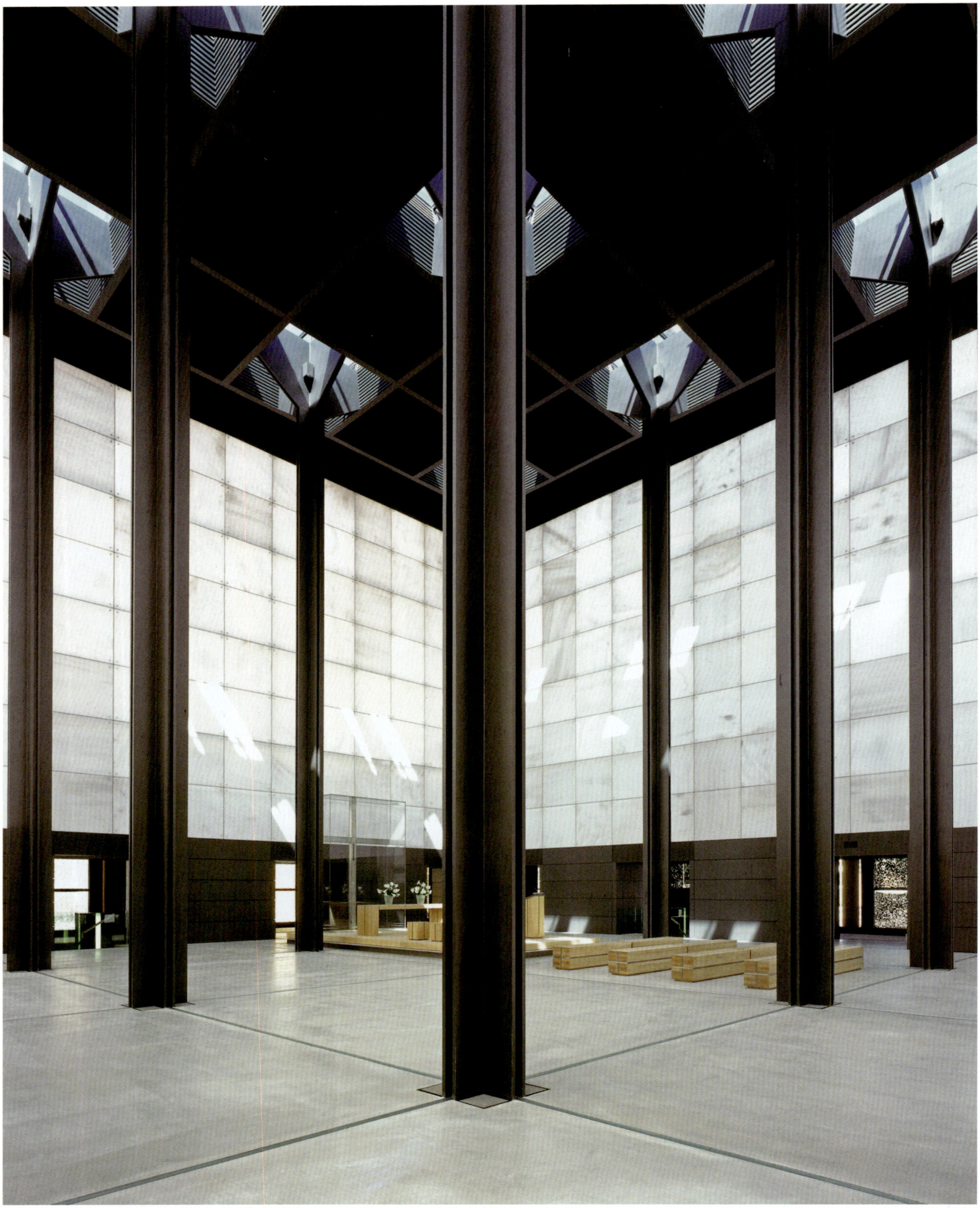

Christ Pavilion, Expo 2000 Volkenroda

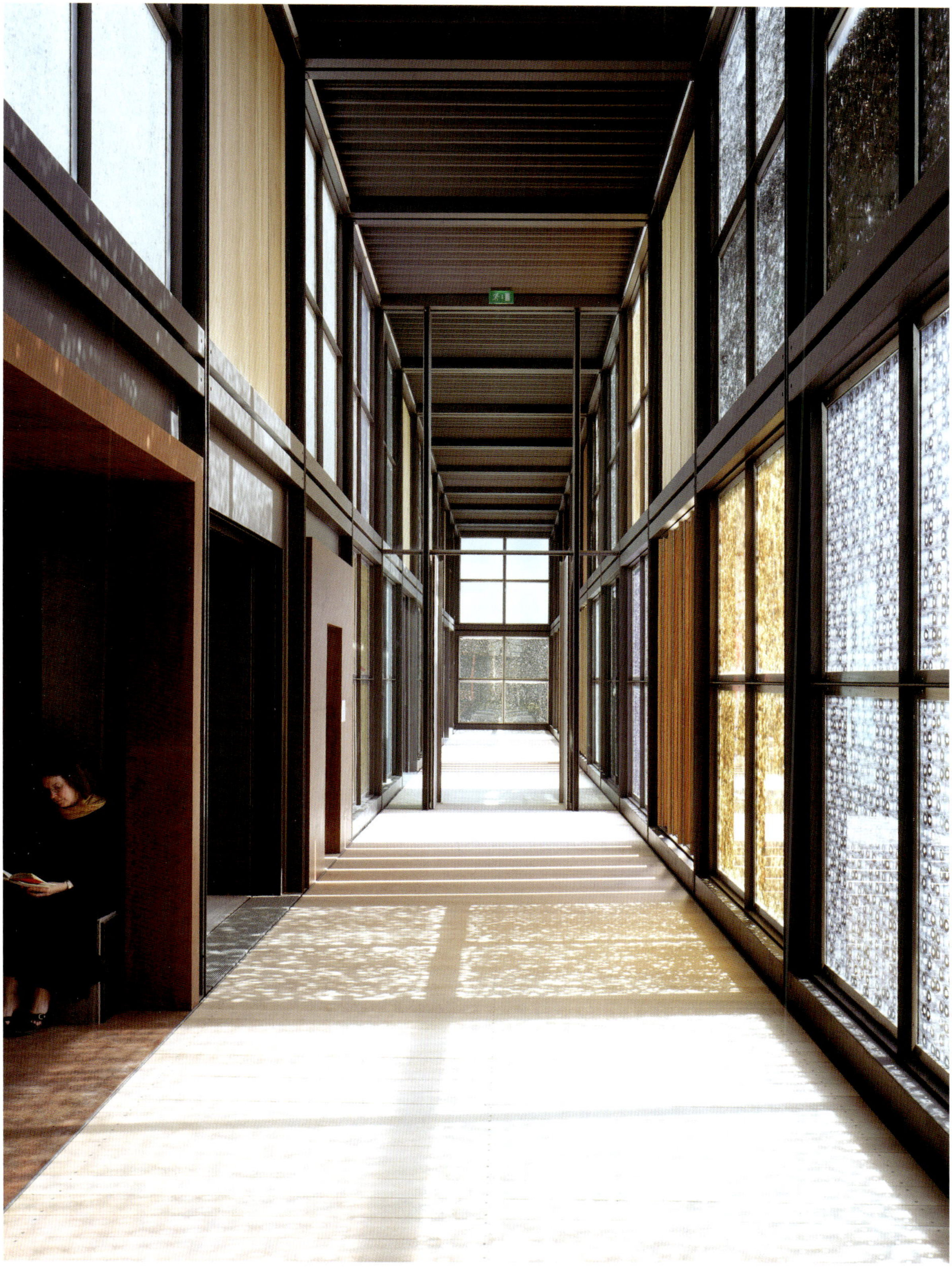

2000年汉诺威世博会基督教馆　沃尔肯罗达

Christ Pavilion, Expo 2000 Volkenroda

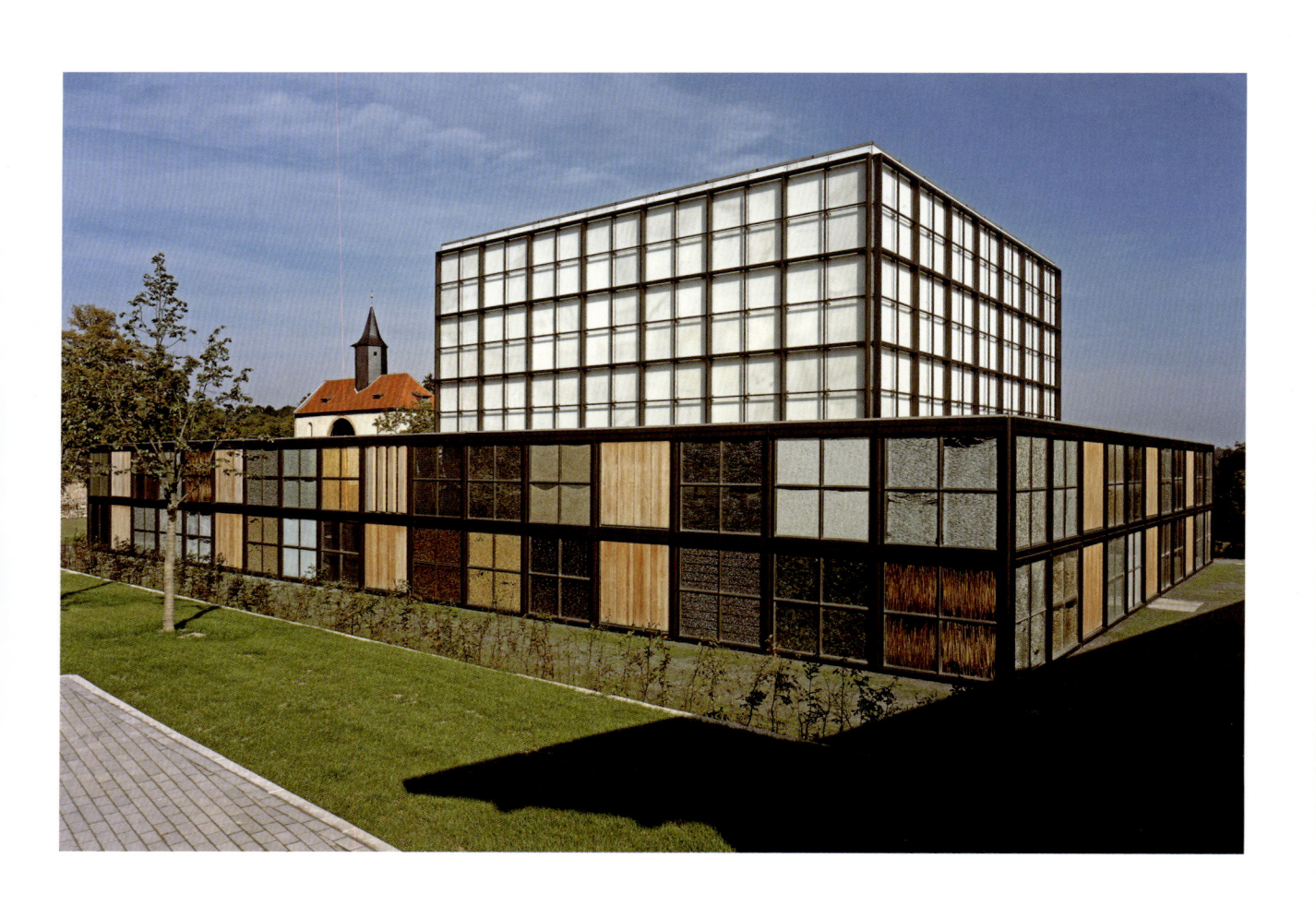

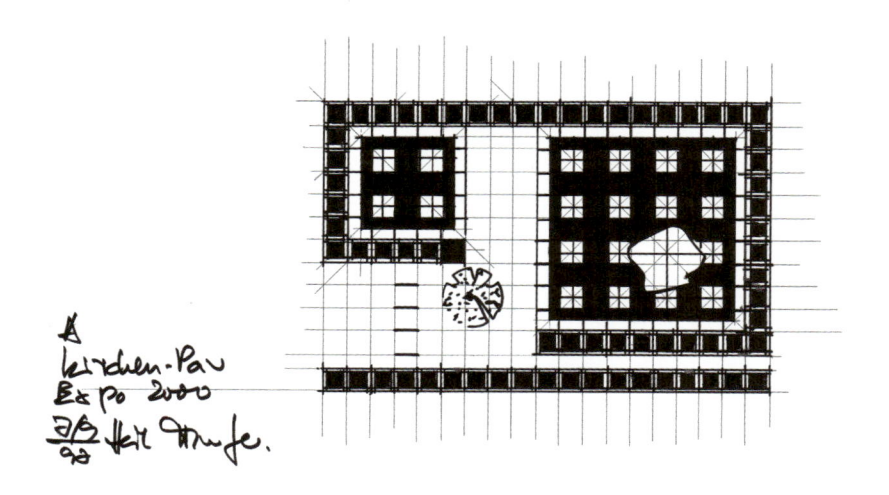

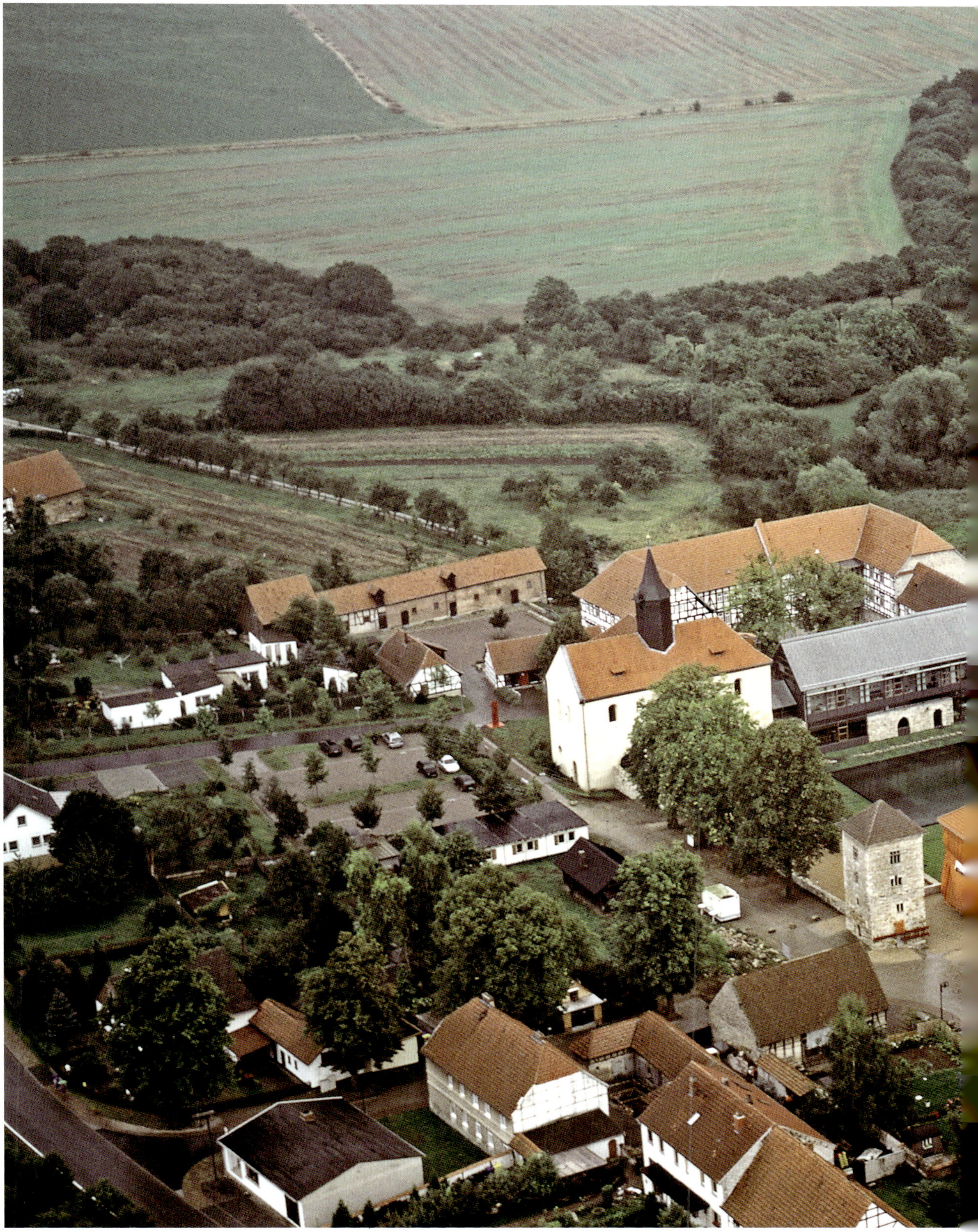

2000年汉诺威世博会基督教馆　沃尔肯罗达

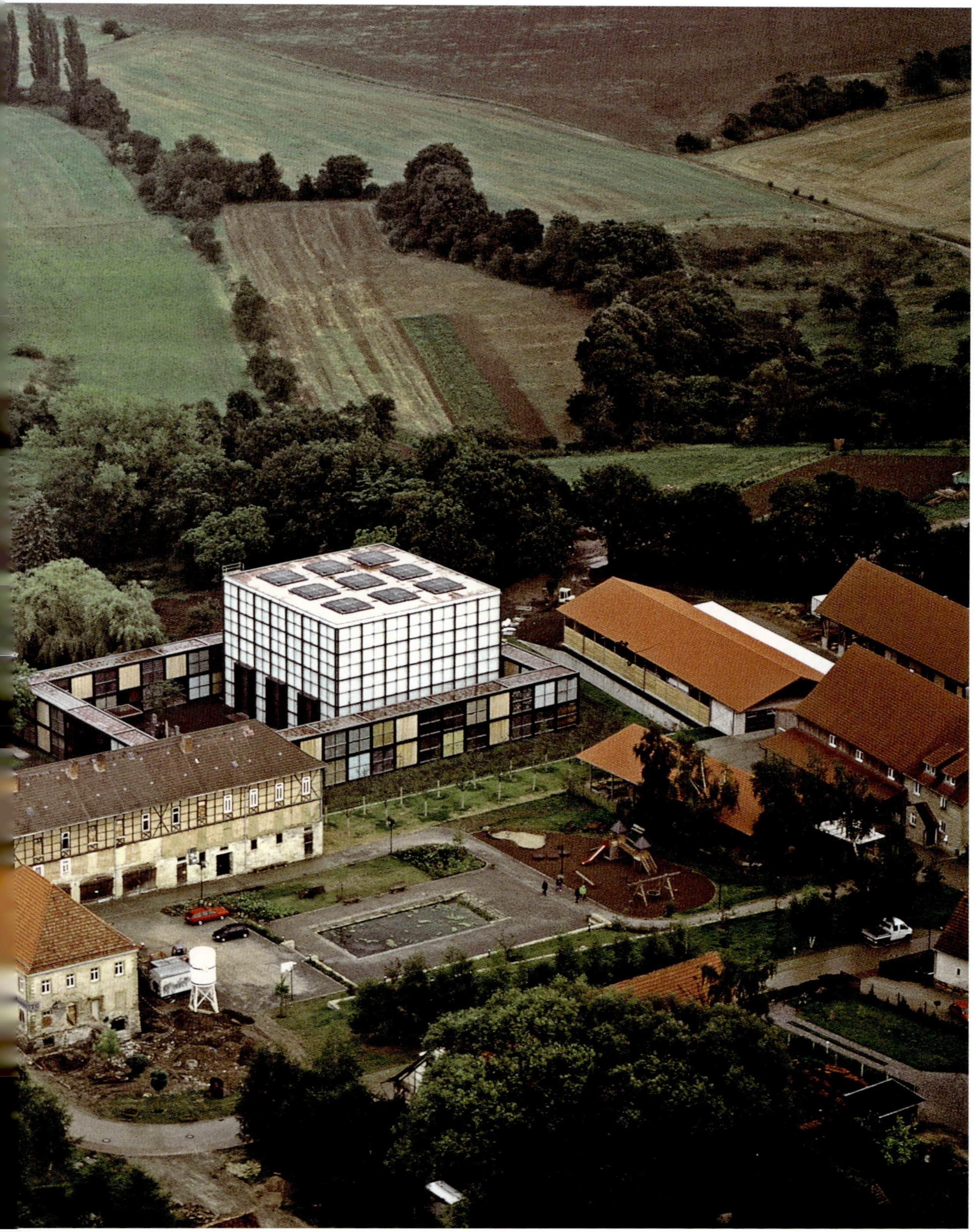

Christ Pavilion, Expo 2000 Volkenroda

322 ²⁶⁴ ↑

里米尼新会展中心
里米尼，意大利

New Trade Fair
Rimini, Italy

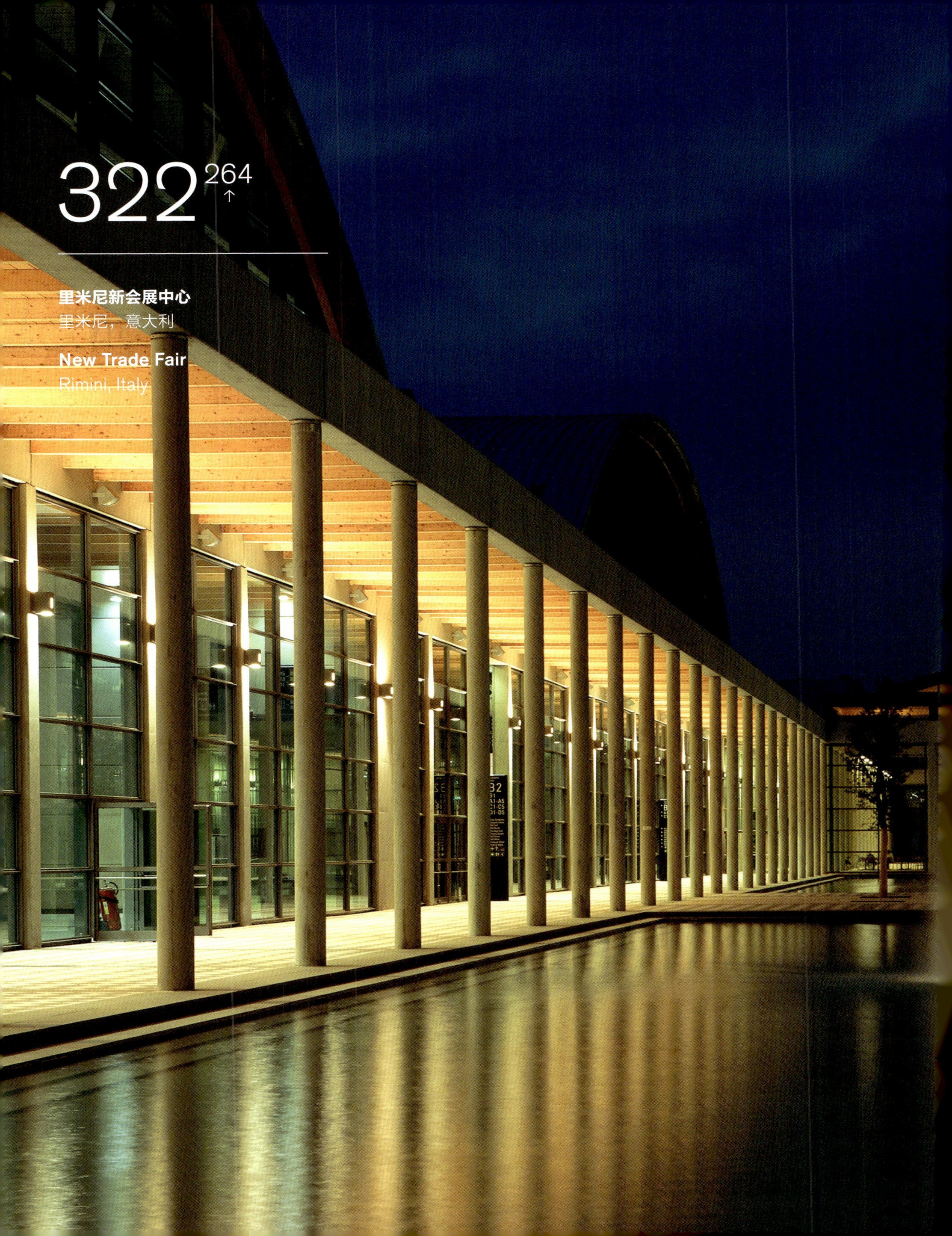

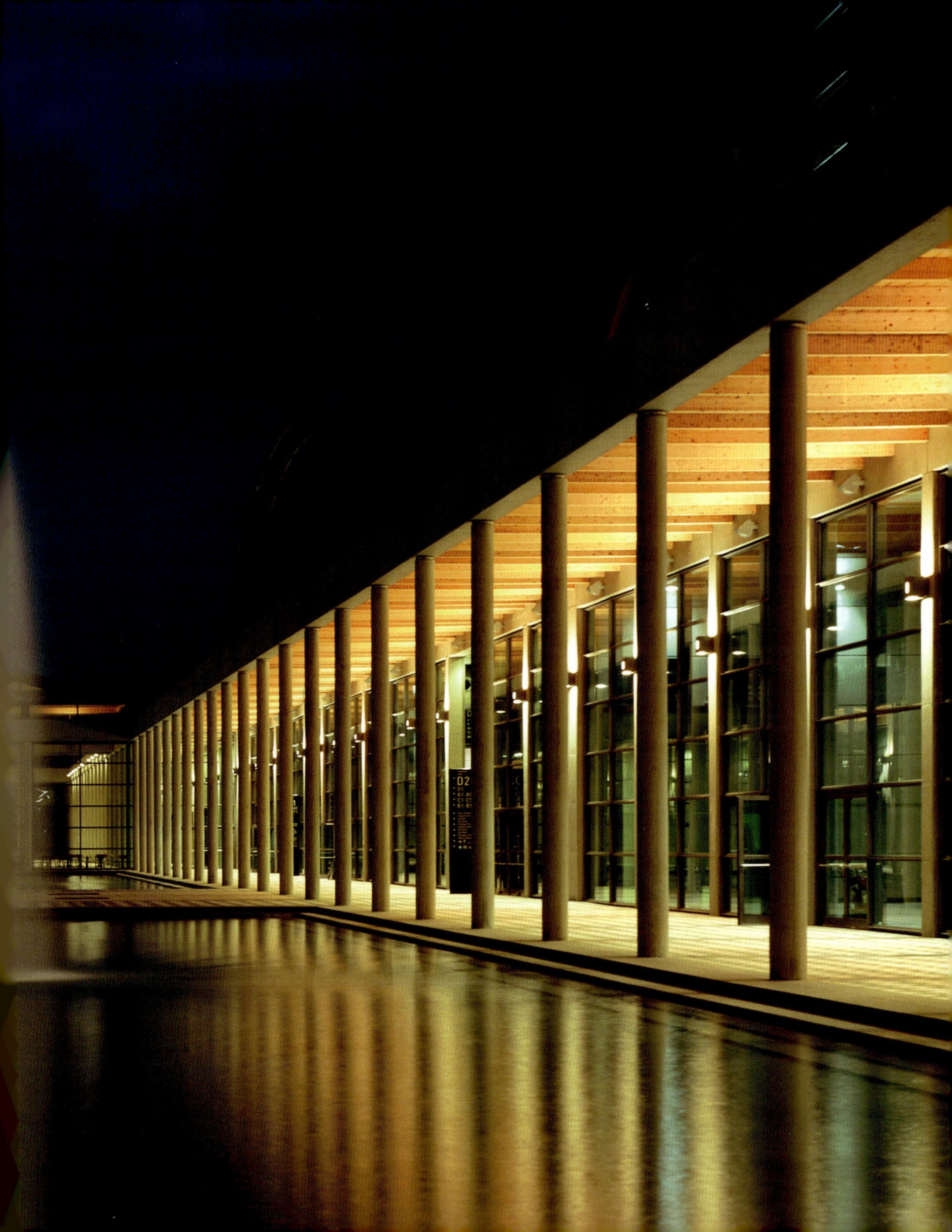
D2

里米尼新会展中心　里米尼

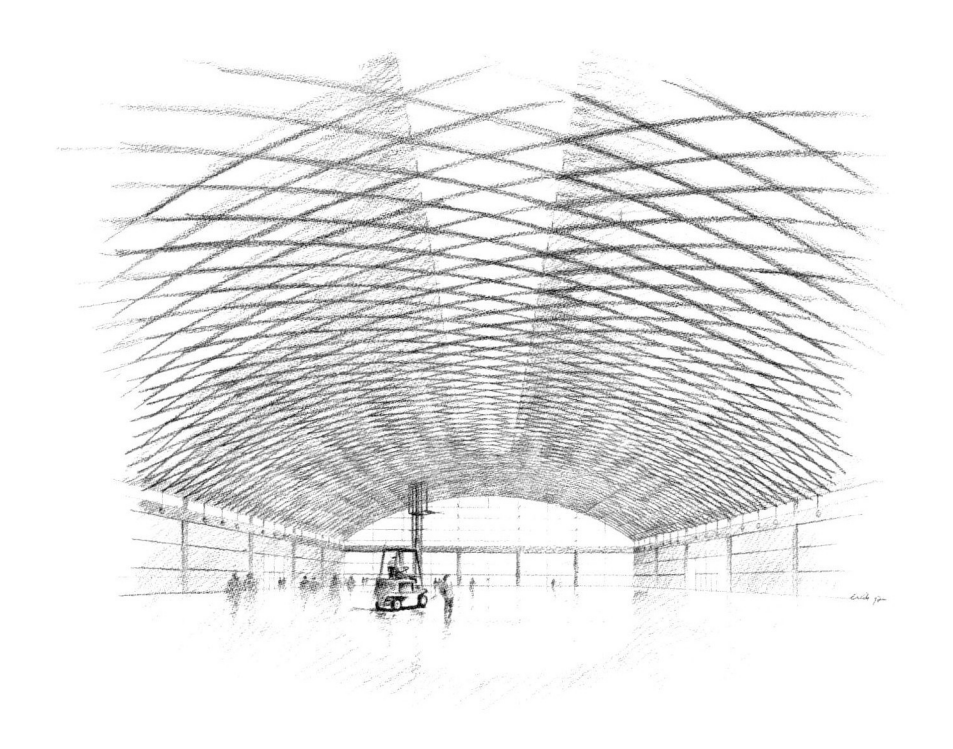

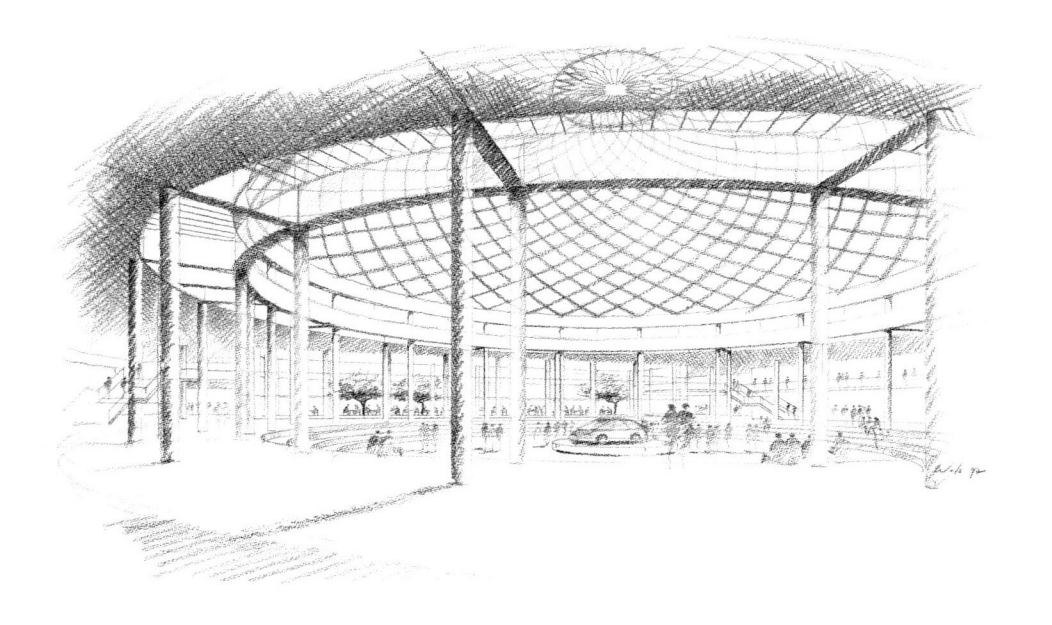

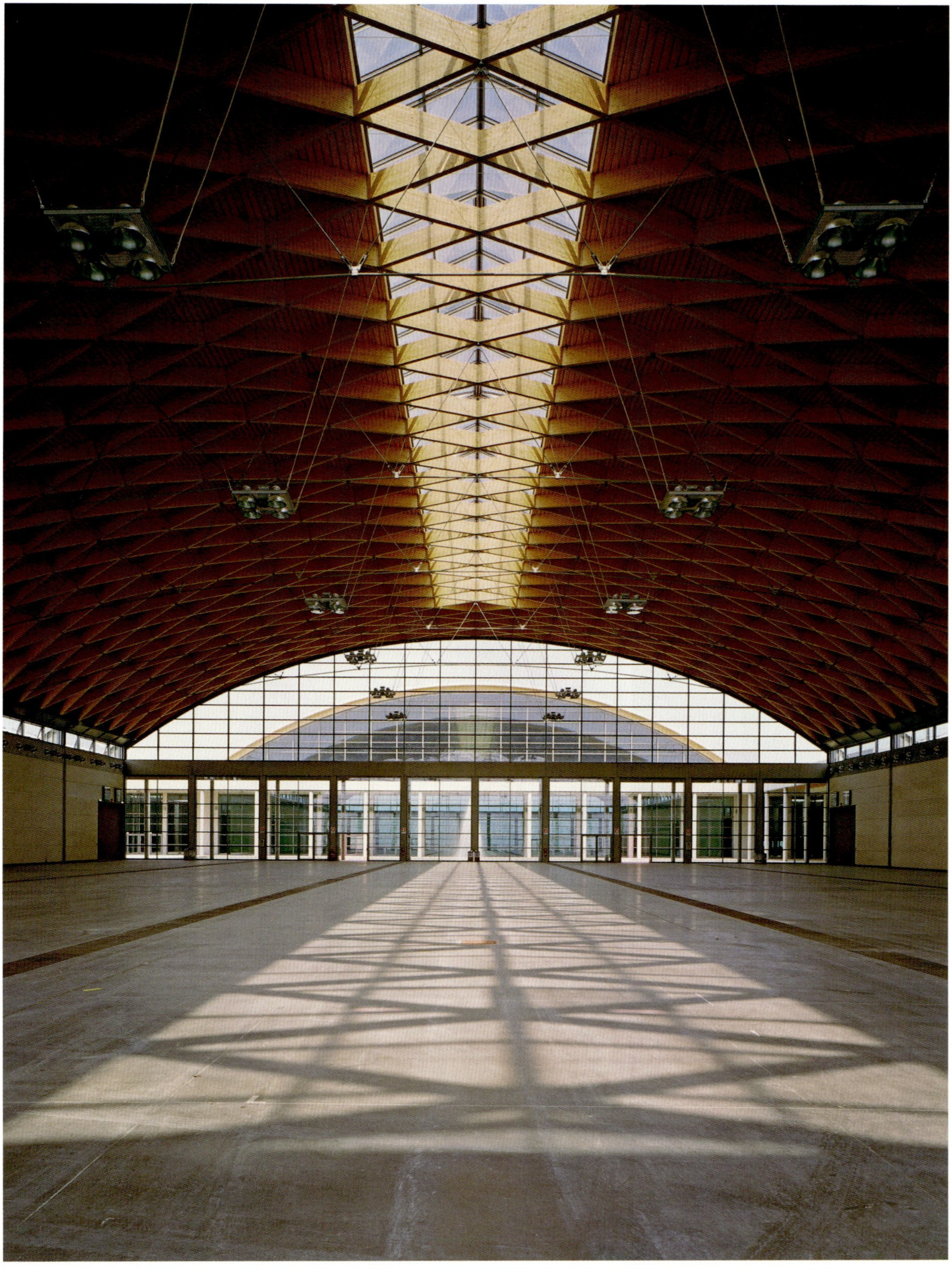

New Trade Fair Rimini

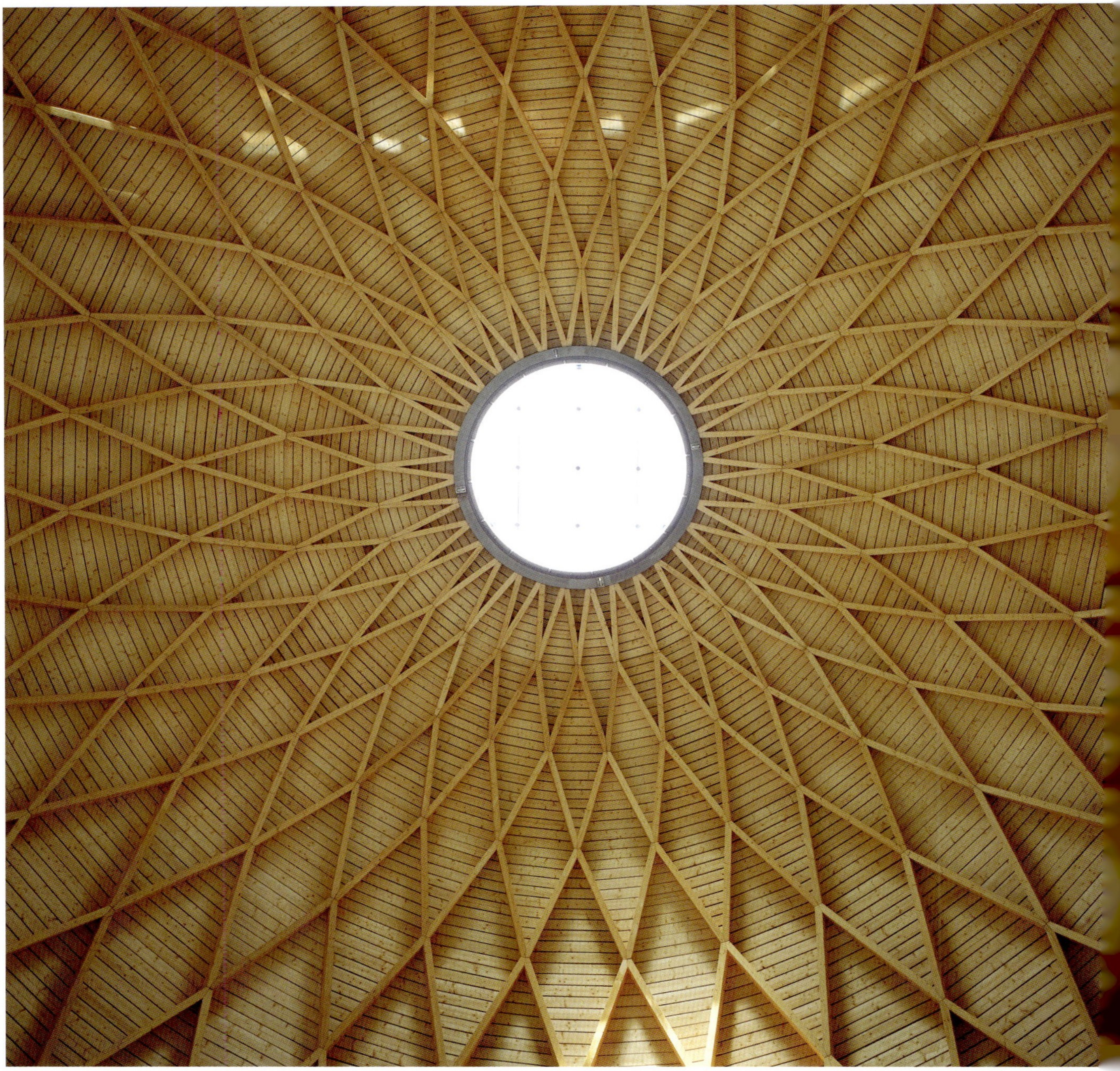

里米尼新会展中心　里米尼

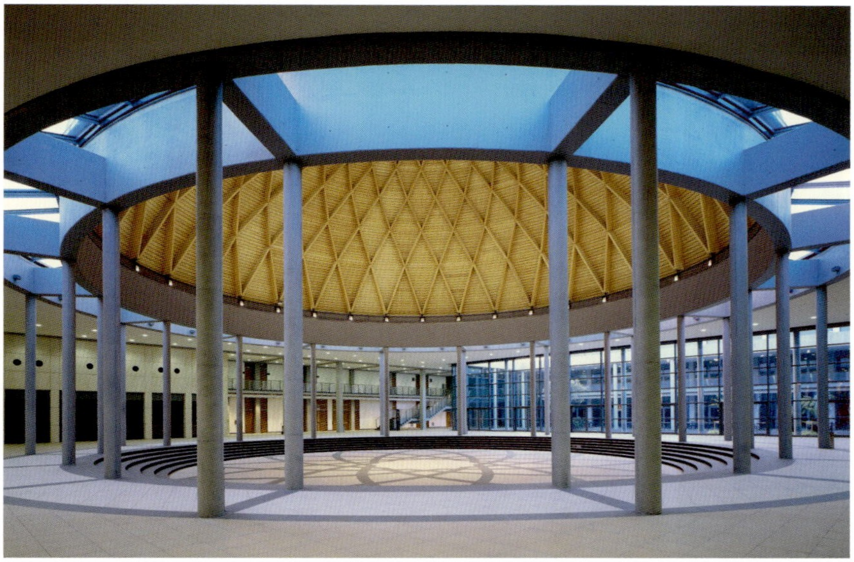

New Trade Fair Rimini

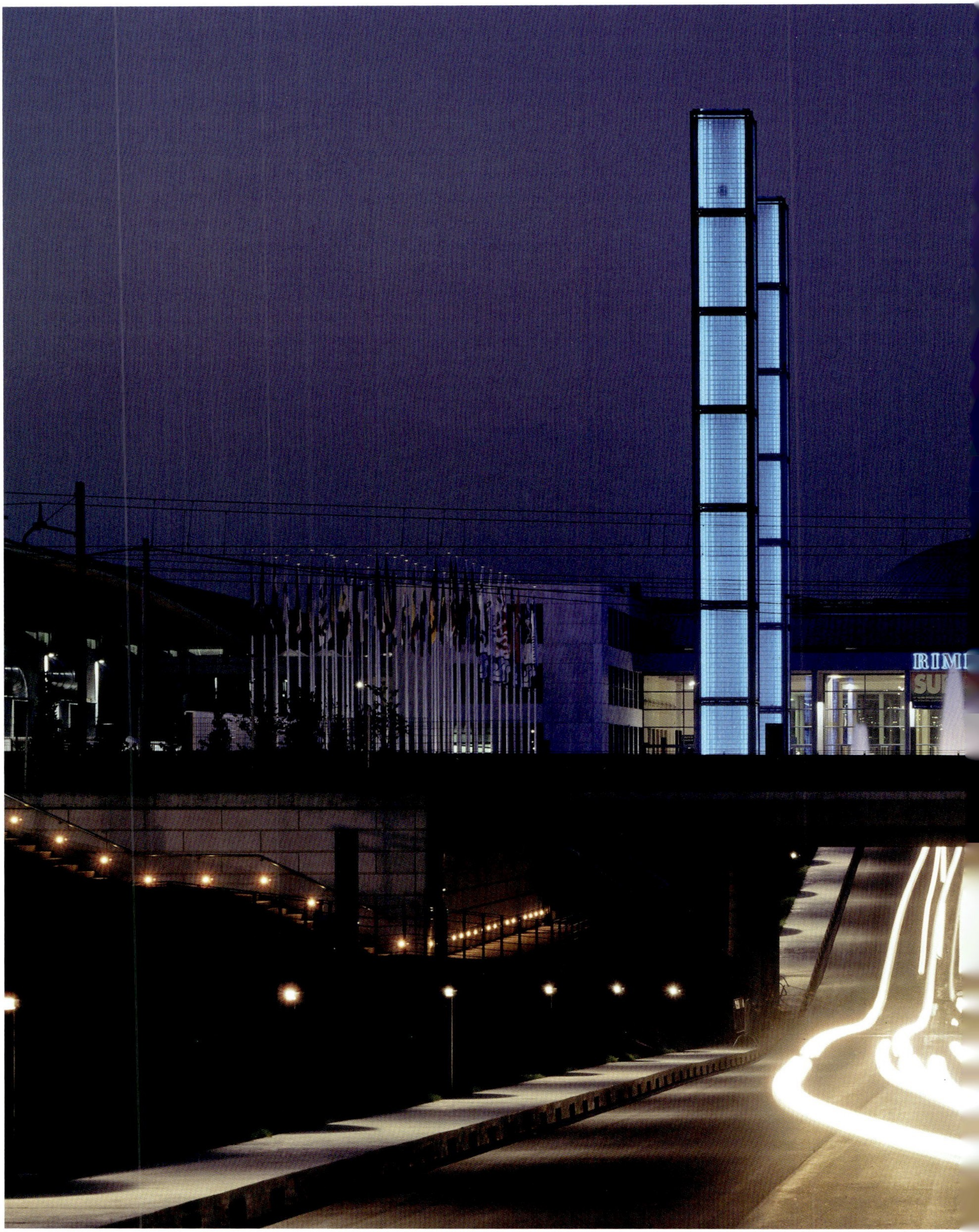

里米尼新会展中心　里米尼

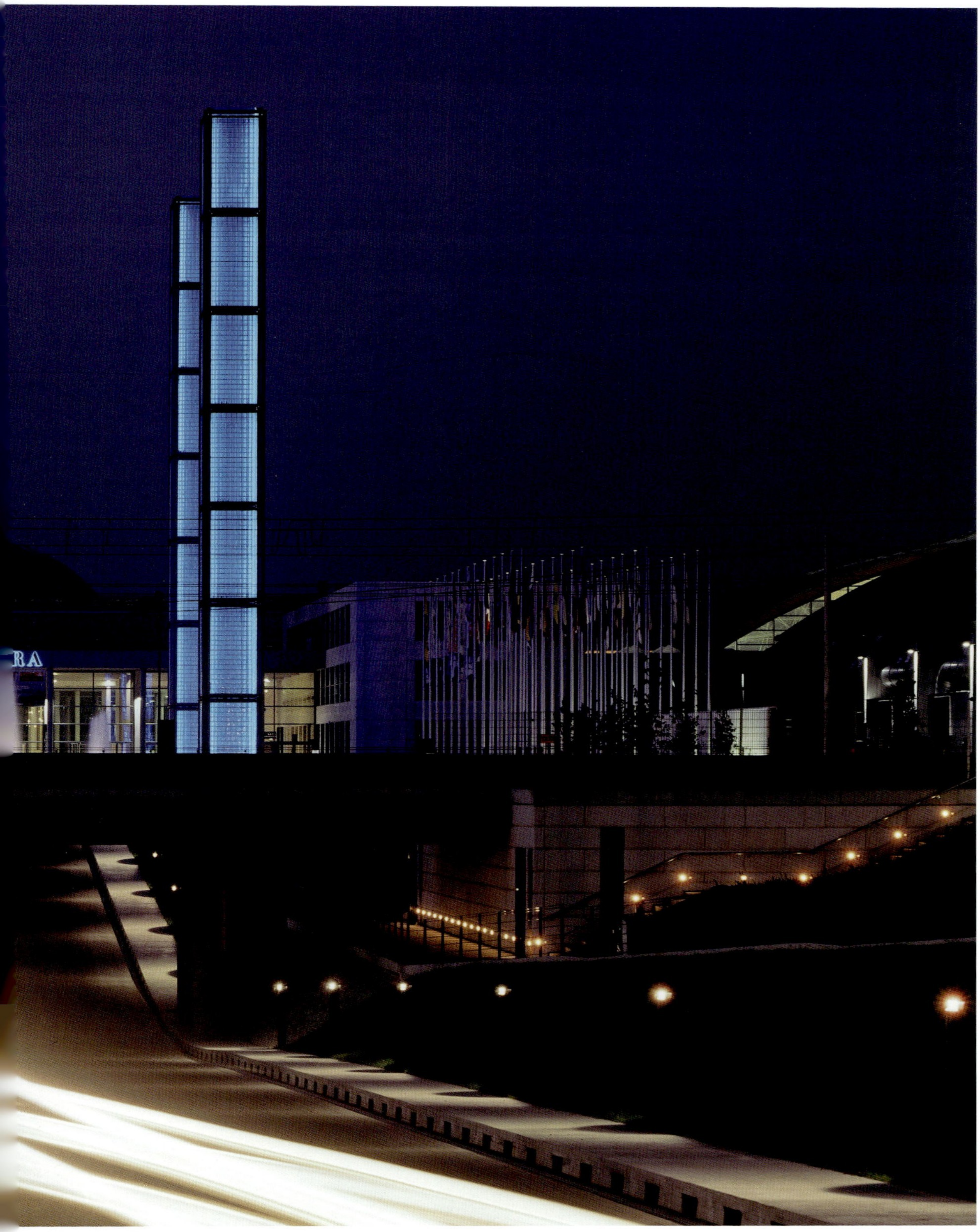

New Trade Fair Rimini

330 ²⁶⁴ ↑

柏林勃兰登堡机场
柏林，德国

Berlin Brandenburg Airport
Berlin, Germany

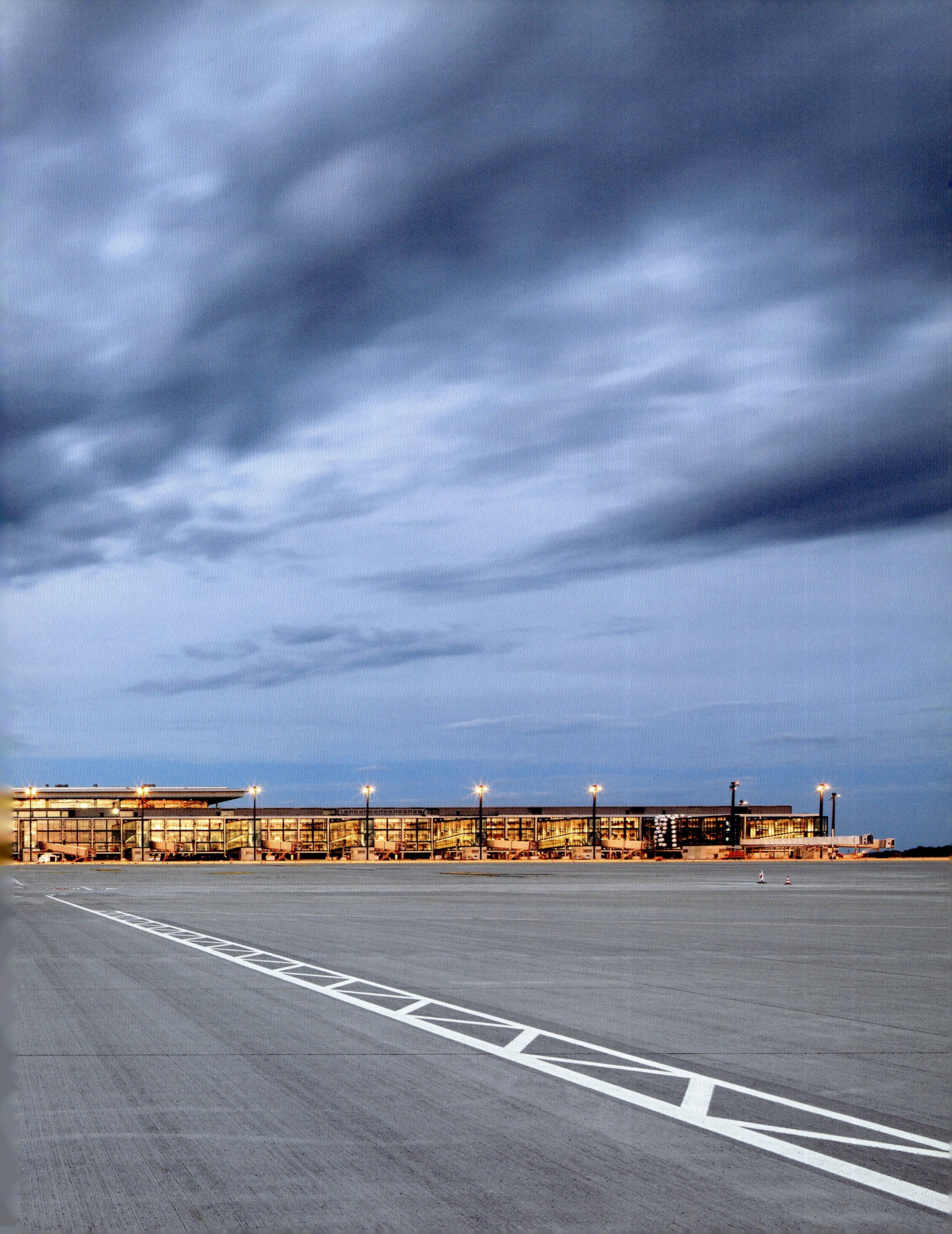

柏林勃兰登堡机场　柏林

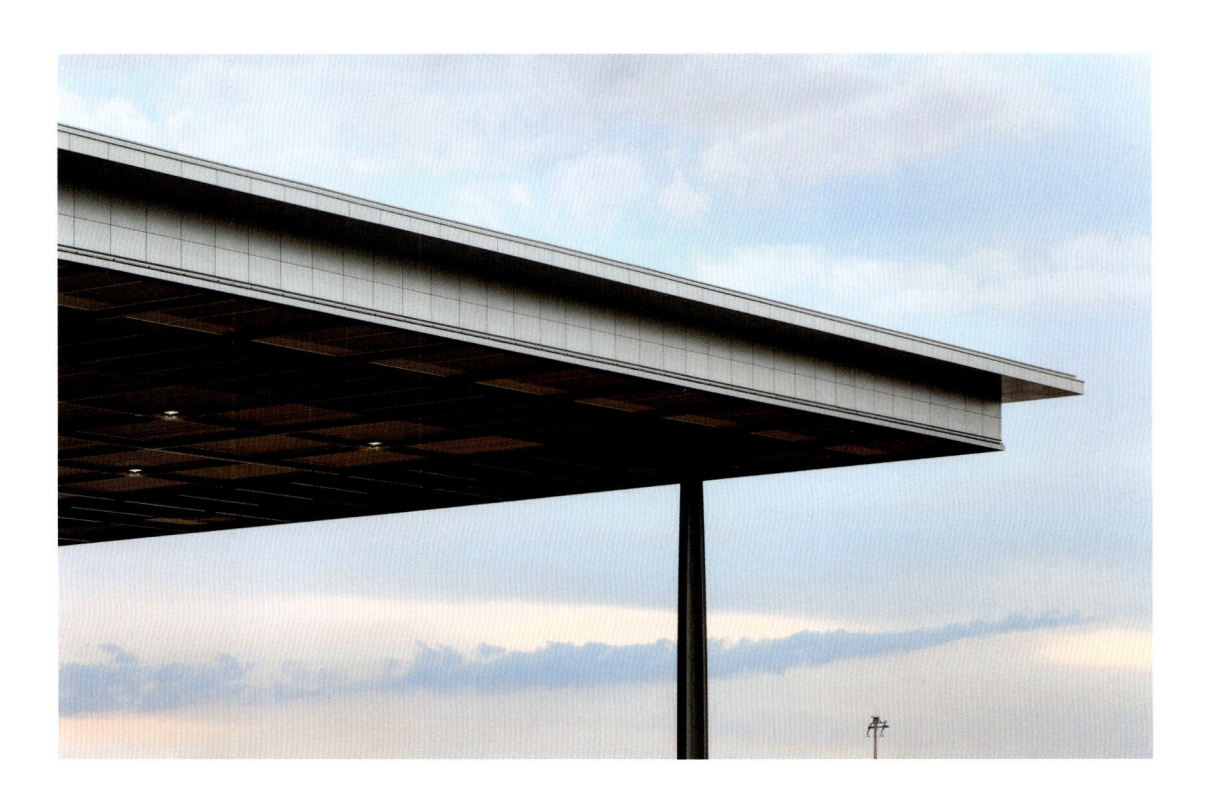

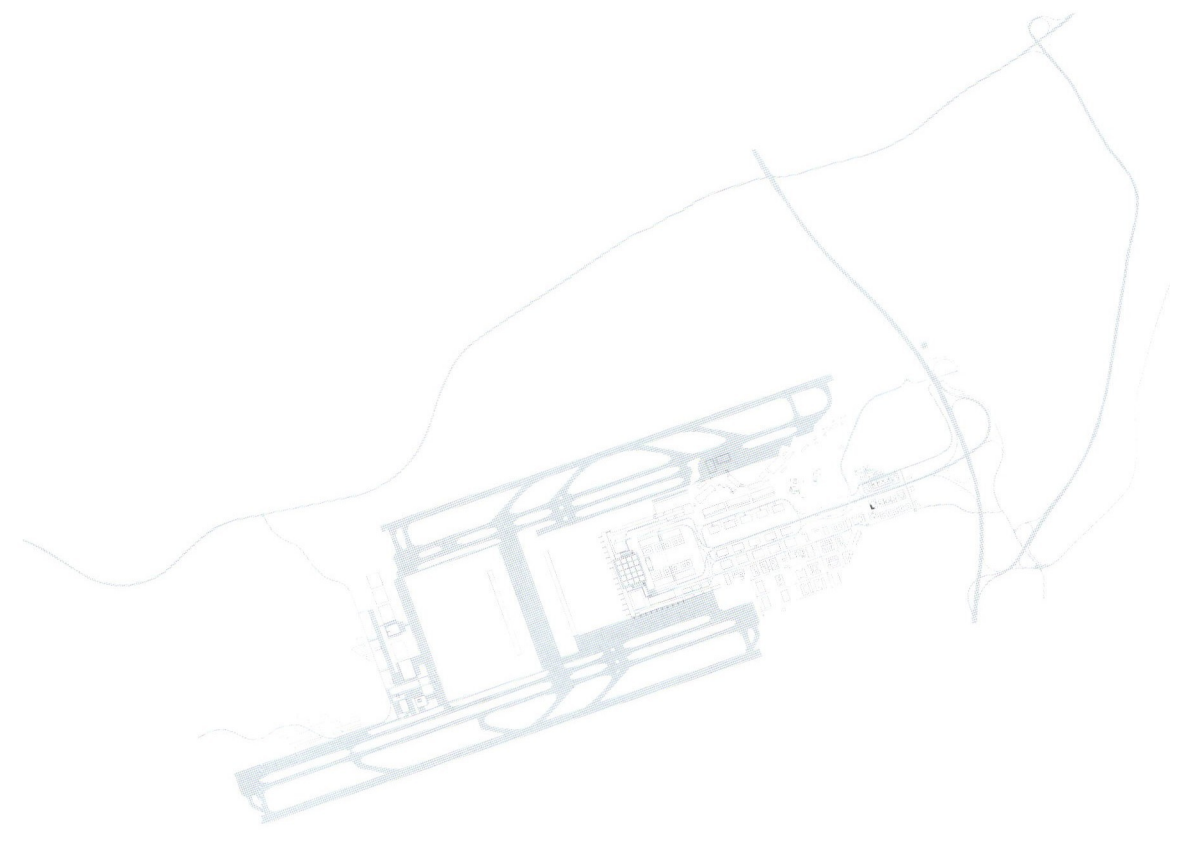

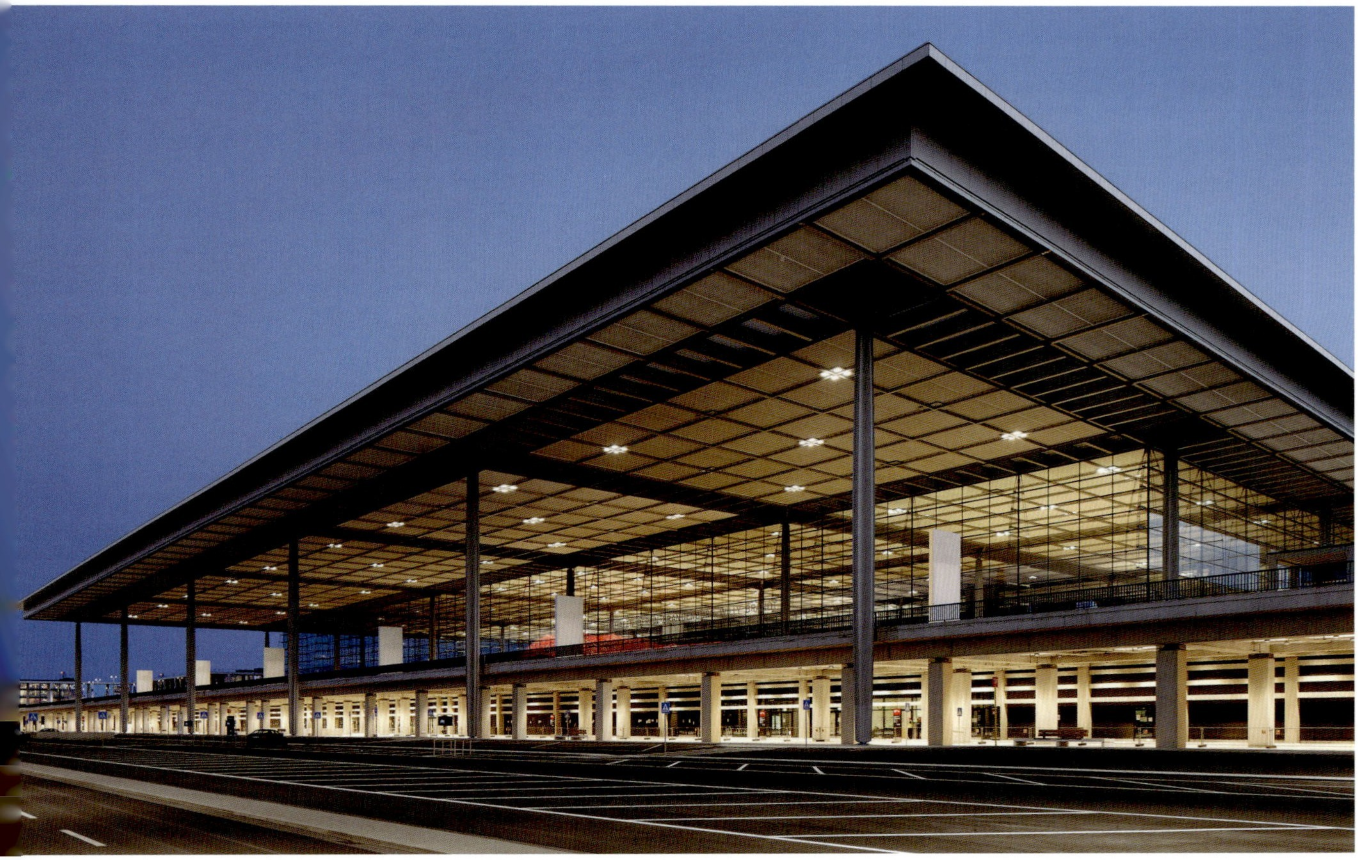

Berlin Brandenburg Airport Berlin

柏林勃兰登堡机场　柏林

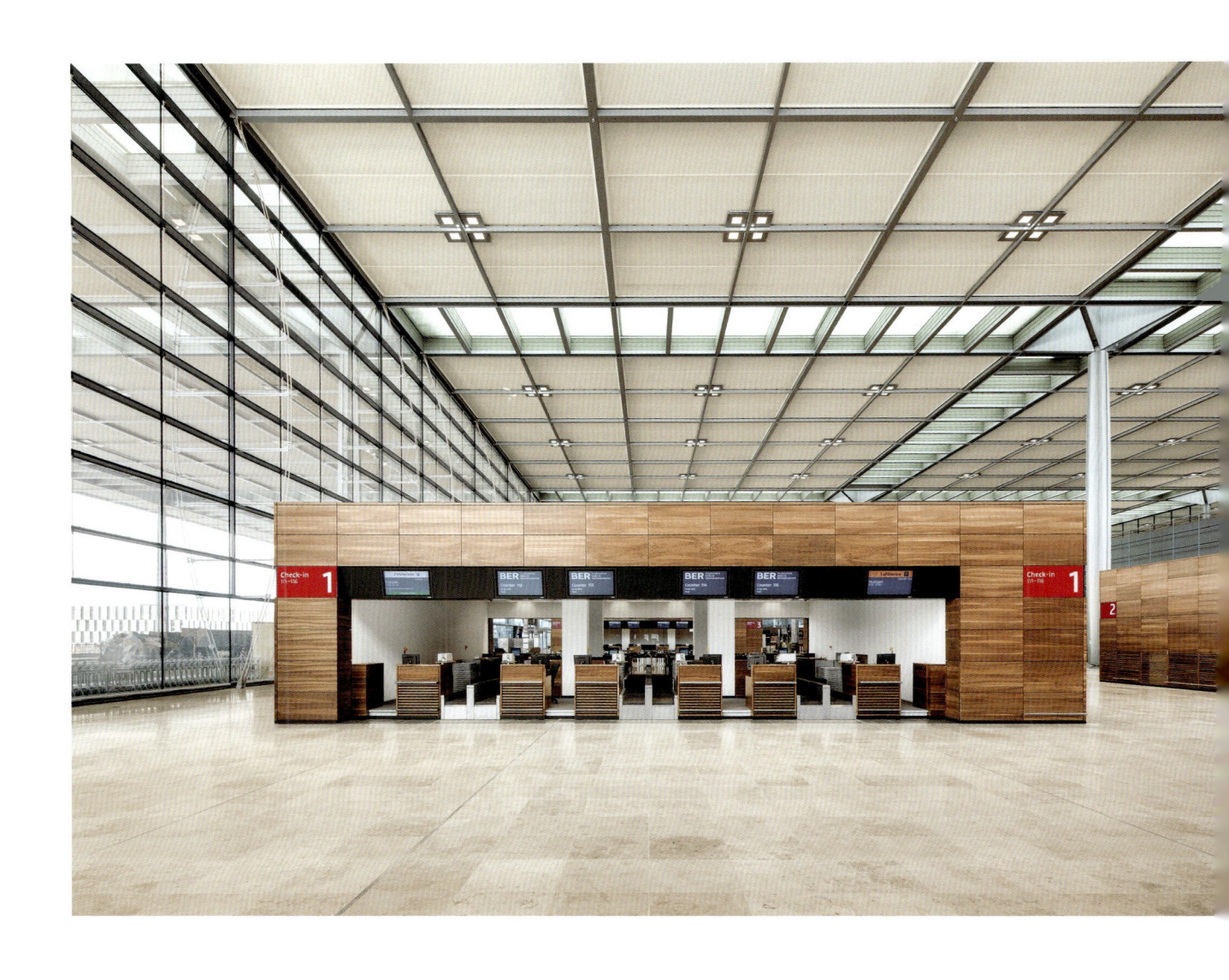

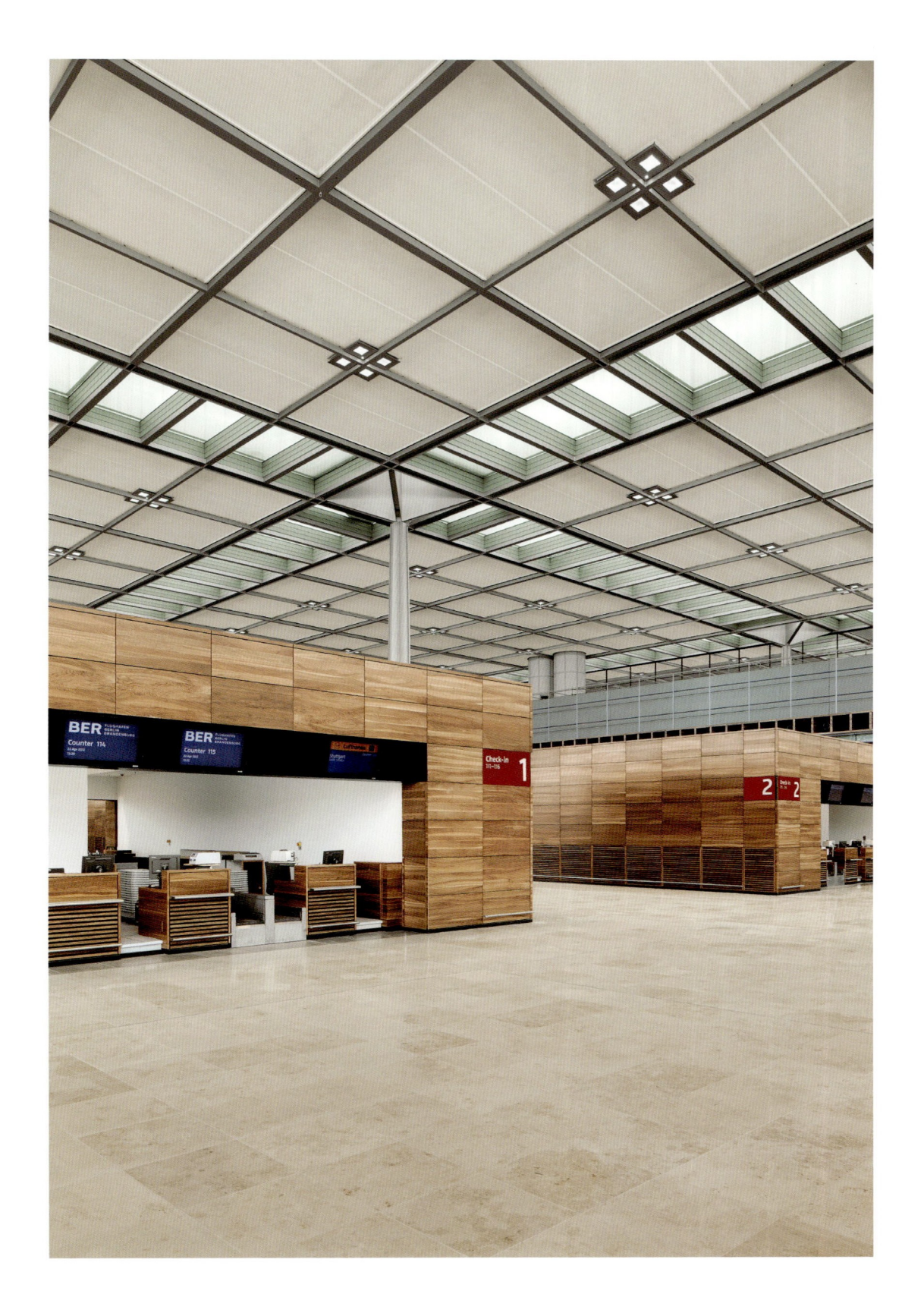

Berlin Brandenburg Airport Berlin

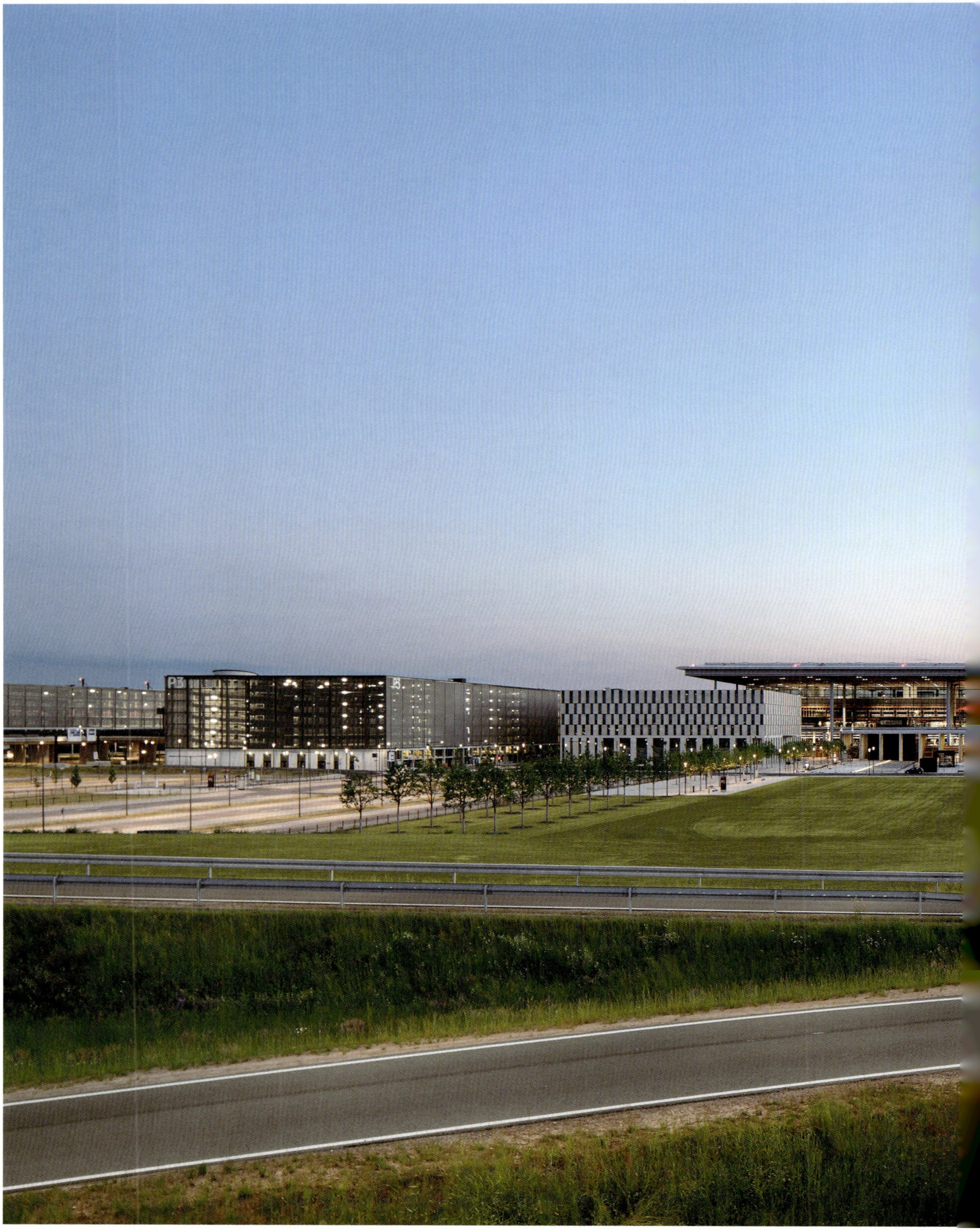

336　柏林勃兰登堡机场　柏林

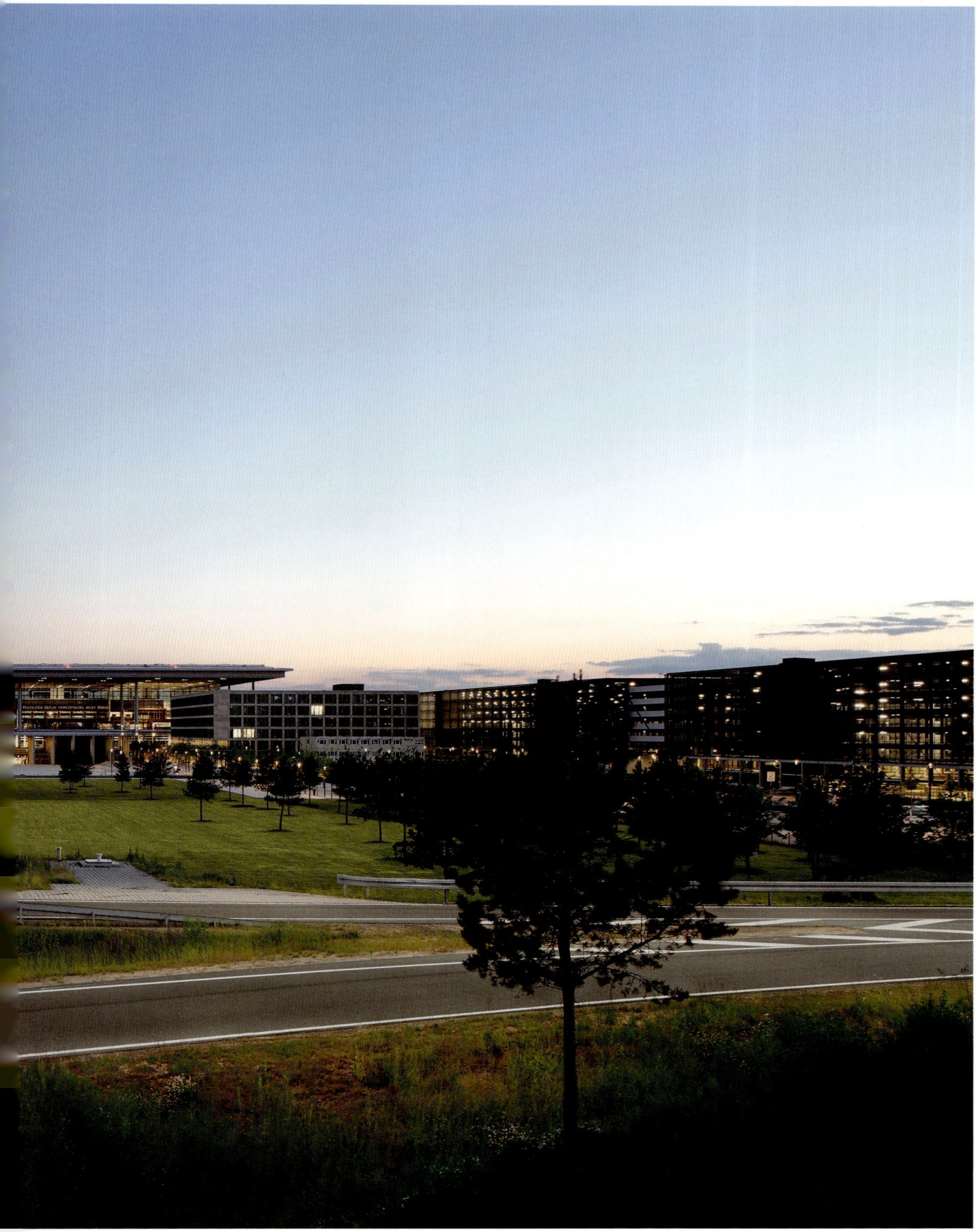

Berlin Brandenburg Airport Berlin

338 ²⁶⁵
↑

柏林奥林匹克体育场改建和屋顶加建工程
柏林，德国

**Olympic Stadium,
Reconstruction and Roofing**
Berlin, Germany

ARCOR ARCOR
IBG-Haus.de
Coca-Cola
WARSTEINER WARSTEINER WARSTEINER
Mercedes-Benz

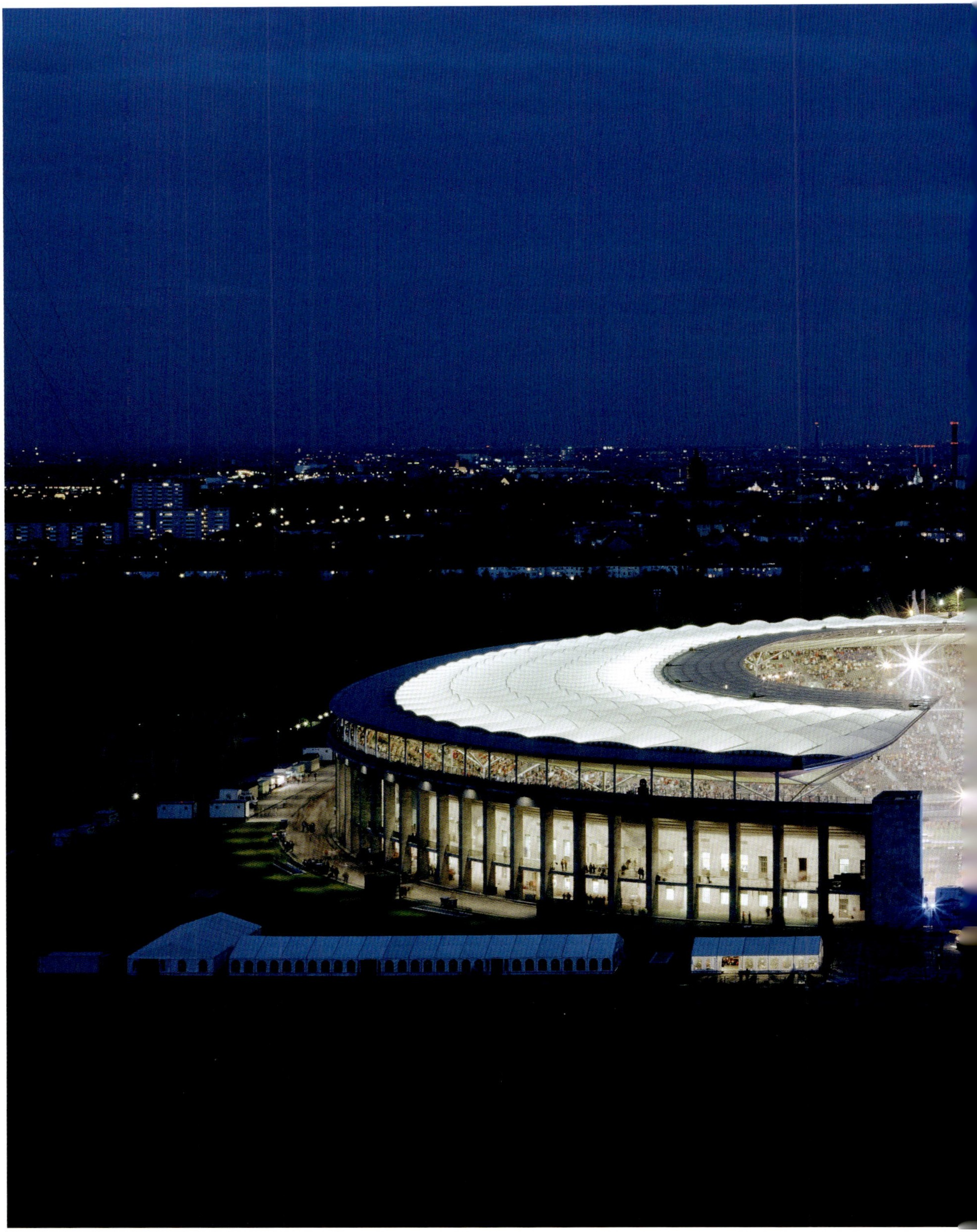

柏林奥林匹克体育场改建和屋顶加建工程　柏林

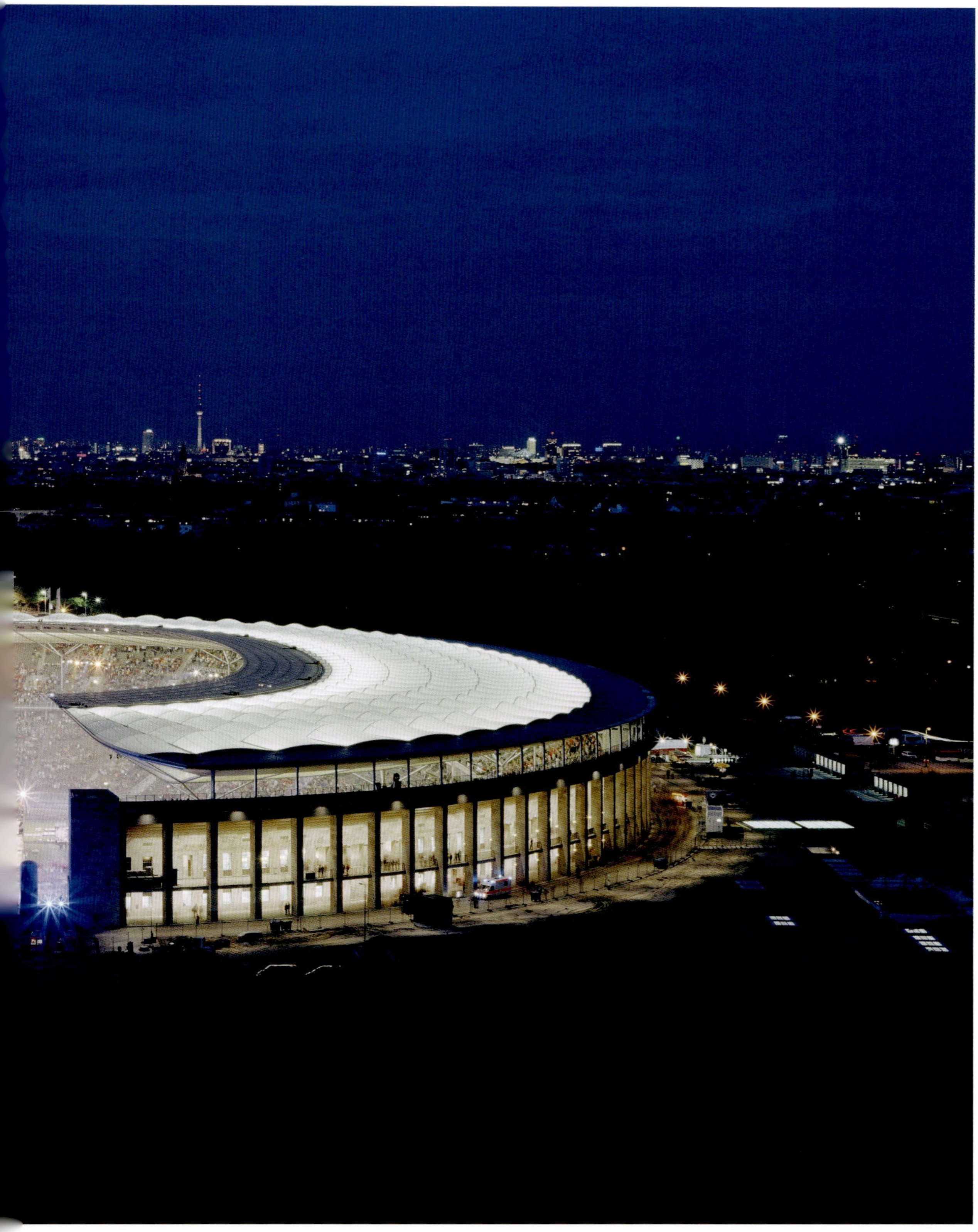

Olympic Stadium, Reconstruction and Roofing Berlin

柏林奥林匹克体育场改建和屋顶加建工程　柏林

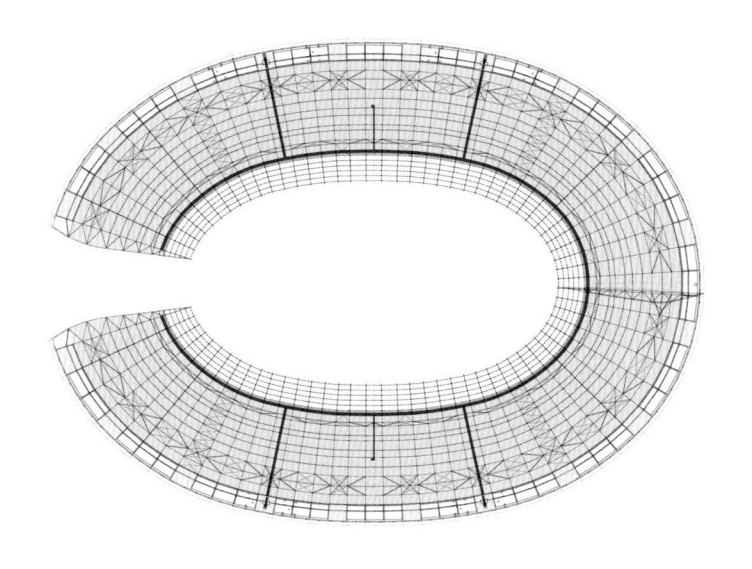

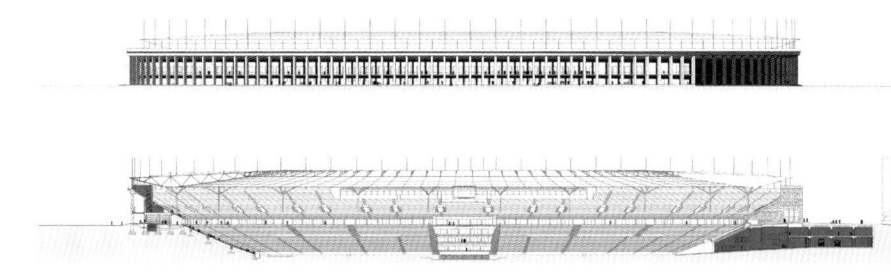

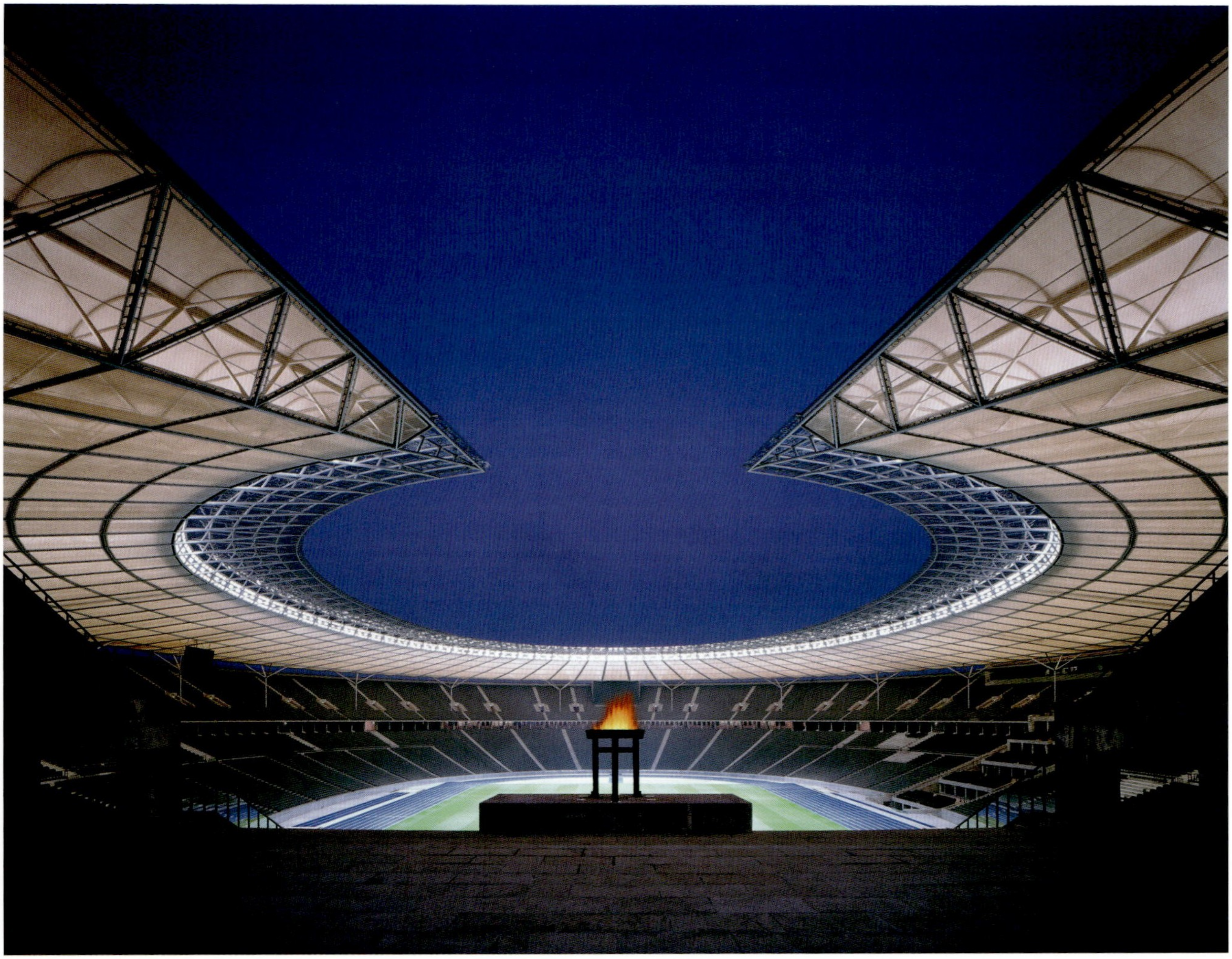

Olympic Stadium, Reconstruction and Roofing Berlin

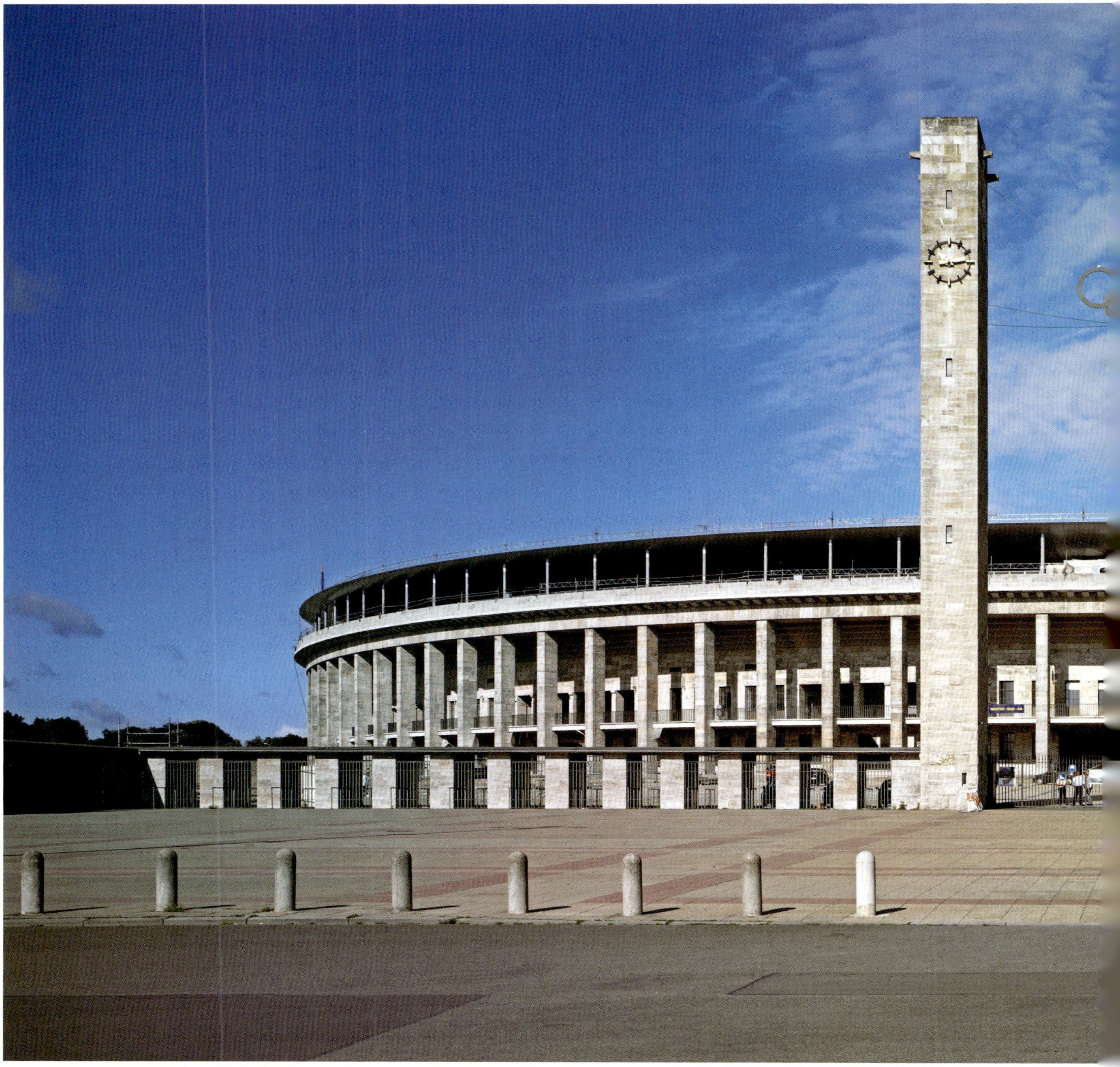

柏林奥林匹克体育场改建和屋顶加建工程　柏林

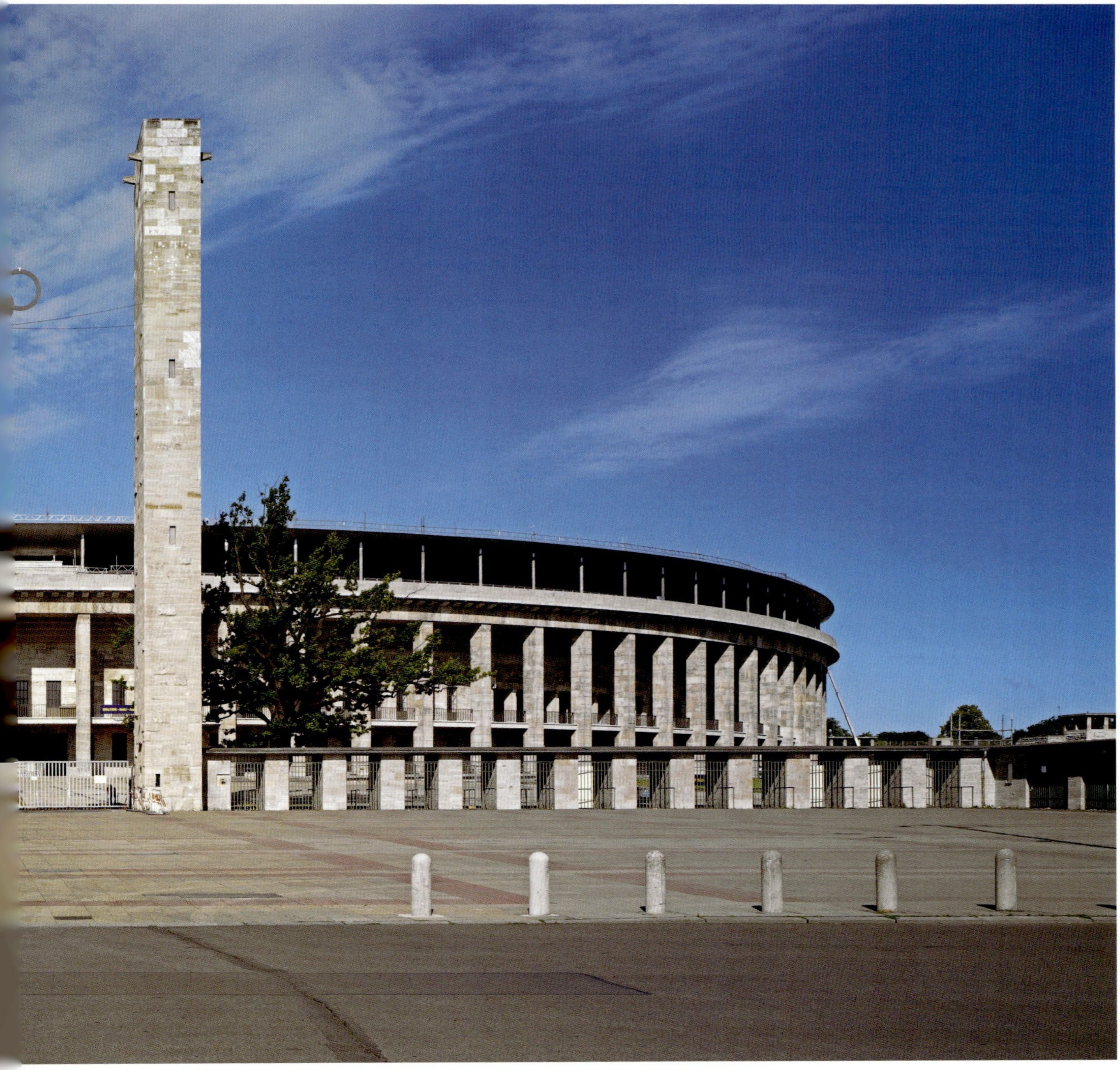

Olympic Stadium, Reconstruction and Roofing Berlin

346 ²⁶⁵

Borgo Trento医院
维罗纳，意大利

Borgo Trento Hospital
Verona, Italy

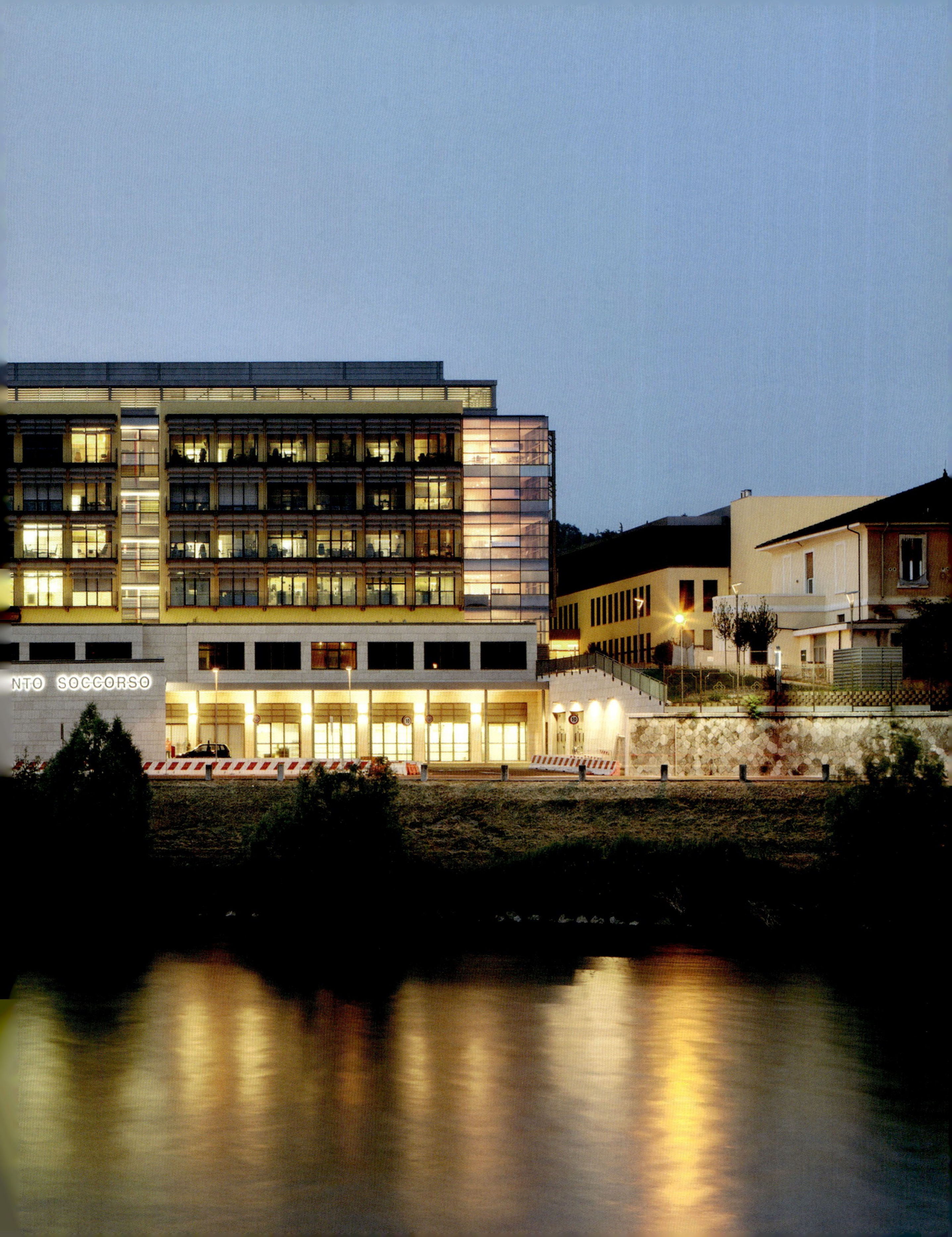
NTO SOCCORSO

Borgo Trento医院　纬罗纳

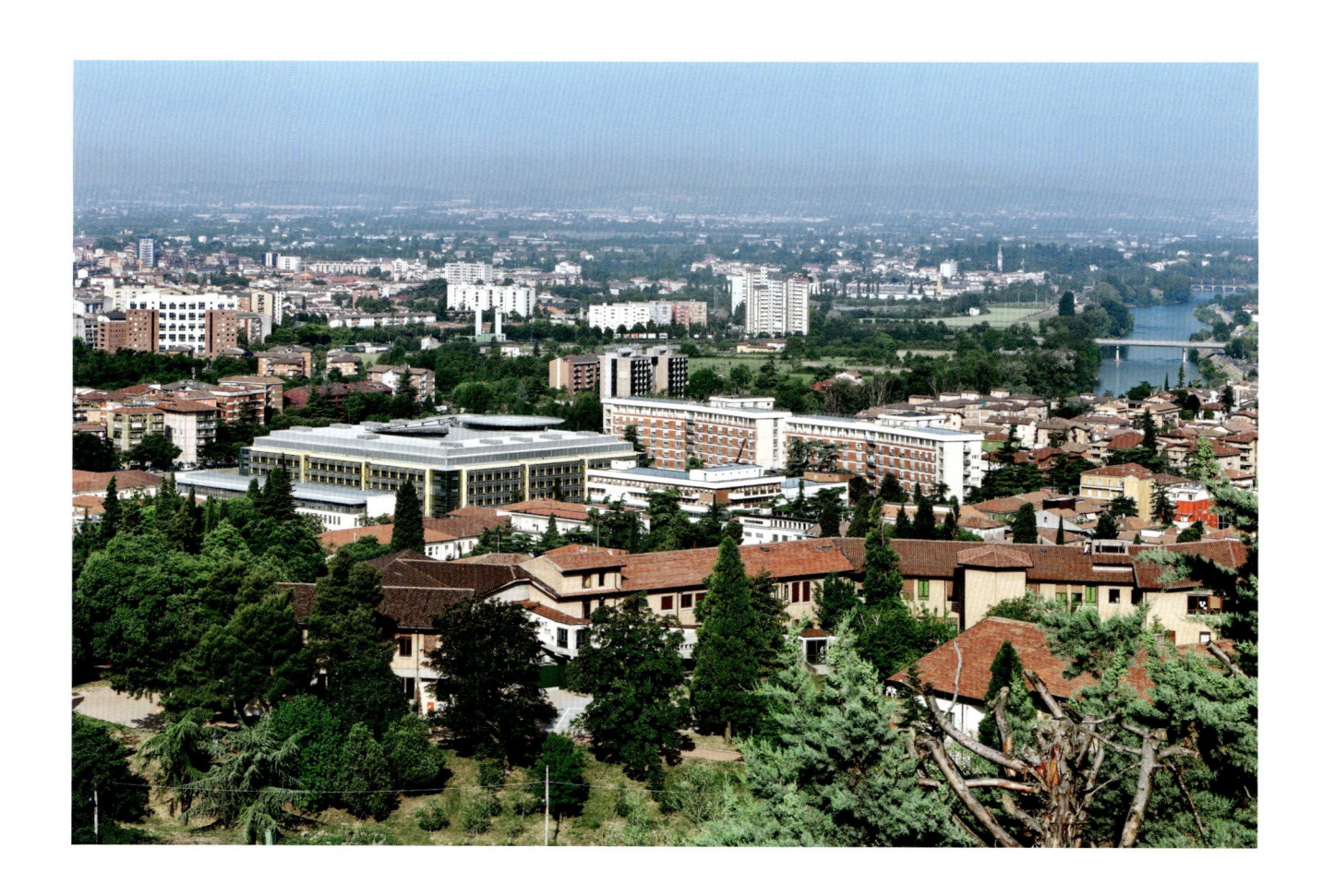

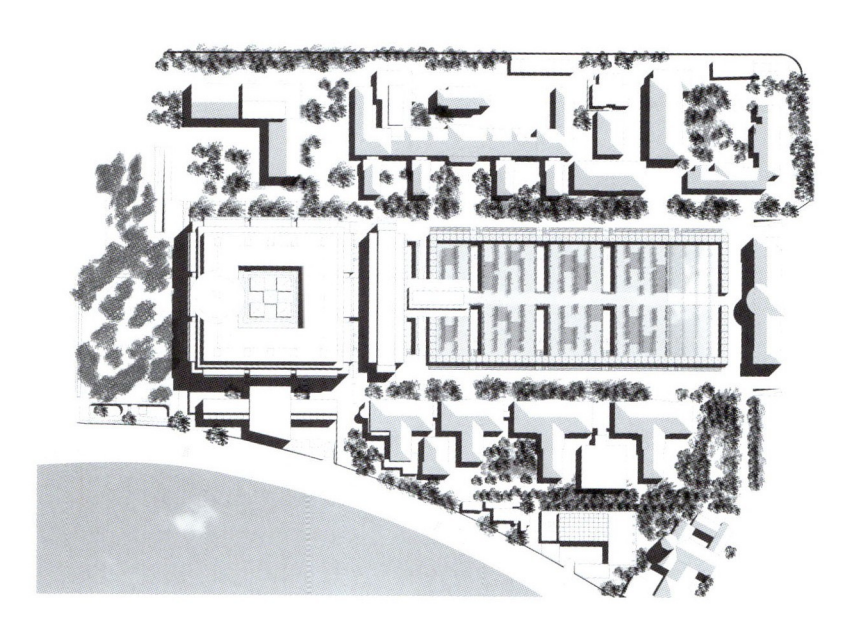

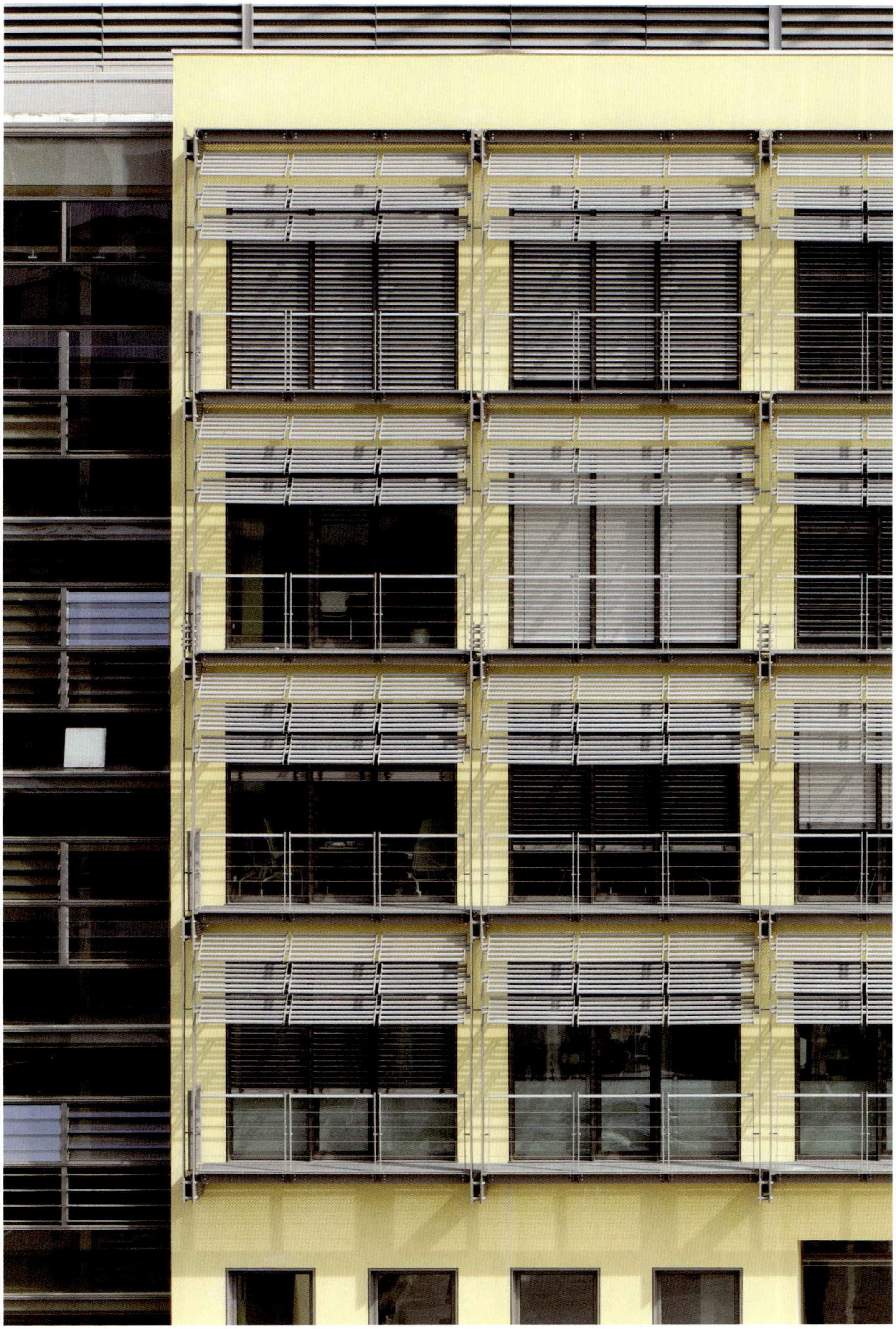

Borgo Trento Hospital Verona

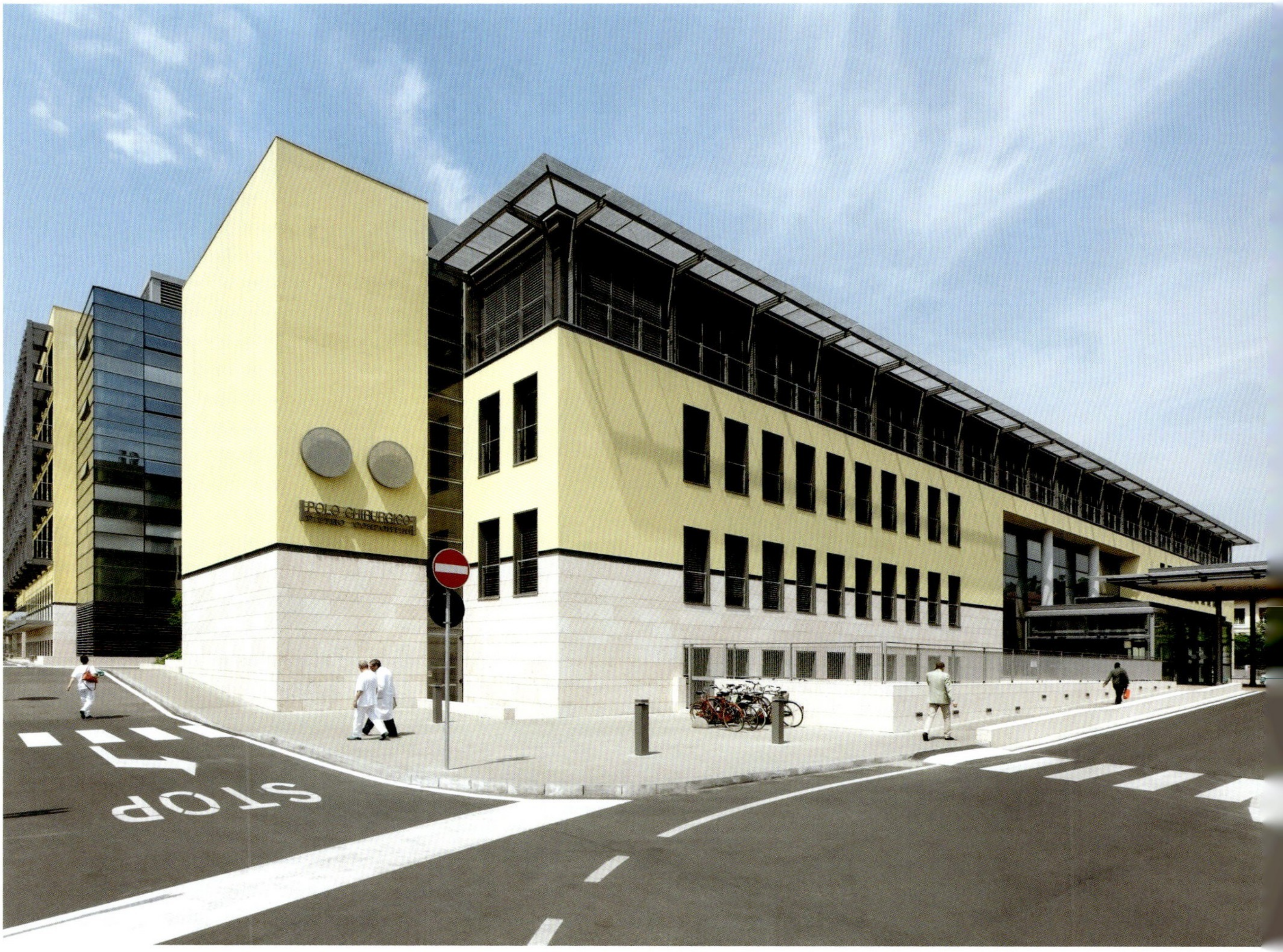
POLO CHIRURGICO
STOP

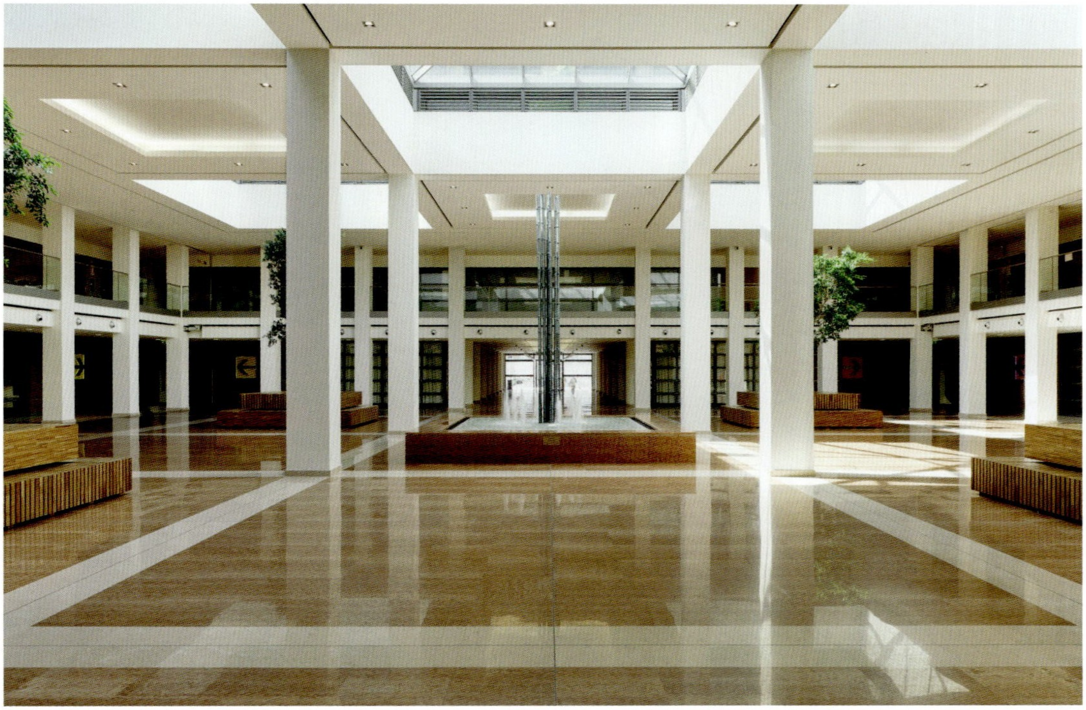

Borgo Trento Hospital Verona

352 ²⁶⁶ ↑

莱茵能量体育场
科隆，德国

RheinEnergie Stadium
Cologne, Germany

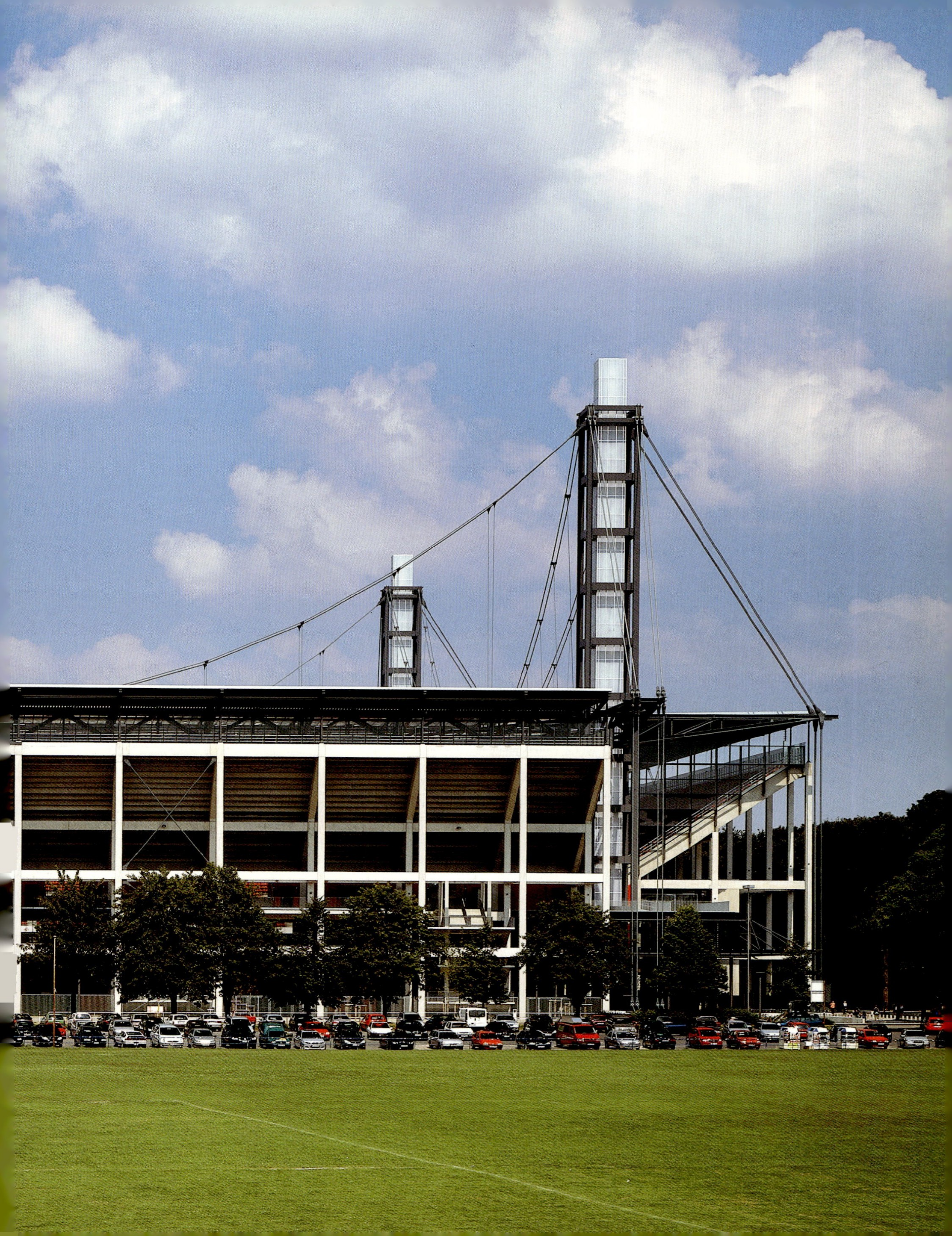

354　莱茵能量体育场　科隆

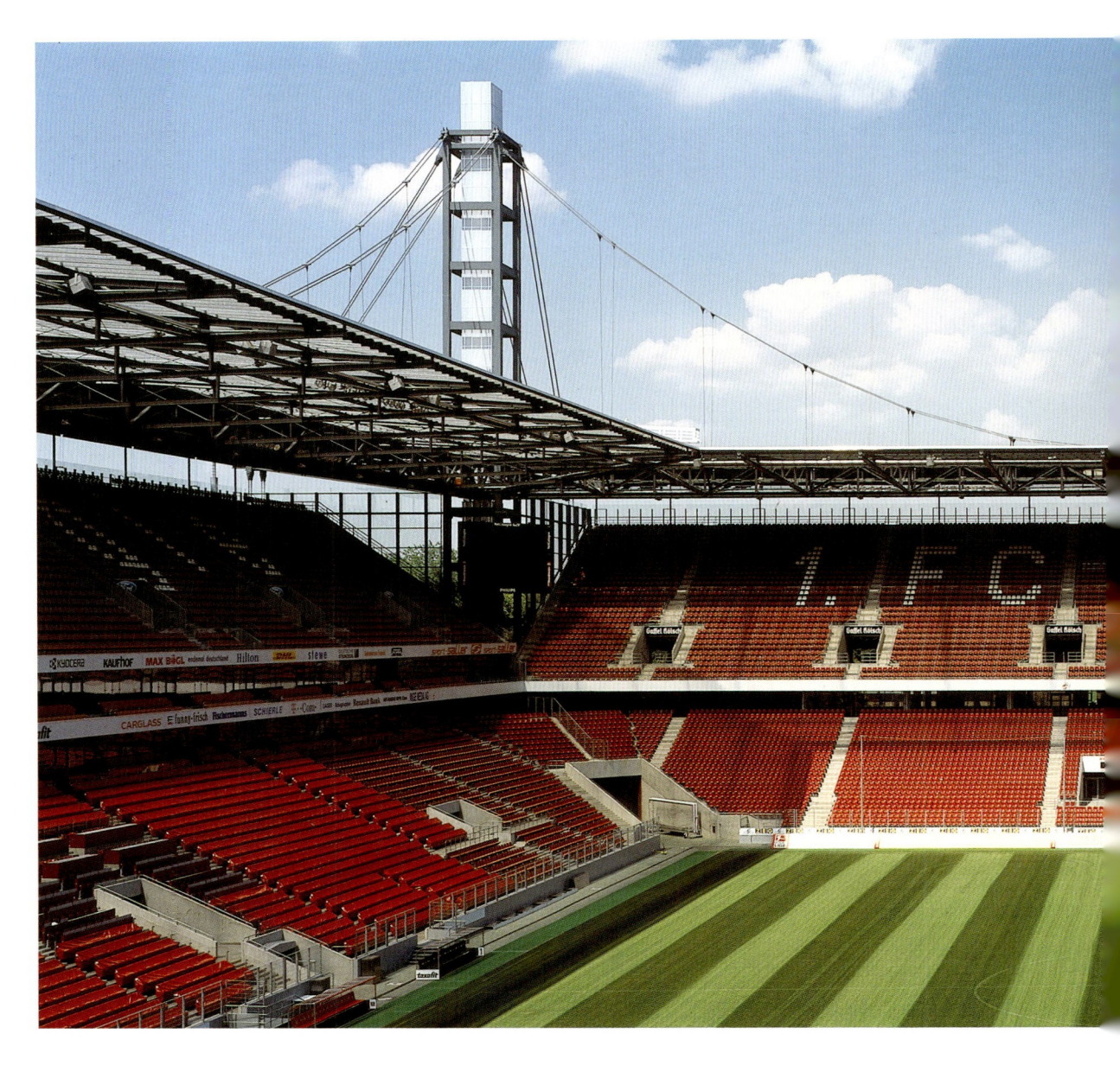

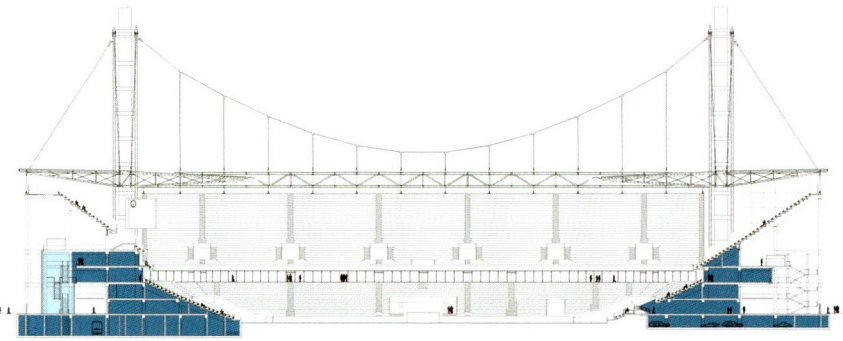

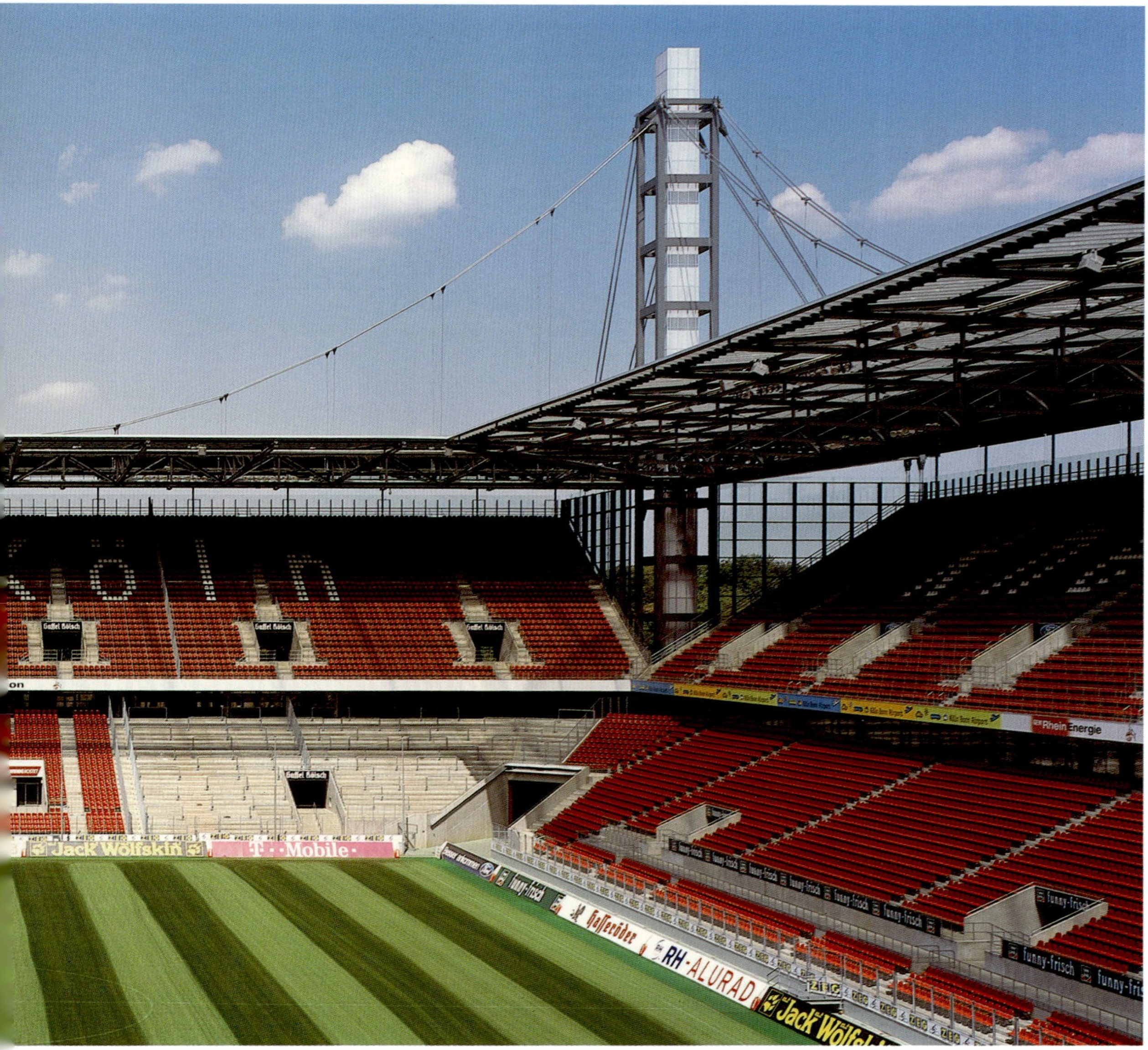

RheinEnergie Stadium Cologne

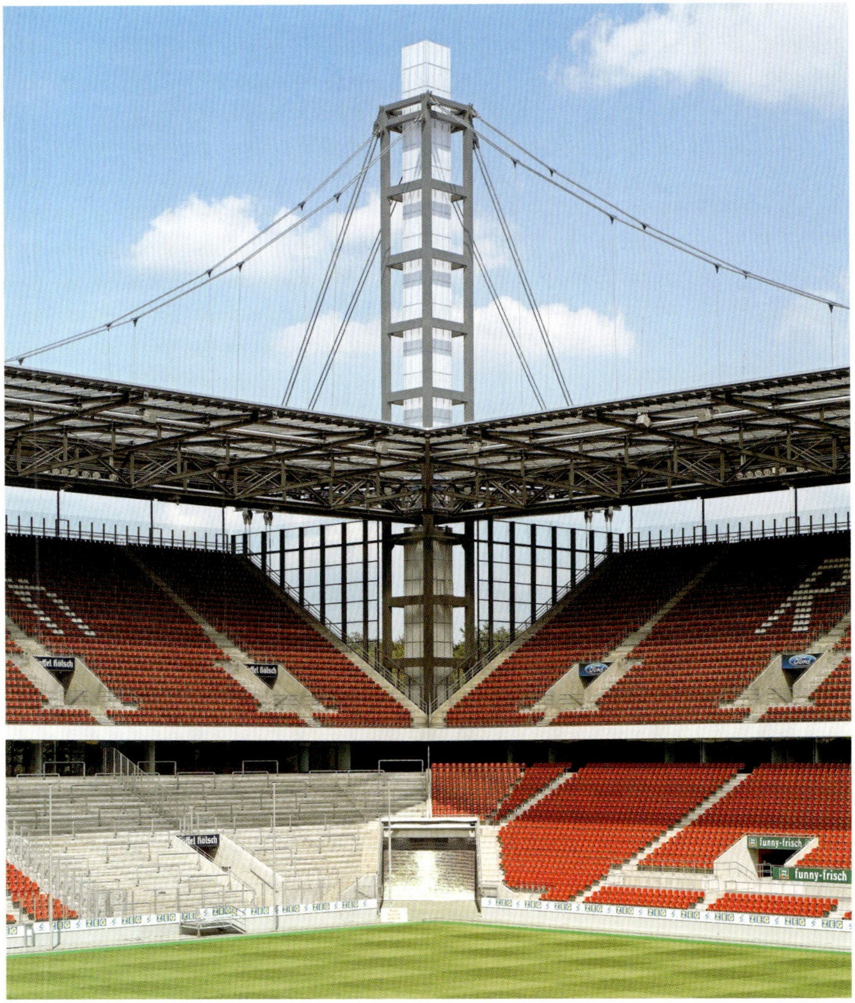

莱茵能量体育场　科隆

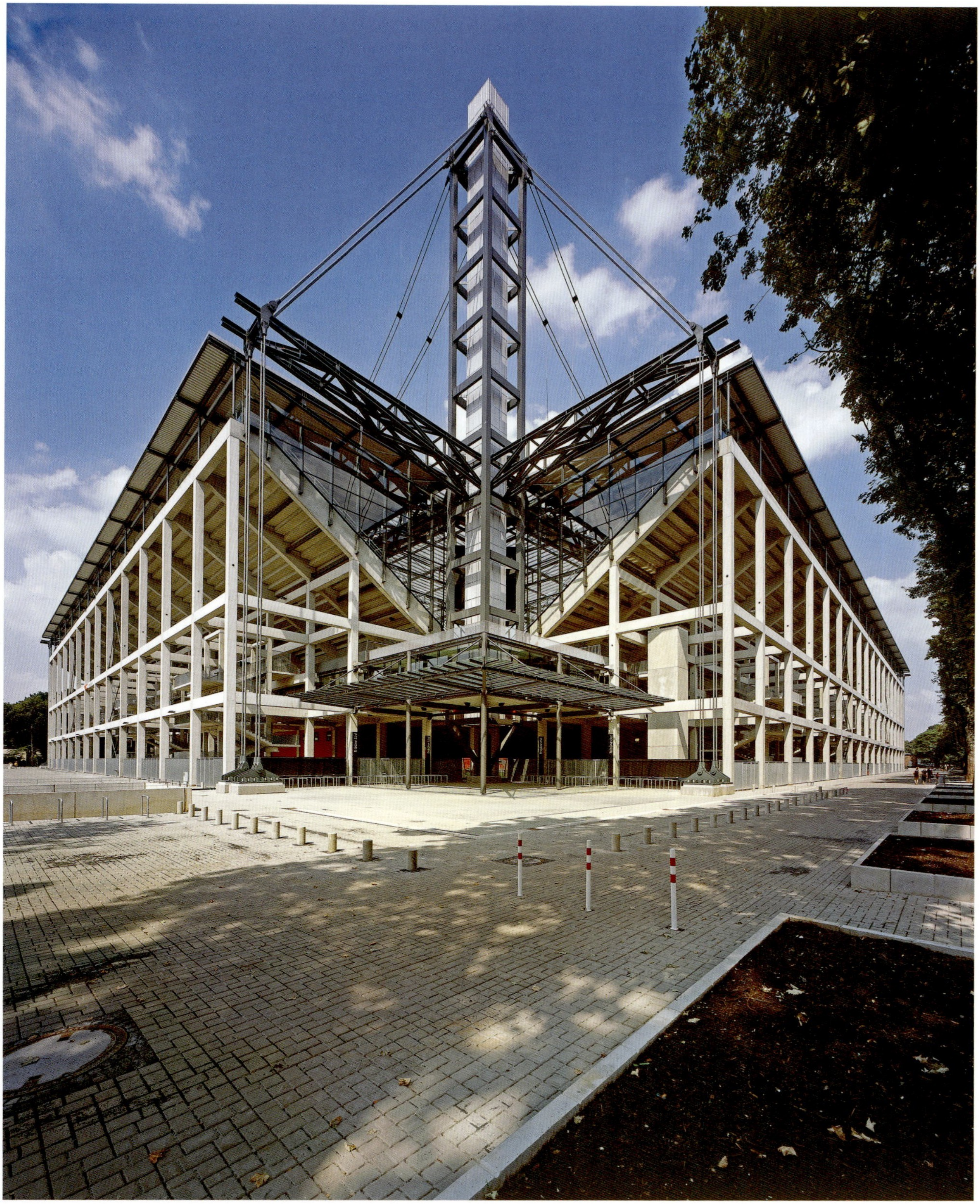

RheinEnergie Stadium Cologne

科隆大学医院心脏中心
科隆，德国

**Cardiac Center
University Clinic of Cologne**
Cologne, Germany

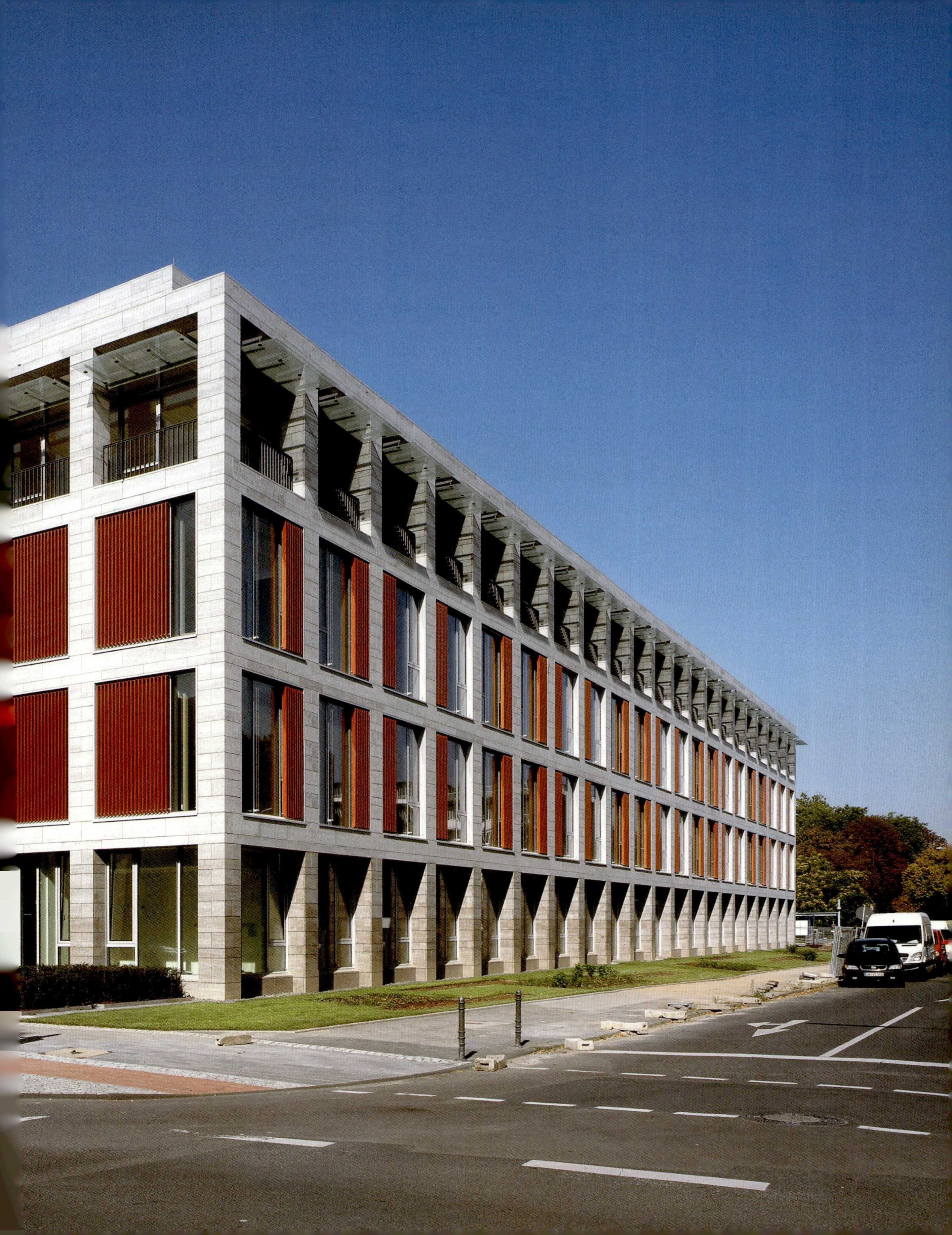

科隆大学医院心脏中心　科隆

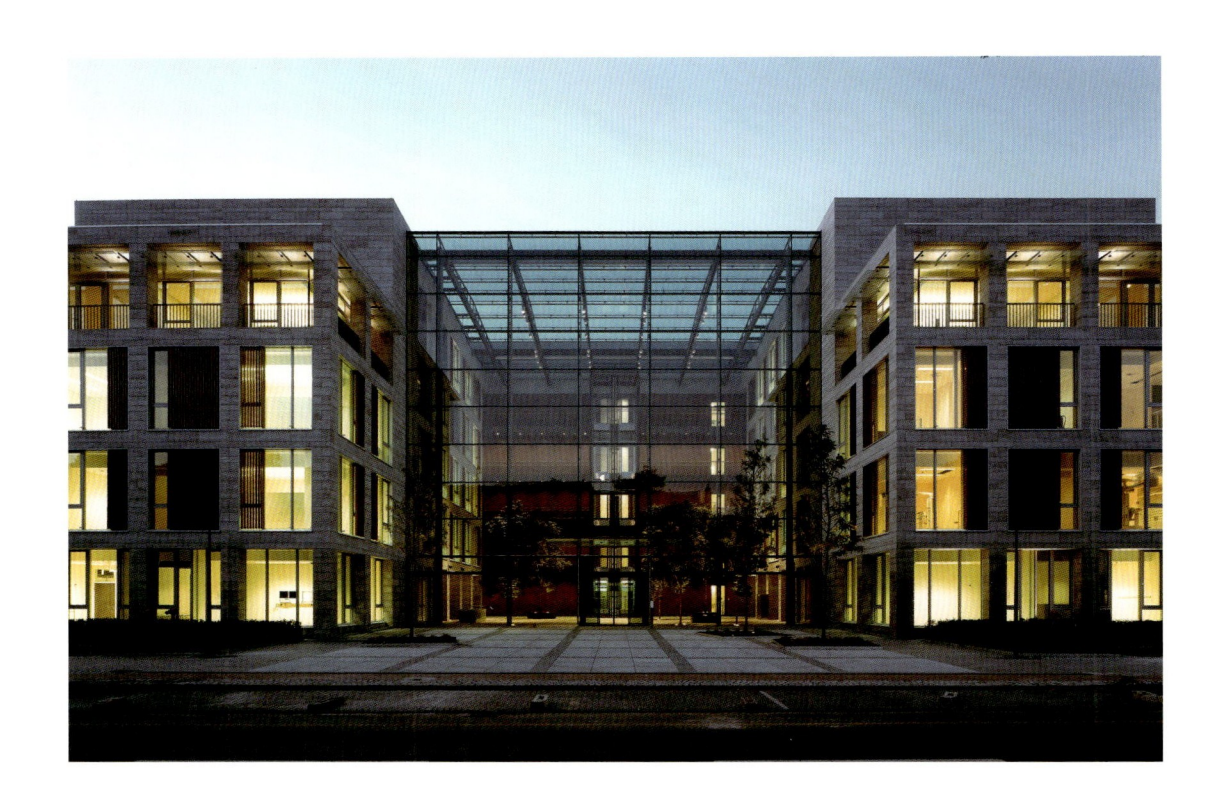

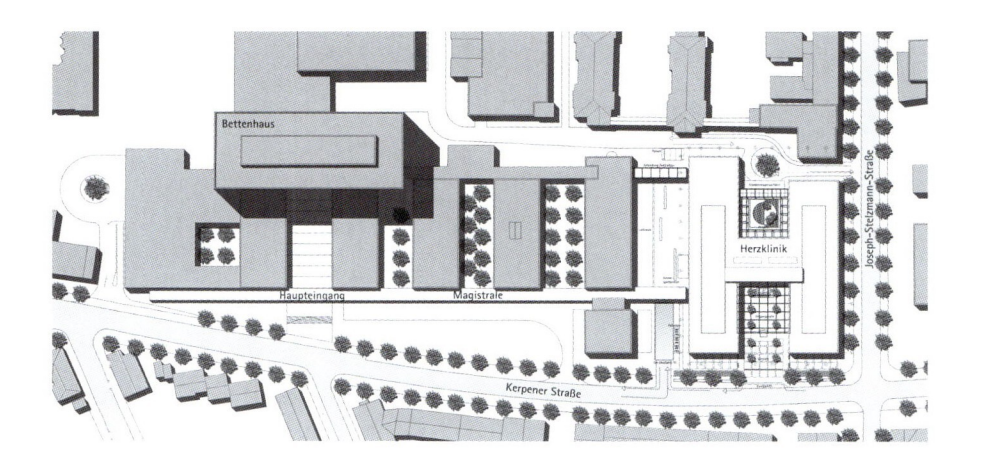

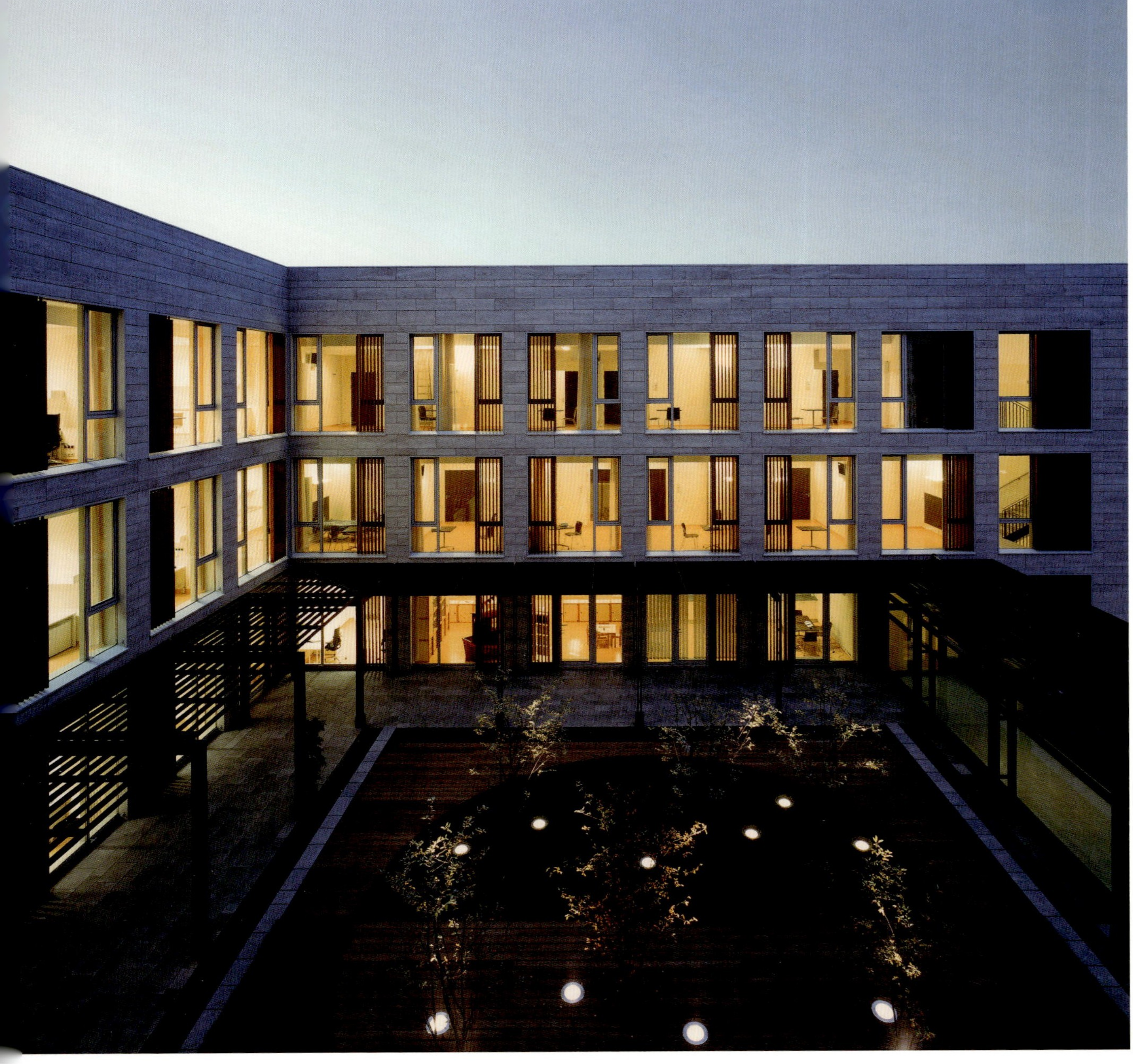

Cardiac Center University Clinic of Cologne Cologne

科隆大学医院心脏中心　科隆

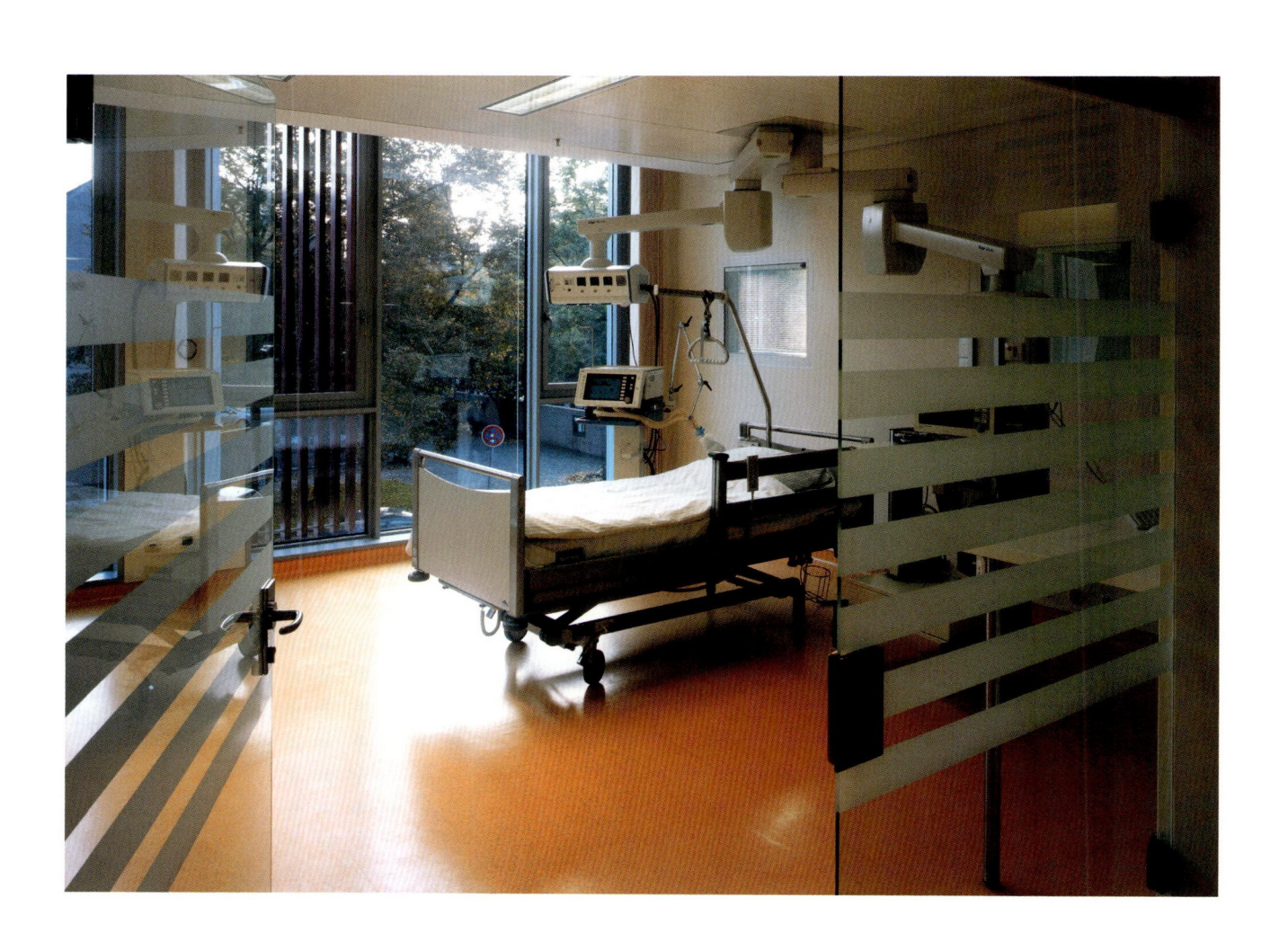

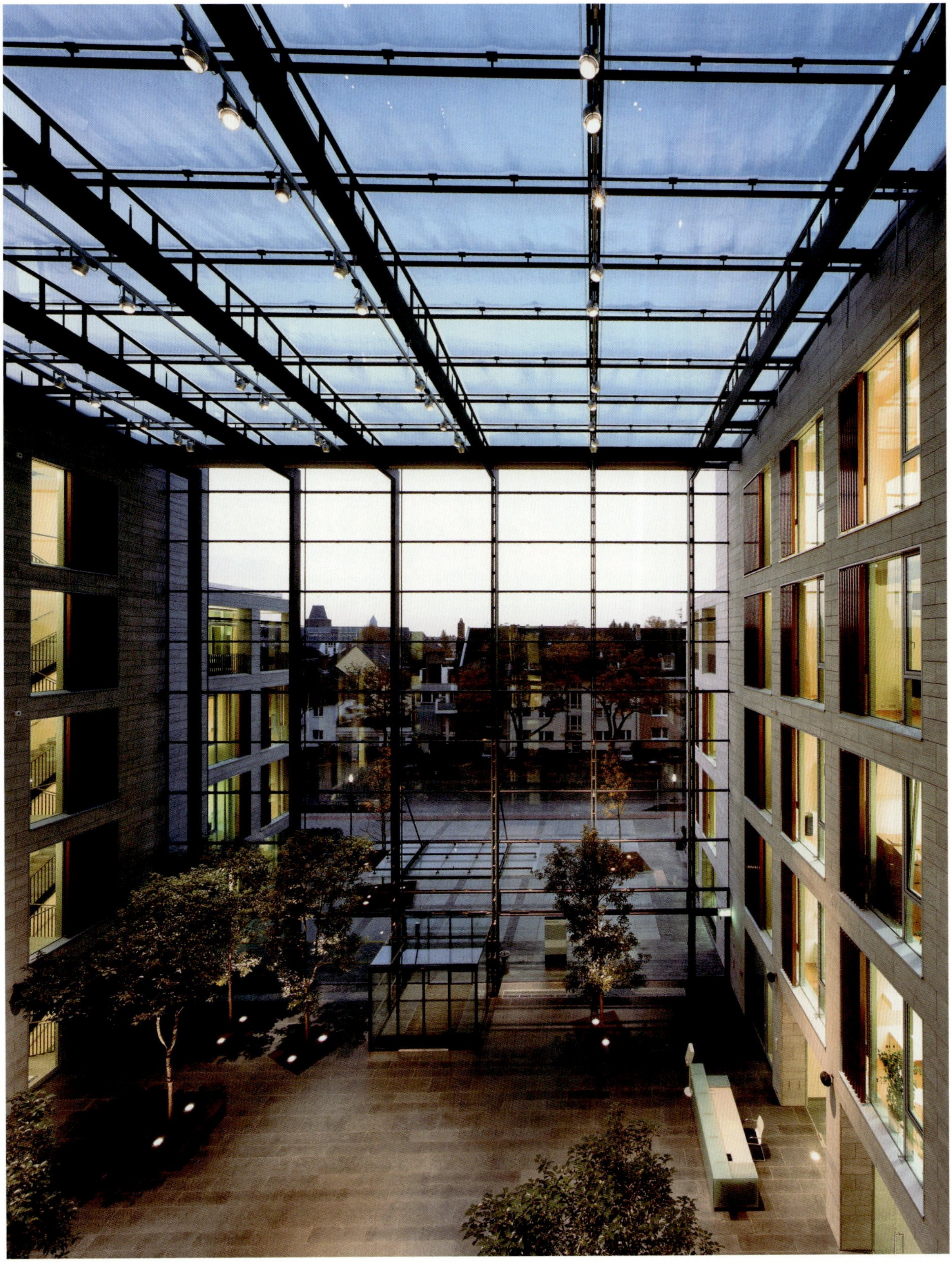

Cardiac Center University Clinic of Cologne Cologne

364 ²⁶⁷ ↑

易北大道别墅
汉堡，德国

Villa at Elbchaussee
Hamburg, Germany

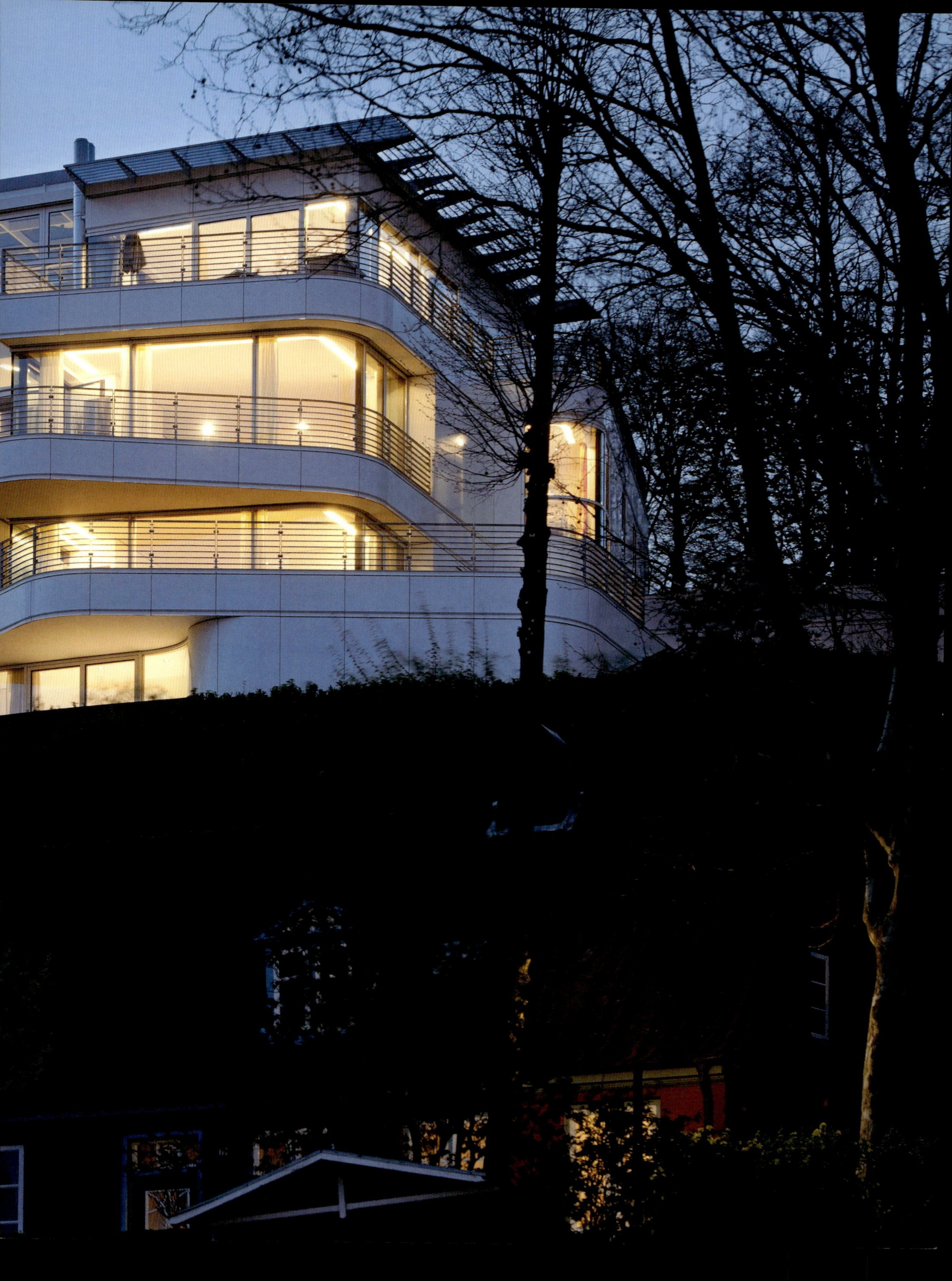

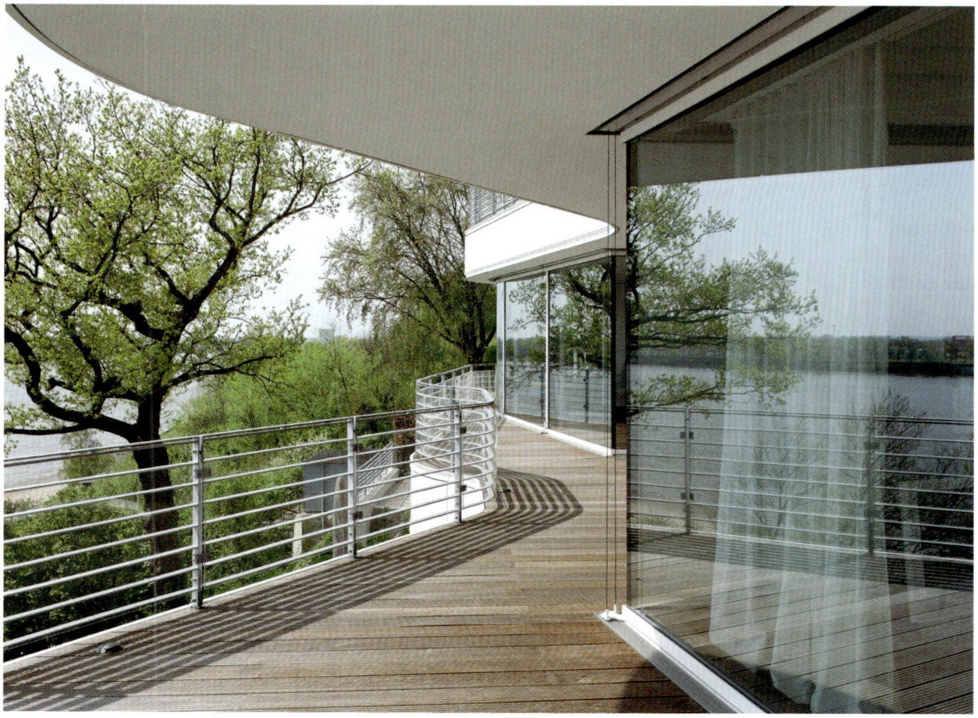

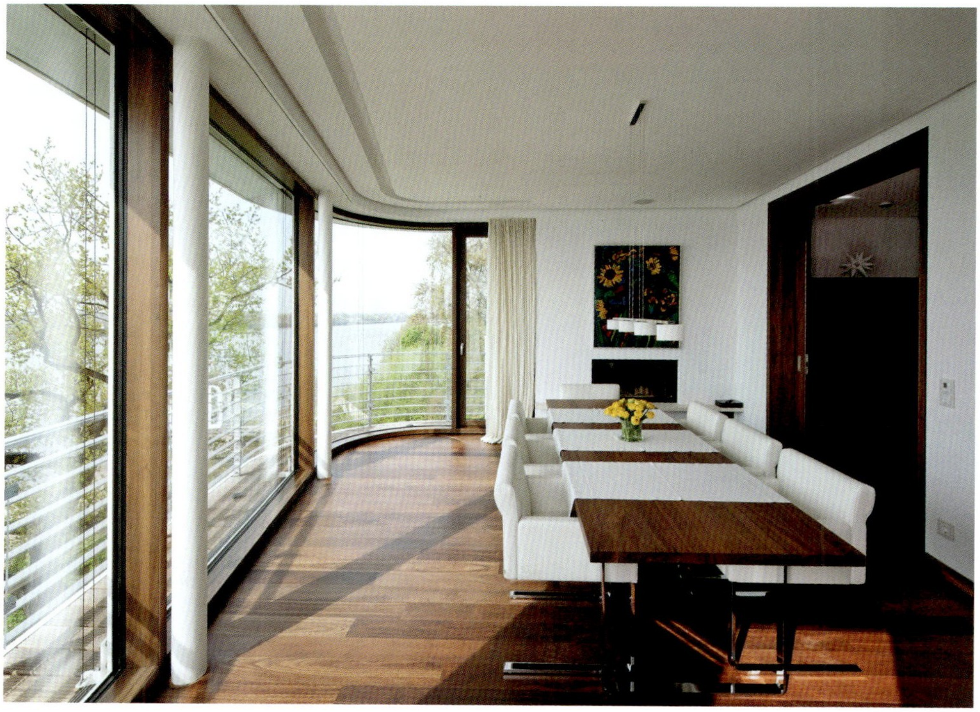

易北大道别墅　汉堡

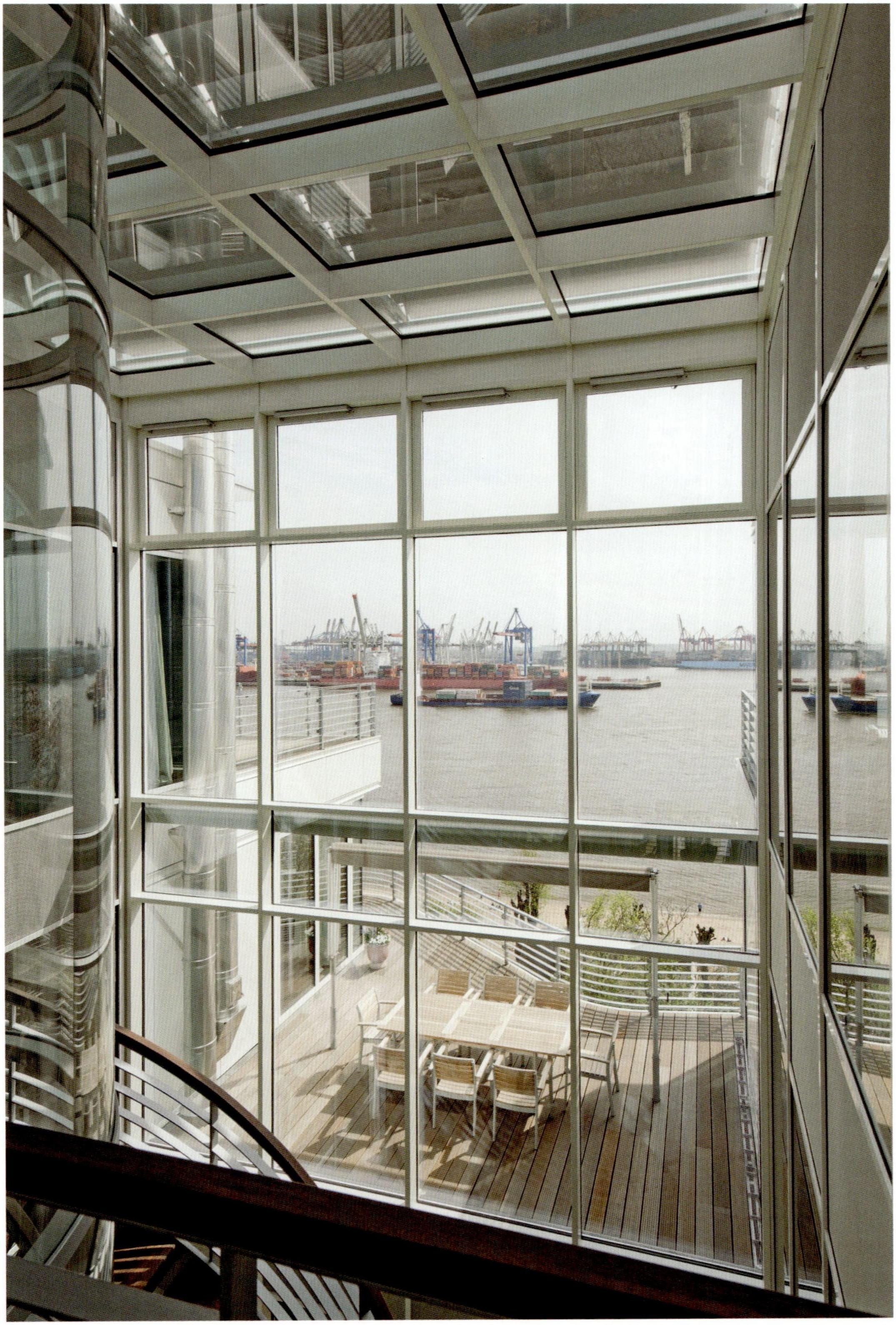

Villa at Elbchaussee Hamburg

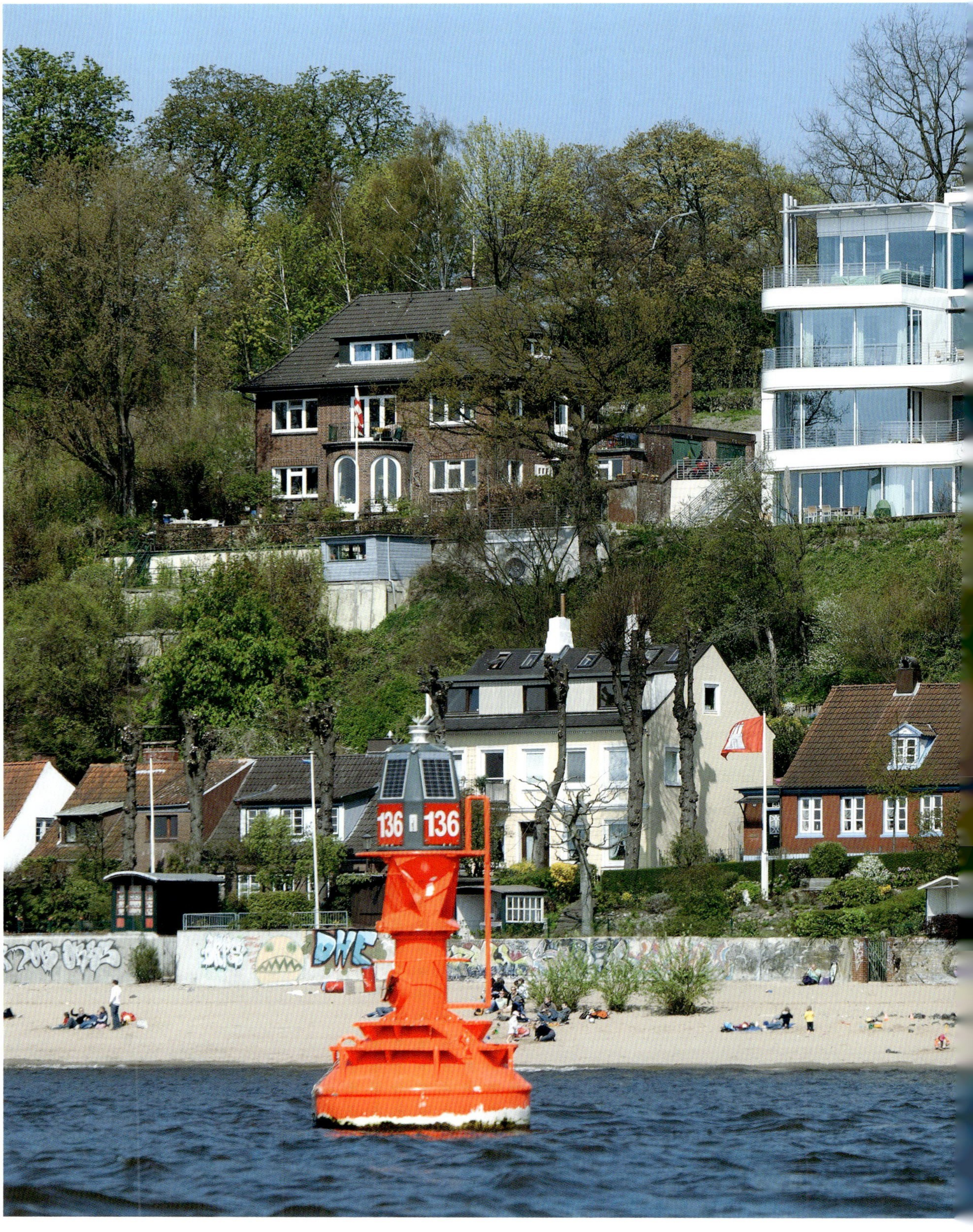

易北大道别墅　汉堡

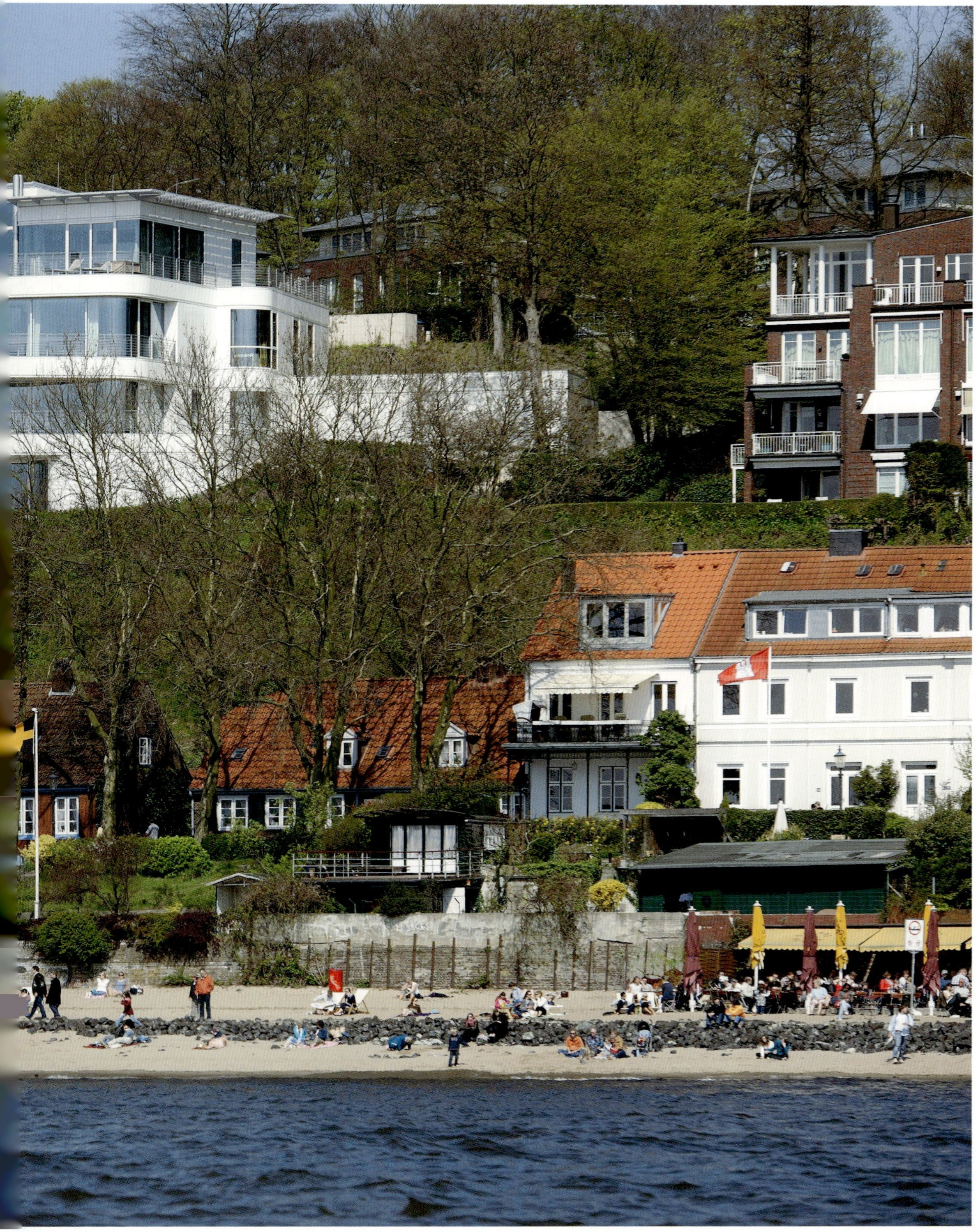

Villa at Elbchaussee Hamburg

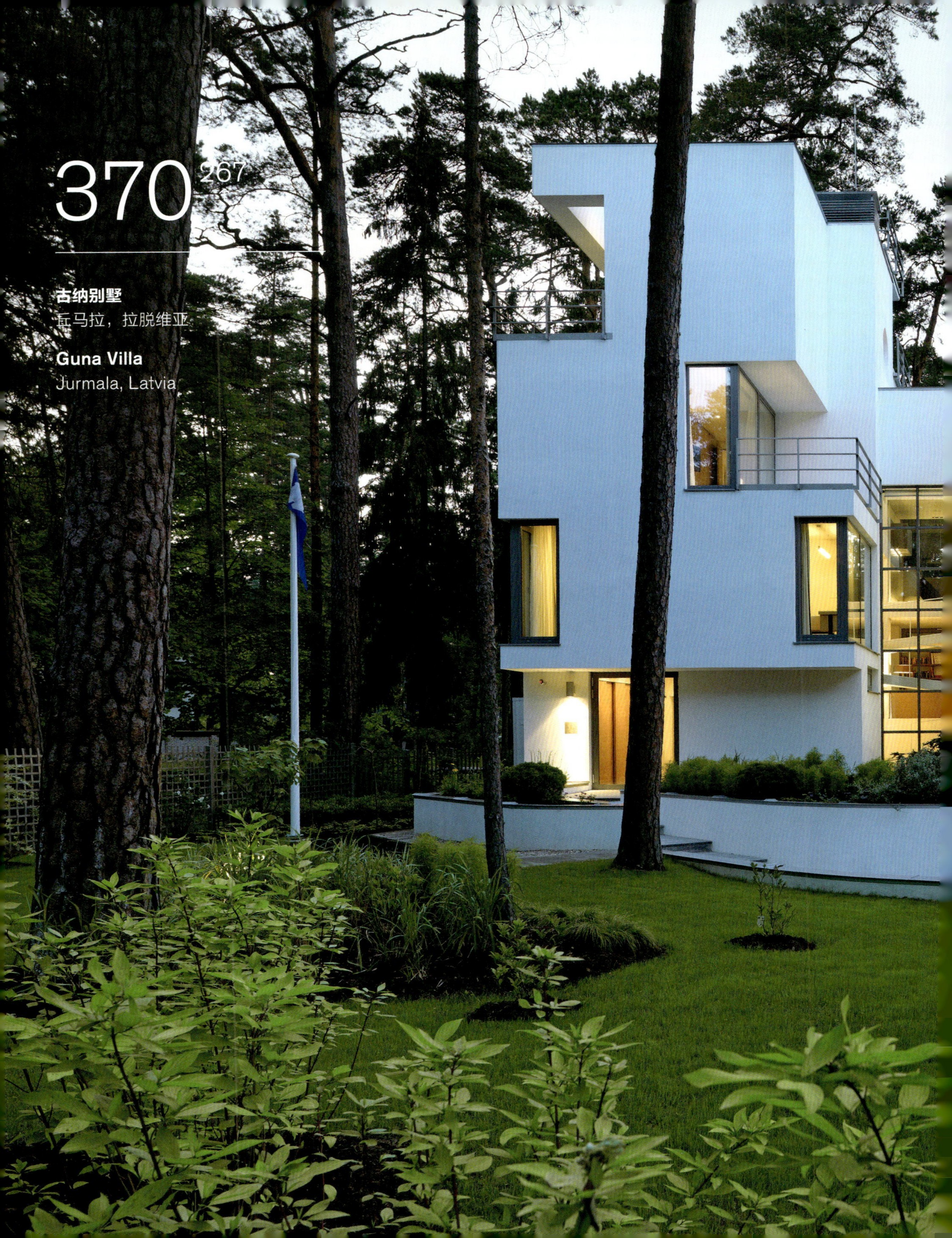

370 [267]

古纳别墅
尤马拉，拉脱维亚

Guna Villa
Jurmala, Latvia

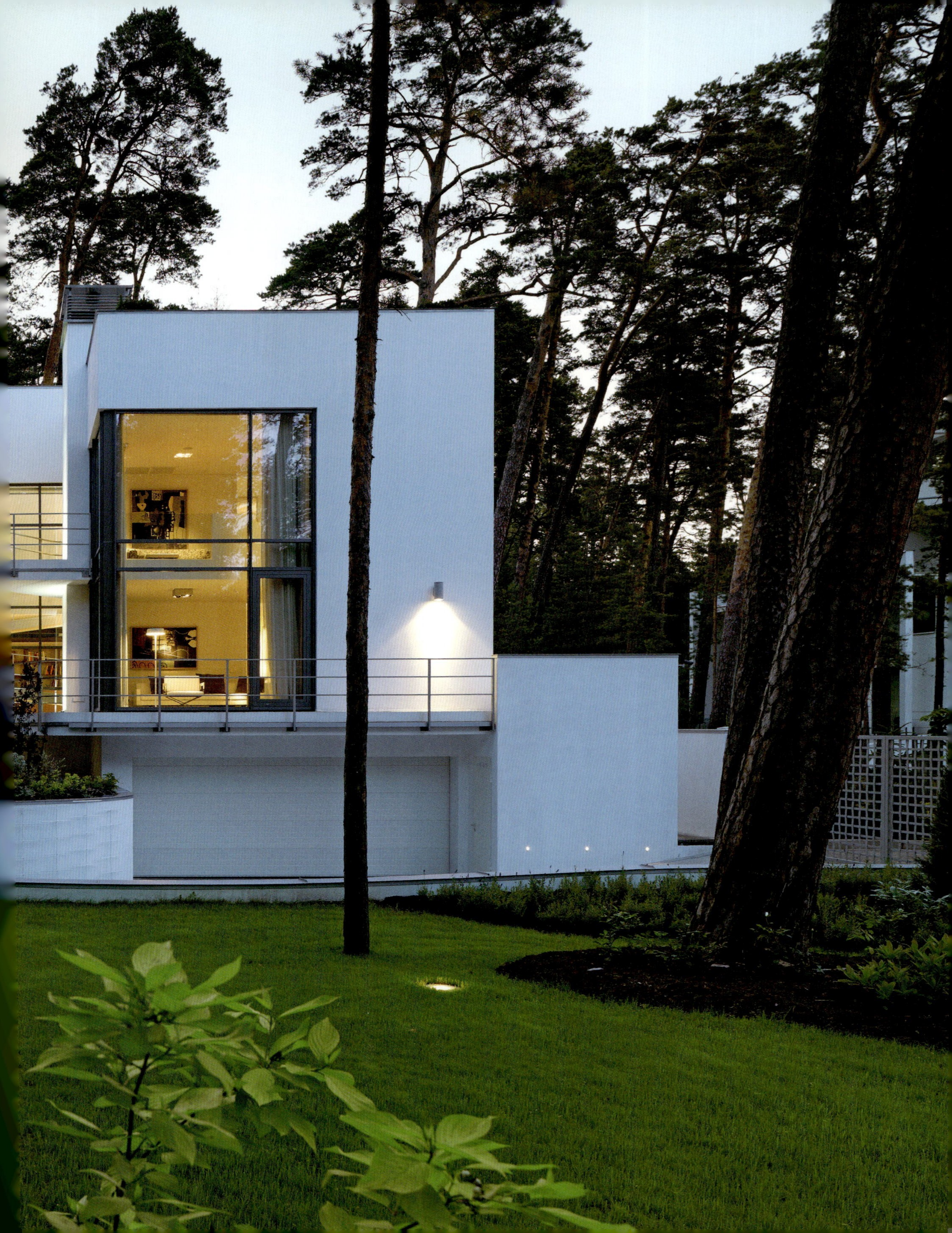

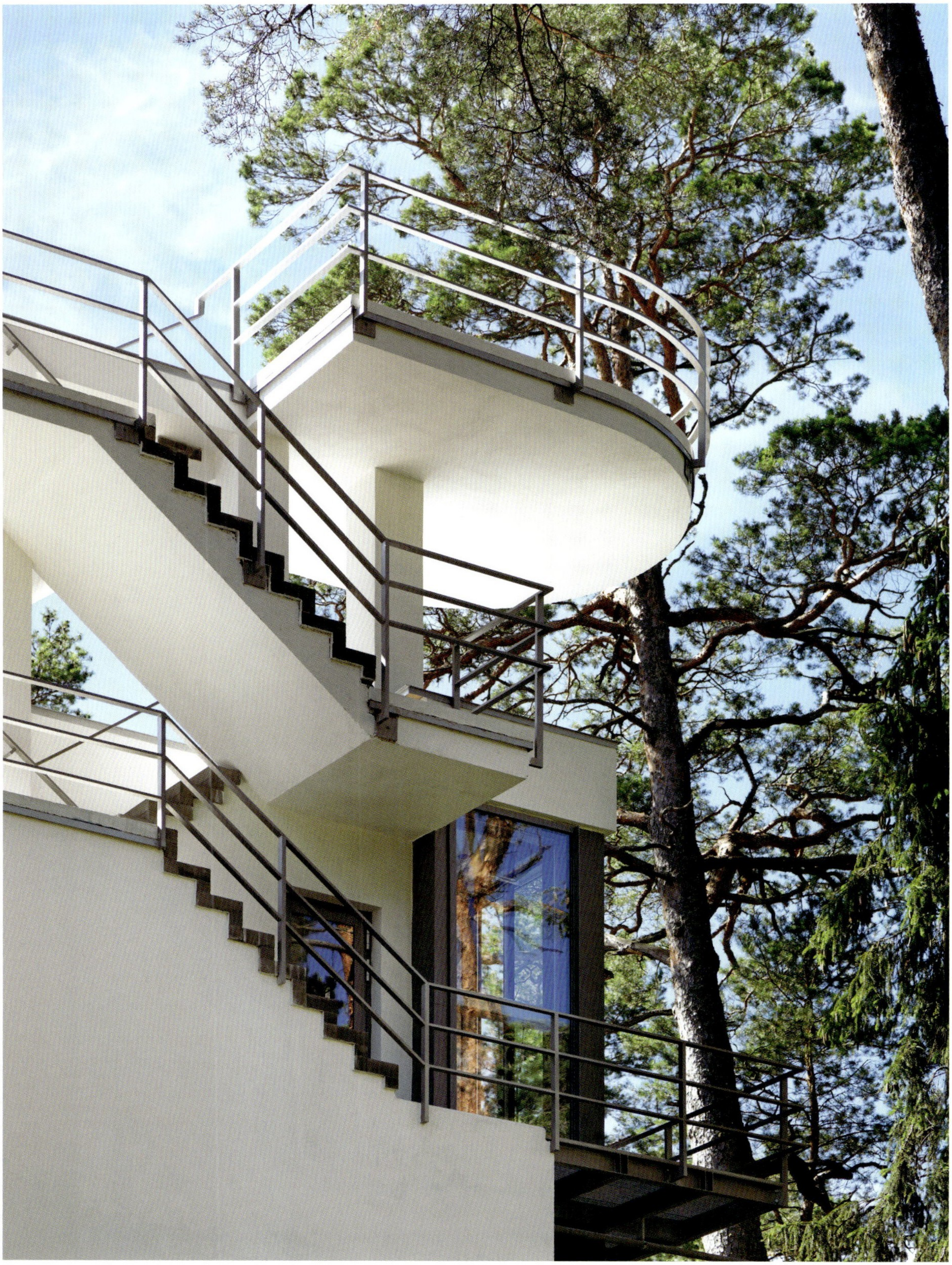

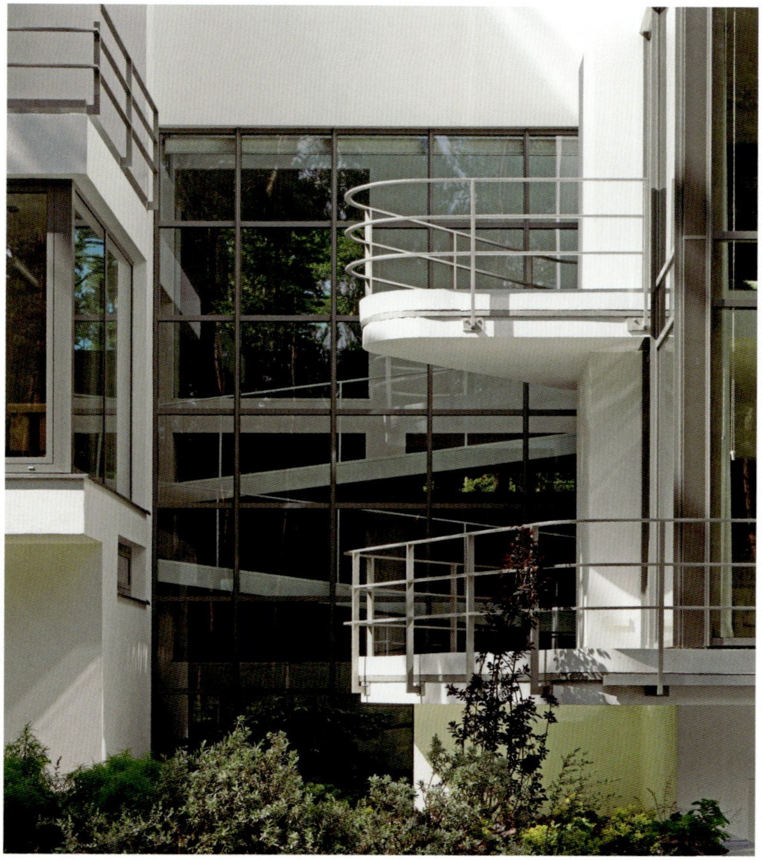

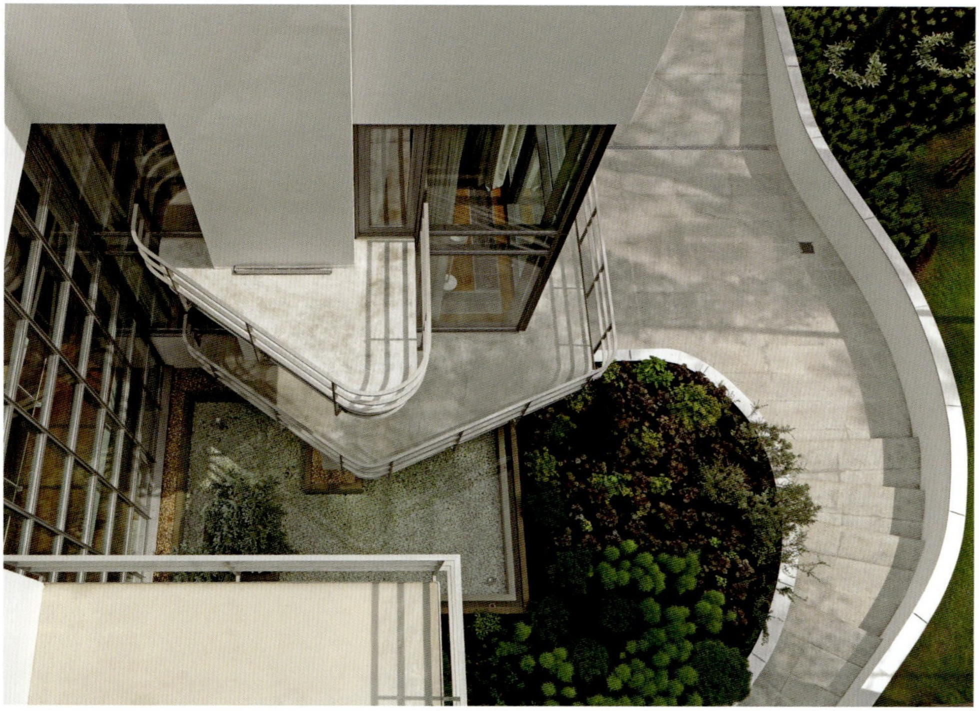

Guna Villa Jurmala 373

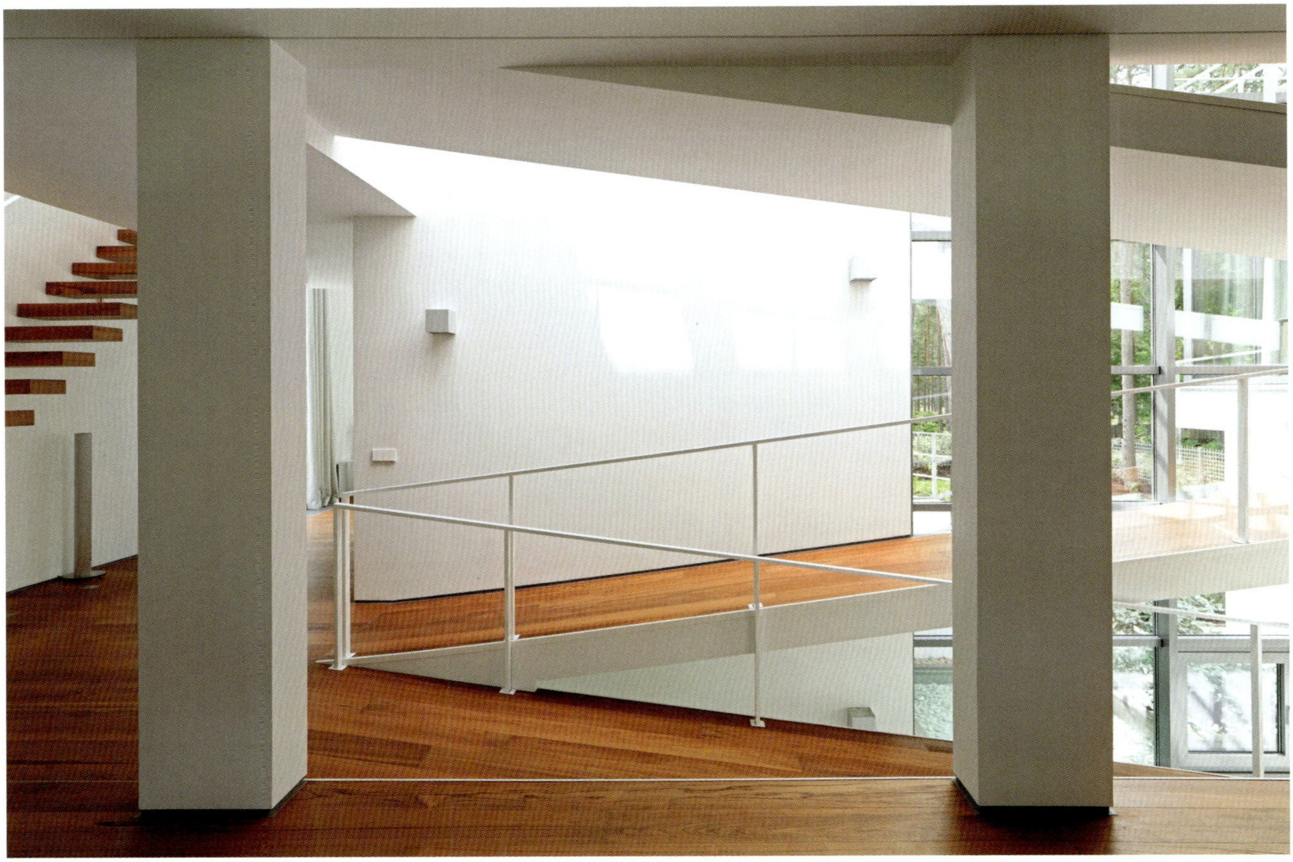

Guna Villa Jurmala

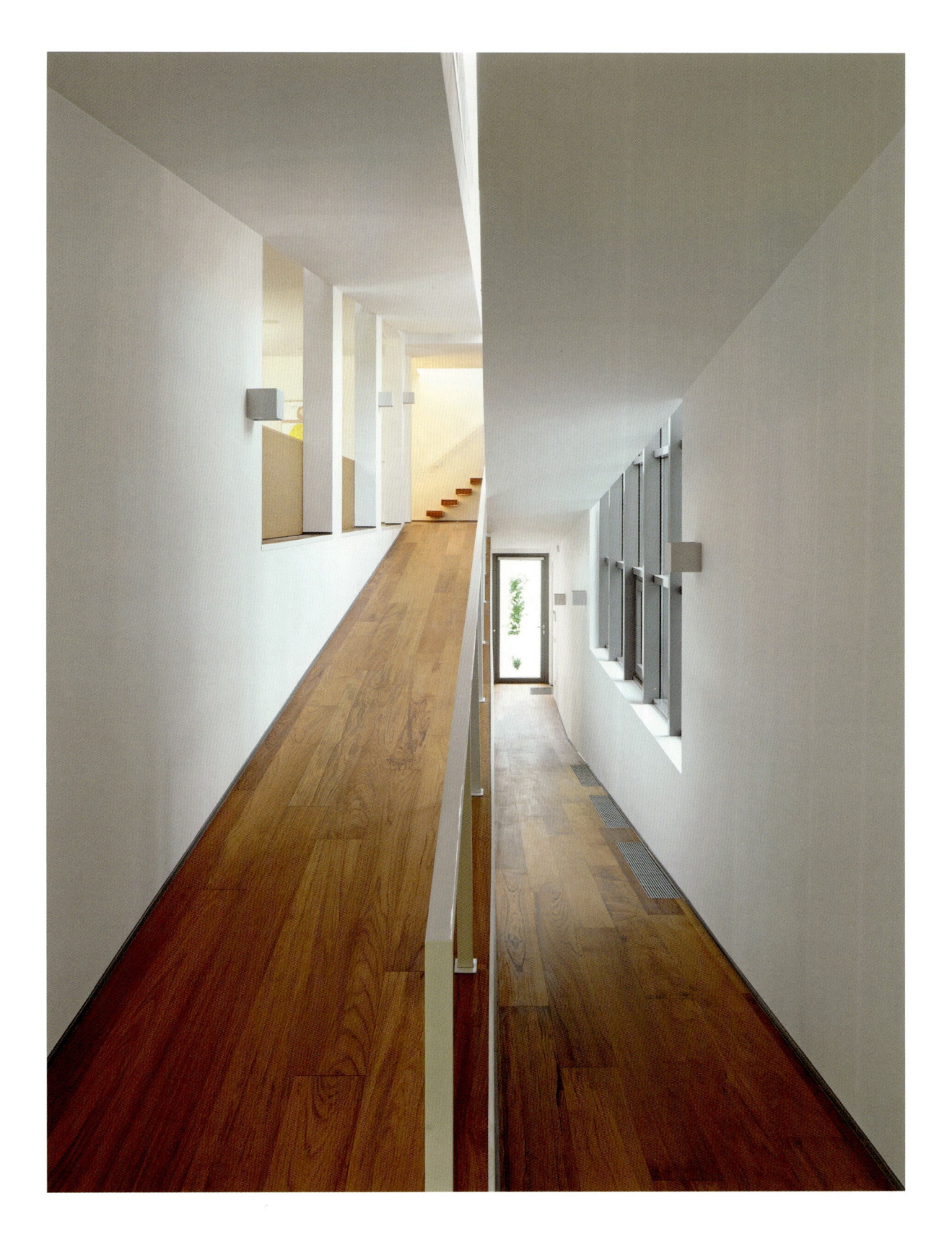

古纳别墅　丘马拉

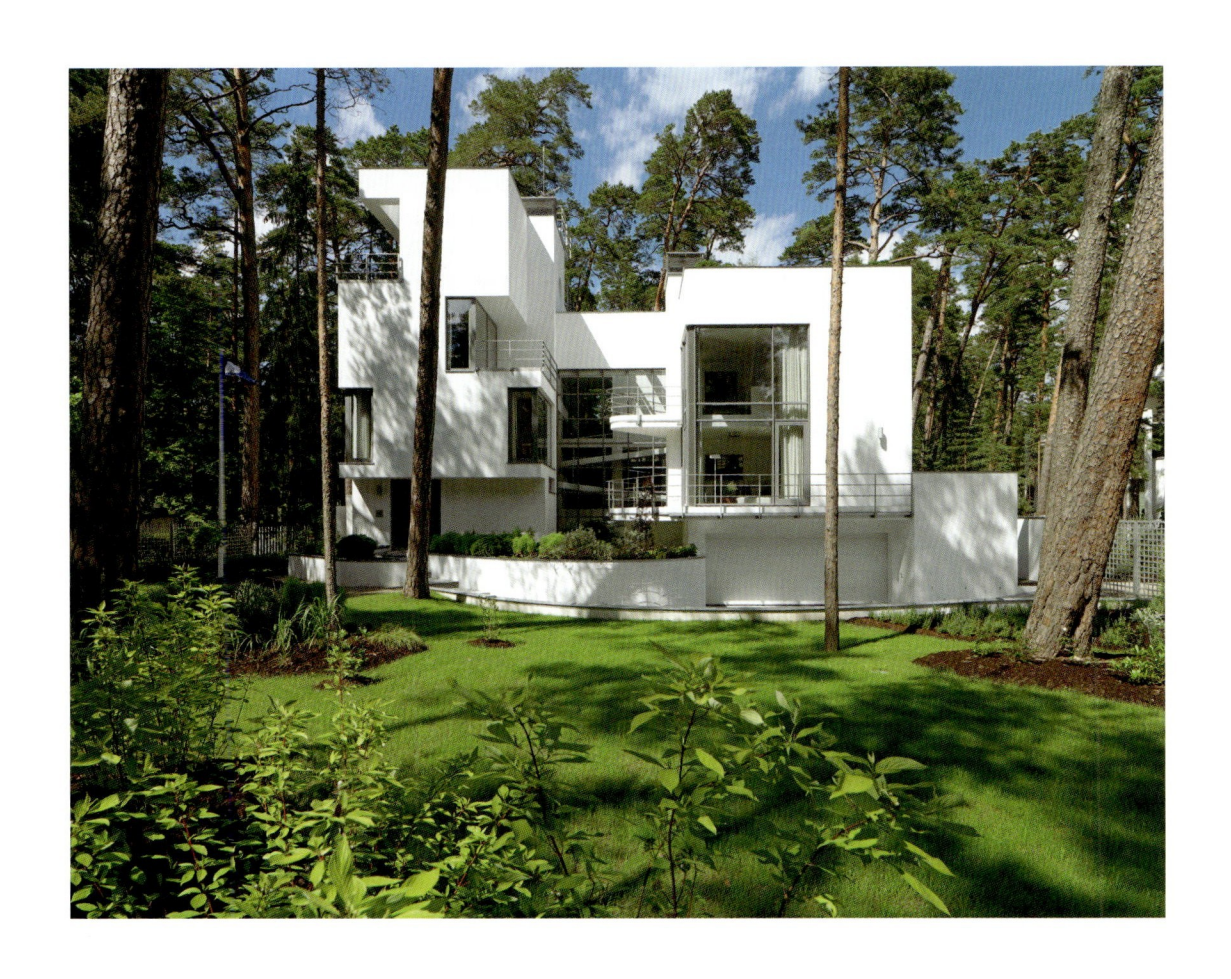

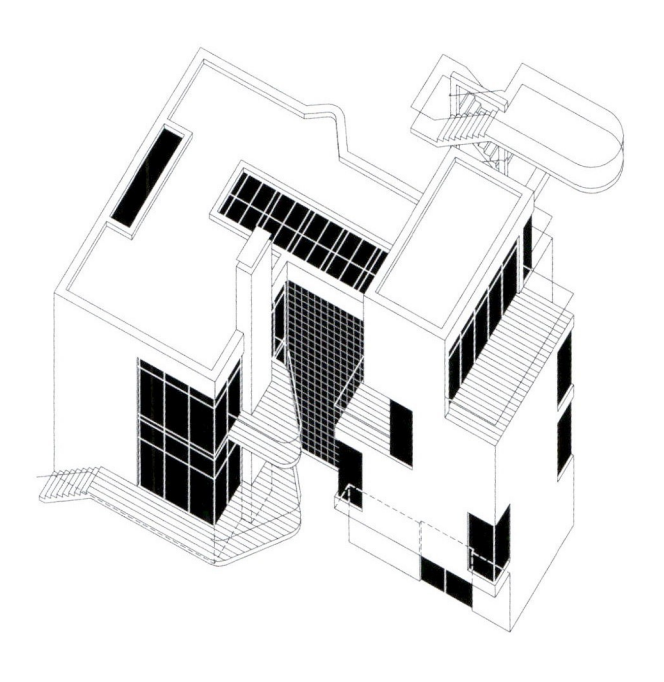

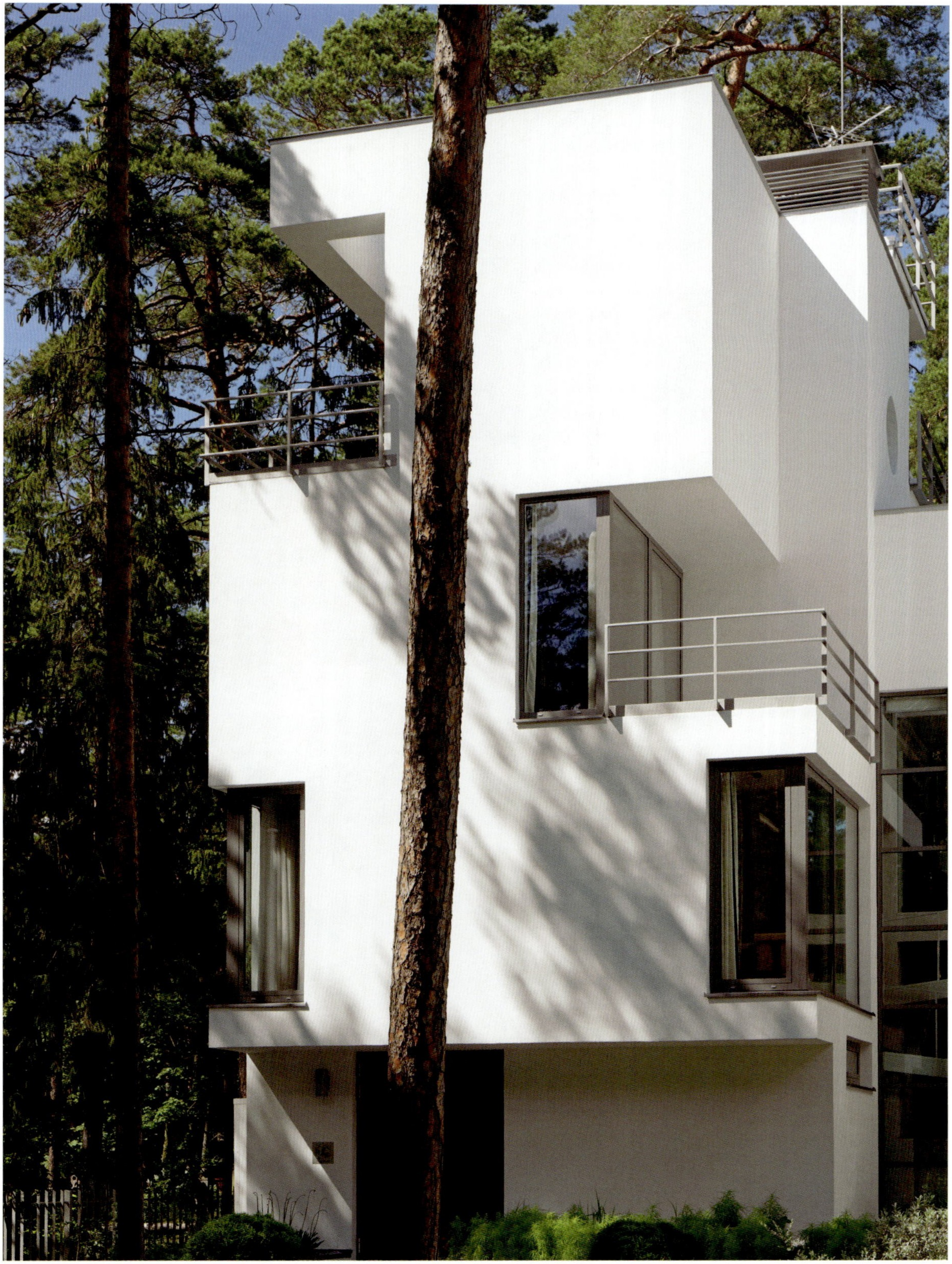

Guna Villa Jurmala

378 268 ↑

鸟类观察站
德国恒洛的格雷斯霍尔姆，德国

Bird-Watching Tower
Graswarder in Heiligenhafen,
Germany

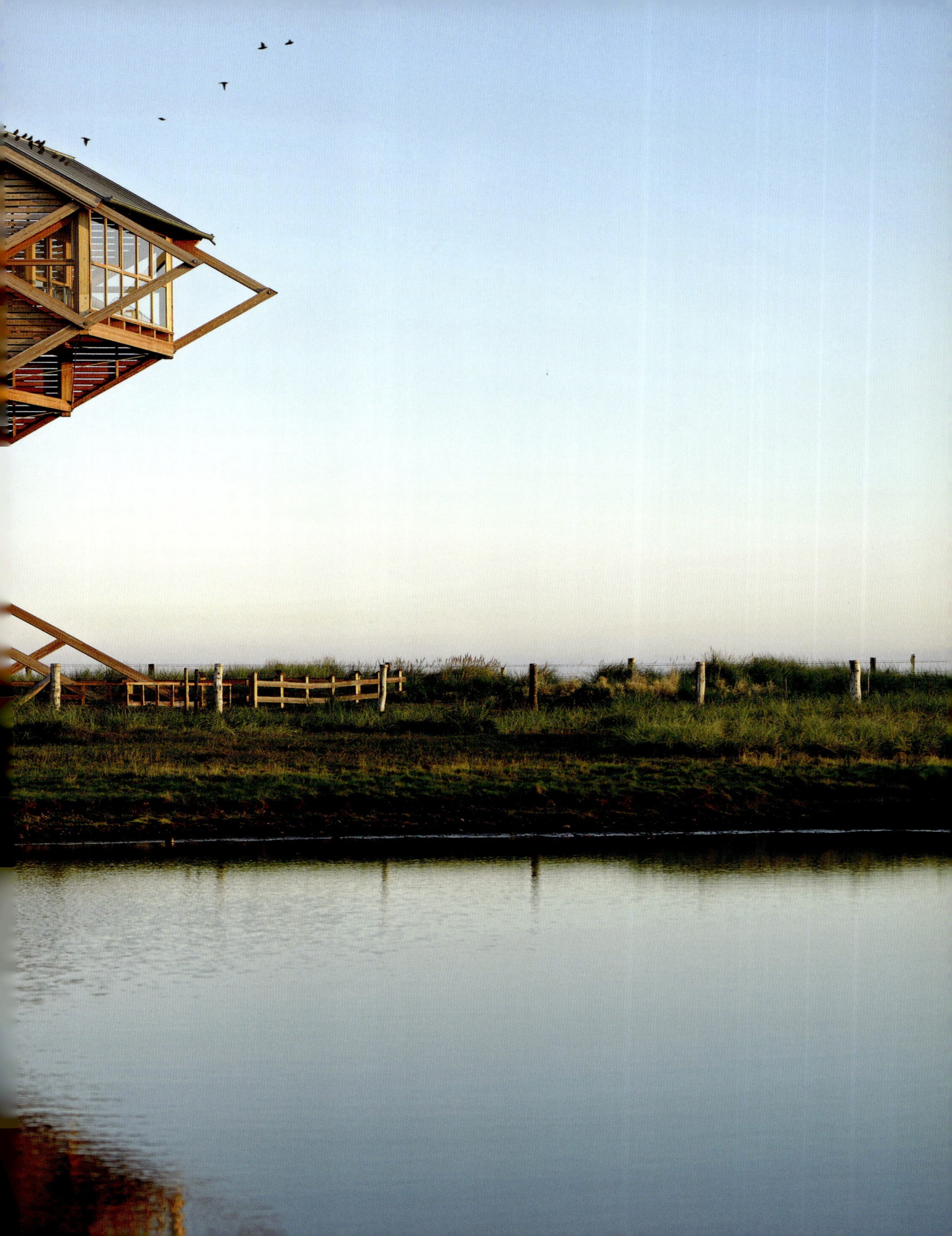

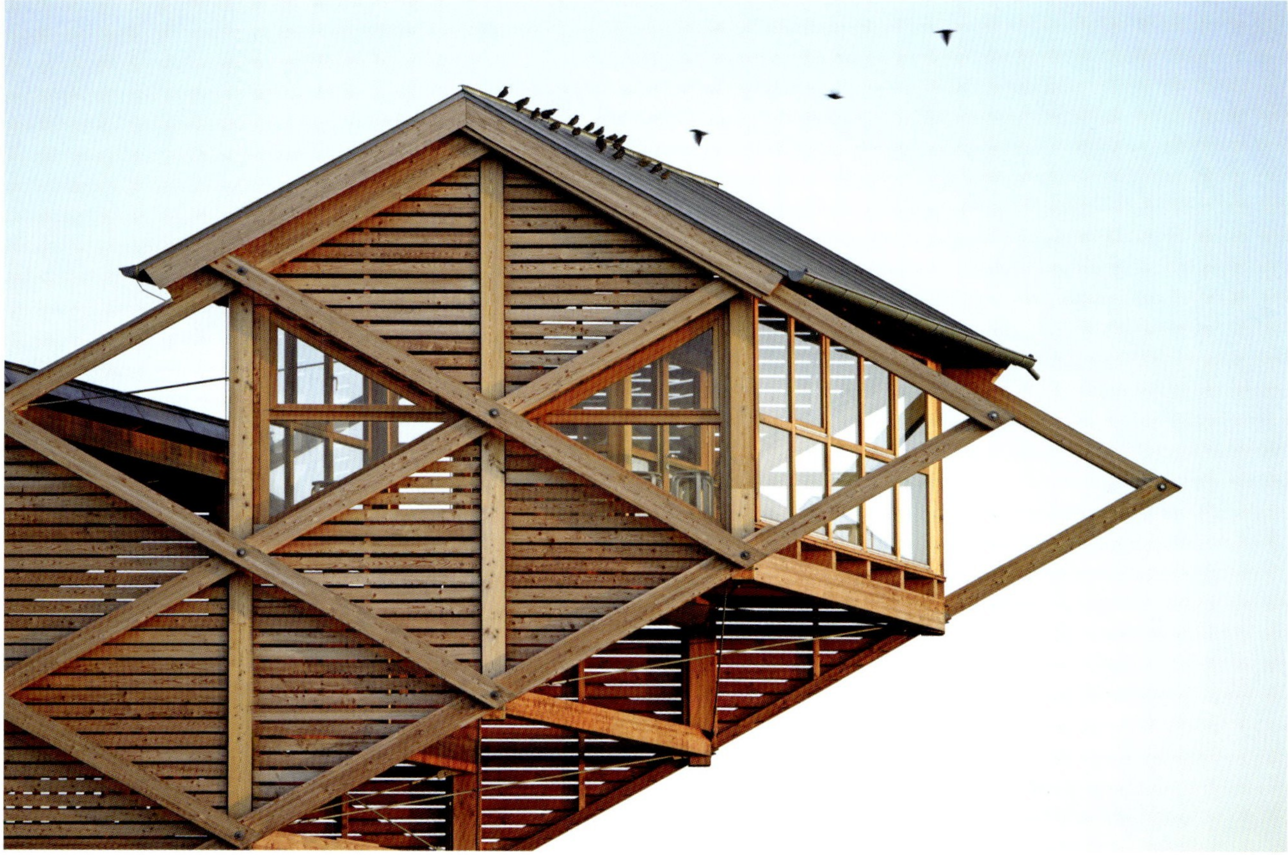

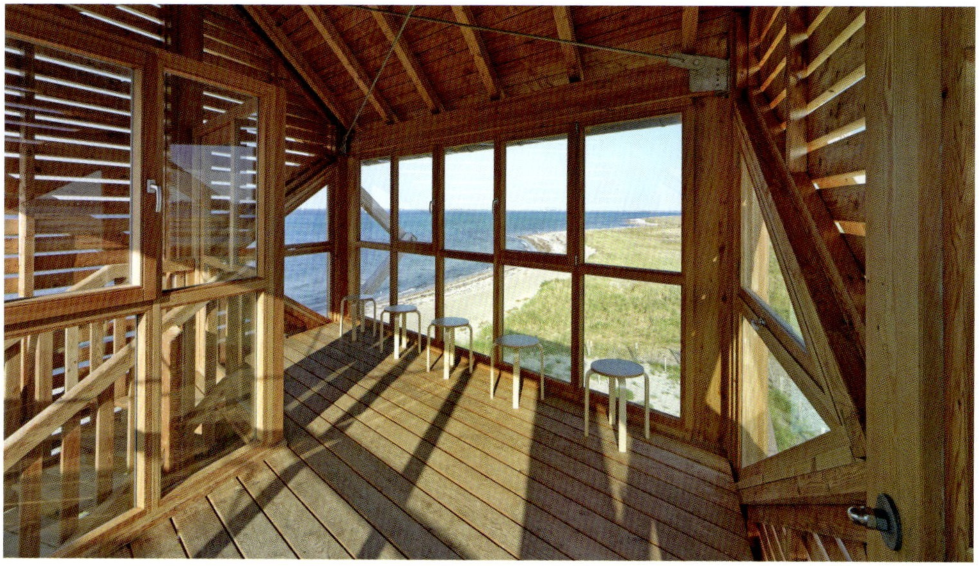

鸟类观察站　海利根港的格拉斯瓦尔德

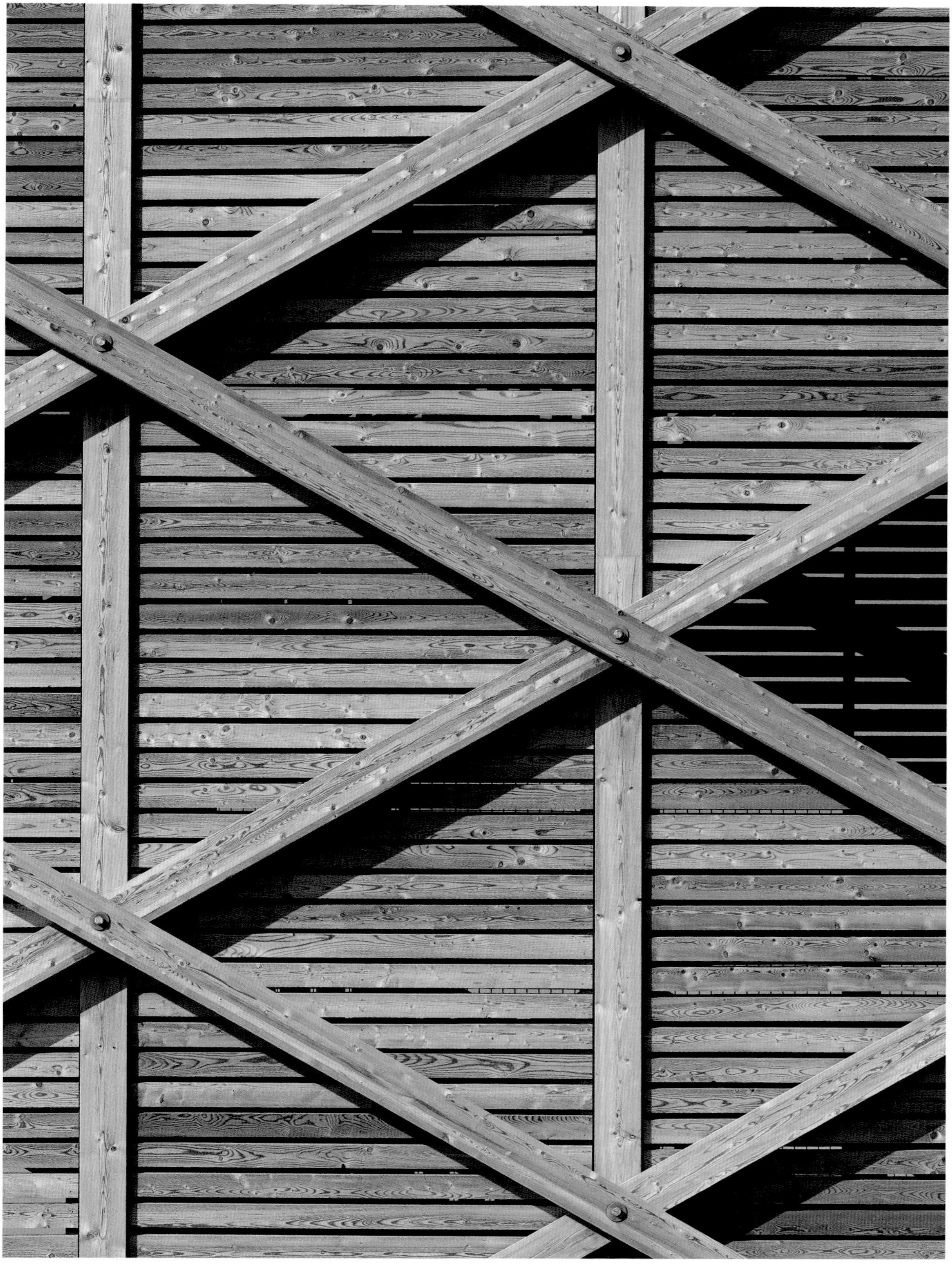

Bird-Watching Tower Graswarder in Heiligenhafen

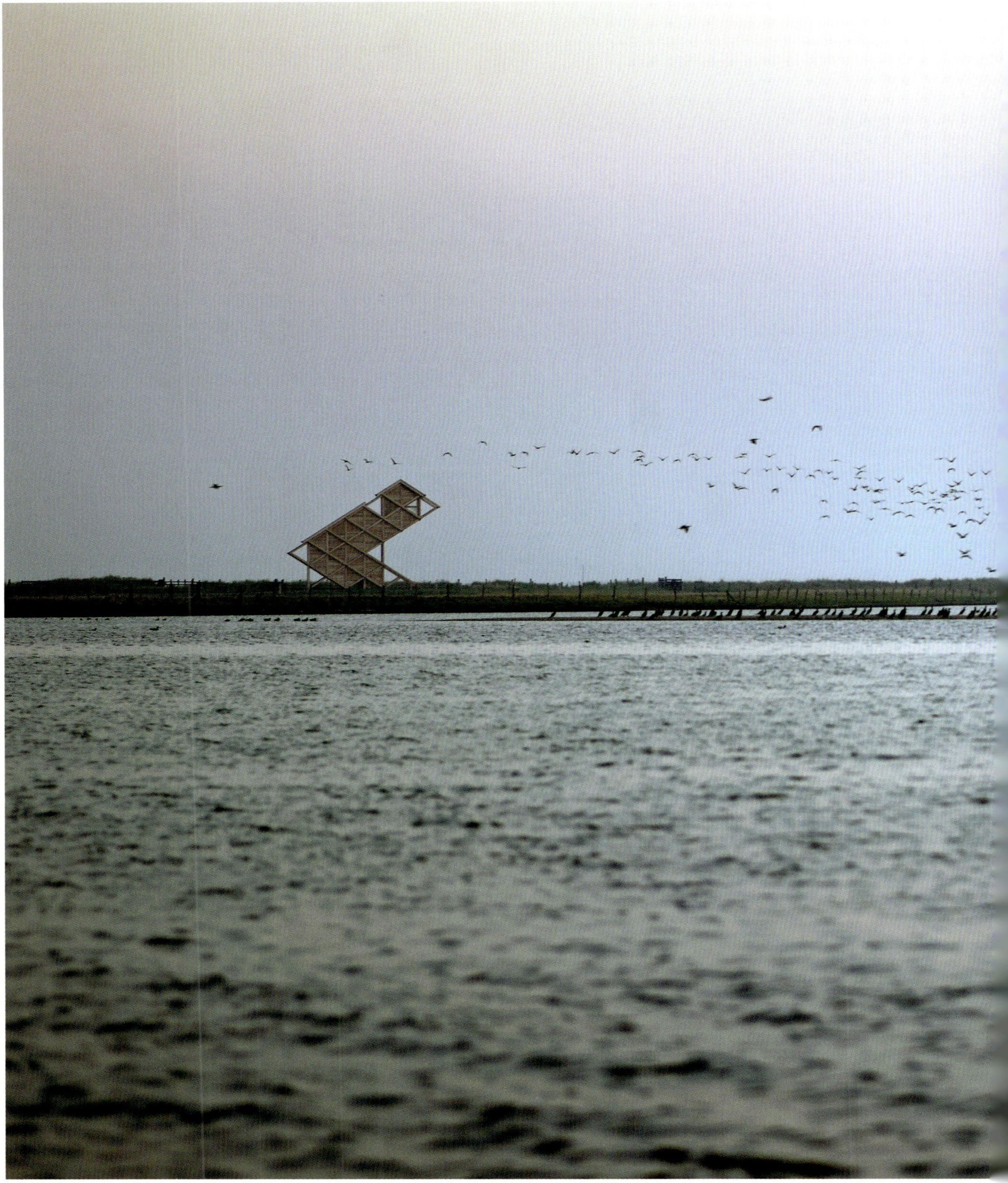

鸟类观察站　海利根港的格拉斯瓦尔德

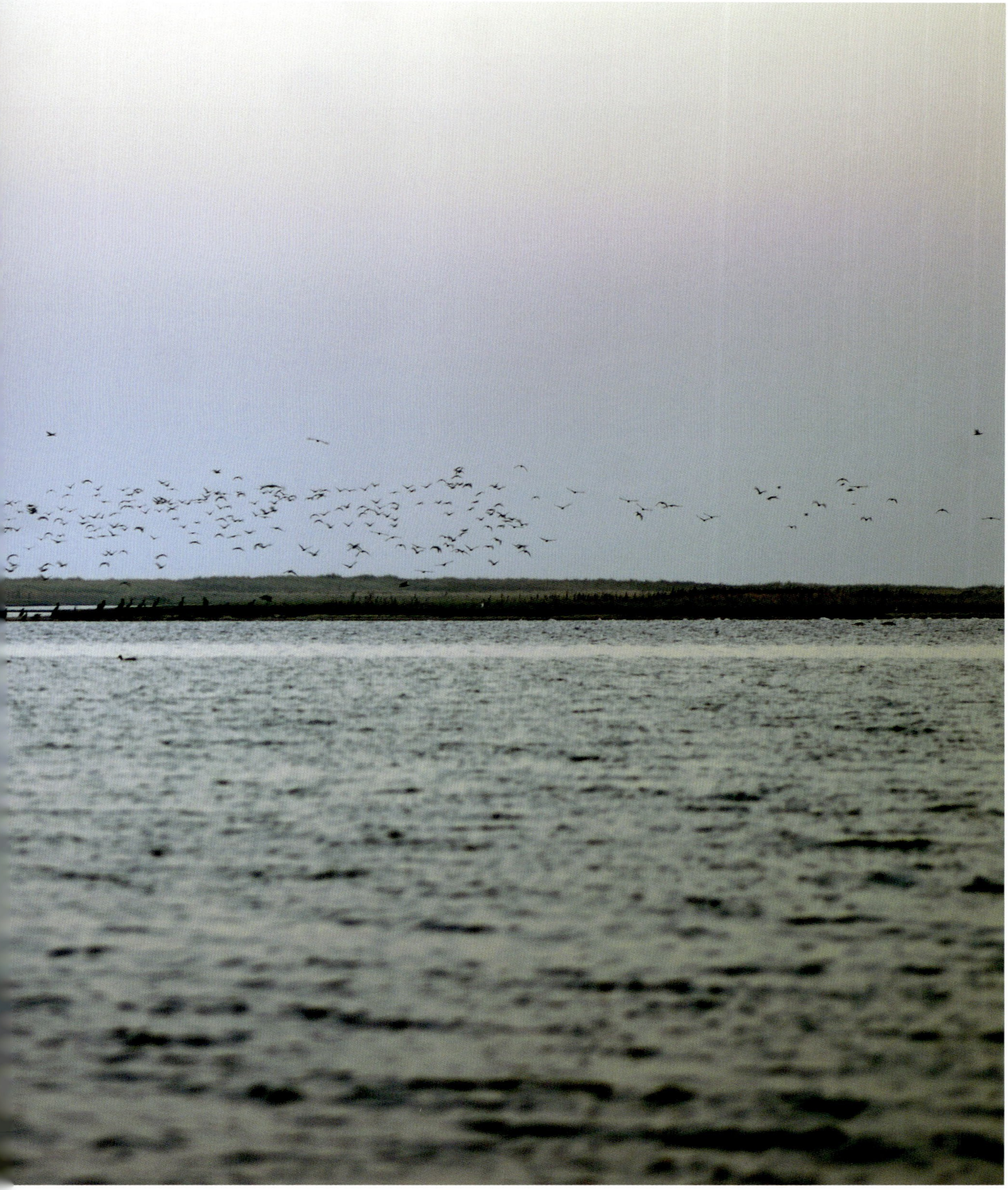

Bird-Watching Tower Graswarder in Heiligenhafen

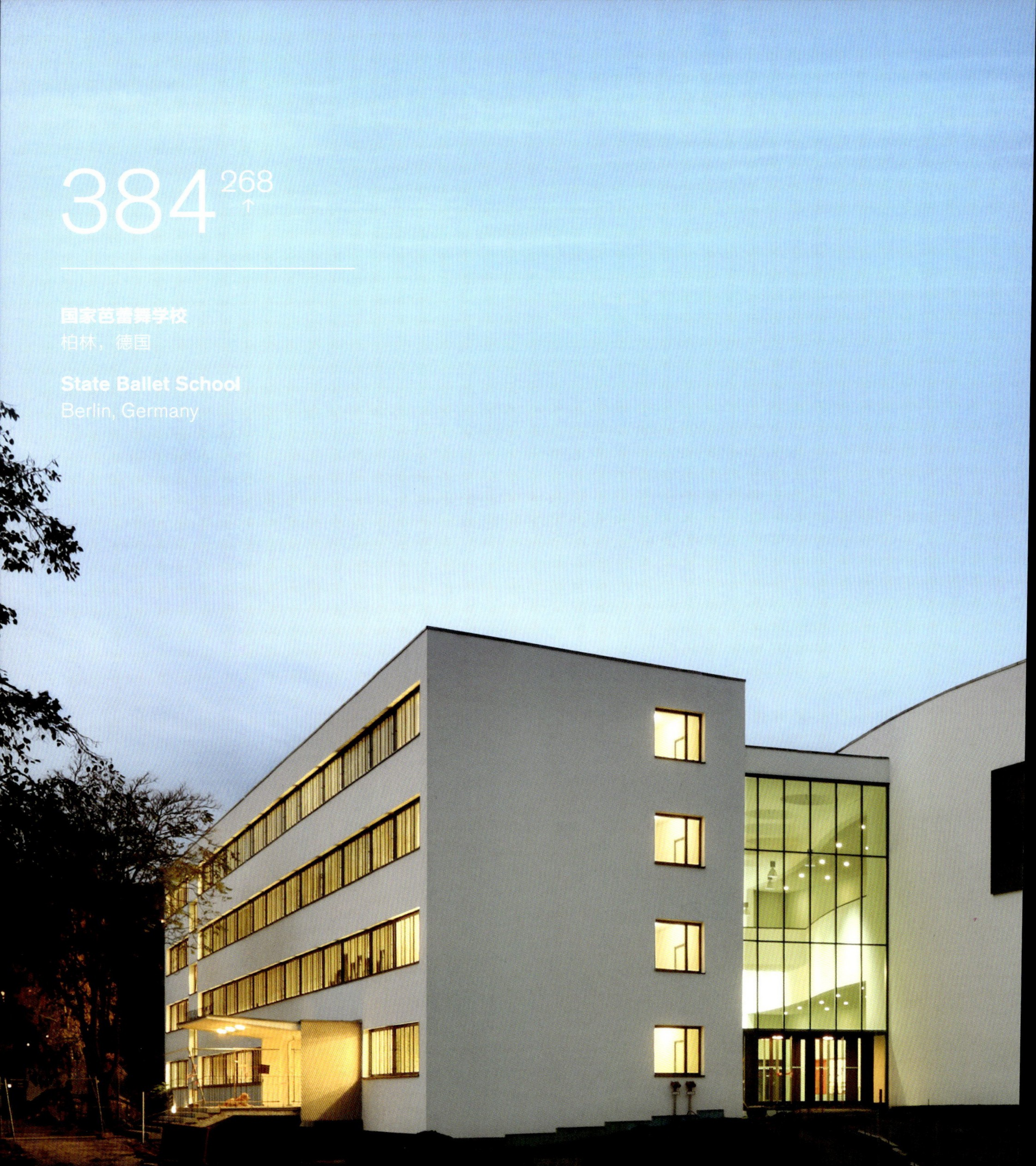

384 ²⁶⁸

国家芭蕾舞学校
柏林，德国

State Ballet School
Berlin, Germany

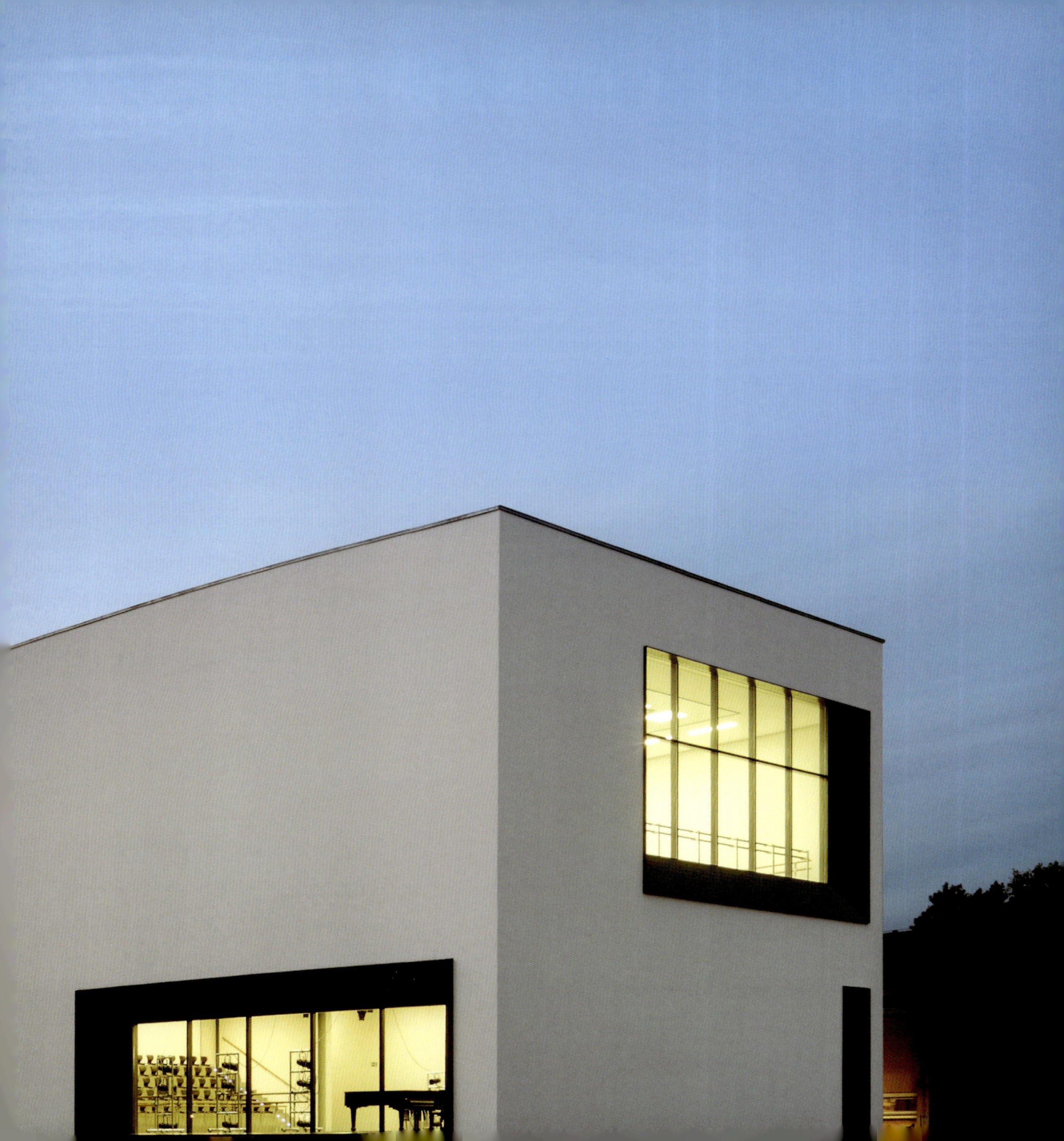

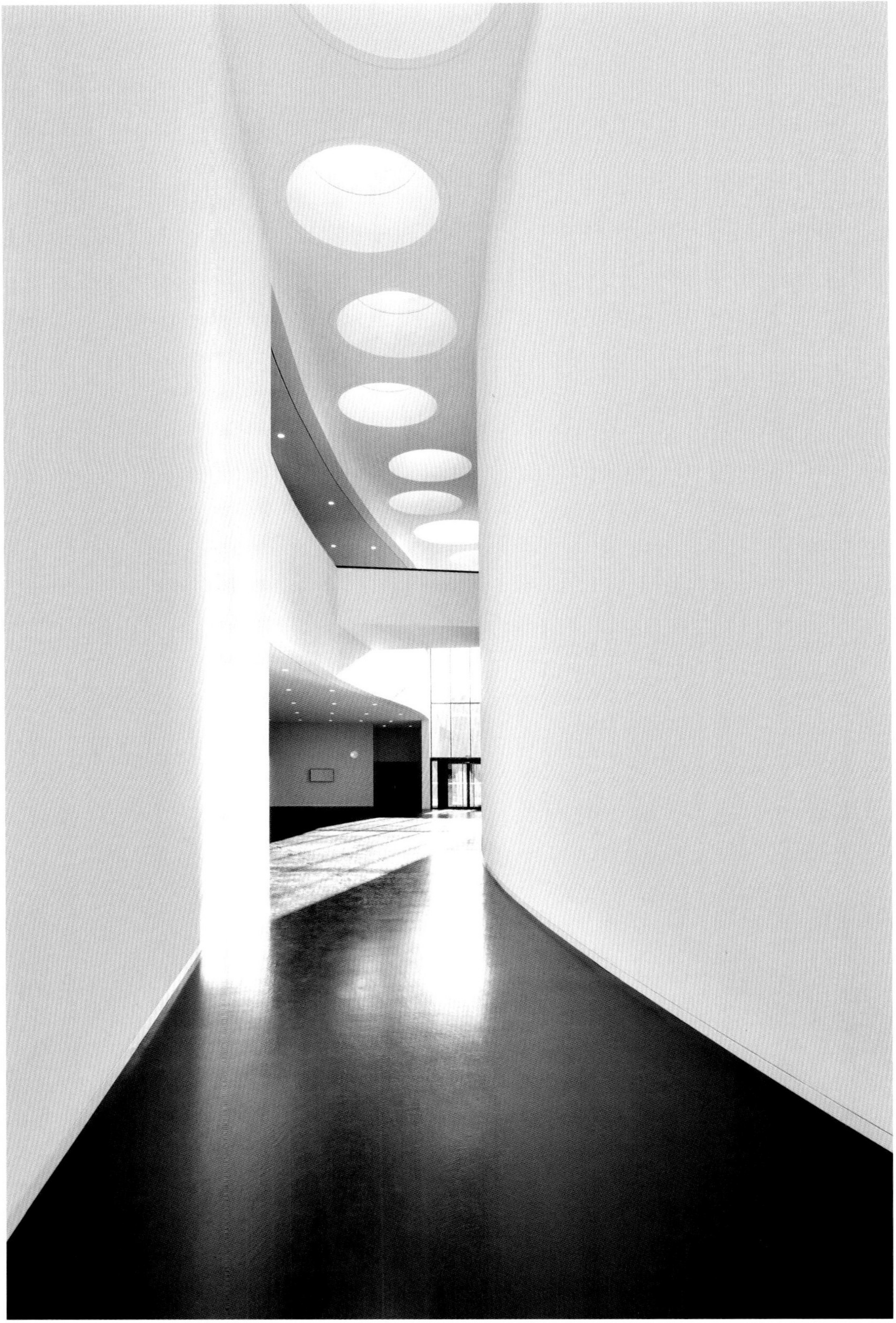

国家芭蕾舞学校　柏林

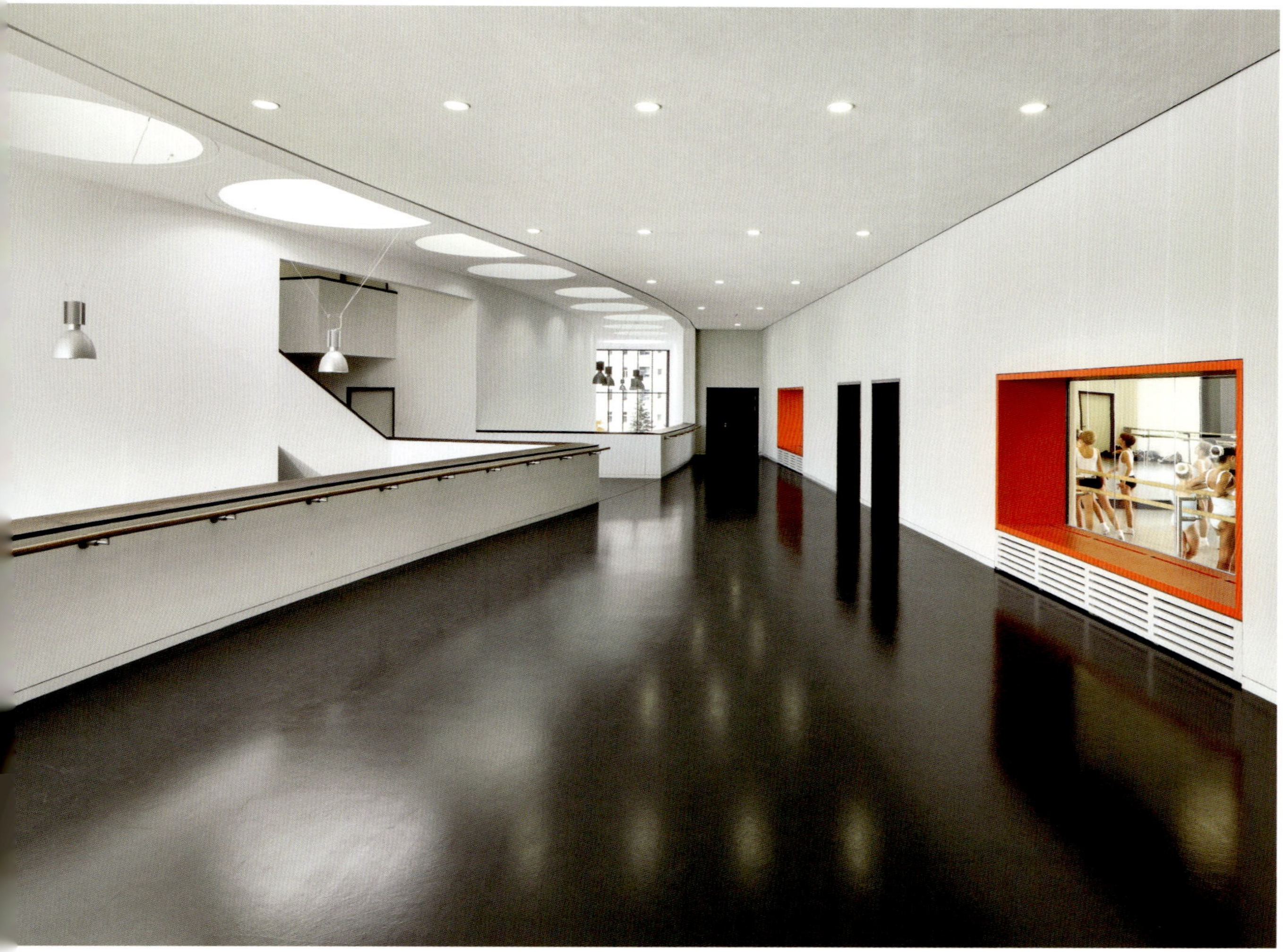

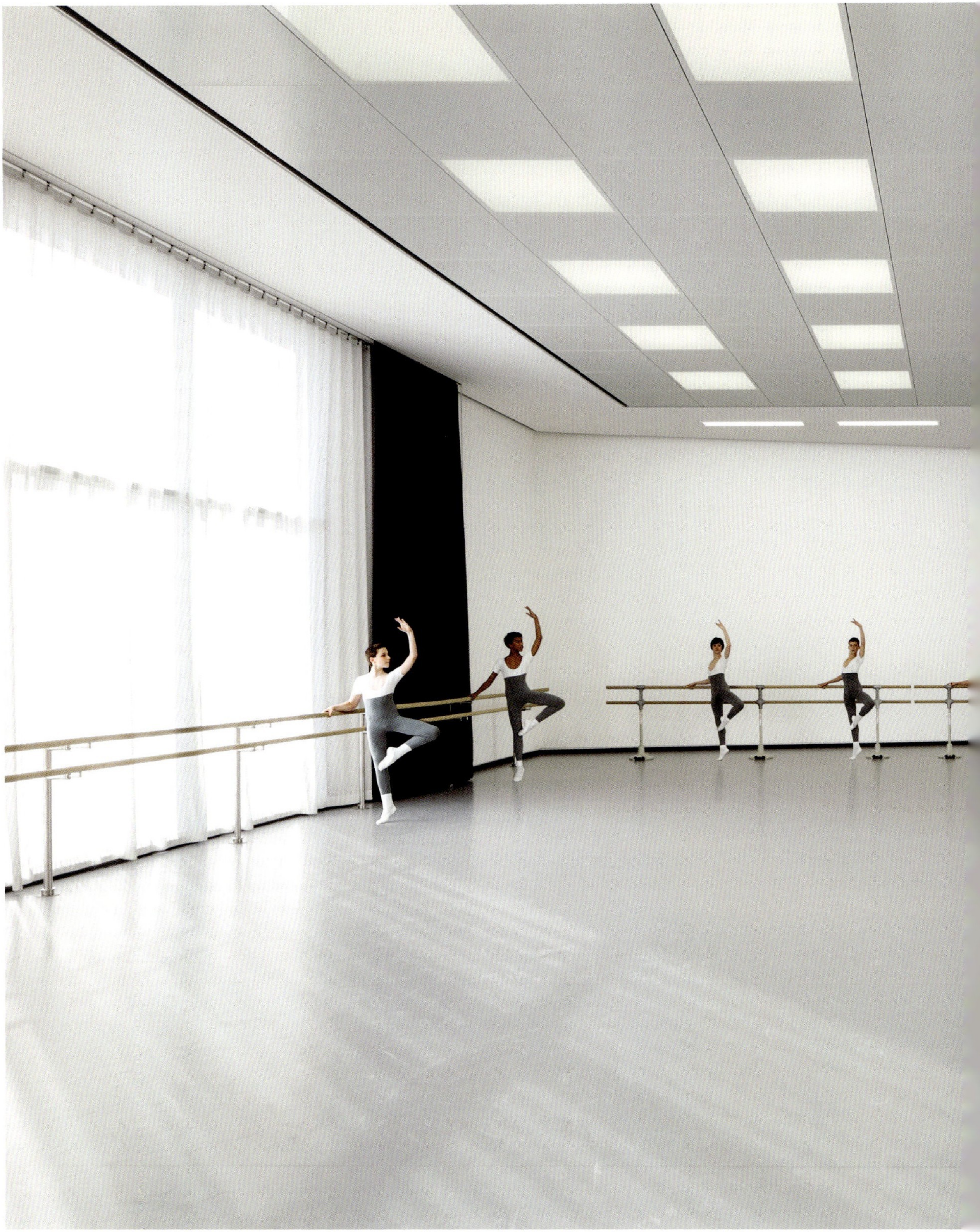

国家芭蕾舞学校　柏林

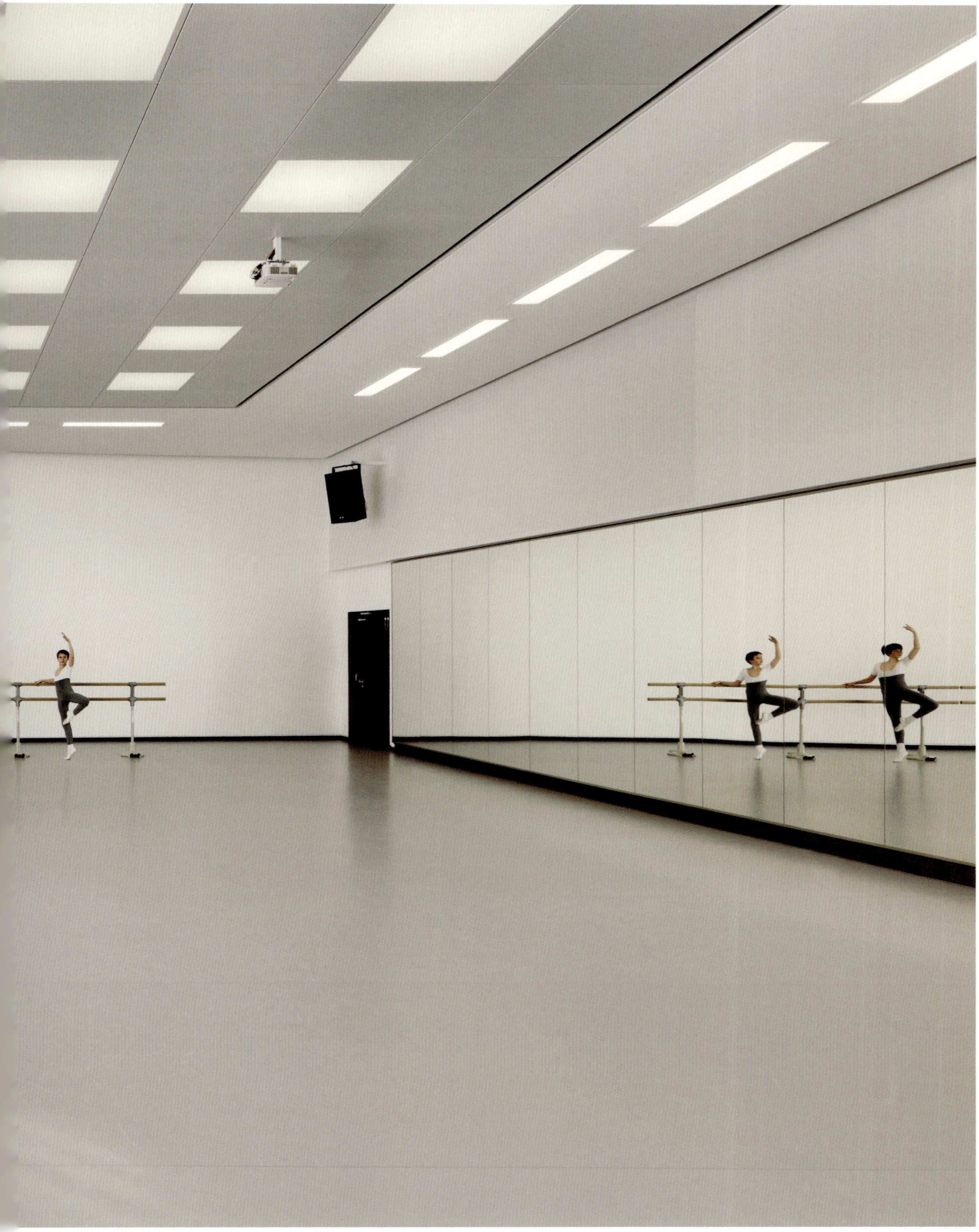

State Ballet School Berlin

390 ²⁶⁹ ↑

德意志银行双塔
法兰克福，德国
Deutsche Bank Twin Towers
Frankfurt, Germany

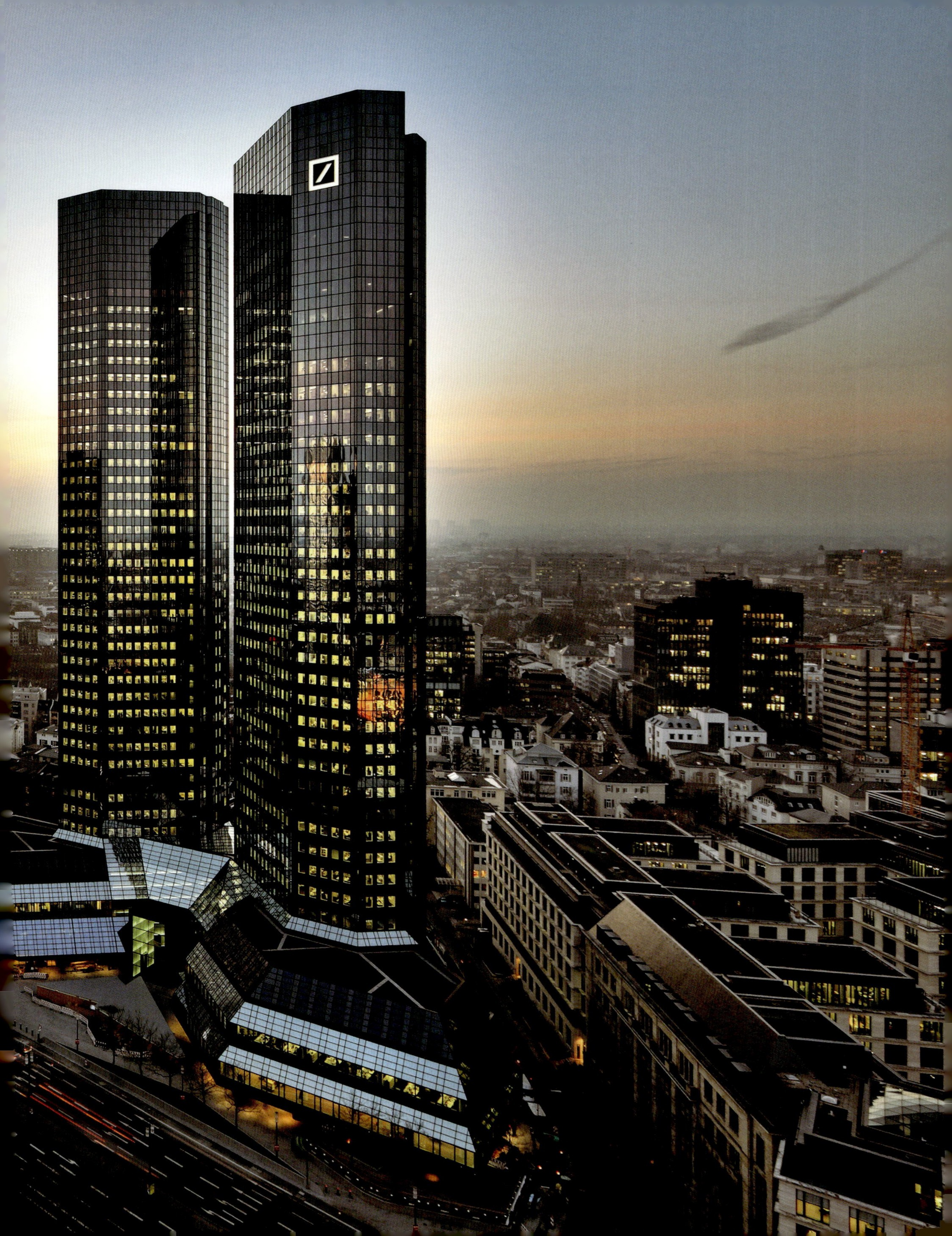

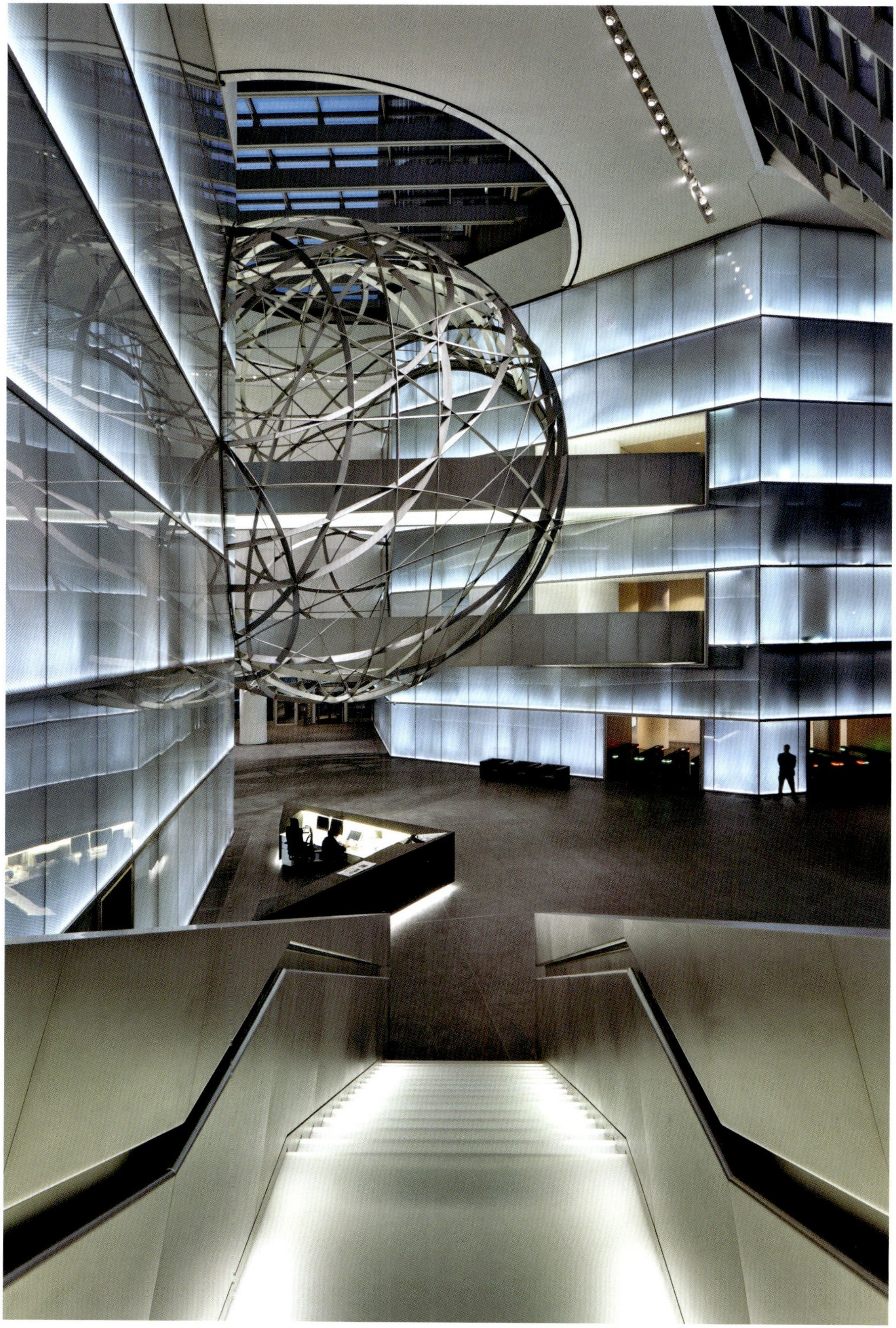

德意志银行双塔　法兰克福

Deutsche Bank Twin Towers Frankfurt

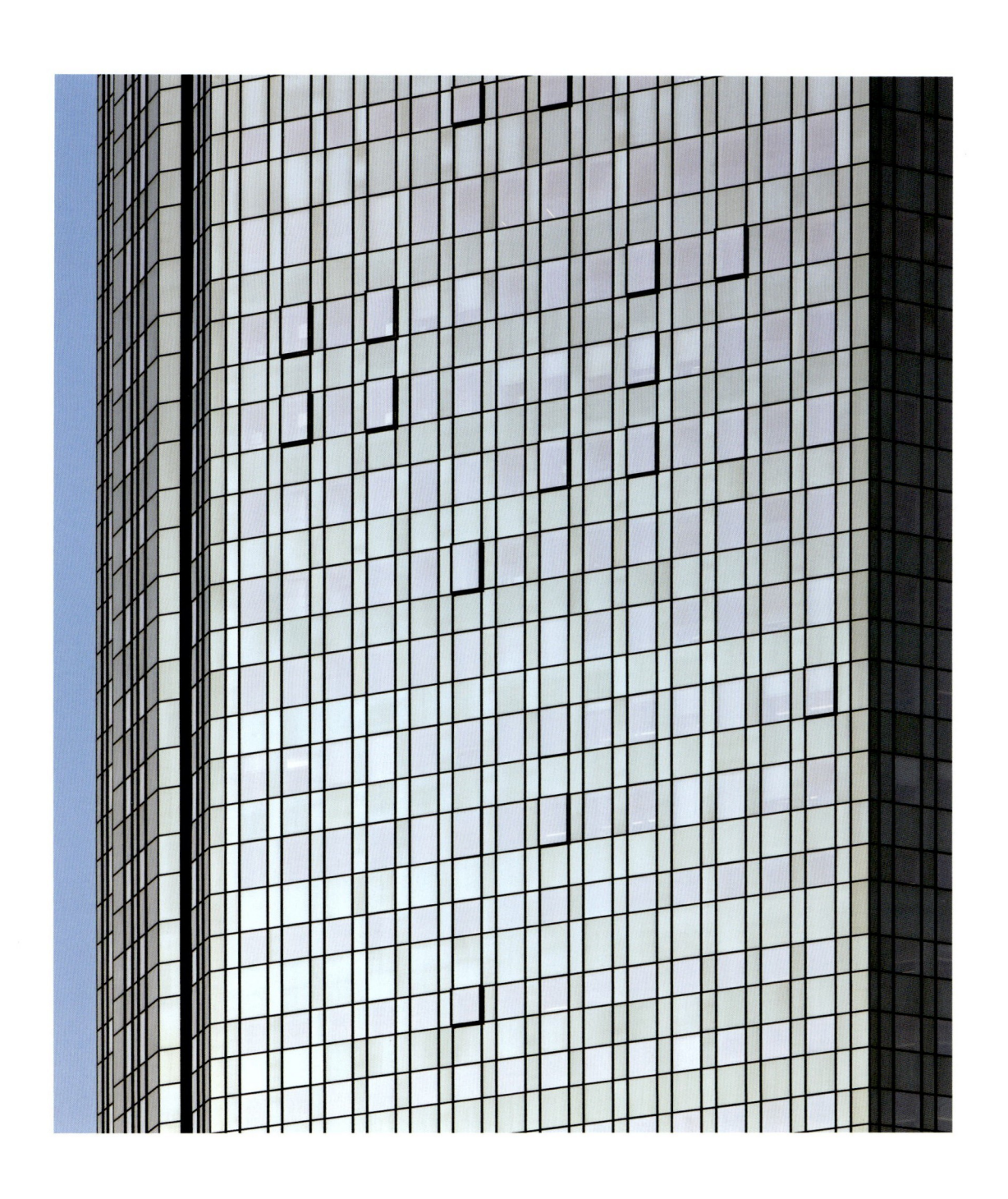

394 ²⁶⁹
↑

国家体育场
华沙，波兰

National Stadium
Warsaw, Poland

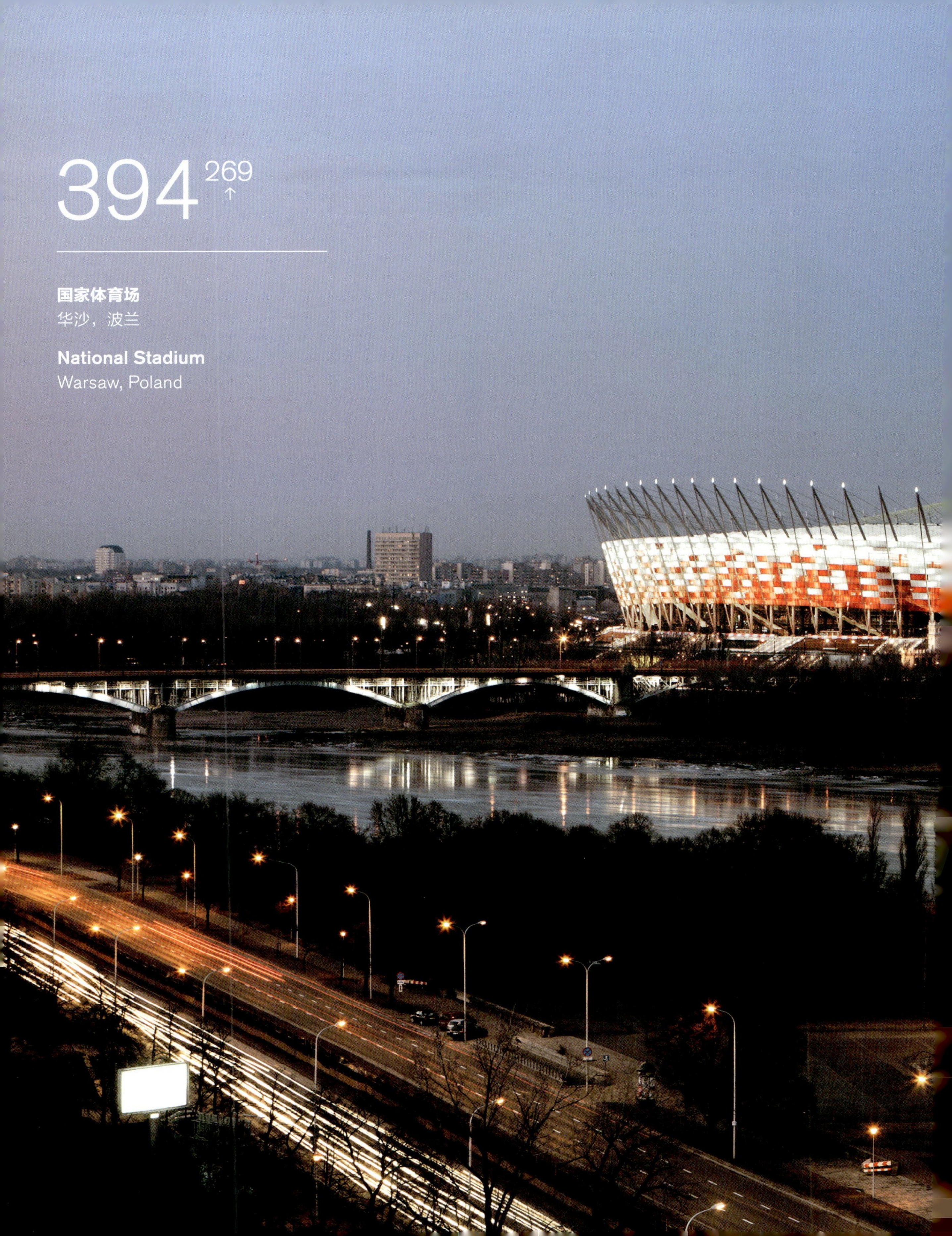

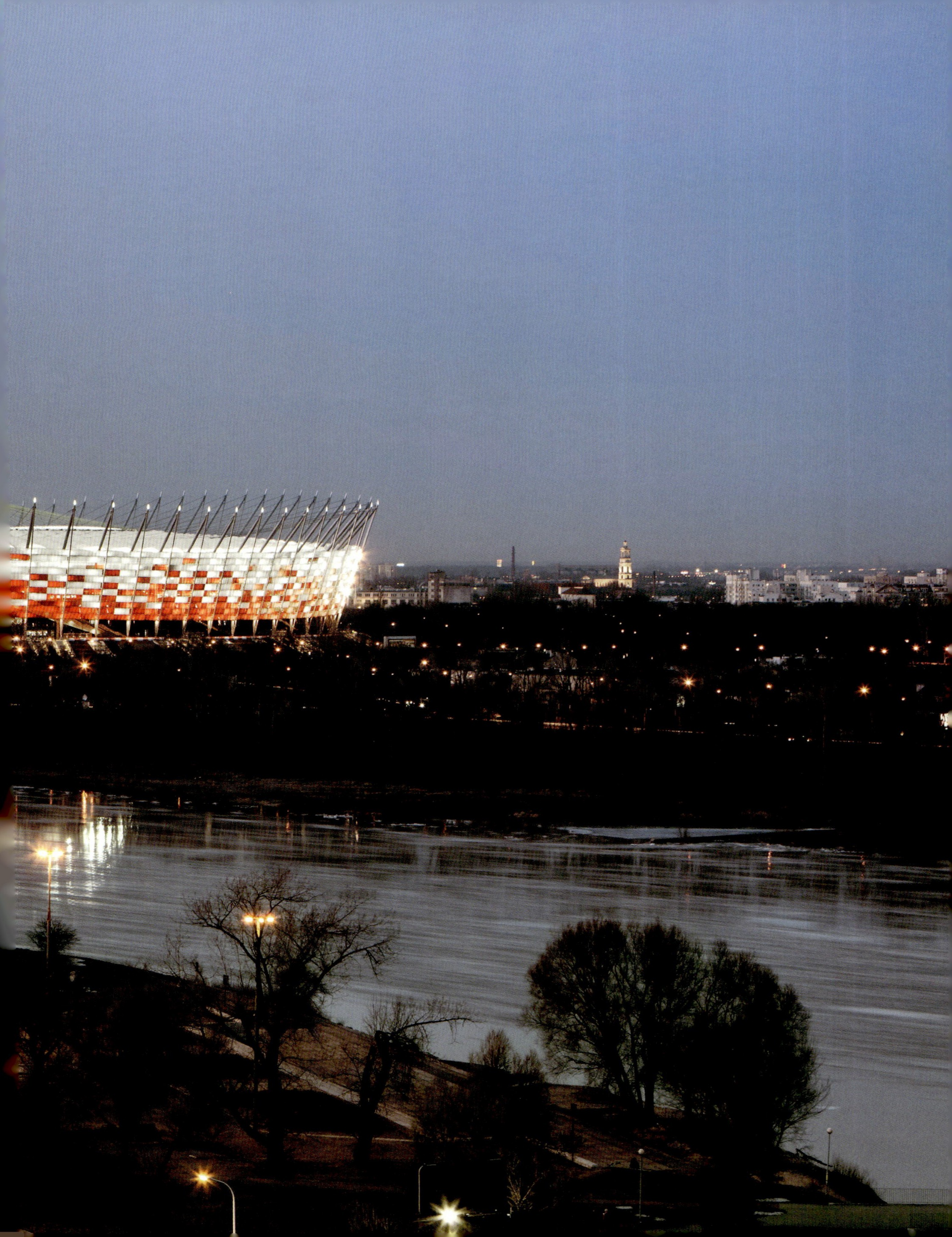

国家体育场　华沙

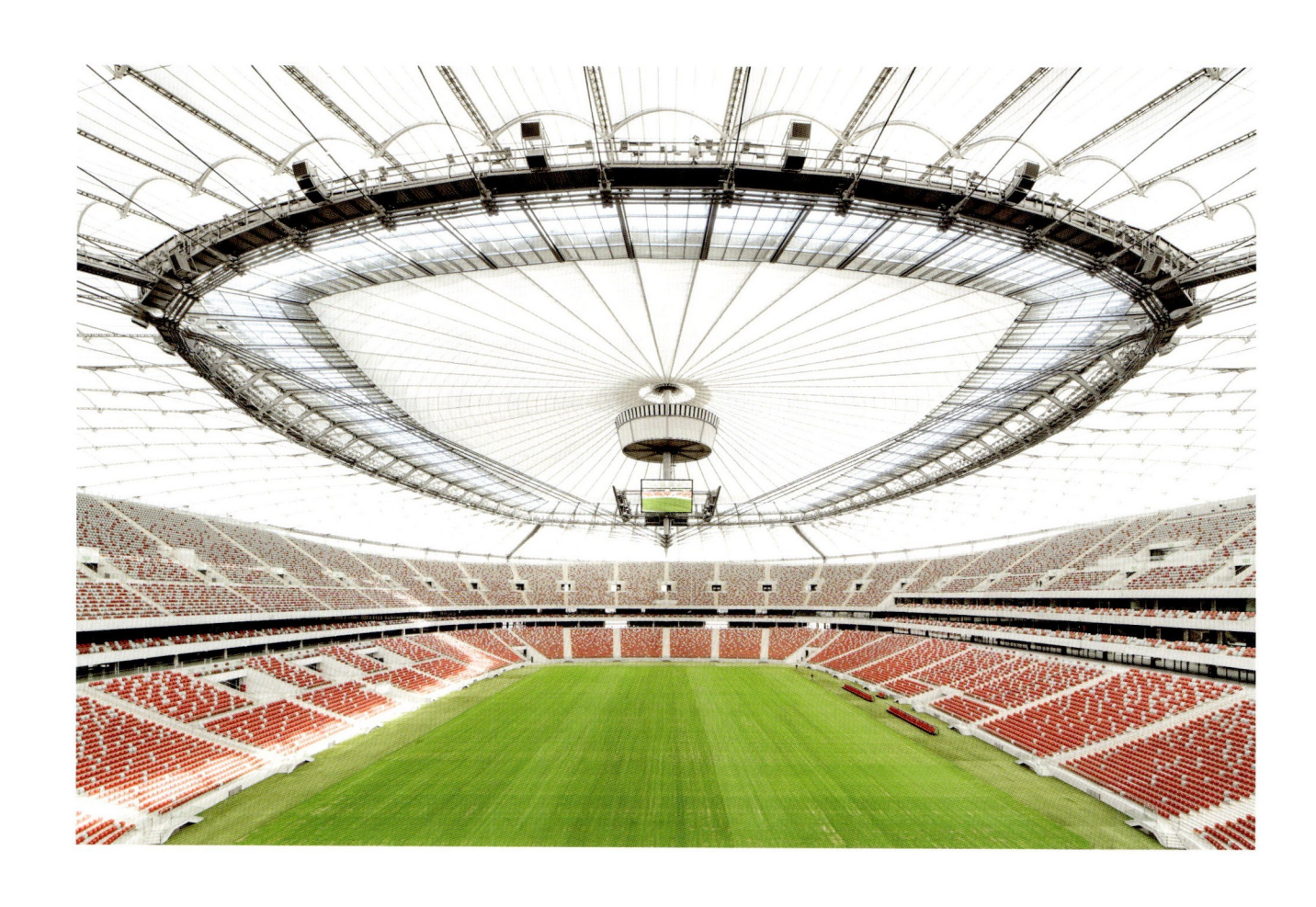

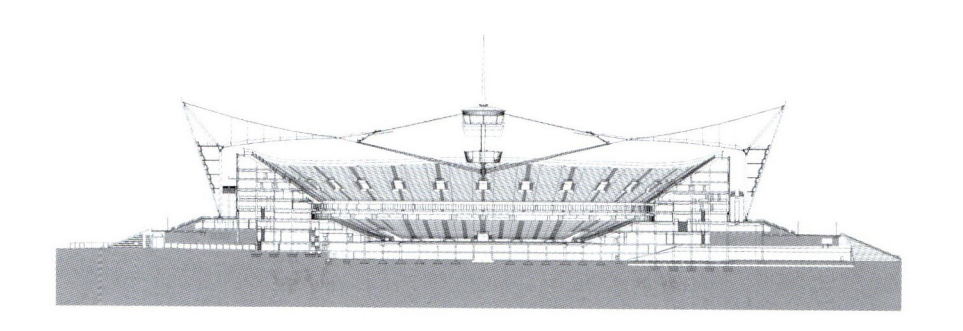

National Stadium Warsaw

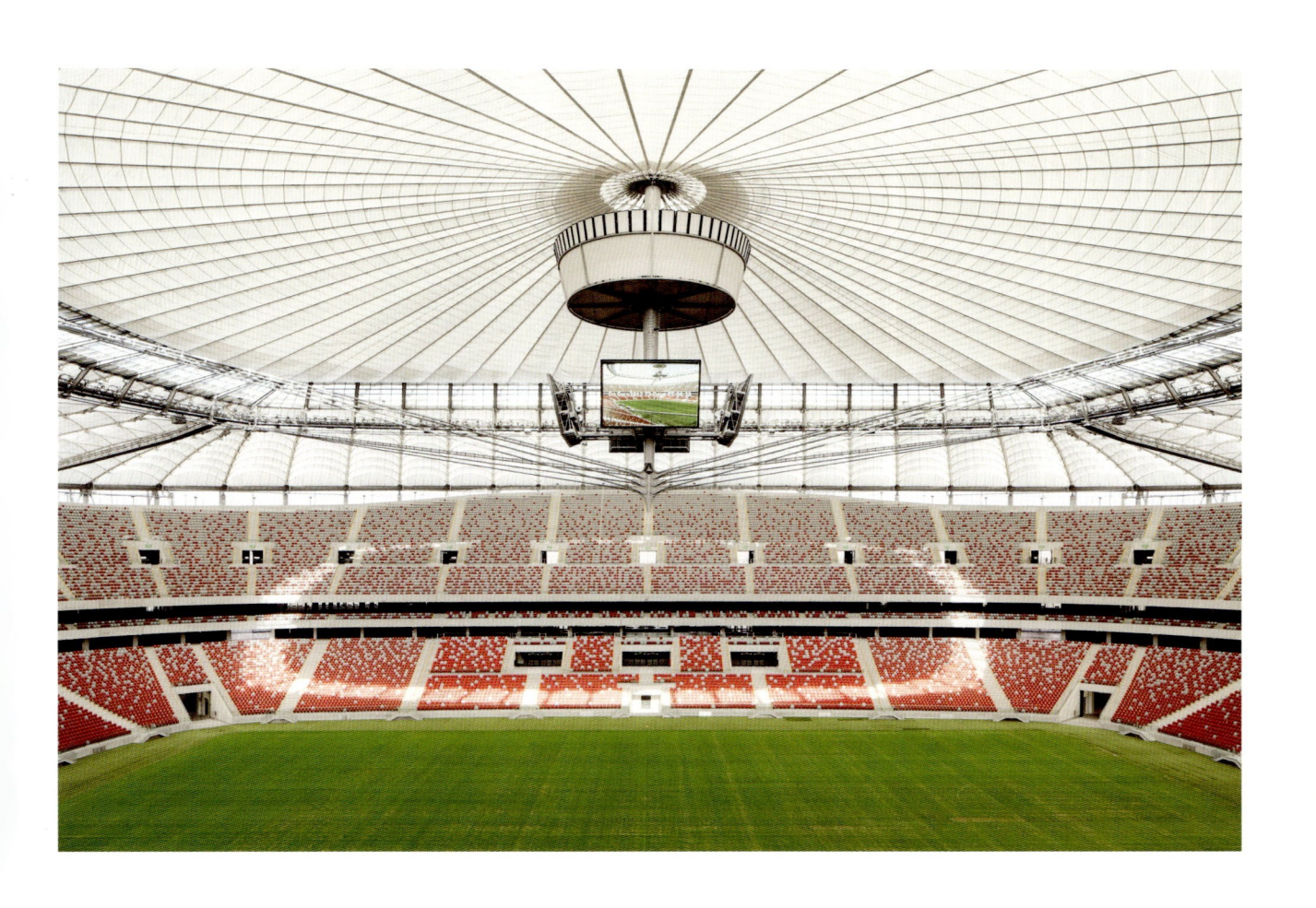

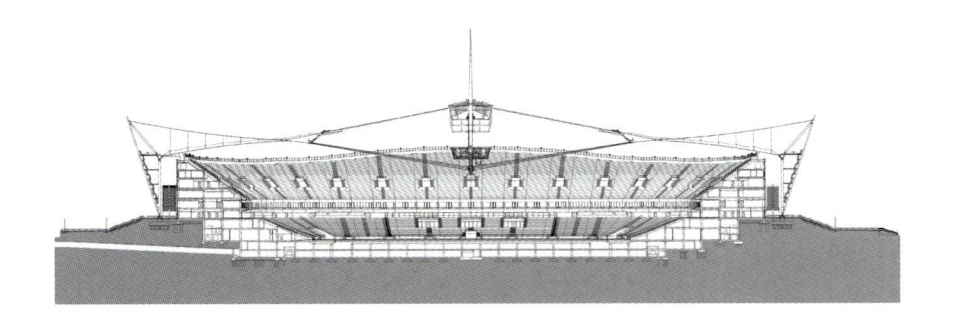

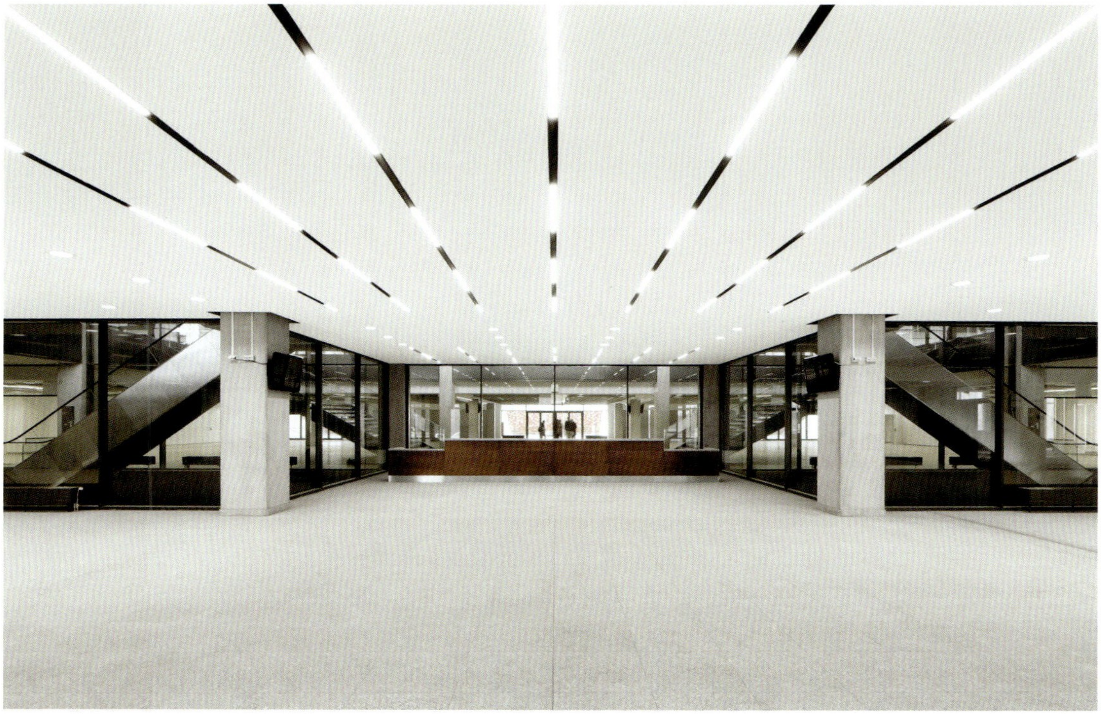

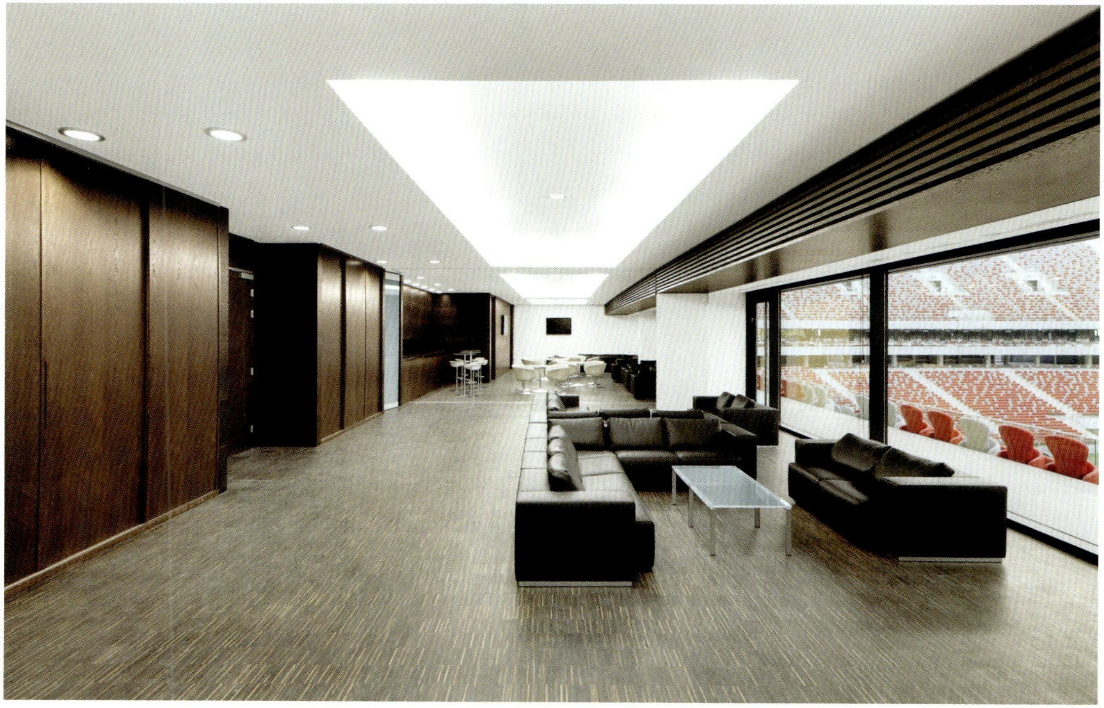

国家体育场 华沙

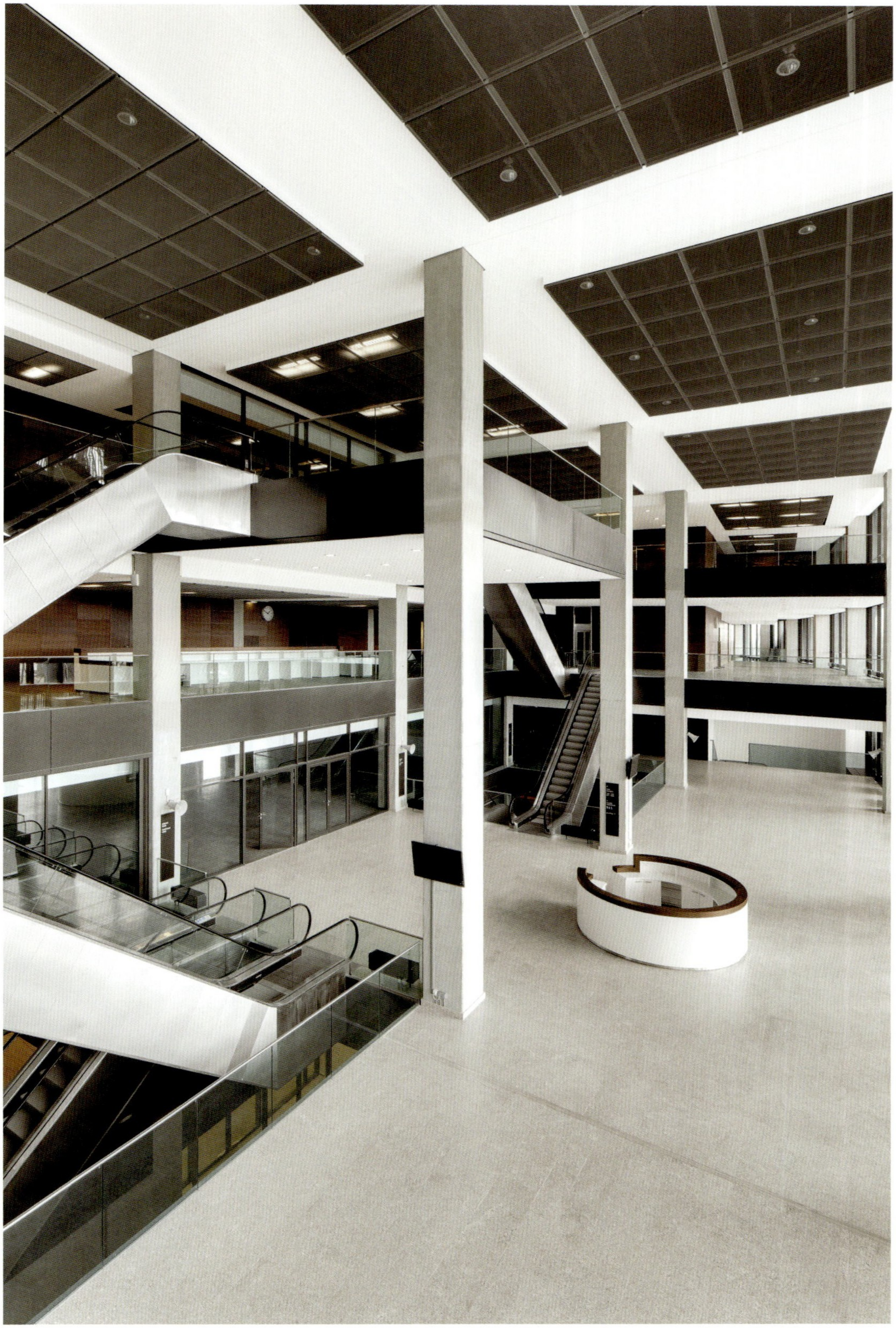

National Stadium Warsaw

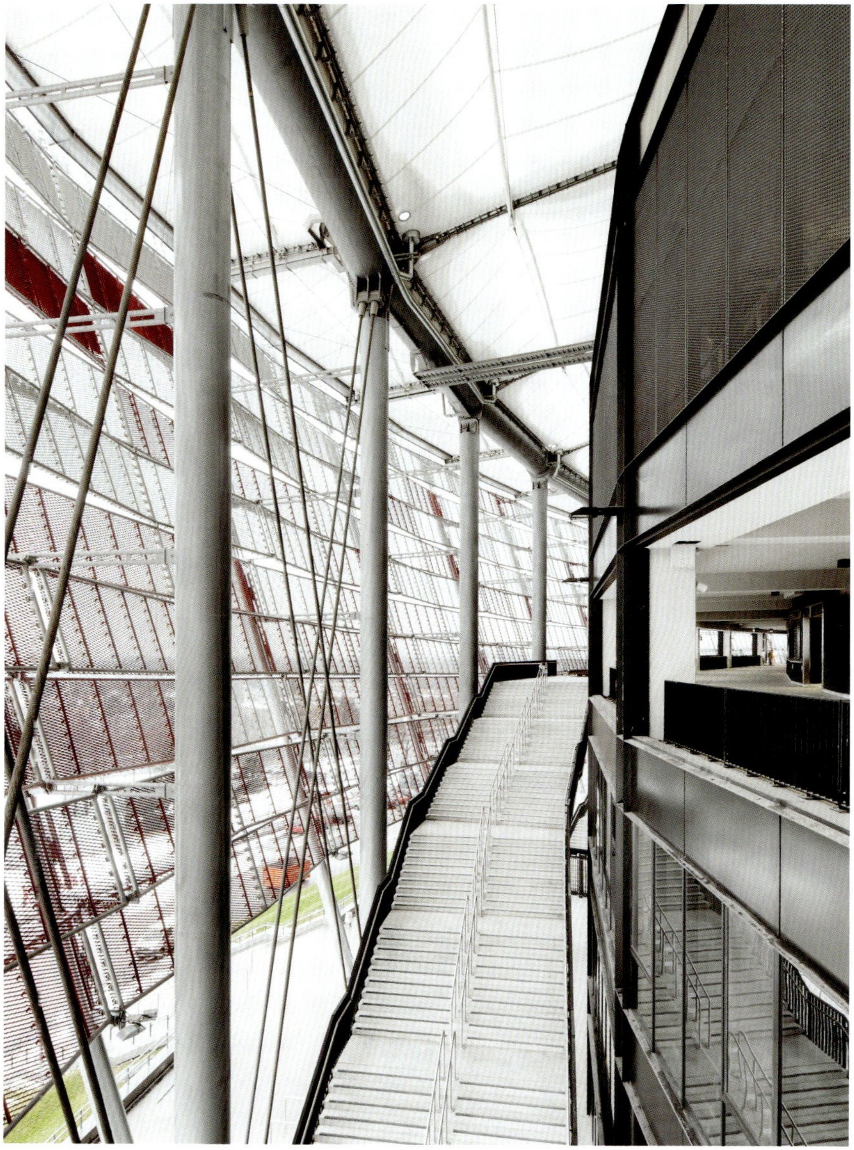

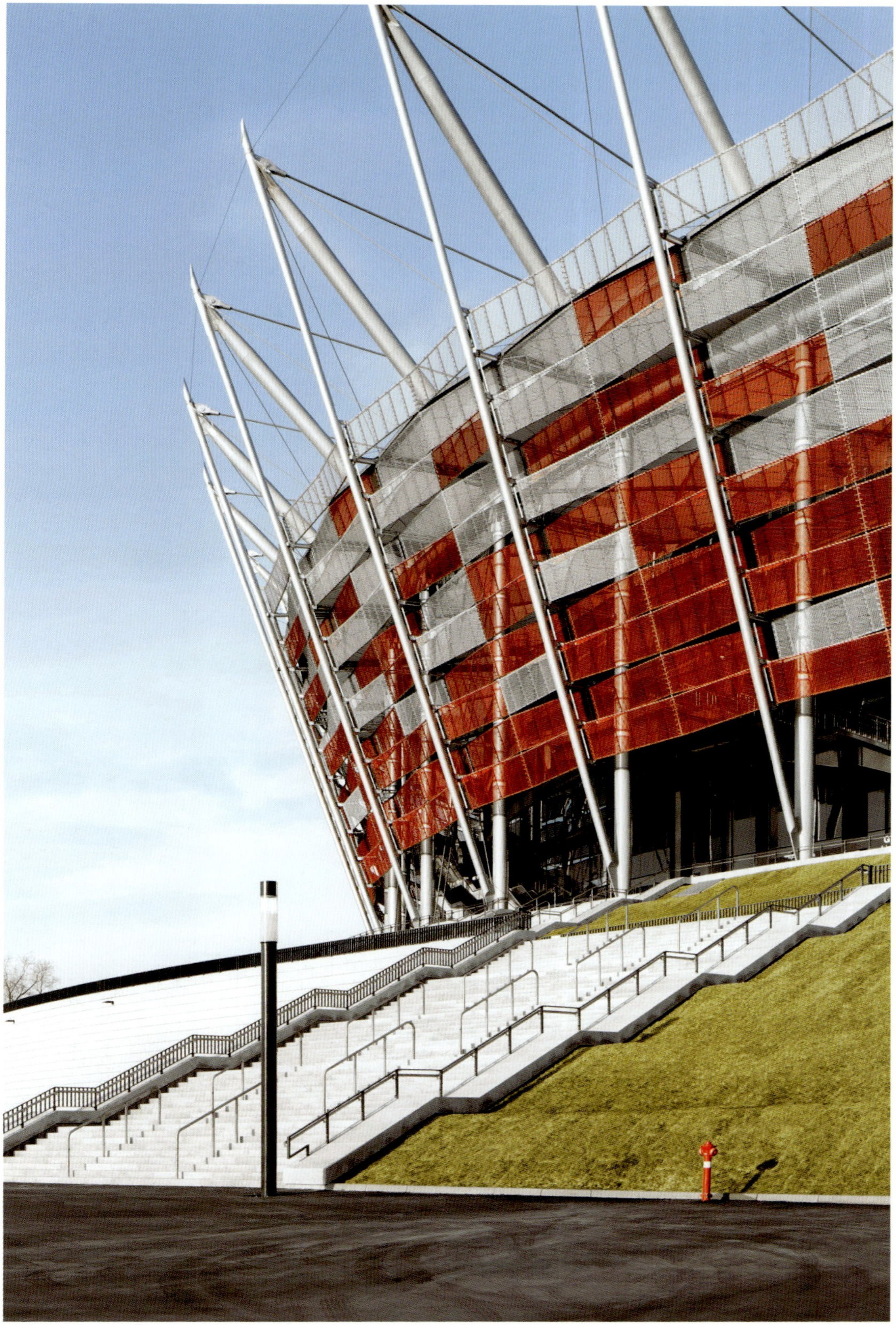

National Stadium Warsaw

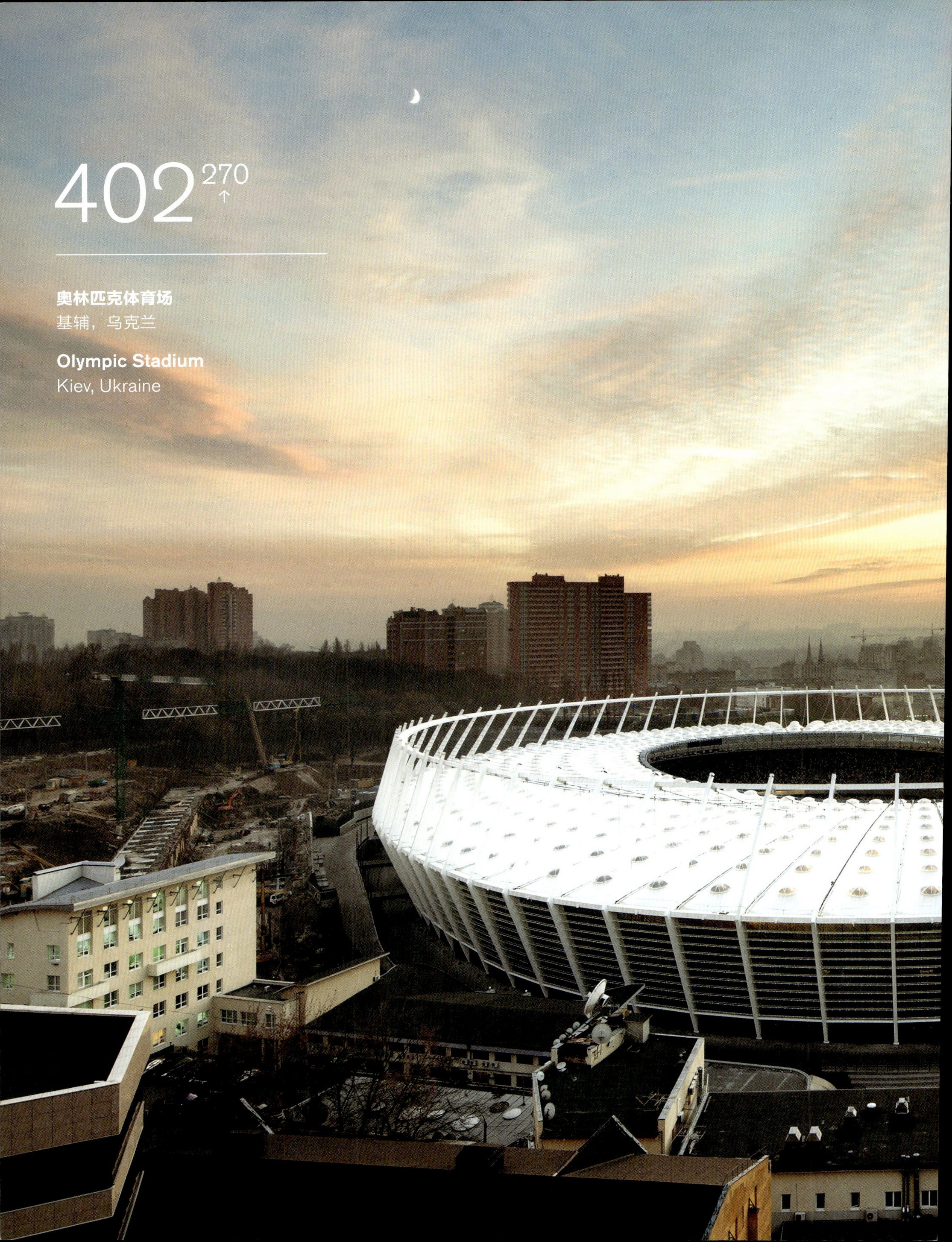

402 ²⁷⁰ ↑

奥林匹克体育场
基辅，乌克兰

Olympic Stadium
Kiev, Ukraine

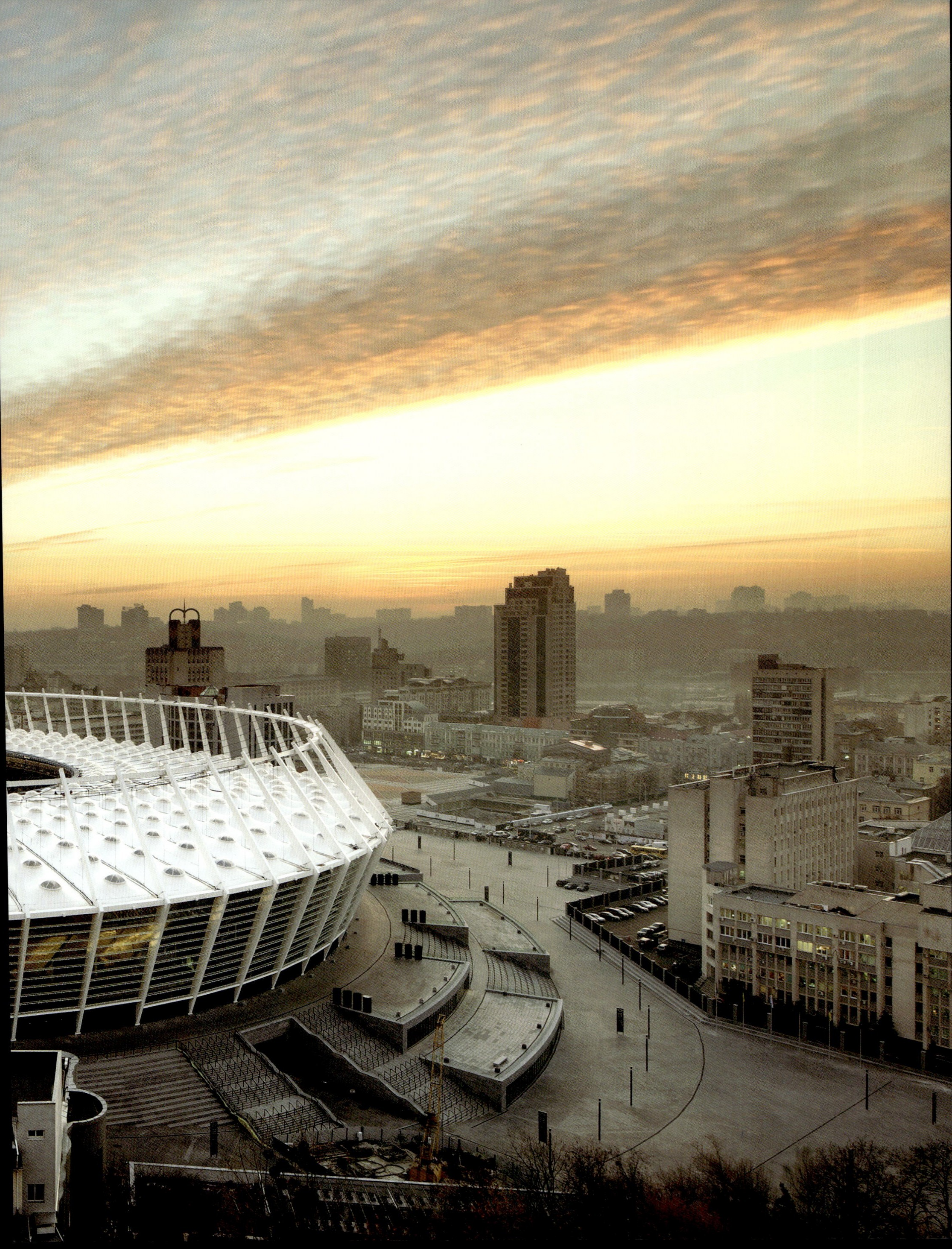

奥林匹克体育场　基辅

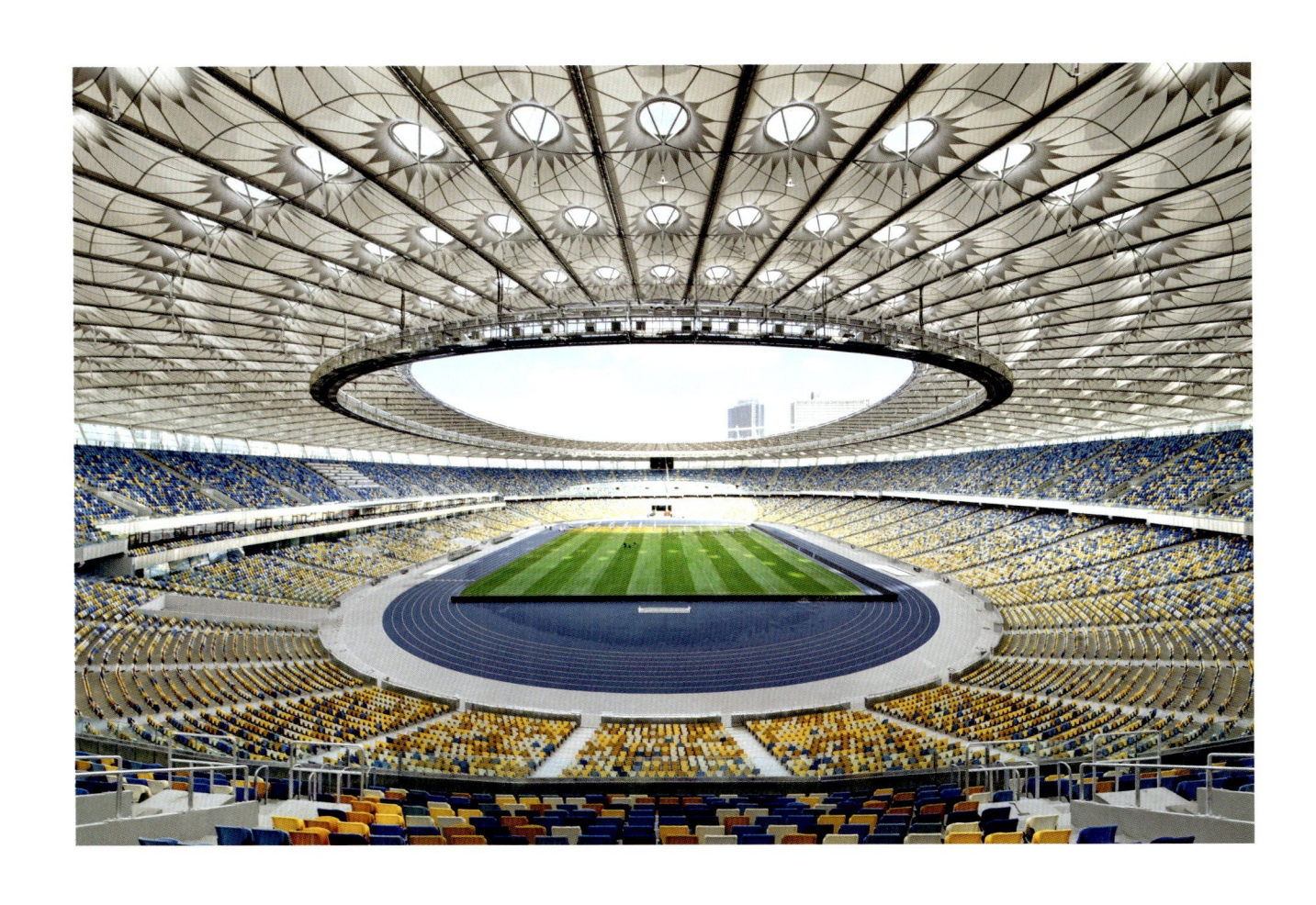

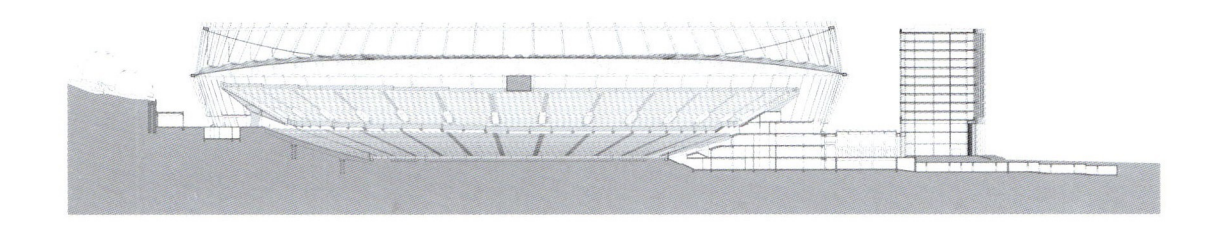

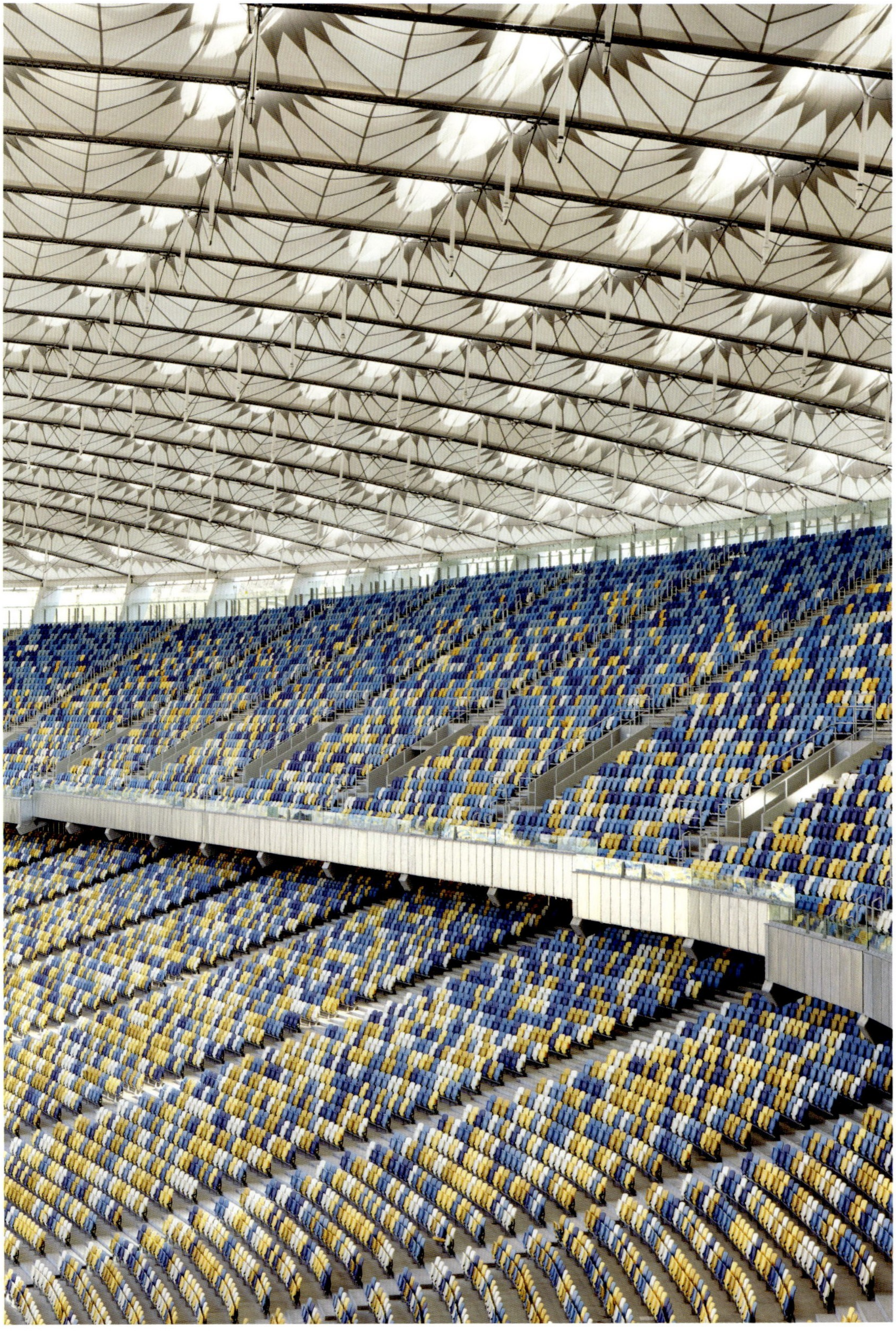

Olympic Stadium Kiev

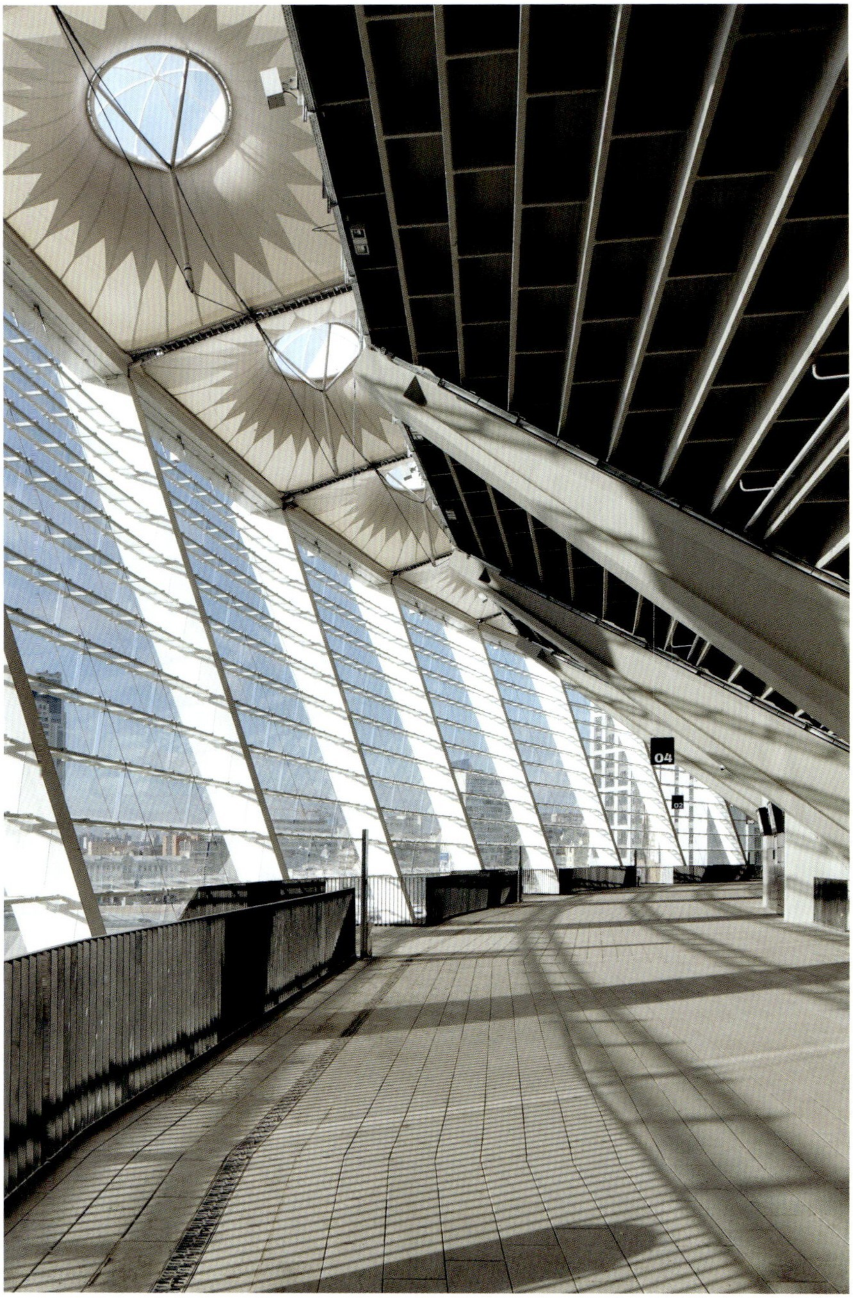

奥林匹克体育场　基辅

Olympic Stadium Kiev

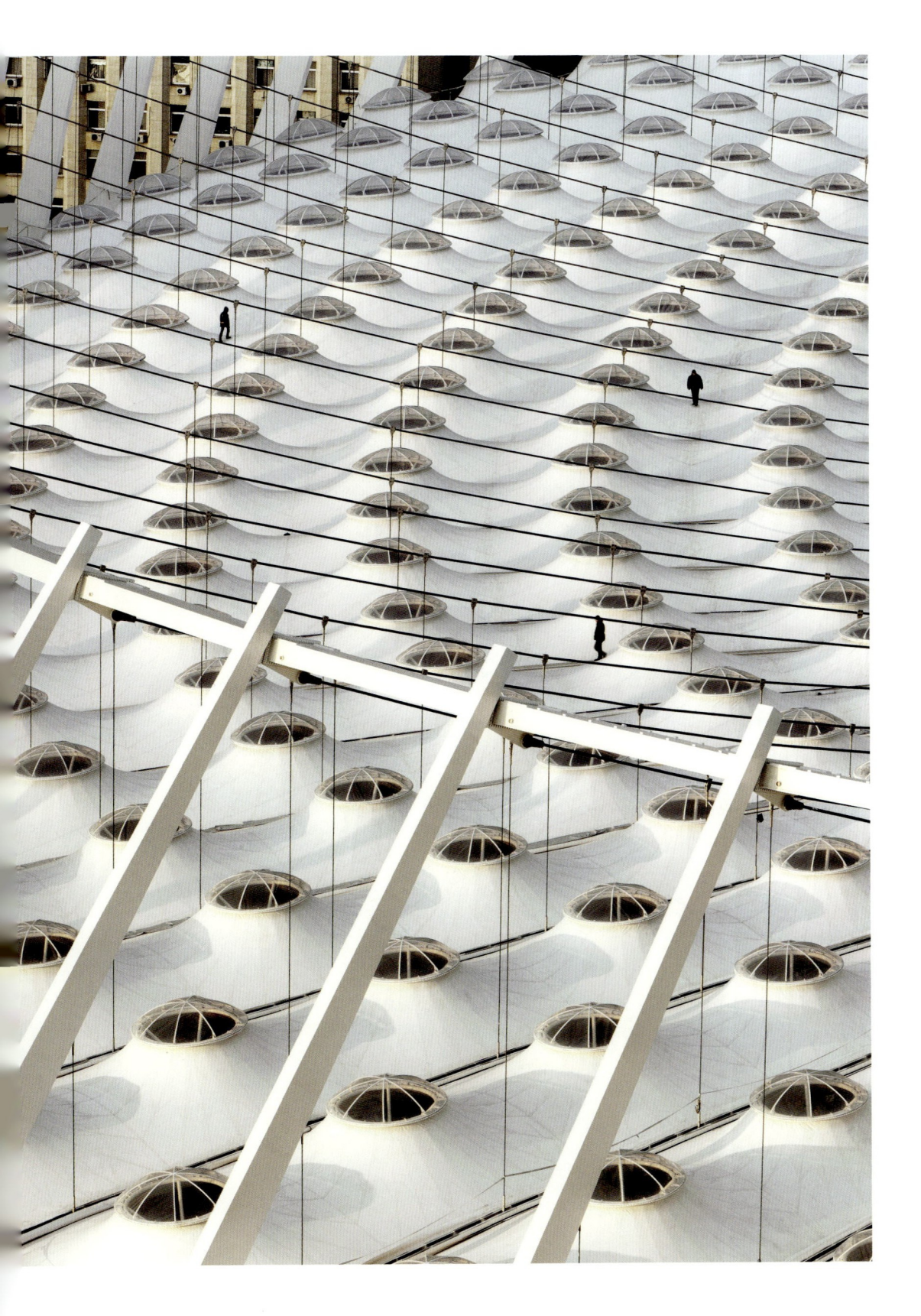

408 270 ↑

德累斯顿文化宫修缮与重建
德累斯顿，德国

**Dresden Kulturpalast,
Renovation and Reconstruction**
Dresden, Germany

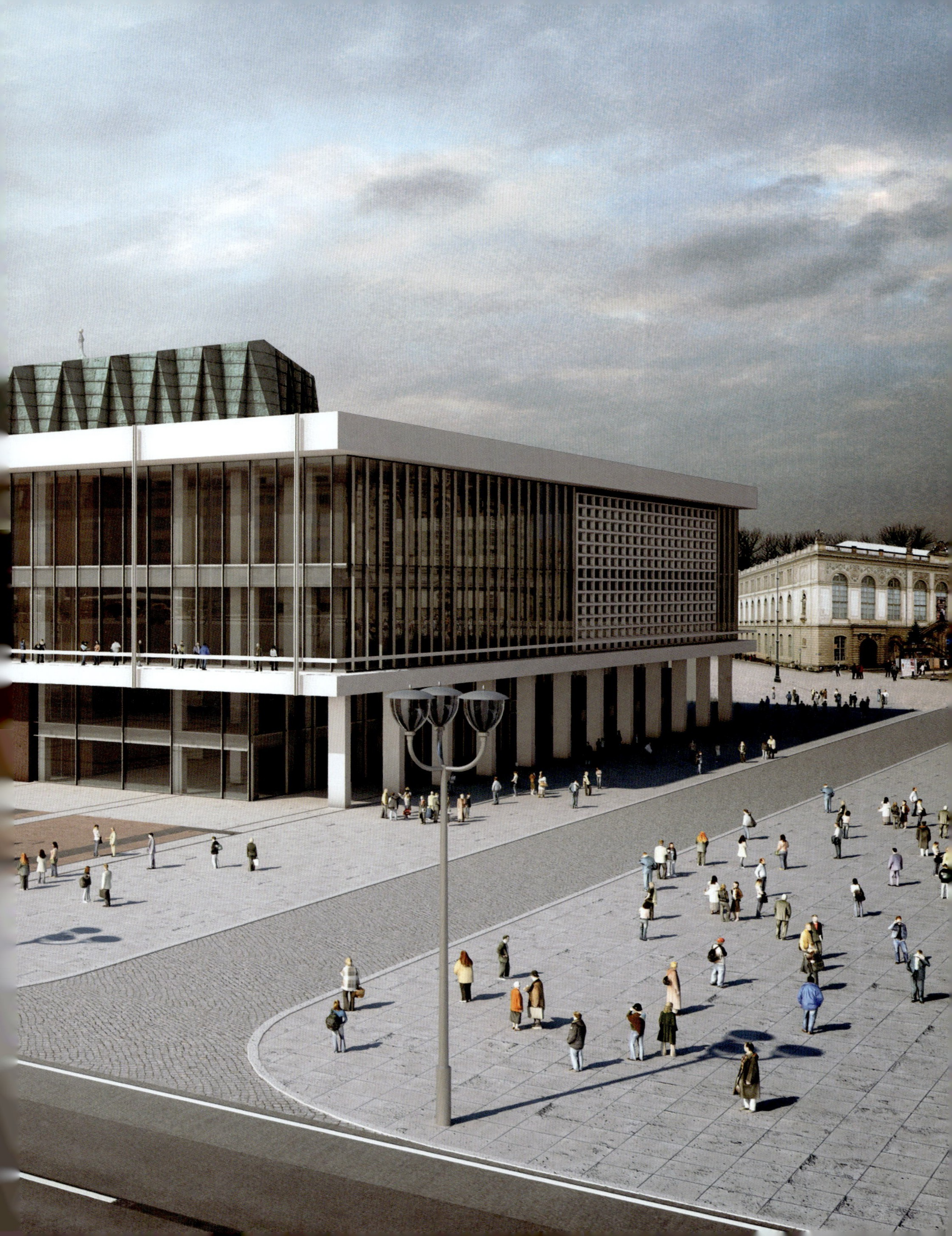

410　德累斯顿文化宫修缮与重建　德累斯顿

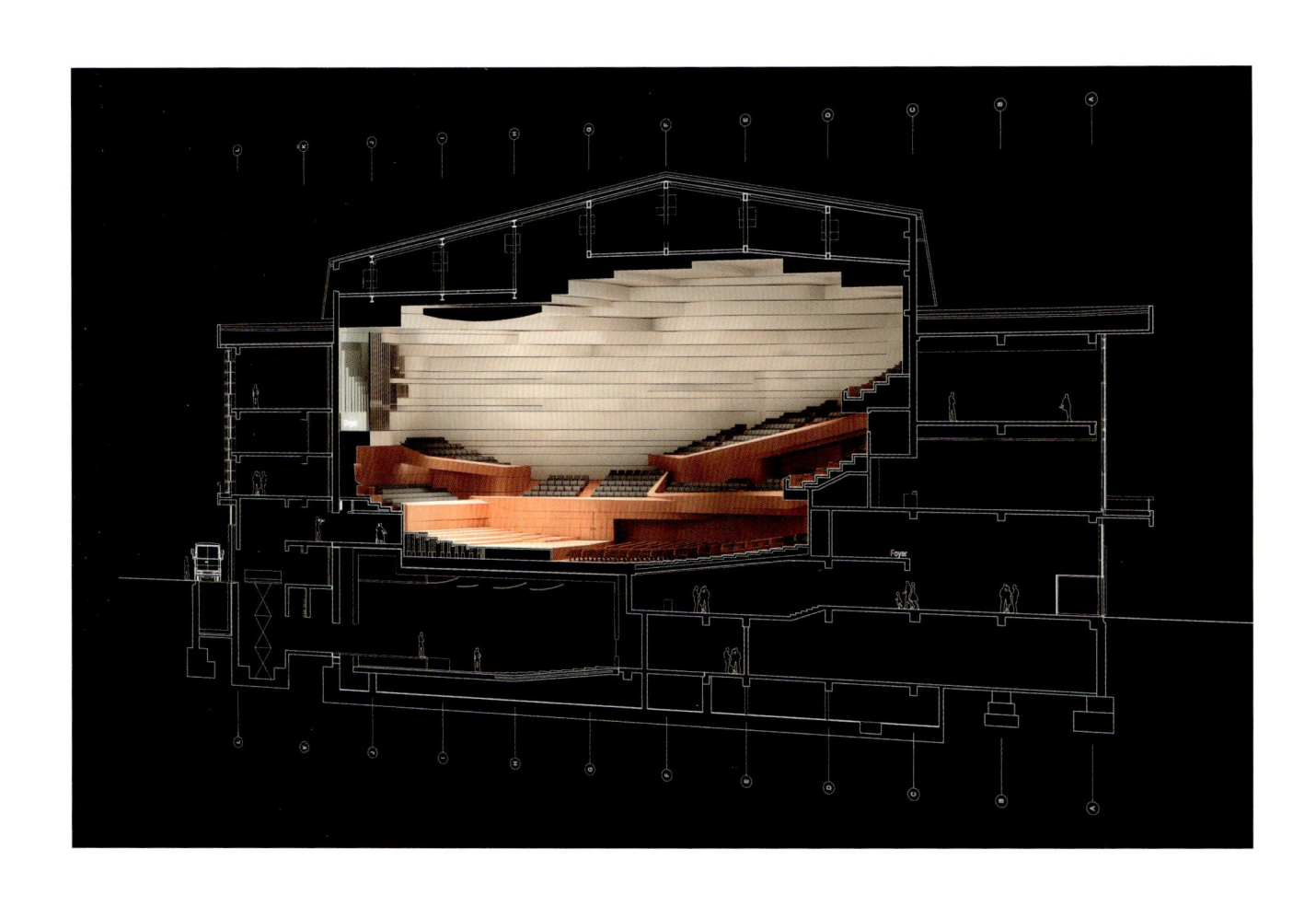

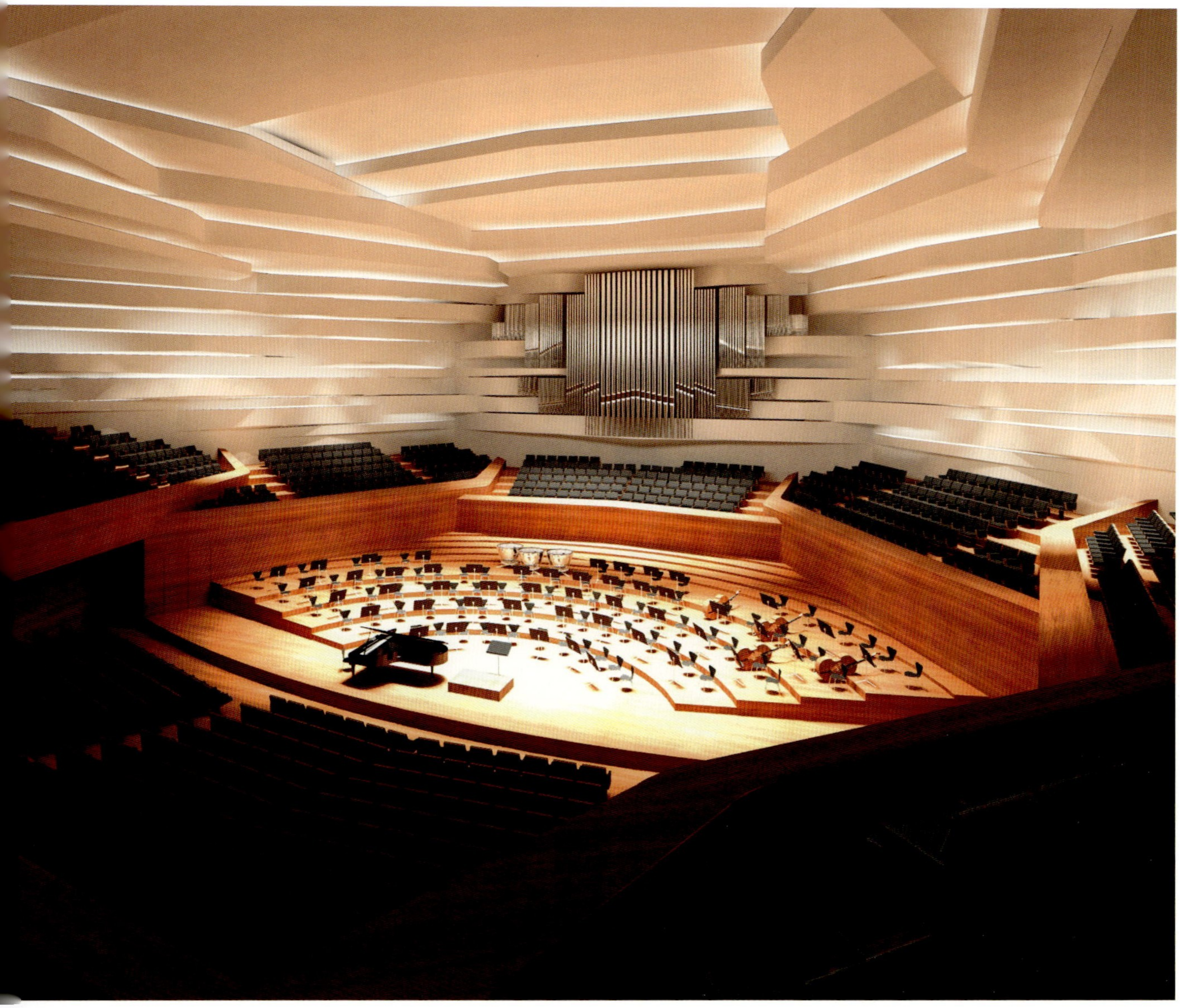

412 ²⁷¹ ↑

TXL⁺总体规划
柏林，德国

TXL⁺
Berlin, Germany

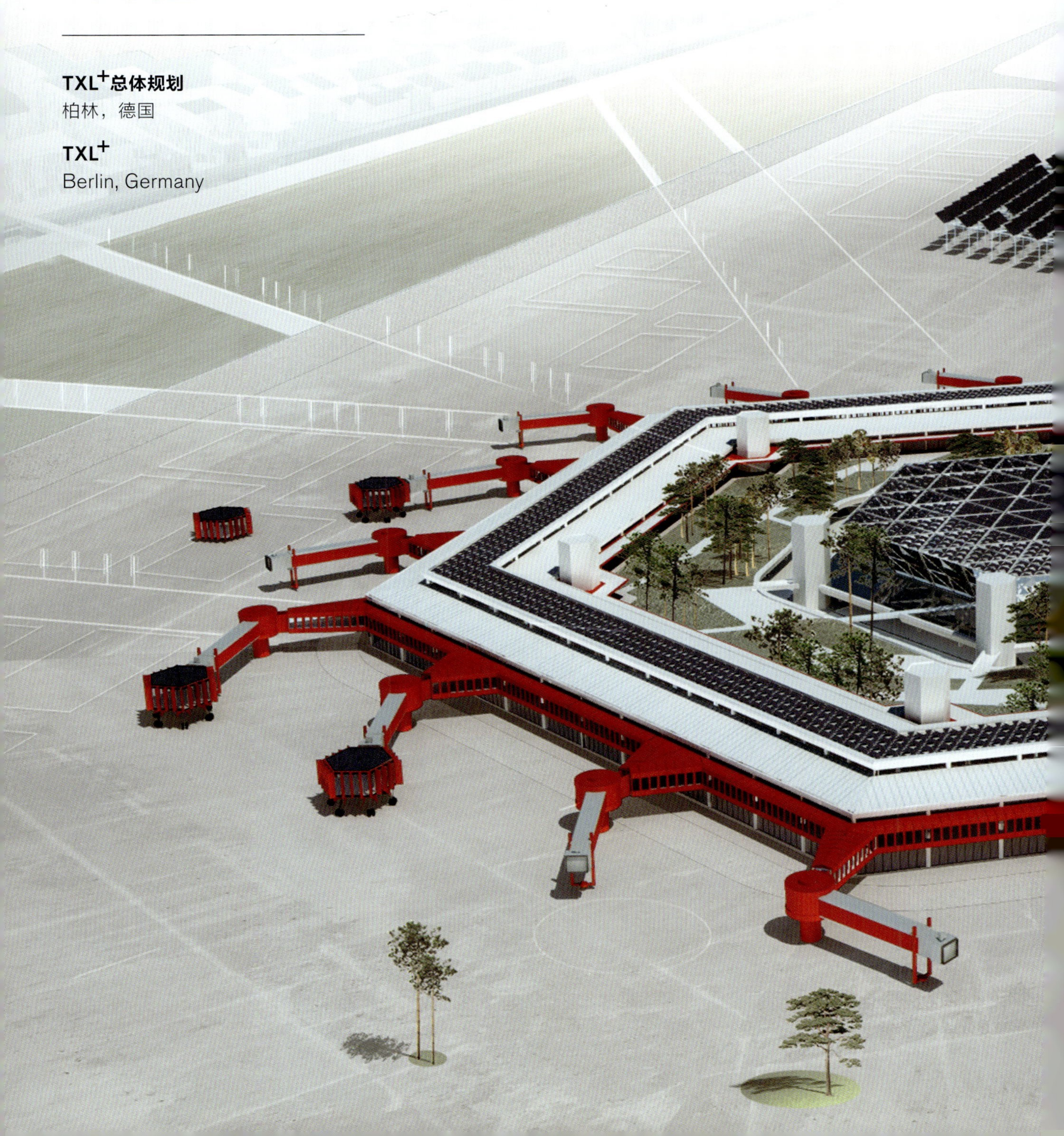

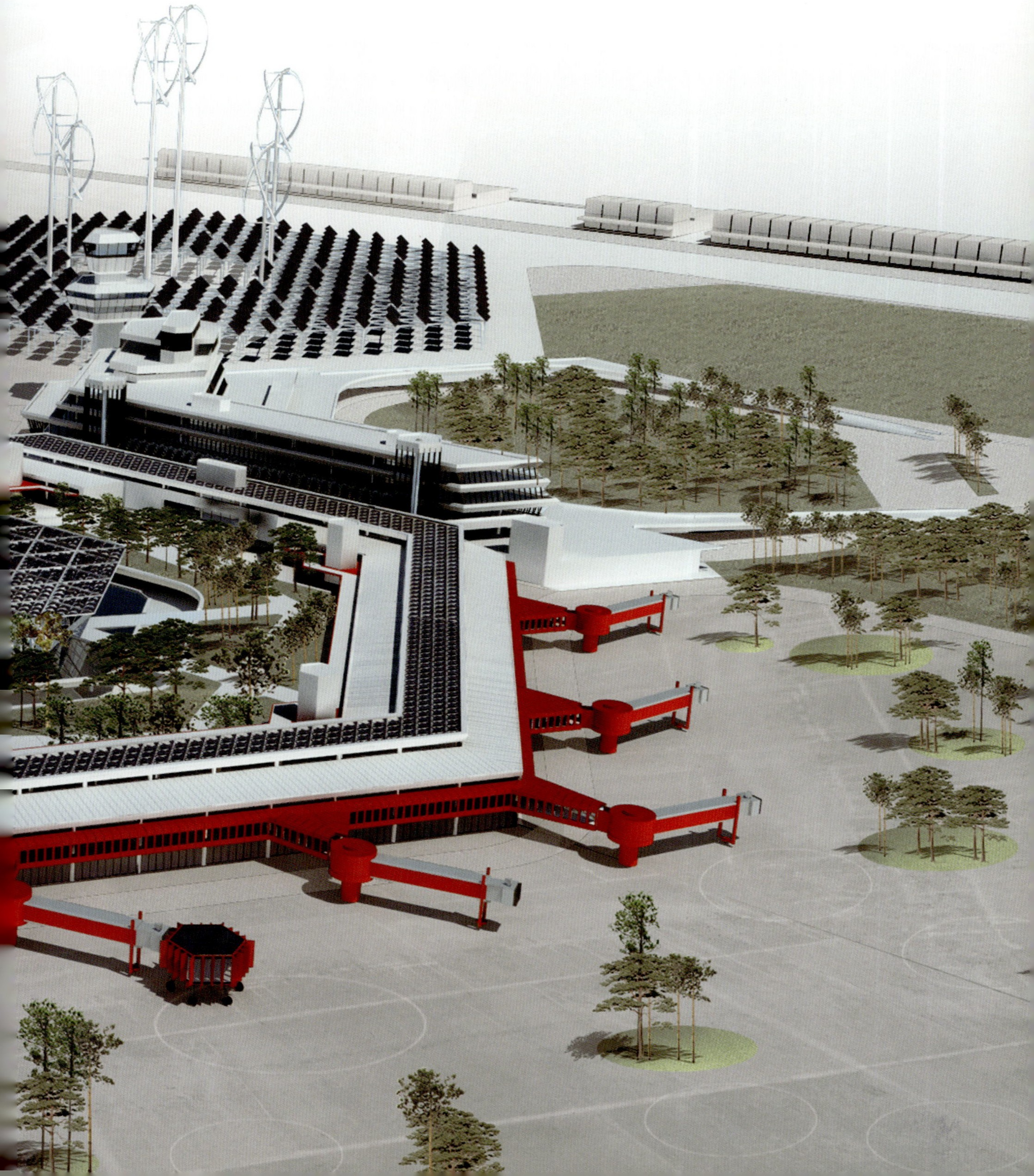

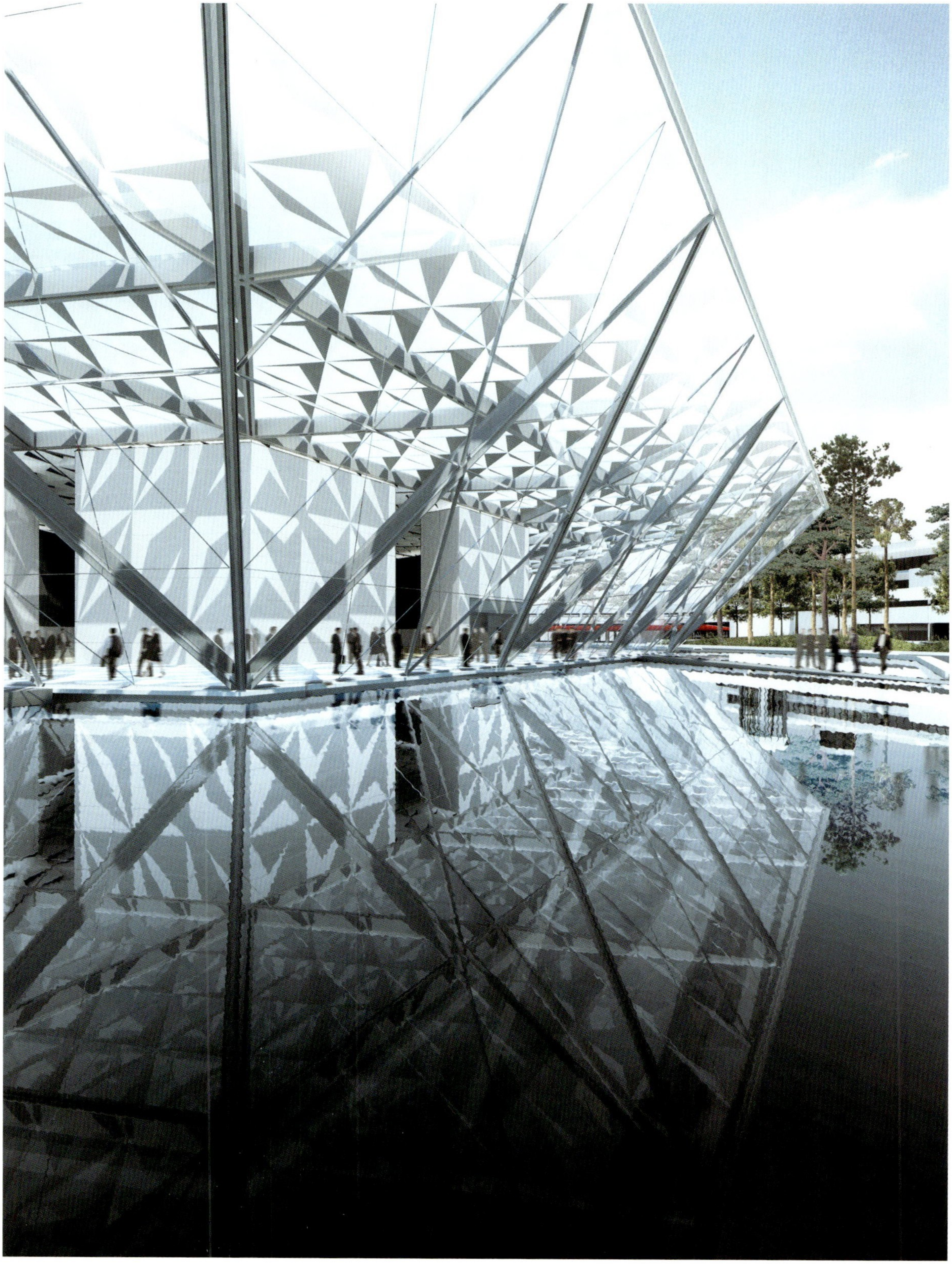

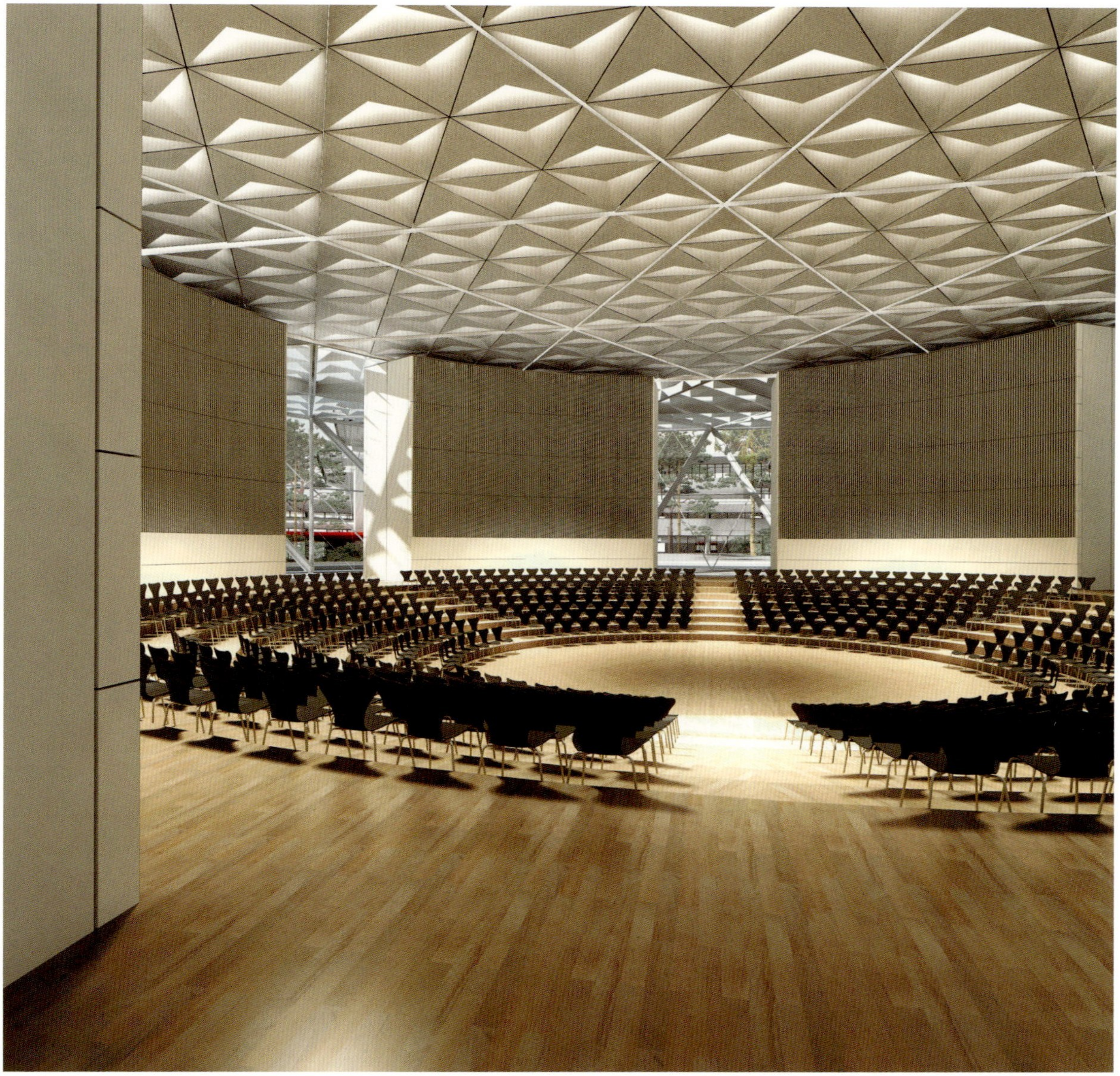

TXL+ Berlin

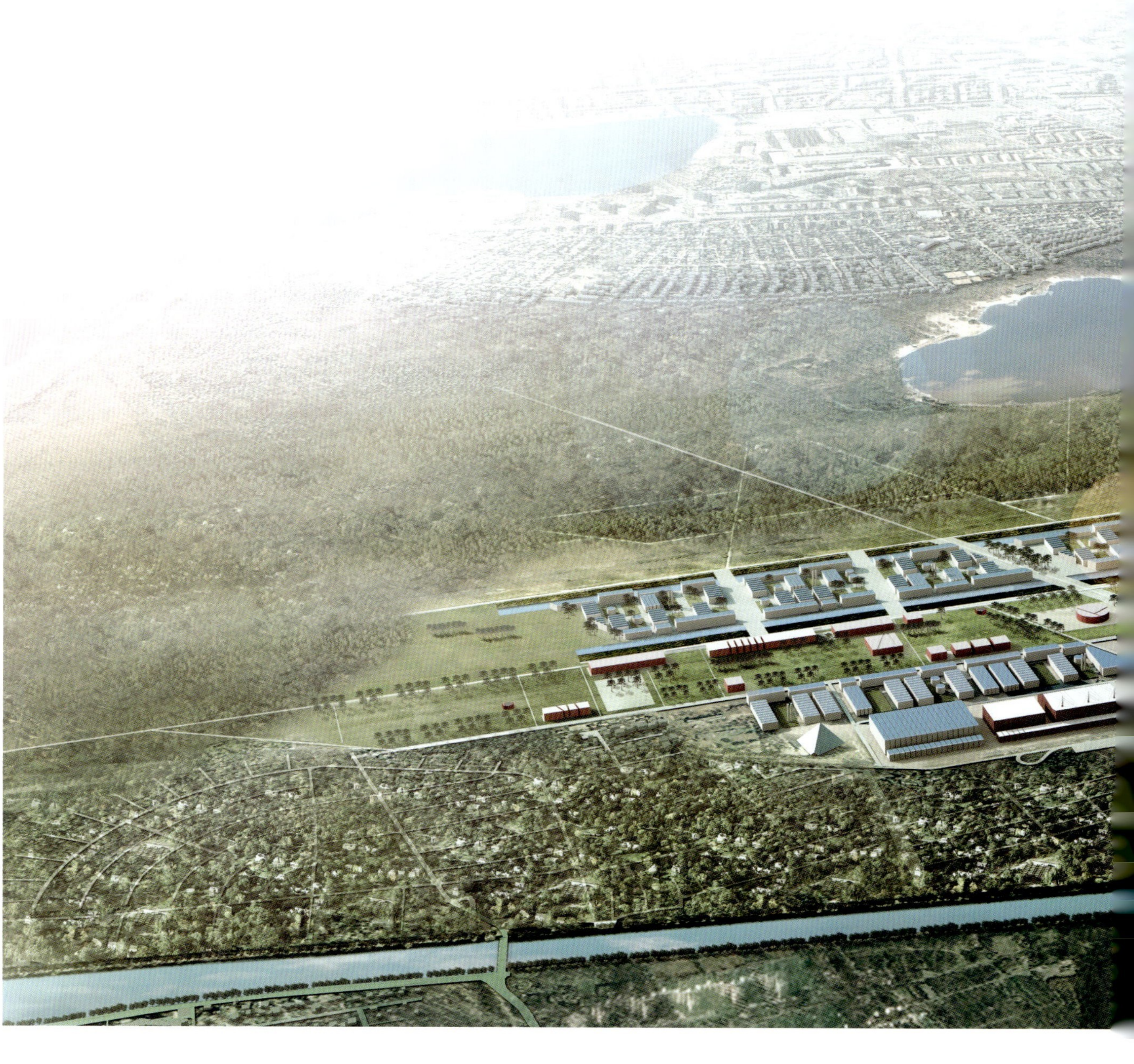

TXL+ 总体规划　柏林

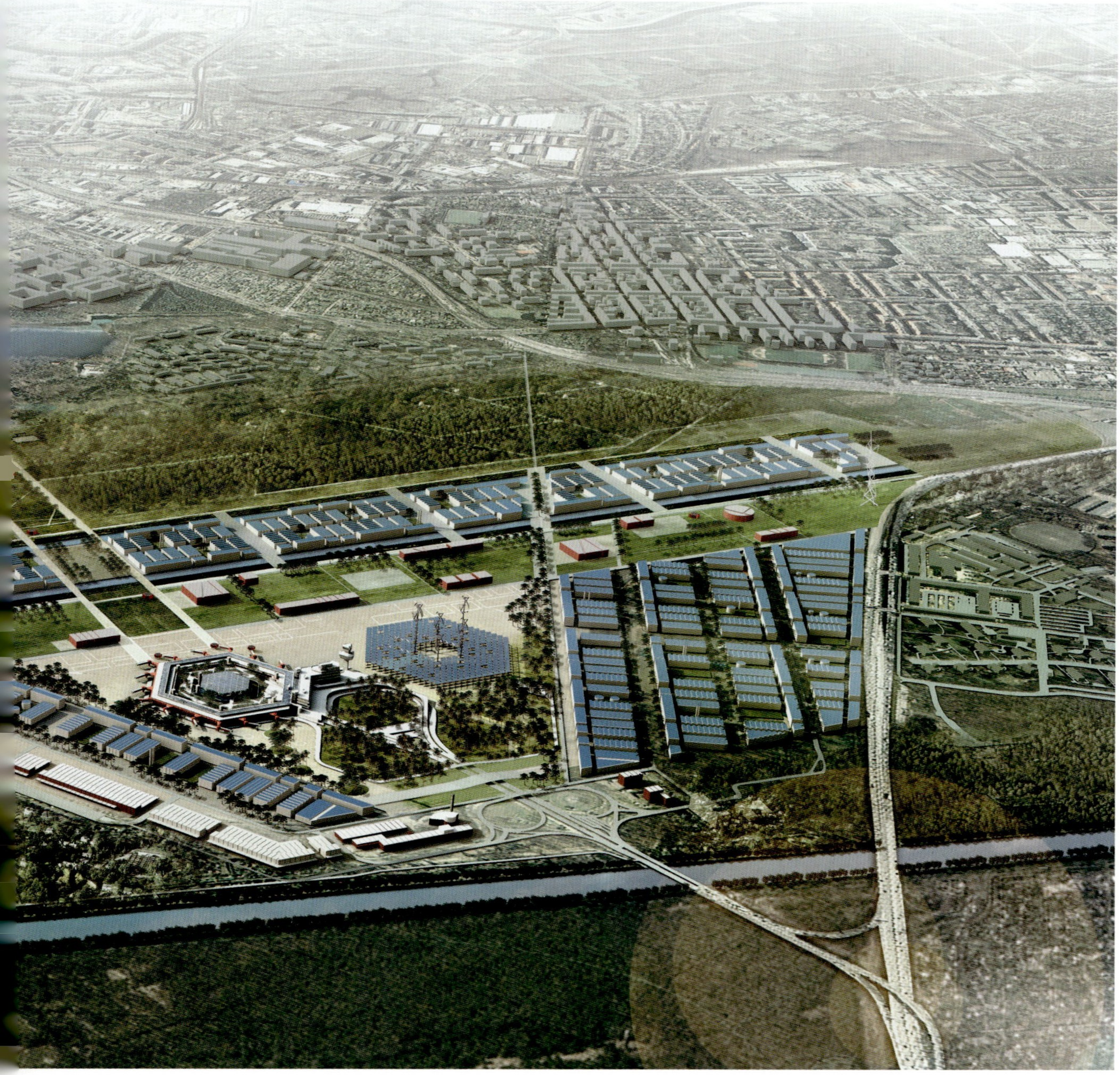

TXL+ Berlin

418 ²⁷¹ ↑

曼海姆美术馆
曼海姆，德国

Kunsthalle Mannheim
Mannheim, Germany

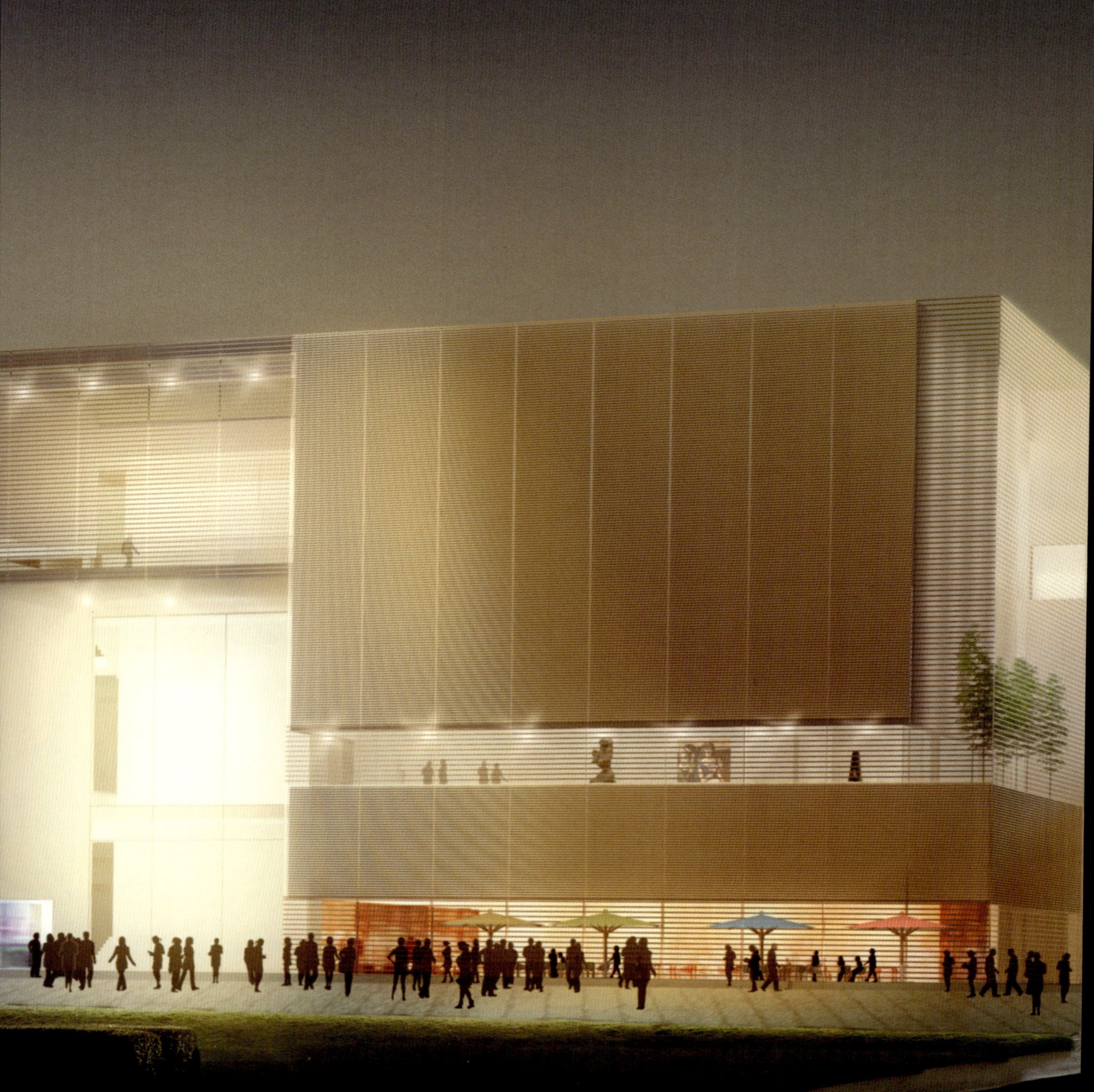

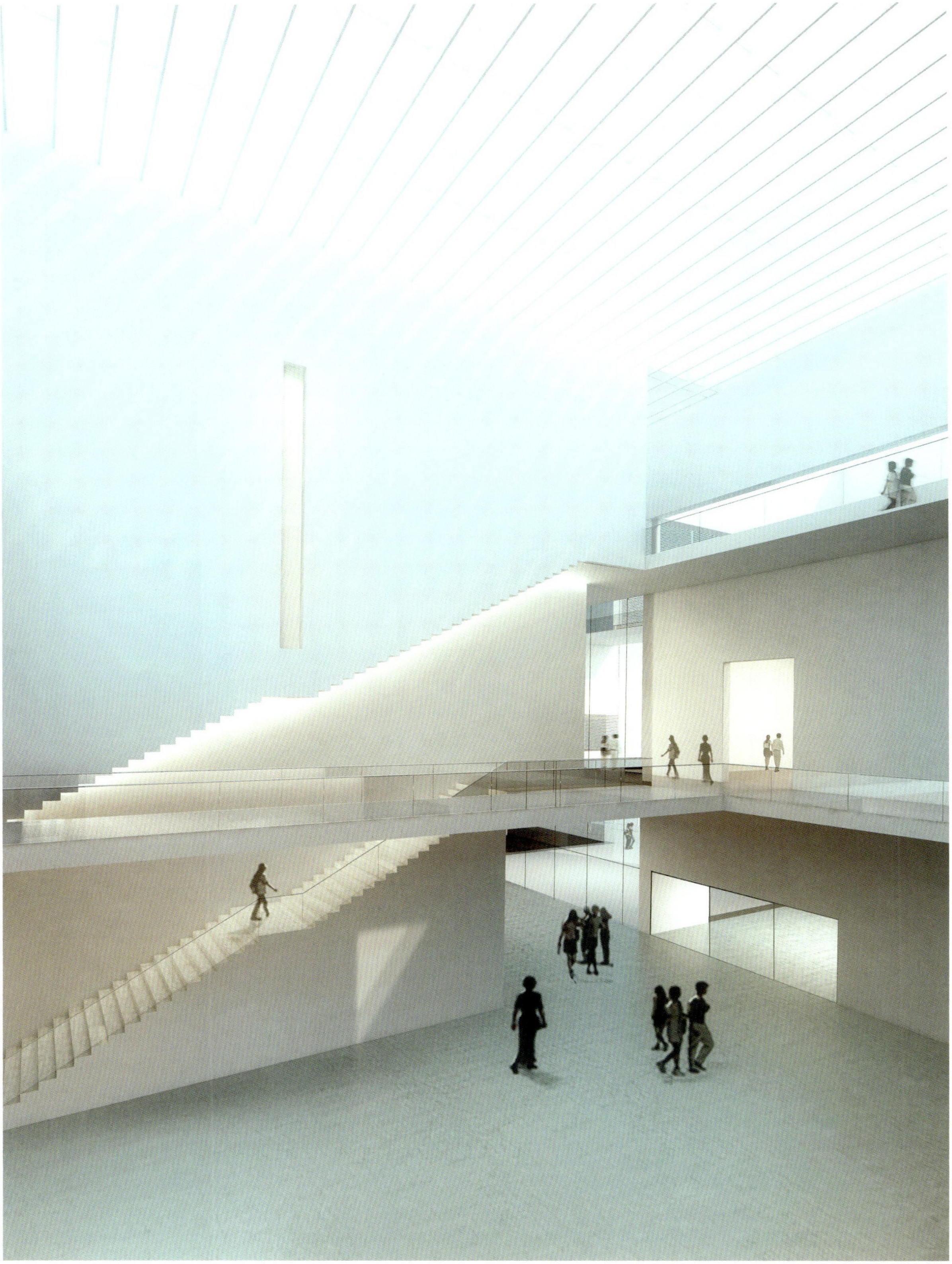

曼海姆美术馆　曼海姆

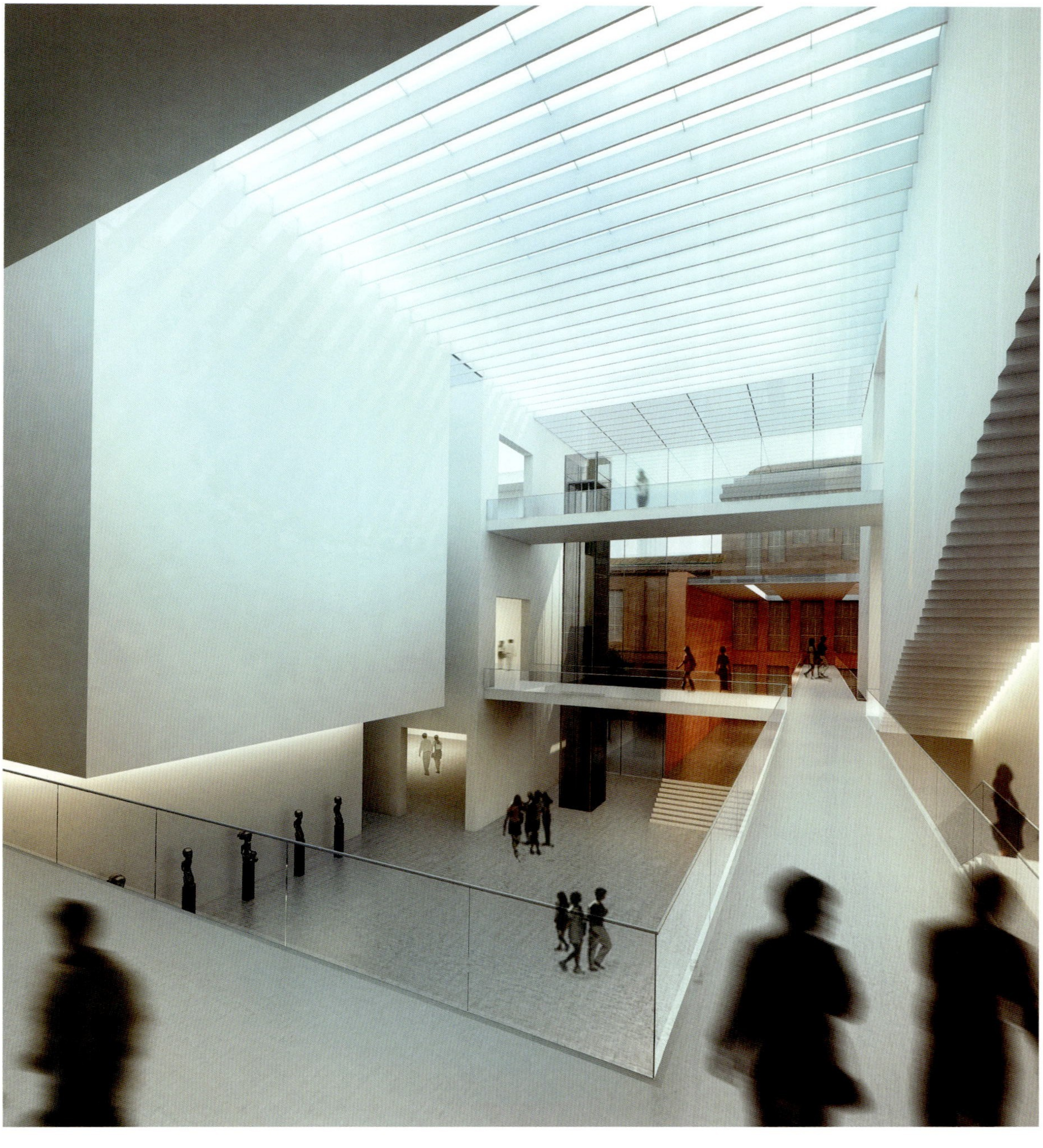

Kunsthalle Mannheim Mannheim

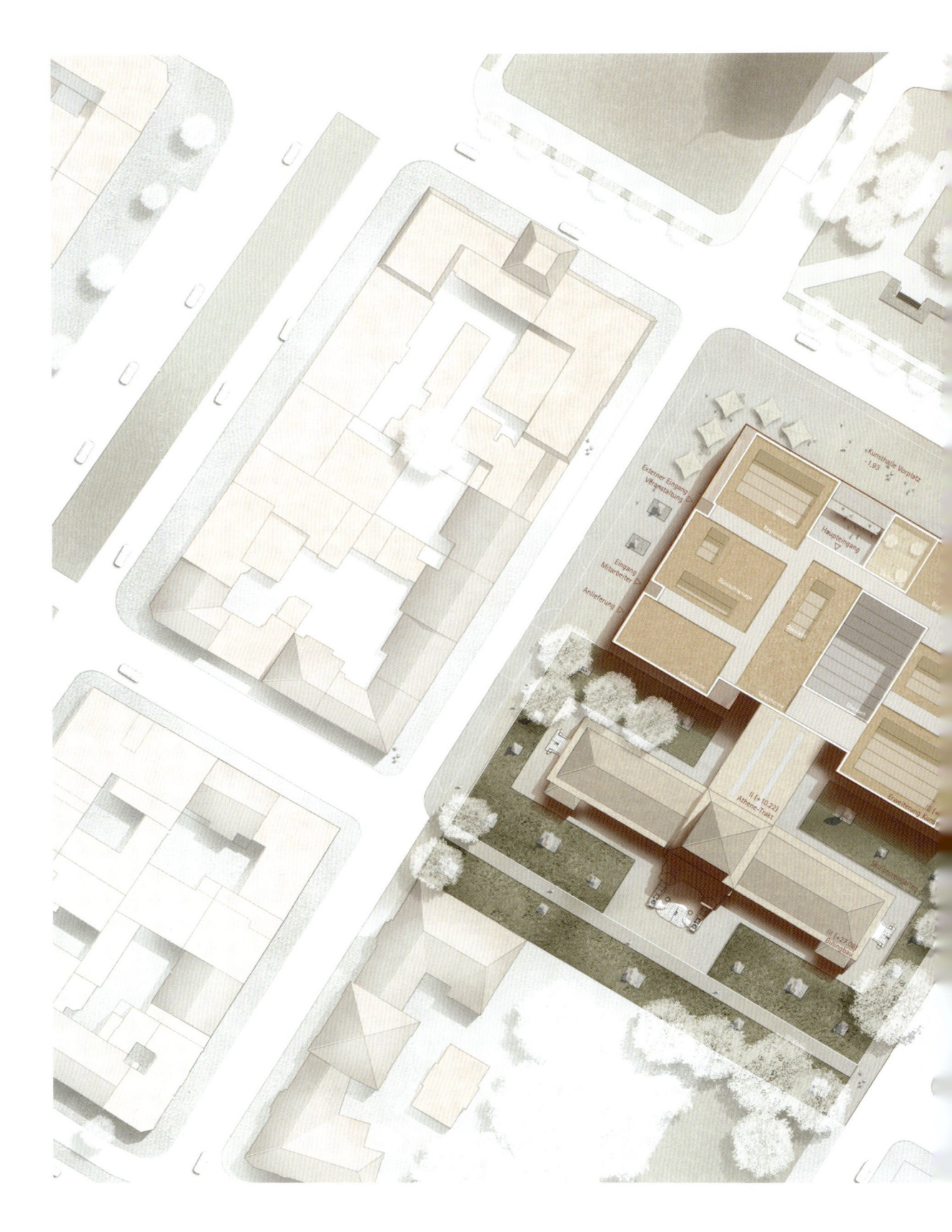

曼海姆美术馆　曼海姆

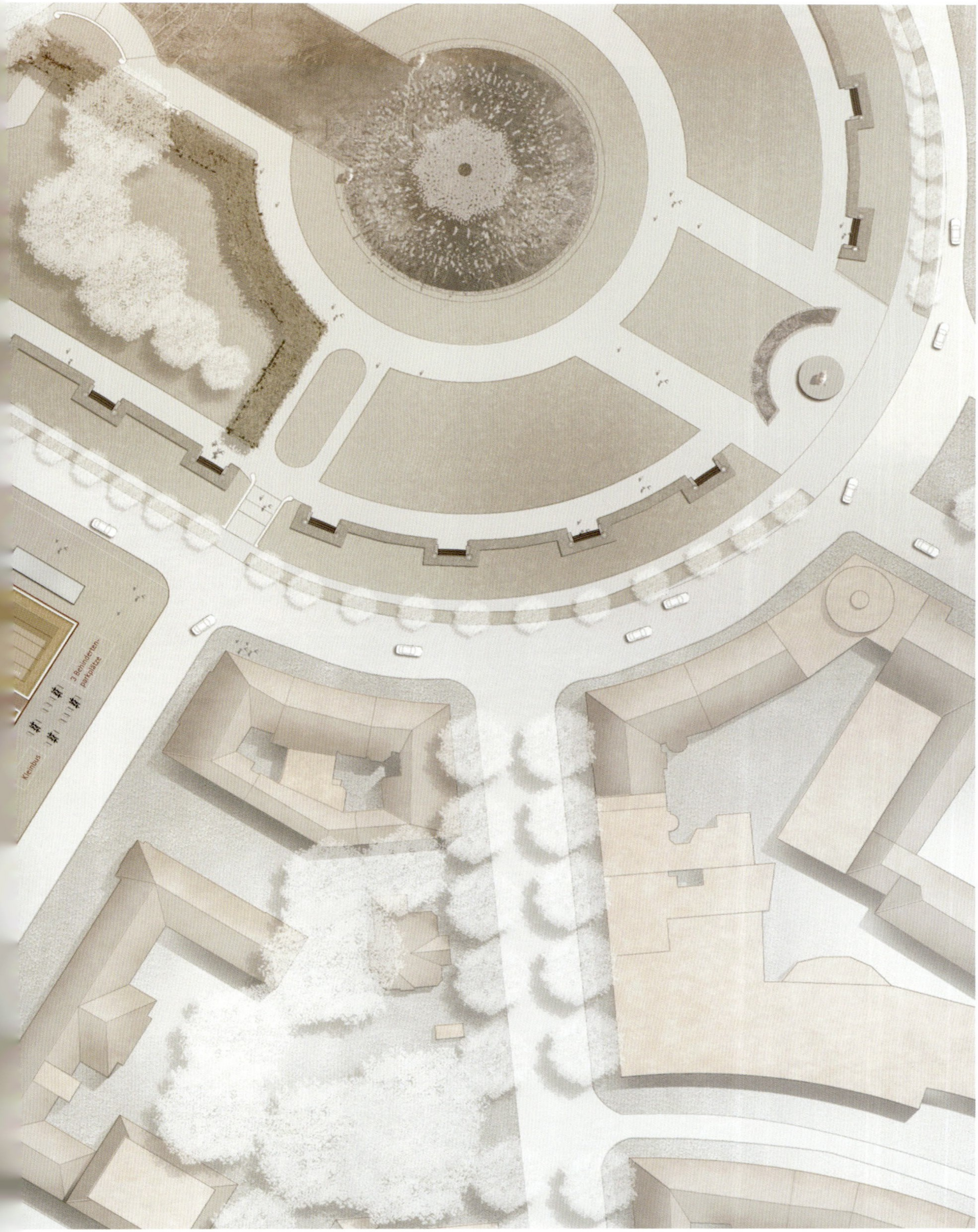

Kunsthalle Mannheim Mannheim 423

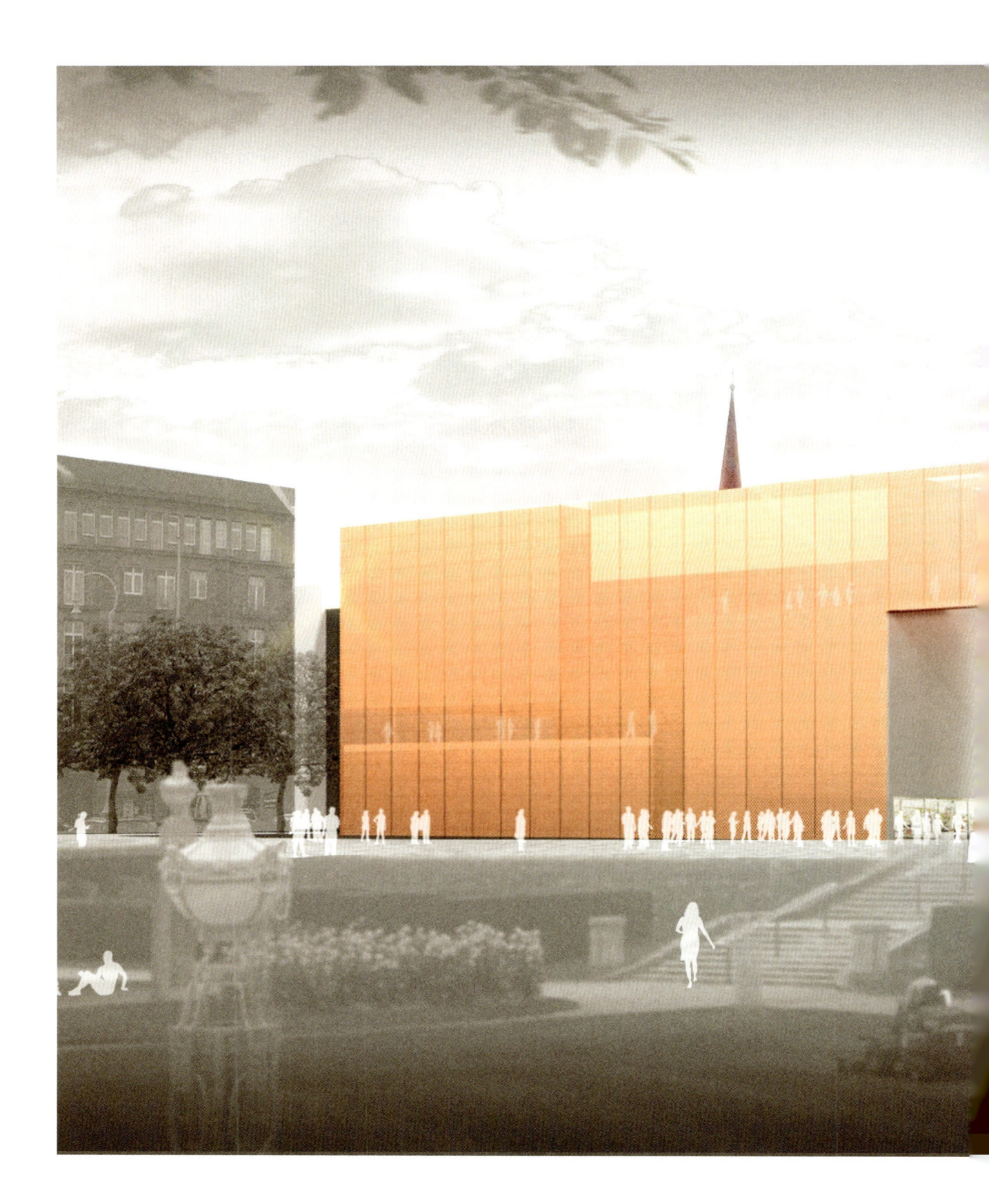

曼海姆美术馆　曼海姆

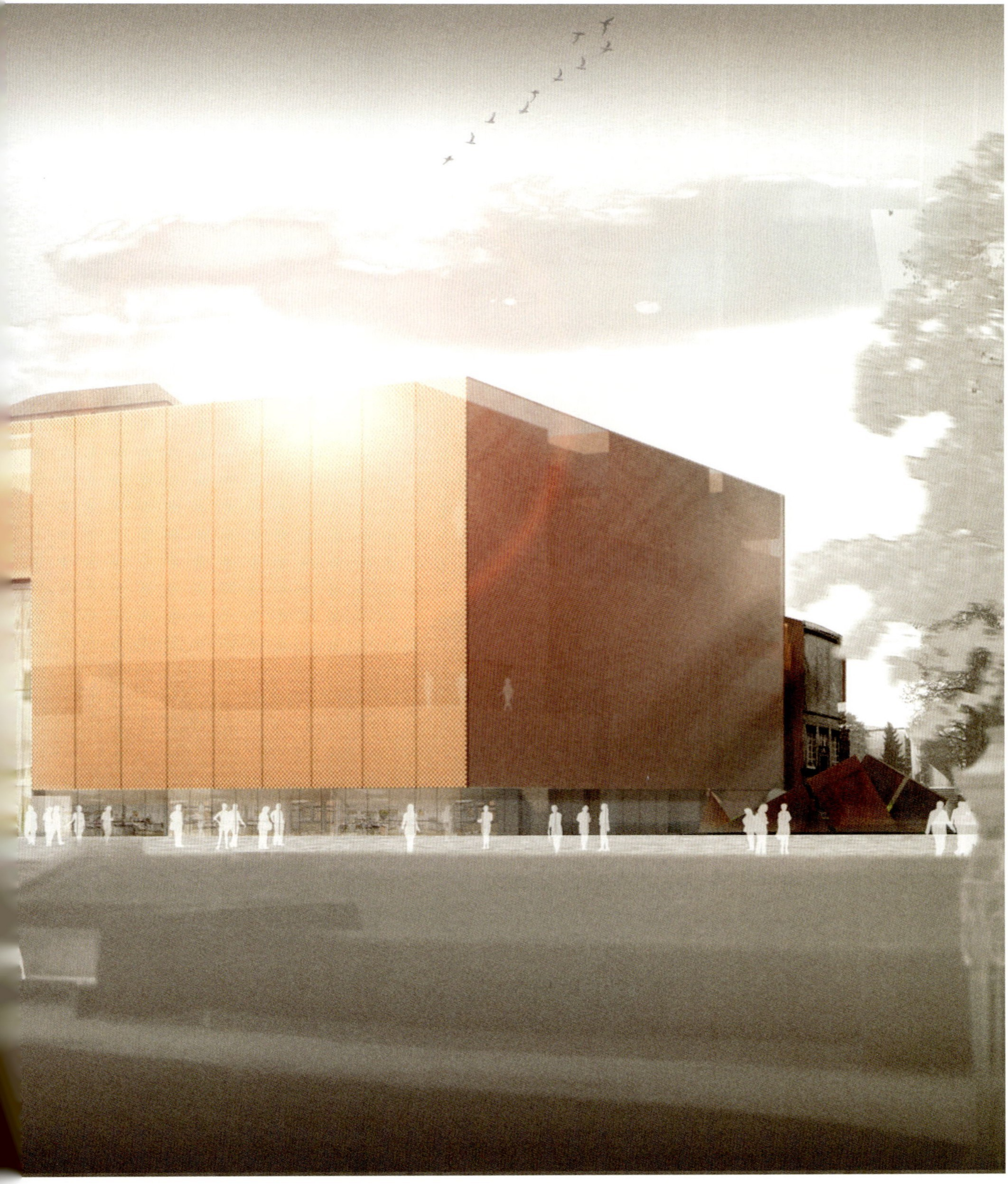

Kunsthalle Mannheim Mannheim

南美洲
South America

巴西 Brazil
巴西利亚 Brasilia
马瑙斯 Manaus
里约热内卢 Rio de Janeiro

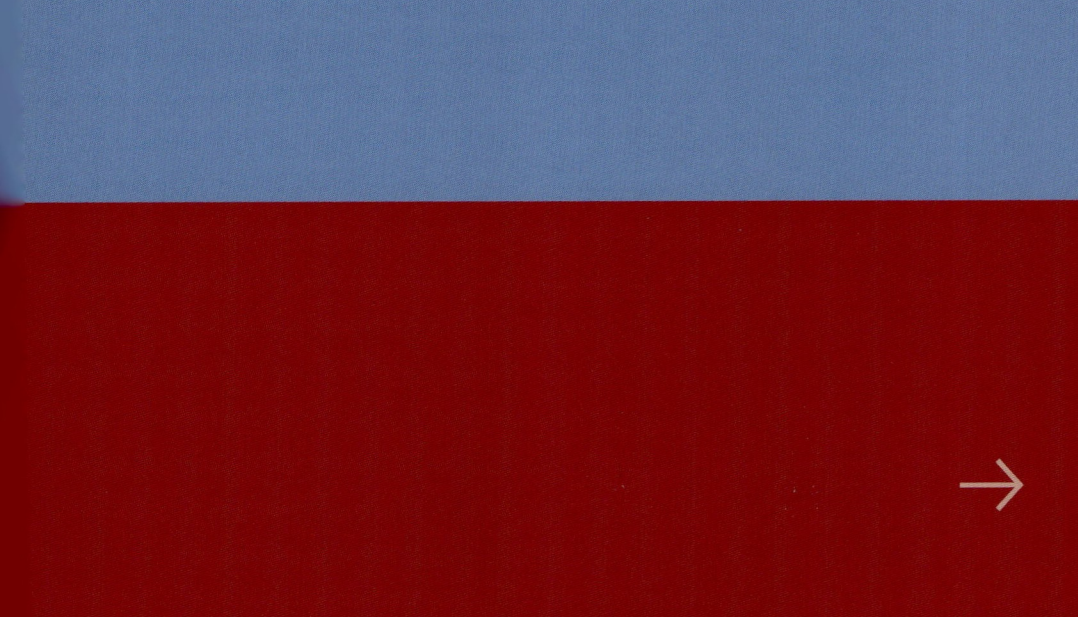

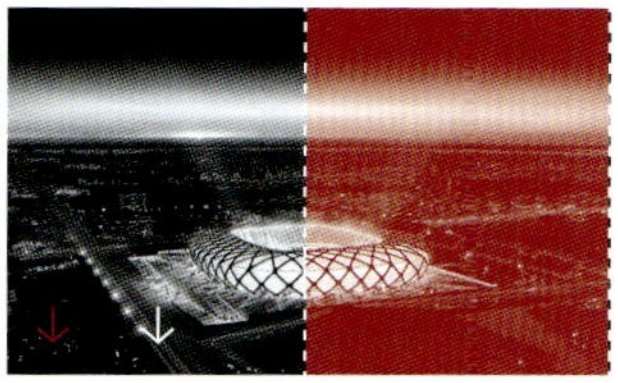

430

亚马逊体育场
马瑙斯，巴西

方案设计：福尔克温·玛格和胡贝特·尼恩霍夫以及马丁·格拉斯 **项目负责人**：马丁·格拉斯，麦克·卡尔森，伯克哈德·皮克 **设计总监gmp巴西**：罗弗·阿曼尼 **合作设计单位**：STADIA, São Paulo; 施莱希工程设计公司 **业主**：Companhia de Desenvolvimento do Estado do Amazonas **建设周期**：2010—2013年 **座席数**：43 500个

设计构想为一个形式简洁但节能高效的体育场，同时还能够反映出其所处特殊地区的环境特色，展现热带雨林多姿多彩的迷人景观。屋面结构由两组互相支撑的悬臂梁构成，蜂窝箱式钢梁同时也是大型的排水管道，可以引流热带雨季巨大的降水量。屋面和外立面由半透明玻璃纤维薄膜覆盖，表面经过低辐射涂层处理，可通过反射热量达到建冷却建筑体的效果。

Arena da Amazônia
Manaus, Brazil

Design Volkwin Marg and Hubert Nienhoff with Martin Glass **Project leaders** Martin Glass with Maike Carlsen and Burkhard Pick **Director gmp do Brasil** Ralf Amann **Co-operation with** STADIA, São Paulo, and schlaich bergermann und partner **Client** Governo do Estado do Amazonas **Construction period** 2010–2013 **Seats** 43,500

With the design of the new Manaus stadium, the aim was to come up with a very simple but highly efficient stadium that would at the same time specifically symbolize the location, particularly the fascination and natural diversity of the tropical rain forest. The roof structure is made up of mutually supporting cantilevers, whose steel hollow core girders function simultaneously as large gutters to drain the immense run-off of tropical rainwater. The fields of the roof and facades consist of translucent fiberglass fabric, whose low-emittance coating reflects heat radiation and thus has a cooling effect.

434

国家体育场
巴西利亚，巴西

方案设计：福尔克温·玛格和胡贝特·尼恩霍夫 **项目负责人**：马丁·格拉斯 **巴西项目负责人**：罗伯特·霍尔姆斯 **设计总监gmp巴西**：罗弗·阿曼尼 **合作设计单位**：施莱希工程设计公司；Castro Mello Arquitetos, São Paulo **业主**：Governo do Distrito Federal **建设周期**：2010—2013年 **座席数**：70 000个

设计目的旨在提供一个理想的解决方案，在强调其在历史以及传统上的重大意义的同时赋予其独特的现代建筑形象。体育场碗状看台由一个环形的广场围绕，全部交通连接设置于广场之内，广场上的"柱林"之上由屋面覆盖。建筑所采用的关键材料为混凝土，再现了巴西利亚的建筑文化。屋面为不规则的圆形悬挂设计，双层结构通过混凝土压力环加以固定。双层结构上层为颜色不同的半透明覆盖件，下层采用背面照明的膜结构。

Estádio Nacional
Brasilia, Brazil

Design Volkwin Marg and Hubert Nienhoff **Project leader** Martin Glass **Project leader, Brazil** Robert Hormes **Director gmp do Brasil** Ralf Amann **Co-operation with** schlaich bergermann und partner; Castro Mello Arquitetos, São Paulo **Client** Governo do Distrito Federal **Construction period** 2010–2013 **Seats** 70,000

The aim of the design is to provide a solution appropriate to the stadium's importance in terms of architectural history, with clear references to the traditions of the site, while at the same time coming up with a distinctive, contemporary configuration. This involves surrounding the bowl of the stadium with a circular esplanade containing all access elements, with the roof resting on the "forest of supports". Key material is concrete, wholly in keeping with Brasília's architectural culture. The roof itself is conceived as a suspended roof with the ideal circular geometry, a double-layer structure held in place by a concrete compression ring. In this, the upper layer consists of sundry translucent covering elements, while the lower layer takes the form of a backlit membrane.

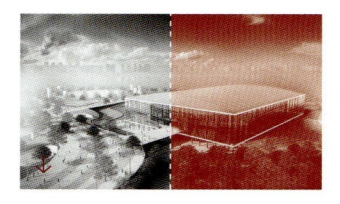

438

2016年奥运会网球及水上运动中心

里约热内卢，巴西

设计： 福尔克温·玛格和胡贝特·尼恩霍夫，2013年 **项目负责人：** 马丁·格拉斯，迈克·卡尔森 **设计总监gmp巴西：** Ralf Amann **里约热内卢项目负责人：** 桑德·图斯特，克劳迪娅·夏普妮 **合作设计单位：** 施莱希工程设计公司; Lumens Engenharia; Sustentech **业主：** Prefeitura da Cidade do Rio de Janeiro **建设周期：** 2014—2015年 **网球中心座席数：** 10 000＋5000＋3000个 **水上运动中心座席数：** 18 000个

2016年夏季奥运会将在巴西里约热内卢举办，这座由gmp设计的网球和水上运动中心位于里约巴拉-达蒂茹卡区内。设计方案在伦敦aecom事务所的前期设计基础上发展而来，场馆可容纳18 000名观众，为一座灵活的临时构建建筑。观众席以及50 m×25 m的泳池上部为半透明的PVC/PES膜结构所覆盖。体育场外立面采用了构造简单的可回收建筑构件确保建筑自然的通风透气，同时赋予体育场令人过目难忘的外部形象。

2016 Olympic Games, Tennis and Aquatic Center

Rio de Janeiro, Brazil

Design Volkwin Marg and Hubert Nienhoff, 2013 **Project leaders, Berlin** Martin Glass, Maike Carlsen **Director gmp do Brasil** Ralf Amann **Project leaders, Rio de Janeiro** Sander Troost, Claudia Chiappini **Co-operation with** schlaich bergermann und partner; Lumens Engenharia; Sustentech **Client** Prefeitura da Cidade do Rio de Janeiro **Construction period** 2014–2015 **Seats, tennis center** 10,000 + 5,000 + 3,000 **Seats, aquatic center** 18,000

For the 2016 Olympic Summer Games in Rio de Janeiro, gmp is designing the Tennis Center and the Aquatic Center in the Barra de Tijuca district of the city. The Aquatic Center is based on a pre-concept by aecom London and consists of a flexible, temporary structure for 18,000 spectators. The spectator stands and the 50 × 25 m pool are covered by a membrane roof made of translucent PVC/PES fabric. Owing to its high degree of permeability, the facade ensures natural ventilation of the stadium combined with uncomplicated re-usability of the various building components, and the characteristic features of the facade ensure a high degree of recognizability.

430 ^{428} ↑

亚马逊体育场
马瑙斯,巴西

Arena da Amazônia
Manaus, Brazil

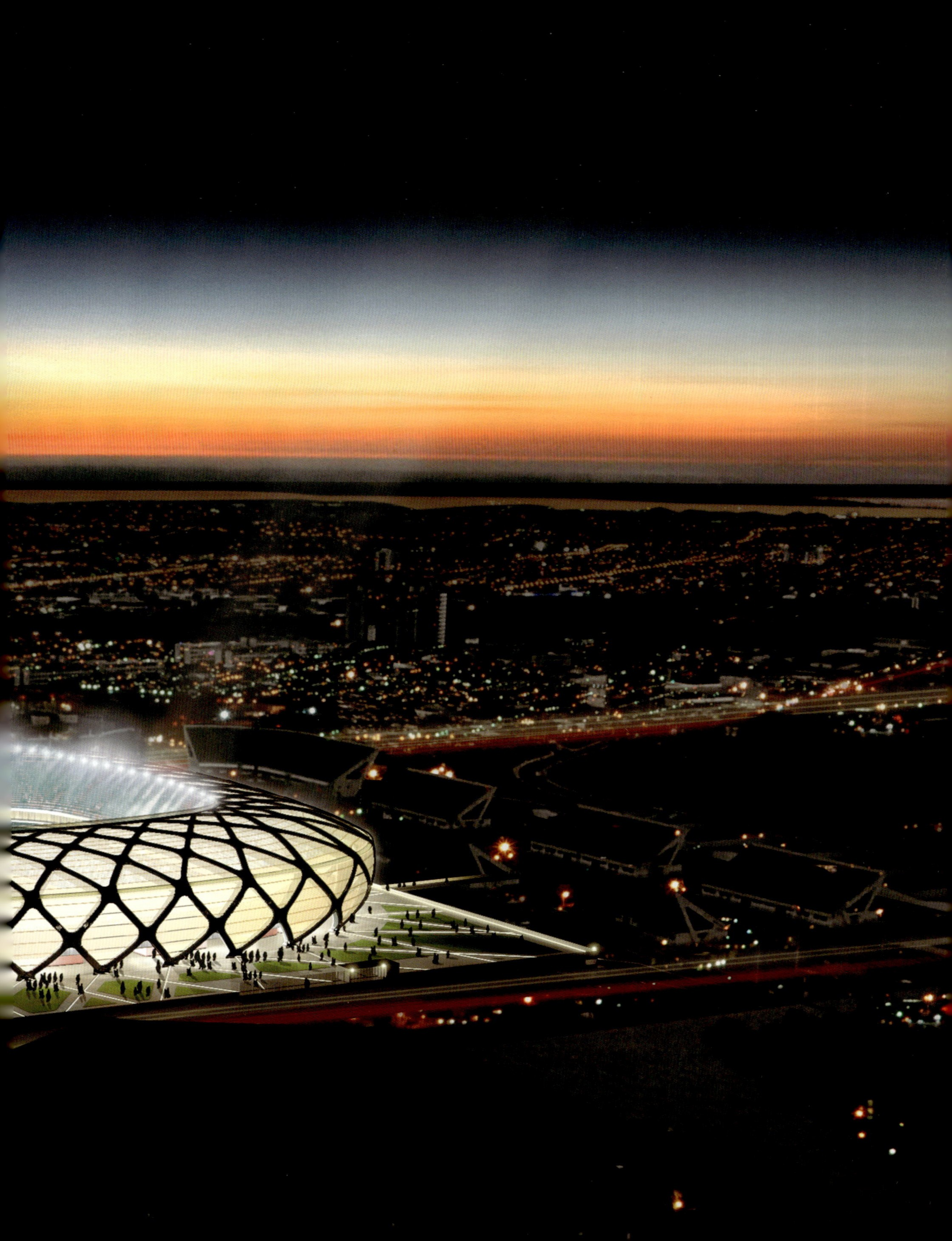

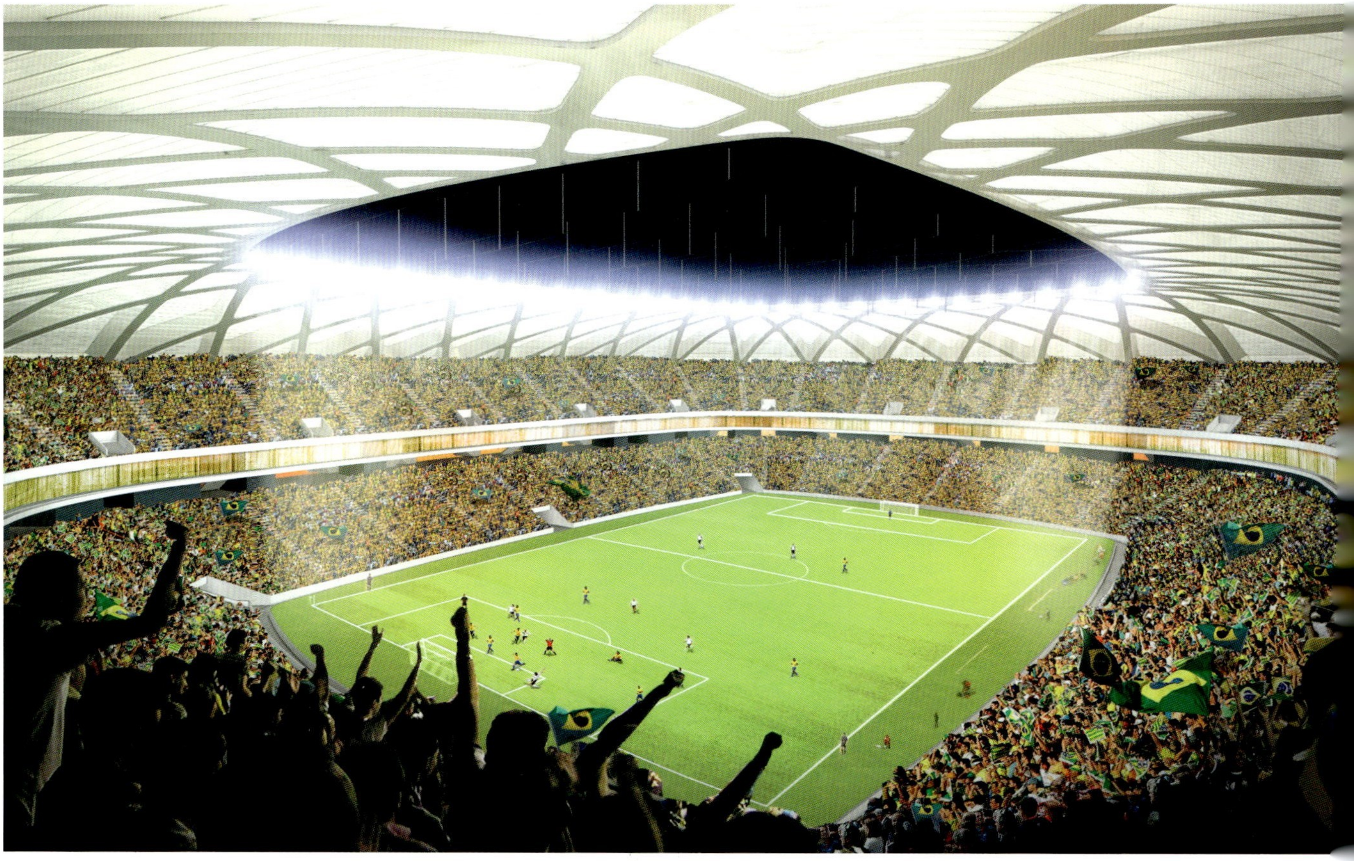

亚马逊体育场 马瑙斯

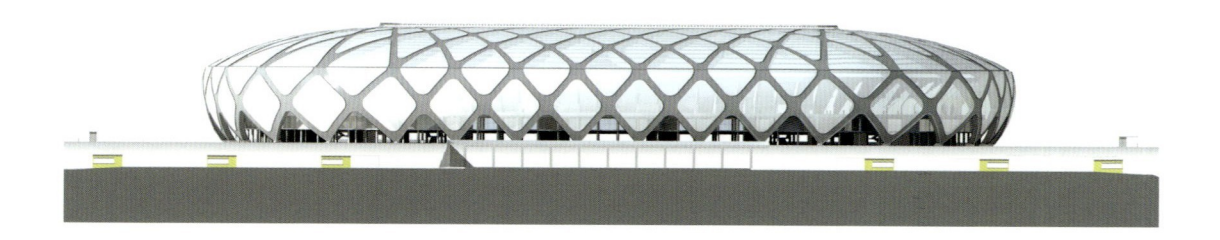

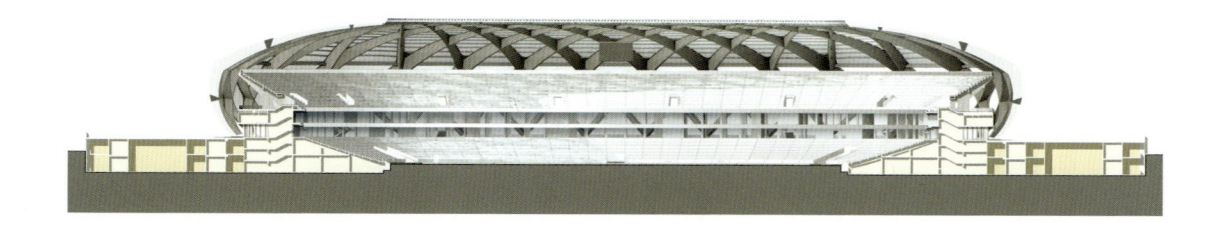

Arena da Amazônia Manaus

434 ^{428} ↑

国家体育场
巴西利亚，巴西

Estádio Nacional
Brasilia, Brazil

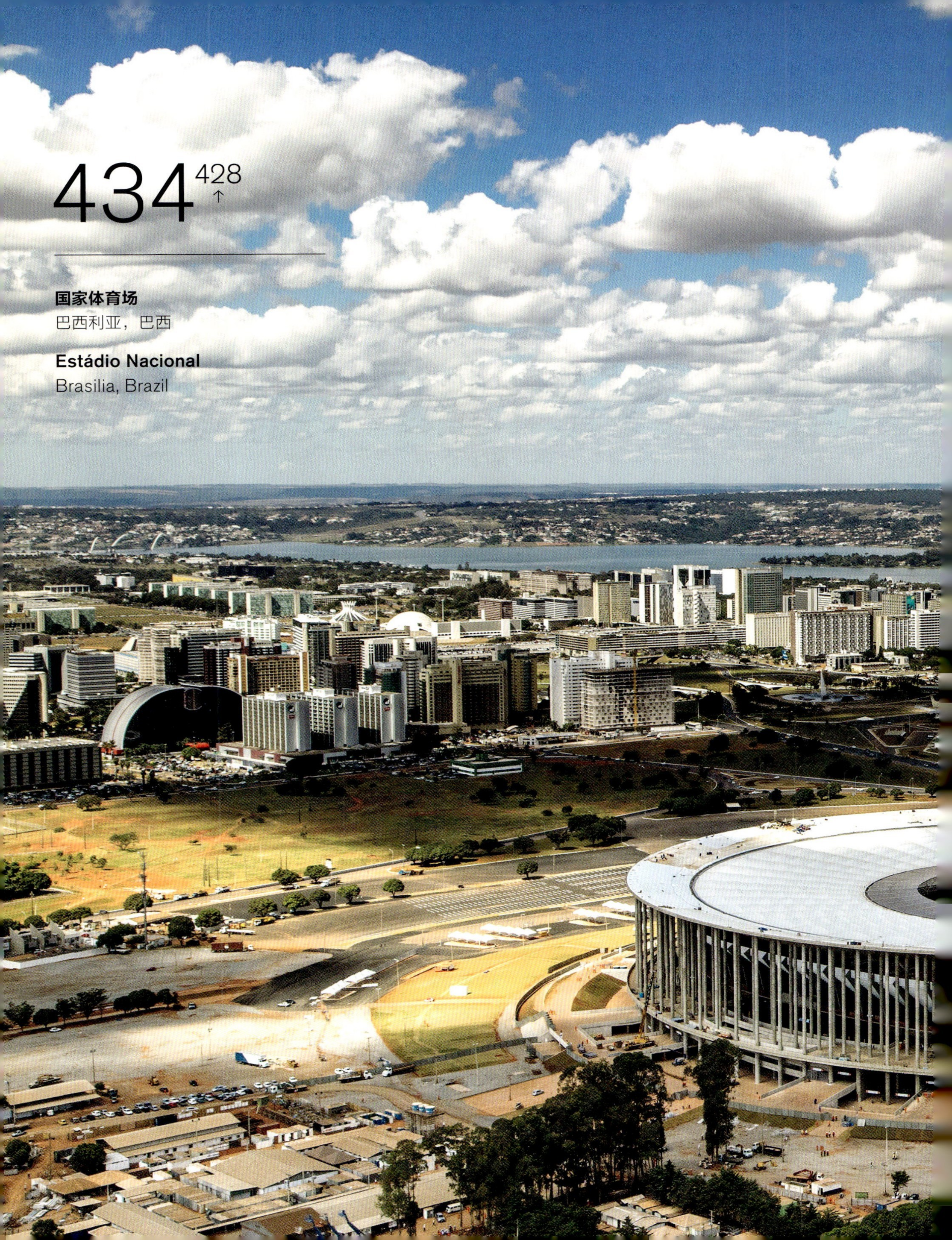

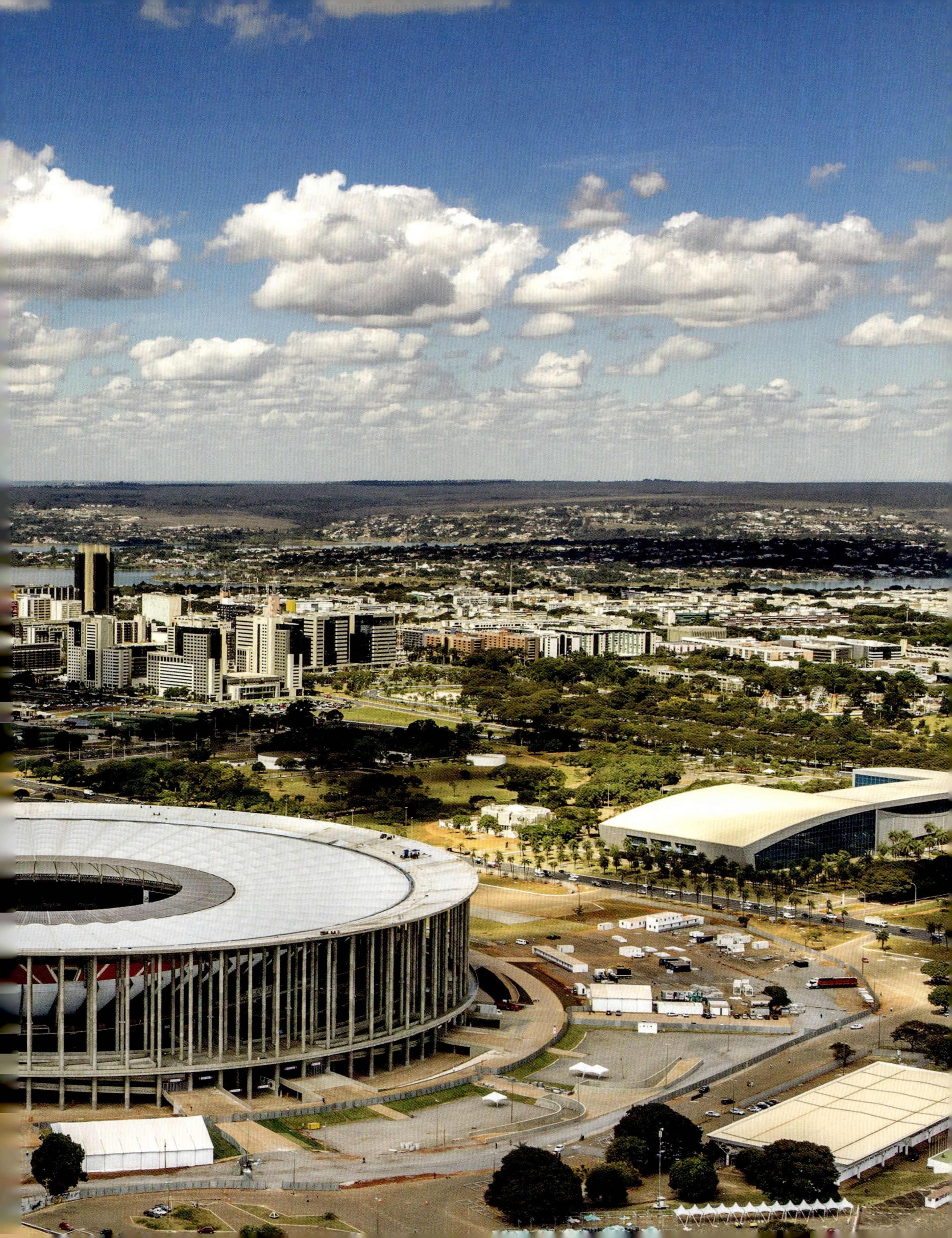

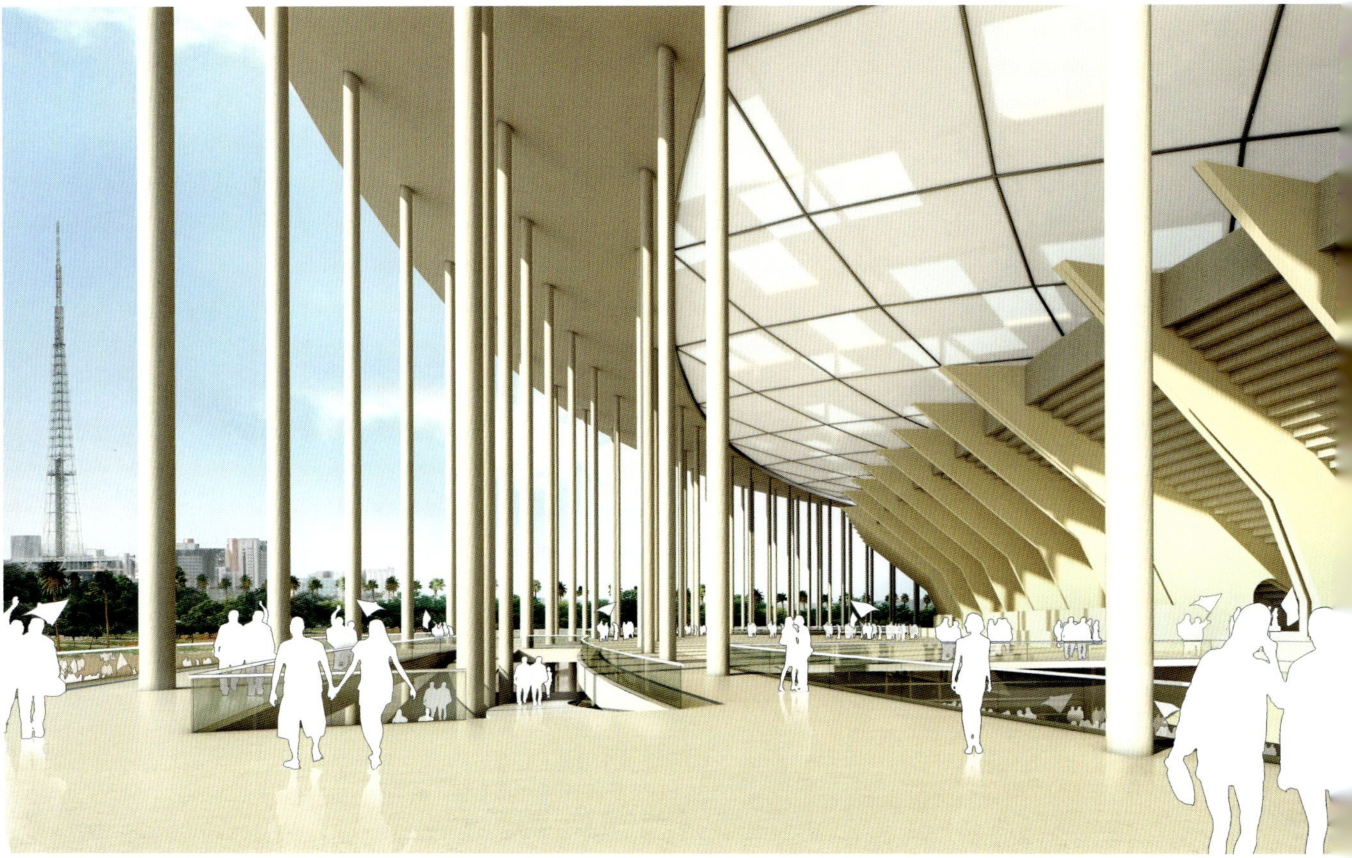

国家体育场 巴西利亚

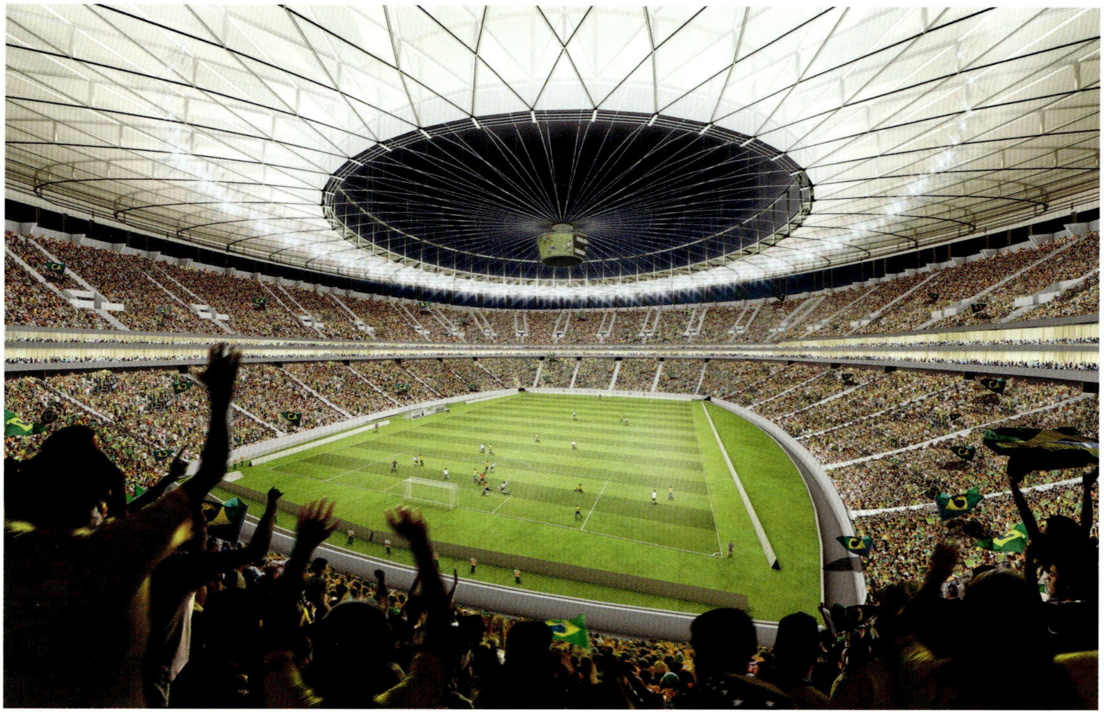

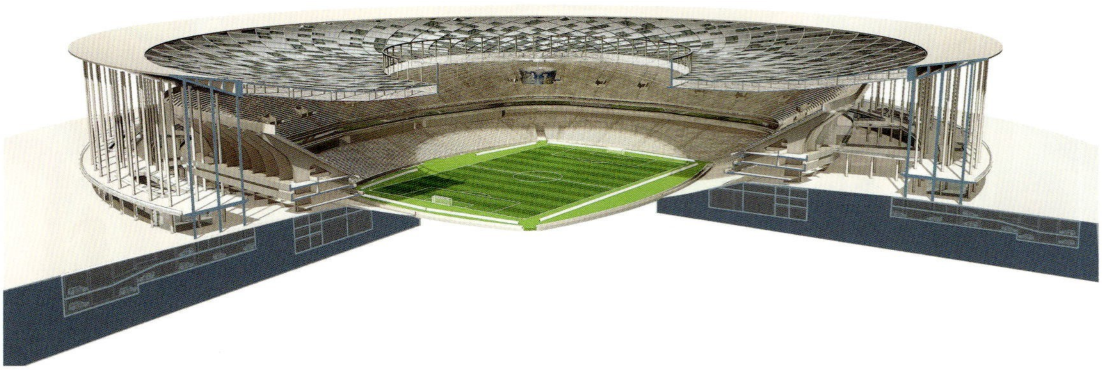

Estádio Nacional Brasilia

438 ⁴²⁹ ↑

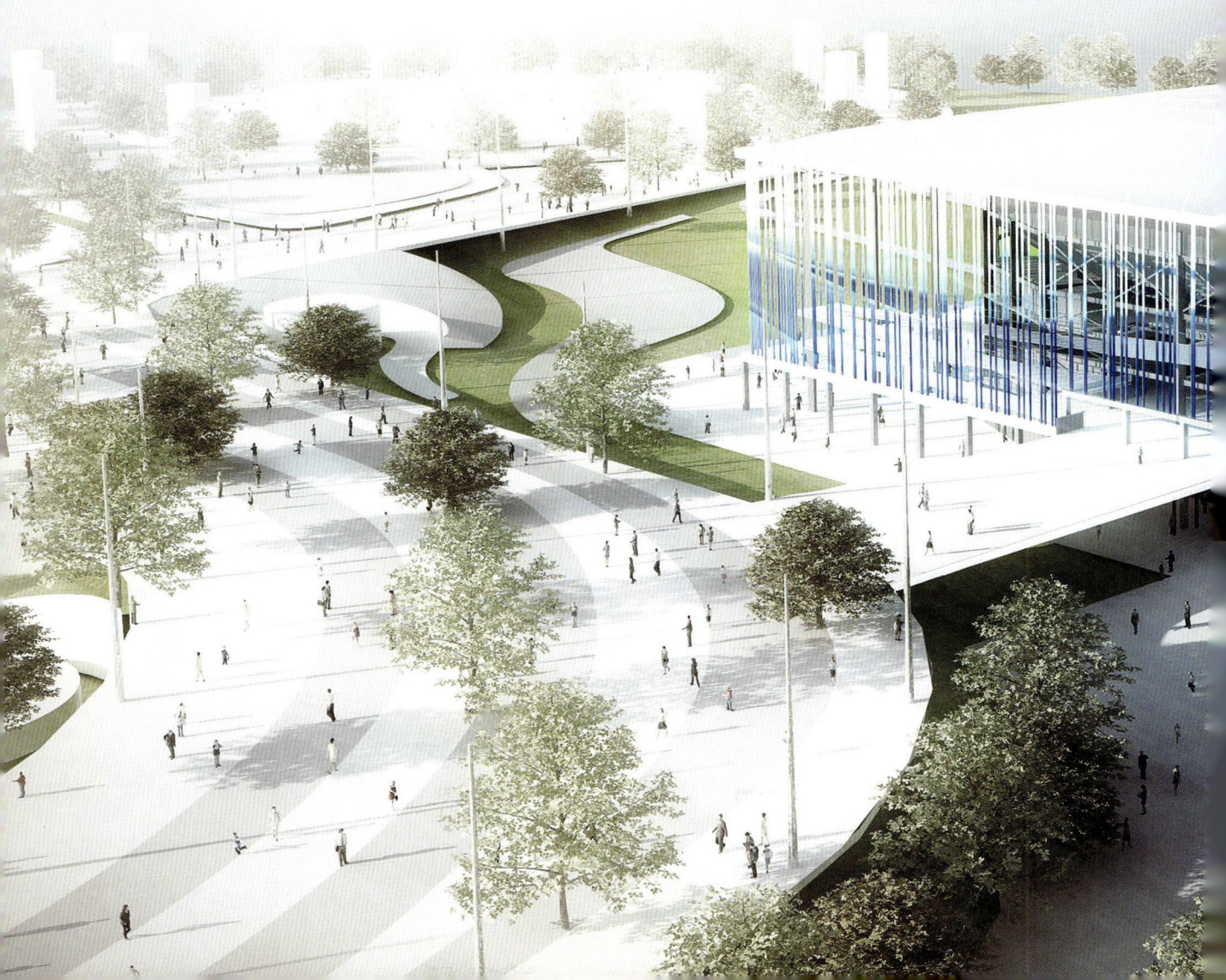

2016年奥运会网球及水上运动中心
里约热内卢，巴西

**2016 Olympic Games,
Tennis and Aquatic Center**
Rio de Janeiro, Brazil

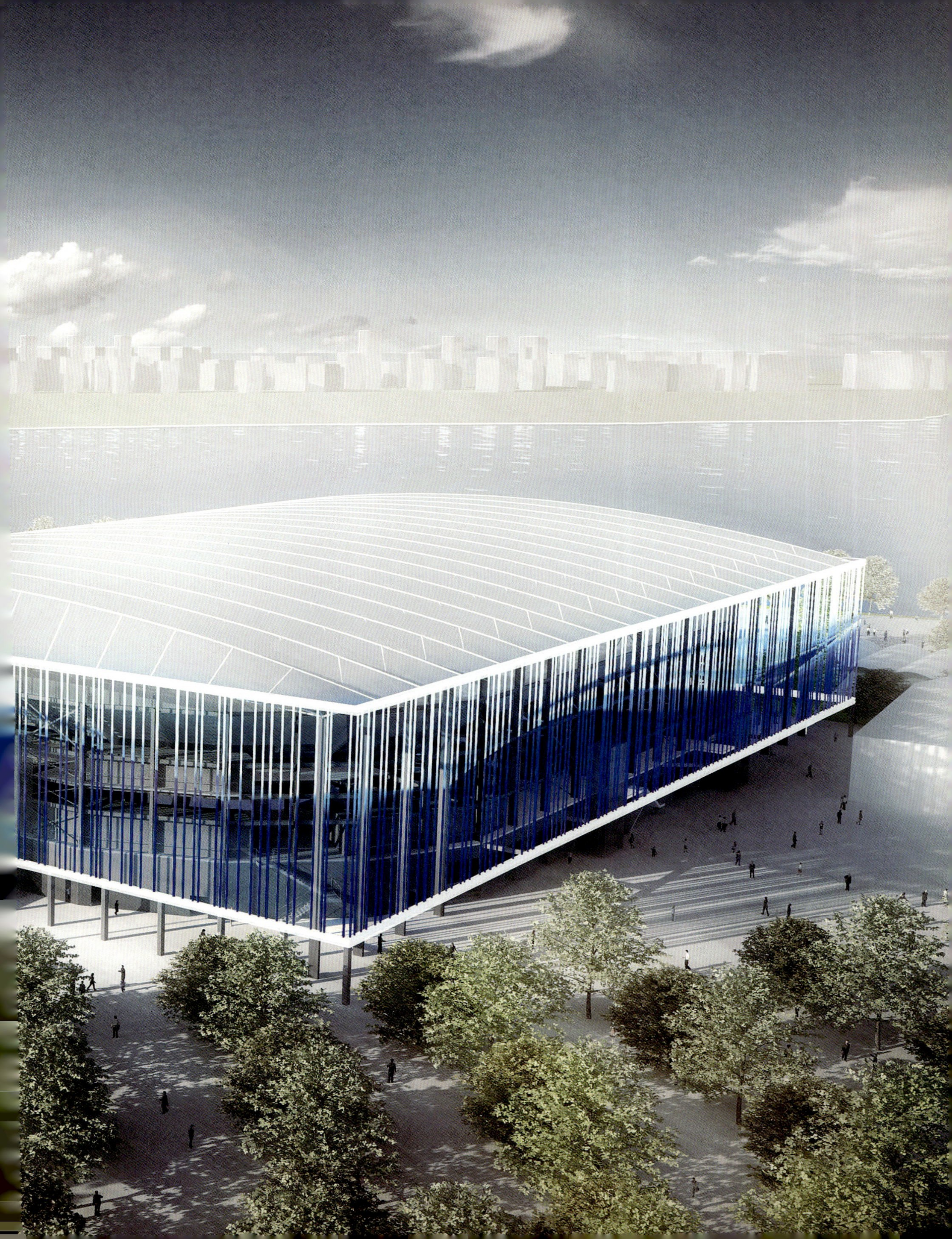

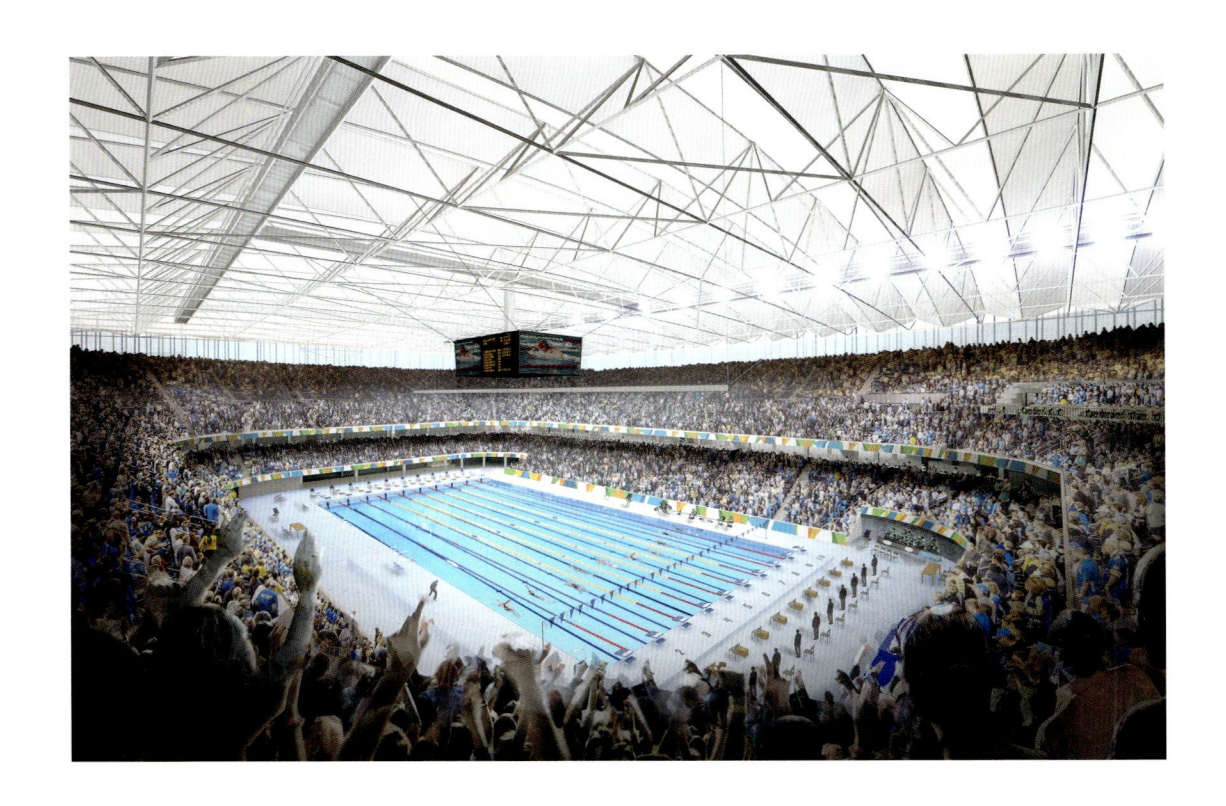

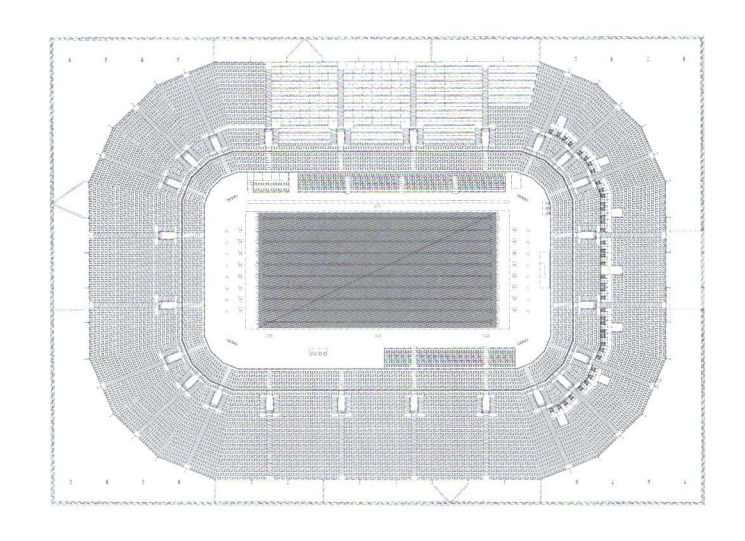

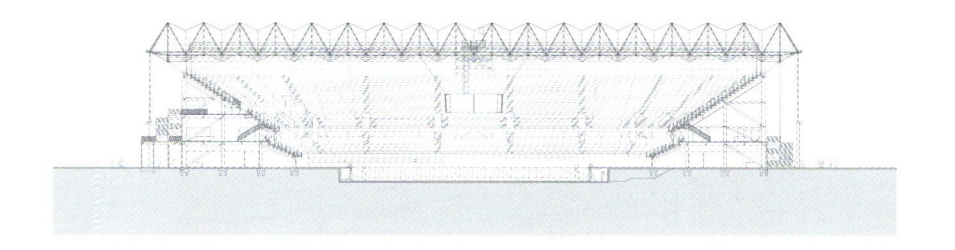

440　**2016年奥运会网球及水上运动中心**　里约热内卢

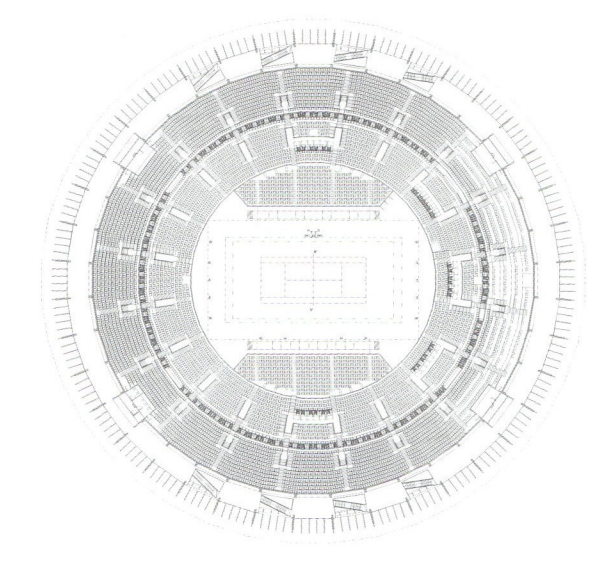

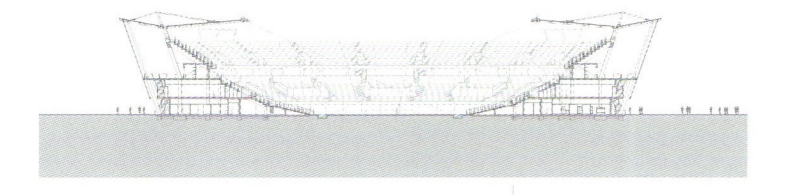

2016 Olympic Games, Tennis and Aquatic Center Rio de Janeiro

Picture Credits

Julia Ackermann
21R, 184/185

Gerhard Aumer
294/295, 320/321

Marcus Bredt
15L, 15R, 16L, 17L, 19L, 23L, 23R, 98/99, 102, 104/105, 106/107, 108, 110, 111, 112, 113, 114/115, 116, 117, 124/125, 126, 127, 146/147, 148, 149T, 150, 151, 152/153, 202/203, 204T, 205, 206, 207, 208, 209, 210/211, 212, 213, 236L, 236R, 237L, 238/239, 240, 241, 244/245, 246, 247, 248/249, 252/253, 254, 255, 256/257, 260L, 262L, 262R, 264R, 265L, 265R, 268R, 269L, 269R, 270L, 272/273, 274, 275, 296/297, 302/303, 304/305, 306/307, 308, 309, 330/331, 332, 333, 334, 335, 336/337, 338/339, 340/341, 346/347, 348, 349, 350, 351, 384/385, 386, 387, 388/389, 390/391, 392, 393, 394/395, 396, 397, 398, 399, 400, 401, 402/403, 404, 405, 406, 407

Busam/Richter
298/299

Fritz Busam
343

Hans Georg Esch
12L, 12R, 16R, 19R, 22R, 38/39, 40/41, 54/55, 56, 57, 58, 59, 60/61, 62T, 63, 64, 65, 66, 67, 100T, 101, 118/119, 120, 121, 122, 123, 154/155, 156, 157, 158, 159, 160, 161, 196/197, 198, 199, 200T, 201, 300/301

Klaus Frahm
261R, 263L, 263R, 264L, 286T, 287T, 290/291, 292, 293, 310/311, 312, 313, 314/315, 322/323, 325, 326, 327, 328/329

Gärtner + Christ
187T

Christian Gahl
11L, 11R, 13L, 13R, 14L, 14R, 18R, 20L, 20R, 21L, 22L, 24L, 42/43, 44, 45, 46, 47, 48/49, 50, 52, 68/69, 71, 72, 73, 74/75, 76, 77T, 78, 79, 80/81, 82/83, 84T, 85, 86, 87, 88, 89, 90/91, 92, 93, 94, 95, 96/97, 138/139, 140, 141, 142, 143, 144, 145, 162/163, 164/165, 166, 167, 168/169, 170/171, 172T, 173, 174, 175, 176/177, 178/179, 180, 181, 182, 183, 188/189, 190, 191T, 192, 193, 194, 195, 214/215, 216T, 217, 218, 219, 220/221

Wolf Dieter Gericke
278, 279

Meinhard von Gerkan
29B, 62B, 77B, 100B, 149B, 187B, 200B, 286B, 319B

gmp Renderings
24R, 25L, 25R, 222/223, 224, 225, 226/227, 228, 229, 230/231, 232, 233, 270R, 271L, 271R, 408/409, 410, 411, 412/413, 414, 415, 416/417, 418/419, 420, 421, 422/423, 424/425, 428L, 429L, 430/431, 432, 436, 437, 438/439, 440, 441

L — left   R — right   T — top   B — bottom

Grinaker-LTA
242/243

Oliver Heissner
288/289

Heiner Leiska
10R, 34/35, 267L, 267R, 268L, 344/345, 356, 364/365, 366, 367, 368/369, 370/371, 372, 373, 374, 375, 376, 377, 378/379, 380, 381, 382/383

Ben McMillan
17R, 51, 53, 128/129, 130, 131, 132/133

Portal da Copa / Tomás Faquini
428R, 434/435

Michael Penner
261L, 284/285

schlaich bergermann und partner
18L, 134/135, 136/137

Jürgen Schmidt
260R, 266L, 266R, 276/277, 280, 281, 283, 316, 317, 318, 319T, 352/353, 354/355, 357, 358/359, 360, 361, 362, 363

Werner Sobek
103L

Stephan Schütz
84B, 164B, 172B, 191B, 216B

Shanghai Urban Planning Administration Bureau
36/37

Jan Siefke
10L, 26/27, 28, 29, 30/31, 32/33, 103R

Bruce Sutherland
250/251

Magdalene Weiss
204B

Peter Wels
324

All plans by
gmp

Some pictures are used more than once.
Multiple credit was omitted.

Picture Credits

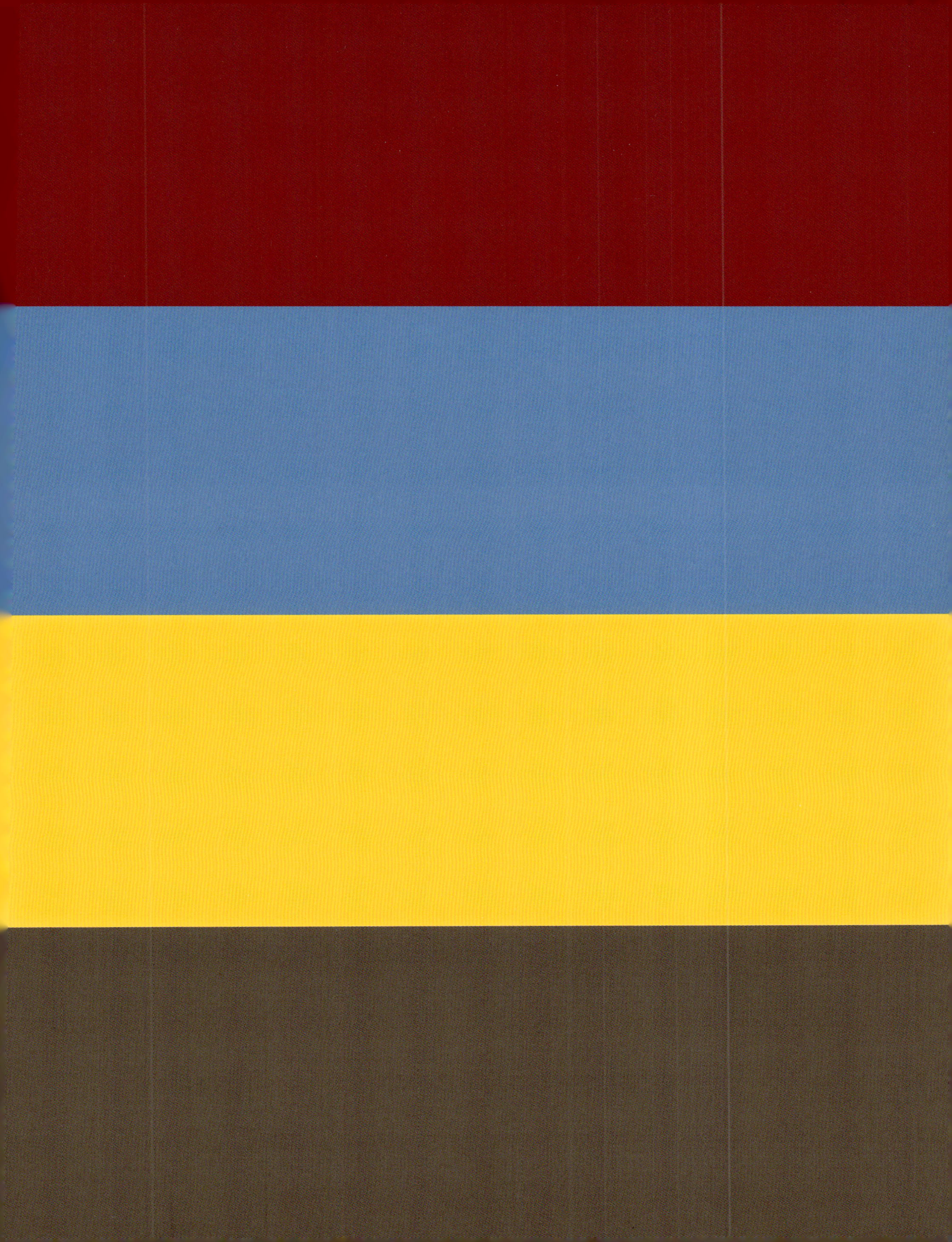